Public Personnel Management

Readings in Contexts and Strategies

Donald E. Klingner

Florida International University

 Mayfield Publishing Company

 International Personnel Management Association

To my family —
Amy, Chris, and Sara.
They are my reasons
for writing.

Copyright ©1981 by Mayfield Publishing Company
First edition 1981

Library of Congress Catalog Card Number: 80-84019
International Standard Book Number: 0-87484-517-3
Manufactured in the United States of America
Mayfield Publishing Company, 285 Hamilton Avenue, Palo
Alto, California 94301

This book was set in Melior by Lehmann Graphics and was
printed and bound by the George Banta Company. Sponsoring
editor was Chuck Murphy, Maggie Cutler supervised editing,
and manuscript editor was Jay Stewart. Nancy Sears supervised
design, and the text and cover were designed by Michael Rogon-
dino. Michelle Hogan supervised production.

Contents

Preface

Many years ago, before I began to study personnel management, a friend raised a philosophical question: What happens to locusts who burrow into the ground and wait seventeen years to emerge only to find when they do that in the meantime they have been covered by a parking lot? It later occurred to me that students sometimes face similar situations. Many of them study a subject for years, finally emerging with a credential only to find that economic conditions have eliminated the demand for the very skills they have developed.

When I was in graduate school, several people tried to discourage me from pursuing the study of public personnel management. They felt the area was an intellectual graveyard, an administrative area devoid of either theory or conflict. Professionally, they believed it represented a much less promising career choice than, say, policy analysis or urban studies.

Since that time, both academicians and practitioners have started to pay more attention to public personnel management. They have explored its connections to political science, public administration and organization theory; and they have developed and tested theories to explain why certain techniques are more effective than others in particular situations. The emergence of both labor-management relations and affirmative action has served to increase the visibility and authority of persons in this field. In short, personnel management has become more respectable academically and more marketable professionally. The Wall Street Journal recently reported, for example, that public personnel management was one of the ten fastest growing occupations in the United States. I do not know whether my career choice was based on foresight or luck. As the hypothetical locust might have done, I can only echo a Vonnegut character (in Slaughterhouse Five) whose phlegmatic reaction to either pleasure or pain is, "and so it goes."

Now, all of a sudden, I look back to find that I have been working in public personnel management since 1968 as a staffing specialist with the federal government, trainer and consultant to numerous organizations, researcher, and professor.

I consider myself extraordinarily lucky to have found a job that I enjoy doing and at which I can make enough money to live comfortably. Personnel management is exciting to me because it symbolizes the eternal conflict between employees and organizations over the relative primacy of such objectives as productivity and job satisfaction. It focuses the political struggle among interest groups for control of public agencies through such activities as affirmative action and labor relations.

The problem is how to reach public personnel management in such a way that students get a clear idea of the techniques and concepts, yet an accurate idea of the underlying ferment of value conflicts as well. One answer is to use both a textbook and a reader because of the unique advantages of each. Readers and textbooks serve different though mutually supportive purposes. A textbook presents one author's view of how public personnel management is done or should be done. It is organized according to the author's view of the topics and reflects his or her assumptions and values. It is conceptually clear, theoretically integrated, and self-contained.

But these strengths can also be weaknesses, for textbooks tend to present stimulating topics in a less than interesting fashion by removing conflicts to achieve clarity and consistency. By contrast, a reader presents many authors' views of a discipline. Each offers a different set of values and assumptions about the field. None of the articles is theoretically integrated, for each author's style context, and assumptions tend to be unique.

By selecting articles that reflect the diversity of the field, the editor of a reader can make it easier for students to pinpoint areas of conflict or change. While it may seem easy to "string together" articles in this fashion, the editor is also responsible for justifying the selections in terms of their topics and positions, analyzing their similarities and differences to make them more apparent to readers, and seeking some unity of style.

This is the first reader I have edited. Looking back on the process, it seems harder to edit a book than to write one. There are so many good articles that some are invariably left out by necessity and others through ignorance. While researching the text for which this reader is an intended companion (*Public Personnel Management: Contexts and Strategies*, Prentice-Hall, 1980), I read between 1,500 and 2,000 books and articles. Yet several of the selections in this reader were suggested by reviewers; I had not come across them myself.

I used several criteria in selecting the articles for this reader. The first was that they explore the range of activities and techniques associated with public personnel management. At least in my view, the articles represent my effort to balance activities such as staffing, rewarding, and employee equity. The second criterion was that they explore both the techniques associated with public personnel management and the values underlying the use of those techniques. For example, techniques for selection can only be appreciated in the light of assumptions about the relationship between public management and political democracy or affirmative action conflicts over the appropriate definition of merit. The third criterion was that articles be selected from a variety of public and private sector personnel journals. These articles are written by both practicing personnel managers and university professors, and this diversity of the journals' styles and authors' backgrounds will hopefully make clear the variety of writing available that is related to public personnel management. Lastly, the articles are intended to be interesting and readable. While the styles differ, each is intended to attract the interest of beginning graduate or undergraduate students. The goal of this selection is to challenge you to question your own knowledge and assumptions about public personnel management.

Public personnel management is, after all, diverse and inconsistent. It is precisely this diversity of values, goals, and circumstances (beneath a facade of value-free reliance on law and uniform techniques) that makes the field so exciting. Welcome, then, to the world of public personnel management. I hope you come to enjoy it as much as I have.

Acknowledgments

Any reader is a group effort. This one is no exception. I would first like to express my appreciation to the authors of the included selections for their efforts. Most of this reader's value is due to the quality of their contributions. In addition, the inclusion of these articles would not have been possible without the gracious consent of the journals in which they had previously been published.

I am grateful to Dean Charles Bonser of the School of Public and Environmental Affairs and to John H. Kragie, assistant dean at Indianapolis, for providing me with the resources necessary to put this reader together. Writing requires blocks of time and considerable support activity. They have been generous with both time and money. In particular, I have become quite dependent upon the secretarial and editorial skills of Alice Williams. Her logical questions and common sense cut down the number of errors considerably. Also, Maria Rincon typed the index.

This reader would not have been possible without the support of two superb editors—Stan Wakefield of Prentice-Hall and Chuck Murphy of Mayfield Publishing Company. Chuck Murphy had many positive suggestions and submitted the reader to an extensive review process that broadened its appeal and improved its quality. Two reviewers contributed valuable suggestions. Felix Nigro of the University of Georgia, one of the "grand old men" of public personnel management, reviewed the entire manuscript. Nicholas Lovrich of Washington State University not only advised in favor of the historical approach used in the first section but also suggested the inclusion of several significant articles I was unaware of. The reader is better for their efforts.

Production of the reader would not have been possible without the help of competent and dedicated professionals at Mayfield Publishing. Pamela Trainer coordinated permissions. Maggie Cutler supervised editorial production. And Jay Stewart edited the manuscript, proving that Petaluma, California, has other graces besides its reputation as the egg capital of the world.

Lastly, I owe a debt of thanks to my wife, Sara, and children, Chris and Amy, for putting up with me while I wrote this. After all, there's no point in doing something you like if you can't share it. I'm glad I have them to be with.

While many others are responsible for this reader's merits, I am responsible for any errors of emphasis or omission.

Introduction

During the early 1900s, public administration theory developed around the assumption of a dichotomy between "politics" and "administration." *Politics* was the dispute over values and objectives of public policy that took place among elected officials and candidates. *Administration* was the process of reaching these objectives through career bureaucrats who were hired and promoted on the basis of their technical skill. Personnel management was widely regarded as the branch of administrative science devoted to refining techniques for the acquisiton and effective utilization of employees, and its objective was increased organizational productivity. In other words, it was something done to employees rather than with them or for them.

The freedom of personnel managers to explore objectives or techniques alternative to those widely used at the time was restricted by public demands that personnel managers support a set of normative expectations collectively known as "the merit system." This system included such principles as open access to public jobs on the basis of ability and performance. Political values such as nepotism, loyalty, responsiveness, or party affiliation were specifically excluded. These merit principles were incorporated into federal and state law and came to control the range of values and behaviors considered acceptable within the emerging profession.

These conditions did much to diminish the attention given public personnel management by academic researchers and theorists, as public policy analysis was considered both more glamorous and theoretically important than the mundane administrative areas where low level bureaucrats made routine decisions on the basis of purely technical considerations clearly based on merit system values. After all, what was the point of developing or testing theory in an area where decision strategies were known and objectives never varied?

In practice, however, things were never as clear as they seemed in theory. By the 1940s, political scientists (with their analysis of the behavior of administrative agencies) and organization theorists (with their study of organizational conflict and decision making) realized that the distinction between politics and administration was fallacious. They began more realistic and profitable investigations of agency responsiveness and discretionary behavior among employees.

Also, the behavioral sciences developed rapidly during the 1930s and 1940s, as exemplified by the Hawthorne studies, which showed the relationship between productivity and social rewards. The emergence of the human relations school of management during the 1950s emphasized the cumulative impact of managerial practices on employees, the importance of employee values and objectives (the informal organization) to organizational productivity, and the need for participative management. These factors, particularly when combined with the spectacular growth of public sector unions, focused personnel management toward employee as well as managerial objectives. Activities such as labor relations, job redesign, career/life planning, compensation, grievances, and concern for occupational safety developed, and these became incorporated into the body of personnel practice.

Finally, the social and political unrest of the 1960s demonstrated that "merit" was an ephemeral concept. Everyone sounded as if they knew what it was, but none could agree on a definition. Suddenly, technical experts in job evaluation and testing found themselves confronted by demands that the definition of merit be expanded to include such factors as seniority, credentials, race, sex, or even political loyalty (now more acceptably labeled "political responsiveness"). These conflicts reinforced what we have always suspected but have usually been unwilling to admit: laws are not impartial but are based on objectives or values held by competing interest groups. In the face of this, it was more productive to examine the values underlying various "merit system" laws and why certain groups supported them than it was to insist upon a value consensus underlying public personnel management. For the practitioner, it is certainly more rewarding to be an administrator who takes risks and mediates among competing interest groups than a technician who merely applies standardized decision rules to predictable situations.

In these respects, public personnel management has certainly grown beyond earlier attempts to define or confine it. It is currently both political and administrative; it seeks to achieve the objectives of management, employees, and outside groups (clients, regulatory agencies, and the media); and it involves conflict rather than consensus over objectives and methods. Despite the uncertainties brought about by these changes, they have undoubtedly made the field more exciting and rewarding. These same changes have led to the development of theories that are both more descriptive and more complex and to the development of techniques that are situational rather than unusual. From our present viewpoint of hindsight, these changes are beneficial.

The public personnel manager's primary role is working with other managers in planning, organizing, staffing, directing, controlling, and rewarding. Planning takes place after the organization's basic objectives have been established by law, and it includes forecasting the number and type of employees needed. Organizing requires the definition of specific jobs within the organization through job classification and evaluation. Directing involves setting performance standards for employees and work units. Controlling takes place through training and management information systems. Rewarding requires connecting performance and rewards through performance evaluation, pay, and benefit systems.

However, this list of functions is incomplete in that it reflects only management-oriented activities, and personnel managers must also be responsive to groups seeking objectives that may differ from those of organizational management: employees and outside groups—unions, regulatory agencies, other interest groups, and the media. Therefore, this list of managerial functions must be augmented by equity functions—employee health and safety, appeal and grievance systems, labor-management relations, affirmative action, and career/life planning. These five activities represent the access of nonmanagerial objectives into public personnel decisions and this has created many of the changes that have occurred in the field since the 1930s.

The readings are arranged in functional categories, therefore, not because they describe the "one best way" to perform a function but because they offer insights into contextual variables as well as skills. For example, the first chapter (on the context of public personnel management) discusses value conflicts that have affected the development of the discipline. Other articles present both current and historical perspectives on activities, thereby showing the evolution of objectives or techniques over time.

Each chapter contains a selection of articles drawn from both public and private personnel management journals. While articles from public sector journals such as *Public Personnel Management* and *Public Administration Review* predominate, many selections from private sector journals have been included because the techniques used by both types of professionals are identical for many activities—job analysis, selection, performance evaluation, and training, for example. While there are also many differences between public and private sector personnel management (chiefly in their contexts and their handling of equity functions), students of public personnel management can learn much from such journals as the *Harvard Business Review*, the *Academy of Management Journal*, *Training and Development Journal*, *Personnel Journal*, *Personnel Psychology*, *Personnel*, and the *Administrative Science Quarterly*. At a time when public personnel managers are seeking contextual solutions, it seems wise to look for private sector applications that may be useful. This is especially true in that entry-level practitioners are likely to be addressing problems involving "nuts and bolts" techniques common to both sectors, as well as problems that relate only to the particular context of public personnel management.

Public
Personnel
Management

1

The Context of Public Personnel Management

The context of public personnel management is political. This means that it involves continuing conflicts over values and objectives. For the most part these conflicts have existed since the emergence of public personnel management as a discipline during the early 1900s and can be traced back from there to the inquiries of the earliest political theorists and philosophers. The following questions have been crucial to the evolution of the discipline:

1. Upon what assumptions about human nature and human interaction should the design of organizations and human resource management systems be based?
2. What are the objectives of a political system?
3. What is the function of a public personnel manager, and what factors affect job performance?

Understandably, answers to these questions have been disputed. The traditional historical perspective was delineated by Frank J. Goodnow in *Politics and Administration*, a classic work in the development of public administration that was first published in 1900. Goodnow's primary thesis was that politics and administration were separable. The former had to do with "... policies or expressions of state will," while the latter concerned "... the execution of these

3

policies."[1] The process of administration involved skills related more closely to science, law, and business than politics, and the objective of administration was efficiency, a goal to be obtained by

> ... the exercise of foresight and discretion, the pursuit of truth, the gathering of information, the maintenance of a strictly impartial attitude toward the individuals with whom they have dealings, and the provision of the most efficient possible administrative organization.[2]

Goodnow concluded that since the bulk of administration was "... unconnected with politics," it should be "... relieved very largely, if not altogether, from the control of political bodies."[3]

Goodnow used personnel management to illustrate the problems that arose with the failure to distinguish administration from politics. In particular, he criticized the "spoils system" for its deleterious effect on the quality of both politics and administration. The phrase *spoils system* described the practice in which elected officials rewarded party loyalists by appointing them to public jobs, routinely discharging employees who had been appointed by the previous party in office. Initially, this system offered the advantages of maintaining strong political parties by inducing popular participation in politics. It had, however, two great faults. Politically it tended to favor the formation of political machines which were

> ... organized not so much for facilitating the expression of the will of the state as for keeping the party in power. It thus aided in making the party an end rather than a means.[4]

Second, as the work of government agencies became more extensive and complicated, the spoils system "... seriously impaired administrative efficiency."[5] In short, for Goodnow, the spoils system exemplified the evils associated with the involvement of politics in what he saw as the essentially value-free and efficient process of personnel administration.

In the first article of this reader, Donald E. Klingner and John Nalbandian disagree with Goodnow's perception that personnel management is a value-free administrative field. They contend that this historical emphasis on political neutrality and value-free choices based upon administrative efficiency has been replaced by the more accurate model of personnel management as a contextual, value-oriented management process influenced by the outcome preferences of employees, managers, and outside groups. They discuss the advantages of this comparative and contextual approach for managers, employees, and students of public personnel management.

Frederick C. Mosher's essay on "Merit, Morality, and Democracy" is drawn from his brilliant book on the relationship between democracy and the values underlying public employment policy. He opposes Professor Goodnow by insisting that personnel management is inseparable from politics to the extent that the achievement of American ideals requires changes in personnel practices. Second, his discussion of administrative morality emphasizes the questions of interest group power and bureaucratic representativeness that were first raised by James Madison two hundred years ago in the *Federalist Papers*. Today, after Watergate and a prolonged era of public cynicism toward the ethics of administrators, these questions are particularly appropriate.

In the third article, Robert T. Golembiewski examines the assumptions about human nature that underlie public personnel management. In particular he looks at the undesirable consequences of these assumptions for supervisory behavior, job analysis, and job design.

Taken together, these first three articles show that public personnel management cannot be separated from public administration, political science, and organization theory and behavior. Granted, these roots are not always visible in a discussion of alternative techniques, but the concepts and value judgments of these fields underlie technical discussions of administrative techniques. There can be no doubt that federal laws, regulations, and grant programs play an increasingly important role in influencing personnel practice at the levels of state and local government. Ray Shapek discusses the impact of these influences on such areas as affirmative action, employee health and safety, and labor-management relations. He makes the point that the combination of federal "carrots and sticks" has required public personnel managers to be much more responsive to the rights of employees and outside groups. Paradoxically, this has made it more difficult for public personnel managers to accomplish organizational objectives, yet it has increased their power within the organization.

As might be expected, commentators have differed on the question of whether or not public personnel management is a profession. Myron D. Fottler and Craig Norrell evaluate the background characteristics and qualifications of state agency personnel directors. They conclude that (a) state agency personnel directors show as high a degree of professionalism as their private sector counterparts, (b) the environment within which state agencies function affects the degree of professionalism and the relative emphasis on different personnel functions, and (c) organizational size affects many factors in the public personnel system.

In the final article of the first chapter, Donald E. Klingner discusses the ways in which personnel management is likely to change in the 1980s. He predicts that changes will occur in the context of personnel management because of a greater emphasis on laws, the demands of competing groups, and the value of human resources. This will lead to changes in the role of the personnel manager, who will gain recognition as a professional and increased potential power within the organization as well as become more directly concerned with organizational effectiveness. Lastly, these changes will increase and diversify the qualifications required of personnel managers in different contexts.

These six articles are not reconcilable; at best they show that the role of the personnel manager is changing and that the personnel function is increasing in importance. A variety of factors—political, economic, social, and technical—influence the performance of personnel activities. These activities, in turn, are based on assumptions about human nature, the purposes of government, and the relationship between politics and personnel management.

NOTES

1. Frank J. Goodnow, *Politics and Administration* (New York: Russell and Russell, 1967), p. 18.

2. Ibid, p. 85.
3. Loc. cit.
4. Ibid, p. 113.
5. Loc. cit.

Personnel Management by Whose Objectives?

Donald E. Klingner

John Nalbandian

Public personnel management, as a field of public administration, has undergone considerable development in the past forty years. Personnel professionals now have a wide range of techniques available that they can apply toward the efficient acquisition, allocation, and development of human resources—human resource planning, job analysis, selection, appraisal, training, and labor-management relations.

The rapid development of these techniques signifies the increasing acceptance of rational, scientific problem solving over previous methods of dealing with employees. However, the advance of rational personnel management has occurred at a cost: by emphasizing the "one best way" to complete a task, personnel professionals have ignored the diversity that exists in reality. Specifically, they have tended to overlook the impact that different organizational objectives and environments have on the effectiveness of personnel management techniques. As a result, many consequences of personnel techniques that affect employees, organization, and environment are defined as falling outside the study and practice of personnel management.

Ideas and concepts drawn from the literature of organization theory and administrative behavior furnish the opportunity to develop a dynamic and realistic view of personnel management. We approach the problem of developing a new theoretical framework in three segments:

1. What values are implied by the current approach to personnel management?
2. What other approach is available?
3. What benefits for academicians, personnel professionals, and employees are associated with the approach developed in this paper?

Donald E. Klingner is an associate professor in the School of Public Affairs & Services at Florida International University. John Nalbandian is an assistant professor of political science at the University of Kansas.

Reprinted from *Public Administration Review* © 1978 by The American Society for Public Administration, 1225 Connecticut Avenue, N.W., Washington, D.C. All rights reserved.

THE PRESENT APPROACH
TO PUBLIC PERSONNEL MANAGEMENT

In the past half century the study of public administration has moved from a discussion of management principles within an organization to analyses of relationships among environmental pressures, organizational structure and technology, and managerial processes. An awareness of the impact of external events on policy outcomes has complicated but enriched our understanding of the tasks and characteristics of "good management." Management is now viewed not just as the art of planning, organizing, staffing, directing, and controlling but also as the rational process of matching the organization's diverse social and technical systems with environmental resources and constraints in order to achieve objectives.[1]

However, personnel management has lagged behind in this developmental process. The focus of inquiry is still directed toward discovering the "one best way" to perform a function rather than toward examining contexts, functions, techniques, and consequences in contingent type arrangements.[2] Several factors contribute to the lag in the development of public personnel theory.

First, much of public personnel administration is dictated by laws, rules, and regulations historically aimed at eliminating political discretion in the management of human resources. For example, according to Rosenbloom,

> The reformer's emphasis on political neutrality led to the enactment of restrictions on the partisan political activities of public employees in a large number of jurisdictions. It also encouraged the development of a position-oriented public personnel administration which attaches rank and salary to positions rather than individuals and thereby makes it somewhat more difficult to exercise political favoritism.[3]

Second, professors of public administration have often viewed public personnel management as a barren area for theoretical study. Historically, it seems that academicians have accepted the view that personnel management consists of the routine application of a practitioner's "bag of tricks." While organizational researchers deal extensively with resource allocation and maintenance questions, they seem to downgrade the role of personnel professionals compared with that of managers or supervisors. The academician's orientation may be a holdover from the administrative-techniques theory prevalent thirty to fifty years ago in that a distinction is drawn between policy level decisions and administration. In this school of thought, when attention is focused on personnel administration, it tends to be toward the development of routinized solutions to personnel management problems.

This orientation on the part of the academician relates to the already mentioned statutory and procedural nature of public personnel. The development of theory in any field requires attention to variables that fluctuate. Simply stated, the theorist attempts to relate the fluctuation in one set of variables to the movement in another. The normative emphasis historically seen in public personnel administration has been to reduce these variations in pursuit of a merit system. Thus, the conditions allowing for the development of theoretical thought in the public personnel field largely have been absent.

The field's legal heritage and the tendency of academicians to view public personnel management as a collection of low level techniques have created a dilemma for personnel managers, and this dilemma is the third factor impeding development of public personnel theory. For despite the shift of administrative theory away from the "one best way" of administration, personnel managers are still implicitly encouraged to believe that this type of solution is both possible and desirable. Since personnel managers are encouraged to view techniques *as if* they were universally applicable and effective in promoting a merit system, the decision to apply them often becomes a routine one involving questions of cost and implementation but not of suitability.[4]

The factors contributing to the lag in the development of public personnel theory have three practical consequences. First, current texts commonly use a sequential discussion of functions pioneered by Glenn Stahl in the 1930s: classification, staffing, motivation, compensation, recruitment, selection and testing, performance evaluation, training, bargaining and grievance procedures, and the role of the central personnel department.[5] There is little continuity, aside from the logic of day-to-day operations, to this sequence. The topics are separate pieces of a puzzle, lacking a conceptual framework. There is no answer to the academician's fundamental question, "How do the pieces fit together?"

Second, personnel managers are implicitly encouraged to ignore the value dimension of their decisions and to support the illusion that personnel management is the value-free application of management-oriented techniques. Yet, this implied assumption stands in remarkable contrast to the highly political atmosphere within which personnel managers actually operate.[6] Rather than there being one best way of personnel management, there are a variety of personnel policy choices, each of which has different outcomes for the employee and client groups competing for scarce organizational resources.

This value dimension of public personnel policy is clearly shown in conflict over issues underlying competing definitions of "merit." Despite universal acceptance of the concept in the abstract, many personnel management questions reflect the continuous battle over which of the following definitions is most appropriate: ability and technical expertise, seniority, credentials, political responsiveness, or social representation.[7] The ambivalence of this key concept has repercussions for selection, promotion, and wage administration, for example, because each of these functions involves distribution of limited resources. Here are a few examples: *Selection*—what relative weight should be placed on ability and social representation in attempting to redress previous patterns of discrimination? During a layoff, what criteria are used to determine who lose jobs first? *Promotion*—what relative weight should be given to ability, seniority, and loyalty in determining promotions? *Wage administration*—should "merit" pay increases be given for increases in seniority or productivity?

As the above examples illustrate, personnel management involves value-laden alternatives; yet administrators are given few guidelines for testing the appropriateness of a given technique under organizational conditions. Current personnel management theory provides no adequate answer to the personnel manager's question, "What action should I take now?"

Third, the implicit focus of personnel management theory on techniques gives scant attention to the cumulative impact on employees. Despite extensive contributions to the knowledge of administrative behavior from research dealing with role theory, expectancy theory, and the psychological contract, there has been little transfer of this knowledge to the body of personnel management practice.

> Industry frequently has tended to give its entire attention to development, adoption, and utilization of personnel techniques and has failed to develop or explore the underlying philosophy. Furthermore, management has been remiss in explaining to employees the rationale inherent in its utilization of such tools even when consciously formulated. This has often led to the failure of techniques or only a partial realization of their potential capabilities because they have been perceived by employees as a means of exploitation or as a means to achieve goals opposed to their best interest.[8]
>
> In personnel relations, management has relied upon authority to achieve cooperation rather than having provided an organizational environment conducive to soliciting the interest, drive, and initiative of employees.[9]

A personnel manager's disregard for the cumulative impact of personnel management decisions on employee aspirations and attitudes can have these organizational consequences: *Job design*—jobs designed to meet present organizational needs may not provide for the development of employee career aspirations. The message sent is that *we* want you now; *you* take care of your future. *Promotion*—a cynical attitude toward authority relationships within the organization can develop where criteria for promotion are not well developed, where they are inequitably applied, or where promotional opportunities are not widely advertised. *Performance evaluation*—there will be little desire to change behavior in the light of performance evaluation feedback if employees believe that organizational rewards are not attached to the evaluation system. Thus, personnel management theory provides no adequate answer to the employee's question, "What can I hope for in this job?"[10]

A NEW APPROACH
TO PUBLIC PERSONNEL MANAGEMENT

If an outdated and artificially value-free conception of personnel management prevails, what is the alternative? One might begin by viewing the dynamics of personnel policy and administration within a decision-making framework in order to conceptually highlight its political, value-oriented context. In addition to this purpose, by focusing the analysis on decision making, we can attempt to transfer learning about management processes in general to personnel management specifically. With this transfer, an effort can be made to show that personnel administration need not be studied and understood as a distinct organizational phenomenon, but rather as an area subject to generally accepted analytical approaches like open systems analysis, functional analysis, or a decision-making approach.

The foundation of our framework is based on James D. Thompson's work. He argues that decision issues involve two major dimensions: (1) beliefs about cause-effect relations and (2) preferences regarding possible outcomes.[11] The resultant matrix, (Fig. 1) slightly modified from Thompson's original, shows four decision issue possibilities (quadrants I–IV) and appropriate problem solving strategies (computation, compromise, judgment, and inspiration).

Preferences regarding possible outcomes

		Agreement	Disagreement
Beliefs about cause and effect relations	Certain	I Computation	II Compromise
	Uncertain	III Judgment	IV Inspiration

Figure 1   Decision-making matrix

Viewing this decision matrix, one can see that personnel issues characterized by agreement on desired outcomes and certainty or relative certainty regarding cause-effect relationships (means to achieve these outcomes) would be the least political (quadrant I). Decision issues falling into other quadrants would be more political: (a) issues where means to ends are known but the outcomes themselves are contended (quadrant II); (b) issues characterized by agreement on desired outcomes but by lack of certainty or relative certainty about the appropriate means to achieve them (quadrant III); and (c) issues where both outcome preferences and appropriate means to achieve them are uncertain (quadrant IV).

One can add dynamism and an evaluative component to this framework by isolating three perspectives that might contend in many personnel decision contexts: (1) the individual employee, (2) organizational management, and (3) outside groups: consumers or even the "public interest."[12] Each of these three frames of reference generates outcome preferences based on its own evaluative criteria: (a) employees seek to maximize the predictability and equity of inducements provided by the organization for their membership and participation;[13] (b) organizational management seeks to maintain and increase environmental supports to meet environmental and internal organizational demands, while maximizing the calculability and predictability of environmental influences;[14] and (c) societal forces commit or withhold support from the organization so as to influence its behavior. Selecting an appropriate quadrant for a decision issue depends on the degree of influence proponents of these viewpoints can muster and on the extent of agreement on issue outcomes and means-end relationships.

Knowing the quadrant that an issue falls into will assist one to understand, explain, and perhaps even predict in a general sense the behaviorial dynamics and type of discussion associated with the issue. In essence, if participants can implicitly categorize an issue or problem into a quadrant, they have effectively "defined" the problem or situation. This agreement on definition acts, in large part, to guide decision making concerning appropriate behavior and the selection of data to be used in solving the problem or carrying out the function of concern. This notion finds its parallel in the work of several writers in different fields: (1) Herbert Simon, who introduces the concepts of "bounded rationality" and "control of decision premises" to help explain coordinated organizational interaction;[15] (2) Erving Goffman, who argues that successful behavior transactions require participant legitimation of each other's behavior;[16] and (3) Eric Berne, whose explanation of transactional analysis asserts that continuing transactions occur in situations of congruent ego states (parallel transactions), while incongruent ego states (mixed transactions) raise a new agenda item revolving around the definition of the situation.[17]

It might be useful at this point to describe briefly general types of behavior and issues one might expect to be associated with each quadrant. If an issue falls into quadrant I, one might expect to see "rational" thinking and evaluation based on concrete kinds of data. The issue might be solved or the function carried out with what March and Simon call programmed decision making,[18] or what Lindblom refers to as the rational comprehensive (root) model.[19] Many phases of job evaluation and wage surveys would fall into quandrant I. In quadrant II, one would expect to see compromise, bargaining, and negotiation taking place between, for example, union and management over wages. In such a case, parties might have a fairly clear idea about the effects of their own and each other's actions while disagreeing over outcome preferences. One might characterize certain kinds of promotion decisions (for example, where one person is responsible for the decision) into quadrant III. In these instances, the desire in the organization or unit to promote a qualified candidate is an agreed upon outcome, while the actions leading to the desired outcome are not always clear. Since these conditions would argue for rational problem solving (outcome preferences being agreed upon) but fail to provide sufficient data to make a programmed decision, one would expect to find a reliance on the judgment of the individual reviewing the candidates. In a group setting, these conditions would lend themselves to consensual rather than compromise or political problem solving. Quadrant IV includes situations that might parallel those found in Emery and Trist's "turbulent field."[20] For example, the issue might be "quality of working life." There might be little agreement among employees, organization, and outside regulatory or pressure groups on what constitutes quality of life and considerable uncertainty or disagreement about what kinds of actions would enhance the quality of working life. This degree of uncertainty led Thompson to designate "inspiration" as the appropriate quadrant IV decision strategy. A quadrant IV issue actually is one that no one knows how to define operationally, let alone resolve. "Quality of working life," for example, is such an abstraction that to deal with it realistically requires its subdivision into component issues of lesser complexity where some common agreement on means and/or ends can be reached. In other words, to improve the quality of working life involves dealing with issues designated as falling into quadrants I, II, and III, which when taken together would affect quality of working life. Even though the fourth quadrant has little operational value—that is, a usable problem solving strategy is not associated with it—its conceptual value should not be overlooked. For its presence indicates that issues falling into this quadrant are complex and can be effectively resolved only when subdivided into several less abstract issues. In addition, it allows one to recognize that using any single decision strategy in dealing with an issue that conceptually falls into quadrant IV would result in premature agreement on goals or methods. This agreement, while appropriate to the other quadrants, would too narrowly define quadrant IV problems and thus hinder their resolution.

So far the discussion of the value-analytical framework has focused on its utility in understanding and explaining behavior involving issues that more or less clearly fall solely into a particular quadrant. Yet it is difficult to find examples that do fall solely into one quadrant or another, and this exercise highlights an intriguing problem associated with human resource management that was introduced earlier. We often act *as if* personnel administration issues, problems, and functions fall within a set of more or less clearly defined boundaries—most often the boundaries set by quadrant I. Indeed, much of personnel administration is subject to programmed decision making and routine technology. In other cases, however, the influence of personnel administrators and theorists—reflecting the organization's value perspective introduced earlier—has enabled them to "impose their will" on their environments by unilaterally assigning a personnel issue to a specific quadrant. This contention connotes nothing derogatory; it simply reflects the continual tension in an open system framework between the organization's need to control its environment (the need for stability) and the need to adapt to it (the need for change). Just as environmental events have unexpected systemic consequences, so organizational managers strive to predict and limit their effects. As outside groups gain influence, the *as if* assumption may begin to crumble, and pressure may begin to develop to redefine issues from quadrant I into other quadrants or to supplant one computational strategy with another designed to achieve a newly agreed upon outcome. The current impact of Occupational Safety and Health Administration regulations and collective bargaining on personnel management illustrates these situations.

At first glance, the value-analytical framework might lead one to believe that the politics of personnel administration is to be found only in quadrants II and IV, where outcome preferences are contended. This would be too limiting an interpretation; politics is also found where employees, organizations, and outside groups disagree on problem definition or, in our analytical scheme, when they fail to agree into which quadrant an issue should be placed. In these cases, the definition of the situation becomes the issue, and the analyst should temporarily superimpose a kind of suprapolitical context on the value-analytical scheme until the real life actors agree on how they define the problem. This temporary movement outside of the framework into the context surrounding it can be illustrated by viewing the hypothetical dynamics of labor-management relations. One can begin at any starting point wherein management makes human resource management decisions and develops techniques that primarily reflect and enhance organization values. Many of these techniques will be reduced to programmed decisions and routine personnel procedures (quadrant I); others will be designated as issues requiring managerial judgment (quadrant III); and still others, as political issues to be bargained by managerial participants (quadrant II). Management has established a zone of employer rights implicitly legitimized through acceptance by all potentially influential and affected parties. At some subsequent time, a union will be established and will challenge the zone of employer rights. This challenge takes place at the suprapolitical level where the union will expect that issues earlier resolved in quadrants I and III by management now be resolved in quadrant II. The challenge is highlighted through focus on specific issues, such as employee work load. Agreements reached will channel particular issues into specific quadrants.

For example, it may be agreed to bargain (II) over wages, utilize seniority to make promotions (I), and to retain management discretion in the area of manpower allocation (III). At a subsequent time the definition of the situation may again be challenged, and its resolution will again take place at the suprapolitical level (for example, when labor desires to move manpower allocation decisions from quadrant III, managerial judgment, to quadrant II, compromise). Again, upon resolution, the issue will be channeled into a quadrant in the value-analytical framework—either remaining in quadrant III or moved, perhaps to quadrant II, as a result of the altered balance of power between contending parties.

We have been arguing that issues, decisions, functions, and behavior associated with human resource management can be understood and explained with the aid of this value-analytical framework. The framework permits personnel specialists to identify expected behavior and to isolate the characteristics of technologies associated with one quadrant more than another; it also assists by highlighting the importance of problem definition issues. Additional examples, such as the issue of selection based on expertise versus political responsiveness, may increase the reader's understanding of the framework. Where merit is defined as technical expertise, certain testing, interviewing, and previous performance analyses are appropriate. Since both outcomes and procedures are generally agreed upon, most such selection decisions would fall into quadrant I, with resolution by computational strategy. The case may be different when one looks at the political appointment process. In cases where political responsiveness is desired but selection criteria are uncertain, a selection decision may require considerable judgment and would fall into quadrant III. Both of these selection examples, one based on expertise and the other on political responsiveness, fall into different quadrants and would be dealt with differently. It is not unusual, however, to find a case where one influential party acts *as if* selection should be based on the former definition of merit (technical expertise) while another acts *as if* it should be based on the latter definition (political responsiveness). This is an example of a problem definition issue. Its resolution takes us temporarily out of the value-analytical matrix and into a political context where the ability to define the situation in one's favor becomes a test of power. This is where the essence of the political nature of personnel administration is found.

Another example, this time regarding affirmative action, is also intended to show that personnel administration can be usefully understood by looking within the quadrants of our framework and also by conceptualizing a suprapolitical context for the decision matrix itself. At some point in an organization's discussion of affirmative action, intraorganizational conflict will focus on two definitions of merit: (1) technical expertise and (2) social representation. In the past few years, this conflict over outcome references has been resolved by attempting to combine both objectives on the grounds that organizations have a need to hire qualified persons and that socially unrepresented groups have a right to be hired preferentially if they meet position qualification standards. An organizational issue concerns the best method for achieving this objective: (a) hiring "quotas" of minorities or (b) establishing "goals" for increasing minority representation and reaching them with "good faith efforts."

This potential conflict situation suggested by the interplay surrounding these methods is complicated by three factors. First, both methods are sometimes implicitly raised simultaneously. Second, court decisions, reflecting a societal level of analysis, often impinge on organizational and individual employee preferences. Third, personnel professionals are often accustomed to view personnel management issues as if they fall into quadrant I (computational decision) and are thus unused to dealing with problem definition conflicts.

What one can observe, then, is two conflicting computational strategies— selection based on expertise and selection based on social representation—

overlapping with the necessarily judgmental aspect of most selection decisions. The combination has the effect of continually deflecting discussion from the substance of the agenda item itself—the actual selection of a candidate—to a discussion of problem definition. Affirmative action discussions have a way of moving back and forth between computational strategy "goals," computational strategy "quotas," judgmental strategy, and a need to redefine the problem itself. Three conclusions follow from these examples.

1. Personnel administration includes issues that fall into each of the four quadrants.

2. Frequently, disputes over substantive objectives mask procedural disputes over which quadrant is the appropriate one in which to resolve an issue.

3. Agreement or lack of it on desired outcomes and degree of certainty regarding knowledge of cause-effect relationships will cue the politican, administrator, citizen, and analyst to the expected dynamics.

BENEFITS OF THE NEW APPROACH

Earlier in the paper the following three questions were posed relating to the field of public personnel administration:

1. Academician: How do the pieces fit together?

2. Practitioner: What action should I take now?

3. Employee: What can I hope for in this job?

Initially, it was suggested that longstanding approaches to public personnel administration could not adequately answer these questions. Then a new framework was presented for the study of public personnel administration. This approach attempts to bring current knowledge of organization theory and administrative behavior to bear on our understanding of the personnel field. Here, organized around the three guiding questions, the benefits of the framework are identified.

The Academician's View

The framework developed in this paper indicates that any personnel management issue, as with any management issue in general, can be classified according to agreement or disagreement on outcomes desired and means of achieving the outcomes. It further suggests that the agreement or disagreement results from interplay of actors at three different levels: environment, organization, and employee. Once the issue is classified, a context is available, signaling the appropriateness of different problem solving strategies: computational, compromise, judgmental, or inspirational.

The analytical scheme proposed here complements other work currently under way in the public personnel field. It may be useful, in seeking to identify the benefits of the new approach, to draw some comparisons. Levine and Nigro[21] have identified a juridical environment, a manpower management environment, a program priority environment, and a manpower policy environment as task environments whose demands impinge on personnel management issues confronting a single agency. They identify organizational and environmental levels of analysis and action and show how interplay between the two levels highlights "cleavages" with resultant strains, conflicts, and contradictions for an agency's top management. Siegel,[22] also utilizing a systems approach, identifies four personnel subsystems—procurement, allocation, development, and sanction—that constitute functional needs to be satisfied by the human resource management system within an agency. He describes each of these functional areas in some detail and notes the systemic relationships between them. The framework proposed in this paper adds to each of these approaches in the following ways.

It poses more explicitly an individual employee level of analysis in addition to organizational and environmental levels. Also, it offers general theoretical guidelines to understanding the driving force at each level. We have argued that individual demands on personnel systems primarily stem from the desire for equity, that organizational demands stem from the desire to control the allocation of resources within the agency and to reduce uncertainty in relationships with task environment elements, and that environmental demands are aimed at moving the agency to produce "socially" desirable outcomes.

Both the Levine and Nigro and the Siegel approaches highlight the strain placed on personnel management due to what might be called substantive differences between the demands coming from actors at different levels of analysis. For example, Levine and Nigro illustrate their argument by showing the strain that results from the agency's desire to establish its own future projects and manpower needs and the priorities established by national policy makers. Importantly, the framework developed in this paper cites another and perhaps even more fundamental source of conflict. Conflict stems not only from differences over outcomes; it also originates in "process" differences. This is the conflict that results when decision makers disagree on the definition of the problem or, in the analytical scheme presented here, the quadrant into which an issue falls. As an example, when an organization uses a *judgmental* strategy to select middle and upper management personnel and a *computational* strategy to select lower-level employees, the desire for a consistent selection procedure brought about by affirmative action mandates will clash directly into a process conflict. The idea of "process" conflict is not well developed in the management field; we are now beginning to analyze data from a project designed to increase our understanding of it.

The Practitioner's View

The framework offers parallel benefits to the practitioner. In deciding, for example, how to perform a particular function, the framework suggests that the personnel manager choose one method over others after evaluating the demands and foreseeable consequences on employees, the organization, and elements of the environment. A review of some of these pressures and functions will demonstrate this point:

1. Employees implicitly argue for jobs that will satisfy higher-order needs as well as lower-order needs (jobs allowing autonomy, responsibility, and advance-

ment), while the organization often prefers standardized, simplified, and specialized jobs that increase managerial control and calculation of production processes.

2. Demands for social equity by racial, ethnic, and sexual minorities precipitate changes in job design, recruitment, selection, promotion, and training, and these can run counter to union demands.

While the framework is primarily aimed at analysis at a specific point in time and with respect to a single issue, it implies that action taken on one personnel issue will affect other issues and that satisfying the demands of actors at one level of action will stimulate demands by actors at other levels. Here are some examples:

1. Efforts to recruit female employees will not result in long-term increases in female staff if the company enters a period of staff reduction and if staff layoff and retention decisions are made on the basis of seniority.

2. An emphasis on entry-level minority recruitment will not result in increases in the number of minority supervisors if promotional criteria are based on seniority; unions may negotiate for promotion on the basis of seniority.

The personnel managers will become aware of themselves as mediators of employee, organization, and environmental interests and demands as reflected in personnel issues. In addition to the conflict stemming from the interplay of forces at each of these levels, the framework alerts personnel managers to conflicts stemming from "process" issues. For example, personnel managers who embark on a job enrichment program must be prepared to mediate conflict among those people responsible for job design, classification, and compensation functions.

The Employee's View

The framework suggests that much of personnel management is political in nature, involving trade-offs among employee, organizational, and environmental demands. Employees, acting individually, clearly carry the least weight in this process. The framework implicitly suggests that employees assess the degree to which their individual job expectations are reflected in organization and environmental actions. If dissatisfied, one would expect to see employees organize more effectively to bring attention to their demands.

To conclude, there are three important concerns facing personnel management today: the academician's interest in developing a theoretical framework that will assist in understanding, explaining, and possibly predicting the behavioral dynamics and discussion surrounding human resource management; the practitioner's concern for selecting appropriate personnel management techniques based on relevant evaluative criteria; and the employee's concern with interpreting how the organization will affect his or her future. A value-analytical framework that views personnel management decisions not as the implementation of general principles such as merit or equity but as choices whose efficacy is determined by their responsiveness to the needs of organizations, employees, and the public provides a suitable frame of reference to deal with these concerns.

NOTES

1. James D. Thompson, *Organizations in Action* (New York: McGraw-Hill, 1967), p. 13.
2. Two exceptions are the systemic approaches taken by Gilbert B. Siegel, *Human Resource Management in Public Organizations: A Systems Approach* (Los Angeles: University Publishers, 1973) and Felix A. Nigro and Lloyd G. Nigro, *The New Public Personnel Administration* (Itasca, Illinois: Peacock, 1976).
3. David H. Rosenbloom, "Public Personnel Administration and the Constitution: An Emergent Approach," *Public Administration Review* 35 (January-February 1975):56.
4. There would seem to be a mutually reinforcing dynamic working here. The academic describes the personnel field in low-level conceptual terms, and the practitioner acts *as if* this were implicitly so. The one case reinforces the other. See Jay M. Shafritz, *Public Personnel Mangement: The Heritage of Civil Service Reform* (New York: Praeger, 1975) for more on this relationship.
5. O. Glenn Stahl, *Public Personnel Administration*, 7th ed. (New York: Harper and Row, 1976).
6. For examples of this applied to position classification, see Michael L. Monroe, "The Position Classifier's Dilemma," *The Bureaucrat*, 4 (July 1975):204–206, and Frank J. Thompson, "Classification as Politics," in *People in Public Service: A Reader in Public Personnel Administration*, 2nd ed. Eds., Robert T. Golembiewski and Michael Cohen, (Itasca, Illinois: Peacock, 1976), pp. 515–29.
7. Loc. cit.
8. Charles Milton, *Ethics and Expediency in Personnel Management* (Columbia: University of South Carolina Press, 1970), p.5.
9. Ibid., p. 163.
10. Versions of the academician's, practitioner's, and employee's questions are originally associated with Immanuel Kant. Wendell G. Holladay's article "The Uses of Knowledge and the Consequences of Knowing." *Key Reporter* 41 (Autumn 1975) brought them to our attention.
11. Thompson, p. 134.
12. Neely Gardner, "Action Training and Research: Something Old and Something New," *Public Administration Review* 34 (March/April 1974):106–15. The three levels of analysis, while perhaps traditional, offer the conceptual benefit of tying into a growing change strategy—action training and research. At its best, AT and R seeks to bring together participants representing each of these three levels to work to identify contentious issues and reach satisfactory courses of action that participants will feel committed to implement.
13. J. Stacy Adams, "Inequity in Social Exchange," in *Advances in Experimental Psychology*, ed. L. Berkowitz (New York: Academic Press, 1965), We have borrowed from Adams's work on equity theory to arrive at this conclusion about employee desires. It is the concept of equity that allows one to understand whether psychological contract between employee and employer is workable. See Edgar Schein, *Organizational Psychology*, 2nd ed. (Englewood Cliffs: Prentice Hall, 1970), p. 12 for discussion of the psychological contract.
14. Thompson, chap. 1. Our belief is that management's primary task, conceptually speaking, is to reduce the force of entropy. To do so, it must focus first and foremost on the organization's environment. From this viewpoint, achieving predictable employee contributions, providing they meet acceptable production standards, is often more important than maximizing employee contributions. Predictability reduces the need to develop contingency plans that might be needed to deal with variable production outcomes, thus simplifying the task of managing.
15. Herbert Simon, *Administrative Behavior*, 2nd ed. (New York: The Free Press, 1956), chaps. 4,5.

16. Erving Goffman, *Presentation of Self in Everyday Life* (New York: Anchor, 1959).
17. Eric Berne, *Games People Play* (New York: Ballentine, 1964), chap. 2.
18. James March and Herbert Simon, *Organizations* (New York: John Wiley & Sons, 1958), pp. 141–47.
19. Charles E. Lindblom, "The Science of Muddling Through," *Public Administration Review* 19 (Spring 1959):80.
20. F. E. Emery and E. L. Trist, "The Causal Texture of Organizational Environments," *Human Relations* 18 (February 1965):21–32.
21. Charles H. Levine and Lloyd G. Nigro, "The Public Personnel System: Can Juridical Administration and Manpower Management Coexist?" *Public Administration Review* 35 (January-February 1975):98–107.
22. Siegel, *Human Resource Management*, loc. cit.

Merit, Morality, and Democracy

Frederick C. Mosher

Over the century that separated the presidencies of Andrew Jackson and Franklin D. Roosevelt, the people of the United States built an ideology which related the public service to their indigenous concepts of democracy in a unique but basically coherent fashion. The ideology came to be known as "merit principles" and the methods devised to give them effect as the "merit system." *Merit* became the administrative expression and foundation of democratic government. As President Theodore Roosevelt said in his first message to Congress in 1901: "The merit system of making appointments is in its essence as democratic and American as the common school system itself." The goals, the norms, and the criteria of merit systems were unambiguous and widely agreed upon. This is attested to by the repetitiveness of countless studies at all levels of government which aimed to strengthen democracy through improved personnel practices. Until World War II few such studies failed to recommend extension of civil service coverage, improved competitive examinations, precise job classifications, and "equal pay for equal work." A neutral, efficient civil service was viewed as not merely desirable; it was essential to democracy itself.

Developments in the second third of the twentieth century have befogged the meaning of merit principles and confused the content of merit systems. The reasons for this growing ambiguity are partly semantic. No doubt many Americans equate

Frederick C. Mosher, now retired, taught at the University of Virginia and the University of California at Berkeley.

From *Democracy and the Public Service* by Frederick C. Mosher. Copyright © 1968 by Oxford University Press, Inc. Reprinted by permission.

the merit system of employment with trappings and practices inherited from the past and held to be of questionable value and declining relevance today: independent civil service commissions, paper and pencil tests, individual job "ownership," unchallengeable job security, paperwork, and red tape. The real sense of "merit principles," however, is a good deal more profound than these popularized views, and the doubts about its current applicability go well beyond questions of semantics. They derive from changes in the society, its ethos, its educational system, its vocational structure—changes so extensive that one wonders whether the old "merit principles" will ever be operational again.

The merit ideology was the progeny of many different parents. Their combination of genes produced an unusual child that, as suggested above, grew into a reasonably solid, consistent, and even handsome adult. Chief among the parents was the Protestant Ethic: respect for, even worship of, work not merely as a practical necessity but as a high moral imperative. As it applies to employment, the word *merit* bears two connotations, both dominantly ethical. One is the sense of deserving and rewarding on the basis of past performance or demonstration (for example, in competitive examination). Work is fundamentally good, desirable, meritorious; the reward for the deserving is the job or the promotion. The second connotation of merit concerns the grounds or criteria of consideration and judgment. A judge considers an argument on its merits; a scientist considers a proposition on its merits; an employing officer considers a prospective or current employee on his or her merits. In all three usages, merits have to do with considerations of intrinsic, relevant value or truth. Negatively, the considerations scrupulously discard any irrelevancies—whether legal technicalities or useless scientific data or factors unrelated to one's worthiness to perform a job of work. In its early days, merit system reform paid more attention to the negative aspect, the elimination of the irrelevancies, than to the positive. The primary extrinsic (irrelevant) ingredient at the beginning was political considerations; others (originally or subsequently) were race, religion, evidence of formal education, family relationship, friendship, and personality attributes.[1] Later, as job specialization developed, so did the sciences of job analysis and aptitude measurement. The positive connotation of merit assumed a more definite shape: the measured capacity to perform a specific type of work.

Beyond the Protestant Ethic, there were a number of other contributors to the unusual character of American ideals of public service merit. Among these some of the principal ones were: heavy stress on the *individual*, measured on his or her own "merits" in competition with everyone else; *egalitarianism*—an open service with equal treatment for all (though within unstated limits) regardless of family, race, religion, social status, formal education, political affiliation; *scientism*—faith that there is a correct solution to every personnel question that can be discovered objectively and scientifically—a best person for each job, a correct placement for each person, an accurate classification for each position, a correct wage for each class, and so on; *separatism*—resting on the double foundation of nonpolitical merit and scientism, personnel work removed from the rest of government and conducted disinterestedly, scientifically, and independently; *unilateralism*—government as sovereign and its decisions, when reached through proper procedures, final.

The Protestant Ethic with respect to work carries no such compelling authority in our society as it once did, particularly among youth and the disadvantaged.

Within the field of public personnel management, professionalism, career systems, and collective bargaining have all challenged the Protestant Ethic and the other parents of merit principles. Some of the elements long considered extrinsic to merit have become part of the "main course": for example, transcripts of educational achievement, professional ascription, membership in appropriate organizations, evidences of political or programmatic sympathy with the public hiring agency, political loyalty, personal "suitability." In fields of employee shortage, there is little competition at entrance or in advancement until one reaches the upper grades. Career systems and labor organizations alike seek to protect their members from the competition of outsiders and also tend to reduce competition among their members on the basis of "merit," substituting the less controversial criterion of seniority. Much of the public service is now careerized, and this means, by and large, that large sectors of it are substantially closed rather than open services. While the scientific drive is on the ascendancy in most fields of knowledge, it seems in personnel administration to be giving ground to the professions, to the universities, and to collective bargaining. Labor organizations are dislodging civil service commissions from their traditional—and still often cherished—posture of independence and driving them into the arms of management. The concept of unilateralism is directly challenged by both collective bargaining and professionalism, each of which demands increasing influence of employees and their organizations upon governmental decisions.

It is interesting that over many decades the development of the civil service, the career systems, the professions, and organized labor had a common enemy—politics and patronage. Perhaps this is why, for the most part, they were accommodating and mutually supportive toward one another.[2] But in the places and to the extent that the common enemy has been beaten back, it has abandoned the battleground to the former allies, who contest with each other. One thing seems clear: the principles of merit and the practices whereby they were given substance are changing and must change a good deal more to remain viable in our society. We can of course continue to use the word, and perhaps we should, but let us not deceive ourselves as to its changing meaning in relation to the determining of merit qualifications; the relations of these to jobs, decisions, and performance in government; the locus of control over job definition and applicant evaluation. We can still have merit systems, but they are not the same as those we inherited from the past and still teach (or delude) ourselves about.

MERIT AND THE UNDERPRIVILEGED

The ideals that gave support to merit principles were of course never fully realized. In fact, given the gross imperfections in American society and its toleration of discrimination and of a more or less permanently underprivileged minority, some of those ideals were, at least in part, mutually incompatible. The concept of equal treatment hardly squares with competitive excellence in employment when a substantial part of the population is effectively denied the opportunity and/or the motivation to compete on an equal basis through cultural and educational impoverishment. The recent awakening of the United States and some of its governments to the problems of racial minorities, poverty, the ghettos, presents another challenge to merit principles and one that promises to grow in the future. There is little agreement about the various strategies that have been suggested to alleviate and hopefully correct the problems or about the vigor with which they should be pursued. But two points are quite clear. First, the nation is committed to doing something; it cannot again bury its head in the sand. Second, a key element in both the short and the long range will be employment.

Among the fastest growing employers in the nation are governments, particularly at the state and local levels where the employment growth rate is running about four times higher than the national average. As federal programs develop for educating, training, and retraining the unemployed and underemployed, there is—and increasingly will be—pressure on the governments to hire substantial numbers of the poor and particularly the products of these programs. Already this pressure has been reflected in efforts to relax or otherwise modify accustomed civil service practices to accommodate this new demand. Among the changes that have been proposed—most of which have already been tried in one jurisdiction or another—are: *restructuring and redesigning work* so that new, lower-level jobs with minimal qualification requirements are created to assist professional and administrative personnel (for example the federal MUST program: Maximum Utilization of Skills and Training); *reexamining and reducing educational and experience requirements* for lower-level positions and eliminating certain disqualifications, such as arrest records; *designing training programs* specifically for governmental types of work, assuring trainees of appointments on completion of training or even appointing them prior to training; *waiving competitive examinations for appointments; systematically developing programs for training and advancement of the poor* in planned, lifetime careers—the "new careers" program; *expanding or improving public services* for the primary purpose of creating new jobs for the underprivileged (for example, the proposal that the post office return to twice-a-day home delivery of mail).

Some of these actions may be taken without doing violence to traditional merit principles. The first one listed, for example, may contribute to overall efficiency by alleviating the pressure for professionals in fields where they are in short supply. But others almost dictate a departure from the traditional criterion of merit and the competitive principle with which it is associated. Insofar as they provide preference in public employment for the poor—and perhaps absolute preference—they are substituting for or adding to merit the criterion of need. It should be noted that this is not the first time that government employment has been used for the primary purpose of benefiting the employees. This practice was widely utilized during the New Deal period, particularly by the WPA (Works Projects Administration). But there is a significant difference. The New Deal programs were conceived and administered as temporary; they provided work for the unemployed until such time as the economy returned to its feet—as it turned out, until World War II. WPA workers acquired no tenure in their jobs. The various undertakings of the poverty program, on the other hand, are intended to provide permanent employment opportunities, hopefully with rising expectations of progressive careers. In those jurisdictions that have civil service laws, the new appointees would acquire civil service status.

It is therefore not surprising that there is a growing feeling among many civil service proponents that they must protect merit principles against the more radical proposals of the poverty program. On the other hand, representatives of the poor in the local councils and of the OEO organizations themselves at all levels are increasingly impatient with civil service for moving too slowly; not creating enough job and career opportunities for the poor; not providing quick, easy, and noncompetitive processes for employment. Further, they can assert with some justice that the civil service claims of equal opportunity and open service never really applied to a substantial minority of the American population. Tensions between the poverty program and civil service are inevitable and will probably grow in the future. How far merit principles must or will "give" in this struggle is a guess. But clearly there will have to be some accommodations made at the bottom of the public employment ladder as well as in the middle.

ADMINISTRATIVE MORALITY

During this period when the traditional principles of merit are being challenged, similar forces are undermining the old articles of faith through which administration and democracy were reconciled. The ideological crutch that segregated policy and politics from administration can today hardly satisfy any but the blind or those who willfully close their eyes. The ideal of objective responsibility is increasingly threatened by both professionalization and unionization with their narrower objectives and their foci upon the welfare and advancement of their own members. At the same time, the idea of representative bureaucracy has acquired a meaning that is not altogether reassuring to the general public interest. Most of the professions are well represented in their appropriate enclaves, as are most of those growing categories of employees who join in collective organizations. Even the poor may now lay some claim to representation in the community councils, though their effectiveness is at least questionable. But who represents that majority of citizens who are not in any of these groups?

The knowledge explosion and the tremendous growth of higher education have greatly enhanced the technical and cognitive capacities of the public service to perform its tasks. At the same time, may they not have weakened its concern for and competence in reaching social decisions responsibly with the full polity in view?

This is essentially a moral question; indeed it is *the* moral question of the public service in American democracy. Among the larger units of American government, the older and more overt violations of individual honesty and trust have been minimized. In terms of the billions of dollars involved in governmental transactions every month, the amount of theft, fraud, bribery, and even expense account padding are today comparatively trivial. Few sectors of American society are more honest and more carefully policed in these regards than the administrative arms of its larger governments.

The harder and infinitely more important issue of administrative morality today attends the reaching of decisions on questions of public policy that involve competitions in loyalty and perspective between broad goals of the polity (the phantom public interest) and the narrower goals of a group, bureau, clientele, or union. Chester I. Barnard defined administrative responsibility as primarily a moral question or, more specifically, as the resolution of competing and conflicting codes—legal, technical, personal, professional, and organizational—in the reaching of individual decisions.[3] Barnard wrote primarily of business administration; students of government would add a less definable but nevertheless all-important code—the public benefit.

The danger is that the developments in the public service of the mid-century decades may be subtly, gradually but profoundly moving the weight toward the partial, the corporate, the professional perspective and away from that of the general interest. In this connection a number of developments noted earlier may be reviewed: the tendency of "elite" professions to dominate the governance of bureaus and other public agencies; the dominance in matters of recruitment, selection, and advancement of professional groups, both in and outside government, and the waning influence of general government (for example, civil service) agencies; the deepening of professional specializations; the development of self-governing professional career systems within public agencies; the corporatism of organized public employees, especially those in professional and subprofessional fields.

The multifarious systems of American government include a variety of built-in institutional and procedural devices to protect against narrowly based, functionally parochial decisions. Most familiar are the divisions and sharing of functions and powers of government among different levels and units; the division and sharing of powers among executive, legislative, and judicial branches; the various devices of executive coordination and control, including particularly the executive budget; and appointive political leadership. Clearly, however, occupational groups can successfully overpass most of these hurdles and in some cases even use them to their own power advantage. The division of official and legitimate power among many satrapies (units of government, executive bureaus, legislative committees) strengthens the influence of the unified occupational group that has a common perspective and objective as well as active participants at all levels and in and outside of many units.

Paul H. Appleby demonstrated, in his lectures on *Morality and Administration in Democratic Government*,[4] that the traditional and popularized protections against immorality in public administration—checks and balances, decentralization, federalism, and others—are a good deal less than effective. In fact their protective value is probably, on balance, negative. Appleby relied instead on two other (and in considerable degree antipodal) institutional mechanisms to assure morality in the public service. One is found in the workings of an open system of politics whereby administrative behavior and decisions must ultimately be judged against their potential influence in the ballot box. Any effort to remove an area of governmental activity from general political responsibility—to "protect" it from politics is, per se, a threat to administrative morality since it encourages the administrator to approach her or his problems narrowly, to minimize or neglect or ignore the general interest.

The second protective mechanism, according to Appleby, is hierarchy within administration which, if effective, forces important decisions to higher levels of determination or at least higher levels of review where perspectives are necessarily broader, less technical and expert, and more political. Unlike most other writers on administration of his time, Appleby minimized the significance of hierarchy as a basis of authority. He liked to quote Chester Barnard to the effect that ". . . experienced and effective administrators prefer not to use authority."[5] Hierarchy, on the other hand, is a means to broaden the perspective for and the responsibility of decision.

The establishment of professional enclaves within public agencies is, of course, a very direct threat to both of Appleby's protective mechanisms: open politics and responsible hierarchy. By removing itself as far as possible from the normal channels of political complaint, debate, and appeal, a professionally dominated agency denies the general public the opportunity for democratic direction and decision. By closing the elite of the hierarchy to all but professionals, it denies assurance of broadly based and disinterested judgment on problems.

Appleby felt, even more vigorously than some of his contemporaries, the danger of experts being "on top rather than on tap." "Perhaps there is no single problem in public administration of moment equal to the reconciliation of the increasing dependence upon experts with an enduring democratic reality."[6] He feared that functional specialization within agencies would result in "relative inattention to the large public" and pointed particularly to one form of this: "preoccupation with subject-matter expertise, as with economics, law, medicine biology, physics. . ."[7]—fields that represent all the professions. Finally, he feared the effects of what I have called career systems of personnel administration—overreliance upon promotions from within, closing the door to outside recruitment, overemphasis upon security and seniority, and so on. Were Appleby writing today, his alarms would no doubt be shriller because some of the recent developments were only on the horizon at the time that he wrote of administrative morality. Professional (as against civil service) control of personnel is now much more evident. Political appointees, the broadly based generalists upon whom he relied so heavily and of whom he was one, are increasingly professionalized and specialized themselves. The knowledge explosion has much more closely linked government professionals with their subject-matter counterparts in the universities and has given a far stronger scientific-expertise flavor to public administration.

In his writings about administrative morality, Paul Appleby addressed himself principally to the institutional arrangements that tended to encourage or to endanger moral behavior. He did not dwell upon the ethical problems of individual public servants or groups thereof. In 1965, this lacuna was eloquently corrected by Stephen K. Bailey in a memorial essay to Appleby.[8] Bailey, building upon precepts drawn from Appleby's writings, teachings and actions, synthesized the essentials of moral behavior in public service in two categories: moral qualities and mental attitudes. The essential moral qualities are three: optimism, courage, and fairness tempered by charity. The words in all three cases are inadequate to the intended meaning. Optimism is the confidence and capacity to deal with ambiguous situations constructively and purposively. Courage is the ability to decide and act in the face of difficulties when withdrawal would be an easier response and the ability to abide by principle even in unpopular causes. Fairness tempered by charity is demanded by the standards of justice and the necessity that value-laden decisions be governed by the public interest.

The "mental attitudes" that Bailey identifies as requisites of personal ethics in the public service are also three in number. All are cognitive in nature, based upon knowledge and understanding and are therefore learnable and teachable. They include recognition of (1) the moral ambiguity of all men and of all public policies; (2) the contextual forces that condition moral priorities in the public service; and (3) the paradoxes of procedures. Under the first of these, Bailey stresses the ambivalence of most public decisions as between personal and private interests and the public interest and, as a corollary, the morally ambivalent effect of public policies. Seldom if ever can a policy be either totally right or totally wrong. In his reference to the awareness of context, Bailey emphasizes the shifting of value priorities, the necessity of flexibility, and the increasing difficulty and complexity of value choices as one rises in the hierarchy. In his reference to procedures, Bailey again stresses flexibility; the use of laws, rules, and procedures to promote fairness and openness; and their abuse to prevent action and to obscure the public interest.

The Barnard-Appleby-Bailey construct of responsibility and morality in public decision making provides a sound base for a philosophy of a public service that is both consistent with and supportive of democracy. The construct contains certain ingredients which, though fairly obvious, are not universally accepted or even recognized. One is that there is a high ethical content in most significant public decisions; public problems do not succumb simply to factual analysis. A second is that the standards of ethical behavior that are applicable and sufficient to a private citizen in his private social relationships are not in themselves adequate for the public decisions of an administrator. The same limitation applies to professional codes of ethics in their applicability to decisions by professionals in the public servic public character of governmental decisions adds complicating dimensions to moral behavior. A third is that public decision problems are seldom black or white in relation to their ethical content and consequences. This is another way of saying that they are difficult and that the "best" solution is seldom without its costs. Finally—and least understood—is the proposition that politics and administrative organization are themselves the best protectors of administrative morality, provided they are open and public.

But if we can accept the Barnard-Appleby-Bailey construct as a philosophic base, how can it be made operational among administrators? Must each one learn it for himself by successive finger burnings—as for the most part Barnard and Appleby and Bailey must have done? Not many administrators are as perceptive and sensitive as these three, and one doubts that such an experiential process would be very effective, even in the very long range. Further, it is clear that some of the central tenets of this view of public morality run directly counter to the doctrine of a number of professions that are important sources of public administrators— probably the majority of them. Most professions are at best ambivalent, at worst downright hostile, toward government in general and politics in particular. Most seek to shield themselves from politics, and this of course means that they oppose open politics. Most oppose the incursion of nonprofessionals into their professional decision-making territory. Most of those that have to do primarily with things rather than people are impatient with ambiguities, compromise, administrative procedure. Those professions that are sciences or that emulate or aspire to be sciences— and this includes the majority of them—emphasize values and processes consistent with the search for absolute knowledge and truth. The exigencies of public problems, imperfectly defined and demanding actions on the basis of partial and often questionable information, are seldom consonant with such values and processes. The recent thrust of many of the professions is not very promising for the development of the kind of administrative morality envisaged by Barnard, Appleby, and Bailey.

DEMOCRACY AND EDUCATION

The winds of change, however, bear other straws, straws that promise new and more meaningful definitions of merit and also a broader and deeper understanding of administrative responsibility. One of these straws is simply the urgency of public problems. The underdeveloped populations of the world are impatient, as are our own minorities, our own impoverished, and our own urban populations. Action will not wait for the completion of data gathering and analysis or for the negotiation of boundaries between occupational monopolies. A second straw is a product of the knowledge explosion itself, which among other things has taught the interconnection of social conditions and the obstinacy of any social problem to respond to a specific, functionally defined solution. The educators by themselves are unable to cope with the problem of education because it goes far beyond teaching. The doctors and the health officers are confronted with the same situation in the area of health, as are the police in the area of crime, the transportation engineers in transportation, the welfare workers in poverty, and all of these in racial discrimination and hostility. Each profession is learning the hard way of its own inadequacies and its underlying dependence upon the methods and understandings of other disciplines. The interdisciplinary and interprofessional approach is no longer a mere academic curio, an interesting but dilettantish experiment. In today's world it is an absolute necessity, for no discipline, no profession can handle even its own problems by itself. This lesson was learned a good many years ago by the natural sciences and the "natural" professions. It is coming later and harder in the social fields, particularly economics, but its ultimate acceptance is inevitable. The interconnection of social problems and the interdependence of disciplines in dealing with them are two sides of the same coin.

Another product of the knowledge explosion has been a growing faith of the society and particularly of its leaders in the value of research to enable us to deal more effectively with our problems. This growth, too, started in the natural sciences and is least questioned there. It has recently spread rapidly in the life and medical sciences. It is beginning to develop in the social sciences. It is interesting, paradoxical, and indeed tragic that government has so tremendously stimulated and supported the physical sciences while giving the back of its hand to those fields of social knowledge upon which government and the society itself most immediately depend. Who first reaches the moon and when he does it are not of overpowering importance. What kind of an earth he returns to is. The problems of Hunter's Point, Selma, Harlem, Lagos, Havana, and Hong Kong are not going to be solved by antiballistic missiles or atomic energy or space spectaculars. They are human problems that can respond only to human remedies. We are only beginning to learn how to analyze these problems and to devise means of coping with them. Social policies must be focused on values, tempered by sympathy, grounded in knowledge.

The higher officials in the public service are products of the colleges and universities and principally of their professional departments and schools. This will be increasingly, even perhaps exclusively true in the future. These persons will have a growing influence in the determination of public policy. Ultimately the possibilities of a truly democratic public service will depend upon the mobility whereby intelligent individuals from all walks of life may progress to higher education and the kind of orientation and education they receive in the universities. On the first point there is evidence of progress, though there is a long way to go. On the second, in spite of centripetal, problem-oriented pressures described earlier, there remains a high and perhaps growing degree of specialization in particular fields accompanied by a declining exposure to and interest in broader social areas, including the context within which each specialization operates.

Merit as traditionally defined is today an anachronism for a large and important part of the public service. In the future, merit will increasingly be measured by professionals against criteria established by the professions and by the universities that spawn them. It will depend in part upon technical and cognitive qualifications in the fields of specialization. The danger is that these will be too large a part of the criteria. Truly meritorious performance in public administration will depend at least equally upon the values, objectives, and moral standards that the administrator brings to his or her decisions and upon his or her ability to weigh the relevant premises judiciously in the approach taken to the problems at hand. The administrator's code can hardly be as simple as the Ten Commandments, the Boy Scout Code, or the code of ethics of any of the professions; decisions will usually require some kind of interpretation of *public* and *public interest* —explicit, implicit, even unconscious.

Such decisions are difficult, complex, and soul testing, for the qualities they demand search the depths of both mind and spirit. As Bailey wrote, "Virtue without understanding can be quite as disastrous as understanding without virtue."[9] Understanding entails a degree of knowledge, a sense of the relationships among phenomena, an appreciation of both social and private values. Most of the ingredients of understanding can be learned, and many of them can be taught. They go well beyond the mastery of scientific method, substantive knowledge, and professional technique. They go beyond the boundaries of the typical profession or the curriculum of the standard professional training course. Yet understanding in this sense must become a major ingredient of public service merit in the future. This will require a degree of modesty and even humility on the part of individual professionals (and professors) about their fields, a curiosity about and an accommodation toward other fields of study and vocation, a sense of the society and the polity and of the relationships between them and the field of occupational concentration.

Governmental agencies have for the most part accepted professional and academic definitions and measurements of merit as applied to specific academic and occupational fields. Most of them have, however, minimized the broader understanding discussed in the preceding paragraph as an element in appointment or advancement. The more difficult, less measurable elements of morality in public decision making have been almost completely ignored in discussions of merit principles, although they may well be the most important criteria of all.

As in our culture in the past and in a good many other civilizations, the nature and quality of the public service depend principally upon the system of education. Almost all of our future public administrators will be college graduates; and within two or three decades, a majority of them will have graduate degrees. Growing numbers of public administrators are returning to graduate schools for refresher courses, mid-career training, and higher degrees. These trends suggest that university faculties will have growing responsibility for preparing and developing public servants both in their technical specialities and in the broader social fields with which their professions interact. The universities, therefore, offer the best hope of making the professions safe for democracy.

NOTES

1. But never have *all* the extrinsic elements been eliminated. Thus, status as a veteran of a foreign war, particularly a disabled veteran, or a widow of a veteran gave (and still gives) one preferment in employment and, in some places, in advancement. Likewise, at one or

another time and place in our history, we have offered employment preference on such nonmerit grounds as sex, age, and physical handicap. Economic need was a qualifying factor for employment in some agencies of the New Deal, and is currently reemerging to challenge merit purism.

2. The same common enemy may also explain the mutually supportive attitudes over the years between the veterans' organizations and civil service. Employment preference on the basis of war experience or disability or widowhood can hardly be reconciled with a "pure" definition of merit. As one student put it: "We know it [veterans' preference] as essentially the negation of merit." (John F. Miller, "Veteran Preference in the Public Service," *Problems of the American Public Service*, Commission of Inquiry on Public Service Personnel [New York:McGraw-Hill, 1935] p. 309.) But both merit and veterans opposed patronage.

3. Chester I. Barnard, *The Functions of the Executive* (Cambridge: Harvard University Press, 1948), chapter XVII.

4. Paul H. Appleby, *Morality and Administration in Democratic Government* (Baton Rouge, Louisiana: Louisiana State University Press, 1952).

5. Ibid., p. 205.

6. Ibid., p. 145.

7. Ibid., p.145.

8. Stephen K. Bailey, "Ethics and the Public Service," in *Public Administration and Democracy: Essays in Honor of Paul H. Appleby*, ed. Roscoe C. Martin (Syracuse, New York: Syracuse University Press, 1965).

9. Ibid., p. 285.

Civil Service and Managing Work:
Some Unintended Consequences

Robert T. Golembiewski

Nature seldom allows us to get what we wish without paying her price. This truism is commonly illustrated by the delicate balance in animal life that often cannot be disturbed to satisfy man's wants (for example, for fox hunting) without demanding something of man in return (for example, by increases in the rabbit population and in crop damage).

The several civil service systems in this country also illustrate this bittersweet combination of intended and unintended consequences. The argument here will not go to the extreme of one observer, in whose judgment the United States Civil Service Commission was the single greatest obstacle to the successful waging of

Robert T. Golembiewski is research professor of political science and management at the University of Georgia.

Reprinted from Robert T. Golembiewski, "Civil Service and Managing Work: Some Unintended Consequences," *American Political Science Review* (February 1962), pp 961–973.

World War II.[1] Rather, the focus here will be on several characteristics of our civil service systems that have, presumably as unintended consequences, an increase in the burdens of managing work. For the most part, the analysis of management problems will derive from the research literature dealing with behavior in organizations, a field of study presently seething with activity.

THE GOAL-MATRIX OF OUR CIVIL SERVICE MOVEMENT

The nature of these unintended consequences is suggested by the matrix of goals or purposes underlying our civil service movement. The primary goal, of course, was the separation of the management of public work from party patronage. Within this overriding goal, Sayre has noted three early subsidiary purposes of our public personnel systems: (a) the guarantee of equal treatment of all employees and all applicants for employment; (b) the application of the logic (or theory) and methods of "scientific management"; and (c) the development of a public career service.[2]

These goals define the field of my present effort. Detailed analysis will demonstrate the significance of the unintended consequences for the management of work, which derive from the ways initially adopted to achieve the work. I take this opportunity to suggest the general nature of these consequences.

Consider first the overall tethers on the management of work implicit in the historical pursuit of the three purposes listed. The guarantee of equal treatment, to begin with, has never quite made peace with the managerially convenient notion that unequal contributions demand unequal reward. To take a recent and characteristic example, the teachers' union in Illinois has lately expressed violent opposition to a proposal for merit pay increases based upon performance. This opposition goes deeper than the convenience of seniority or of hours of graduate study as objective criteria for pay increases and far deeper than the blatant protectionism of hacks. However lofty the motives, the effect is clear. In practice, the struggle toward the "equal treatment" goal virtually forced public personnel systems into a monumental preoccupation with technique and mechanics. As Sayre concludes:

> Its main effect has been to move personnel administration, in the words of Gordon Clapp, "into the cold objective atmosphere of tests, scores, weighted indices, and split-digit rankings" so completely that "these technical trappings have become symbols of the merit system."[3]

The management of work pays a stiff price for such technical elegance. Work is notoriously insensitive to such easy capture, and the most subtly contrived managerial rewards and punishments might be frustrated by an awkward distribution of test scores. Moreover, these technical trappings put powerful weapons into the hands of "staff" people. That more than one "line" manager has been stymied by one of these "split-digit rankings" without, moreover, accepting the results as divinely ordained does nothing to lessen the often intense jurisdictional tugs-of-war encouraged by the traditional "line-staff" distinction. These tensions are apt to be increased by the time lag inherent in centralized administrative systems, and public personnel systems are usually operated centrally.

The logic and methods of "scientific management," second, tended to condemn managers to a treadmill even as it aided them. Scientific management was imported from the "practical" world of business where its impact was enormous.[4]

But the impact was not one way. Thus there is no denying the useful revolution in viewing work that the methods of scientific management sparked. However, as recent research particularly demonstrates, the assumptions in the logic (or theory) of scientific management concerning man and his work were mechanistic carica-tures.[5] Consequently, the manager tended to be less effective in direct relation to the degree that he patterned his behavior on the logic of the approach. That is, the reasonable methods of scientific management were often guided by an inadequate theory. Consequently, the usefulness of engineering a task with the methods of scientific management must be differentiated sharply from the usefulness of or-ganizing a task's component sequential steps in terms of the theory of scientific management.[6]

The establishment of a public career service, third, also tended to have unin-tended and unfavorable consequences that counterbalanced the favorable and intended consequences. As Sayre put it,

> Stated in its most positive terms, this objective represents an effort to provide the conditions of work which will attract and hold a public service of op-timum talents. In its negative aspects, the goal has been translated into an elaborate system of protectionism. In the area of methodology, the negative connotations have slowly but surely won the dominant position. . . .[7]

Such protectionism, of course, would often bind the manager severely even as it safeguarded him or her (and their subordinates) from arbitrary removal.

In sum, then, striving toward the purposes of civil service movement had its general costs. Three more specific sets of restrictions that burden the management of work in our civil service systems will concern us presently. These costs of our civil service systems, however, must be kept in perspective. Today we can profit from hindsight and a sophisticated research literature. The efforts to achieve the separation of the civil service from patronage, in contrast, came before enough was known about the conceptual and operational problems of the description of organi-zation, personality, or "position" to preclude an uncomplicated Tinker Toy ap-proach to all three of these elements of personnel administration. That is, simple assumptions took the place of an understanding of empirical phenomena which were at least more complex than and often essentially different from the assump-tions.

Consequently, the early approach to public personnel administration is under-standable, if inadequate. The compulsions of life could not wait on the scientific explanation of the universe. However, necessity should not be suffered to be a virtue, lest the original simplistic assumptions become too deeply buried under a specialized literature. Students of public personnel administration, fortunately, have done considerable self-critical work of late. The determined if preliminary efforts since World War II to outgrow its early biases are a leading feature of the reorientation currently under way in public administration.[8]

SUPERVISORY POWER AND CIVIL SERVICE

Perhaps the most rewarding clue to supervisory effectiveness in recent research exploits the "power" concept. "Power" refers, in general, to the ability to control the job environment. Getting recommendations for promotion accepted, for example, indicates that a supervisor has relatively high power. "Power" thus conceptually complements "authority," which refers to the degree to which the formal organization legitimates a supervisor's control of the job environment. Typically, all supervisors at the same level monitoring similar operations have similar authority; yet typically, these supervisors will differ in their power.

Power seems to be related to effective supervisory performance, whether it is exercised upwards, as influence with superiors, or downwards, as control of the specific job site. Pelz, for example, studied some fifty measures of supervisory practices and attitudes without finding any marked correlations with employee morale and attitudes. When the influence of a supervisor with his or her superior was specified, however, rather sharp differences were observed. High supervisory power was associated with effective performance.[9] Consequently, as Likert concluded, a supervisor must be an effective subordinate as well as an effective superior.[10] Otherwise, a supervisor cannot be expected to influence his or her subordinates consistently.

Similarly, power expressed as control of the job site is associated with effective performance. Likert provides much supporting data. A comparison between the top third and the bottom third of departments (ranked in terms of productivity) is particularly relevant here. Personnel in the top departments, in contrast with those in the bottom departments, uniformly attributed greater influence over "what goes on in your department" to these four sources: higher management, plant management, department manager, and the workers themselves. Moreover, the top departments also desired that greater influence be exercised by all four sources than did the bottom departments. Significantly, the greatest differences between the top and bottom departments are in the power attributed to department managers (their primary supervisors) and in the power they desired that department managers exercise.[11] These are reasonable results. A low-power supervisor has little leverage for motivating his or her people via control over the job site. That is, the workers have little reason to take him or her seriously.

If the reasons for the importance of supervisory power to effective performance seem clear enough, our civil service systems do little to ease the burdens of managing work via increases in supervisory power. This is particularly lamentable because much evidence suggests that the "power" variable may be influenced substantially by the design of the job, by the organizational structure (of which more later), and by training. The supervisor's personality, in short, does not appear to be the crucial (or major) factor in determining power.

Although only empirical research can establish the point definitely, there seems to be ample evidence of this failure in civil service systems to respond to the need of facilitating the management of work by increasing supervisory power. On the broadest level, the first and third primary goals of the civil service movement certainly do not encourage supervisory power, and (as will be demonstrated) the application of the logic and methods of scientific management has the same effect.

To become more specific, these limitations on supervisory power have many practical impacts. For example, first-line supervisors seem to have less control over hiring and firing than their counterparts in business. The difficulty in business organizations of firing or reductions-in-force need not be underplayed, but the elaborate review procedures and the novel "bumping" arrangements often found in our civil service systems [12] probably admit of less flexibility in public agencies even on the part of officials at relatively high organizational levels. Raw turnover ratios seem to support this position.[13] Similarly, the emphasis upon seniority in promotions and pay increases in the public service plus the failures of supervisory rating of employee performance[14]—both common in our civil service systems—suggest that the environment in public agencies has not been conducive to the general heightening of supervisory power.

Some counterforces are at work, although they do not promise imminent change in the present condition of limited encouragement of supervisory power. Thus the federal program for rewarding superior performance permits a modest increase in supervisory power. Even in this case, however, many agencies have apparently preferred to ride very close herd over the recommendations of lower-level supervisors or (in at least one case of which I have personal knowledge) to neglect the immediate supervisor altogether. Thus this program not only died aborning as an opportunity to increase supervisory power, but its administration may also reduce that power even further.

All this, be it noted, is not by way of an argument for arbitrary managerial or supervisory action. Just such abuses, of course, supplied motivation for the restraints emphasized above. The stress here, rather, is upon ways of reinforcing formal authority so as to permit greater effectiveness consistent with the policies of an agency. Just as in the case of any delegation, attempts to increase supervisory power imply training and the development of suitable overhead controls. Moreover, "power" in the relevant research does not imply heavy-handed coercive techniques, which most subjects interpret as lack of control of the environment. Evidence such as that reviewed below (see footnotes 48–51) supports this point. The task of inducing high supervisory power, then, is more delicate than a mere reversal of gears toward the "spoils system" or advocacy of an administrative law of the jungle.

JOB DESIGN AND CIVIL SERVICE

Similarly, our civil service systems tend to limit the potential for increasing managerial effectiveness implicit in job design. The second primary goal noted above is the chief culprit, with strong support from the goal of "equal treatment." Their interaction in increasing managerial burdens can be illustrated in two ways, by considering specific job content and by considering the place of the job in the broad organizational structure.

In its doctrine about simplifying job content, particularly, the logic of scientific management makes difficulties for managing work effectively. As in industry, at low organization levels the process of routinization has often been carried too far in the public service. The effects of "job enlargement" on employee performance, at least in business concerns, [15] suggest the contribution to effective management that may be gained by adding content to a worker's responsibilities. This may be accomplished by increasing the scope of jobs or by rotating individuals through several jobs.[16] The crucial factor does not seem to be the number of task elements given to an individual or the complexity of these elements. Patently, a job could become too complex. Rather, the significant point seems to be that various techniques of job enlargement, when they work, work because they increase the worker's control over his or her job environment.[17] Hence we see the success of plans for increasing the employee's control over factors that are not in the normal flow of work, such as that often called "bottom-up management."[18]

The effects of "job enlargement" may be explained in terms of the earlier analysis. In Likert's study, as already noted, employees in high-producing units felt that they themselves exercised and desired more power over their work than did individuals in low-producing units. This is consistent with the favorable effects on output commonly reported in the "job enlargement" literature, while it suggests an apparent paradox. Note that Hi-Pro units ranked themselves *and* three levels of supervisors as higher on "power" than did Lo-Pro units. This might seem curious but only if one assumes that there is only so much "power" to be had, so that what superiors gain subordinates must lose. The fact seems to be, on the contrary, that a high-power supervisor can afford to (and usually does) allow subordinates to exercise greater power too.[19] A low-power supervisor is in such an insecure position that he or she can seldom be so generous. The real paradox, then, is that the apparently most straightforward way of adding to one's power is often the most direct way of reducing it. The common mechanical conceptions of organized activity implicit in scientific management discourage such thinking.

The often marked consequences of job enlargement may be illustrated briefly. Machine operations in an industrial concern, for example, had been plagued by an array of difficulties: productivity and quality were falling, and tension between operators and inspectors was growing. The crucial factor was that the tool in this particular operation, when dulled to a certain point, would suddenly begin producing pieces that did not meet specifications. Inspectors were not always able to spot such sudden deteriorations in the product quickly, and operators (inspection not being *their* job) did not always cease work even when the quality was obviously unacceptable. Inspection reports helped little when they did come, the operators marking them down as "ancient history." The solution was easy. Simple gauges were given to operators to make periodic checks on their production, and the operators were allowed to decide when it was necessary to resharpen their cutting tools. The consequences: runs of defective products became shorter and less frequent; the nagging tension between inspectors and operators was reduced; and output zoomed. Examples need not be confined to industrial operations. In a paperwork operation, similarly, a rather simple change increased output by 30 percent and reduced employee turnover by 70 percent.[20]

Although the design of the job could be an important means of reducing the problems of managing work, our civil service systems do not encourage the exploitation of such techniques as job enlargement. Consider only one feature that has an inhibiting effect, the very detailed job descriptions common in the public service. That these are an important part of the mechanisms for guaranteeing equal treatment of employees and for developing a career service does little to encourage flexibility in job design. Employee unions and the civil service commission staff can make much of these job descriptions, even in cases in which employees solidly favor changes of a job-enlargement sort. The difficulty is not necessarily avoided by job descriptions that conclude: "or other duties the supervisor may designate." Custom, employee unions, and an overprotective civil service commission can void such open-ended descriptions.

Perhaps, however, this leans too heavily on personal (and limited) experience. Some administrators no doubt pay little attention to detailed job descriptions, except for such purposes as convincing the civil service commission that an individual deserves a multistep promotion. And it could be argued that the significant point is not whether detailed job descriptions exist, but whether strong employee unions exist. Even in such cases, however, the detailed job description is part of the institutional framework within which management and union must function.

In determining the place of the job in the broad organizational pattern, our civil service systems also increase the problems of managing work. Consider two characteristics that tend to dominate patterns of organization in the public service: a limited span of control and organization by function or (at lower levels) by process. These characteristics largely derive from the impact of scientific management upon public personnel administration. Analysis of these two characteristics is particularly useful because it demonstrates, among other features, their tendency to reduce supervisory power.

The analysis of these two characteristics is facilitated by some simplified graphics.[21] Figure 1A presents the orthodox organization of functions (or processes) A, B, C—which may be taken to be any components whose integration is required to perform some administrative task—under the condition of a limited span of control. Figure 1B presents the more unorthodox organization by product (or discrete subassembly), which permits a far broader span of control.

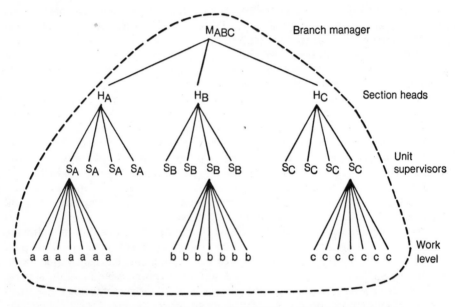

Figure 1A   Functional (process) organization with narrow span of control

The functional model, with modest reservations, can be considered the pattern for government organizing. This does not do full justice to the diversity of actual organizational arrangements, admittedly. Various factors—size, pressure of work, geography, and the like—have encouraged significant deviations from the functional model. Thus, long ago the Justice Department surrendered the fancy of having every government lawyer in the department. The functional model, however, is commonly encountered in practice, and it is certainly the most commonly prescribed model in the literature, as in the Hoover Commission's *Report on the General Management of the Executive Branch.*

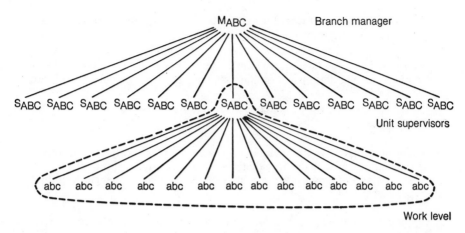

M_{ABC} Branch manager

S_{ABC} S_{ABC} S_{ABC} S_{ABC} S_{ABC} S_{ABC} S_{ABC} S_{ABC} S_{ABC} S_{ABC} S_{ABC} S_{ABC} S_{ABC} Unit supervisors

abc abc abc abc abc abc abc abc abc abc abc abc abc abc   Work level

Figure 1B   Product (discrete subassembly) organization with broad span of control

The following contrast of the functional model with the product model, then, requires that two points be kept in mind. First, the functional model does not guide all public organizing, but it is nonetheless influential. Second, the product model will not always be a feasible alternative, although it often will be. In other words, the contrast has much to recommend it, although hardly everything. Thus, although the analysis may have an either-or flavor, many other factors would serve to soften the contrast in practice and would guide the choice in specific cases of the functional model, the product model, or combinations of the two.

These simple variations in the organization of jobs in larger structures can have profound consequences for the management of work. In general, the type of structure common in most public agencies (see Figure 1A) incurs substantial costs avoided by the less familiar structure in Figure 1B. These costs derive from three features associated with these two patterns of structure: job enlargement, the size of the "managerial entity," and supervisory power.

First, to point up the obvious. Figure 1B is based upon job enlargement at all levels. Each employee at the work level in Figure 1B performs all three components of the task, and each supervisor's responsibilities encompass all three. Figure 1A's emphasis upon routinization limits the scope and perhaps thereby the effectiveness of the management of work. Of course, there are some limits on the functions or processes (A, B, C, . . .) that may be strung together. In general, however, the limits seem to be very broad indeed.[22]

Second, the "managerial entity" is vastly larger in Figure 1A than in Figure 1B. The size of the managerial entity can have profound consequences. It may appear, for instance, that the structure in Figure 1B puts too much strain on the capacities of management because of the apparently greater demands it imposes upon the supervisors. In reality, however, structures such as that in Figure 1A often imply greater (and different) demands upon management talent. Figure 1B structures reduce in significant ways the management burden carried by M_{ABC} and the supervisors as well. The difficulties faced by M_{ABC} in structures like that in Figure 1A cause considerable problems for supervisors, for example, by tending to reduce their supervisory power. Many of the problems associated with sizable organizations more generally derive not from the aggregate size of the organization but from the size of its component managerial entities. Thus the manager in our hypothetical organization in Figure 1A directs the work of 99 employees and encounters the difficulties to be enumerated below; the manager in Figure 1B oversees the work of 195 employees, yet significant problems facing the mangement of work are reduced.

The "managerial entity" concept warrants further analysis. Worthy defines it in these terms:

> The administrative unit can be no smaller than that portion of the organization falling within the jurisdiction of an individual who controls enough elements of the total process to make effective decisions regarding the total process.[23]

A high-level managerial entity might be organized around some total product, for example, water resource development in the Kings River Valley. The processing by each of several competing teams of all categories of mail received by the Government Printing Office, with each team handling all correspondence from writers whose names begin with designated letters of the alphabet, illustrates the kind of discrete subassembly around which a low-level managerial entity could be organized.

At whatever level of organization, then, a managerial entity contains that parcel of process components necessary for the performance of some discrete task. The areas enclosed by the heavy dotted lines in the two figures above symbolize managerial entities. Interpretively, any S_{ABC} in Figure 1B can "get all the way around" our hypothetical administrative task. In Figure 1A, in contrast, only M_{ABC} can do this job. M_{ABC} in Figure 1A has a managerial entity that contains one hundred individuals; that of S_{ABC} contains only fifteen.

Many of the problems in sizable organizations derive from the failure to restrict the size of the organization's managerial entities. Haire's analogy seems apt in this connection. He suggested the mushrooming problems caused by the growth in the size of organizations via the "square-cube law" applied to the story of Jack and the Beanstalk.

> . . . Jack had nothing to fear from the Giant. If he were, as he is pictured, ten times as large as a man and proportioned like one, Jack was perfectly safe. The Giant's mass would be 10^3 or a thousand times a man's, because he was ten times as big in every dimension. However, the cross section of his leg bones would have increased in only two dimensions, and they would be 10^2 or a hundred times as big as a man's. A human bone simply will not support ten times its normal load, and the Giant, in walking, would break his legs and be helpless.[24]

In a similar way, arithmetic increases in the size of the managerial entity seem to generate exponential increases in the problems of the management of work. Meeting these increases in size within the framework of the type of organization structure in Figure 1A does nothing to reduce these difficulties.

This general position can be elaborated. The size of the managerial entity, in sum, is likely to affect such significant features of administration as the time lag between the perception of a problem and action on it, which influences supervisory power; the style of supervision; the measurement and the motivation of performance; and the training of subordinates.

Patently, first, decisions will tend to be pushed upward in an organization such as that in Figure 1A; for only M_{ABC} oversees all of the components that require integration. As a result, delegation to supervisors is all but restricted to routine matters, that is, those that involve the single component supervised by any supervisor and only that component.

The separation of decision making from the action level often has significant costs. Overloading upper levels may make time pressure a very serious factor, the more so if the stakes are high. A shutdown in any of the sections in Figure 1A might cause output to drop as low as zero. The manager, then, is under great pressure to assure that A, B, and C are integrated, and he or she is likely to exert that pressure downward. This does not encourage upward communication, in turn, which is difficult enough in the "tall" organization described in Figure 1A. (Notice that Figure 1B, with 69 percent more people, has one less organizational level than Figure 1A.) The efforts of the manager to fight the daily battle of integration of the components of her or his operation and to get the information required for the job will finally tend to undercut any efforts by the supervisors to gain high power. The common development of large "staff" units complements this tendency.

In contrast, decisions in Figure 1B organizations would strongly tend to be forced down to the action level and certainly at least to the level of S_{ABC}. Indeed, M_{ABC} may have no other reasonable alternative, given his or her broad span of control. Upward communication and supervisory power will often be affected favorably. M_{ABC}, consequently, should be freed from the unremitting pressure of integration implicit in a Figure 1A structure. Downtime at any work station, for example, will not cause difficulty throughout the managerial entity. Output would fall at most by $1/N$. The manager therefore could devote her- or himself to motivating superior performance, to training and counseling and the like rather than attempting to eliminate the possibility of error.

These comments on decision making also suggest that the two types of structures encourage different styles of supervision. The structure in Figure 1A encourages "close supervision," that is, detailed instructions, persistent attempts to direct and observe performance and the like. The limited span of control of course permits this, and the pressure for the integration of the task components may force it. The structure in Figure 1B encourages "general supervision," that is, monitoring performance in terms of results with considerable freedom for the employee so long as he or she is performing up to standard. Close supervision of janitors, for example, would require such directions as, "You will sweep from left to right, forty strokes per minute," and correspondingly close checks on performance. General supervision, in contrast, would assume competency and give such instructions as: "Sweep the floors in such time that you are able to get your other work done and so that the floor will reflect x units of light from a refractometer." The refractometer provides the check on performance. Acknowledgedly, this goes a little far. All of the components of general supervision are there, however, especially the measure of performance.

Structures of the type in Figure 1A pay a heavy cost to the degree that they in fact do encourage close supervision. In one study, for example, less than 30 percent of the work teams whose first-level or second-level supervisors practiced close supervision had high output. Whereas nearly 70 percent of the work units receiving only general supervision had high output.[25]

The reader may suppose, then, that the manager and supervisors in a Figure 1B organization would face an impossible task in motivating and measuring performance. For general supervision must be based upon performance standards, and what will keep standards high if the supervisor "gets off their backs?" But the several units headed by an S_{ABC}, each performing the same task, obviously set the stage for a relative measure of performance. They are in competition with each other, which tends to keep performance high. This would complement the added contributions to be expected because of the job enlargement practiced in 1B-type structures. At the same time, reduced "line-staff" conflict seems implied by this potential for motivation and measurement, "staff" development being in large part due to top-level management's difficulties in motivating and, especially, measuring performance.

Figure 1A organizations do not offer the same possibilities. One might try to encourage competition within, for example, some S_A unit or between the S_A units and the S_B units. But competition of that sort, as experimental studies suggest, is not likely to aid performance on most tasks,[26] since the tasks themselves are not comparable and may indeed be incommensurable. The point may be driven home by considering this proposition: Assembling all As (or Bs or Cs) in organizationally separate units encourages the restriction of output and invites substantial jurisdictional conflict when the responsibility for an error must be assigned. Much evidence supports this proposition.[27] Responsibility is far more difficult to assign in a 1A-type structure, for at least three inspections would be required to permit accurate assignment of praise or blame, one after each of the component operations. Figure 1B organizations would require only one such inspection. Such considerations, and there are many others, attest to the difficulties of motivating and measuring performance in Figure 1A organizations.

These features of Figure 1B organizations suggest a way out of the objection that public agencies are not guided by "profit" and that performance measurement is therefore difficult. In Figure 1A organizations in business, the measurement of macroscopic profit does little to determine the often crucial measurement of the effectiveness of constituent units. Hence, many business enterprises have approached the type of organization sketched in Figure 1B by establishing "individual profit centers" within (for example) a plant. Their services are then "sold" internally, sometimes with the useful provision that outside purchase is possible if price or quality are not considered appropriate by the "buyer."[28] This encourages self-discipline of both "buyer" and "seller." Comptroller W. J. McNeil worked for years to install arrangements of this sort in the Department of Defense for the provision of common procurement of goods and services as a means of economy and of strengthening the secretary's hand.

In any case, Figure 1B organizations seem to have a definite advantage in the training of subordinates. Patently, S_{ABC} faces training challenges not available to S_A (or S_B or S_C) in the normal course of events. Reasonably, then, organizational structures such as that in Figure 1B should tend toward the early elimination of those without management ability, while it would attract the more able. Reasonably, then, high satisfaction and output should characterize Figure 1B organizations. These expectations are indeed supported by some research in the Sears, Roebuck chain[29] and elsewhere.[30]

Despite these (and other) advantages of 1B structures, our public personnel systems do not provide a congenial home for them. The dominant emphasis in these systems—and it is no doubt often a necessary emphasis—is negative rather than positive. As one observer with high-level experience in both government and industry noted.[31]

> ... no matter how well briefed on federal service peculiarities the private business executive may be, one of the first things he notices in public admin- istration is this emphasis on procedure and routine. This emphasis is admit- tedly necessary and desirable provided it does not make method an end in itself. When it does, over-organized bewilderment results. The newcomer to top management positions in the federal service frequently feels that the organization and methods set up with the laudable idea of keeping him from doing wrong actually result in making it excessively difficult to do right.

This emphasis, despite its legitimacy, seems to have been overdone at all levels. Overdone or not, it is valuable to know what it costs to preserve the emphasis in Figure 1A structures.

Generations of organization theorists have labored hard to preserve the fiction of the unity of command in our public affairs, this being the very slender thread by which we demonstrate that the electorate really does control the administration through its election of the president. One may judge the impact of this theory upon supervisory practices from the longevity of the logically consistent but unrealistic notion that politics and administration are somehow separate. This notion, of course, is the keystone of our civil service systems. Their failure to respect the realities of delegation hardly augurs for better treatment of this matter at lower organization levels. Comfortable as the fiction of unity of command may be to many, multiline relations exist. We can chose to neglect this datum for various reasons, as the Hoover Commission did in arguing for a structure such as that in Figure 1A.[32] But this neglect may prove embarrassing,[33] and it is very likely that our theoretical simplism has a high cost. Long ago Gaus put the argument for a multiline view in these convincing terms:

> Such a theory. . . is the only one which fits the facts of contemporary delega- tion of wide discretionary power by electorates, constitutions, and legisla- tures to the administrators [who] must, of necessity, determine some part of the purpose and a large part of the means whereby it will be achieved in the modern state.[34]

Finally, the accepted pattern of organization in public agencies (as well as in business concerns) is functional. This reflects the historic strength of the model sketched in Figure 1A and suggests the barriers that will restrain attempts to approach the Figure 1B model in organizing.

JOB DESCRIPTION AND CIVIL SERVICE

It says worlds, while it avoids an enormous complexity, to note that our civil service systems are typically based upon a duties classification as opposed to a rank classification. Public personnel specialists have gone in for a duties classification with a sometimes uncritical zeal. As Nigro explains,

In a duties classification, the beginning point is a detailed analysis of the tasks required in the individual position. In fact, the tendency in the United States has been to make fairly minute investigations of job content.[35]

The emphasis need not be exaggerated, for the specialists have providently refrained from stressing the content of all jobs. The handling of secretarial positions—whose importance is usually measured by secretaries and bosses in terms of what the boss does rather than what the secretary does—is perhaps the most striking illustration of what has been called the "realistic" approach to classification.[36] But the bias of job description in this country has not moved very far from the classic expression it was given, for example, in the 1932 classification plan for Philadelphia. Nigro called this "one of the best books of specifications on record." It listed twenty individual classes of clerks, for each of which specifications had been developed. Specifications were also stated for thirty additional classes of principal and chief clerks in the various city departments.[37]

The inspirations for this emphasis on job description in our public personnel systems seem clear enough. The logic and methods of scientific management—which encouraged the view of organization as a "delicate mechanism" of gearlike "positions" whose drive shaft was the line of command—clearly had their influence. Moreover, position classification provides the bases for equal treatment, general formal policies and procedures regarding recruitment, salary, promotions, and the like. Finally, position classification encourages the attempt to group similar jobs into a reasonable number of classes, subclasses, and so on. This provided a ladderlike framework upon which a permanent career service could be built.

Despite its contribution to achieving the goals of our civil service movement, the American approach to job description has its unintended costs. Some obvious costs will be considered immediately, and subsequent analysis will consider one less obvious set of costs in some detail.

First, since one product of position classification was to be a manageable number of classes, this required a procrustean neglect of distinguishing job characteristics. Second, the position approach became the victim of its own imprecise terms. Consider the common observation that the "position" is the "universal building block of all organizations."[38] The observation has a certain validity, since all organizations contain positions. It tended to mislead the unwary, however, into supposing that "organization" is only a set of positions. The temptation to think of organization as some massive mechanical structure of positions linked by lines of authority was strong, since it apparently served to simplify the problems of personnel work.

Third, the emphasis upon a duties classification implies a substantial rigidity. Consider the difficulties of dealing with the many positions that have a kind of life cycle, with stages that impose varying demands on the incumbent. Developing an administrative role may be a very delicate task, while playing the role thereafter may be child's play. This phenomenon is difficult to accommodate within the framework of most of our public personnel systems. Some adaptations may be made quickly enough, but often it is necessary to waste "big" people on jobs too small for them or to give "small" people jobs too big for them. Similarly, the emphasis upon a duties classification makes it difficult to utilize positions for training purposes without the stretching of a point or two by the position analyst. The traditional question—What does the incumbent do?—is not appropriate for such positions, for he or she may, in fact, contribute little toward immediate task performance.

The abortive struggles toward a Senior Civil Service and then a Career Executive Program for the federal government reflect the tenacity of the grip of these two types of inflexibilities.[39] It was intended that the highly mobile and select corps of administrators in such programs would be used in both of the ways alluded to above, that is, as experienced "fire fighters" and as trainees getting the "big picture." The rank-in-job bias in our civil service systems played not a little part in the lack of action.

Fourth and finally, the approach via a duties classification taken in this country is not the only available one. Indeed, in public administration it appears that only Canada and Brazil follow our example closely. Many personnel systems—public and business—emphasize broad and general classes rather than narrow and detailed ones. Some of the spirit claimed for the British civil service, for example, is suggested by this open-end description of the few grades of "scientific officer" in Her Majesty's Service.[40]

> It is not possible to define with precision the duties of the various grades but, broadly speaking, the duties of the grades above principal scientific officer include responsibility for the administration and direction of scientific work while the principal scientific officer and lower grades concentrate on the scientific work itself. . . .
>
> But the posts of senior principal scientific officer and above may, with Treasury authority, be created for outstanding individual research workers.

Not infrequently, on the business side, executives will take the more extreme ground that they will not tolerate even an organization chart at their level lest it force them into patterns of action that may become inappropriate, just as these patterns develop a vested interest in protecting personnel.

This general approach to job description has its virtues. For example, by all accounts the British achieve great flexibility, avoid the sometimes gross artificialities of more "precise" efforts, and (one supposes) increase the power of the supervisors whose discretion is obviously emphasized. Their approach also seems to avoid the situation that haunts position analysts and outside observers alike: that an Einstein would have the same grade as any other physicist doing "similar work."

These problems of the American approach are well enough known, although they do not prove the inferiority of a detailed approach to job description in the lower classifications. These problems may have profound consequences for the management of work. At its worst, taking the mechanical aspects of job description too seriously can disrupt the flow of work. Moderation on the part of both "line" and "staff" seems indicated. The decentralization of much personnel work in the federal service suggests that just such a mature moderation has set in.

Other factors encourage a diluted devotion to the methods and theory implicit in the duties classification in this country. Here let us consider only this feature: it is not obvious that the common attempts at precision are precise about all (or most) of the elements of work that are important. This should encourage a healthy skepticism in developing and administering duties classifications. For, first, the technology of duties classification cannot support great precision now, nor is it likely to do so in the immediate future. Second, if a duties classification purports to describe the behaviors required for the effective performance of an organization's work, existing efforts commonly miss many significant possibilities. If it merely codifies existing practices, it may not be worthy of vigorous support, for duties classifications are at least implicitly prescriptive.

The specific dimensions that characterize tasks are but imprecisely known. The usual guidelines for classification—level in the hierarchy, formal authority and responsibility, funds administered, and the like—are not sufficient for doing the job tidily. For example, they do not take into account whether Supervisor X is the informal as well as formal leader of his or her work unit. It is impractical and unjust to treat Supervisor X's job as the same whatever the answer to this question. Moreover, if a job description is prescriptive, a supervisor's socioemotional performance cannot be overlooked. We may fairly ask of an approach that preaches and seeks precision, Precision about what?

The question remains, what is significant in describing a task? It is a disarming question. Existing research does not suggest that it has an obvious or an uncomplicated answer. Factor analysis, a sophisticated mathematical technique, perhaps offers the most hope of developing a set of dimensions that will permit us to describe jobs precisely. A technical discussion of factor analysis can hardly be attempted here. In general, however, the technique permits an initial judgment as to the number of independent dimensions necessary to account for the variation in some batch of scores (for example, in rankings by several analysts of jobs in terms of the discretion they require incumbents to exercise). The technique has been utilized to isolate the various kinds of intellectural abilities measured by intelligence tests. There is no way to solve such problems a priori. Factor analysis, in sum, might well complement and direct the enormous amount of observation that normally goes into developing a duties classification and into keeping it current.

Applications of factor analysis to job description suggest the problems that must be met. The technique, for example, has been applied to the ratings of a very large number of characteristics of various jobs. Existing results do not suggest that a synthesis is imminent. A simple manual task, for example, required only a few factors to describe it in one study.[41] Another factor analysis of more complex tasks isolated twenty-three factors.[42] Yet only seven factors were considered necessary to describe the four thousand jobs listed by the U. S. Employment Service.[43] Thus existing work does not suggest a clear pattern. To further complicate matters, there seem to be "families" of tasks for which individual sets of factor dimensions probably must be developed.[44]

Despite the inconclusiveness of such factor analytical work, two points seem clear. First, the dimensions isolated thus far do not closely resemble the guidelines implicit in much classification work. In fact, the factors need not have any obvious connection with "common sense" notions.[45] Second, the isolation of such factors is only the initial step. Factor analysis provides a rough map of those things that are important descriptively. Successful prediction, however, is the crucial test. Such validatory work might take this form: If the task has dimensions a and d, individuals with such-and-such training, proficiency, attitudes, and personality will prove to be high producers.

Even this preliminary factorial work has clear implications for our public personnel systems. Duties classification will have limited usefulness to the degree that task dimensions are not developed and the validatory work referred to above is not undertaken. The interim question of whether the pursuit of precision about characteristics—which may or may not be functionally important in describing the task—is worthwhile must probably remain open. The answer is not obviously in the affirmative. A fundamental reevaluation of the common approach to job description in this country seems required while we await the scientific explanation that will permit great precision. It would seem useful to attempt to test whether general classification provides savings beyond the reach of the detailed classification.

If there must be detail in job description, many factors could fruitfully be included in the usual duties classification. One such is the style of supervision. Different jobs seem compatible with different styles of supervision. On the available evidence, general statements under this head must be tentative, largely because we know so little about the dimensions along which tasks differ. An example, however, may be hazarded. Provisionally, jobs could be conceived of as differing in the degrees to which their performance is programmed and to which their successful performance requires interpersonal cooperation. When a task is unprogrammed and requires high interpersonal cooperation, a permissive supervisory style has seemed most appropriate for those subjects tested. An authoritarian supervisory style will cause the least socioemotional dislocation on tasks that are highly programmed and require little interpersonal cooperation.[46] These are general relations, indeed, and require much specification of intervening conditions. Similarly, individuals with differing personality characteristics tend to perform most effectively under different supervisory styles.[47] Meeting the needs of employees via an appropriate supervisory style would probably serve to increase the power of supervisors or at least to provide supervisors with a favorable environment in which to seek high power.[48]

The specification of such factors as the supervisory style congenial to a job is particularly important because the logic of scientific management encourages the choice of a generally inappropriate style. Thus close supervision—which is consistent with this theory—seems to be associated with high output in only a minority of cases, as already noted. If one had to make a choice between the two types of supervision, then, it is not crystal clear that one would be well advised to obey the logic of scientific management.

This analysis can be extended. Close supervision, patently, is encouraged by a structure such as that in Figure 1A. Supervisory pressure would seem to be most directly applicable in this model, which in turn might suggest high supervisory power. However, things do not seem to happen this way often. Likert reports that the more "unreasonable pressure" reportedly exerted by a supervisor, the less the power attributed to that supervisor.[49] Moreover, evidence suggests that greater supervisory pressure serves to isolate the supervisor from his or her workers by increasing the danger of communication.[50] In addition, pressure seems inversely related to output. For example, ten of eleven departments in Likert's study that reported little outside pressure to control the pace of work were above-average producers. Nine of ten departments reporting great pressure were below-average producers.[51] Reasonably, then, job descriptions might well profit from the specification of such job-relevant factors as the style of supervision.

This discussion of two approaches to job description—through those factors normally included and through those factors often neglected—permits of simple summary. There seem to be very substantial costs of commission and omission in the job descriptions common in our civil service systems. These costs complicate the management of work, however nicely the systems fit the three core goals underlying the American approach to public personnel administration.

SUMMARY

Our federal Civil Service Commission has been accustomed to serve more than one master. As one commentator noted:

> "For whom does the Civil Service Commission work?" We used to reply, "Well, we think it works first for its congressional committees, second for the status employees, third for the American Legion in support of veterans' preference laws, fourth for civil service employees' unions, and possibly fifth for the President." Since the end of World War II, the President has moved up in this list, but it is difficult to tell just how far.[52]

The analysis above, in essence, argues that yet another master requires service, the development of a work environment within which a professional manager can do her or his most effective job. Substantial revisions in traditional thinking and technique about our civil service systems will be required to that end.

NOTES

1. John Fisher, "Let's Go Back to the Spoils System" reproduced in part in *Ideas and Issues in Public Administration*, ed. Dwight Waldo (New York, 1953), pp. 200–01.

2. Wallace Sayre, "The Triumph of Technique Over Purpose." *Public Administration Review* 8 (Spring 1948): 134–35.

3. Ibid, p. 134.

4. Dwight Waldo, *The Administrative State* (New York, 1948), pp. 47–64.

5. See my *Behavior and Organization* (Chicago: Rand McNally, 1962), esp. chaps. 1–4.

6. See my "Organizing Work: Techniques and Theories." *Advanced Management —Office Executive* 1 (June 1962): 26–31.

7. Ibid., pp. 134–35.

8. The outlines of this reorientation are drawn sharply in O. Glenn Stahl, *Public Personnel Administration* (New York, 1956), pp. 577–82.

9. Donald C. Pelz, "Interaction and Attitudes between Scientists and Auxiliary Staff," *Administrative Science Quarterly* 4 (December 1959): 321–36, and 4 (March 1960): 410–25.

10. Rensis Likert, *New Patterns of Management* (New York, 1961), p. 114.

11. Ibid., pp. 56–57.

12. James E. Drury, *The Displaced Career Executive Program* (Inter-University Case Program, University of Alabama Press, 1952).

13. Stahl, p. 473.

14. Felix Nigro, *Public Personnel Administration* (New York, 1959), p. 295.

15. Chris Argyris, *Personality and Organization* (New York, 1957), pp. 177–87, summarizes many relevant studies.

16. Ibid., p. 177.

17. Ibid., p. 180.

18. William Givin, *Bottom-Up Management* (New York, 1949).

19. The point has been amply demonstrated in experimental situations. See James G. March, "Influence Measurement in Experimental and Semi-Experimental Groups," *Sociometry* 19 (March 1956): 26–71.

20. Peter F. Drucker, *The Practice of Management* (New York, 1954), pp. 291–92.
21. The parent of this analysis may be found in James C. Worthy, *Big Business and Free Men* (New York, 1959), pp. 90–99.
22. The point is supported by the example in Drucker, p. 291. See also Argyris, pp. 177–87.
23. Worthy, pp. 92–93.
24. Mason Haire, ed., *Modern Organization Theory* (New York: John Wiley & Sons, 1959), pp. 273–74.
25. Dorwin Cartwright and Alvin Zander, eds., *Group Dynamics* (Evanston, 1953), esp. pp. 617–19.
26. Robert T. Golembiewski, *The Small Group: An Analysis of Research Concepts and Operations* (University of Chicago Press, 1962), pp. 202–04.
27. Eliot D. Chapple and Leonard R. Sayles, *The Measure of Management* (New York, 1961), pp. 18–45.
28. W. H. Mylander, "Management by Executive Committee," *Harvard Business Review* 33 (May 1950): 51–58.
29. See William F. Whyte, *Man and Organization* (Homewood, Ill.: Richard D. Irwin, Inc. 1959), pp. 11–16.
30. Ernest Dale, "Centralization versus Decentralization," *Advanced Management* 21 (June 1956): 15.
31. Marver Bernstein, *The Job of the Federal Executive* (Washington, D.C.: Brookings Institution, 1958), pp. 34–35.
32. Hoover Commission, *Report on the General Management of the Executive Branch* (Washington, D.C., 1949), pp. 1, 3–4.
33. As, for example, in *Morgan vs. United States*, 298 U.S. 468, where the secretary of agriculture was rebuked for deciding a case he had not heard in person.
34. In John Gaus, Leonard D. White, and Marshall E. Dimock, *The Frontiers of Public Administration* (University of Chicago Press, 1940), p. 91.
35. Nigro, p. 85.
36. Julius E. Eitington, "Injecting Realism into Classification," *Public Personnel Administration* 15 (March 1952): 31–35.
37. Nigro, pp. 98–99.
38. Leonard D. White, *Introduction to the Study of Public Administration* (New York, 1948), p. 28.
39. Paul P. Van Riper, "The Senior Civil Service and the Career System," *Public Administration Review* 18 (Summer 1958): 189–200.
40. Royal Commission on the Civil Service, *Introductory Factual Memorandum on the Civil Service* (London: Her Majesty's Stationery Office, 1953), p. 54.
41. A. W. Melton, *Apparatus Tests*, AAF Aviation Psychological Program, Research Report No. 4 (Washington, D. C.: Government Printing Office, 1947).
42. L. L. McQuitty, C. Wrigley, and E. L. Gaier, "An Approach to Isolating Dimensions of Job Success," *Journal of Applied Psychology* 38 (1954): 227–32.
43. E. J. McCormick, R. H. Finn, and C. D. Scherps, "Patterns of Job Requirements," *Journal of Applied Psychology* 41 (1957): 358–64.
44. Launer F. Carter, William Haythorn, and Margaret Howell, "A Further Investigation of the Criteria of Leadership," *Journal of Abnormal and Social Psychology* 45 (1950): 350–58.
45. The naming of factors is not always an easy task, for any factor normally has "loadings" of several variables. Hence the sometimes exotic designations of factorial structures.
46. Robert T. Golembiewski, "Three Styles of Leadership and Their Uses" *Personnel* 38 (July-August 1961): 28–39.
47. Allen D. Calvin, Frederick K. Hoffman, and Edgar L. Harden, "The Effect of Intelligence

and Social Atmosphere on Group Problem-Solving Behavior," *Journal of Social Psychology*, 45 (February 1957): 61–74.

48. Likert, pp. 93–94.

49. Ibid., pp. 56–57.

50. Ibid., p. 45.

51. Ibid., p. 20.

52. Bernstein, p. 76.

Federal Influences in State and Local Personnel Management: The System in Transition

Raymond A. Shapek

The first half of the 1970s had a devastating impact on the federal system, and more is promised for the last half. The pressures and forces exerted by the energy crises, concomitant inflation, recession, unemployment, and the inactivity of federal policy initiative brought about with the demise of the Nixon Administration have altered traditional modes of governmental operation to the point that previous methodologies, indices, and methods of economic prediction no longer apply. The concept of federalism and the Nixon appellation, "New Federalism," have been submerged in the malaise of a state in transition. However, one certainty remains steadfast: federal actions (or inactions) will have an increasing effect on the administrative operation of state and local governments.

We are now in a period of transition, and the total impact of the factors mentioned above cannot be measured. However, significant changes are occurring in the area of personnel resource management at the state and local levels as a result of federal influences. Three factors have made personnel resource management a crucial issue for state and local governments in the 1970s:

1. *The rapid growth of state and local government employment and payroll costs have made human resources the most costly segment of government.* State and local governments registered an increase of 14 percent in payroll costs last year alone—the largest increase since 1958.

2. *The enactment of national laws has complicated the role of public managers.* Public policy enactments related to equal employment opportunity (EEO), occupational health and safety, fair labor standards, labor-management rela-

Raymond A. Shapek is chairman of the Department of Public Administration at Kent State University.

Reprinted from Raymond A. Shapek, "Federal Influences in State and Local Personnel Management: The System in Transition," *Public Personnel Management* (January-February 1976), 41–49.

tions, and other personnel related measures have become more and more significant to state and local governments.

3. *New and extended management responsibilities have resulted from increasingly complex rules and regulations in federal grants-in-aid.* Grant application, administrative requirements, and funding and resource allocation decision making require better, more efficient personnel practices. State and local administrators are forced to seek improvements in personnel selection techniques, position classification and pay plans, employee training, and so on. In short, we have witnessed a resurgence in application of the concept of "merit" as a means of responding to pressures for increased efficiency and productivity.

It is within these three areas—the effects of state and local governmental growth, the complications brought about by national laws, and increased demands on state and local management requiring greater sophistication in personnel practices—that federal influences on state and local personnel management systems can be explored.

EFFECTS OF STATE AND
LOCAL GOVERNMENTAL GROWTH

The growing interdependence of the state and local sectors, the national government, and of course the national economy can be measured by the changes that have taken place in the last twenty years. The fiscal and personnel impacts are manifested in the following:

1. Civilian domestic expenditures (including Social Security) increased dramatically from 12.9 percent GNP to 25.4 percent in 1974. Federal aid to state and local governments increased from .8 percent of GNP in 1954 to 3.1 percent of GNP in 1974.

2. Federal aid, which accounted for 11.4 percent of state-local general revenue in 1954, expanded to 26.5 percent of state-local general revenue in 1974.

3. State aid to local governments, over half of which is for education, has increased steadily from 41.7 percent of locally derived revenue in 1954 to 57.5 percent in 1974.

4. General civilian government employment now accounts for 14.6 percent of the nation's employed labor force. Four-fifths of this employment is in the state-local sector.

5. During the period 1955–1973 employment at the state-local level increased by 117.5 percent compared to 17.1 percent at the federal level and 35.8 percent in the private sector.

6. Average annual earnings of state-local employees have increased almost as rapidly as earnings of federal employees and now exceed earnings in private industry by 6 percent.[1]

State and local government is growing and accounting for a greater share of our fiscal resources. The greatest part of state and local expenditures (outside of capital improvements) is for wages. The largest increases in wages have been in the public sector. State and local government employment reached 12.95 million in 1975 and is increasing rapidly, while federal government employment (excluding the military) remained relatively stable at 2.82 million persons. Wayne Anderson, executive director of the Advisory Commission on Intergovernmental Relations (ACIR) noted that public sector expenditures will exceed two-thirds of the GNP by the year 2000, given the present rate of growth, and most of this growth will be in state and local governments. The 1975 U.S. budget recommended federal domestic grants-in-aid of $56 billion for 1976 compared to $13 billion in 1966. Total outlays for assistance to individuals will rise from $140 billion in 1974 to $173 billion in 1975 and to $190 billion in 1976.

Through the 1960s the rapid growth of state and local governments was in part a response to the demands for more and better services. The federal response was more grant-in-aid programs. However, there was ultimately a recognition that the federal government alone could not logically meet this need—responsibility must be shifted back to the "provider" level. By necessity, the concept of "New Federalism" emerged.

The panoply of administrative programs formulated by the Office of Management and Budget (the OMB circulars, the Federal Regional Councils, Federal Assistance Review, and others) and acts by Congress (a series of bloc grants) were attempts to devolve and decentralize program administration in order to promote more initiative and responsibility at the state and local levels. However, the programs were also designed to promote federal goals and were controlled through federal postaudit and evaluation procedures.

Almost every grant program passed by Congress has been subject to administrative rules and regulations promulgating federal intervention in state and local government personnel management practices (as well as in other areas). For example, the Federal Assistance Review Task Force, under the leadership of OMB, surveyed 221 grant programs and discovered 172 specific instances of requirements or procedures related to personnel administration.[2] While some devolution and decentralization has taken place in the administrative process, the personnel resource area has become increasingly subject to federal impositions. These complexities are reflected especially well in several national laws imposing national objectives on state and local governments.

COMPLICATIONS BROUGHT
ABOUT BY NATIONAL LAWS

Within the host of measures enacted by Congress that impact on state and local personnel management systems, three have been of significant consequence to personnel administration not only in terms of dollars but also in terms of social impact.[3] The first of these is the Comprehensive Employment and Training Act (CETA) and a series of other programs administered by the Department of Labor (DOL). The second of these actions is the potpourri of measures leading to the extension of collective bargaining into the public sector. The third is the resurgence of public conscientiousness over the rights of minorities reflected in passage of the Equal Employment Opportunity Act.

CETA and Other DOL Programs

CETA was designed to reduce in number the almost ten thousand (nationwide) existing fragmented manpower efforts aimed at similar problems. It was signed into law by President Nixon on December 28, 1973.[4] CETA's purpose was to (further) transfer responsibility and resources for manpower programs to states and localities with minimal federal intervention in program design or operation.

Although CETA has successfully consolidated efforts in labor management development under the old categorical approach, it has also changed the nature of the relationships between the DOL and state and local governments. On the positive side, the grants can be channeled through the 430 "prime sponsors" (general purpose governments serving populations of over 100,000 persons) and tailored more specifically by the recipients to meet their unique needs. However, the role of the state is minimized. Overall, CETA is a form of special revenue sharing.

Most of the controversy over CETA at the state and local levels has been in Titles II and VI.[5] Title VI was hastily passed by Congress in December 1974 to alleviate the pressures of unemployment and the recession. Title VI funds were earmarked to relieve critical unemployment on a temporary, short-term basis. However, Congress mandated priority for certain groups, such as minorities, veterans, and the elderly. State and local governments have reflected some dissatisfaction with this procedure and have felt that it has served to circumvent merit procedures in hiring. In some jurisdictions, local politicians have used Title VI for political ends, and in others they have manipulated personnel hiring to relieve the local payroll burden. In the latter instance, some permanent employees were released and temporary Title VI personnel hired. Needless to say, the unions were not pleased.

Developments in three other labor programs proved of great importance in 1973. First, state actions in the federal-state unemployment insurance program indicated a trend toward elimination of discriminatory provisions regarding women workers. A second program followed three years of experience under the Occupational Safety and Health Act of 1970. On the federal side, three new agencies were formulated, the Occupational Safety and Health Administration (OSHA) in the Department of Labor, the National Institute of Occupational Safety and Health (NIOSH) in the Department of Health, Education, and Welfare, and the independent Occupational Safety and Health Review Commission. These agencies employ nearly two thousand persons for research, inspection, enforcement, training, and administration of tasks involving occupational safety and health nationwide. By the end of 1973, sixteen states had implemented plans "at least as effective" as the federal program, four others had been approved by OSHA, and twenty-seven others were under review. The sixteen active plans employed the services of almost four thousand employees.

The third significant labor development related to advances following passage of the Age Discrimination in Employment Act in 1967. The purpose of the act was to promote employment of "experienced" workers between the ages of forty and sixty-four by prohibiting discrimination on the basis of age in hiring and job retention, equity in compensation, and other terms, conditions, and privileges of employment. Voluntary compliance changed discriminating practices affecting forty thousand jobs; administrative actions brought nearly $2 million in damages to over one thousand workers, and there have been 160 civil court cases since the start of the program.

Another piece of legislation, which is administered by the DOL, is the extension of the Equal Pay Act of 1963[6] as it is affected by the Fair Labor Standards Act (FLSA) extension to state and local governments.[7] The extension of the Equal Pay Act of 1963 requires the same pay for men and women doingsubstantially the same work and requiring substantially equal skill, effort, and responsibility under similar working conditions in the same establishment. "Equal" does not mean "identical," but jobs compared under the act must be substantially similar. Where discrimination is found to exist, pay for the lower must be raised to equal that for the higher paid sex.

Collective Bargaining

The significant growth in public sector employment has been accompanied by increased responsibilities and pressures on public agency personnel directors. A recent International City Management Association (ICMA) survey revealed that city personnel directors now spend approximately 12 percent of their time on labor-management related activities. This represents their second greatest commitment of time to any one area. Public unions more than doubled in size in the 1960s and exceeded (in proportion) the number of employees who have joined industrial unions. Membership in the leading government employee union, the American Federation of State, County, and Municipal Employees (AFSCME) rose from 250,000 in 1964 to 700,000 in 1974. Federal intervention in the realm of collective bargaining has helped to stimulate organizational militance—even in smaller jurisdictions—which began with earlier experiences in the cities of New York, Philadelphia, and Cincinnati.[8]

Federal labor-management policy changed significantly in 1962 when President Kennedy issued E.O. 10988 supporting union recognition in the public sector. The unions hailed this action while state and local elected and administrative officials condemned it.[9] Further modification to federal policy took place with E.O. 11491, which became effective on October 29, 1969. Although significant changes occurred with President Nixon's order—wages, salaries, and other substantive issues remained outside the scope of "negotiable" items.

Within the states, before 1959, there was no statutory obligation for public managers to deal collectively with employees. Following Wisconsin's initiative in that year, nearly every state (forty) has granted some type of employee union recognition measure or has been forced to alter personnel agency policies as a result of federal grants-in-aid requirements.[10] Over two-thirds of the local governments (291 cities) responding to a recent ICMA survey reported collective bargaining arrangements with local employee associations. One problem has been that most cities must work with more than one bargaining unit. The average is five but reaches 242 in New York City.[11]

U.S. Supreme Court decisions have also impacted on the collective bargaining activities of state and local governments. The validity of the Hatch Act, which prohibited partisan political activity by state employees paid with federal funds, was upheld. Also upheld was the state's right to limit the political activity of all other state employees.[12] On the other hand, the Supreme Court invalidated a provision of New York State Civil Service Law denying permanent competitive positions to noncitizens. Perhaps the most significant Supreme Court action was Chief Justice Warren Burger's temporary stay on the implementation of the Fair Labor Standards Amendments of 1974 as applied to state and local governments.[13] Allan Pritchard, executive vice-president of the National League of Cities, criticizes sponsors of FLSA for failing to consider the increased personnel costs to the cities (now 80 percent of the local budget), especially in the area of overtime pay to fire fighters. The impact will be a forced reduction in duty hours as well as a forced reorganization of local fire services to emphasize fire prevention and code enforcement instead of fire suppression.[14]

The concept of collective bargaining poses some threat to the principle of merit systems in personnel administration in at least three other areas—compulsory union membership, seniority promotion, and pay structures in job classification. Compulsory union membership (closed or union shops) may discourage competition for positions and inhibit the entry of persons opposed to union membership. Seniority promotions negate the use of performance evaluation and written tests as indices of achievement and criteria for promotion. In actual practice, however, the concept of seniority promotion is applied even in the best of merit systems. Also, the merit principle of "equal pay for equal work" may be more contingent upon political factors than on technical evaluation and rates set by experts. The multiplier effect on local wage structures from jurisdiction to jurisdiction, when outside factors intervene, is obvious. Starting, median, and maximum wage rates in smaller cities with labor unions or employee associations are significantly higher than in cities without these organizations. Besides raising labor costs, the union effect on the management of local government appears to be significant.[15]

Equal Employment Opportunity

The third significant area of federal laws affecting personnel management at the state and local levels is in the area of equal employment opportunities for minorities and women. With the 1972 passage of the Equal Employment Opportunity Act (EEOA), state and local governments became subject to the provisions of Title VII of the Civil Rights Act of 1964 prohibiting discrimination in employment practices.[16] Under the EEOA, the courts are authorized to enjoin unlawful conduct and to order affirmative relief, including back pay for up to two years prior to the filing of a charge of discrimination. Affirmative action (under the EEOA) was not intended to mean "preferential treatment" to minority groups or women; it was meant to reinforce true merit employment concepts by assuming that individuals from all segments of society have an equal opportunity to enter public service on the basis of open competition and advance according to relative ability.[17]

"Affirmative action" means a vigorous effort to eliminate not only the more obvious instances of discrimination but also subtle forms such as (class or race biased) selection and promotion standards and tests that favor one race over another. The clash of this concept with merit principles is one of the most contentious and disputed in personnel systems today. On the one hand, it is poor practice to hire other than the best-qualified applicant for a job. On the other hand, it is (equally) unfair to deny employment or promotion when a deficiency in qualifications exists because of past discriminatory practices or systemic deficiencies.[18]

What is the answer to a recent complaint that the admissions test for policeman in the District of Columbia discriminates against black candidates because a lower percentage of black applicants (compared to whites) passed the test?[19]

The counterreaction to this phenomenon is the indignation of majority group members who claim reverse discrimination. The U.S. Supreme Court refusal to address this question, in spite of its volatility, came in *Defunis* v. *Odegaard* when a divided court declared the case moot.[20] The problem is both ethical and moral. Mr. Justice Brennan, in his dissenting opinion, reflected the serious nature of the questions involved:

> . . . In endeavoring to dispose of this case as moot, the Court clearly dismisses the public interest. The constitutional issues which are avoided today concern vast numbers of people, organizations and colleges and universities, as evidenced by the filing of twenty-six *amici curiae* briefs. Few constitutional questions in recent history have stirred as much debate, and they will not disappear. They must inevitably return to the federal courts and again to this court. . .

The entire field of personnel testing has been ensnared in the qualification and selection dilemma. Thus, personnel testing has been dragged into the courts as part of the larger issue. The 1971 U.S. Supreme Court decision of *Griggs* v. *Duke Power Co.* has had a significant impact on selection criteria and evaluation techniques of state and local government employers.[21] The *Griggs* decision defined employment tests or practices unlawful if a disparate effect on persons of different races can be demonstrated. Additionally, selection tests must be job related or accurate predictors of job performance.[22] Unfortunately, all merit systems are not guarantees of equal employment opportunity, and there is no such thing as perfect validity in a test.

Although the percentage of minority persons in federal, state, and local employment roughly corresponds to the percentage of minority persons in the U.S. population, the distribution of minorities by job level is poor. Women and other minorities remain concentrated in the lower level jobs and their movement upward has been slow.

The question of equal employment opportunity for all is related to the quest for quality in the public personnel system. Unfortunately, there is evidence that many state and local agencies have not seriously pursued affirmative action objectives and that discrimination in employment practices is extensive.[23] It has recently been traced to extend to programs funded by general revenue sharing, especially in smaller units of government.

The enforcement of equal opportunity employment at the federal level has been vigorous. Federal monitoring of state and local systems subject to the EEOA has produced significant change, and more changes are yet to come.[24] The Equal Employment Opportunity Commission (EEOC) has approximately two thousand five hundred employees to investigate complaints (for all governments having at least fifteen employees). EEOC investigators are assisted by a large civil rights division in the Department of Justice, the civil rights enforcement capability (unit) of HEW and other federal agencies administering federal grant programs.

In spite of the negative factors noted earlier, state and local governments are moving toward greater effectiveness in combatting discrimination in employment. Human rights agencies have been established in forty states and the District of

Columbia—at least four hundred such agencies exist at the substate level in thirty-four of these states. These actions indicate a receptivity for change as well as an adjustment to external federal pressures. However, the recent legal attention to minority rights and employment practices has increased the burden on state and local personnel managers.

INCREASED DEMANDS ON
STATE AND LOCAL PERSONNEL MANAGERS

The final portion of this report centers on impacts on state and local personnel systems that have resulted from the forces mentioned at the outset, which demand not only increased sophistication in personnel practices but greater utility, productivity, and cost effectiveness in personnel recruitment, selection, promotion, pay policies, and other employment practices. In the absence of consistent state action, the federal government has moved to apply uniform personnel practices throughout the public sector work force based on the assumption that application of merit principles will lead to more efficient, effective government.[25]

Federal intrusion is not viewed by all to be desirable. Robert Craig, of the National Association of Counties, opposes federal intervention as "inappropriate because it usurps local prerogatives, it dictates use of tax revenues used by state and local government, and it violates the intergovernmental partnership."[26]

Others desire greater federal intervention. AFSCME president, Jerry Wurf, states that "only fourteen states have come up with labor relations laws (for public employees) that can even be described as fair. None of them gives public employees parity with their counterparts in private industry . . . No one pattern prevails among the fifty states and eighty thousand governmental units, save one: that public employees are nowhere the equals of working or private industry."[27] Wurf calls for federal action and leadership.

Regardless of the controversy generated, federal intrusions in state and local personnel systems, for good or bad, are a viable and growing force. The most obvious manifestation of federal action is in imposition of federal "merit system" standards.

Merit System

The evolution of the merit system dates back to the Social Security Act of 1935, which required a state plan for proper and efficient administration of the various title programs (with certain prohibitions):

> A State plan . . . must . . . provide such methods of administration (including methods relating to the establishment and maintenance of personnel standards on a merit basis, except that the Secretary shall exercise no authority with respect to the selection, tenure of office, and compensation of any individual employed in accordance with such methods) as are found by the Secretary to be necessary for the proper and efficient operation of the plan. . . .

Abuses within the system were common.[28] In one state each employee was required to "contribute" $100 of his or her salary to the incumbent political party in order to retain his or her job. Retention in or obtaining a position was a subject of political manipulation rather than capability to do the job. Recognizing this, the Social Security Board encouraged the establishment of merit systems for the grants-in-aid programs under the Social Security Act but had no legislative authority to require them.

By 1939 the necessity for merit standards was recognized by Congress, and the act was amended to require a merit system of personnel administration in three public assistance programs—crippled children's services, maternal and adult health, and the unemployment compensation programs. Merit systems were supposed to encourage efficiency as well as to provide protection to the states and their citizens and were not meant as an encroachment by the federal government.[29]

Merit systems, used synonymously with "civil service" means that employees hired are: (1) recruited and selected through competitive examination, (2) appointed to jobs classified according to duties, responsibilities, and degree of difficulty, (3) paid salaries equivalent to those paid for jobs of equivalent responsibility and difficulty, (4) eligible for promotion based on capacity and performance, (5) subject to dismissal only for cause, such as inefficiency or improper conduct on the job, and assured of equal treatment on all personnel actions regardless of political or religious affiliation, race, national origin, or any other nonmerit factor.[30]

Since these standards were originally issued, there have been a number of significant changes:

1. *1948.* The standards were updated and reissued as a joint document (the original standards had been issued separately by the Public Health Service, the Children's Bureau in Labor, and the Social Security Board). The principle of "substantial conformity" was extended to nonstatewide merit systems.

2. *1963.* The standards were revised to reflect national policy on discrimination on the basis of race, national origin, or other nonmerit factors.

3. *1971.* The standards were again revised to emphasize the options available to state and local governments to encourage innovation and allow for diversity in the design and management of their own individual systems of personnel administration. The most significant changes were the following: (a) provision for affirmative action to achieve equal employment opportunity; (b) the addition of specific prohibitions of discrimination based on age, sex, or physical disability; (c) strengthened the provisions on appeals of alleged discrimination; (d) provided for practices to facilitate the career employment of the disadvantaged; (e) recognized the right of employees to organize; (f) clarified the flexibility of state and local governments to establish a wide variety of types of merit organizations and liberalized state options; (g) provided a new section on career advancement and a new section on cooperation between merit systems to facilitate maximum utilization of manpower and to increase opportunities for employee mobility.

4. *1971.* The Intergovernmental Personnel Act of 1970 was signed into law and the responsibility for administration of the standards was transferred from the Department of Health, Education and Welfare to the U.S. Civil Service Commission.

Intergovernmental Personnel Act of 1970 (IPA)

Perhaps the most significant merit enactment was the passage of the Intergovernmental Personnel Act of 1970.[31] IPA's purpose was to strengthen and increase the ability of state and local governments to participate in the federal system. Through a system of formula grants, state and local governments are encouraged to upgrade the capacity and effectiveness of their personnel systems within their own priorities.[32] Additionally, IPA provides technical assistance; temporary assignments of personnel between the federal government and state and local governments or universities; admission of state and local government employees to federal training programs; development of cooperative recruiting and examining efforts; and administration of merit employment standards applicable to about thirty federal grants-in-aid programs (including over 70 percent of all federal grant funds). IPA also authorizes the U.S. Civil Service Commission to make grants to state and local governments to improve their personnel management and training.* An average of five hundred projects have been funded each year, ranging from training programs for newly elected governors and state legislators to developing a personnel system for a small city.

In most states, the IPA grant program is shaped by an advisory council made up of state and local government officials. The council develops annual priorities and plans for their state's share of the IPA formula grant funds (80 percent of the total appropriation). This plan is then reviewed and approved by the state's chief executive and sent to the U.S. Civil Service Commission's regional office for funding. USCSC's ten regional offices offer consultation on applications; they monitor and evaluate program performance and insure that grantees comply with matching, audit, civil rights, and other program requirements.[33] The USCSC also awards discretionary funds (20 percent of the total appropriation) based on applications sent to it directly by states and localities. Roughly half of the discretionary funds are allocated by the regional offices.

In its short history, IPA has had significant impact on state and local personnel systems, especially considering its modest size. Some of the more significant accomplishments include the following:

1. *Personnel management technical assistance.* Over seven thousand contacts have been made with state and local jurisdictions by USCSC staff, who recommended an estimated fifteen thousand improvements in personnel administration. Over half of the improvements support equal employment opportunity.

2. *Intergovernmental mobility.* 1,382 persons in the federal, state, local, and university work force accepted temporary assignments under this program as of April 30, 1974. Nearly 40 percent were state and local government and university staff on assignment to the federal agencies. These assignments represented a salary investment of over $19 million, 70 percent of it paid by the federal government.[34]

---

*EDITOR'S NOTE: The Civil Service Commission was replaced in January 1979 by the U.S. Office of Personnel Management, which is now responsible for IPA activities.

3. *Intergovernmental training.* Over thirty-five thousand state and local government employees attended USCSC-sponsored training programs in the past three years.

4. *Cooperative recruiting and examining.* Currently, eighteen Intergovernmental Job Information Centers operate throughout the country, offering single-source information for state, county, municipal, and federal jobs. In addition, twelve intergovernmental examining arrangements are in operation.

IPA's grant program has become one of the most respected and praised federal grants-in-aid programs passed by Congress. Its success, however, has generated a much larger demand for assistance by states and local governments than its appropriation levels will concede. It is estimated that IPA funding meets only one-half of 1 percent of the total potential demand for personnel improvement funding assistance. Given its current appropriation level of $15 million, IPA will probably continue to be a small, narrowly gauged grant program designed to stimulate and tantalize personnel improvement at the state and local levels. If expanded, however, it could parallel the phenomenal growth of state and local governments, expanding to meet the new challenges, needs, innovations, and demands of the late 1970s. Today, IPA is only a small remedial measure providing a modicum of relief from the growing pressure of federal influences on state and local personnel systems. Reading recent federal legislative enactments carefully (for example, the Housing and Community Development Act of 1974, changes to the HUD 701 program, the Fair Labor Standards Act and so on), there is obviously a tightening of federal control and increased stress on compliance with federal objectives. "New Federalism" is dead, and the pendulum has begun an increasingly rapid swing in the opposite direction.

NOTES

1. Advisory Commission on Intergovernmental Relations (ACIR), *Trends in Fiscal Federalism: 1954–1974,* "M-86 (Washington, D.C.: U.S. Government Printing Office, February 1975), pp. 1–3. Also, David B. Walker, "How Fares Federalism on the Mid-Seventies," *The Annals* (November 1974): 17–31.

2. Subcommittee on Intergovernmental Relations of the Committee on Government Operations, U.S. Senate, *More Effective Public Service: The First Report to the President and the Congress by the Advisory Council on Intergovernmental Personnel Policy—January 1973* (Washington, D.C.: U.S. Government Printing Office, March 1974), p.70

3. At least twenty-five other major pieces of legislation contain federal requirements for personnel standards. See the Advisory Council on Intergovernmental Personnel Policy, *More Effective Public Service: The First Report to the President and the Congress by the Advisory Council on Intergovernmental Personnel Policy—January 1973* (Washington, D.C.: U.S. Government Printing Office, March 1974), pp. 77–8.

4. Public Law 93-203.

5. Guidelines issued by the U.S. Civil Service Commission provide that applications for financial assistance under CETA must include provisions insuring that agencies will ". . . undertake analysis of job descriptions and . . . revisions of qualification requirements at all levels of employment . . . with a view toward removing artificial barriers to public employment . . ." and further "assurances that the program will . . . contribute to the elimination of artificial barriers to employment and occupational advancement . . ." See CETA Title II, Sec. 205 (c), (18) and (21); also Bureau of Intergov-

ernmental Personnel Programs, *Guidelines for Evaluation of Employment Practices under the Comprehensive Employment and Training Act* (Washington, D.C.: U.S. Civil Service Commission, July 1974).

6. Other DOL programs included Institutional Training under the Manpower Development and Training Act, the Job Opportunities in the Business Sector Program, the Neighborhood Youth Corps, Operation Mainstream, Public Service Careers, the Concentrated Employment Program, the Job Corps, the Work Incentive Program, Public Employment Program, and the Pilot Comprehensive Manpower Programs. For more detailed federal impact information related to DOL programs, see U.S. Department of Labor Manpower Administration, *Manpower Report of the President* (Washington, D.C.: U.S. Government Printing Office, April 1974), pp. 37–66.

7. Federal assistance efforts related to state and local compliance with the FLSA are aimed at: (1) programs to assure nondiscrimination because of age; (2) review of state and local personnel systems to eliminate built-in barriers to hiring, promoting, and retaining of older workers; (3) helping state and local governments to establish and maintain appropriate information and record systems; see footnote 13.

8. Mayor Robert F. Wagner permitted limited use of collective negotiations by city employees in 1958; Philadelphia has had labor agreements with provisions for union security and exclusive recognition since 1939; employee organizations have enjoyed de facto recognition of employee organizations since 1951. See also, National Governors Conference, *Report of Task Force on State and Local Government Labor Relations* (Chicago: Public Personnel Association, 1967), and ACIR, *Labor-Management Policies for State and Local Governments*, A-35 (Washington, D.C.: Government Printing Office, September 1969) for background material on impacts of collective bargaining activities on cities.

9. See Jerry Wurf, "Unions Enter City Hall," *Public Management* (September 1966) for the AFSCME perspective. The Advisory Council on Intergovernmental Personnel Policy concluded fifteen recommendations in the area of labor-management relations as a condition to receiving Federal grant-in-aid. Op. cit.

10. Keith Ocheltree, "Developments in State Personnel Systems," in the Council of State Governments, *The Book of the States 1974–75*, Vol. XX (Lexington, Kentucky: 1974), pp. 120–28. In spite of impressive union gains, their chief weapon, the right to strike, is still outlawed in all but three states (Hawaii, Pennsylvania, and Vermont). Although federal union employees have no "right to strike," this privilege was strongly urged in a recent address by W. J. Usery, Jr., special assistant to the president and director, Federal Mediation and Conciliation Service. See "Collective Bargaining in the Federal Sector: Preparing for Change," an address presented to the Collective Bargaining Symposium for Labor Relations Executives, July 8, 1974.

11. Andrew W. Boesel, "Local Personnel Management Organizational Problems and Operating Practices," in *The Municipal Yearbook 1974* (Washington, D.C.: International City Management Association, 1974), p. 89.

12. The Federal Political Activities Act (5 U.S.C., 1501-1508) was amended by Section 401 of the Federal Election Campaign Act (October 15, 1974) to remove the restrictions on active state and local employee participation in political campaigns and to permit an employee to be a candidate for nonpartisan elective office. State and local merit prohibitions against improper use of authority and coercion of employees continue to apply.

13. U.S. Supreme Court, No. A-553, *National League of Cities, et al. v. Peter J. Brennon, Secretary of Labor, December 13, 1974*. The temporary stay covered all parts of the FLSA applied to state and local governments, including those which became effective on May 1, 1974. This includes the minimum wage and overtime provisions of the FLSA, extension of the Age Discrimination in Employment Act of 1967, and the Equal Pay Act of 1972.

14. Allen E. Pritchard, Jr., "Editorial, Issues in Personnel Management," *Network News* (Washington, D.C.: National Training and Development Service, Winter 1975), p. Z. Government action and the failure to consider concomitant required actions by state

and local governments has become a cause of increasing concern in the reality of today's rampant inflation. New pressures are being exerted to force Congress to assess the costs and impacts of socially desirable requirements imposed on state and local government regulation. See, for example, "The Inflationary Costs," *Washington Post* (March 5, 1975), p. A-14.

15. David Stanley, *Managing Local Government Under Union Presence* (Washington, D.C.: Brookings Institute, 1972). See also *Urban Data Service Report* (Washington, D.C.: International City Management Association, January 1975), p. 8.

16. Although federal laws and administrative regulations prohibiting employment discrimination on the part of state and local governments existed for some years prior to 1972, the EEO Act of 1972 added powerful enforcement powers. The EEOC may investigate charges of employment discrimination, and, if no conciliation is achieved, the Department of Justice may bring suit against the offending agency.

17. For guidance on affirmative action, see Bureau of Intergovernmental Personnel Programs, *Equal Employment Opportunity in State and Local Governments—A Guide for Affirmative Action* (Washington, D.C.: U.S. Government Printing Office, Revised, November 1972); *Equal Employment Opportunity and Affirmative Action* (Durham, New Hampshire: New England Municipal Center, 1973); *Affirmative Action Guide for Washington Local Governments* Information Bulletin #349, (Seattle: Washington Local Government Personnel Institute and the Association of Washington Cities, 1973).

18. The courts have sought to provide relief to all members of groups found to have suffered from discriminatory employment systems, going to the extent of providing remedial relief to alleviate the "present effects " of "past discrimination," *U.S.* v. *U.S. Steel Corp.*, 5EPD, 8619 (May 3, 1973); *Carter* v. *Gallagher*, 452 F.2d 315 (8th Cir., 1971). Strongly implied is the promotion of minorities to adjust racial employment balances with "diminished" regard for the concept of merit.

19. William Rasberry, editorial comment, *Washington Post* (March 19, 1974), p. A-23. The police entrance examination for the District of Columbia was found to be discriminatory by a three judge U.S. district court. Two factors determine the decision: (1) disproportionate results—blacks were failing the exam at four times the rate of whites, and (2) the administration failed to prove the exam was job related. This case applied also to the FSEE (now PACE). The concept of "merit" is related to who scores best on an examination. What does not follow is to say that a slightly higher score will predict better job performance—this has been called the merit trap.

20. The court delayed a decision in this area by selecting a moot case for review.

21. 401 U.S. 424, 433. For an encapsulated review of fifty-eight significant civil rights court cases dealing with personnel administration, see Bureau of Intergovernmental Personnel Programs, USCSC, *Equal Employment Opportunity Court Cases* (Washington, D.C.: U.S. Government Printing Office, March 1974).

22. U.S. Commission on Civil Rights, *For all the People . . . By All the People* (Washington, D.C.: 1969).

23. For discussions of the objectives of merit selection, see Earl J. Reeves, "Making Equality of Employment Opportunity a Reality on the Federal Service," *Public Administration Review*, 30 (January/February 1970): 43–49; and Samual Krislov, *The Negro in Federal Employment* (Minneapolis: University of Minnesota Press, 1967); and Management Information Service, *Increasing Minority Employment by Affirmative Action Program* (Washington, D.C.: International City Management Association, 1972).

24. For example, IPA-funded affirmative action projects in eleven States for fiscal year 1974 totaled $647,073 (with match). As a result of this emphasis, 95 percent of the sixty-state merit systems and four hundred federal grant assisted agencies now have affirmative action plans.

25. For a listing of programs covered by statutes and regulations relating to a merit system, see the Advisory Council on Intergovernmental Personnel Policy, pp. 77–78.

26. Quoted in ACIR, *Federalism in 1974: The Tension of Interdependence*, M-89 (Washington, D.C.: February 1975) p. 13.

27. Ibid.

28. At the time only nine states had general civil service systems, and several of these were not functioning effectively.

29. All states accepted the standards as issued, and by 1940 most states had merit systems in operation. States not having a statewide civil service system had merit system covering agencies that receive Federal grants-in-aid.

30. These goals are set forth in terms of objectives of the Intergovernmental Personnel Act. See U.S. Civil Service Commission, *On the Move: Personnel Systems Improvements in State and Local Governments.* BIPP 152–38 (March 1974).

31. Public Law 91–648.

32. All but six states utilize state plans to outline personnel management objectives. The states without plans are Alaska, Delaware, Idaho, New Hampshire, Rhode Island, and Vermont. All of these states with the exception of Alaska have single IPA plans that include all local governments. These six have not adopted statewide plans because of their historical and traditional approaches to dealing with their local governments. In some instances, the state government is unwilling to assume responsibility for administering a state-local program. In others, skepticism over state involvement in local affairs is an issue. The IPA does not *require* a state plan.

33. The matching ratio will revert to 50-50 unless amendments restoring the original formula are passed by Congress.

34. For more detailed analysis of the extent and utilization of the mobility provisions of the IPA, see, U.S. Civil Service Commission, *The IPA Governmental Assignment Program: 1974 Report,* BIPP 152-44 (October 1974); *Guidelines on Personnel Mobility* (June 1971); "Memorandum to the Heads of Departments and Agencies," dated August 25, 1971, from President Nixon; U.S. Civil Service Commission, "A Report to the President" (September 1, 1972); and U.S. Civil Service Commission, "Questions and Answers" (February 1973).

State Government Personnel Directors: A Comparative Analysis of Their Background Characteristics and Qualifications

Myron D. Fottler

Craig Norrell

One of the key issues discussed in the personnel management literature in recent years has been "professionalization." To what degree are personnel managers true professionals? Professional training, career and a common body of knowledge are three criteria of a profession. An examination of the background characteristics and qualifications of personnel managers is one approach to determining the degree of "professionalization." However, while a significant amount of research has been done on the background characteristics of private sector personnel directors,[1] much less has been done with their public sector counterparts. Nor is there much information on how or why the degree of professionalism varies in different areas of the country, in different types of public organizations, and in organizations of varying size. This is surprising in view of the significance of personnel costs in public expenditures and the increased sophistication being required of public personnel managers in response to societal demands and legal pressures.

Due to the wide variety of educational backgrounds found among personnel managers, the shifting into and out of the field to other specialties, and an alleged lack of a generalized body of knowledge, some believe that personnel management will never be a true profession.[2] This is reinforced by the desire of many organizations to maintain a commitment to the organization (managerial model) rather than to the profession (professional model).[3] Lack of professionalism may be even more of an issue in the public sector than the private.

One author feels that public personnel managers are not and will not be fully professional as long as personnel management remains unintegrated with the basic management processes in government and the managers themselves are short-termers who do not expect to spend their entire careers in personnel management.[4]

PREVIOUS RESEARCH

Only two previous studies have focused upon the background characteristics and qualifications of personnel managers in public agencies. The first study, by Jones,

Myron D. Fottler is associate professor of human resources management in the Graduate School of Business, University of Alabama. Craig Norrell is in the M.B.A. program at the University of Alabama.

Reprinted from Myron D. Fottler and Craig Norrell, "State Government Personnel Directors: A Comparative Analysis of Their Background Characteristics and Qualifications," *Public Personnel Management* (January-February 1979), 17–25.

examined 160 federal government personnel managers in a regional city in grade levels GS-9 to GS-13.[5] That study did not differentiate the different levels nor did it relate background characteristics to other variables such as organization size. The second study, by Fottler and Townsend, examined personnel directors of various public agencies in the state of Iowa.[6] Among these were state agencies, city and county governments, and public school districts.

An examination of these studies, as well as previous studies of the private sector, reveals several problems inherent in any attempt to generalize the results. First, different levels of personnel managers (personnel directors and personnel managers) are studied. In some cases these different levels are combined in the statistical analysis.[7] Second, the nature of the employing organization has often either not been specified or data for diverse organizations have been combined. It is therefore impossible to disentangle the relationship among various organizational characteristics (size, level of government, mission) and professionalism. Third, the background characteristics and qualifications studied have been diverse. There is no single set of variables that have been studied in all the previous research.

DATA AND METHODOLOGY

The present study analyzes information concerning state government personnel directors in Alabama (1978) and Iowa (1977). The directors of seventeen Alabama state agencies and ten Iowa state agencies are included in the sample. Personal interviews were conducted with personnel directors of all seventeen state agencies in the state of Alabama. These departments were Agriculture and Industry, Alcohol and Beverage Control, Corrections, Education, Forestry, Health, Highway, Industrial Relations, Insurance, Mental Health, Military, Pardon and Parole, Pensions and Security, Personnel, Public Safety, Public Service, and Revenue. These individuals were members of the Personnel Officer's Council. Of the seventeen directors studied, eleven had personnel responsibilities for 1,000 or more employees, three for 250–999 employees, and three for 1–249 employees.

The variables examined were the same examined in a previous study of Iowa public personnel managers by the senior author.[8] These included age, sex, education, previous personnel experience, personnel as sole function, years in present position, years in personnel work, ratio of personnel workers per 1,000 employees, college major, and courses specified as most helpful on the job. The Iowa study was based on data gathered through a mail questionnaire responded to by ten of the twelve state government agencies in the state. Thus, the data reported in this study will focus exclusively on personnel *directors* rather than all managers involved in the personnel function.

A comparison of Alabama and Iowa provides some data on two states that exhibit both similarities and differences. Both states are approximately equal in population and in the proportion of the population in urban, suburban, and rural areas. However, Alabama is located in the South rather than the Midwest, has lower per capita income, and may have a more "conservative" political ideology. A good example of the latter is the fact that Iowa has had a Public Employment Relations Act for about four years, whereas Alabama is not even considering such legislation.

In sum, the present study constitutes a partial replication of the Iowa study focusing upon state agencies. These data should allow us to determine which background factors are constant and which are variable in different public agencies. It may also provide some insight into the relative degree of public professionalization in different areas of the country. Where personnel data are available, comparisons with previous studies of the private sector will also be made.

RESULTS AND DISCUSSIONS

Table 1 shows the background characteristics of state government personnel directors for the total sample of public personnel directors as well as a breakdown by state and size grouping. The mean age is approximately fifty and 85 percent are male. Approximately one-third hold graduate degrees, while 85 percent have bachelor's degrees. Almost 90 percent have held a previous job in personnel, and 78 percent are involved in personnel as their sole function. These individuals have spent an average of fifteen years in personnel work and almost seven years in their present position. The ratio of personnel employees (excluding clerical) per 1,000 employees is approximately two.

Contrary to the views of some critics of the public personnel role.[9] these data are supportive of a high degree of professionalism among public sector personnel directors. This is more true of previous personnel experience than education, as two-thirds lack a graduate degree. These data indicate public personnel directors in state agencies are not short-termers. A permanent career commitment to public personnel management is indicated.

With a few exceptions, these results are also consistent with similar data generated in the private sector.[10] One exception was sex. Whereas previous research has shown 96–100 percent of private sector directors to be male, only 85 percent of these public sector personnel managers are male. While such data are only suggestive, they may indicate that the public sector is more open than the private sector to females in high-level positions.

The other exception is the ratio of personnel workers per 1,000 employees. Studies of the private sector have shown that ratio to vary from 5 to 9, whereas these data for the public sector show an average ratio of 1.8. The explanation may lie in the existence of a Civil Service Commission in state government that handles many of the personnel functions which must be performed internally in private companies. It may also reflect the relatively small size of private companies studied (x each 259 employees), since smaller companies tend to have a higher ratio of personnel employees per 1,000 employees (due to their inability to utilize economics of scale). Nevertheless, the data reported here is not consistent with a view that public sector organizations are more "bureaucratic" than private sector organizations.

There were several significant differences between the two states. Alabama's personnel directors are older and less educated than those in Iowa. Merit may play a greater role and politics a lesser role in the appointment of personnel directors in Iowa as compared to Alabama. An alternative explanation is that experience receives relatively heavier weight and education relatively less weight in the recruitment of personnel directors in Alabama. Some evidence for this interpretation is the fact that the mean years experience in personnel work was seventeen years in Alabama compared to thirteen years in Iowa.

One surprising finding is that while none of the state personnel directors in

Iowa were female, four of the Alabama directors (24 percent) were female. Although there is no obvious reason why females should be more readily accepted in Alabama, it may be that the salaries or power of the personnel director are lower in Alabama. Since these variables were not the focus of the present study, such a relationship is merely conjecture. An interesting sidelight of the Alabama data is the fact that the female directors had a mean age of sixty and had spent nineteen years in personnel work. Yet only 50 percent had a college degree, and only 50 percent had personnel as their sole function. This provides some support for the view that the personnel role in Alabama may be less "professionalized" than in Iowa.

Finally, there was also a significant difference in the ratio of personnel employees per 1,000 employees, with Alabama employing fewer. This finding is also consistent with the previous finding. If the personnel role is considered primarily clerical, the ratio of (nonclerical) personnel employees should presumably be lower. The Alabama personnel directors interviewed indicated that emphasis was placed on technical clerical workers within Alabama's personnel system. If such employees were included in the calculation of the personnel ratio, the ratio would equal 3.1. The interviewers also indicated that Alabama's agency personnel directors work in close conjunction with the State Personnel Department whose staff provides valuable support.

Size also provides some interesting contrasts. The larger agencies have a significantly higher probability of employing a male personnel director. Since there is a positive correlation between size of agency and salary of the personnel director[12] it may be that females are accepted for lower paying, but not higher paying, personnel directorships. The larger employers also tend to recruit individuals with previous personnel experience and more years of such experience. This may reflect a higher salary schedule and therefore a larger candidate pool for the directorships of large agencies.

As might be expected, personnel constitutes the sole function of all of the personnel directors in larger agencies, but only 46 percent of the personnel directors in smaller agencies indicated that personnel was their sole function. This reflects the fact that personnel becomes a more specialized management function as the size of an agency grows.[13] Small agencies may not have the volume of activity in personnel to justify hiring a full-time person whose sole duty is personnel. Finally, the data in Table 1 show that the ratio of personnel employees per 1,000 employees declines as agency size increases. This negative relationship between organization size and the personnel ratio has been found in other studies and undoubtedly reflects economics of scale.[14]

Table 2 indicates the college major of state government personnel directors for the higher degrees attained. The most prevalent majors were industrial relations or personnel (26 percent) and social sciences (26 percent). Law (11 percent), other business (7 percent), and public administration (7 percent) were also heavily represented. Approximately one-third of the subjects had majored in business (either industrial relations or other). Fifteen percent of the directors studied were not college graduates. Previous studies of the private sector indicate 17–30 percent had majored in personnel/industrial relations, while 40–50 percent had majored in business.[15] The college majors of the public personnel managers is quite comparable to that found for the private sector. The only exception is that the private sector managers appear to have a higher proportion of business degree holders and a

Table 1 Background characteristics of state government personnel directors, by state and size of government unit

Background characteristics	Total Sample	State		Size	
		Alabama	Iowa	1–999 Employees	1000+ Employees
	(n = 27)	(n = 17)	(n = 10)	(n = 11)	(n = 16)
Mean age	49.8	53.3*	44.0 *	49.2	50.3
Proportion Male	85.2	76.5**	100.00**	72.7**	93.8 **
Proportion with bachelor's degree	85.2	76.5**	100.00**	81.8	87.5
Proportion with graduate degree	33.3	29.4*	40.0 *	36.4	43.8
Proportion with previous personnel experience	88.5	88.2	90.0	72.7**	100.00**
Proportion with personnel as sole function	77.8	76.5	80.0	45.5**	100.00**
Mean years in present position	6.6	7.0	5.9	6.5	.7.2
Mean years in personnel work	15.3	16.6	13.2	13.4*	16.7 *
Ratio of personnel workers per 1,000 employees	1.8	1.4**	2.6 **	2.5*	1.3 *
Mean number of employees	1929	1770*	2200*	439**	3018**

* t–values for differences statistically significant at p < .05
** t–values for differences statistically significant at p < .01

Table 2 College major of state government personnel directors for highest degree attained, by state and size of government unit (percentage distribution)

College major	Total Sample	State Alabama	State Iowa	Size 1–999 Employees	Size 1000+ Employees
	(n = 27)	(n = 17)	(n = 10)	(n = 11)	(n = 16)
Industrial relations/ personnel	25.9	17.6**	40.00**	9.1**	37.5**
Social sciences (economics, psychology, sociology, political science)	25.9	29.4	20.0	45.4**	12.5**
Law	11.1	11.8	10.0	18.2*	6.2*
Other business majors (general business, accounting, finance, marketing)	7.4	11.8	0.0	0.0	12.5
Public administration	7.4	5.9	10.0	0.0	12.5
Physical sciences	3.7	0.0	10.0	9.1	0.0
Education	3.7	0.0	10.0	0.0	6.2
Noncollege graduate	14.9	23.5*	0.0	18.2	12.5
Totals	100.0	100.0	100.0	100.0	99.9

Table 3 College courses specified by state government personnel directors as most helpful, by state and size of government unit (percentage distribution)

Courses	Total Sample	State Alabama	State Iowa	Size 1–999 Employees	Size 1000+ Employees
	(n = 102)	(n = 71)	(n = 31)	(n = 43)	(n = 59)
Industrial relations/ personnel	21.5	18.3*	29.0*	20.9	22.0
Public administration	16.7	22.6**	3.3**	16.3	17.0
Statistics	16.7	21.1**	6.4**	18.6	15.2
Other business courses	11.7	11.3	12.9	14.0	10.2
Psychology and sociology	10.8	9.9	12.9	9.3	11.8
Organization behavior	6.9	5.6	9.7	4.6	8.5
Economics	6.9	4.2*	12.9*	7.0	6.8
Law	5.9	5.6	6.4	7.0	5.1
Education	2.9	1.4	6.5	2.3	3.4
	100.0	100.0	100.0	100.0	100.0

smaller proportion of social science majors. This is not surprising since most business schools have a private sector orientation (although this situation has been slowly changing in recent years).

Comparison of Alabama and Iowa indicate that there are significant differences in the proportion of college graduates and the proportion of industrial relations/ personnel graduates in the two states. As indicated previously, none of the Iowa personnel directors were without a degree, whereas almost one-fourth of Alabama's personnel directors were not college graduates. This reflects a greater emphasis on experience in selecting personnel directors in the Alabama State government. The greater proportion of industrial relations/personnel degrees in Iowa may reflect the existence of a statute allowing state government employees to engage in collective bargaining. It may also reflect a greater amount of union activity generally in Iowa and the consequent greater proportion of college graduates with an industrial relations major.

Industrial relations/personnel majors are also more prevalent in larger state agencies. This may reflect a higher degree of "professionalism" in the larger agencies. Individuals who major in this field in college may have more of a career commitment to the field than those who major in other subjects. Conversely, the high proportion of social science majors in smaller agencies may reflect a larger element of chance in the career patterns of personnel directors in smaller agencies. The higher proportion of law graduates in smaller agencies may reflect the fact that lawyers are viewed as specialists and do not generally become personnel directors in larger agencies that can afford to employ a lawyer on staff. Smaller agencies that cannot afford to hire a legal specialist tend to hire a lawyer as director and then use the individual for both general and specialized personnel functions.

Table 3 shows the courses that state government personnel directors specified as most helpful to themselves and to an individual contemplating entering the public personnel management field. The twenty-seven directors mentioned a total of 102 courses or an average of approximately 3.8 courses per respondent. The most frequently mentioned courses were industrial relations/personnel, public administration, and statistics. Other business courses, psychology, and sociology were also mentioned frequently. Previous studies in the private sector have emphasized all of these courses with the exception of public administration and statistics. Reasons for the inclusion of public administration courses by public personnel directors (but not private sector personnel directors) are rather obvious.

The greater emphasis on statistics in the public sector surveys may reflect differences in the institutional environment at the time when the surveys were conducted. The private sector studies in which helpful courses were discussed were reported in 1969 and 1970.[16] By contrast, these public sector surveys were conducted in 1977 and 1978. Affirmative action was a much more significant factor in the late 1970s than it was in the late 1960s. As a result, test validation is a major concern. Such validation cannot be implemented or evaluated if the personnel manager is unaware of statistical concepts and techniques.

Several differences in course selection between Alabama and Iowa are also noted in Table 3. Industrial relations/personnel courses were given greater emphasis in Iowa due to the passage of a Public Employment Relations Act in 1974. The Alabama personnel directors indicated that they did not expect passage of a similar law in Alabama within the next five years. Reasons for the greater emphasis on the public administration in Alabama are not clear. If state government in Alabama is more politicized than that in Iowa, then perhaps the respondents felt courses in public administration might provide students with more political sophistication. Alabama's greater emphasis on statistics may reflect the fact that Alabama directors considered test validation to be their most serious problem. In fact, Alabama had more occupational examinations validated and approved by the EEOC than any other state government at the time of this writing. In Iowa successful implementation of the collective bargaining law was considered the top priority. Size of the state agency apparently is not a crucial determinant of necessary courses for a personnel director.

CONCLUSIONS AND IMPLICATIONS

Several conclusions are possible on the basis of data presented here and in previous studies. However, given the great diversity of public and private sector organizations in the United States, these should be considered as hypotheses for further testing rather than firm statements of fact.

First, state government personnel directors appear to exhibit as high a degree of professionalism as their private sector counterparts. The data for both are quite comparable, and each exhibits long experience in personnel work, study of similar course work relevant to the field, and very high proportions of degree holders. Perhaps increasing the proportion of graduate degree holders might increase professionalism in the future. Over time, this appears to be occurring. Whether or not public sector personnel directors have the degree of autonomy necessary to operate their departments in a truly professional manner is an issue that is addressed elsewhere.[17] More decentralization of power and autonomy to the various departments may be necessary to foster professionalism among the state government personnel directors.

Second, the environment within which state agencies function affects the degree of professionalism and the relative emphasis on different personnel functions. States that want to foster professionalism should emphasize education as a major criteria. Those that want to foster an organizational orientation may wish to give greater emphasis to experience. States that centralize most of the more important personnel functions can also expect to find lesser degrees of professionalism among the personnel directors in the individual agencies. The priorities existing in each state government will determine both the degree of professionalism and the degree to which various skills, attributes, and background factors are emphasized. The existence of collective bargaining statutes or the concern with test validation will affect both the types of individuals recruited as personnel directors and the personnel priorities of the agency.

Finally, organizational size affects many factors in the public personnel system. Among the most important are the rewards, perceived prestige, the quality and professionalism of personnel directors, the degree of specialization, and economies of scale. Larger government agencies appear to attract more highly qualified personnel directors since their size allows greater rewards, more specialization, and economies of scale. Much more research comparing the personnel function in the public and private sectors and in different public sector organizations is needed before definitive conclusions can be drawn.

NOTES

1. For example, see William F. Glueck, "Directors for Departments of Organization: Their Educational Achievement and Career Patterns," *MSU Business Topics* 17 (Winter 1969): 44–54 and Dalton E. McFarland, *Company Officers Assess the Personnel Function.* AMA Research Study No. 74 (New York City: American Management Association, 1969).

2. George Ritzer and Harrison M. Trice, *An Occupation in Conflict: A Study of the Personnel Manager* (Ithaca, New York: New York State School of Industrial and Labor Relations, Cornell University, 1969).

3. See John B. Miner and Mary G. Miner, "Managerial Characteristics of Personnel Managers," *Industrial Relations* 15 (May 1976): 225–34.

4. See Jay M. Shafritz, *Public Personnel Management: The Heritage of Civil Service Reform* (New York City: Praeger Publishers, 1975), pp. 108–115.

5. William A. Jones, Jr., "Occupational Perceptions of Federal Personnel Administrators in a Regional City," *Public Personnel Management* 5 (January-February 1976): 52–59.

6. Myron D. Fottler and Norman A. Townsend, "Characteristics of Public and Private Personnel Directors," *Public Personnel Management* 6 (July-August 1977): 250–58.

7. See Miner and Miner.

8. See Fottler and Townsend.

9. See Shafritz.

10. For a convenient summary of previous research in the private sector, see Fottler and Townsend, Table 1.

11. See Bruce E. Despelder, *Ratio of Staff to Line Personnel* (Columbus, Ohio State University, Bureau of Business Research, 1962).

12. Alton W. Baker, *Personnel Management in Small Plants* (Columbus, Ohio: State University, Bureau of Business Research, 1955).

13. When an organization grows in the private sector, personnel functions are assigned to one employee or manager, first on a part-time basis and then full time. Studies have found that private organizations employ a full-time personnel director when there are 100–200 employees. See Baker and Despelder. The same phenomenon appears to apply to the public sector.

14. See Despelder.

15. See Fottler and Townsend.

16. See O. Jeff Harris, "Personnel Administrators: The Truth About Their Backgrounds," *MSU Business Topics* 17 (Winter 1969): 22–29 and Thomas L. Wheeler, "Graduate Business Education for Personnel Management Executives," *Personnel Journal* 49 (November 1970): 932–34.

17. See Shafritz.

The Role of Personnel Management in the 1980s

Donald E. Klingner

This paper was originally prepared for presentation at the Mid-Continent Conference in New Personnel Management at the University of Kansas, Lawrence, Kansas, June 1, 1979.

The end of each decade seems to serve as a signal to commentators that it is time to set pen to paper. Just as surely as March brings robins, 1980 will bring speeches and articles predicting the ways in which personnel management is to change during the coming decade. This article is no exception; it will discuss four areas of personnel management that have begun to change over the past decade. First, the context of personnel management—the conditions, values, and laws influencing it—have changed. This has led to three other changes: (1) an increase in the number and variety of personnel managers; (2) a potential increase in their responsibilities and power within organizations; and (3) changing entry requirements and career patterns for members of the profession.

All of these changes are revolutionary in that they involve fundamental alterations in the nature of personnel management. While some of them may have been predictable ten or twenty years ago, their emergence is recent, considering that personnel management did not even exist one hundred years ago.

CHANGING CONTEXT

The context of personnel management is determined by the values, conditions, and events that affect personnel activities. Several changes are apparent here, including (a) a continuing shift from closed to open system models of the personnel function, (b) disputes over goals and methods, (c) the increasing importance of law, (d) a blurring of the distinction between public and private sectors, and (e) the increased value of human resources.

Traditionally, personnel management was a staff function that served to assist line management in the procurement, allocation, development, maintenance, and sanctioning of human resources. Most simply stated, its objective was to make people productive. While this goal is still valid, in the past it was always pursued from a management perspective. Now it is evident that personnel managers must also be cognizant of the goals and interests of two groups beside management: employees and external pressure groups (unions, media, government regulators, legislatures, and special interest groups). These two groups have been responsible for the addition of several new areas of concern to the personnel manager's responsibilities: affirmative action, labor-management relations, appeal and grievance systems, employee health and safety, and career/life planning.[1]

Reprinted from Donald E. Klingner, "The Role of Personnel Management in the 1980s," *The Personnel Administrator* (September 1979).

The resultant enlargement of the personnel function has intensified disputes over goals and methods appropriate to given situations. More and more, questions are settled "politically" in a contest of opposing values, rather than through management's choice of the most efficient solution for reaching a unanimous goal. For example, the *Weber* case (*Weber* v. *United Steelworkers of America*) has raised the issue of whether preferential reassignment of blacks constitutes reverse discrimination against whites. Or fines against steel manufacturers for OSHA violations raise the question of whether safety is a worthwhile objective if it means that increased costs will spur relocation of the plant to a different community. In this respect, personnel managers are like automobile manufacturers: Not only must the car they make sell, it must also be safe, economical, and advertised fairly.

The references to court cases indicate that as the objectives of personnel management become increasingly disputed among these three groups— management, employees, and external pressure groups—such questions are more likely to be resolved outside the organization than inside it. This has resulted in a host of laws, court decisions, and administrative regulations that guide, bind, and frustrate personnel managers. In the private sector, the Wagner Act and the Taft-Hartley Act have defined the conditions under which unions may organize, bargain collectively, and administer contracts. In the public sector, the "strings" attached to federal grants-in-aid heavily restrict personnel practice by requiring recipients to classify jobs, staff them, and evaluate employees according to merit system standards. As in most political situations, these laws are seldom clear. The *Sears* case, an attempt to force federal agencies to clarify their conflicting affirmative action goals, represents a valiant attempt by a major retailer to bring order out of chaos. Yet it is fairly safe to predict that affirmative action agencies will continue to enforce conflicting demands that organizations hire more veterans (without discriminating against females) and blacks (without discriminating against whites). Why? Because each agency represents a different value rather than representing "the government" as Sears would prefer.

In the past, it was possible to draw a distinction between the private and public sectors on the grounds that the former existed to make a profit while the latter provided socially desirable goods and resources. Despite the virtues of "free enterprise," a close reading of American economic history shows that business has long clamored for some government regulation to restrict competition and regulate the market. For example, the Federal Trade Commission was established to enforce self-regulation of advertising practices; and the Food and Drug Administration was initially intended to promote agricultural exports by having the federal government certify their quality. The increasing power of employees and external interest groups has also hastened the trend toward accepting the social responsibilities of business. Under the influence of popular sentiment, captured in acts like the Jarvis-Gann Initiative in California, public agencies are moving to develop measures of productivity. Any contemporary management journal is filled with discussions of "cost containment" and "zero-based budgeting." The public-versus-private dichotomy is also complicated by the growth of quasi-public industries that are closely regulated regardless of ownership: banks, insurance companies, schools, and hospitals. The result is a mixture of socialism and regulated state capitalism, which means that public and private personnel management can be less easily differentiated in terms of objectives or methods.[2]

These trends are occurring against a backdrop of increasing complexity of work methods. Organizations require more skilled persons with more specialized skills than at any time in history. This means that the costs of acquiring, maintaining, utilizing, and replacing human resources are increasing. If it costs $5,000 to select one manager and $15,000 to train him or her on the job for six months, then 100 percent turnover in that position costs the organization $20,000 annually per manager. The waste of human resources, like the waste of money, is increasingly recognized as a burden for the organization.

INCREASED NUMBERS AND DIVERSITY

The changing context of personnel management is causing three other changes. The first of these is an increase in the number and diversity of personnel managers. According to a recent *Wall Street Journal* article, personnel management is among the ten fastest growing occupations in the United States. This growth is due to the factors discussed above. Certainly, increases in federal regulation have increased the need for specialists in labor relations, occupational safety and health, and affirmative action. The increased cost of *mis*managing human resources has led to the development of specialized techniques for selection, performance evaluation, promotion, and training. The proliferation of subspecialties and the increasingly political nature of the personnel function (as an interpreter of regulations and a mediator among the interests of competing groups) has led to a relative increase in budget and personnel within the organization.[3] In short, personnel managers have learned to their advantage that there is a brighter future for them as managers than as technicians.

This growth in the number and power of personnel managers is also due to increases in the types of personnel managers. At least four identifiable types of personnel professionals exist: in-house, central staff agency, regulatory commission, and consultant. Each has a different organizational base, different values, and different objectives.

In-house personnel managers are primarily responsible for helping supervisors and line managers reach company goals. They are normally caught between the conflicting demands of the company supervisors (for quick and compliant approval of personnel actions) and employees (for maximum opportunity for promotion) and top management (to keep the organization out of trouble).

Central staff agency personnel are responsible for performing centralized functions, such as job evaluation, recruitment, testing, record keeping, training, or retirement, for a number of separate organizations. They are created either to ensure compliance with merit system regulations (particularly in the public sector), or to gain the benefits of economies of scale. These personnel are more likely to regard themselves either as defenders of "merit" or as proponents of efficiency. They are apt to be less sympathetic to the needs of the agency manager than are their in-house counterparts. Since both centralization and decentralization have opposite advantages. the tension between these two types of systems can be expected to continue. In an era of corporate expansion, greater centralization of functions will typically occur because of the greater efficiency of large-scale recruitment and testing. In an era of retrenchment, as is occurring now in the federal government, decentralization will occur because of the need to develop diversified agency responses to peculiar problems.

The third type of personnel manager, the member of a regulatory commission, is most frequently found in the public sector. This person evaluates the personnel decisions of subsidiary personnel departments for compliance with regulations, particularly in cases involving a grievance or disciplinary action. Included in this category would be labor-management-relations mediation agencies, merit review boards, and the new federal Merit Systems Protection Board.

The increasing complexity of personnel activities has increased the number of consultants offering services to government and industry. These outside experts usually offer services in areas subject to heated disputes over objectives (where the services of an impartial adviser are considered helpful) or in areas requiring experience or resources beyond the scope of the organization's in-house staff (for example, extensive job reevaluation or training). The growing body of research literature in personnel management is largely due to the ability of consultants to combine services to client organizations with data collection and analysis.

INCREASED RESPONSIBILITIES

The changing context of personnel management has led to a second change in the nature of the profession. At least potentially, the responsibilities of the personnel manager have expanded, but it is important to emphasize that this increased responsibility is potential rather than actual. Its realization depends on whether or not personnel managers perceive these new responsibilities as their domain and whether they have the power to defend their claims. Three growth areas are evident.

First, personnel managers are increasingly expected to mediate among the competing objectives of organizational units, employees, and outside groups.[4] For example, human resource forecasts are based on assumptions about the relative power of departments and affirmative action compliance requirements. As a mediator among conflicting interests, the personnel manager has more influence than a technician working toward known objectives does.

Second, personnel managers are responsible for interpreting government regulations, developing new techniques in compliance with them, and (if need be) defending the organization should government investigators question its personnel practices.[5] This responsiblity has increased the professional status of personnel managers, since the expertise required to make sense of regulations is great, as is the risk of failure. Recently, for example, the personnel manager of a large electronics firm met regulations issued by the Office of Federal Contract Compliance Programs by hiring two Indian engineers. Not long after their probationary period had passed, a routine EEOC investigation revealed that they should not have been included in the company's affirmative action compliance data because they were Asian rather than native American Indian. The personnel manager was fired. Personnel managers are thus often expected to comply with confusing and contradictory regulations enforced by competing agencies and are held responsible for failure to do so.

Third, the increased complexity of personnel management means that personnel managers will be held responsible for developing, implementing, and evaluating programs in support of line management in at least five new areas: (1) job humanization, (2) performance-oriented compensation, (3) flexible work schedules, (4) flexible compensation plans, and (5) career/life planning. [6,7,8] Job humanization refers to the matching of technological work methods with human needs. It can include job enrichment, job enlargement, or job rotation. Performance-oriented compensation is based on the concept of equity but is oriented toward outcomes of work rather than job descriptions. Flexible work schedules, popularly called "flexitime," are an answer to parking problems, traffic congestion, and the variability of employees' biological clocks. Yet it may be difficult to institute this kind of program without sacrificing control, communications, and efficient administration of time and leave regulations. Flexible compensation plans allow employees to select benefits from a range of alternatives, up to a certain dollar value. However, critical problems with flexible compensation plans remain in such areas as administrative efficiency and conformance with IRS regulations. Lastly, career/life planning is the other side of human resource planning. Rather than asking what the organization's human resource needs are, the personnel manager must meet the employees' needs for vocational counseling, coping with job stress, and preparing for retirement. The potential alternatives are cynicism, alcoholism, and on-the-job retirement.

The involvement of the personnel manager in these five problem areas means that she or he must collect data for planning and evaluating programs. This may include job satisfaction, turnover, sick leave abuse, productivity, or other measures of human resource utilization. When these data are used to develop new programs or evaluate current ones, the result is action research: the systematic use of data for evaluative and planning purposes.

NEW QUALIFICATIONS, NEW CAREERS

These changes lead to our final topic—the personnel manager of the 1980s. What will be his or her qualifications and career pattern? Five somewhat contradictory trends emerge from a view of future personnel managers: (1) increased regulatory orientation, (2) increased quantitative orientation, (3) increased humanist orientation, (4) increased professionalism, and (5) increased managerial competence.

First, personnel managers are required to know laws, regulations, and case law related to labor relations and affirmative action. Because (as the discussion of the context indicates) these laws are often confusing and contradictory, personnel managers need to be skilled not only in following regulations but also in interpreting them and working with outside compliance agencies to administer them. Second, personnel managers are expected to possess technical skills in data collection, analysis, and interpretation for purposes of managerial control. These skills include statistics, computer programming, research methods, and accounting. For example, the development of empirical test validation techniques requires knowledge of inferential statistics. In order to receive information about the differential pass rate on a test for blacks and whites, the personnel manager must have sufficient understanding of personnel management information-system data requirements to request the appropriate reports. To evaluate the effectiveness of an affirmative action program, the personnel manager must be able to develop research designs comparing present and former utilization of human resources. The evaluation of the cost effectiveness of the implemented program requires comparing the cost of the program against the cost of underutilization of human resources.

Third, personnel managers are required to have knowledge of social science theory and research related to the humanization of work. They are still expected to be "people oriented," though this orientation is perhaps more technological than during the "human relations" era of the 1950s and 1960s. Today, specialists at job redesign, flexible compensation, and productivity bargaining are expected to be concerned with both the quality of work life (employee motivation and job satisfaction) and organizational effectiveness (turnover, absenteeism, and employee productivity). While the objective may still be the ideal convergence of individual and organizational goals, the climate and jargon fit the "austere 1980s" rather than the "self-actualizing 1960s."

Fourth, these three trends—greater emphasis on interpretation of laws, technical skills, and humanization of work—have vastly increased the professional status of personnel management as an occupation. Ten years ago it was possible to debate whether personnel management was an occupation (a cluster of jobs with similar tasks and qualifications) or a profession (more explicit self-identification, stricter entrance requirements, credentials and training).[9] Today it is evident that a profession has emerged. There are several professional personnel management associations with thousands of members, and there are also many respected personnel journals. Hundreds of schools and departments (of business administration, public administration, and psychology) offer course work or degrees in personnel management and its subspecialties.

A variety of people will be drawn into personnel management because they are attracted to different values or objectives within the field. Those with a legal background will be attracted because of its regulatory aspects. Those with a technical or quantitative orientation (business, statistics, data processing, or economics) will be attracted to its accounting and control functions. And those with a humanistic orientation (sociology, psychology, education, political science, or philosophy) will find comfort in its orientation toward human development in organizations.

These two trends—professionalization and diversity—will lead to stronger attempts to formalize entrance requirements and model career patterns for the profession.[10,11,12] At the same time, these trends will prevent agreement on the precise nature of these requirements and patterns. For the near future, personnel managers will agree only that their profession involves a mixture of art, science, and professional practice. However, it can be increasingly expected that top level personnel managers will have a broad base of skills, as demonstrated by their experience in company programs such as sales, manufacturing, or finance.[13]

It is ironic that traditional personnel managers have often resisted trends that have subsequently become responsible for the growth of their profession. The legal, technical, and humanistic aspects of personnel management have injected controversy into areas of personnel such as selection and job design that were once considered the domain of technicians. Yet these influences (external legal requirements, managerial demands for increased productivity, and employee concerns with the humanization of work) have led to the emergence of personnel managers as *managers*. In short, they now share responsibility for mediating among groups and mobilizing organizational resources toward greater productivity. This, then, is the fifth and final emergent trend in personnel management qualifications and career patterns. By participating to a greater extent (with other managers) in helping maintain organizational productivity and effectiveness, personnel managers will become more adept at the traditional skills of bureaucratic infighting. They will learn to maintain and extend domain, protect budgets and "turf," and utilize scarce resources toward competing objectives. In effect, they will behave increasingly like managers rather than technicians.

Having been in the field for over ten years, I have mixed feelings about these changes. I hope that we can become professional without becoming smug, that we can become technically competent without losing common sense, and that we can enter into the process of management without losing our faith that the needs of people and organizations can indeed converge and, further, that we can help make this happen.

NOTES

1. Donald E. Klingner and John Nalbandian, "Personnel Management by Whose Objectives?" *Public Administration Review* 38, 4 (July-August 1978): 366–72.

2. Frank J. Thompson, "Are P.A. Graduates any Different? A Preliminary Look at Public Personnel Officials," *Public Personnel Management* (May-June 1978): 198–204.

3. Fred K. Foulkes and Henry M. Morgan, "Organizing and Staffing the Personnel Function," *Harvard Business Review* (May-June 1977): 142–54.

4. James M. Mitchell and Rolfe Schroeder, "Future Shock for Personnel Administration," *Public Personnel Management* (July-August 1974): 265–69.

5. Thelma Hunt, "Critical Issues Facing Personnel Administrators Today," *Public Personnel Management* (November-December 1974): 464–72.

6. Fred K. Foulkes, "The Expanding Role of the Personnel Function," *Harvard Business Review* (March-April 1975): 71–84.

7. Edwin H. Burack and Edwin L. Miller, "The Personnel Function in Transition," *Management Review* (March 1977): 50–53.

8. Bernard M. Bass, "Organizational Life in the '70s and Beyond," *Personnel Psychology* 25 (1972): 19–30.

9. Thomas H. Patten, Jr., "Is Personnel Administration a Profession?" *Personnel Administration* (March-April 1968): 39–48.

10. Dan Prock and Bob Henson, "The Educational Needs of and the Future Labor Market Demand for Human Resource Managers," *Personnel Journal* (December 1977): 602–07.

11. David L. Austin, "Portrait of a Personnel Executive: More Participation," *The Personnel Administrator* (August 1978): 58–63.

12. Myron D. Fottler and Norman A. Townsend, "Characteristics of Public and Private Personnel Directors," *Public Personnel Management* (July-August 1977), 250–58.

13. ———, "The Specifications for a Top Human Resources Officer . . . A Personnel Symposium," *Personnel* (May-June 1978): 24–31.

2

Planning and Public Personnel Management

Planning is necessary for the management of human resources in organizations, and three personnel activities are particularly involved: human resource planning, organizational development, and the design of personnel systems. The first allows organizations to estimate future employee needs and to develop programs—selection, promotion, or training—to meet those needs. The second is a process that uses knowledge and techniques from the behavioral sciences to increase organizational effectiveness by integrating individual desires for growth and development with the organizational objective of productivity improvement. It is, in effect, planned organizational change involving human resources. The third includes the changing of personnel processes or structures to meet organizational goals within environmental constraints.

Addressing the topic of organizational human resource planning, Milton Drandell evaluates several alternative human resource forecasting techniques: collective opinion, analysis of historical data, and more sophisticated techniques such as exponential smoothing. He emphasizes that the choice of a forecasting technique depends upon the size of the agency, the qualifications of forecasters, and the resources available. While some readers may find this article technical, it is a lucid discussion of the comparative advantages of quantitative and nonquantitative forecasting techniques.

The first article on organization development is by Edgar Schein. As an organizational psychologist, he considers the human element to be of increasing importance to organizations because peoples' skills are needed in design and marketing. Managers need to select the right kind of employees and to recognize the effect of changed lifestyles on organizational work habits. The personnel manager's job is to coordinate the matching of employee and organizational needs from the line manager up to top management. This article not only provides a conceptual focus for human resource planning, it also connects this with career/life planning by showing how personnel managers can meet employee needs as well as organizational goals.

Ellis Hillmar's analysis of the similarities between organization development (OD) and management by objectives (MBO) takes Schein's concept further. He considers both OD and MBO to be concerned with the increased effectiveness of human resources, through work systems, to meet organizational goals. In addition to a fine review of the values and concepts of both fields, he presents several examples of their harmony in the real world of planned organizational change.

The fundamental question, beyond the validity of the link between organizational and employee needs, that Schein and Hillmar propose is the question of whether OD can measurably increase employee productivity. John Kimberly and Warren Nielsen evaluate the success of an OD project in a plant that had been plagued by decreasing employee production standards and profits and increasing grievances and absenteeism. Employees from the plant manager on down were involved in a multistep process of problem diagnosis, data collection, change recommendation, action planning, and team building. The results, however, neither supported nor refuted the assumption that OD causes productivity increases. While increases in quality and profit did occur, increases in quantity of production did not. This factor was felt to be outside the control of plant management, dependent instead upon corporate policy and market conditions. Besides serving as an excellent OD case study, this article shows why personnel managers must be familiar with research methods in order to assess the desirability of proposed organizational changes.

One of the most momentous changes in public personnel management in the last century was the demise of the U.S. Civil Service Commission in 1979 and the division of its functions among the Equal Employment Opportunity Commission and two new agencies (the Office of Personnel Management and the Merit Systems Protection Board). In the final article of Chapter 2, Steven Knudsen, Larry Jakus, and Maida Metz discuss the reasons for this change, describe the change process, and evaluate its probable impact on federal personnel management. It is important to realize that the change process they describe is an example of the applicability of organization development to a personnel system. Because it analyzes the values and objectives of various professionals inside and outside the commission, this article is a noteworthy example of the politics of public personnel management.

A Composite Forecasting Methodology for Manpower Planning Utilizing Objective and Subjective Criteria

Milton Drandell

The author would like to express his appreciation to Trygve Dahle of the Defense Contract Administration Services Region, Los Angeles, for his kind help and assistance in this research. He would also like to thank Professor R. Hal Mason, UCLA Graduate School of Management, and Professors Geraldine Ellerbrock and Paul Zivkovich, School of Business and Social Sciences, California Polytechnic State University, San Luis Obispo, for their helpful comments.

The agencies in the Contract Administration Services (CAS) of the federal government are concerned with the administration of contracts between the government and industry. The goods produced under these contracts vary from clothing and food to sophisticated electronic equipment and space vehicles. They cover virtually every commodity and product produced by American industry. The dollar value of these contracts is substantial; therefore, their administration from the time negotiation has been completed to the time of delivery is of extreme importance.

The incidence of these contracts is based on many factors of a political, social, and economic nature involving congressional and executive action. The forecast of contracts that will be received for administration by one of the geographical regional offices is an exogenous variable whose probability distribution is difficult to obtain. A large manpower force is necessary to administer the contracts, and such a force must be relatively stable to be effective. Thus the problem in manpower planning is to determine a suitable level of personnel to handle the existing contracts and those forecast for the future. What is desired is an equitable balance between the requirements and the means to respond to those requirements.

The administration of the contracts is broken down into three elements referred to as contracts received, contracts shipped, and contracts on hand, the last being the inventory of those currently being administered. These three are referred to as leading indicators in the sense of their importance to the system. There are other indicators to be considered—nine were involved in the study—but these three are the most important. Of these, contracts received, the exogenous variable over which the administrators have no control, is the most difficult to predict. Figures 1 and 2 depict the time series behavior of the first two of these indicators.

Milton Drandell is an associate professor in the School of Business and Social Sciences, California Polytechnic State University, San Luis Obispo, California.

Reprinted from Milton Drandell, "A Composite Forecasting Methodology for Manpower Planning Utilizing Objective and Subjective Criteria," *Academy of Management Journal.* Vol. 18, No. 3 (September 1975), 510–19.

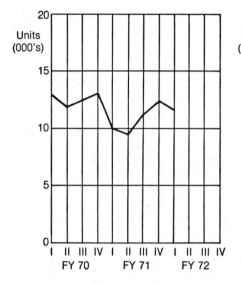

Figure 1 Prime and support contracts received—Quarterly

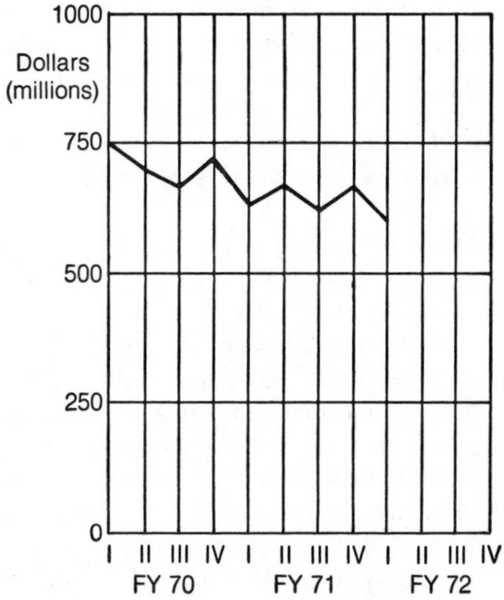

Figure 2 Dollar value of material inspected and released for shipment—Quarterly

This paper concerns itself with one of the regions charged with the responsibility for the administration of the contracts residing there. The methodology developed deals with the indicators themselves. Once a forecast of these has been made, determination of manpower requirements can be readily determined.

THE APPROACH TO FORECASTING

The method of attack in determining the best approach to a particular problem in forecasting is primarily a function of the organization involved. To attempt a scale of sophistication greater than, or less than, that which an organization is capable of ingesting is to invite disaster. This is true even when an organization is large and wealthy in resources with a large computer complex and staff. If the methodology and the output produced is beyond the willingness or capabilities of the organization to grasp, understand, and implement, then little if anything is gained from the development of a sophisticated model. I have seen such large and comprehensive models fail in very large organizations and yet succeed in a comparatively small organization. One management could accept and implement the approach; the other could not. One management was brought into the development of the methodology; the other was not. It was management, not the size of the organization, that was the key to success.

A study of the organization and its people, then, is of utmost importance if a forecasting methodology, particularly one involving a quantitative and computer approach, is to succeed. People supply the data; people interpret and use the output results. No matter what the degree of sophistication involved, people make the system work. The purpose was to study the CAS organization and determine what approach would have the best chance of success.

Collective Opinion Approach

The most common form of forecasting methodology today is that of collective opinion. Basically, this involves the synthesis of all information available to management into a qualitative and essentially nonquantititive form. It should not be taken lightly merely because it is not a quantitative or computer-oriented approach. It involves the value judgments of individuals highly knowledgeable in their fields and possessing an intuitive sense related to problems not easily put into mathematical form. Carried through to a more sophisticated level, this becomes the so-called Delphi method used today, particularly for the long-range forecast. Where the basic variables affecting the forecast are not known explicitly and where even if known their probability distributions are difficult to construct, the method of collective opinion and the Delphi method subjectively express the fears, hopes, and aspirations of the forecaster as she or he looks into the future. Often an analysis of these subjective beliefs is as good or better than what is achieved by a more sophisticated quantitative approach.

A technique moving beyond the collective opinion approach involves the analysis of past parameters and historical data in order to construct ex post probability distributions. Then, as Hertz (6) has shown, these past probability distributions can be combined by means of a simulation approach into an overall collective probability distribution. Individual probability distributions for the future behavior of the variables can also be constructed subjectively and included in the simulation process. There are many variations to the above approaches in the use of past objective and future subjective data (3, 5). Their specific use depends on the application involved. Finally, there are the sophisticated mathematical models, the mathematical programming approach. These models are the most difficult to design and implement, and they do not necessarily produce the greatest return. The entire range of possibilities was studied in the analysis of the problem of forecasting manpower requirements in CAS.

THE METHODOLOGY SELECTED

A time-sharing system does not lend itself in general to a large-scale mathematical approach. A study showed that to develop such a model would be very difficult and the results obtained would be of questionable value. It was decided to use the particular resources the organization possessed; thus, to rely on collective opinion, a great amount of past data, and a remote time-sharing system with a resident set of statistical and mathematical programs. The methodology now became clear. A subjective analysis of the future would be combined with an objective analysis of the past to produce a composite forecast incorporating the best of both possible worlds. No other approach seemed to fit the problem better than this.

One of the most common techniques used in forecasting methodology is that of regression analysis. This technique does not perform well where time series are concerned. Regression analysis was tried, with the indicators as dependent variables and parameters other than time as the independent variables. No suitable set of independent variables could be found that would behave satisfactorily, using past data to test this approach.

Exponential smoothing (ES), a method of weighted averages, has been used successfully in inventory control with time as the independent variable, and it has also been used in other time series analyses (2). It has some definite advantages over regression analysis, and the time-sharing system contained a sophisticated exponential smoothing program (4). It was decided to test this technique as the one to analyze the past data—the objective part of the composite forecast.

EXPONENTIAL SMOOTHING

Exponential smoothing is a method of weighted averages. Whereas regression analysis assigns the same weights to all the data, ES has the ability to vary the weights and give more credence to the more current data than to data from the more distant past. This is a desirable objective since the former have much more validity for future behavior than the latter do. The general advantages of ES are:

1. Only the current value of the indicator and the forecast for the current period are needed to make the forecast for the next time period.

2. Cyclical and seasonal factors can be included in the forecast. The computer program provides for this (4).

3. The weights given to present and more immediate past demands are different than those assigned to the demands of the more distant past. (Here demand is the actual value of the indicator for a certain point in time.)

4. The time-sharing system provides for rapid change as needed in a dynamic analysis.

The basic formula for exponential smoothing is given by:

Forecast for next period = forecast for current period $+\alpha$ (Current period demand $-$ forecast for current period),

where α is a number between 0 and 1.

If F_{i+1} = forecast for next period

F_i = forecast for current period

D_i = Current period demand or value of the variable,

the above equation can be expressed simply as

$$F_{i+1} = F_i + \alpha(D_i - F_i), 0 < \alpha < 1.$$

This equation states that the forecast for the next or (i+1) period is equal to the current forecast plus a fraction of the difference between the current demand and the forecast for the current period. This difference could be positive, negative, or zero.

The more usual form for the formula is given by

$$F_{i+1} = \alpha \cdot D_i + (1 - \alpha)F_i.$$

It can be shown that the current (or old) forecast F_i can itself be expressed in terms of the previous demand D_{i-1}, the previous forecast F_{i-1}, and various powers of α. Continuing in this fashion, it finally can be shown that the forecast F_{i+1} is equal to a sum of previous demand occurrences, each multiplied by various powers of α for as many past history demands as are available. These powers of α are the weights given to the past demand histories, and these weights decrease as a function of time depending upon the initial value of α. For a more complete discussion of the mathematics involved, see Exhibit 1.

To show the effects on the forecast F_{i+1} for various values of α, say for $\alpha=.3$ and $\alpha=.7$, the following are weights assigned to the demands for several past periods.

Table 1 Weights assigned to past period n

α	Demand Weight	1	2	3	n 4	5	6	7
.3	.3	.21	.1470	.1029	.0720	.0504	.0353	.0247
.7	.7	.21	.0630	.0189	.0057	.0017	.0005	.0002

For $\alpha=.3$, seven periods in the past plus the current period account for better than 94 percent of the total weight. For $\alpha=.7$, three past periods plus the current period account for more than 99 percent of the total. Thus the flexibility of the approach is evident, and it is also obvious that a judicious choice of α is necessary. This choice depends on the data and what one assesses the future to hold. The final decision is obtained by analyzing many computer runs and testing ex post the effects of various α's, which was done here. A most important aspect of the time-sharing computer approach is that changes can easily be incorporated into the model on an immediate basis.

Testing the Exponential Smoothing Hypothesis

The ES technique was tested using past data. It was soon found that an α of .3 represented the past best. This also agreed intuitively with what was felt by many to be optimal based on the number of factors involved. Management agreed that approximately six or seven quarterly time periods in the past would provide the most information, with the weights distributed as shown in the example above.

Using $\alpha=.3$ and the past monthly history of each indicator for fiscal year (FY) 1971, a number of test runs were made. The forecasts generated were then compared to the actual occurrence of these indicators in the past. Although ES concerns itself with forecasting the demand primarily for the next period ahead, the computer program used also had the ability to forecast beyond that based on an analysis of the data. This forecast, of course, was not as accurate as the forecast for the next or $(i+1)$ period; yet it served a useful purpose in forecasting on the required yearly basis.

The results obtained indicated in general a difference between actual and predictive behavior of less than 10 percent. Similar results were achieved in forecasts of secondary indicators. In a number of the cases where the error was greater than 10 percent, there was an explanation; namely, had a more detailed analysis been made beforehand, adjustments could have been made to the input data to reflect foreseen abnormal conditions. This reinforced the decision to include in any final forecasting procedure elements of a subjective nature that could not be determined from an analysis of past history.

The reason for the excellent behavior of the ES approach is that the independent variable of time has inherent in it all the parameters that affect the dependent variable, the indicator itself. This was for the short term, four quarters ahead, for which the ES technique works well. Furthermore, the ES computer program had the ability to analyze cyclical and seasonal behavior, an important consideration. It was decided that the ES technique would form the basis for the quantitative analysis of the past.

THE COMPOSITE FORECAST

The following procedure was developed to achieve the forecasting methodology desired. First, a forecast using ES was made based on past data alone. Subjective predictive estimates were then made by management in the form of expected, high, and low values. Special forms were developed for this purpose. The exponential smoothing forecasts were not shown to those making the subjective estimates. The forecasts were made for the four quarters of the year ahead.

A linear regression analysis was then performed on these sixteen points to produce the final composite forecast for each indicator. The regression analysis basically served to average out the four points for each of the quarters. The composite forecast was then based on ES to analyze the past and on subjective estimates to analyze the future. The technique is shown graphically in Figure 3. The final quarterly forecasts lie on the linear function.

This approach combines the past and the future, a desirable objective. In the past, the forecasts made by management were point estimates that were essentially expected values. However, basically, stochastic variables having associated probability distributions difficult to obtain were involved. Those making the point forecasts had essentially a range of values in mind, even though these were not expressed quantitatively. In an attempt to capture this range of beliefs, the high and low values were obtained.

Testing the Composite Approach

In order to test the composite approach methodology as opposed to actual performance behavior, an analysis of past data was first made. The point estimates that had been made for fiscal year (FY) 1971 for nine indicators were taken and a reasonable arbitrary amount added to each value to achieve high and low values. These served as if they had been the subjective estimates made at that time. An analysis then was performed on data for the period 1969–1970 in order to obtain an ES forecast for FY 1971. A composite forecast was then made for FY 1971 as described. The three forecasting techniques—the subjective estimates made in the usual fashion, the ES method alone, and the composite forecast—were then ranked in terms of the number of times they were nearest to the actual occurrence of the indicators. Since nine indicators and four quarters of fiscal year 1971 were in-

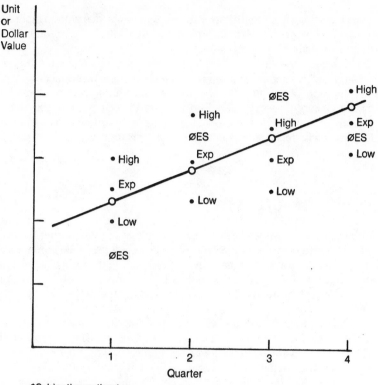

*Subjective estimates.
Ø = Forecast provided by exponential smoothing.
O = Composite forecast value generated by regression analysis.

Figure 3   Forecast estimates

volved, there was a total of thirty-six observations. The results of this test are presented in the top section of Table 2.

It can be seen from Table 2 that a forecast using ES alone based on historical data, namely Technique II, would have outperformed the standard method of subjective estimates, Technique I, by better than two to one. The composite forecast, Technique III, was in first place nine times, compared with eight for I and nineteen for II. Of course, the better the subjective estimates and the ES forecasts, the better the composite forecast. The composite forecast was never last. On the other hand, Technique I was in last place twenty-two times and Technique II was last fourteen times. The composite forecast was in first and second place a total of thirty-six times, far better than the other two techniques.

A composite forecast was then made at the end of FY 1971 for the first and second quarters of FY 1972. This was based on subjective estimates made by management and an ES forecast for the same period. The comparison between the forecast and the actual performance of the indicators for the first two quarters of FY 1972 is shown in the bottom section of Table 2. Here again the composite forecast was superior. It was in first and second place seventeen times, in last place only one time, a performance superior to the other two techniques. Certainly both these tests together with others that were made speak well for the composite forecast approach.

Table 2 Comparative analysis of forecasting techniques

Quarterly analysis
for FY 1971 for nine indicators

Number of Forecasts:	I	Techniques[a] II	III
In first place	8	19	9
In second place	6	3	27
In third place	22	14	0

Analysis for 1, 2 Q FY 1972

Number of Forecasts:	I	Techniques[a] II	III
In first place	8	5	5
In second place	3	3	12
In third place	7	10	1

[a]I—Standard method using subjective estimates only; II—Exponential smoothing method using past history only; III—Composite forecast using I and II.

CONCLUSION

The composite approach worked well for several reasons. Among these was the fact that CAS management played an active role. The computer time-sharing system provided an excellent means for developing, testing, and implementing the program. The behavior of the past was well explained by the exponential smoothing technique. The subjective or collective opinion approach worked well in supplying estimates of the future.

It is possible to vary the procedures by assigning different weights to the various elements. For example, the ES forecasts for each quarter based on past data alone could be given an assigned weight of γ. The three subjective estimates for each quarter could then be averaged, using the concept of the Beta function, to produce an expected value E, with $E=(a+4m+b)/6$, where a is the optimistic estimate, m is the most likely estimate, and b is the pessimistic estimate. The value E could now be given the weight δ, with γ, $\delta>0$, $\gamma+\delta=1$. This permits the user to assign different weights to the two separate forecasts depending upon his estimate of their relative worth. The regression analysis blending procedure is now applied to the adjusted values $(\gamma_i(ES)_i+\delta_iE_i)$, $i=1,2,3,4$, for the four quarters ahead.

The blending of the past and the future makes for a meaningful forecast, one not only more substantive in nature but one which also can be more readily explained and understood.

EXHIBIT I

Exponential Smoothing

Exponential smoothing is a method of exponentially weighted moving averages. The basic formula is

$$F_{i+1}=F_i+\alpha(D_i-F_i), \tag{1}$$

where F_i is the forecast for the ith period, D_i is the demand (value of the variable) for the ith period, α is a value such that $0 < \alpha < 1$.

Equation (1) can be rewritten as

$$F_{i+1} = \alpha \cdot D_i + (1-\alpha)F_i, \qquad (2)$$

which is its usual form.

Equation (2) is the forecast for the $(i+1)$ period in terms of the demand and forecast for the ith period, namely D_i and F_i. The forecast F_i itself involves a demand and forecast for the previous or $(i-1)$ period. More explicitly, this states that

$$F_i = \alpha \cdot D_{i-1} + (1-\alpha)F_{i-1}.$$

On substituting the right hand side of the equation above for F_i in (2),

$$F_{i+1} = \alpha \cdot D_i + (1-\alpha) \cdot \{ \alpha \cdot D_{i-1} + (1-\alpha)F_{i-1} \},$$

which upon simplifying becomes

$$F_{i+1} = \alpha \cdot D_i + \alpha(1-\alpha)D_{i-1} + (1-\alpha)^2 F_{i-1}.$$

This states simply that the forecast for the $(i+1)$ or next period is a function of the demand D_i in the current period plus the demand D_{i-1} and forecast F_{i-1} of the previous period, each multiplied by powers of α, which are essentially the weights given to these periods.

Now again the forecast for the $(i-1)$ period, F_{i-1}, itself depends on the demand D_{i-2} and the forecast F_{i-2} for the previous or $(i-2)$ period, and so on.

Continuing backwards in this manner,

$$F_{i+1} = \alpha \cdot D_1 + \alpha(i-\alpha)D_{i+1} + \alpha(1-\alpha)^2 D_{i-2} + \ldots + \alpha(i-\alpha)^n D_{i-n} + (1-\alpha)^{n+1} F_{i-n}.$$

Thus the forecast is a series of exponentially weighted values of the current and past demands plus a last term which is a weighted value of the forecast for the preceding nth period. Furthermore, since $0 < \alpha < 1$, the effect on F_{i+1} of each term in the series decreases as n increases, this rate of decrease being a function of α and n. If it is assumed that there are as many past demand histories as desired—namely, an infinite series—then a weighted average of the past demands in the ordinary sense is possible since

$$\alpha + \alpha(1-\alpha) + \alpha(1-\alpha)^2 + \alpha(1-\alpha)^3 + \ldots = 1.$$

REFERENCES

1. Box, G. E., and G. W. Jenkins. *Times Series Analysis.* San Francisco: Holden-Day, 1970.
2. Brown, G. B. *Smoothing, Forecasting and Prediction.* Englewood Cliffs, N.J.: Prentice-Hall, 1963.

3. De La Vallee Poussin, D. C., and N. S. Sarofim. "Leading Indicators: A Tool for Corporate Forecasting," *Sloan Management Review* 14, 3 (1973).

4. General Electric Time-Sharing Systems. *Marketing and Economic Forecasting* 1969.

5. Groff, G. K. "Empirical Comparison of Models for Short Range Planning," *Journal of the Institute of Management Sciences* 20 (1973): 22–31.

6. Hertz, D. B. "Investment Policies That Pay Off," *Harvard Business Review* 46, 1 (1968): 96–104.

7. Koontz, H., and C. O'Donnell. *Essentials of Management.* New York: McGraw-Hill, 1974.

8. Regels, C. C. "Exponential Forecasting: Some New Variations," *Journal of the Institute of Management Sciences* 10, 5 (1969).

9. Roman, D. O. "Technological Forecasting in the Decision Process," *Academy of Management Journal* 13 (1970):127–38.

Increasing Organizational Effectiveness through Better Human Resource Planning and Development

Edgar H. Schein

Much of the research on which this paper is based was done under the sponsorship of the Group Psychology branch of the Office of Naval Research. Their generous support has made continuing work in this area possible. I would also like to thank my colleagues, Lotte Bailyn and John Van Maanen, for many of the ideas expressed in this paper.

INTRODUCTION

In this article I would like to address two basic questions. First, why is human resource planning and development becoming increasingly important as a determinant of organizational effectiveness? Second, what are the major components of a human resource planning and career development system and how should these components be linked for maximum organizational effectiveness?

The field of personnel management has for some time addressed issues such as these, and much of the technology of planning for and managing human resources has been worked out to a considerable degree.[1] Nevertheless there continues to be in organizations a failure, particularly on the part of line managers and functional managers in areas other than personnel, to recognize the true importance of planning for and managing human resources. This paper is not intended to be a review

Reprinted from Edgar H. Schein, "Increasing Organizational Effectiveness Through Better Human Resource Planning and Development," *Sloan Management Review*, Vol. 18, No. 1, 1–21.

of what is known but rather a kind of position paper for line managers to bring to their attention some important and all too often neglected issues. These issues are important for organizational *effectiveness*, quite apart from their relevance to the issue of humanizing work or improving the quality of working life.[2] The observations and analyses made below are based on several kinds of information:

1. Formal research on management development, career development, and human development through the adult life cycle conducted in the Sloan School and at other places for the past several decades;[3]

2. Analysis of consulting relationships, field observations, and other involvements over the past several decades with all kinds of organizations dealing with the planning for and implementation of human resource development programs and organization development projects.[4]

WHY IS HUMAN RESOURCE PLANNING AND DEVELOPMENT (HRPD) INCREASINGLY IMPORTANT?

The Changing Managerial Job

The first answer to the question is simple, though paradoxical. Organizations are becoming more dependent upon people because they are increasingly involved in more complex technologies and are attempting to function in more complex economic, political, and sociocultural environments. The more different technical skills there are involved in the design, manufacture, marketing, and sales of a product, the more vulnerable the organization will be to critical shortages of the right kinds of human resources. The more complex the process, the higher the interdependence among the various specialists. The higher the interdependence, the greater the need for effective integration of all the specialities because the entire process is only as strong as its weakest link.

In simpler technologies, managers could often compensate for the technical or communication failures of their subordinates. General managers today are much more dependent upon their technically trained subordinates because they usually do not understand the details of the engineering, marketing, financial, and other decisions that their subordinates are making. Even general managers who grew up in finance may find that since their day the field of finance has outrun them, and their subordinates are using models and methods they cannot entirely understand.

What all this means for the general manager is that he or she cannot any longer safely make decisions alone; he or she cannot get enough information digested within his or her own head to be the integrator and decision maker. Instead, managers find themselves increasingly having to manage the *process* of decision making, bringing the right people together around the right questions or problems, stimulating open discussion, insuring that all relevant information surfaces and is critically assessed, managing the emotional ups and downs of prima donnas, and insuring that out of all this human and interpersonal process, a good decision will result.

As I have watched processes like these in management groups, I am struck by the fact that *the decision emerges out of the interplay*. It is hard to pin down who had the idea and who made the decision. The general manager in this setting is *accountable* for the decision, but rarely would I describe the process as one in which he or she actually makes the decision, except in the sense of recognizing when the right answer has been achieved, ratifying that answer, announcing it, and following up on its implementation.

If the managerial job is increasingly moving in the direction I have indicated, managers of the future will have to be much more skilled in how to:

1. Select and train their subordinates
2. Design and run meetings and groups of all sorts
3. Deal with all kinds of conflict between strong individuals and groups
4. Influence and negotiate from a low power base
5. Integrate the efforts of very diverse technical specialists

And if the above image of what is happening to organizations has any generality, it will force the field of human resource management increasingly to center stage. The more complex organizations become, the more they will be vulnerable to human error. They will not necessarily employ more people, but they will employ more sophisticated highly trained people both in managerial and in individual contributor staff roles. The price of low motivation, turnover, poor productivity, sabotage, and intraorganizational conflict will be higher in such organizations. Therefore it will become a matter of *economic necessity* to improve human resource planning and development systems.

Changing Social Values

A second reason why human resource planning and development will become more central and important is that changing social values regarding the role of work will make it more complicated to manage people. There are several kinds of research findings and observations that illustrate this point. First, my own longitudinal research of a panel of Sloan School graduates of the 1960s strongly suggests that we have put much too much emphasis on the traditional success syndrome of "climbing the corporate ladder."[5] Some alumni indeed want to rise to high-level general manager positions, but many others want to exercise their particular technical or functional competence and only rise to levels of functional management or senior staff roles with minimal managerial responsibility. Some want security, others are seeking nonorganizational careers as teachers or consultants, while a few are becoming entrepreneurs. I have called these patterns of motivation, talent, and values "career anchors" and believe that they serve to stabilize and constrain the career in predictable ways. The implication is obvious—organizations must develop multiple ladders and multiple reward systems to deal with different types of people.[6]

Second, studies of young people entering organizations in the last several decades suggest that work and career are not as central a life preoccupation as was once the case. Perhaps because of a prolonged period of economic affluence, people see more options for themselves and are increasingly exercising those options. In particular, one sees more concern with a balanced life in which work, family, and self-development play a more equal role.[7] Third, closely linked to the above trend is the increase in the number of women in organizations, which will have its major impact through the increase of dual career families. As opportunities for women open up, we will see more new lifestyles in young couples that will affect the organization's options as to moving people geographically, joint employment, joint career management, family support, and so on.[8]

Fourth, research evidence is beginning to accumulate that personal growth and development is a lifelong process and that predictable issues and crises come up in every decade of our lives. Organizations will have to be much more aware of what these issues are, how work and family interact, and how to manage people at different ages. The current "hot button" is *mid-career crisis;* but the more research we do, the more we find developmental crises at *all* ages and stages.[9]

An excellent summary of what is happening in the world of values, technology, and management is provided in a recent text by Elmer Burack:

> The leading edge of change in the future will include the new technologies of information, production, and management, interlaced with considerable so-cial dislocation and shifts in manpower inputs. These developments are without precedent in our industrial history.
>
> Technological and social changes have created a need for more educa-tion, training, and skill at all managerial and support levels. The lowering of barriers to employment based on sex and race introduces new kinds of manpower problems for management officials. Seniority is coming to mean relatively less in relation to the comprehension of problems, processes, and approaches. The newer manpower elements and work technologies have shifted institutional arrangements: the locus of decision making is altered, role relationships among workers and supervisors are changed (often becom-ing more collegial), and the need to respond to changing routines has become commonplace. . . .
>
> These shifts have been supported by more demanding customer re-quirements, increasing government surveillance (from product quality to antipollution measures), and more widespread use of computers, shifting power bases to the holders of specialized knowledge skills.[10]

In order for HRPD systems to become more responsive and capable of handling such growing complexity, they must contain all the necessary components, must be based on correct assumptions, and must be adequately integrated.

COMPONENTS OF A HUMAN RESOURCE PLANNING AND DEVELOPMENT SYSTEM

The major problem with existing HRPD systems is that they are fragmented, incom-plete, and sometimes built on faulty assumptions about human or organizational growth. *Human* growth takes place through successive encounters with one's environment. As the person encounters a new situation, she or he is forced to try new responses to deal with that situation. Learning takes place as a function of how those responses work out and the results they achieve. If successful in coping with the situation, the person enlarges his or her repertory of responses; if not, the person must try alternate responses until the situation has been dealt with. If none of the active coping responses works, the person sometimes falls back on retreating from the new situation or denying that there is a problem to be solved. These responses are defensive and growth limiting.

The implication is that for growth to occur, people basically need two things: *new challenges* that are within the range of their coping responses, and *knowledge of results*, information on how their responses to the challenge have worked out. If the tasks and challenges are too easy or too hard, the person will be demotivated and cease to grow. If the information is not available on how well the person's responses are working, the person cannot grow in a systematic, valid direction but is forced into guessing or trying to infer information from ambiguous signals.

Organizational growth similarly takes place through successful coping with the internal and external environment.[11] But since the organization is a complex system of human, material, financial, and informational resources, one must consider how each of those areas can be properly managed toward organizational effectiveness. In this article I will only deal with human resources.

In order for the organization to have the capacity to perform effectively over a period of time, it must be able to plan for, recruit, manage, develop, measure, dispose of, and replace human resources as warranted by the tasks to be done. The most important of these functions is the planning function, since task requirements are likely to change as the complexity and turbulence of the organization's environment increase. In other words, a key assumption underlying organizational growth is that the nature of jobs will change over time, which means that such changes must be continuously monitored in order to insure that the right kinds of human resources can be recruited or developed to do those jobs. Many of the activities, such as recruitment, selection, performance appraisal, and so on, presume that some planning process has occurred that makes it possible to assess whether or not those activities are meeting *organizational needs*, quite apart from whether they are facilitating the individual's growth.

In an ideal HRPD system, one would seek to match the organization's needs for human resources with the individual's needs for personal career growth and development. One can then depict the basic system as involving both individual and organizational planning and a series of matching activities that are designed to facilitate mutual need satisfaction. If we further assume that both individual and organizational needs change over time, we can depict this process as a developmental one as in Figure 1.

In the right-hand column, we show the basic stages of the individual career through the life cycle. While not everyone will go through these stages in the manner depicted, there is growing evidence that for organizational careers in particular, these stages reasonably depict the movement of people through their adult lives.[12] Given those developmental assumptions, the left-hand side of the diagram shows the organizational planning activities that must occur if human resources are to be managed in an optimal way and if changing job requirements are to be properly assessed and continuously monitored. The middle column shows the various matching activities that have to occur at various career stages.

The components of an effective HRPD system can now be derived from the diagram. *First*, in the organization there have to be the overall planning components shown on the left-hand side of Figure 1. *Second*, there have to be components that insure an adequate process of staffing the organization. *Third*, there have to be components that plan for and monitor growth and development. *Fourth*, there have to be components that facilitate the actual process of the growth and development of

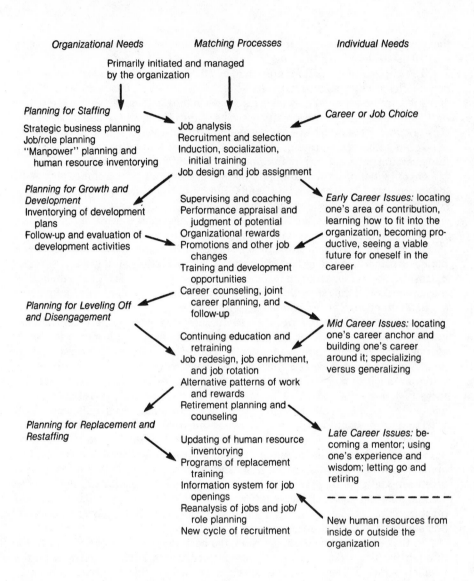

Figure 1   A developmental model of human resource planning and development

the people who are brought into the organization; this growth and development must be organized to meet *both* the needs of the organization and the needs of the individuals within it. *Fifth*, there have to be components that deal with decreasing effectiveness, leveling off, obsolescence of skills, turnover, retirement, and other phenomena that reflect the need for either a new growth direction or a process of disengagement of the person from his or her job. *Finally*, there have to be components which insure that as some people move out of jobs, others are available to fill those jobs; and as new jobs arise, people are available with the requisite skills to fill them. In the remainder of this article I would like to comment on each of these six sets of components and indicate where and how they should be linked to each other.

Overall Planning Components

The function of these components is to insure that the organization has an adequate basis for selecting its human resources and developing them toward the fulfillment of organizational goals.

Strategic Business Planning   These activities are designed to determine the organization's goals, priorities, future directions, products, markets growth rate, geographical location, and organization structure or design. This process should lead logically into the next two planning activities, but it is often disconnected from them because it is located in a different part of the organization or is staffed by people with different orientations and backgrounds.

Job/Role Planning   These activities are designed to determine what actually needs to be done at every level of the organization (up through top management) to fulfill the organization's goals and tasks. This activity can be thought of as a dynamic kind of job analysis where a continual review is made of the skills, knowledge, values, etc., which are presently needed in the organization and will be needed in the future. The focus is on the predictable consequences of the strategic planning for managerial roles, specialist roles, and skill mixes which may be needed to get the mission accomplished. If the organization already has a satisfactory system of job descriptions, this activity would concern itself with how those jobs will evolve and change, and what new jobs or roles will evolve in the future.[13]

This component is often missing completely in organizations or is carried out only for lower-level jobs. From a planning point of view, it is probably most important for the highest level jobs—how the nature of general and functional management will change as the organization faces new technologies, new social values, and new environmental conditions.

"Manpower Planning" and Human Resource Inventorying   These activities draw on the job/role descriptions generated in job/role planning and assess the capabilities of the present human resources against those plans or requirements. These activities may be focused on the numbers of people in given categories and are often designed to insure that under given assumptions of growth there will be an adequate supply of people in those categories. Or the process may focus more on how to insure that certain scarce skills which will be needed will in fact be available, leading to more sophisticated programs of recruitment or human resource development. For example, the inventorying process at high levels may reveal the need for a new type of general manager with broad integrative capacities, which may further reveal the need to start a development program to insure that such managers will be available five to ten years down the road.

These first three component activities are all geared to identifying the *organization's* needs in the human resource area. They are difficult to do, and tools are only now beginning to be developed for job/role planning.[14] In most organizations I have dealt with, the three areas, if they exist at all, are not linked to each other organizationally. Strategic planning is likely to exist in the office of the president. Job/role planning is likely to be an offshoot of some management development activities in personnel. And human resource inventorying is likely to be a specialized subsection within personnel. Typically, no one is accountable for bringing these activities together even on an ad hoc basis.

This situation reflects an erroneous assumption about growth and development that I want to mention at this time. The assumption is that if the organization develops its *present* human resources, it will be able to fill whatever job demands may arise in the future. Thus do we find elaborate human resource planning systems in organizations, but they plan for the present people in the organization, not for the organization per se. If there are no major changes in job requirements as the organization grows and develops, this system will work. But if jobs themselves change, it is no longer safe to assume that today's human resources, with development plans based on *today's* job requirements, will produce the people needed in some future situation. Therefore, I am asserting that more job/role planning must be done independent of the present people in the organization.

The subsequent components to be discussed, which focus on the matching of individual and organizational needs, all assume that some sort of basic planning activities such as those described have been carried out. They may not be very formal, or they may be highly decentralized (for example, every supervisor who has an open slot might make his or her own decision of what sort of person to hire based on private assumptions about strategic business planning and job/role planning). Obviously, the more turbulent the environment, the greater the vulnerability of the organization if it does not centralize and coordinate its various planning activities and generate its HRPD system from those plans.

Staffing Processes

The function of these processes is to insure that the organization acquires the human resources necessary to fulfill its goals.

Job Analysis If the organizational planning has been done adequately, the next component of the HRPD system is to actually specify what jobs need to be filled and what skills and so on are needed to do those jobs. Some organizations go through this process very formally; others do it in an informal unprogrammed manner, but it must occur in some form in order to specify what kind of recruitment to do and how to select people from among the recruits.

Recruitment and Selection This activity involves the actual process of going out to find people to fulfill jobs and developing systems for deciding which of those people to hire. This component may be very formal including testing, assessment, and other aids to the selection process. If this component is seen as part of a total HRPD system, it will alert management to the fact that the recruitment selection system communicates to future employees something about the nature of the organization and its approach to people. All too often this component sends incorrect messages or turns off future employees or builds incorrect stereotypes which make subsequent supervision more difficult.[15]

Induction, Socialization, and Initial Training. Once the employee has been hired, there ensues a period during which he or she learns the ropes, learns how to get along in the organization, how to work, how to fit in, how to master the particulars of the job, and so on. Once again, it is important that the activities which make up this component are seen as part of a total process with long-range consequences for the attitudes of the employee.[16] The goal of these processes should be to facilitate the employees becoming productive and useful members of the organization both in the short run and in terms of long-range potential.

Job Design and Job Assignment   One of the most crucial components of staffing is the actual design of the job that is given to the new employee and the manner in which the assignment is actually made. The issue is how to provide *optimal challenge*, a set of activities that will be neither too hard nor too easy for the new employee and neither too meaningless nor too risky from the point of view of the organization. If the job is too easy or meaningless, the employee may become demotivated; if the job is too hard and/or involves too much responsibility and risk from the point of view of the organization, the employee will become too anxious, frustrated, or angry to perform at an optimal level. Some organizations have set up training programs for supervisors to help them to design optimally challenging work assignments.[17]

These four components are geared to insuring that the work of the organization will be performed. They tend to be processes that have to be performed by line managers and personnel staff specialists together. Line managers have the basic information about jobs and skill requirements; personnel specialists have the interviewing, recruiting and assessment skills to aid in the selection process. In an optimal system these functions will be closely coordinated, particularly to insure that the recruiting process provides accurate information to the employee about the nature of the organization and the actual work that he or she will be doing in it. Recruiters also need good information on the long-range human resource plans so that these can be taken into account in the selection of new employees.

Development Planning

It is not enough to get good human resources in the door. Some planning activities have to concern themselves with how employees who may be spending thirty to forty years of their total life in a given organization will make a contribution for all of that time, will remain motivated and productive, and will maintain a reasonable level of job satisfaction.

Inventorying of Development Plans   Whether or not the process is highly formalized, there is in most organizations some effort to plan for the growth and development of all employees. The planning component that is often missing is some kind of pulling together of this information into a centralized inventory that permits coordination and evaluation of the development activities. Individual supervisors may have clear ideas of what they will do with and for their subordinates, but this information may never be collected, making it impossible to determine whether the individual plans of supervisors are connected in any way. Whether it is done by department, division, or total company, some effort to collect such information and to think through its implications would be of great value to furthering the total development of employees at all levels.

Follow-up and Evaluation of Development Activities   I have observed two symptoms of insufficient planning in this area: one, development plans are made for individual employees and are written down but are never implemented; and two, if they are implemented, they are never evaluated either in relation to the individual's own needs for growth or in relation to the organization's needs for new skills. Some system should exist to insure that plans are implemented and that activities are evaluated against both individual and organizational goals.

Career Development Processes

This label is deliberately broad to cover all of the major processes of managing human resources during their period of growth and peak productivity, a period that may be several decades in length. These processes must match the organization's needs for work with the individual's needs for a productive and satisfying work career. The system must provide for some kind of forward movement for the employee through some succession of jobs, whether these involve promotion, lateral movement to new functions, or simply new assignments within a given area.[18] The system must be based on both the organization's need to fill jobs as they open up and employees' needs to have some sense of progress in their working lives.

Supervision and Coaching   By far the most important component in this area is the actual process of supervising, guiding, coaching, and monitoring. It is in this context that the work assignment and feedback processes which make learning possible occur, and it is the boss who plays the key role in molding the employee to the organization. There is considerable evidence that the first boss is especially crucial in giving new employees a good start in their careers[19] and that training of supervisors in how to handle new employees is a valuable organizational investment.

Performance Appraisal and Judgment of Potential   This component is part of the general process of supervision but stands out as such an important part of that process that it must be treated separately. In most organizations there is some effort to standardize and formalize a process of appraisal above and beyond the normal performance feedback that is expected on a day-to-day basis. Such systems serve a number of functions—to justify salary increases, promotions, and other formal organizational actions with respect to the employee; to provide information for human resource inventories or at least written records of past accomplishments for the employee's personnel folder; and to provide a basis for annual or semiannual formal reviews between boss and subordinate to supplement day-to-day feedback and to facilitate information exchange for career planning and counseling. In some organizations so little day-to-day feedback occurs that the *formal* system bears the burden of providing the employees with knowledge of how they are doing and what they can look forward to. Since knowledge of results—of how one is doing—is a crucial component of any development process, it is important for organizations to monitor how well and how frequently feedback is actually given.

One of the major dilemmas in this area is whether to have a single system that provides both feedback for the growth and development of the employee and information for the organization's planning systems. The dilemma arises because the information that the planning system requires (for example, how much potential does this employee have to rise in the organization?) may be the kind of information that neither the boss nor the planner wants to share with the employee. The more potent and more accurate the information, the less likely it is to be fed back to the employee in anything other than very vague terms.

On the other hand, the detailed work-oriented, day-to-day feedback the employee needs for growth and development may be too cumbersome to record as part of a selection-oriented appraisal system. If hundreds of employees are to be compared, there is strong pressure in the system toward more general kinds of judgments, traits, rankings, numerical estimates of ultimate potential, and the like. One way of resolving this dilemma that some companies have found successful is to develop two separate systems—one oriented toward performance improvement and the growth of the employee and the other one oriented toward a more global assessment of the employee for future planning purposes and involving judgments that may not be shared with the employee except in general terms.

A second dilemma arises around the identification of the employee's "development needs" and how the information is linked to other development activities. If the development needs are stated in relation to the planning system, the employee may never get the feedback of what his or her needs may have been perceived to be, and, worse, no one may implement any program to deal with those needs if the planning system is not well linked with line management.

Two further problems arise from this potential lack of linkage. One, if the individual does not get good feedback around developmental needs, he or she remains uninvolved in their own development and potentially becomes complacent. We pay lip service to the statement that only the individual can develop himself or herself but then deprive the individual of the very information that would make sensible self-development possible. Two, the development needs as stated for the various employees in the organization may have nothing to do with the organization's needs for certain kinds of human resources in the future. All too often there is complete lack of linkage between the strategic or business planning function and the human resource development function resulting in potentially willy-nilly individual development based on today's needs and individual managers' stereotypes of what will be needed in the future.

Organizational Rewards—Pay, Benefits, Perquisites, Promotion, and Recognition   Entire books have been written about all the problems and subtleties of how to link organizational rewards to the other components of a HRPD system to insure both short-run and long-run human effectiveness. For purposes of this paper I wish to point out only one major issue—how to insure that organizational rewards are linked to *both* the needs of the individual and the needs of the organization for effective performance and development of potential. All too often the reward system is neither responsive to the individual employee nor to the organization, being driven more by criteria of elegance, consistency, and what other organizations are doing. If the linkage is to be established, line managers must actively work with compensation experts to develop a joint philosophy and set of goals based on an understanding of both what the organization is trying to reward and what the employee needs actually are. As organizational careers become more varied and as social values surrounding work change, reward systems will probably have to become much more flexible both in time (people at different career stages may need different things) and by type of career (functional specialists may need different things than general managers).

Promotions and Other Job Changes   There is ample evidence that what keeps human growth and effectiveness going is continuing optimal challenge.[20] Such challenge can be provided for some members of the organization through promotion to higher levels where more responsible jobs are available. The promotion opportunities are limited for most members of the organization, however, because the pyramid narrows at the top. An effective HRPD system will, therefore, concentrate on developing career paths, systems of job rotation, changing assignments, temporary assignments, and other lateral job moves that insure continuing growth of all human resources.

One of the key characteristics of an optimally challenging job is that it both draws on the person's abilities and skills and that it has opportunities for "closure." The employee must be in the job long enough to be involved and to see the results of her or his efforts. Systems of rotation that move the person too rapidly either prevent initial involvement (as in the rotational training program) or prevent closure by transferring the person to a new job before the effects of her or his decisions can be assessed. I have heard many "fast track" executives complain that their self-confidence was low because they never really could see the results of their efforts. Too often we move people too fast in order to "fill slots" and thereby undermine their development.

Organizational planning systems that generate "slots" to be filled must be coordinated with development planning systems that concern themselves with the optimal growth of the human resources. Sometimes it is better in the long run for the organization not to fill an empty slot in order to keep a manager in another job where he or she is just beginning to develop. One way of insuring such linkage is to monitor these processes by means of a "development committee" composed of both line managers and personnel specialists. In such a group the needs of the organization and the needs of the people can be balanced against each other in the context of the long-range goals of the organization.

Training and Development Opportunities   Most organizations recognize that periods of formal training, sabbaticals, executive development programs outside of the company, and other educational activities are necessary in the total process of human growth and development. The important point about these activities is that they should be carefully linked both to the needs of the individual and to the needs of the organization. The individual should want to go to the program because she or he can see how the educational activity fits into the total career. The organization should send the person because the training fits into some concept of future career development. It should not be undertaken simply as a generalized "good thing" or because other companies are doing it. As much as possible, the training and educational activities should be tied to job/role planning. For example, many companies began to use university executive development programs because of an explicit recognition that future managers would require a broader perspective on various problems and that such "broadening" could best be achieved in the university programs.

Career Counseling, Joint Career Planning, Follow-up, and Evaluation   Inasmuch as the growth and development that may be desired can only come from within the individual himself or herself, it is important that the organization provide some means for individual employees at all levels to become more proactive about their careers and some mechanisms for joint dialogue, counseling, and career planning.[21] This process ideally should be linked to performance appraisal because it is in that context that the boss can review with the subordinate the future potential, development needs, strengths, weaknesses, career options, and so on. Often the boss is not trained in counseling but does possess some of the key information that the employee needs to initiate any kind of career planning. More formal counseling could then be supplied by the personnel development staff or outside the organization altogether.

The important point to recognize is that employees cannot manage their own growth development without information on how their own needs, talents, values, and plans mesh with the opportunity structure of the organization. Even though the organization may only have imperfect, uncertain information about the future, the individual is better off knowing that than making erroneous assumptions about the future based on no information at all. It is true that the organization cannot make commitments, nor should it unless required to by legislation or contract. But the sharing of information if properly done is not the same as making commitments or setting up false expectations.

If the organization can open up the communication channel between employees, their bosses, and whoever is managing the human resource system, the groundwork is laid for realistic individual development planning. Whatever is decided about training, next steps, special assignments, rotation, and so forth, should be jointly decided by the individual and the appropriate organizational resource (probably the supervisor and someone from personnel specializing in career development). Each step must fit into the employee's life plan and must be tied into *organizational needs*. The organization should be neither a humanistic charity nor an indoctrination center. Instead, it should be a vehicle for meeting the needs of both society and individuals.

Whatever is decided should not merely be written down but executed. If there are implementation problems, the development plan should be renegotiated. Whatever developmental actions are taken, it is essential that they be followed up and evaluated by both the person and the organization to determine what, if anything, was achieved. It is shocking to discover how many companies invest in major activities such as university executive development programs and then never determine for themselves what was accomplished. In some instances, they make no plans to talk to the individual before or after the program, so that it is not even possible to determine what the activity meant to the participant or what might be an appropriate next assignment for him or her following the program.

I can summarize the above analysis best by emphasizing the two places where I feel there is the most fragmentation and violation of growth assumptions. *First*, too many of the activities occur without the involvement of the person who is "being developed" and therefore may well end up being self-defeating. This is particularly true of job assignments and performance appraisal where too little involvement and feedback occur. *Second*, too much of the human resource system functions as a personnel *selection* system unconnected to either the needs of the organization or the needs of the individual. All too often it is only a system for short-run replacement of people in standard type jobs. The key planning functions are not linked in solidly and hence do not influence the system to the degree they should.

Planning for and Managing Disengagement

The planning and management processes which will be briefly reviewed here are counterparts of ones that have already been discussed but are focused on a different problem—the problem of the late career, loss of motivation, obsolescence, and ultimately retirement. Organizations must recognize that there are various options available to deal with this range of problems beyond the obvious ones of either terminating the employee or engaging in elaborate measures to "remotivate" people who may have lost work involvement.

Continuing Education and Retraining   These activities have their greatest potential if the employee is motivated and if there is some clear connection between what is to be learned and what the employee's current or future job assignments require in the way of skills. More and more organizations are finding out that it is better to provide challenging work first and only then the training to perform that work once the employee sees the needs for it. Obviously, for this linkage to work well, continuous dialogue is needed between employees and their managers. For those employees who have leveled off, have lost work involvement but are still doing high quality work, other solutions such as those described below are more applicable.

Job Redesign, Job Enrichment, and Job Rotation   This section is an extension of the arguments made earlier on job changes in general applied to the particular problems of leveled-off employees. In some recent research, it has been suggested that job enrichment and other efforts to redesign work to increase motivation and performance may only work during the first few years on a job.[23] Beyond that the employee becomes "unresponsive" to the job characteristics themselves and pays more attention to surrounding factors such as the nature of supervision, relationships with co-workers, pay, and other extrinsic characteristics. In other words, before organizations attempt to "cure" leveled-off employees by remotivating them through job redesign or rotation, they should examine whether those employees are still in a responsive mode or not. On the other hand, one can argue that there is nothing wrong with less motivated, less involved employees so long as the quality of what they are doing meets the organizational standards.[24]

Alternative Patterns of Work and Rewards   Because of the changing needs and values of employees in recent decades, more and more organizations have begun to experiment with alternative work patterns, such as flexible working hours, part-time work, sabbaticals or other longer periods of time off, several people filling one job, dual employment of spouses with more extensive child-care programs, and so on. Along with these experiments have come others on flexible reward systems in which employees can choose between a raise; some time off; special retirement, medical, or insurance benefits; and other efforts to make multiple career ladders a viable reality. These programs apply to employees at all career stages but are especially relevant to people in mid and late career stages where their own perception of their career and life goals may be undergoing important changes.

None of those innovations should be attempted without first clearly establishing a HRPD system that takes care of the organization's needs as well as the needs of employees and links them to each other. There can be little growth and development for employees at any level in an *organization* that is sick and stagnant. It is in the best interests of both the individual and the organization to have a healthy organization that can provide opportunities for growth.

Retirement Planning and Counseling   As part of any effective HRPD system, there must be a clear planning function that forecasts who will retire and feeds this information into both the replacement staffing system and the counseling functions so that the employees who will be retiring can be prepared for this often traumatic career stage. Employees need counseling not only with the mechanical and financial aspects of retirement but also to prepare them psychologically for the time when they will no longer have a clear organizational base or job as part of their identity. For some people, it may make sense to spread the period of retirement over a number of years by using part-time work or special assignments to help both the individual and the organization to get benefits from this period.

The counseling function here, as in other times during the career, probably involves special skills and must be provided by specialists. However, the line manager continues to play a key role as a provider of job challenge, feedback, and information about what is ahead for any given employee. Seminars for line managers on how to handle the special problems of preretirement employees would probably be of great value as part of their managerial training.

Planning for and Managing Replacement and Restaffing

With this step the HRPD cycle closes back upon itself. This function must be concerned with such issues as:

1. Updating the human resource inventory as retirements or terminations occur.

2. Instituting special programs of orientation or training for new incumbents to specific jobs as those jobs open up.

3. Managing the information system on what jobs are available and determining how to match this information to the human resources available in order to determine whether to replace from within the organization or to go outside with a new recruiting program.

4. Continuously reanalyzing jobs to insure that the new incumbent is properly

prepared for both what the job now requires and will require in the future.

How these processes are managed links to the other parts of the system through the implicit messages that are sent to employees. For example, a company that decides to publicly post all of its unfilled jobs is clearly sending a message that it expects internal recruitment and supports self-development activities. A company that manages restaffing in a very secret manner gets across a message that employees might as well be complacent and passive about their careers because they cannot influence them anyway.

SUMMARY AND CONCLUSIONS

I have tried to argue in this article that human resource planning and development is becoming an increasingly important function in organizations, that this function consists of multiple components, and that these components must be managed by *both* line managers and staff specialists. I have tried to show that the various planning activities are closely linked to the actual processes of supervision, job assignment, training, and so on and that those processes must be designed to match the needs of the organization with the needs of the employees throughout their evolving careers, whether or not those careers involve hierarchical promotions. I have also argued that the various components are linked to each other and must be seen as a total system if it is to be effective. The total system must be managed as a system to insure coordination between the planning functions and the implementation functions.

I hope it is clear from what has been said above that an effective human resource planning and development system is integral to the functioning of the organization and must, therefore, be a central concern of line management. Many of the activities require specialist help, but the accountabilities must rest squarely with line supervisors and top management. It is they who control the opportunities and the rewards. It is the job assignment system and the feedback that employees get that is the ultimate raw material for growth and development. Whoever designs and manages the system, it will not help the organization to become more effective unless that system is *owned* by line management.

NOTES

1. See Pigors and Myers (24) and Burack (10).
2. See Hackman and Suttle (13), and Meltzer and Wickert (21).
3. See McGregor (20), Bennis (6), Pigors and Myers (24), Schein (29), Van Maanen (36), Bailyn and Schein (4), and Katz (18).
4. See Beckhard (5), Bennis (6), Schein (28), Galbraith (12), Lesieur (19), and Alfred (1).
5. See Schein (31).
6. See Schein (32).
7. See Bailyn and Schein (4), Myers (22), Van Maanen, Bailyn, and Schein (38), and Roeber (25).
8. See Van Maanen and Schein (39), Bailyn (3) and (2), and Kanter (17).
9. See Sheehy (33), Troll (35), Kalish (16), and Pearse and Pelzer (23).

10. See Burack (10), pp. 402–03.

11. See Schein (29).

12. See Dalton and Thompson (11), Super and Bohn (34), Hall (14), and Schein (32).

13. See Schein (32).

14. See Schein (32).

15. See Schein (26) and (32).

16. See Schein (27), and Van Maanen (36).

17. See Schein (26).

18. See Schein (30) and (32).

19. See Schein (26), Bray, Campbell, and Grant (9), Berlew and Hall (8), and Hall (14).

20. See Dalton and Thompson (11), and Katz (18).

21. See Heidke (15).

22. See Bailyn (2)

23. See Katz (18).

24. See Bailyn (2).

REFERENCES

1. Alfred, T. "Checkers of Choice in Manpower Management." *Harvard Business Review*, January-February (1967):157–69.

2. Bailyn, L. "Involvement and Accommodations in Technical Careers." In *Organizational Careers: Some New Perspectives*, edited by J. Van Maanen. New York: John Wiley & Sons, 1977.

3. Bailyn, L. "Career and Family Orientations of Husbands and Wives in Relation to Marital Happiness." *Human Relations* (1970): 97–113.

4. Bailyn, L., and E. H. Schein, "Life/Career Considerations as Indicators of Quality of Employment." In *Measuring Work Quality for Social Reporting*, edited by A. D. Biderman and T. F. Drury. New York: Sage Publications, 1976.

5. Beckhard, R. D. *Organization Development: Strategies and Models*. Reading, MA: Addison-Wesley, 1969.

6. Bennis, W. G. *Changing Organizations*. New York: McGraw-Hill, 1966.

7. Bennis, W. G. *Organization Development: Its Nature, Origins, and Prospects*. Reading, MA: Addison-Wesley, 1969.

8. Berlew, D., and D. T. Hall. "The Socialization of Managers." *Administrative Science Quarterly* 11 (1966): 207–23.

9. Bray, D. W., R. J. Campbell, and D. E. Grant. *Formative Years in Business*. New York: John Wiley & Sons, 1974.

10. Burack, E. *Organization Analysis*. Hinsdale, IL: Dryden, 1975.

11. Dalton, G. W. and P. H. Thompson. "Are R&D Organizations Obsolete?" *Harvard Business Review*, (November-December 1976): 105–116.

12. Galbraith, J. *Designing Complex Organizations*. Reading, MA: Addison-Wesley, 1973.

13. Hackman, J. R., and J. L. Suttle, *Improving Life at Work*. Los Angeles: Goodyear, 1977.

14. Hall, D. T. *Careers in Organizations*. Los Angeles: Goodyear, 1976.

15. Heidke, R. *Career Pro-Activity of Middle Managers*. Master's thesis, Massachusetts Institute of Technology, 1977.

16. Kalish, R. A. *Late Adulthood: Perspectives on Aging*. Monterey, CA: Brooks-Cole, 1975.

17. Kanter, R. M. *Work and Family in the United States*. New York: Russell Sage, 1977.

18. Katz, R. "Job Enrichment: Some Career Considerations." In *Organizational Careers: Some New Perspectives*, edited by J. Van Maanen. New York: John Wiley & Sons, 1977.

19. Lesieur, F. G. *The Scanlon Plan*. New York: John Wiley & Sons, 1958.

20. McGregor, D. *The Human Side of Enterprise*. New York: McGraw-Hill, 1960.

21. Meltzer, H., and F. R. Wickert. *Humanizing Organizational Behavior*. Springfield, IL: Charles C. Thomas, 1976.

22. Myers, C. A. "Management and the Employee." In *Social Responsibility and the Business Predicament*, edited by J. W. McKie. Washington, D.C.: Brookings, 1974.

23. Pearse, R. F. and B. P. Pelzer. *Self-directed Change for the Mid-Career Manager*. New York: AMACOM, 1975.

24. Pigors, P., and C. A. Myers. *Personnel Administration*. 8th ed. New York: McGraw-Hill, 1977.

25. Roeber, R. J. C. *The Organization in a Changing Environment*. Reading, MA: Addison-Wesley, 1973.

26. Schein, E. H. "How to Break in the College Graduate." *Harvard Business Review* (1964): 68–76.

27. Schein, E. H. Organizational Socialization and the Profession of Management. *Industrial Management Review* (Winter 1968): 1–16.

28. Schein, E. H. *Process Consultation: Its Role in Organization Development*. Reading, MA: Addison-Wesley, 1969.

29. Schein, E. H. *Organizational Psychology*. Englewood Cliffs, NJ: Prentice-Hall, 1970.

30. Schein, E. H. The Individual, the Organization, and the Career: A Conceptual Scheme, *Journal of Applied Behavioral Science* 7 (1971): 401–26.

31. Schein, E. H. "How 'Career Anchors' Hold Executives to Their Career Paths." *Personnel* 52, 3 (1975): 11–24.

32. Schein, E. H. *The Individual, the Organization and the Career: Toward Greater Human Effectiveness*. Reading, MA: Addison-Wesley, forthcoming.

33. Sheehy, G. "Catch 30 and Other Predictable Crises of Growing Up Adult." *New York Magazine*, February 1974, pp. 30–44.

34. Super, D. E., and M. J. Bohn. *Occupational Psychology*. Belmont, CA: Wadsworth, 1970.

35. Troll, L. E. *Early and Middle Adulthood*. Monterey, CA: Brooks-Cole, 1975.

36. Van Maanen, J. "Breaking In: Socialization to Work." In *Handbook of Work, Organization, and Society*, edited by R. Dubin. Chicago: Rand McNally, 1976.

37. Van Maanen, J., ed. *Organizational Careers: Some New Perspectives*. New York: John Wiley & Sons, 1977.

38. Van Maanen, J., L. Bailyn, and E. H. Schein. "The Shape of Things to Come: A New Look at Organizational Careers." In *Perspectives on Behavior in Organizations*, edited by J. R. Hackman, E. E. Lawler, and L. W. Porter. New York: McGraw-Hill, 1977.

39. Van Maanen, J., and E. H. Schein. "Improving the Quality of Work Life: Career Development." In *Improving Life at Work*, edited by J. R. Hackman and J. L. Suttle. Los Angeles: Goodyear, 1977.

Where OD and MBO Meet

Ellis D. Hillmar

Many practitioners, consultants, and students of both organization development (OD) and management by objectives (MBO) perceive these as separate and distinct technologies. In an earlier article, Arthur C. Beck, Jr., and I took the position that it didn't make much difference where you started in implementing one or the other, for you would soon need to have the other to be truly successful.[1] This article will examine the confluence of these major forces in the ever-changing world of today's organization.

WHAT IS OD ALL ABOUT?

A recent publication defined OD as a planned, managed systematic process to change the culture, systems, and behavior of an organization in order to improve the organization's effectiveness in solving its problems and achieving its objectives.[2] Inherent in this definition are many of the aspects of the MBO process: planned, managed, achieving objectives, and so on.

OD and MBO both emerged in the management literature during the early days of the humanistic movement. Early OD efforts grew out of personal development laboratories in human relations training. Quite naturally, then, much of the focus was oriented toward people and their interpersonal relationships in small groups within the organization. This correlated with early MBO efforts, which also had a high individual orientation for motivation and performance appraisal applications. Howell referred to this as Stage I MBO.[3]

In more recent years, the growth and development of OD practitioners has tended to include less and less of the human relations predominance and more of a systems and task orientation. This has been more supportive of a similar growth in MBO—Howell's Stage II[4]—in which the emphasis switches to developing organizational goals and integrating the individual manager's needs. This continuing growth and expansion has tended to create considerable confusion as to what OD is all about. In the early days, it was relatively easy to stereotype it as "sensitivity training ... whatever that is." With the increased emphasis on systemic approaches, however, that is no longer possible. This difference, human relations versus systems, also represents one of the major issues in choosing the approach to and use of OD technology, for their implementation activities are usually quite different.[5]

Ellis D. Hillmar is assistant director, Management Center, Institute for Business and Community Development, University of Richmond, Virginia.

Reproduced by special permission from the April 1975 *Training and Development Journal.*

IS OD FOR REAL?

Managers seem to have a basic concern about OD: Is it for real or just another fad? OD comes with the depth and change orientation of behavioral science, the complexity of multidisciplines and a certain amount of mystique. Since it tends to deal with a whole system, it almost defies any serious attempt to evaluate its true value because of the many variables. Thus, most OD efforts are currently justified on limited identifiable results and significant theoretical concepts. However, there is an increasing ground swell of positive experiences which are providing substantial evidence that something real is happening for the participants in most OD applications.

Because of its nature, OD's boundaries can include almost anything happening in the organization. When the focus is on improving effectiveness, problem solving, achieving objectives, managing, systemic process, or behavior, OD interventions might fall into any (or all) of the following types of activity: team building, job design/enrichment, goal setting, problem solving, work climate/environment, decision making, managing differences/conflict, process consultation, diagnosis and feedback, organization/physical structure, interpersonal skills, values clarification, transactional analysis, managing accountability, helping relationships.

GESTALT AND OPEN SYSTEMS

Two additional development forms that are getting increased attention within OD are *Gestalt techniques* and *open systems concepts*. The Gestalt approach emphasizes that individuals need to develop their own internal support system rather than being so dependent on group/team (outside) support. This is sometimes a "painful" process, as with most personal growth experiences, but it helps the person to know his or her own potential and increases coping ability within organizational reality.

An "open system" organization is one in which there is full recognition of the presence and impact on the organization of the total environment. In this situation, the organization is viewed as a system with inputs-transformation process(es)-outputs. Any one or all of these may be affected by forces from outside the organization such as government or clients. An open system plans for the impact, whereas a closed system tends to ignore the impact on the premise that it is outside of the system and "they" have the problem, not us. The methodology of working with open systems concepts includes many activities that are part of a results oriented MBO process.

In an OD application, there are many issues and concerns to be resolved by the consultant and/or the organization. From the above listed alternatives, one obvious question is, Where do we start? Other issues not mentioned thus far would include: the use of a consultant and whether that consultant should be internal or external, the role of "top" management, the definition of who is the client organization, the relationship of OD work to more traditional training or management development, whether the emphasis will be on task (what) or process (how) issues, and who initiates and manages the change process? Resolving these issues is part of developing a psychological contract, matching expectations, between and among the various parties involved relative to what results are desired.

HOW DOES OD GET
INTO AN MBO APPLICATION?

When an organization begins to conceive of MBO as its management process rather than another control technique, the need for OD increases rapidly and dramatically. Though the "theory" literature continues to emphasize the management aspects, case studies and research data tend to indicate that relatively few organizations apply it in that manner. There is much stronger evidence to support Pellissier's observation that most American organizations tend to use MBO for control or administration rather than organizational management.[6]

Most MBO texts seem to have been written based on a set of assumptions that include participative management as an operational reality. Also, managers are expected to have a full range of behavioral skills and competencies. I find both of these to be far from reality. Many organizations and managers seem to think that just allowing individuals to set their own objectives, which are then "collected" to represent the organization's goals, is participative management. This is "permissiveness" at best and "abdication" at worst. Another variation exists with boss-imposed or management-imposed objectives to which the subordinate "agrees." Though agreeing implies some form of participation, this is not the essence of participative management or goal setting.

For several years I have been amazed at the number of organizations that indicated they had management by objectives, for it just didn't check out with my sampling. Kindall and Schuster[7] seem to have clarified the true situation: There is relatively little participative MBO in which the boss and subordinate agree in advance on what the results should be.

Several factors, however, seem to indicate a positive shift toward MBO becoming a true management process: (a) increased awareness of the disparity as documented in a growing number of journal articles; (b) more managers who are willing to confront existing organizational norms of control versus management; and (c) increased knowledge and understanding of behavioral science and OD skills and technology.

In his article, "Critical Issues in MBO," Carvalho has set the stage for the need for MBO and OD to come together.[8] First, he identified MBO as a *concept* in which people should know, before they start working toward them, what kinds and amounts of results they want to achieve. Then, he goes on to describe how the application of the concept is affected by the organization's behavioral patterns and systems for handling power distribution in the organization and making decisions relative to objectives and the allocation of its resources. These are basic issues in organization development. Thus, the theory base for MBO and OD meet when we begin to work the issue of how to apply the concept of MBO to groups and organizations.

ORGANIZATION FOR RESULTS

As an organization begins to take on the reality of "second generation" MBO (Howell's Stage II), it must come to grips with both MBO and OD in some significantly different ways. Taking a systemic approach to the integration of the theory base leads to a synergistic transcendence that moves beyond merely having both concepts functioning in the same organization. Inherent in such a program is the commitment to manage for results by objectives and develop the effectiveness of the organization through a planned change and growth process in which the desired results are clearly stated. An essential ingredient of integration activities is a clear understanding of values at both the organization and invididual levels. This will be a significant effort for most since little has been done here. The organization—management—must examine its philosophy and assumptions about people, operations, and management style in order to set out the underlying values that will help managers and employees focus the organization's energy toward creating the agreed upon result.

A truly participative MBO application creates a need for individuals to have greater awareness of their own values in order to more realistically establish personal goals and to function with more personal power. Humble has made reference to the need for recognizing and including personal goals in an organization's goal setting process.[9]

Myers and Myers,[10] Hughes and Flowers[11] have provided an indication of the potential managerial impact of personal values for working. My experience in working with both types of values clarification indicates considerable importance for both MBO and OD applications.

An important characteristic of this second generation MBO is the shift in emphasis from individual to organizational results. This creates considerable pressure for OD skills. Now there are individual, work group, and intergroup concerns to be managed, most of which are basic OD issues. In this context, too, there is much greater need for defining the results to be achieved by the organization. This tends to create quite a different perception of what results really are.

Napier and Gershenfeld deal with this issue and the nature of the interactive relationship within the group.[12] An important understanding here is that though individual achievement is still very important, the individual's needs and goals are distinctively different from overall organization needs and goals. Further, even if you were to add up all the individual needs and goals, they would not be expected to equate directly to the organization goals.

This second generation application, then, moves MBO into a group process which requires managerial skills that are not readily available in most of our highly structured, directive management systems. Basic group skills that will be necessary for group or team goal setting are: problem solving; management of the helping relationship, differences, and accountability; and planning, particularly in the open systems concept.

UNDERHILL MODEL

At the Institute for Business and Community Development of the University of Richmond where we have been working to integrate various pieces of both MBO and OD, Dr. R. S. Underhill has developed a model (Fig. 1) that has been quite helpful in working with various client systems to diagnose and plan applications strategy and training/development needs. This model identifies five major areas of interest that are potential entry points for working with an organization when taking a systemic approach. Two of these areas, MBO and OD, have been covered above in some depth, though the goal-setting process within MBO/R (our acronym

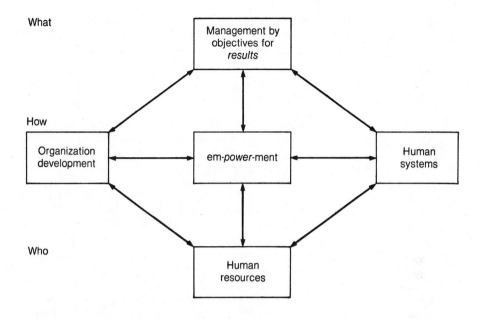

Figure 1   Entry points for diagnosis and planning

for management by objectives for results) moves to much greater depth than simply writing objectives. The remaining areas are closely related and supportive of achieving the integration that seems to have the greatest potential for organization effectiveness. In this application, the person, a human being, is extremely important, and in these areas we must seek to satisfy a variety of human needs.

One area is concerned with the *human resource* and deals with personal values and personal growth issues that develop and affirm the self concept of the individual within the group or organization. A second area is that of *human systems*. Under this category, we are seeking to assure that the systems within the organization are human oriented. Such systems would be concerned with developing policies, procedures, organizational structure, and operations that were supportive of individuals in achieving organizational results rather than just perpetuating individual activities. The third area has to do with *power* or, more appropriately, the em*pow*erment of the individual. It is only through "personal" power that the fullest potential of the organization will ultimately be realized so that we can move to the third generation application that Howell has described.[13] We have drawn primarily on the work of John Talbot (an OD consultant) for our theory base in em*pow*erment diagnosis and application.

This form of personal power relies on working a variety of OD issues to develop psychological contracts on how power will be utilized in a way that is not based on hierarchical authority. As you can see in the illustration, empowerment is the core, the central issue. Unless the interconnecting channels are open with minimum resistance in the system, not much flow of energy will occur in the organization.

This model in its greater depth provides a theory base for empowering the system to establish the organization results desired, to develop the organization to maintain the process, and to *manage* by objectives to achieve those results.

ACHIEVING EFFECTIVENESS

Earlier I indicated that the theory base for OD and MBO meet when we consider applying MBO in the context of groups working toward organizational effectiveness. It is on the human side of results where OD and MBO come together—as concepts. But it is actually in the people of an organization that OD and MBO meet, when they function as groups or teams to achieve organizational results through an MBO process that is supportive of their movement toward satisfying their own personal needs as well. How each person perceives his or her reality will have a marked effect on the meeting of MBO and OD and their success or failure in the organization. If we are to achieve organizational effectiveness, I believe we must work with the focus on organization results and use systems knowledge to help us develop a supportive interpersonal process. In this situation, as we analyze, diagnose, plan, implement, and evaluate, the phrase *think systems* would force us to constantly test the data to validate that we were considering the system issues of who-how-what. In Figure 1, you can identify the interrelationships of these three issues. Too often organization concerns stop after what-how and forget the need to include the person. Similarly, many individuals on their independence or ego trips never get beyond who-how to the reality of the organization's what—results.

DEVELOP DIFFERENT PERCEPTIONS

In order to manage this approach, we need to develop some different perceptions of the process of management and the organization. The increasing application of OD and behavioral technology and its integration with MBO having an organization focus is moving many people into new dimensions of organization life. One quickly comes to grips with the need to think and conceptualize at the "whole" or holistic level. In this situation, you have to be able to move almost instantly from a level of concern for the whole organization to a level of concern for the whole individual. It is like listening and responding to the vibration of a symphony orchestra while at the same time being able to identify with the instruments in first one section, then another.

When you begin to experience this meeting of MBO and OD, I believe that the other issues in our model (Fig. 1) will have new meaning for you and will receive much greater attention and understanding. With the increasing technology in all areas of development and management, our tool kit is running over. For MBO and OD to meet in people—in you—it means "You really gotta wanna" put it to work. It is a demanding process which requires managerial skills and effort, but that personal investment yields high levels of organizational and individual achievement—results.

NOTES

1. Arthur C. Beck, Jr. and Ellis D. Hillmar, "OD to MBO or MBO to OD: Does it Make a Difference," *Personnel Journal* (November, 1972): 827–34.

2. Harold M. F. Rush, *Organization Development: A Reconnaissance* (New York: The Conference Board, 1973), 2.

3. Robert A. Howell, "Managing by Objectives—A Three-Stage System," *Business Horizons* (February 1970): 42–43.

4. Ibid., 43–44.

5. S. R. Ganesh, "Choosing an OD Consultant," *Business Horizons* (October 1971): 49–55.

6. Raymond F. Pellissier, "Why MBO Works Better in Britain," *Management by Objectives Journal* 2, 2: 4–7.

7. Fred E. Schuster and Alva F. Kindall, "Management by Objectives—Where We Stand Today, A Survey of the Fortune 500," *Human Resource Management* 13 (Spring 1974): 8–11.

8. Gerald F. Carvalho, "Critical Issues in MBO," a paper presented to Mountain Plains Management Conference and available through *Management by Objectives Newsletter*, (1974): 1–9.

9. John W. Humble, *How to Manage by Objectives* (New York: AMACOM, 1973), 5–6.

10. M. Scott Myers and Susan S. Myers, "Adapting to the New Work Ethic," *The Business Quarterly* (Winter 1973): 48–58.

11. Charles L. Hughes and Vincent S. Flowers, "Shaping Personnel Strategies to Disparate Value Systems," *Personnel* (March/April 1973): 8–23.

12. Rodney W. Napier and Matti K. Gershenfeld, *Groups: Theory and Experience* (Boston: Houghton-Mifflin Company, 1973), 106–07.

13. Howell, 44–45.

Organization Development and Change in Organizational Performance

John R. Kimberly

Warren R. Nielsen

This research was supported, in part, by the Institute of Labor and Industrial Relations at the University of Illinois, Champaign. The authors would like to acknowledge the comments of an anonymous reviewer and those of George Graen, Michael Moch, and Louis Pondy on previous drafts of this paper.

This study examined the impact of an organization development (OD) effort on organizational performance using a model of causal linkages in planned change that appears to underlie the OD approach to organizational intervention. Significant positive changes in target group attitudes and perceptions were found, as was significant positive change in quality of output and in profit. No change in the levels of productivity was found, and a strong positive correlation between those levels and levels for the industry as a whole was interpreted as indicating that this particular index of performance was outside the direct control of plant management and more a function of corporate policy and market conditions.

Organization development, a philosophy of and technology for producing organizational change, has been implemented in a variety of organizations. Growing out of the human relations tradition in the forties and fifties, it is actually a pastiche of techniques developed in the behavioral sciences that focus on problems of organizational learning, motivation, problem solving, communications, and interpersonal relations. While it is misleading to speak of OD as a clearly defined and integrated approach to producing change (21), its proponents (7, 4, 6, 27, 12, 14) argue that it can lead to improved organizational effectiveness and health.

Given the importance of change in the literature on organizations and the prevalence of OD in management circles, there is a surprising lack of systematic evidence regarding its efficacy, particularly in terms of its impact on organizational performance. With certain exceptions (29, 26, 8, 30, 28, 19, 9), most of the evidence to date consists of testimonials, anecdotes, and impressions or research focused on changes in attitudes toward and perceptions of organizational reality. This evidence is generally favorable: that is, it attests to the success of OD interventions in producing change in positive directions. Less numerous, however, are studies of change in measures of organizational performance, as Friedlander and Brown (16)

John R. Kimberly is an assistant professor of sociology at the University of Illinois in Urbana-Champaign. Warren R. Nielsen is an assistant professor in the Department of Management at the University of Nebraska at Lincoln.

Reprinted from John R. Kimberly and Warren R. Nielsen, "Organization Development and Change in Human Performance," *Administrative Science Quarterly*, Vol. 20, No. 2 (June 1975), 191–206.

in their extensive review of the literature have pointed out. The purpose of this article is to begin to fill that gap.

RESEARCH SETTING

The study on which this article is based involved the implementation of a planned change program in an automotive division of a large multiplant, multidivisional corporation. The plant employed approximately 2,600 hourly and 200 salaried employees; work was organized on an assembly-line basis. Parts were furnished by other plants of the parent corporation, with the employees assembling the final product. The plant operated with three separate shifts. Shifts one and two were responsible for building the product and the third shift repaired those units that were unacceptable upon final inspection. There were five basic hierarchical levels in the organization made up of hourly employees, foremen, general foremen, assistant superintendents, and superintendents. A plant manager oversaw the total plant operation.

There were a number of factors that influenced the management of the plant to embark on an OD program. First, the plant was a major unit in a division that had been considered very successful in the past but which in recent years was experiencing decreases in production, quality, and profits and increases in absenteeism, turnover, and grievance rates. Second, there was a general feeling in the plant that supervisors and managers were not working together and that the level of teamwork had decreased. Third, many managers believed that the first-line supervisors did not see themselves as a part of the team and some effort was needed to rectify this situation. Finally, the plant manager appeared to have a genuine concern for improving the performance of the organization.

Although members of plant management did not think that their values were in conflict with those underlying OD, they did not enter into the change project because of a particular commitment to OD values. Rather, they felt that OD and its accompanying methods and techniques might be a vehicle for improving organizational effectiveness, and they agreed to try it on that basis. The plant manager, production superintendents, and the change agents decided that the OD effort should be concentrated on the production group since this group's performance was most directly related to the performance of the organization as a whole. All production supervisors—foremen and general foremen—and managers, assistant superintendents, and superintendents, as well as the plant manager, therefore, participated in various phases of the OD program, which began in January 1970 and continued formally, with the use of outside assistance, through March 1971.

CHANGE PROGRAM

A brief summary of the OD program used in the organization includes the following seven phases.[1]

1. Initial diagnosis: The diagnosis consisted of three stages. First a series of interviews was held with a sample of fifteen supervisory and managerial personnel including the plant manager and his immediate staff. Second,

group meetings were held with those interviewed to examine the results and to determine problem areas and priorities. Finally, the plant manager, his immediate staff, and the external consultants met to finalize the change design.

2. Team skills training: Foremen, general foremen, assistant superintendents, and superintendents participated with their peers in groups of approximately twenty-five individuals in a series of experience-based exercises during a two-and-a-half-day workshop.

3. Data collection: Immediately following the team skills training, all foremen completed two questionnaires. The first concentrated on organizational health and effectiveness and the second asked them to describe the behavior of their immediate supervisor—general foremen or assistant superintendents.

4. Data confrontation: In this phase, various work groups were asked to review the data described above and determine problem areas, establish priorities in these areas, and develop some preliminary recommendations for change.

5. Action planning: Based on the data and conversation during the data confrontation, each group developed some recommendations for change and plans for the changes to be implemented. The plans included what should be changed, who should be responsible, and when the action should be completed.

6. Team building: Each natural work group in the entire system, including the plant manager and his immediate staff of superintendents, then met for two days. The agenda consisted of identifying blocks to effectiveness for the specific group and the development of change goals and plans to accomplish the desired changes.

7. Intergroup building: This phase consisted of two-day meetings between groups that were interdependent in the plant. The groups met for the purpose of establishing mutual understanding and cooperation and to enhance collaboration on shared goals or problems.

The sequence in which the interventions occurred is outlined in Table 1.

RESEARCH DESIGN

One criterion for judging the utility of any research design is its ability to rule out the possibility of alternative explanations. From an experimental point of view, it would be highly desirable to design the research using controls that would make it possible to isolate the effects of treatment conditions—the OD interventions—on the dependent variables—changes in perceptions of organizational climate and supervisory behavior and change in productivity, quality, and performance to budget. In this case, however, as in most field research, ideal procedures specified by formal canons of experimental design had to be modified to meet situational constraints. Three particular constraints were present. First, the change program had been initiated and was well along before this phase of research was developed. Second, the fact that the interventions were plant-wide precluded the establishment of internal controls, although such control would have had to occur after the program. Finally, the plant itself was structurally different from other plants in the parent corporation, which made the use of another plant in the system as a control for the organizational performance data questionable. Hence, what emerged was a

Table 1 Change program sequence

Intervention	Initiated	Completed
Initial diagnosis	12-01-69	12-31-69
Team skills training	01-09-70	02-28-70
Data collection	01-10-70	03-01-70
Data confrontation	05-09-70	08-19-70
Action planning	09-01-70	12-31-70
Team building	01-01-71	02-01-71
Intergroup building	02-02-71	02-28-71
Data collection	03-15-71	03-15-71

post hoc design combining elements of what Campbell and Stanley (10) have called a "One Group Pretest Posttest Design" and a "Time Series Experiment." This quasi-experimental design, used in conjunction with industry-wide data for the time period in question, enables one to begin to deal with the issue of alternative explanations, albeit on less than ideal terms.

Data were collected from the management subsystem or target group of the organization regarding perceptions of organizational climate and supervisory behavior just before and immediately after the involvement of the outside consultants in the OD program. These data, collected anonymously at two times, were used to measure the extent of change in the managerial subsystem as a whole. Two questionnaires were employed. One was developed by Douglas McGregor for use in team building and asked the respondents to rate such factors as trust, support, communication, understanding of objectives, commitment to objectives, handling of conflict, utilization of resources, control methods, and organizational environment. The second, developed by Ed Nevis for use in OD projects and modified for this study, asked employees to describe the behavior of their immediate supervisors relative to listening, expressing ideas to others, influence style, decision making, relations with others, task orientation, handling of conflict, willingness to change, problem solving, and self-development.

Indices of organizational performance—namely, production rate, quality levels, and performance to budget—were compiled on a daily basis for the fifteen months before, the fourteen months during, and the twelve months after the interventions. These data meet the criteria for a modified time-series experiment design. Within the limitations of this design, therefore, the impact of the OD interventions on the organization that is the setting for the study could be considered. Longitudinal data on hard measures of organizational performance are generally absent in the literature on organizational development; by contrast with what is in the literature, the approach used here—though developed after the change program had been initiated—has a variety of advantages, both theoretical and empirical.

HYPOTHESES

The model used to generate testable hypotheses about the impact of the interventions was based on an assumption about causal linkages in an organization that is central to the OD approach to organizational change. Since the interventions were explicitly designed to produce change in the attitudes, perceptions, and behaviors of the individuals who were participants in the change program, this change was called first-order change. Change of this sort may produce changes in the attitudes, perceptions, and behaviors of other individuals in other parts of the organization (for instance, reducing absenteeism among hourly employees) as a consequence of the interdependencies that exist or are created between subsystems in the organization. This was called second-order change. Finally, change in indices of the performance of the organization as a whole, indices that reflect aggregated individual behaviors, may occur as a consequence of first-order change alone or the combination of first- and second-order change. At the start of any planned change program of this type, therefore, it is posited that first-order change should be temporally antecedent to other kinds of change. Thus, it is argued that change in the attitudes, perceptions, and behaviors within the OD target subsystem is a necessary condition for the attribution of changes in other organizational indices to the interventions. Over time, however, because of the nature of the interdependencies among organizational variables and feedback mechanisms inherent in the change program itself, there will be reciprocal causation.

The model developed, therefore, was based on what was perceived to be a major assumption about causal linkages that is inherent in the technology of OD in general and that is reflected in, among others, the work of Argyris (1, 2), Likert (24), and Blake and Mouton (7). The merits of the model itself are not argued here; alternative models, in fact, may capture the complexity of causal relations more effectively. It is argued, however, that this model is a reasonable approximation of that used explicitly or intuitively by most OD change agents and for that reason its tenability should be examined empirically. Schematically, the model is outlined in Figure 1.

It is assumed that the impact of the OD interventions on attitudes, perceptions, and behaviors within the target subsystem can be directly tested. If change in the predicted direction occurs, the impact of the interventions on other organizational variables can be indirectly tested. A finding of no change in the target subsystem would mean that (a) any changes observed in other organizational variables could not reasonably be attributed to the interventions or (b) that if changes in perfor-

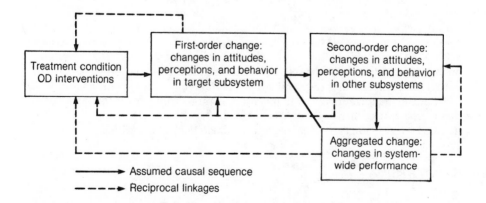

Figure 1   Causal linkages in planned change

mance were observed in the absence of change in the target subsystem, the causal assumption should be seriously questioned. If change in the predicted direction occurred, the attribution of change in other variables to the interventions would become more plausible. Using this approach, the following hypotheses were tested.

Direct Test

As a consequence of the OD change program, (1A) significant positive change will be produced in perceptions of organizational climate within the target subsystem, and (1B) significant positive change will be produced in perceptions of supervisory behavior within the target subsystem.

Indirect Test

As a consequence of the OD change program, (2A) significant increases in units produced will be observed, (2B) significant decreases in the variance in units produced will be observed, (3A) significant increases in the level of the quality index will be observed, (3B) significant decreases in the variance in the quality index will be observed, and (4) significant increases in the profit index will be observed.

There is a great deal of literature (5, 15) that constitutes the theoretical basis from which hypotheses 1A and 1B are generated. The hypotheses about changes in production and quality rates need some further discussion, however. Changes in both the absolute level and in the variance around that level are hypothesized. Based on the kinds of impacts OD interventions are designed to produce, changes in both measures logically could be expected. Positive changes in organizational climate and supervisory behavior could be expected to lead to better planning, more cooperation, and improved problem solving and to the discussion and adoption of new ideas that would, in turn, lead to an increase in the total volume of organizational outputs, as well as increases in the predictability of the flow of outputs from period to period.

RESULTS

The approach used to conceptualize the process of change requires that analysis of change in perceptions within the target subsystem precede analysis of change in organizational performance. To determine whether significant perceptual change took place between pre-1970 and post-1971 measurement, separate t-tests were computed for each item on the two questionnaires regarding organizational climate and supervisory behavior. In each case, one-tail tests of significance were used, since the direction of change was hypothesized. The sample consisted of responses from approximately ninety production foremen. The results of these tests are presented in Tables 2 and 3.[2]

The analysis performed on the data pertaining to organizational climate indicates that the pre-1970 and post-1971 period means for all items differed more than might be expected by chance—the items showing the least change were significant

Table 2 Organizational climate

Item	January 1970 (N=90)		March 1971 (N=87)		t-value
	X̄	SD	X̄	SD	
Trust	3.73	1.48	4.78	1.14	5.09[a]
Support	3.76	1.74	4.36	1.48	2.37[b]
Open communications	3.04	1.61	4.64	1.38	6.83[a]
Understanding of objectives	4.52	1.42	5.29	1.27	3.64[a]
Commitment to objectives	4.40	1.49	5.17	1.26	3.58[a]
Handling of conflict	3.79	1.54	4.91	1.36	4.88[a]
Utilization of member resources	3.80	1.67	4.78	1.35	4.14[a]
Self-direction, autonomy	3.20	1.85	4.77	1.51	5.88[a]
Supportive environment	3.24	1.76	4.56	1.36	5.28[a]

[a] $p < .0005$
[b] $p < .01$

Table 3 Supervisory behavior

Item	January 1970 (N=90)		March 1971 (N=87)		t-value
	X̄	SD	X̄	SD	
Listening	3.45	1.73	4.48	1.56	3.90[a]
Expressing ideas to others	4.14	1.78	5.07	1.35	3.60[a]
Influence	2.85	1.50	4.05	1.80	4.55[a]
Decision making	3.43	1.55	4.40	1.63	3.82[a]
Relations with others	2.85	1.61	3.86	1.66	3.82[a]
Task orientation	4.20	1.46	4.85	1.45	2.76[b]
Handling of conflict	3.71	1.76	4.33	1.85	2.14[c]
Willingness to change	4.28	1.40	5.00	1.36	3.26[b]
Problem solving	3.30	1.80	4.25	1.93	3.06[b]
Self-development	3.24	1.90	4.01	1.62	2.71[b]

[a] $p < .0005$
[b] $p < .005$
[c] $p < .025$

at the .01 level. In addition, the change for all items was in the predicted direction. The data relative to organizational climate suggested that after the OD program, the organizational participants perceived greater levels of trust and support in the target subsystem, conflicts were handled more openly, and the skills and resources of the participants were more fully utilized. In addition, they saw greater opportunities for autonomy and self-direction.

The supervisory behavior data are consistent with the data on organizational climate in that pre- and postmeans, for all items comprising this variable, differed more than might be expected by chance and changed in the predicted direction. After the initiation of the OD program, the first-line supervisors perceived their managers as encouraging more subordinate involvement in such activities as plan-

Table 4 Production rates by periods

Period	X̄	SD	t-value
Day shift			
Before vs. during	14,039–11,649	2,639–3,234	2.19[a]
During vs. after	11,649–13,442	3,234–1,394	1.77[b]
Before vs. after	14,039–13,442	2,639–1,394	.71 NS
Night shift			
Before vs. during	13,706–11,446	2,718–3,080	2.09[a]
During vs. after	11,446–13,371	3,080–1,563	1.94[b]
Before vs. after	13,706–13,371	2,718–1,563	.38 NS

X̄= Average number of units produced per month.
[a] $p < .025$
[b] $p < .05$

ning, decision making, and direction of group activities. The managers were also perceived as making a greater effort to hear and understand the subordinates' positions on problems and work goals as well as making increased use of subordinates' skills in problem solving.

The results provided strong support for the hypothesis that significant positive change would be observed in perceptions of organizational climate and supervisory behavior within the target subsystem. As Campbell and Dunnette (11) have pointed out, there is a variety of problems associated with data of this sort, particularly in an $N = 1$ design. Clearly, all of them have not been solved here. The results, however, suggested that it would be appropriate to analyze the hard performance data and examine indirectly the impact of the OD interventions on organizational outcomes. Had change in the target subsystem not occurred, it would not have been reasonable to attribute changes in organizational performance to the change program, at least in terms of the theoretical rationale of OD.

Data regarding the rate of production were collected on a daily basis and then averaged across the forty-one months and the three time periods. The analysis is based on separate t-tests for this index that were performed on the period data— before, during, and after—to determine if significant change had taken place. In each case, one-tail tests of significance were used. A separate analysis of the data was performed for both the day and night shifts of the organization. Table 4 presents the results of these tests.

The results suggest two conclusions. First, the production rate for both shifts declined from the period before the OD program and then recovered in the period after it. The monthly production rates data (see Figure 2) indicate that the decline had begun in late 1968 and continued for seven months into the change program. At this point, the production rates began to improve and continued improving throughout the period following the program. Second, there are significant differences between the periods before and during and those during and after the intervention but not between the periods before and after. The production rate had not increased; it had only recovered to previous levels.

These results provide no support for hypothesis 2A. In an attempt to understand the lack of support, a secondary analysis was undertaken. The analysis was

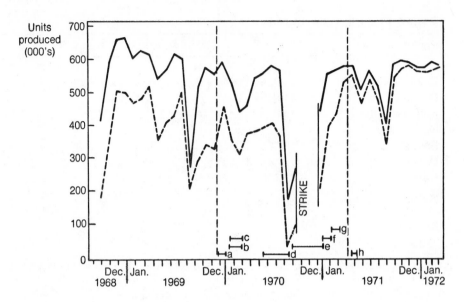

Figure 2 Production rates and quality levels (average daily rate and level per month)

stimulated by the notion that rates of production might be outside the control of the plant studied and more a function of market conditions and corporate policy. If this were the case, the OD interventions and the kinds of change they produce could not be expected to be related to change in this particular variable. Accordingly, rates of production in the plant—number of units produced per month—were compared with rates of production for the same period measured in the same way for the industry as a whole. It was hypothesized that if the preceding were in fact the case, the two rates would be highly correlated. The results of this analysis are presented in Table 5. The results of the correlation analysis indicate that the level of production in the plant is closely related to that of the industry. The recovery made by the plant while engaged in the OD program almost duplicates that made in the industry as a whole, apparently as a result of market conditions.

The second hypothesis about organizational performance advanced was that if

Table 5 Plant-industry correlation analysis

Period	Plant X̄	Plant SD	Industry X̄	Industry SD	Correlation[a]
Before	53,524.4	10,337.6	660,714.1	138,531.6	.93 (N=16)
During	42,996.9	15,685.4	582,263.1	143,043.6	.93 (N=13)
After	45,700.5	8,256.3	644,293.1	104,129.8	.90 (N=12)
Total time	47,896.5	12,431.8	631,033.2	132,268.9	.90 (N=41)

[a]Sample size is the number of months in each time period.

Table 6 Changes in the variance in the production index

| | 95 percent confidence intervals Before | | After variance |
	Upper limit	Lower limit	
Day shift	16,678,003	3,797,901	1,945,467
Night shift	17,865,355	4,395,611	2,442,969

the OD program improved planning, decision making, problem solving, and use of internal resources, there would be a reduction in the amount of variance in levels of production. To test the hypothesis, an analysis of the variance in the production rate was performed. The variance for the index was computed, and 95 percent confidence intervals were established. Following the procedure outlined in Hays (18, pp. 344–347), the confidence intervals were then used as a basis for determining whether there was reason to believe that the variance in the production index for the periods before and after the program were drawn from the same population. Table 6 presents the confidence intervals for the variance for the periods before intervention by shift and the variance in production levels in the period after.

For both the day and the night shifts, the lower limits of the 95 percent confidence interval for the period before are higher than the variance in the period after. It is unlikely, therefore, that the variance in the period after would fall within the boundaries of the period before. This in turn, would indicate that there is reason to believe that the variances before and after are not drawn from the same population. In addition, the F-ratios for both shifts were significant at the .05 level. This being the case, the results are consistent with the hypothesis that the variance in production would decrease as a consequence of the OD interventions. The reduction in the variance in production levels began during the OD program and continued after its completion.

Data regarding the level of quality were collected on a daily basis and then averaged across the forty-one months and the three time periods. The analysis is based on separate t-tests for this index—average number of units produced per month that did not require repair or rework—which were performed on the period data—before, during, and after—to determine if significant change had taken place. In each case, one-tail tests of significance were used. A separate analysis of the data was performed for both the day and night shifts of the organization. Table 7 presents the results of these tests.

The data outlined in Table 7 indicate several things. First, the number of quality units that were produced on both shifts declined significantly from the period before the OD program and then increased significantly in the period after. Second, as might be expected, the decrease in quality units parallels the decrease in total units produced that is shown in Table 4. Third, whereas the production rate had only recovered to previous levels, the number of quality units produced in the period after increased significantly—.01 for the day and .005 for the night shift— relative to the period before. The quality-quantity ratio increased from 71/100 to 92/100 for the day shift and from 69/100 to 92/100 for the night shift. The interventions, therefore, appear to have had a positive and measurable effect on levels of quality in the plant.

A more graphic representation of the relation between the time series data—

Table 7 Quality units by periods

Shift	Period	X̄	SD	t-value
	Before vs. during	10,133– 7,984	2,673–3,413	1.90[a]
Day	During vs. after	7,984–12,494	3,413–1,696	4.13[b]
	Before vs. after	10,133–12,494	2,673–1,696	2.68[c]
	Before vs. during	9,539– 8,070	2,657–2,823	1.44[d]
Night	During vs. after	8,070–12,362	2,823–1,642	5.59[b]
	Before vs. after	9,539–12,362	2,657–1,642	3.24[e]

X̄ = Average number of units produced per month not requiring repair or rework.
[a] $p < .05$
[b] $p < .0005$
[c] $p < .01$
[d] $p < .10$
[e] $p < .005$

Table 8 Changes in the variance in the quality index

	95 percent confidence intervals Before		After variance
	Upper limit	Lower limit	
Day shift	17,124,280	3,899,163	2,876,077
Night shift	16,909,725	3,850,669	2,695,506

production and quality levels—and the interventions used is found in Figure 2. In this graph, only data for the day shift are presented, since there were no appreciable differences between shifts. The relatively dramatic dips in production levels in the month of August are a consequence of annual model changeovers. The strike referred to on the graph took place in another part of the corporation but closed down the plant under investigation for the time period indicated.

To test the hypothesis that as a result of the OD change effort significant decreases in the variance in the quality levels would occur, the variance for the index was computed and confidence intervals were established—95 percent. The confidence intervals were then used as a basis for determining whether there was reason to believe that the variances in the quality index for the period before and after were drawn from the same population. Table 8 presents the confidence intervals for the variance for the period before by shift and the variance in quality levels in the period after.

For both the day and night shifts, the lower limits of the 95 percent confidence interval for the period before are higher than the variance in the period after. Therefore, on the basis of this test, it would appear unlikely that the variance in the period after would fall within the boundaries of the period before. In other words, the variance in the period after appears to be significantly lower than in the period before. The F-ratios for both shifts were significant at the .07 level.

The final hypothesis tested focused on the relation between the change program and profit. It was hypothesized that if the OD program led to improved managerial and supervisory skills, these changes would ultimately be reflected in changes in the profit index of the organization. To test this hypothesis, monthly

Table 9 Profit or loss by period

Period	X̄	SD	t-value
Before vs. during	−116,995 − −133,700	165,089 − 185,514	.25 NS
During vs. after	−133,700 − + 19,983	185,514 − 84,649	2.63[a]
Before vs. after	−116,995 − + 19,983	165,089 − 84,649	2.62[a]

X̄=Average monthly profit or loss.
[a]$p < .01$

profit or loss data for this index were averaged across the three time periods, and separate t-tests were performed to determine if significant change had taken place. Table 9 presents the results of these tests.

These results indicate that the profit index, which was already in a negative position, declined from the period before the OD program and then moved to a positive position in the period after. As Figure 3 indicates, the monthly profit level

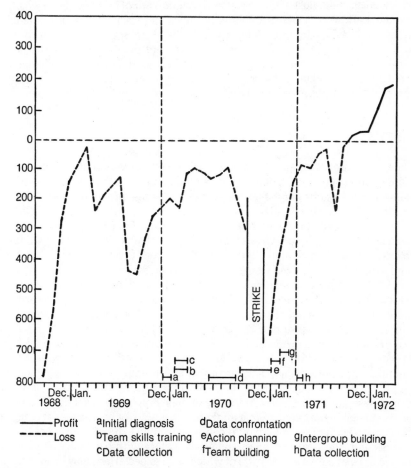

Figure 3 Profit and loss (performance to budget)

had begun to decline in late 1968 and continued until approximately the midpoint of the change effort. At this stage, the index began to improve and continued to improve throughout the period after. This trend is reflected in the fact that there are significant differences between the means for the periods during and after the program and those before and after but not between those for the periods before and during.

Given these results, the major issue in the analysis was the extent to which change in the profit index within the organization was related to trends in the industry as a whole. This issue was critical, since the rate of production was found to be highly correlated with that of the industry. To explore it, a secondary analysis was undertaken. Monthly profit or loss data for the plant were standardized and correlated with the rate of profit for the same period for the industry as a whole. It was hypothesized that if profit was a function of external market conditions and/or corporate policy, the two rates would be highly correlated. The correlation for the forty-one-month period was .48, as contrasted with the correlation of .90 for the production data. This correlation explains 24 percent of the variance in profit, which means that most of the variance, therefore, cannot be attributed to changes in market conditions or policy. Thus, it becomes more plausible to attribute change in the profit level to internal changes within the plant. Significant change did occur in the production variance, quality variance, and quality levels; and it appears highly probable that the changes in these indices contributed to the change in the profit index. This being the case, it can be concluded that the OD program did contribute to an improved profit position.

DISCUSSION

The results presented suggest two important conclusions about organization development as an organizational change modality. First, they indicate—given the limitations of the design—that the particular change program analyzed here did result in improved organizational performance, as well as positive change in attitudes and perceptions within the target subsystem. Changes in attitudes and perception of individuals were accompanied by changes in behavior, which were reflected in turn in changes in organizational performance. Thus, it can be concluded that OD can indeed result in directed change.

While comparative assessment of the two classes of indicators is problematic, it does appear that the extent of the impact of the program was more modest on the system performance indices than on the attitudes and perceptions of the employees. The difference in impact may be accounted for by (a) the fact that the OD program was not an attempt to manipulate the performance indices directly and (b) by expectation effects (23). The prime focus was on the attitudes, behavior, and skills of supervisory and managerial personnel, and the program was designed on the explicit assumption that changes in them would ultimately lead to positive change in system-wide performance. At this point, it is impossible to determine how much of the change in the target system might be accounted for by learning or expectation effects or whether this trend would continue over an extended period of time.

Second, the results suggest some parameters within which OD may be expected to be effective and outside of which such expectations may be unwarranted. These conclusions go beyond the data at this point and the interpretation is speculative, but the assumptions are reasonable. The data indicate that perceptions of organizationally anchored phenomena—organizational climate and supervisory behavior—improved. Further, they indicate that production variance decreased, rates of quality increased, variance in quality decreased, and profits increased. Finally, there was no change in rates of production. While this latter finding was unexpected, the fact that the plant production figures were highly correlated with industry production figures for the same period led to the conclusion that rates of production are likely to be largely determined externally, by corporate policy and market conditions. Since neither of these is within the direct control of the group most directly affected by the OD program, there is no reason to expect that these rates should be affected by the interventions. Later discussion with the plant manager and his immediate staff suggested that this interpretation corresponded closely to their perception of reality.

What emerges from this combination of hypothesis testing and post hoc interpretation is the importance of target group control over variables used to assess the impact of OD interventions. Use of inappropriate indices of impact can create unrealistic expectations, both on the part of the researcher and, more important, on the part of the participants in the change program itself. The decision about what can realistically be expected must come from the participants and evaluation must be made, at least in part, in terms of the kinds of results that they determine are significant. The notion of control is important, therefore, from the dual perspective of participants and observers. It is reasonable to expect that the managerial group in the study could influence quality levels within the plant; it is much less reasonable to expect that they could directly influence rates of production in the context in which they were operating. This finding may also have implications beyond the area of organization development. For example, managerial control may be a critical variable in the failure or success of other organizational change strategies. It may also be that the internal characteristics of an organization are more important in achieving organizational change than the particular strategy employed to produce that change. In any case the finding strongly suggests that performance in human systems is affected by a complex interplay of external as well as internal factors and that performance models which exclude either set of constraints or which are based on oversimplified causal assumptions about the directness of links between interventions and outcomes are inadequate. Much of the activity that is currently under way under the rubric of organization development is based on a closed-system approach, that is, an approach that focuses almost exclusively on internal dynamics. Because the model developed here was designed to reflect assumptions about causal linkages that are prevalent in the field, it is, in a very real sense, a closed-system model. There is an increasing awareness on the part of organizational analysts of the importance of the external environment, however, and those involved in developing planned change strategies will undoubtedly begin to make wider use of open-systems approaches in their work. As these shifts from the use of closed- systems to open-systems strategies occur, the model used here will have to be modified to take this movement into account.

The findings and interpretations presented here are based on one series of interventions in one industrial plant and on a research design that has both advantages and limitations. Thus, some questions remain which are discussed in detail elsewhere (22). Also, the approach to the analysis and interpretation of the data presented in this article were determined by a particular model that approximates the one used either explicity or intuitively by many in the field of OD. The results of the analyses do provide some support for the tenability of the model as an abstract representation of the causal linkages involved in planned organizational change. Further support or contradictory evidence must await the results of similar studies in other organizational settings. In considering its utility, however, it is not suggested that it serve as a general model of organizational change. If, for examle, one were interested in examining the relation between changes in what Hall (17) has called the general environment and changes in organizational structure, a different model would be appropriate.

Further research on the relative efficacy of planned change efforts might profitably focus on at least two fronts. First, additional studies should be undertaken to explore the tenability of the present model more rigorously. For example, this study would have been stronger if it had been deliberately planned from the very start and it was possible to deal more effectively with the problems of control groups and soft measure instrumentation. Second, alternative models must be developed and tested in a variety of organizational settings. Only through increased efforts in careful monitoring of change processes over time can there be an understanding of the nature of planned change efforts and how to enhance their effectiveness.

NOTES

1. For a more complete description of these methods and techniques, see Fordyce and Weil (13), Margulies and Raia (25), and French and Bell (14).

2. It would have been desirable to have control group scores on these items to serve as a benchmark and to help deal with the potentially confounding influences of regression, history, and maturation effects. In the absence of a control group, however, the results of a study by Hribal (20) in the same corporation provide insight into the nature of the movement on the team effectiveness questionnaire. He found that (1) there was significant positive movement over time on all items in the questionnaire in his experimental group; (2) with one exception, there were no significant differences between the means on the items in the experimental group at time 2 and the control group, measured at only one point in time; and (3) the means for the control group were lower than those for the experimental group at time 2 on seven out of nine items. Had the reverse been true, the regression argument would have been more persuasive. Thus, in the absence of formal controls, these results—combined with the fact that performance in the plant under study was in a downward trend in the period before initiation of the change program—suggest that the effects noted above are likely to account for only a small portion of the observed variability.

REFERENCES

1. Argyris, Chris. *Interpersonal Competence and Organizational Effectiveness.* Homewood, Ill.: Irwin Dorsey, 1962.

2. ———. *Management and Organization Development: The Path from Xa to Yb.* New York: McGraw-Hill, 1971.

3. Beckhard, Richard. "An Organization Improvement Program in a Decentralized Organization." *Journal of Applied Behavioral Science* 2 (1966): 3–25.

4. ———. *Strategies of Organizational Development.* Reading, Mass.: Addison-Wesley, 1969.

5. Beer, Michael, and S. W. Kleisath. "The Effects of the Managerial Grid Lab on Organiza-

tional Leadership Dimensions. In *Research on the Impact of Using Different Laboratory Methods for Interpersonal and Organizational Change*, edited by S. S. Zalkind. Symposium presented at the American Psychological Association, 1967.

6. Bennis, Warren G. *The Nature of Organization Development*. Reading, Mass.: Addison-Wesley, 1969.

7. Blake, Robert R., and Jane S. Mouton. *Corporate Excellence Through Grid Organizational Development*. Houston: Gulf, 1968.

8. Blumberg, A., and Robert T. Golembiewski. "Confrontation as a Training Design in Complex Organizations. *Journal of Applied Behavioral Science* 3 (1967): 525–47.

9. Bowers, David G. "OD Techniques and Their Results in 23 Organizations: The Michigan ICL Study." *Journal of Applied Behavioral Science* 9 (1973): 21–43.

10. Campbell, Donald T., and J. C. Stanley. *Experimental and Quasi-Experimental Design for Research*. Chicago: Rand-McNally, 1966.

11. Campbell, J. P., and Marvin D. Dunnette. "Effectiveness of T-Group Experiences in Managerial Training and Development." *Psychological Bulletin* 70: 73–104.

12. Dalton, Gene W., Paul R. Lawrence, and Larry E. Griener. *Organizational Change and Development*. Homewood, Ill.: Irwin Dorsey, 1970.

13. Fordyce, J. K., and R. Weil. *Managing with People*. Reading, Mass.: Addison-Wesley, 1971.

14. French, Wendell L., and G. H. Bell. *Organization Development*. Englewood Cliffs, N.J.: Prentice-Hall, 1973.

15. Friedlander, Frank. "The Impact of Organizational Training Laboratories upon the Effectiveness and Interaction of Ongoing Work Groups." *Personal Psychology* 20 (1967): 289–307.

16. Friedlander, Frank, and L. Dave Brown. "Organization Development," *Annual Review of Psychology* 25 (1974): 313–40.

17. Hall, Richard H. *Organizations: Structure and Process*. Englewood Cliffs. N.J.: Prentice-Hall, 1973.

18. Hays, W. L. *Statistics for Psychologists*. New York: Holt, Rinehart and Winston, 1963.

19. Hill, P. *Towards a New Philosophy of Management*. New York: Barnes and Noble, 1971.

20. Hribal, James F. *An Investigation of the Impact of an Organization Development Program in a Production Control Organization: A Post Intervention Measurement and Analysis Approach*. Unpublished master's thesis. University of Illinois, Urbana, 1973.

21. Kegan, Daniel L. "Organization Development: Description, Issues and Some Research Results." *Academy of Management Journal* 14 (1971): 453–64.

22. Kimberly, John R., and Warren R. Nielsen. "The Impact of Organizational Development on Organizational Productivity: An Empirical Analysis." Proceedings: Midwest Academy of Management, Chicago, 1973.

23. King, Albert S. "Expectation Effects in Organizational Change." *Administrative Science Quarterly* 19 (1974): 221–30.

24. Likert, Rensis. *The Human Organization: Its Management and Value*. New York: McGraw-Hill, 1967.

25. Margulies, N., and A. P. Raia. *Organization Development: Values, Process and Technology*. New York: McGraw-Hill, 1972.

26. Marrow, Alfred J., David G. Bowers, and Stanley Seashore. *Management by Participation*. New York: Harper & Row, 1967.

27. Schein, Edgar H. *Process Consultation: Its Role in Organization Development*. Reading, Mass.: Addison-Wesley, 1969.

28. Seashore, Stanley E., and David G. Bowers. "Durability of Organizational Change." *American Psychologist*. 25 (1970): 227–33.

29. Trist, Eric L., G. W. Higgin, H. Murray, and A. B. Pollock. *Organizational Choice*. London: Tavistock, 1963.

30. Zand, D. E., F. T. Steele, and S. S. Zalkind. "The Impact of an Organizational Development Program on Perceptions of Interpersonal Group and Organization Function." *Journal of Applied Behavioral Science* 5 (1969): 393–410.

The Civil Service Reform Act of 1978

Steven Knudsen

Larry Jakus

Maida Metz

The Civil Service Reform Act of 1978 was enacted to create a legal framework for rules and procedures that would improve the performance of federal civilian employees. Improved performance brought about by personnel changes was believed crucial to improving government effectiveness. The Reform Act signed into law on October 15, 1978, changed the government's structure of personnel administration. The reform consisted of two parts; the Reorganization Plan and the Civil Service Reform Act.

The Reorganization Plan divided the Civil Service Commission (CSC) into two parts: the Office of Personnel Management (OPM) and the Merit Systems Protection Board (MSPB). The OPM was charged with developing personnel management practices and regulations while the MSPB was given responsibility for protecting the system from political abuse and assuring that merit principles were adhered to.

Major tenets of the act included:

1. Delegation of personnel powers from the OPM agency staff to line agencies.

2. Creation of the Senior Executive Service (SES), a new grade classification for most of the government's top managers (GS levels 16, 17, and 18 and executive levels IV and V). Managers in the SES would be assigned where needed throughout the federal government and would be given substantial bonuses for meritorious performance.

3. Institution of merit pay for middle-level managers (GS levels 13–15). Based on performance evaluations, the manager can receive salary bonuses and cash awards up to $25,000.

4. Creation of a simpler process for firing an incompetent employee and provision of additional protection for "whistle-blowers."

5. Legislation of certain federal employee rights for the first time: the right to

Reprinted from Steven Knudsen, Larry Jakus, and Maida Metz, "The Civil Service Reform Act of 1978," *Public Personnel Management* (May-June 1979), 170–81.

unionize and the right to arbitrate. The legislation upgrades the collective bargaining rights from Executive Order to statutory law.

Implementation of the reforms was not defined in the law as it is the responsibility of the executive branch. Because of the recent passage of the act, implementation is only now beginning. Accordingly, it is premature to judge whether the behavior of federal employees will be altered and how this will impact government effectiveness.

Our analysis of the civil service reform process is divided into five sections. The first section explains the pressures that led to the decision to undertake civil service reform and reasons for the successful passage of the act at this time. The second section describes the change process itself. The change process has two dimensions. The first is the process by which a personnel management project, headed by Dwight Ink, studied the problem and made recommendations. The second is the process by which the Reform Act, a derivative of the task force recommendations, was affected by congressional law making.

The third section describes what has been done to implement the legislation. The fourth section describes how the change effort will be internally evaluated by the government. And the final section is followed by our prognosis for successful implementation.

PRESSURES FOR CHANGE

Criticism of the government bureaucracy has been intensifying in recent years, and many of the problems had been attributed to the civil service laws. A decision to undertake civil service reform was made prior to a detailed analysis and diagnosis of the problems with the federal government and the extent to which the civil service laws were responsible. It was believed that a performance audit of every government program, as is performed on selected programs periodically by the U.S. General Accounting Office was not possible. Such an undertaking would have been gargantuan in scope and, therefore, virtually impossible due to its complexity.

It was felt, nonetheless, that many of the problems were traceable to the lack of effective personnel laws. Problems attributed to the personnel laws included the following:

1. Administrations believed that entrenched bureaucracies had frustrated the administration's efforts in carrying out policy.
2. Most government managers expressed dissatisfaction with the current system.
3. The Nixon administration had found a way to circumvent the rules and procedures within the system. These were enumerated in the *Malek Manual*, a series of procedures developed by Nixon staffer Alan May.
4. The public felt that there was an inordinate amount of deadwood in the system resulting from managers' inability to fire incompetent employees.
5. The Civil Service Commission (CSC) was forced to act in the often conflicting roles as personnel development officer and protector of merit principles. Many felt this conflict resulted in inadequate performance of both roles.

The following events conspired in 1978 to make passage of the reform possible:

1. Much of the needed background work had been done by previous administrations in earlier attempts to amend the civil service laws. Civil service reform had been a consideration of administrations since 1937. Many of the elements of the 1978 Reform Act had germinated during earlier administrations.

2. There was a consensus from people who worked in the system that band-aid modifications to the system would not work, because they attacked only part of the problem and would result in more "confusion, profusion, and red tape."

3. Public disillusionment with government had been increasing steadily over the last decade. Attempts to clean up the federal bureaucracy automatically gained the support of the public. Movements such as Proposition 13 in California further sensitized the public to the process of government reform. Although the public knew little of the substance of the reform, the sentiment for "reform" itself was strong.

4. The president set up a task force to manage the change effort. The task force process served a dual function in effecting the change process. It contributed specific recommendations around which the Reform Act was developed and was also responsible for bringing large numbers of diverse individuals, groups and organizations into the change process. This created a sense of involvement and commitment while broadening the base of support for a reform.

5. Carter's campaign promise to improve and reorganize the federal bureaucracy drew public attention to bureaucratic problems. The executive office actively worked to make the reform a national issue.

6. Committee structure and membership in Congress had recently changed, which eliminated several congressional impediments to reform. In the Senate, the old Post Office and Civil Service Committee was reorganized into the Government Affairs Committee at the close of the Ninety-fourth Congress (1976). The new committee was considered much more open to legislation affecting personnel laws. In the House Post Office and Civil Service Committee, Rep. Morris K. Udall was able to assume leadership for this bill. He is considered an expert in getting legislation through committee. Without his forceful leadership, it is less likely that legislation would have been enacted.

7. The administration's timing of the policy process was key to the success of the change effort. For example: (a) Congress had failed thus far to give Carter any substantial domestic legislation and as a result, Congress was willing to support Carter. Furthermore, it was perceived to be a nonpartisan issue. (b) The Reform Act was brought before Congress in the second half of the session when the legislators were pressed for time. This helped forestall much of the debate and polarization common to the Panama Canal Treaty or the Energy Bill. (c) The act was voted on shortly before the November elections. "Government reform" was a safe issue to vote yes on and politically risky to oppose.

8. Very stringent time constraints throughout the change process generated and sustained momentum while limiting the ability of resistive elements to organize and frustrate the process.

THE CHANGE PROCESS

The change process began in earnest when President Carter established the Personnel Management Project in May of 1977. The president appointed Dwight Ink to head the project. Ink was chosen because of his long experience with the federal bureaucracy, his reputation for honesty, and his willingness to undertake a project that had experienced failure in previous attempts. Mr. Ink followed a model for change that he had used successfully in the past. The model's characteristics and the reasoning behind these characteristics are as follows:

1. The change agent (Ink) would have the freedom to direct the project as he saw fit. As such, he was not given a written charter prescribing procedures to be followed. In the end, Ink would be accountable for the recommendations contained in the final report.

2. The change process would respect the laws regarding reform but would bypass rules and procedures that would have directed reform activity. Ink believed that rules and regulations, which existed to protect the process from abuse, served to unnecessarily constrain the process. It was important to remove the process from the ordinary channels due to time pressures and to assure that all relevant information would be utilized. Ink created a special project group within the CSC to coordinate the project. Several bureaus in the CSC and the Office of Management and Budget (OMB) were completely bypassed by this new group.

3. The scope of the study would be broad. A wide-ranging debate over civil service reform would be sure to encompass all important issues, while it would also be of more interest to lawmakers, the public, and other people important to the change process. This would motivate them to become involved in the process.

4. The process to develop reform legislation would be an open process that would be led by people with demonstrated expertise. Ink believed that this expertise, coupled with openness which assured that all points of view would be represented, increased credibility in the process. This in turn would reduce resistance to the reforms recommended.

Ink saw the real problem with government bureaucracy lying in the historic growth of red tape which destroyed individual accountability for decisions. The myriad of rules and regulations both impeded efficiency and made the process so complex and incomprehensible that corruption of the system became inevitable. Ink believed that clear effective laws could improve the civil service system if they provided management more flexibility and provided additional safeguards against abuse. A management analysis team traced a sample of individuals through the hiring and firing process. These studies demonstrated how the current rules and procedures coupled with the lack of clear legislative mandates for effective personnel administration impeded good personnel management. One case study described an eighteen-month attempt by an agency to fire a clerk typist, which only ended with the clerk typist's resignation. This study received extensive media attention and became a rallying cry for reform.

In order to make diagnosis of the problems of the civil service system manageable, Ink and his staff first identified twenty-six areas of government personnel policy concern. They grouped these twenty-six areas into nine topic areas. Ink organized task forces around each topic area that would be responsible for diagnosing the problems, developing support for the change, and designing recommendations within its jurisdiction.

The task forces were grouped around these topic areas:

1. Composition and dynamics of the federal work force.
2. Senior executive service.
3. The staffing process.
4. Equal employment opportunity and affirmative action.
5. Job evaluation, pay and benefit systems.
6. Labor-management relations.
7. Development of employees, supervisors, managers, and executives.
8. Roles, functions and organization for personnel management.
9. Federal, state, and local interaction in personnel management.

Each task force met for a maximum of ninety days. Their initial products consisted of option papers that were circulated among over eight hundred interested groups and individuals for comment. The option papers were redrawn in response to the public input and circulated a second time for comment.

The task forces presented their final recommendations in a series of reports. Dwight Ink drew on these reports to develop the final staff report, which he sent to Alan Campbell, chairman of the Civil Service Commission, and Wayne Granquist from OMB. The final staff report contained 125 recommendations for changes in personnel practices, which called for legislation or an executive order for implementation. The few cases where Ink's recommendations differed from the task force conclusions were indicated in the report.

Additional elements of the task force process had important impacts on the change effort. These elements and their impacts are outlined below.

1. Membership in the task forces was drawn primarily from the ranks of government managers. "This avoided the process of relying solely on outside 'experts' who might have had to spend most of the study period learning the problems with little time left for solutions. Further, the heavy involvement of careerists means that there are a number of people in the system who understand the reasons for the recommendations and can help implement whatever recommendations may be approved by the president and Congress." (Dwight Ink)

2. The location of all the task forces on the same floor of a single building contributed to the success of the task force efforts. The location at Buzzard's Point removed all task force members from other commitments. The close physical contact between task forces allowed for instant and frequent communication on what were often complex interrelated issues.

3. The short time allocated for task force work, necessary for civil service reform to meet the timetables of the legislative session, indirectly assisted the change effort. The short time frame created an atmosphere in which momentum could develop. In addition, the ninety-day limit on task force activity made it

possible for Ink to recruit task force leaders inside and outside of government who would have been unable to commit themselves for longer periods.

4. Input was solicited through public hearings that allowed more people to involve themselves in the change process. This broadened the base of public involvement in the change effort beyond the eight hundred individuals and groups that received task force option papers for comment.

5. The task force process helped establish credibility in the change effort. Credibility was a major concern since civil service reform had been attempted by previous administrations without success. The reaction of several government employees unions to initial approaches by Dwight Ink demonstrated a lack of credibility. At initial contacts these unions felt that the task force efforts were a "smoke screen" for something else. It wasn't until the option papers were written and being circulated that the unions felt that the reform should be taken seriously. At that point it was too late to assume an active role in the process.

Due to time constraints, the task forces primarily utilized existing information pertinent to their studies rather than conducting original research. As a result, their recommendations did not radically differ from those of previous administrations. Thus, it cannot be argued that the originality of the task force findings were responsible for the widespread acceptance of the reforms. Rather, it was the task force process itself that engendered the support necessary for implementing their recommendations.

The Congressional change process formally began in March of 1978. Seven months of congressional acion on the bill followed before the final act was signed by the president. The administration was willing to compromise certain provisions of the act to get the bill through Congress. Several of these accommodations significantly altered certain provisions of the initial bill as indicated below.

Veterans Preference

Veterans have received significant preference in hiring under the old civil service law. The consensus of the task force and public opinion was that this privilege should be reduced since: (1) veterans status gave no particular qualification for most jobs; (2) minorities and women were perceived to be discriminated against because of the preference; (3) the rationale under which there had been a need for preference, the readjustment to civilian life after warfare, was no longer relevant. The task force recommendations that were incorporated into the president's bill would have diminished preference for many veterans. The veterans lobby, however, objected, and the bill was amended to reestablish most of the former provisions.

Union Rights

Consideration of union rights was a potential roadblock to passage of the Reform Act. There was concern that united opposition by unions would bring defeat of the bill. On the other side, there was the concern that conservatives would block any bill that increased the power of unions. It gained the support of congressmen on both sides by establishing union existence as a matter of law (previously unions had existed by Executive Order). The reform also created the Federal Labor Relations Authority (FLRA), which would arbitrate labor-management disputes. However, the bill did not expand the overall scope of collective bargaining.

The reform bill had the support of the leadership of the American Federation of Government Employees (AFGE), an affiliate of the AFL-CIO. The AFL-CIO leadership saw the legal codification of union rights and the creation of the FLRA as important steps in the unionization of the federal work force. However, the bill was opposed by the other federal employee unions and by the membership of the AFGE local since it was seen to increase the politicization of the federal personnel system. They also felt that the overall bill increased constraints upon union bargaining. The support of the bill by the AFGE served to diffuse union opposition and was a factor in the successful passage of the Reform Act.

Merit Protection

Bernard Rosen, chairman of the CSC during the Nixon and Ford administrations and unofficial representative of the government bureaucrats against the reform, was able to have the Reform Act amended to reflect his views. His amendments forced several significant changes designed to increase merit protection. He achieved these alterations despite opposition by Dwight Ink and several other key people in the change process.

Finally, the Carter administration's "multi-million dollar campaign" was necessary to get Congress to act on the legislation. This effort was necessary since support for the reform was broad but not deep. The president and/or cabinet members contacted heads of large corporations, big city mayors, and the governor of every state to encourage them to pressure their congressmen to support the bill. Simultaneous press releases and communications aimed at highlighting popular aspects of the bill gained public support and alerted prestigious groups to elements of the bill they supported. These efforts brought about the support of such groups as Common Cause, the Chamber of Commerce, the Business Roundtable, and the public-interest research group headed by Ralph Nader.

IMPLEMENTATION

Throughout the execution of the change strategies described in the previous sections, much emphasis was placed on the importance of minimizing potential resistance so as to aid implementation of the bill. Yet, while "everyone was concerned with implementation," it was only after the passage of the bill that specific plans began to be formulated. The leadership of the Civil Service Commission has recently held meetings in which they have identified four areas requiring special attention: the SES, merit pay, delegation of personnel authority to agencies, and R and D demonstration authority. Additional planning has produced the time frame around which the implementation of the reform shall be based:

Table 1 Implementation of reform

January 1	New reorganization formally into effect. Agencies give strength requests for SES; MPB organization into effect
January 13	Effective legislative date
March 1	SES allocations
March 15	Incumbents given option to enter SES
June 11	Decisions made
July 13	Effective

Within these parameters, the secretariat (the core group within OPM charged with interim responsibility for implementation) has turned its attention to writing regulations to implement the legislation.

An initial move toward active preparation for the actual implementation came in the form of a recent meeting in Ocean City, Maryland. Five hundred individuals were present, 75 percent of whom were agency program managers, while the remaining 25 percent were personnel officers. The objectives of this meeting were threefold. First, the importance and significance of the bill was impressed upon those attending. The second objective was to educate the managers about the true contents of the bill and the ensuing change, in the belief that with increased understanding would come increased acceptance. And third, as this group was vitally affected by the bill, they were asked for feedback and input into the implementation process. The meeting is considered by many present to have been a success and is now the basis for future meetings to be held by each agency.

Another area of active preparation for implementation is one identified by Dwight Ink as paramount: performance appraisals. A conference on compensation and appraisal has been scheduled for the near future. In addition, individuals within the commission, assisted by experts in industry and academia, have begun to devise criteria by which to evaluate an individual's performance within the context of his or her work. Criteria must also be developed to evaluate managers within their managerial role. This in turn requires an evaluation of the accomplishment of the respective agency. This is an important departure from the previous system, which involved evaluating all individuals within the same grade classification on the same government-wide skills.

Although these are strong and positive (albeit isolated) contributions to the implementation process, many tasks have yet to be attended to. Specific regulations and procedures have yet to be finalized, personnel staffing has not yet been settled, and presidential appointments to the directorship of agencies are still being anxiously awaited. Extensive planning within certain areas has thus been hampered. To provide continuity, ad hoc committees have been formed that will stay on subsequent to the anticipated presidential appointments.

But most notable is the lack of a defined transition process. When questioned concerning implementation, individuals knowledgeable about the reform bill expounded upon the changes to be achieved, but no mention was made about the recognition of a need for a defined and planned transition stage. It was inferred several times that once in effect in January, things would proceed until complaints were received. It should be mentioned, though, that plans have been made to maintain open communication channels with the agencies to provide a more direct means of expressing these concerns.

Given the situation described above, there are several factors vital to the success of the implementation process. It is important to maintain enthusiasm and momentum. Any dysfunctional resistance that can be foreseen should be diminished and/or overcome. Actions to contribute to this effort would include further (more widespread) education to continue to reduce the resistance generated by ambiguity and uncertainty. Perhaps most important to reducing resistance is an actual change in the self-image presently sustained by management. Described as victims of the bureaucracy, the managers (bureaucrats) must recognize that the expectations placed on them have changed. Whereas before they felt they were not expected to be innovative or risk-takers, the reforms place increased emphasis on creativity, dynamic leadership, and accountability for agency performance. Managers must change their self-perceptions and thus actions to match those being held of them by their superiors as well as the general public. This may be encouraged by the correlations between such actions and their salary.

Also vital to the successful implementation of the reform is the careful development of actual performance appraisals. For SES members, the performance of the agency under their supervision is to be a key consideration in their compensation and must therefore be treated with heightened sensitivity and forethought. A system resembling management by objectives (MBO) is presently planned for the SES. The OPM has set up guidelines within which each agency will define its own evaluation criteria, subject to OPM approval. These guidelines include a meeting between an individual and her or his superior to establish objectives and goals for the individual and her or his agency. Feedback must also be given in a formal interview supported by a written evaluation. Therefore, it can be seen that there have been positive steps toward implementation, although the process has not benefited from extensive preplanning.

EVALUATION

The evaluation of the change effort embodied in the civil service reform is a process in itself. Because Congress has the option to dissolve the SES in five years, the evaluation of the reform is presently a five-year strategy. Thus far, this effort does not appear to be a matter of high priority. This is indicated by the fact that there has been no budget assigned to the project and those organizing the effort have been working with "small potatoes" funding. Further, it was not until after the act was signed that an individual (an academician trained in political science) was brought in to design the evaluative criteria. Although unfamiliar with the reform and its intricacies and working with a five-year strategy, this individual's sabbatical has only been scheduled to last one year.

The task at hand is to evaluate the "success" of the reform, which calls for recognition of improvement in the effectiveness of governmental agencies. Progress has been made in the establishment of both the priorities and the work groups required to develop them. The three most important areas were determined to be the SES, merit pay, and discipline.

Based on these, an extensive process of consultation was begun to establish objective measures around which the evaluation would be structured. Contacts with individual agencies were undertaken to obtain accurate profiles of the objectives of each particular agency, as they vary drastically (from "no bad cows" in the Department of Agriculture to "no tax evasion" in the IRS). These procedures are also recognized as a way to create a vested interest and thus a willingness to work with what is finally adopted.

Members of the academic world and experienced managers from industry, as well as private practitioners and consultants, were consulted on effective evaluative criteria and procedures for gathering them. Input from these sources is being pooled with that received from organizational development personnel internal to the commission to produce measures and measurement techniques. These will be used to monitor improvement within the agencies, one measure of the success of the reforms.

For these measures of improvement to be meaningful, they must be applied against a baseline evaluation derived through utilization of the same evaluative techniques. The urgency of establishing a baseline has somewhat affected the choice of techniques, stressing those that are available now. Those that are expected to be used include personal self-assessment, interviews of both the agency and its constituents and client groups, productivity measures presently available, and the annual work-force survey on quality of work life that is presently in use. It is recognized that self-assessment and interviews can be less effective at uncovering the existence of true problems and their depth. However, it is felt that the new reward structure based on improvement may encourage openness concerning existing problems.

Having completed this, another decision to be made is which of the periodic evaluative efforts to contract out to private practitioners. It is not presently the desire of the government to internally generate the large majority of the data it desires.

The ultimate value of the above described process will be the extent to which OPM utilizes the analyzed results, thereby completing the feedback loop. If they consider the results credible, they will actively incorporate them in modifying their personnel policies.

CONCLUSION

Although implementation of the reforms is just beginning, the change process to date has been extremely successful. A prime factor in the success so far was the skill with which the present state was "unfrozen," that is, the degree to which the motivation to change was developed. The forces for change in large organizations today tend to originate outside the organizations, and the government is no exception. These pressures were strong and included public demands for lower taxes and better service, increasing public distrust of the bureaucracy, increased power of unions and special interest groups as well as the election to high office of those advocating change (Carter). The increase in these pressures since Watergate created sufficient discomfort with the present state to start the change process moving but were by no means adequate to maintain momentum. There was still the need to reduce resistance and develop commitment to the change effort.

The strategy for reducing resistance and developing commitment was largely responsible for achieving the first reform of the civil service system since its inception in 1883. Overall, numerous proven methods were employed to obtain commitment in the diagnosis and problem-solving stages of the change. These included problem finding activities (widespread circulation of option papers for comment), educational activities (public hearings), the treatment of hurting systems (greatest attention was toward personnel policies), and attention to the reward structure (merit and bonus pay).

Further, the task force process adhered to many of the proven steps to reduce resistance to change. The task groups were composed primarily of managers who will now feel that the change is their own: there was visible and strong commitment from the top (Carter); there was emphasis on reduction of red tape to make managers' jobs easier; and the diagnostic efforts incorporated extensive feedback from affected groups.

Care was also taken in the design of the change process. In recognizing that proper diagnosis of the problems required a clear picture of the present state, a management analysis team was organized to do just that. The eighteen-month process to fire the clerk typist mentioned earlier was one of many types of personnel actions documented by the team to obtain an accurate picture of the present situation.

In spite of the support and commitment developed through the task force process, it remained to get the Reform Act passed by Congress. In this second phase of the process, there was a necessity for compromise. It was only after negotiating these compromises that the "critical mass" of support necessary to implement the reforms was achieved.

The problem diagnosis and acceptance of the system-wide change goals must be considered a remarkable success in the context of the federal government. However, successful implementation of the reforms is by no means assured. Positive steps have been taken. It has been determined whose commitment must be obtained for the reforms to succeed (managers as a whole), the actions necessary to obtain their commitment (meetings such as Ocean City to explain the reform and seek advice on writing regulations), and the monitoring system required to assess progress (evaluation criteria and techniques). However, it remains to be seen whether the reforms will in fact receive the support from managers necessary to integrate the desired responses (as reflected in the reforms) into managers' task and value orientations.

Certain factors tend to make the prognosis for change less than positive:

1. The change was largely developed from the top down, but success will depend on middle-level and upper-level managers. If the level of dissatisfaction among these managers is not high enough, there will be insufficient commitment to the reforms and thus an inability to integrate the reforms into the system.

2. There appears to be a widespread belief that informal evidence of success (or lack of success) will be fairly obvious, which could cause formal evaluation to be glossed over.

3. Government change has been likened to trying to make an imprint in a bog; only constant pressure can maintain the imprint. There is a real question whether the administration can maintain the momentum for the five years considered necessary for implementation of the reforms and refreezing of the system. First, the administration may change and a new one may bring with it

new priorities. Second, the average tenure for political appointees is two years, often insufficient time to develop and implement priorities. Third, program decisions have become the top priority for many agency managers, and personnel administration is a lesser concern, particularly when faced with budget cutbacks. In addition, evaluation of personnel for pay purposes runs counter to the egalitarian norms of the government.

In spite of the above, several substantial factors promote a favorable prognosis for success. The environment is highly supportive (both the administration and the public), and widespread enthusiasm and optimism is evident among the reform advocates. Also, there remains a strong perception among almost all concerned of the need for the change. Finally, as the reforms are implemented, government service and effectiveness should improve. If this results in a renewed sense of faith in bureaucracy by the public and managers themselves, it should go a long way toward integrating the reforms into the system and improving the overall organizational health of the federal government.

REFERENCES

Interviews:

Berlin, Seymour. Federal consultant and originator of the concept of the Senior Executive Service.

Goldenberg, Edie. Special assistant to Jules Sugarman, the Civil Service Commission director for Policy Analysis and Review. Ms. Goldenberg was in charge of developing procedures for evaluating the reform.

Ingram, Claudia, and Claude Barsfield. Staff Members of the Senate Committee on Government Affairs.

Ink, Dwight. Director, President's Personnel Management Project.

McCloskey, Ronald. Staff member for the House Post Office and Civil Service Committee.

Rosen, Bernard. Past chairman of the Civil Service Commission.

Sugiyama, Jim, and Joe Howe. Assistants to Dwight Ink for the president's Personnel Management Project.

Tobias, Robert. General Council, National Treasury Employees Union.

Literature:

Conference Report on Public Personnel Management Reform, January 23, 1978, U.S. Civil Service Commission, May 1978, Washington, D.C.

Cooper, Ann. Six articles in the Congressional Quarterly: "Carter Plan to Streamline Civil Service Moves Slowly Toward Senate, House Votes." (July 15, 1978): 1777–84.
"Carter Civil Service Plan: Battered but Alive." (July 22, 1978): 1839–41 and 1890–94.
"Civil Service Reorganization Plan Approved." (August 12, 1978): 2125–29.
"Carter Military Bill Veto Could Slow Senate Action on Civil Service Measure." (August 19, 1978): 2174.
"Senate Approves Carter Civil Service Reforms." (August 26, 1978): 2239 and 2299.
"Civil Service Reforms Likely This Year." (September 16, 1978): 2458–62.

Couturier, Jean J. "The Quiet Revolution in Public Personnel Laws." Public Personnel Management (May-June 1976).

Fialka, John J. A three-part series entitled, "The War on the Bureaucracy." *Washington Star*, June 4, 5, 6, 1978.

Lebo, Harlan. "The Administration's All Out Effort on Civil Service Reform." *National Journal Reports* (May 27, 1978): 837–38.

Ink, Dwight. "Who Creates Bureaucratic Chaos?" *Exchange* Vol. V, Issue IX, 1976. Reprinted from the Washington Star, July 29, 1976.

National Journal issue entitled "The Embattled Bureaucrat." (Sept. 30, 1978) No. 39. This issue contains four articles on the federal bureaucracy.

Personnel Management Project, Vol. 1, Executive Summary and Recommendations. December 1977.

Personnel Management Project, Vol. 3, Supplementary Materials. December 1977.

Rosen, Bernard. "How a Reform Bill Critic Was Won Over." *Federal Times* (October 23, 1978): 13.

Section Analysis to Accompany a Bill Entitled, "Civil Service Reform Act of 1978."

U.S. Congress (95-2) Senate Government Affairs Committee, *Civil Service Reform Act of 1978 and Reorganization Plan Number 2 of 1978*, hearings, April 6, 7, 10, 12, 13, 19, 20, 27 and May 3, 4, 5, 9, 1978. Appendix June 1978, Government Printing Office, Washington, D.C.

3

Organizing, Staffing, and Public Personnel Management

The organizing and staffing functions have long been considered basic to public personnel management. Organizing, viewed most broadly, is the process of dividing organizational activities into sets of tasks to be performed by employees occupying individual positions. This process requires the public personnel manager to break down agency objectives into separate position activities and objectives. Equity and administrative efficiency dictate that the comparative worth of jobs be evaluated and that jobs be classified according to the type of work and amount of responsibility they involve.

Because job evaluation results in the specification of minimum qualifications for a position, it becomes the basis for other management-oriented personnel activities such as recruitment, selection, performance evaluation, and training. Yet employees and outside groups are also interested because of its impact on selection, promotion, affirmative action, labor relations and career/life planning. The controversial nature of many staffing decisions and the fact that beginning personnel professionals are quite likely to serve as job analysts or application raters makes it important to understand the staffing function. Each of the four articles in this section addresses different aspects of the job evaluation and selection process.

Kenneth Woods points out that job evaluation—the ranking of jobs for pay purposes—is closely related to other organizational processes such as organization development (OD) and management by objectives (MBO). He evaluates both sides of the controversy over whether to pay people based on the worth of the job they hold or the quality of their performance in that job. Based on the British experience with nationwide wage-price guidelines, he suggests ways in which job evaluation can augment collective bargaining for wage-determination purposes. In many ways, the experience of the British with both inflation and recession can serve as useful examples to American public administrators who face similar situations.

Job analysis is intimately connected to selection in that the validation of selection techniques requires that they be related to the skills, knowledge, or abilities needed to perform essential job tasks. Thus, job analysis must specify not only the type of work performed but also the performance standards required. How this can be done, given the variability of jobs and the need for administrative uniformity, is the topic addressed by Erich Prien. Because of the problems associated with job-specific performance standards, he recommends a job evaluation approach using both task and worker methods.

Although more difficult to develop and administer than traditional job descriptions which focus on employee activities, results-oriented job descriptions (RODs) have many advantages. They give employees a clearer understanding of performance expectations, enable employees and supervisors to evaluate employee performance objectively, and assist managers in tying employee objectives to organizational objectives through MBO systems. The third article in this section, by Donald E. Klingner, evaluates the feasibility of RODs and their effect on the role of the personnel manager.

Staffing involves the recruitment, selection, orientation, and promotion of employees. Because these processes determine who gets jobs, they are subject to a great deal of controversy. No other personnel function is characterized by such apparent agreement as that people should be hired or promoted on the basis of ability but also by such bitter disagreement about how ability should be determined. An article by Frank Dyer highlights this controversy by discussing the impact of affirmative action guidelines on the recruitment and selection process. These guidelines require that tests be validated unless they do not have an adverse impact on protected groups. However, most small-sized or medium-sized agencies rely on tests that may be discriminatory, yet these agencies do not have either the resources or numbers of employees necessary to conduct an empirical validation study. One alternative, according to this author, is to use higher pass rates for nonprotected than for protected class applicants. However, this alternative is less feasible if reverse discrimination is a problem. While this article is somewhat technical because of its reliance on statistical analysis of adverse impact and selection decisions, it does show the extent to which selection techniques are affected by constantly changing laws, case law, and administrative regulations.

The importance of valid and inexpensive selection techniques has led to much innovation in this area, including such techniques as panel interviews and assessment centers. By far the most commonly used selection device, however, is still the job application—a standardized record of an applicant's education, training, and experience. In the final article of this section, Edward L. Levine and Abram Flory III examine the use of job applications to see how related they actually are to job performance. Their exploratory study concludes that applications are more reliable and valid than interviews, despite the emphasis placed on the interview by both employers and applicants.

Job Evaluation: More than Just a Management Technique

Kenneth Woods

How are judgments and decisions affecting employees to be made if a balance is to be kept between justice and cost effectiveness, between managerial accountability for results and managerial accountability for sound employee relations? The chronic anxiety implicit in this question for employers and managers is not lessened by the accumulating risk of legal action; more and more they appear not *like* judges, but *before* them. Job evaluation is a matter of judgment. It is a more or less systematic way of making judgments about jobs. It concerns decisions that employers have to make and that fundamentally affect their employees as people. It goes, therefore, to the heart of the question with which this paragraph started.

In the context of this question, I shall be considering job evaluation as process rather than technique and in particular as a social and participative process, catalytic as well as analytic. I shall look first at its value within organizations for purposes other than pay and then at its use across organizations or sectors as a basis for pay determination. Attitudes are of the essence throughout.

Getting attitudes right can be critically important but never easy. Leadership or charisma may be the answer, but they are not always ready at hand. As a participative process, job evaluation can unobtrusively help to liquefy attitudes, reduce misunderstandings, and resolve conflicts in a way that is not resented and is seen as businesslike and purposeful. It cannot work if attitudes are against it; if they are amenable, it can work on them.

Job evaluation can be a practical starting point for organization development. If the approach is designed and implemented with OD objectives in mind, then OD objectives can be achieved or at least promoted. It can and should be part of the OD panoply.

Many of the attitude problems that inhibit the effectiveness of organizations have to do with job or role perceptions. They may arise from misunderstandings about roles, implicit refusal to recognize changes in the relative importance of roles, or a confused amalgam of chemical reactions against people mixed up with misunderstandings about roles. Where roles are not defined or understood, tension and insecurity and parochial politics flourish. Sorting out problems of job definition and relativities can often dispose of the root cause and in doing so lessen some of the related tensions and uncertainties. A number of features of job evaluation as a social and participative process make this possible:

1. It provides an acceptable reason—for example a better pay structure—for

Reprinted from Kenneth Woods, "Job Evaluation: More than Just a Management Technique," *Personnel Management*, Vol. 8 (November 1976), 27–29.

entering into a social situation and spending time on discussions that may otherwise be rejected as trivial or irrelevant.

2. The focus on jobs enables participants to talk and make judgments about things with personal implications for themselves and others, from which they would otherwise tend to shy away.

3. It provides a discipline and structure for dealing with complex matters of judgment, which make the process feasible and even enjoyable. Job evaluation can have some of the fascination of a game, if played right, and that can be valuable.

4. It provides a language, which makes possible communication about complex matters otherwise very difficult to articulate.

5. The process involves a sensitive balance between inherent negotiating and political elements on one side and an overt search for a rationale on the other. It would be idle to pretend that negotiating postures can be excluded, but they can be tempered by a judicious probing for relevant facts and arguments. Through this process, the perceptions and values of people can be changed in a gradual, evolutionary way without upsetting stability. Relativities between jobs are likely to be changed in the direction that reason demands but only so far as the people concerned can stomach.

JOINT PROBLEM SOLVING

The 1976 Industrial Personnel Management (IPM) survey of job evaluation[1] showed that while the establishment of a "fair" pay structure was by far the most commonly stated reason for introducing job evaluation, other aims and benefits were acknowledged by a significant proportion of respondents; 35 percent, for example, felt that job evaluation had "helped to decrease industrial relations problems." As many as 37 percent had joint union and management evaluation committees. Where unions or other employee representatives are directly involved in the evaluation process, there is an opportunity for achieving genuine participation in practice and for developing a working relationship in which unions are not simply making claims on the employers but are participating with them in a joint problem-solving and decision-making exercise that has a vital bearing on differentials and other negotiable issues. This in the long term can be an even more significant benefit than the smoothing away of friction points in industrial relations through a more soundly based pay structure.

Pay and employee relations are not the only areas affected. The potential uses of job evaluation for man-job matching, career development, performance evaluation, and organizational analysis have been well rehearsed. Another possible consequence, which will seem a boon to some but not to others, is that the door may be opened for the personnel function into wider management processes and enable it to influence positively the way an organization is run. It would then be poised to fulfill what Brian Holland calls the "catalytic" role of personnel management—that it should be "provoking or assisting changes which help the organization and its employees to remain in some kind of harmony of objectives."[2]

It would indeed take a very long recipe to set out all the ingredients needed if job evaluation is to make the best possible impact across the board. For starters it must: (a) be effectively calibrated with related management systems and processes; (b) be based on explicit criteria, which together provide a logically coherent view of each job as a whole and an analysis of jobs that explains them in terms of purpose rather than activities; (c) encourage a questioning approach and require a rationale for the judgments made, in order to avoid the barren confrontation of unsupported assertions; (d) achieve a balance between structure and open-endedness—enough structure to generate confidence and maintain consistency, enough open-endedness to avoid rigidity and the subordination of judgment and common sense to the "system"; and above all, (e) be appropriate and acceptable—appropriate to its own objectives and to the situation, acceptable at all stages (design, introduction, and so on).

Management has to maintain a balance between its own assessment of what is appropriate and what appears to be acceptable. It must have regard to the reasons, implicit as well as explicit, for introducing job evaluation and to facets of the situation likely to influence the workability of particular approaches. An organization with a general climate of openness, for example, is unlikely to be satsified if a few members of management go into a huddle and keep the whole evaluation thing to themselves.

Resistance may come from managers or from unions, for good or for bad reasons. A manager who sets great store on his or her personal freedom to operate by whim, caprice, or tantrum will not welcome any move to define his or her accountability or even that of subordinates. A union may proclaim a general aversion for job evaluation, but it may be an aversion well founded in experience of badly run schemes. The sponsors must be alive to the bounds of acceptability but at the same time recognize that they can be shifted by effective communication. Understanding is a precondition of acceptance, though not a guarantee of it.

Implementation can be phased. The first stage, for example, may be a detailed examination of a particular job or group of jobs or it may be an analysis of the activities of a particular department or company and the context in which it operates as a means of getting people to talk about and examine relevant issues objectively. Decisions can then be made about the next stage on the basis of reactions to the first. What is appropriate and acceptable is likely to change from time to time, even in the same organization, because of changes in the situation, people's attitudes, and their skill and responsibility in making structured judgments.

What is of overriding importance is that unrealistic expectations should not be allowed to develop. If they are, an approach that is acceptable at the beginning may end up by causing more damage to relations and pay structures than if nothing at all had been attempted.

While recognizing that job evaluation is almost invariably used as a basis for determining pay, I see a clear distinction between job evaluation—which includes the analysis of jobs and assessment of relativities between them—and job pricing. Others take a different view. Professor Paterson, for example, includes "the establishment of fair pay based on job grading" in his definition of job evaluation.[3] Pay determination is influenced by a number of factors, which feature either not at all or very differently in job evaluation: the ability to pay, market factors, union power and negotiating pressures, the sociopolitical constraints on pay levels and differentials, which have now in the era of joint government and Trades Union Congress negotiations assumed greater importance than ever before.

Job evaluation says something about the relationship that is desirable between the pay of jobs on the basis of their position in a national pattern of job relativities, but what it says is both limited and conditional. It may say that job X is greater or smaller than job Y and therefore ought to be paid more, other things being equal, but does not say by how much more; this is a function of an organization's policy on differentials and the gradient of the pay line. The actual pay awarded to an individual within this pay policy is conditional upon market and individual factors, which have to be reconciled with the relativities suggested by evaluation.

PRICE TAG

Market values attach to people, whereas job evaluation measures the relative importance of jobs. The market is concerned with the price tag of knowledge and skills in a particular supply and demand situation, whereas job evaluation is concerned with how knowledge and skills are used in a working context and with the relative value of their use to an employing organization.

Acceptability of job evaluation as used for pay determination depends, as is often said, on fairness and equity. But fairness is a very elusive concept. It is probably impossible to reconcile all conflicts between the apparent requirements of equity and the real-life constraints of the situation. People are not predisposed to accept easy answers to the question: "Why should I be paid less than Charlie?" What is to be done if one employer cannot afford to pay as much as another or if the value of the work is manifestly less to one employer than to another?

Notions of fairness or equity are based on comparisons, however invidious. Brian Livy suggests that job evaluation itself "is based on comparison, comparison with other jobs, comparison against a standard, or by comparing the amount of a factor present in a given set of jobs."[4] I do not dissent from this but hasten to draw a distinction between the kinds of comparisons across industries or sectors. Comparisons are used by unions as a basis for leapfrogging claims and by employers as a basis for salary surveys, one of the most notable examples being the work of the Pay Research Unit of the Civil Service, which operates on the Priestley "principle of fair comparison."

In the words of the relativities report: "Job comparisons establish similarities in jobs so that the pay for similar jobs can be compared from one employer to another."[5] A signal danger of highlighting similarities is that important differences may be ignored. These differences may be the content of the jobs themselves or in the structures, value systems, and environments of the employing organizations. To say that job A is like job B on the basis of functional similarity in specified respects is not to say that it is "equal in size" to job B.

Justifying the proposition that job A is the same size as or bigger or smaller than job B becomes more difficult as one crosses functional, departmental, or company frontiers. There is a natural tendency for comparing organizations to superimpose their own values on the rest of the world. This can produce quite anomalous results. An organization which, for example, values policy formulation more highly than the management of resources is likely to take a very different view of the world from one which places a high premium on executive responsibility and getting things done. If all the relevant organizations come together as equals and agree amongst themselves, that is a different matter.

Evidence on industry-wide or national job evaluation schemes, particularly in Sweden and the Netherlands, suggests that benefits can be gained from nationally sponsored schemes, provided that they are not too inflexibly linked with pay controls. The evidence discussed below is derived from the National Board for Prices and Incomes.[6]

Sweden, with its strong tradition of centralization in industrial relations, has six major industry-wide schemes covering manual workers. Pay is associated with job evaluation results in different ways, varying from a fixed pay and point tariff in one industry to complete freedom in the translation of points to pay in another. Both unions and employers are involved from the center and appear generally satisfied that the exercise is worthwhile.

In the Netherlands, a standardized national scheme for manual workers was introduced in the early 1950s, with a "wage line" set by the government. In 1968 guidelines for wage increases were discontinued, and job evaluation ceased to be an instrument of national wage control between industries but is still widely used as a basis for fixing differentials. Thus the advantages of job evaluation within industries or firms were retained, without allowing the equal pay for equal work principle to override imperfections in the labor market or differences in the ability of organizations to pay. Wage control had forced the less profitable firms to pay as much as the most profitable, which in turn were prevented from investing more in remuneration, even when they were short of labor.

As with individual organizations, there are dangers in too rigid an association of job evaluation and pay. I would therefore treat with caution the suggestion made by Richard Stokes[7] that a national council for the regulation of differentials should "develop a national job evaluation system" as a sideline to its main task of apportioning additions to the national pay bill between employment groups as proposed by Wilfred Brown. It would be difficult to avoid a direct link between evaluation and pay, resulting in a stalemate in which there was little possibility of changing either pay or evaluation independently of the other. In the Soviet Union, where virtually all workers are state employees and where representative jobs throughout industry are graded by a state committee, provision is made for differences in pay for comparable workers as between different industries, different regions, and even different establishments. But systematic differentiation of that kind in the pay of jobs awarded the same points on a national job evaluation scheme would be difficult to sustain here in a relatively free bargaining situation where the presumption of equal pay for equal work is too well entrenched in the public psyche to be easily dislodged. It underlies all comparability claims and the "principle of fair comparison" and is reflected in statute, not only in the Equal Pay Act but also to some degree in the Employment Protection Act.

Any attempt to introduce greater discipline into national pay deliberations must encounter problems of acceptability. Unions that enjoy great negotiating strength may feel that their bargaining freedom is likely to be weakened by a systematic job evaluation approach. On the other hand, one of the main challenges facing the United Kingdom is to make the exercise of union power "responsible" — to mellow the dizzy freedom of claim making with an understanding and acceptance of the need for an appropriate relationship between the claims made and the economic performance both of the employing organization and of the country as a whole. Union power to force a change in the distribution of income must by some acceptable means be tempered by a feeling of responsibility for the total amount of wealth available for distribution and the productivity improvements required to increase it. Such responsibility does not diminish power—it makes it firmer and more constructively directed. In Sweden this acceptance of responsibility has long been a feature of the political and industrial relations scene. The current pattern of negotiations on national pay policies between the government and the Trades Union Congress could be a significant move in that direction here.

There are plenty of hints about the likely contents of Phase Three of this incomes policy, and job evaluation features amongst them. Rushing headlong into a national job evaluation scheme would be disastrous, but it would be no bad thing to encourage job evaluation within firms or individual organizations, provided that the right ingredients are there. What really needs to be stimulated, both in the private and the public sectors, is a more rigorous and questioning approach to the whole subject of manpower utilization and what people are paid for, together with the disciplined focus on jobs and their purposes that job evaluation should demand. There needs to be greater emphasis on jobs, job requirements, and practical objectives rather than status, formal qualifications, or negotiating muscle. Measurement and study of activities or methods are useful management aids but always the focus should be first on why activities are performed and only second on what or how. In too many areas of employment the fundamental question of purpose, the question of why this or that job exists, is never asked at all, let alone answered.

NOTES

1. "Job Evaluation in Practice." Information Report 21, Industrial Personnel Management, 1976.
2. B. J. Holland, "Who Is in Charge of Personnel Management?" *Management Services in Government* (May 1975).
3. T. T. Paterson, *Job Evaluation* (London: Business Books, 1972).
4. B. Livy, *Job Evaluation,* (London: Allen & Unwin, 1975).
5. "Relativities," *Pay Board Advisory Report 2*, HMSO Cmnd 5535, 1974.
6. "Job Evaluation," *NBPI Report 83* (Supplement), HMSO CMND 3772—1, 1975.
7. Richard Stokes, "Ineffective Incomes Policies: The Great British Obsession," *Personnel Management* (September 1975).

The Function of Job Analysis in Content Validation

Erich P. Prien

Although job analysis is an essential feature of almost every activity engaged in by industrial-organizational psychologists, the subject is treated in textbooks in a manner which suggests that any fool can do it and thus it is a task that can be delegated to the lowest level technician. This is quite contradictory to the position taken by Otis (11) in explicating and defending the practice, and it is clearly at variance with the statements in the EEOC Selection Guidelines (however vague these statements may be) admonishing the researcher to do a *thorough* job analysis in test selection and in criterion development. Job analysis for these purposes is not accomplished by rummaging around in an organization; it is accomplished by applying highly systematic and precise methods. This is particularly salient for the content validation strategy in which the formal evidence is the "paper trail" as compared to a statistical analysis.

While Zerga (16) has listed twenty different uses for job analysis and Morsh (9) has identified nine different methods, there has been no attempt to systematically couple use with method or to evaluate the relative efficacy of methods for a particular use, such as in content validation research. The major industrial texts mention the topic of "job analysis" and name the various approaches, but none provides the detailed treatment necessary for someone to actually learn how to do it. There are a few exceptions: Flanagan's critical incident technique (3), Otis and Leukart's text on job evaluation (12), and the Civil Service Commission's Handbook for Analyzing Jobs (15). The latter two published treatments of job analysis pertain to job evaluation and compensation and are only marginally useful for other purposes. Most recently though, two how-to-do-it manuals have appeared specifically pertaining to the job element method of job analysis for selection test construction and development via content validity. One is a popularized review of the Civil Service Commission job element method (Minnesota Department of Personnel [1974]) and the other is a more precisely detailed treatment (Great Lakes Assessment Council [undated]), which follows essentially the same format and procedure. Both of these manuals provide instructions and examples for the collection and processing of job analysis data through to the development of content valid selection tests. However, neither manual provides much of a research base to support the technique. Thus, both manuals simply reflect the imperfect state of the art as is appropriate for a workbook. In a more critical sense, there is a comparatively limited research data base for the job element approach to job analysis (task-KSAP test) although it is now receiving increasing application in industry.

In spite of the fact that relevant questions have not been raised in the context of nonempirical, job analysis-*based* validation, there has been considerable research

Reprinted from Erich P. Prien, "The Function of Job Analysis in Content Validation," *Personnel Psychology*, Vol. 30 (1977) 172.

in the area of job analysis itself (13). But the degree of clarity and the extent of our knowledge about what we are doing and what we have accomplished leaves a lot to be desired. For this reason, I am unwilling to rest comfortably with the statement in the EEOC Selection Guidelines to the effect that "any method of job analysis will be acceptable," or with the assumption that face validity judgments are the equivalent of empirical validity. Thus, I am particularly anxious when we consider the content validity approach to developing a personnel selection procedure.

In the previous review of the research literature we suggested that there were basic questions which had not been answered or for which only partial answers were available. These questions concerned:

1. Reliability and validity of job description information.
2. Relationships between job functions and individual difference character-istics.
3. Relationships between job functions and performance behavior or style.
4. Relationships between function characteristics (time, emphasis, and so on) and individual differences.
5. Evolution of function components (jobs).
6. Research designs essential to obtaining answers to pragmatic questions.

Clearly Ronan and I took the position that accomplishment in the area of research on job analysis had approximated little more than a pilot effort, particu-larly with reference to personnel selection and even more so with reference to content validity. During the past five years, additional research results have ac-cumulated, but only a few studies appear to advance the state of the art. (By *advance*, I mean provide better answers to the questions previously raised.)

Our questions at that time grew out of our concern with the technology of job analysis; but in the context of content validity, only three remain salient: (1) reliability and validity, (2) job functions and individual differences, and (3) the perennial question of research designs needed to produce appropriate information. For my purpose here I would add a fourth question or issue, namely, that of the *sufficiency* of job analysis information. The remainder of this paper will deal with these four questions.

First, the question of reliability should be viewed in the context of the type of job analysis involved. For example, the reliability of worker-oriented methods appears to have been firmly established. Both McCormick (8) and Fleishman (4) report reliability coefficients for their instruments in the magnitude range expected for commerical maximum performance tests. Reliability here is in terms of inter-rater agreement or of a composite of judgments made using a multidimensional instrument. Most of the worker-oriented research approaches are based on the notion that there exists a finite set of dimensions—a taxonomy of aptitudes, abili-ties, or characteristics—that can be used to describe a job and that accounts for the variability in job performance effectiveness. While there are differences in the instruments used in systematic research programs now in existence, they are identical in requiring the reporter to interpret observations or make judgments regarding the individual difference characteristic involved in performing a job. For example, a service station attendant should rate high on McCormick's PAQ dimen-sion A-1, watching devices/materials for information, and on Fleishman's Task

Abilities Scales (TAS), "flexibility of closure" and "selective attention." The point is that these judgments would be made on the basis of observing the attendant servicing a car—putting gas in the tank, checking oil level, tire pressure, belts and wires, and so on. Because the aptitude profiles produced by these job analysis techniques are directly convertible to a set of test items, it could be argued that worker-oriented approaches to job analysis are the most directly applicable to the content validity problem.

Task-oriented methods using questionnaires such as job inventories or checklists of occupational tasks have a longer history of use but have not received the "institutional" research attention given the PAQ or the TAS. Task-oriented questionnaires contain items usually describing the work activities of a family of jobs such as Hemphill's Executive Position Description Questionnaire (5) or Lawshe's Clerical Task Inventory (7). The reliability data for task-oriented job analysis is far less impressive, but the conditions under which they are obtained are quite different. Specifically, the reported reliability of task-oriented questionnaires is usually calculated using the position incumbent and superior descriptions prior to any reconciliation and using unselected items. (Here we are now obtaining considerably higher reliabilities with a standardized questionnaire.) The product of this approach to job analysis is not directly convertible to a set of test items. For example, the service station attendant "visually checks engine compartment for maintenance and/or service needs" describes a job activity, but to construct a test that will logically differentiate the more and less effective attendants requires a judgment, that intuitive leap we talk about. Is that individual difference "perceptual speed," "visual acuity," "knowledge of automotive engines and accessories," or some other unnamed individual difference characteristic?[1] The judgment process is identical to that performed using the worker-oriented questionnaire, but with the task-oriented questionnaire each judgment is linked to a specific act. To the extent that there is some redundancy of individual difference requirements for tasks, the repeated judgment should produce a reasonably reliable estimate of the required characteristics.

Validity of obtained data is obviously more difficult to ascertain and the question has two facets: namely, do the instruments measure the named dimensions and are those characteristics essential to successful job performance? Validity of the worker-oriented job analysis is clearly supported by the results obtained by both McCormick and Fleishman. The validity of the PAQ as a measure of attribute requirements has been established using both an occupational classification criterion (test scores of job incumbents versus others) and GATB validity coefficients as criteria. PAQ profile scores predict both criteria at well above chance levels. Further support for the underlying aptitude dimensions (construct validity?) is obtained by relating expert judgments of those dimensions to empirical data, again across a large sample of jobs. The TAS directly represent the dimensions of the abilities taxonomy, but the scale anchor statements are expressed as job acts. Construct validity is established by relating scale ratings to empirical data across a wide variety of laboratory tasks. For example, for a task rated high on a dimension, a measure of that characteristic is a valid predictor of task success. In general, the research results are clear and convincing. The PAQ and the TAS measure what they are supposed to measure (the dimensions of their respective taxonomies of individual difference characteristics) and what is measured is related to variability in success.

The validity of task-oriented job analysis also has two facets, each of which must be approached differently. The first question of validity concerns the relation of the reported position composition and the "real" position. The second question concerns the underlying aptitudes and/or abilities that are derived from the *base* data. Evidence concerning the first question of validity is limited and sometimes indirect, being in the form of measures of profile similarity for different raters describing the same job, factorial congruence, and occupational criterion group studies. Task-oriented questionnaires do differentiate jobs within the groups intended, and the differences are consistent with the criterion group characteristics (chief executive officers have higher scores on "long-range planning" than do middle management). Validity in the sense of measuring the underlying aptitudes or abilities is a more difficult problem. The assumption is that performance on a particular task is a function of a specific individual difference characteristic or some unique combination of characteristics. This issue is the substance of question two concerning job functions and individual differences.

Research directed toward answering question two can be described only as sophomoric because of the weakness of the typical design. Several attempts were made to correlate job dimension scores with test scores of the position incumbent on the assumption that employees are essentially in positions corresponding to their abilities and the reverse. This design requires the assumption that some form of selectivity and/or selective retention accompanies job placement. Occupational classification rather than job performance becomes the criterion. While occupational classification may be an appropriate criterion for interest inventories, it is a questionable criterion for maximum performance measures. The more robust test, relating performance variability specific to a job function and test scores, has been used in only a few instances with mixed results. Thus, at the present time, it cannot be stated with certainty that task-oriented questionnaire dimensions are related in any meaningful way to individual differences (14, 6). This is the point at which I've had some second thoughts about the work I've done and the position I've taken in the past; namely, that the task-oriented approach was the best way to go about job analysis. The concentration of programmatic research has been on the worker-oriented approach to job analysis. The data produced can be more or less directly translated into individual difference measure instruments within the scope of the given taxonomy (Fleishman's work represents the ultimate expression of this condition). The task-oriented job analysis requires either that long intuitive leap to the individual difference requirements or the accumulation of massive amounts of empirical data. Considering the apparent complexity of occupation-specific dimensions, the latter task might well be impossible.

I have commented indirectly in the paragraphs above on question six concerning research methodology. While the research done so far has produced taxonomies of either individual or job characteristics, there are a variety of other specific questions concerning both worker- and task-oriented questionnaries that remain partially or wholly unanswered. The basic questions that remain to be investigated concern judgment strategies of those who complete questionnaires, rating scales used in questionnaires and the structure of jobs and work. In a more pragmatic vein, there has been a paucity of research asing the *part-job* method where validation samples are identified across all jobs based on job analysis. Also, considering the importance of methods of job analysis, it is surprising that no one has yet systematically compared methods across a sample of jobs. Brumback et al. (1) used five methods of job analysis but studied only three jobs. It is evident that different purposes for which job analysis is conducted require unique data, but it appears to me that knowledge of the products of methods and their interrelations would aid our understanding of the nature of work.

This brings me to the final question, that of sufficiency (and contamination) of job analysis data. I have no empirical data base here, just my own observation. It appears to me that worker-oriented job analysis data (this includes the critical incident technique) is more vulnerable to contamination and/or being insufficient than task-oriented job analysis data. In situations where I have used both task-oriented and worker-oriented approaches, I have attempted to reconcile the data obtained using a task-oriented method with the data obtained using a work-oriented method. In performing the comparisons, I've used both thematic analyses categories and individual items to construct a matrix. Uniformly I have difficulty reconciling the two approaches because the worker-oriented data contains items without parallel in the task-oriented items or the reverse.

The crunch comes in the test construction for any position having specific job content knowledge requirements. The worker-oriented job analysis approach does not provide a data base (nor does the critical incident technique without another intuitive leap) for "content valid" selection instruments. Thus, it appears that the development of "content valid" selection tests encompassing the full range of job-specific knowledge and the underlying aptitudes and/or abilities will require the use of task-oriented job analysis and some form of worker-oriented analysis. If my observation is correct, content valid tests based on worker-oriented job analysis alone are likely to include irrelevant items which produce test score variance that in turn carries over into personnel decision. We have been using a crude form of content validity to select experimental tests for empirical validation for many years, and I don't think anyone would argue with the observation that more of those experimental tests fall by the wayside than demonstrate significant validities.

In summary, the research on job analysis and on the application of that data to the problem of selection test construction has grown out of its infancy. However, there is insufficient evidence for the sole use of any method for the construction of a content valid test. Thus, in order to account for issues of specfic job content knowledge and contamination of worker-oriented data, I propose that multiple methods of job analysis be used and specifically that a task-oriented approach be used in selection research.

NOTE

1. I am ignoring here the distinction of content and construct validation because the distinction is nebulous and at the moment somewhat arbitrary.

REFERENCES

1. Brumback, G. B., T. Romashko, C. P. Hahn, and E. A. Fleishman, *Model Procedures for Job Analysis, Test Development, and Validation*. Washington, D.C.: American Institutes for Research, 1974.
2. Drauden, G. M., and N. G. Peterson, *A Domain Sampling Approach to Job Analysis*. Minnesota Department of Personnel Test Validation Center, April 1974.

3. Flanagan, J. C. "The Critical Incident Technique." *Psychological Bulletin* 51, 4 (1954): 327–58.

4. Fleishman, E. A. "On the Relation between Abilities, Learning, and Human Performance." *American Psychologist*, 27 (1972): 1017–32.

5. Hemphill, J. K. *Dimensions of Executive Positions.* Research Monograph Number 89, Bureau of Business Research, the Ohio State University, 1960.

6. Jones, M. A. "An Across-Organization Study of Manager Characteristics and Performance." Unpublished Ph.D. dissertation, Memphis State University, 1975.

7. Lawshe, C. H. "Individual's Job Questionnaire Checklist of Office Operations." Purdue University Bookstore, 1975.

8. McCormick, E. J., P. R. Jeanneret, and R. C. Mecham. "A Study of Job Characteristics and Job Dimensions as Based on the Position Analysis Questionnaire (PAQ)." *Journal of Applied Psychology Monograph* 56, 4 (1972): 347–68.

9. Morsh, J. E. "Job Analysis in the United States Air Force." *Personnel Psychology* 17 (1964): 7–17.

10. Mussio, S. J., and M. K. Smith. *Content Validity: A Procedural Manual.* Chicago: International Personnel Management Association, (undated).

11. Otis, J. L. Whose Criterion? Presidential address to Division 14 of the American Psychological Association, 1953.

12. Otis, J. L., and R. H. Leukart. *Job Evaluation.* Englewood Cliffs, N.J.: Prentice-Hall, Inc., (1954).

13. Prien, E. P., and W. W. Ronan. "Job Analyses: A Review of Research Findings." *Personnel Psychology* 24, 3 (1971): 371–96.

14. Rusmore, J. T. "Identification of Aptitudes Associated with Two Criteria of Management. Success for Twenty Theoretically Defined Jobs." Criterion Conference, Edward Henry, ed. Pinehurst, North Carolina: The Richardson Foundation, 1967.

15. U. S. Department of Labor. *Handbook for Analyzing Jobs.* Washington, D.C., 1972.

16. Zegra, J. E. "Job Analyses, A Resume and Bibliography." *Journal of Applied Psychology,* 27 (1943): 249–67.

When the Traditional Job Description Is Not Enough

Donald E. Klingner

Most personnel managers agree that job descriptions are an important part of the personnel function.[1] Job descriptions are the basis for many other personnel activities, such as human resource planning, recruitment, and position management. Yet these same personnel managers may also admit to one another that the traditional job description is not related to the most basic need of the organization and its employees—improving productivity.

This dilemma is important because it affects the way personnel managers view the personnel function. It can be clarified by answering these questions:

1. What are the traditional purposes of job analysis and evaluation?
2. What organizational and employee needs are not met by traditional job analysis and evaluation methods?
3. What can be done to improve job description and evaluation?
4. How will this affect managers, employees, and personnel managers?

TRADITIONAL JOB ANALYSIS AND EVALUATION

Job analysis is the process of recording information about the work performed by an employee. It is done by observing or interviewing the worker, with the corroboration of the supervisor. It results in a *job description*—a written statement of the employee's duties. It may also include a qualifications standard, which specifies the minimum education and/or experience an employee needs to perform the position's duties satisfactorily.

Job classification is the process of categorizing positions according to the type of work performed, the type of skill required, or other job-related factors. Classification simplifies job analysis, for it means that a standardized job description and qualifications standard can be written for an entire group of positions. A job, therefore, is actually a group of positions that are sufficiently alike with respect to their duties and qualifications to justify their being covered by a single job description.

Two classification methods are commonly used:

1. The Department of Labor categorizes jobs into thousands of occupations catalogued in the *Dictionary of Occupational Titles*. Sidney Fine and other human resource specialists developed the method, which is based on worker functions, work fields, work methods, work products, and worker traits needed for each occupation.[2]
2. The position analysis questionnaire, developed by Ernest J. McCormick and various associates, categorizes jobs in terms of the elements or traits needed to perform the jobs well.[3]

Job evaluation is the comparison of jobs for pay purposes. Jobs may be measured against an absolute scale of difficulty or relative to other jobs. These comparisons are used to justify differences in the pay rate of each job. The following methods are the most commonly used:

1. *Whole-job ranking* compares jobs based on their importance to the organization relative to the chief executive's job. It is usually heavily influenced by the status of the incumbent.[4]
2. *Classification ranking* compares jobs against an absolute predefined scale, which qualitatively defines different skill levels. Each job is assigned a pay level based on the amount of skill required, as shown by the wording of the job description.[5]
3. *Factor methods* evaluate jobs by ranking them relative to each other. However, factor methods are much more complex than whole-job ranking in that several

factors relevant to job difficulty are used (such as physical conditions, risks, and qualifications required). Factors are weighted in importance, each job is ranked on each factor, and quantitative rankings are then obtained by multiplying the factor weight times the rank on each factor.[6]

4. *Point methods* evaluate jobs quantitatively by using a predetermined number of factors, similar to the factor method. However, the point method divides each factor into several qualitative levels of difficulty and assigns point values to each level. By weighting the factors, deciding the qualitative level a job merits on each factor, and multiplying the factor weight times the quality level, a quantitative score for each job can be computed. These point values are finally translated into pay differentials.[7]

Of these four methods, only the last three are recommended as defensible to employees on the basis of equity. Classification ranking is used by the federal government; factor ranking and point methods are used by most large corporations and by many state and local governments.

Job classification and evaluation are necessary for many personnel activities.

1. *Human resource planning:* They enable the organization to catalog the number and type of positions in each unit, to plan for future growth, and to predict future human resource needs.

2. *Position management:* By cataloging the type, number, and grade level of jobs in each organizational unit, the personnel department can help control the cost of personnel resources.

3. *Recruitment:* They enable the personnel department to routinely advertise for jobs that have frequent turnover.

4. *Testing:* By identifying the type of skill required for satisfactory performance of a job, the organization can begin to validate aptitude or ability tests used for selection purposes.

PROBLEMS WITH TRADITIONAL METHODS

Figure 1 is an example of a traditional job description. Note that it specifies the organizational unit to which this position is responsible, the general duties performed by the incumbent, and the minimum qualifications required for eligibility.

This job description is deficient in two respects: it does not specify the performance expected of the employee, and it does not specify the linking or enabling relationship between standards, skills, and minimum qualifications. This job description lists the general duties performed by any number of administrative assistants. Because it applies to a range of positions, it is necessarily vague concerning the nature of the typing, reports, meetings, and correspondence involved. The employee may be working in a foundry, a personnel office, or a chemical supply house. In each case, specific duties will differ. The last entry, "other duties as assigned," leaves the job description open to any additions the supervisor may propose.

Second, there are no clues provided concerning the conditions under which

Administrative assistant
Responsibilities: works under the direction of the
supervisor, operations control section

Duties:

Types correspondence and reports
Compiles reports
Maintains inventory of supplies
Arranges meetings and conferences for the supervisor
Handles routine correspondence
Other duties as assigned

Qualifications:

High school degree or equivalent
Type 40 wpm
Two years experience in a secretarial position or equivalent education

Figure 1 Typical job description

the job is to be performed. Is an electric typewriter available or not? How large is the filing system and is it current and accurate? How much correspondence is there to answer? Do all duties occur continuously, or do some require more work at certain times? What guidelines or instructions are available to aid the employee? What working conditions make task performance easier or harder?

Most critically, there are no standards set for minimally acceptable employee performance of each of the job's duties. This omission is basic to the distinction between job evaluation and performance evaluation. The former is the process of evaluating job worth, while the latter is the process of measuring the performance level of an employee in that job. While this distinction is accepted by most personnel managers, most managers and employees feel that in practice it is difficult to separate an abstract "job" from the concrete performance of its incumbent. The above job description does not specify the quantity, quality, or timeliness of service required, nor does it set these standards in the light of varying conditions. For example, it may be easy for a salesperson to increase sales 10 percent annually in an industry growing by 20 percent annually. It is more difficult to achieve the same sales increase in a declining market.

Moreover, traditional job descriptions specify a general set of minimum qualifications for each position. If jobs have been classified according to the type of skill required, these minimum qualifications may be based on skills required to perform duties. In general, however, traditional methods blur the following logical sequence of relationships between tasks, standards, skills, and qualifications:

1. Each job task must be performed at certain minimal standards for the organization to function.

2. Certain skills, knowledge, and abilities enable the employee to perform a task up to standard.

3. Certain minimum qualifications ensure that the employee will have these skills, knowledge, and abilities.

These two problems reduce the usefulness of job descriptions to organizational planners, program managers, and employees. Organizational planners are handicapped because such traditional job descriptions describe only the personnel inputs into a job and not the resultant outputs. That is, they do not specify how many employees would be needed to produce outputs at a given level of quantity, quality, or timeliness. Because traditional job descriptions do not lend themselves to open systems analysis or contingency planning, they do not meet the increasing need to measure program outputs relative to inputs, rather than measuring only inputs.[8] Legislators and executives are less willing to assume, as they may have in the past, that an agency will provide 10 percent more services if it is allocated 10 percent more employees. Output-oriented job descriptions are analogous to program budgets, while traditional job descriptions resemble input-oriented line-item budgets. Clearly, the line-item approach is useful for control purposes, while the program approach is more useful for productivity improvement.[9]

Managers, in their turn, are handicapped because they cannot readily use such job descriptions for recruitment, orientation, MBO goal setting, or performance evaluation. If new employees are recruited on the basis of the brief description of duties and qualifications given in the traditional job description, then extensive interviewing by managers may be needed to select those applicants most qualified for a particular job. Orientation will require clarification of the job description to fit the particular organizational context, and it may be incomplete because of other demands on the manager's time. If the organization uses MBO goal setting and evaluation procedures, these will occur independently of the position's job description. This means that job descriptions will be used only by the personnel department for human resource planning, recruitment, and position management, while managers will control and evaluate employee performance by an unrelated set of MBO procedures. If MBO is not used, then performance evaluation will probably be based on employees' job-related personality traits rather than on outputs.[10]

Employees are generally unable to use traditional job descriptions for orientation, performance improvement, or career planning.[11] Because they give only a brief description of duties, employees must wait to learn about working conditions and standards until they have been hired. Yet this may be too late; unclear or inequitable psychological contracts are a cause of much unrest between employees and organizations. Evaluating employees without giving them clear performance expectations is a sure way to increase anxiety and frustration.[12] Lastly, employees cannot use traditional job descriptions for career/life planning because they do not specify how increases in minimum qualifications are related to increases in skills required for satisfactory task performance. It is easiest for employees to accept the qualifications for a position and to strive to meet them through upward mobility programs if these linkages are more apparent.

Personnel managers and the personnel management function itself are most seriously affected by the limited usefulness of traditional job descriptions. Because traditional job descriptions are best suited to cataloging and managing positions, they are regarded as irrelevant to productivity improvement by program planners, managers, and employees.[13] Inevitably, they tend to be regarded in the same light as inventories of office equipment or the updating of civil defense plans—something that must be maintained as a bureaucratic necessity but which is not a useful tool for accomplishing primary organizational or employee goals. This perceived uselessness of job descriptions affects other personnel activities as well. If personnel managers consider job descriptions one of the most important personnel activities, and if job descriptions are in fact useless for managers and employees, it follows logically that other personnel activities are equally unimportant. This logic is frequently used to belittle performance evaluation, job analysis, training demand surveys, and other items of the personnel manager's stock in trade.[14]

Therefore, the primary result of these deficiencies in traditional job evaluation is to divorce personnel management from those organizational activities that are concerned with inputs, outputs, and enlironmental relationships—primarily program planning, budgeting, and program evaluation. As a result, personnel management is viewed as a series of low-level operational techniques that are used mainly for organizational maintenance purposes.

HOW TO IMPROVE JOB DESCRIPTIONS AND EVALUATIONS

Obviously, job descriptions would be more useful if they clarified the organization's expectations of employees and the linkages between tasks, standards, skills, and minimum qualifications. These improved, results-oriented job descriptions (RODs) would contain the following information:

1. *Tasks*: What behaviors, duties, or functions are important to the employee's job?

2. *Conditions*: How often is a task done? What conditions make the task easier or harder to complete? What written or supervisory instructions are available to aid the employee in performing a task?

3. *Standards*: What objective performance expectations are attached to each task? These standards of quantity, quality, and timeliness should relate meaningfully to organizational objectives.

4. *SKAs*: What skills, knowledge, and abilities are required to perform each task at the minimally acceptable standard?

5. *Qualifications*: What education and/or experience (length, level, and type) are needed to ensure that employees will have the necessary SKAs for task performance?

Three examples of results-oriented job descriptions are shown in Figure 2.

These RODs provide clearer organizational expectations to employees. They encourage supervisors and employees to recognize that both standards and rewards can be contingent upon conditions. For example, a secretary can type neater copy more quickly on an electric than on a manual typewriter. In the second example, an increase in the local crime rate might cause a temporary increase in each probation officer's caseload from sixty to seventy-five clients. If this happens, it could be expected that the quality, length, or frequency of weekly visits would be reduced and that the judge would accept fewer than seventy-five percent of their presentence recommendations. In the third example, standards might vary with the total sales volume of the company, the experience of the salesperson, or market conditions.

SKAs are tied to task performance, and minimum qualifications are elated to them using content or face validation methods. As performance standards vary, it is probable that SKAs would vary in corresponding fashion as would minimum

Typist/Receptionist		
Tasks	**Conditions**	**Standards**
Type letters	When asked to by supervisor; using an IBM Selectric typewriter; according to the office style manual	All letters error-free; completed by 5 P.M. if assigned before 3 P.M.
Greet visitors	As they arrive, referring them to five executives with whom they have scheduled appointments	No complaints from visitors referred to the wrong office or waiting before being referred

Skills, knowledge, and abilities required:
Ability to type 40 wpm
Ability to use Selectric typewriter
Knowledge of office style manual
Courtesy

Minimum qualifications:
High school degree or equivalent
Six months' experience as a typist or an equivalent performance test

Salesperson		
Tasks	**Conditions**	**Standards**
Sell plumbing fixtures	Over an eleven-state area; to hardware retailers	$250,000 annually
Retain current customers	375 existing customers	95 percent of current customers reorder each year

Skills, knowledge and abilities required:
Knowledge of plumbing fixtures
Knowledge of contractors and purchasers
Ability to sell
Ability to work independently

Minimum qualifications:
High school graduation or equivalent
Two years' experience selling plumbing fixtures
Proven sales record (equivalent territory and sales volume)

Juvenile Probation Officer		
Tasks	**Conditions**	**Standards**
Meet with probationers weekly to assess their current behavior	Caseload of not more than 60 appointments scheduled by receptionist; supervisor will help with difficult cases; use procedures stated in rules and regulations	All probationers must be seen weekly; those showing evidence of continued criminal activity or lack of a job will be reported to supervisor
Prepare presentence reports on clients	When requested by the judge; average of 5 per week, per instructions issued by judge; supervisor will review and approve	Your reports will be complete and accurate as determined by the judge; he/she will accept 75 percent of presentence recommendations

Skills, knowledge and abilities required:
Knowledge of the factors contributing to criminal behavior
Ability to counsel probationers
Ability to write clear and concise probation reports
Knowledge of judge's sentencing habits for particular types of offenders and offenses
Knowledge of law concerning probation

Minimum qualifications:
High school degree or equivalent; plus four years' experience working with juvenile offenders or a B.S. degree in criminal justice, psychology, or counseling
Able to pass a multiple choice test on relevant probation law
Possess a valid driver's license

Figure 2　Results-oriented descriptions (RODs)

qualifications. For example, a probation officer handling more difficult cases and working without direct supervision would need more skill in counseling probationers and writing presentence investigation reports. wthis would probably require more experience, more related education, or a more successful counseling record.

HOW DO RODS AFFECT ORGANIZATIONS?

Results-oriented job descriptions focus on performance standards, the conditions that differentiate jobs and the linkages between standards, SKAs, and qualifications. In so doing, they resolve many of the problems attributed to traditional job descriptions:

1. They give the program planner a means of relating personnel inputs to organizational outputs.

2. They give managers a means of orienting new employees to performance expectations, setting MBO goals, and evaluating employee performance objectively.

3. They give employees a clearer idea of organizational performance improvement expectations and of the minimum qualifications for promotion or reassignment.

4. They increase the impact of personnel managers on organization and employee productivity rather than merely on position management and control.

While they are useful for these purposes, RODs appear to have some serious disadvantages: (1) changes in conditions and standards require constant rewriting of RODs; (2) each position requires a different ROD; (3) some positions do not have measurable performance standards; and (4) RODs cannot be used to classify jobs for human resources planning purposes or to evaluate them for pay comparability purposes.

First, it is inevitable that conditions affecting task performance will change. Won't this require that RODs be rewritten frequently to specify these changed conditions and standards, thereby causing an unmanageable paperwork load for supervisors and the personnel department? On the other hand, most communication between employees and supervisors concerns unforeseen changes in organizational goals, employee tasks, environmental conditions, and performance standards. Integrating RODs into the organizational planning and evaluation system does mean an increase in time spent on writing job descriptions, but it may not mean an increase in time spent on organizational communications. What will occur, in fact, is a new focus of communication on those changes in goals or conditions that affect employee performance standards. Moreover, most organizations do not change objectives frequently.[15] The use of a new job description method will not in itself increase the rate of organizational change.

Second, much of the previous analysis has emphasized that different positions within a job will have different conditions and standards. Won't this lead to a proliferation of different position descriptions for similar positions? The answer to this question depends on the position. It will not do so where groups of employees perform similar tasks under similar conditions. It will where they do not. For example, a group of claims examiners who were assigned clients on a random basis using identical methods and equipment and having equal experience could be expected to evaluate claims according to the same standard. But if employees worked in different locations, had different tasks, and used different equipment, then their standards would differ. While some increase in the number of position descriptions would occur under RODs, there would not be a separate description for each position.

Third, many supervisors and job analysts consider it difficult to establish individual performance expectations where groups of employees must work closely together. There are two possible responses to this problem: (1) to establish (as part of the conditions statements attached to a task) the nature and extent of mutual expectations that one position's successful task completion requires of others or (2) to develop work group performance expectations which assume that mutual interdependencies exist. The first solution, while cumbersome to develop or revise, may be useful in clarifying the key points on which work group members need to build communications and trust. The second solution, while it ignores interdependencies explicitly, is more often more useful in group incentive situations (project teams), where it is difficult to evaluate the relative effectiveness of individual members' contributions in the absence of a completed product or service.

The last objection is the most serious from the personnel manager's viewpoint. Job descriptions are used not only to clarify expectations for each position but also to classify jobs for human resource planning purposes and to evaluate them for pay comparabilty purposes. How could these vital functions be accomplished using RODs? The answer is to continue using those aspects of traditional job analysis that are necessary for these purposes. Personnel managers could continue to group jobs into occupational classes based on the type of work performed. Traditional job evaluation methods could then be used to determine the pay ranges appropriate to each position, and employee performance relative to objectives specified in the ROD would be used to "fine tune" the system within pay ranges. This would give managers some other basis besides seniority for awarding or withholding within-grade increases and would also resolve the conflict over the relative importance of job evaluation and performance evaluation in setting pay.

By tying skills, knowledge, and abilities to tasks and validating minimum qualifications as enablers to task performance, linkages could be established between positions to aid in career/life planning, promotion assessment, and upward mobility. Here again, the relationship between RODs and traditional evaluation methods would be complementary. Traditional methods would show an organization's job structure, and clusters of RODs (grouped by occupation) would show how increasing qualifications were related to SKAs and SKAs to task performance.

Adopting RODs means that organizations will use two types of job descriptions—traditional and performance oriented. There is a justifiable tendency to reject proposed solutions that are more complicated than current techniques. However, this tendency also reflects a desire to return to an era when personnel management techniques were simpler and more uniform than they are today. Yet our experience usually shows that diverse techniques are necessary.[16] Most authorities recommend different performance evaluation methods for different purposes (that is, performance improvement or reward allocation). They also recommend a variety of selection methods, such as performance tests, biodata review, or probationary appointments, for different types of positions. Because job analysis and evaluation are used for several different purposes—performance improvement chief among them—we need to accept the use of different methods.

NOTES

1. Jonathan S. Rakich, "Job Descriptions: Key Element in the Personnel Subsystem," *Personnel Journal* 51, 1 (January 1972): 46.

2. Sidney A. Fine, "Functional Job Analysis: An Approach to a Technology for Manpower Planning." *Personnel Journal* 53, 1 (November 1974): 813–18.

3. Ernest J. McCormick, Joseph W. Cunningham, and George C. Thornton, "The Prediction of Job Requirements by a Structured Job Analyis Procedure," *Personnel Psychology* XX (1967): 431–40.

4. Richard I. Henderson, *Compensation Management* (Reston, Va: Reston Publishing Co., Inc., 1976), 132–37, 171–77.

5. Robert E. Sibson, *Compensation* (New York: AMACOM, 1974), 34–35, 38–43.

6. John A. Patton, C. L. Littlefield, and Stanley A. Self, *Job Evaluation* (Homewood, Ill., Richard D. Irwin, Inc., 1964), 192, 193.

7. Lawrence L. Epperson, "The Dynamics of Factor Comparison/Point Evaluation," *Public Personnel Management* (January-February 1975): 38–48.

8. Allan Schick, "The Road to PPB, The Stages of Budget Reform" in *Public Budgeting and Finance*, ed. Robert T. Golembiewski (Itasca, Ill.: Peacock, 1968), 523.

9. Jerry McCaffery, "MBO and the Federal Budgetary Process," *Public Administration Review* (January-February 1976): 36.

10. Alan H. Locher and Kenneth S. Teel, "Performance Appraisal—A Survey of Current Practices," *Personnel Journal* (May 1977): 247.

11. Frank P. Sherwood and William J. Page, Jr., "MBO and Public Management," *Public Administration Review* (January-February 1976): 29.

12. John C. Aplin and Peter P. Schoderbek, "How to Measure MBO," *Public Personnel Management* (March 1976): 89.

13. Bernard H. Baum and Peter F. Sorensen, Jr., "A 'Total' Approach to Job Classification," *Personnel Journal* (January 1969): 31–32.

14. Robert L. Malone and Donald J. Petersen, "Personnel Effectiveness: Its Dimensions and Development," *Personnel Journal* (October 1977): 498–501.

15. Patricia Cain Smith and L. M. Kendall, "Retranslation of Expectations: An Approach to the Construction of Unambiguous Anchors for Rating Scales," *Journal of Applied Psychology* 2 (1963): 149–55.

16. Edgar H. Schein, "Changing Role of the Personnel Manager," *Journal of the College and University Personnel Association* 26, 3 (July-August 1975): 14–19.

An Alternative to Validating Selection Tests

Frank J. Dyer

About five or six years ago, shortly after the Supreme Court decision in *Griggs* v. *Duke Power*, many companies dropped their testing programs for fear of being charged with discrimination in hiring. In many of these cases, objective selection testing for production and clerical entry-level jobs was replaced by interviewing. The short-term gain was relative immunity from test-related discrimination charges. The long-term effects are now beginning to appear. Employees hired in the absence of objective entry-level standards are now bidding up into more responsi-

Frank J. Dyer is a senior research associate for the Psychological Corporation in New York City.

ble jobs where poor performance can have a devastating effect on operations. Employers would like to see standards reinstituted at some level because general quality of the work force, including nonminorities, has suffered.

Where jobs require minimal levels of specific abilities, subjective interviews cannot separate the good prospects from the poor ones. This isn't at all surprising since experienced interviewing trainers will tell you that modern interviewing techniques were not designed to assess clerical ability, mechanical skills, or computational proficiency. Good interviewers rely on test data for this information.

This brings us full circle. When it comes to jobs that require specific measurable abilities, business can't get away from the need for objective tests. But the risk of discrimination still exists. Without solid scientific evidence demonstrating the validity of the tests, you are open to discrimination charges. Unfortunately, validation research is not feasible in many smaller organizations. This situation is known in psychological parlance as a double bind. The double bind under consideration certainly doesn't do much to lessen managerial stress but merely underlines management's need for a selection strategy that includes a positive affirmative action stance and still singles out employees with good production potential.

The proposed solution is based on a thorough reading of EEOC and FEA guidelines and on precedent developed in more than one hundred published court decisions relating to selection. Its philosophy may be stated in a single sentence: Insofar as Title VII is concerned, you are free to use any test you choose without having to produce evidence of its validity so long as the total selection procedure does not have an adverse effect on protected groups.

Two definitions seem to be in order. *Total selection procedure:* This translates as "bottom line," or the actual number of hires and rejects after candidates have been given all tests, interviews and other screening devices used in making the final decision. This means that you may legally use an unvalidated test to eliminate a sizeable percentage of any particular group, as long as other components of the total selection process compensate in such a way that there is no adverse effect in final hiring decisions.[1] *Adverse effect:* According to Federal Executive Agency Guidelines, this is defined as a selection rate for a protected group (minorities or women) that is less than 80 percent of the selection rate for the group with the highest rate (usually whites or males). Smaller differences in selection rates may also be considered as constituting adverse effect where these differences are statistically significant or where they are felt to be significant in practical terms. While the EEOC Guidelines do not define adverse effect specifically, compliance officers generally employ "the 80 percent rule" in practice.

Legal decisions, however, often rely upon population statistics in deciding whether or not adverse effects exist. Regardless of selection ratios, if the percentage of women or minorities in an employer's work force does not correspond to population percentages (usually defined in terms of U.S. Census Bureau Standard Metropolitan Statistical Area, or SMSA), a judgment of adverse effect is entirely possible in trial situations. Therefore, the personnel manager must take a hard look at hiring figures and at the population statistics for a local area to make certain that selection procedures do not result in adverse effect. There is no way to avoid making detailed percentage comparisons. But if you do your homework and find that the within-group percentages are approximately equal, you eliminate the need to conduct a formal validation study of your tests. Such a study is not legally necessary if adverse effect doesn't exist.

BRINGING THE PERCENTAGES INTO LINE

What if analysis reveals what appear to be significant percentage differences? In that case several questions should be considered. For instance:

1. What would be the effect on union relations of lowering test standards for protected groups to bring selection percentages into line?
2. Can your own staff perform a validation study?
3. Is there a sufficient number of employees at the same level within each job title to conduct a criteria-related validation study?
4. What would be the effect on productivity if differential cutoffs were set?

If your firm is like most small- or medium-sized organizations considering testing, you should come up with the following answers:

1. You could probably get differential standards by the union for entry-level hiring without much trouble.
2. You do not have the in-house resources to conduct a criteria-related study.
3. You may not have a sample of sufficient size to conduct a criteria-related study.

If you are in this position, then setting differential cutoffs to bring the percentages into line is the strategy of choice. Rather than ignoring the question of job-related abilities, the use of appropriate selection tests with differential cutoffs will determine the best candidates within each group. In fact, this procedure will represent a positive step toward implementation of both short-term and long-term affirmative action plans. It will create expanded opportunities for minorities at entry level and will greatly increase the probability that new hires will be promotable when selections for higher-level positions are made. Additionally, affirmative steps such as this do not violate the antipreference provisions of Title VII or of Executive Order 11246.[2]

But what about the effect on productivity? Lowering standards for certain applicants will naturally give you a less able group of hires than if you were to use a single standard. Luckily, this situation is not inevitable. For illustration's sake, let's say you've been using a clerical ability test to select at entry level. You and your supervisors think the test is great; there are no complaints about new hires who score at least at the fiftieth percentile for industry norms. On the other hand, your company lacks resources with which to validate the test, and you want to do something about cutoff scores in order to eliminate any adverse effect. You also want to maintain harmonious relations with the supervisors who appreciate the good people you send them.

Figure 1 represents test distributions for protected (A) and nonprotected (B) applicant groups. Ideally, you would set the cutoff score at the level indicated for satisfactory performance. This would admit 50 percent of the applicants from Group B but only 16 percent of the applicants from protected Group A. If you lowered the cutoff for A to the point indicated by the dotted line, you would eliminate adverse effect, but a much smaller percentage of selectees from A would be satisfactory performers.

Figure 2 presents a more desirable solution that also eliminates adverse effect.

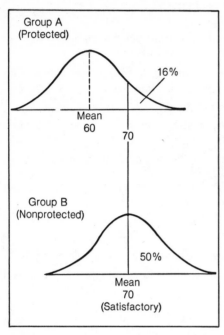

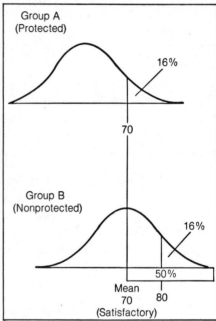

Figure 1   **Figure 2**

The solid line represents the cutoff for Group A, accepting 16 percent of this group. Under an assumption of substantial "true" validity for the test, these selectees may be expected to have a high probability of success. The broken line in Figure 2 represents the new cutoff for nonprotected Group B, *adjusted upwards*. Selectees from this group may be expected to have very good chances for success. The overall quality of selectees is at least as good, if not better, than that which would result from using the original cutoff score for both groups. Thus, by being slightly more selective, an organization may use a test without creating adverse effect while maintaining high performance quality. This can be done if there is an adequatesupply of capable applicants from nonprotected groups. The chief costs would be in examiner and processing time, since more applicants must be seen, given the smaller percentages accepted, in order to achieve the same number of new hires relative to the old cutoffs.

In periods when the supply of applicants is limited because of unfavorable labor market conditions, the above principle may be applied in modified form. Figure 3 uses equal selection rates of 30 percent for protected and nonprotected groups, with passing scores adjusted downward for the former and upward for the latter group within five raw score points of the original cutoff. The larger percentage of acceptances, as compared to the strategy in Figure 2, requires that fewer applicants be processed to fill all positions.

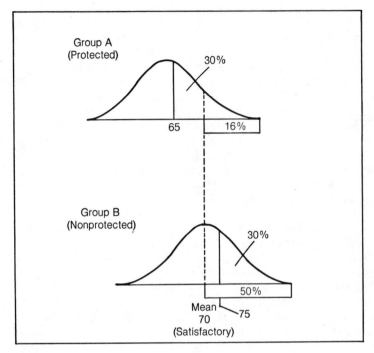

Figure 3

THE WISDOM OF TEST VALIDATION

As may be seen from the foregoing, a formal empirical test validation study is not mandatory in order to stay within the law. It is, however, something that one ought to do where possible. The motivation for doing a validation study should be effective business operation rather than fear of legal department pressure. Hastily performed studies, devised with the primary purpose of generating legal evidence, have seldom managed to achieve even that limited objective, let alone provide meaningful information for improving personnel decisions. You can stay out of court by validating your tests and avoiding adverse effect—by using research as a scientific tool rather than as a weapon of the legal department. And where validation research by professional psychologists is not possible, there are sound techniques by which personnel can establish the appropriateness of entry-level tests with a reasonable degree of certainty.

The first step is a job analysis, implemented through a review of existing position descriptions and follow-up interviews with supervisors and incumbents. This information may than be used to make careful inferences about skill and ability requirements. The next step is to choose tests that are designed to measure these skills and abilities. Specificity is the key here: a general mental ability test is appropriate where general reasoning ability is a salient job requirement, but more often tests of specific computational, clerical, mechanical, or motor skills are closer to the mark. Once you have chosen some tentative predictors, read the test manuals to find out if these instruments have shown validity for jobs similar to those in your organization. The convergence of job analysis and test manual information should give reasonable assurance that the tests measure needed skills. Coupled with this method of choosing appropriate tests, the affirmative action techniques outlined above will result in meaningful, job-related selection without adverse effect and therefore without the need for legal validation.

Where empirical validation is feasible, or becomes feasible after the organization has collected data over a period of time, you may wish to hire a research consultant. The costs involved in conducting a local validation study are usually justified by the increased employee productivity resulting from accurate selection. Properly conducted research pays off but only when it is well planned and free of the time constraints that so often mar the value of studies undertaken "on the eve of trial."

It is tempting to speculate on what might happen if at some future time the Supreme Court should decide that preventing "reverse discrimination" is more important than taking affirmative action on behalf of women and minorities. Such a decision would probably make it illegal to relax selection standards for any particular group of applicants. However, some of the basic principles of differential cutoff and test validation would still hold. Employers would still be obligated to select the best people, whether from combined or separate applicant pools. Firms that are not in a position to conduct local validation studies would still be able to satisfy societal and legal requirements through careful study and monitoring of their selection data. Finally, where jobs require specific identifiable skills, a scientifically constructed measure of these skills is the best way to select employees—no matter what the Supreme Court may rule.

NOTES

1. See *Smith* v. *Troyan* 10 FEP Cases 1380 and FEA 1976 Guidelines, Section 4b.
2. *Questions and Answers on the Federal Executive Agency Guidelines on Employee Selection Procedures*, Question 10, 529.

Evaluation of Job Applications—
A Conceptual Framework

Edward L. Levine

Abram Flory III

An assumption often expressed within the field of personnel selection holds that the interview is the most often used selection technique.[1] This is untrue. The most widely used selection technique is the evaluation of the job application blank or the resume. Such evaluations may take place as part of the interviewing process itself or as a prelude to further screening, whether it be in the form of a written test, an interview, or some other means of assessment. In the public sector, particularly where formal merit systems have been instituted, a review of job applications is done to determine whether an individual meets minimum qualifications for a position. If minimum qualifications are not met, then the applicant is barred from any further consideration. For literally hundreds of job classes in various governmental jurisdictions, an evaluation of background training and experience, which is usually referred to as a T and E (training and experience) or E and E (education and experience) evaluation, may constitute the sole scoring and ranking method used to screen for a vacant position. Indeed, judgmental methods used in such evaluations may be highly elaborate and detailed.[2] In the private sector, to judge by the reported literature, application evaluation may take the form of global judgments of suitability primarily by an interviewer or scoring by means of some empirical weighting schema.[3] To provide some idea of the frequency of usage of applications, Carlson's extrapolation may be employed.[4] Thus, if an arbitrary assumption is made that 50 percent of those filing applications or resumes are ultimately interviewed, then over one billion applications and resumes per year are prepared and screened in the United States.

Yet despite its universality, the evaluation of applications for personnel selection and placement has not been researched in a systematic fashion to any great extent. Research has been done on the empirically weighted application, usually for predicting turnover.[5] However, evidence has recently been presented to show that this technique may be less efficacious than previously thought.[6] Moreover, the use of weighted application blanks has long been questioned on grounds of its atheoretical orientation. It is indeed a puzzlement as to what the legal implications of previously used, presumably valid, items might be. For example, Scollay found that

Edward L. Levine is director of the Selection Resource Center in Arizona. Abram Flory III is manager of personnel operations and employee/labor relations for the State of Arizona.

Reprinted from Edward L. Levine and Abram Flory III, "Evaluation of Job Applications: A Conceptual Framework," pp 378—385. Copyright 1975 by Public Personnel Management.

the most valid items for predicting a salary increase criterion were: "If subject's father dead, subject's age at time," and "Mother's occupation."[7]

More recent research on application evaluation has focused on factors affecting the quality of evaluations as opposed to the method of evaluation per se. There have been investigations in a variety of settings utilizing a wide array of personal history information, which reveal that:

1. Evaluations are more reliable if raters are given detailed job information.[8]
2. Evaluations are affected, though probably to a small extent, by the operation of a contrast effect.[9]
3. Evaluations are more stable when the quality of the information available to raters is good.[10]
4. Evaluations are differentially affected by both information content and favorability of information, with unfavorable information having a greater effect.[11]
5. Experienced evaluators appear to be more reliable than inexperienced evaluators, though Langdale and Weitz did not corroborate this finding.[12]

When method of application evaluation itself is the issue of concern, very little is available other than the standard approaches of empirically keying the items.[13] The few extant studies dealing with method of evaluation other than empirical weighting have demonstrated that projective evaluation of application information could validly predict performance and tenure.[14] More recently Cleff developed a set of dimensions to describe both people and jobs and then used a computerized matching process to select.[15] His reported validity and reliability for the system appear very promising.

Our review of the literature led to the conclusion that the fragmentary nature of the research in this area was not conducive to the growth of a systematized body of knowledge. In addition, the scope of reported research on application evaluation is relatively limited given the importance of the technique in personnel selection. A preliminary conceptual framework is proposed in Table 1 in the supposition that it may foster more programmatic theory and research.

Table 1 A conceptual schema for classifying methods of evaluating job applications

I. Job relatedness							
High				Low			
II. Depth of interpretation							
Surface characteristics		Inferred traits		Surface characteristics		Inferred traits	
III. General method of evaluation							
Judg- mental	Statis- tical	Judg- mental	Statis- tical	Judg- mental	Statis- tical	Judg- mental	Statis- tical
1	2	3	4	5	6	7	8

Three variables have been selected for emphasis: job relatedness of information, depth of interpretation, and general method of evaluation. These factors have been dichotomized for ease of presentation, though all three are theoretically continuous variables. *Job relatedness* refers to the extent to which information gathered is job related on its face (for example, place of residence is not job related, career history is). *Depth of interpretation* refers to whether the application information is utilized to measure underlying traits and constructs or whether it is evaluated directly (for example, when membership in civic groups is used as an index of sociability, a trait, or "deep" interpretation is made; whereas, when it is keyed empirically to an aspect of job performance or turnover, it is a "surface" characteristic).

General method of evaluation is the means by which information is combined to arrive at an evaluation or prediction.[16] Statistical methods are those in which scores or predictions are arrived at by formulas or stringent rules. Judgmental methods are those in which a rater combines the information in some less structured fashion. For example, an empirically keyed bio data blank is a statistical method, whereas an analysis by an interviewer of the extent of match between an applicant and the job is judgmental.

There are other dimensions that may be incorporated into the schema. One in particular is proffered by Carlson who distinguishes among scoring and evaluation of information, prediction of future performance, or the actual employment decision.[17] Also, within each appropriate cell it is possible to identify a number of methods, judgmental or statistical, by which to combine information. However, the heuristic value of the framework may be reduced if the schema is made overly complex at this point.

What are the manifestations of the eight cells that result from all combinations of the factors in Table 1? Perhaps an example for each would assist in clarifying the schema.

Cell 1: high job relatedness, surface characteristics, judgmental evaluation. A personnel analyst reviews the background training and work history to determine the extent of match between prior positions and the position applied for. The closer the match, the higher the score.

Cell 2: high job relatedness, surface characteristics, statistical evaluation. Individuals fill out blanks on what job tasks they can do and would like to do. Supervisors fill out parallel checklists that pertain to their jobs. A punch-card sorter is then employed to determine those applicants who match best with the position, with sorts conducted on most important tasks, next most important, and so on.

Cell 3: high job relatedness, inferred traits, judgmental evaluation. Background work history is reviewed by an interviewer, who notes pattern of positions as indicators of an individual's orientation with regard to people, data, and equipment. The interviewer then judges how well this orientation fits that called for on the job.

Cell 4: high job relatedness, inferred traits, statistical evaluation. A career history index is factor analyzed and factor scores computed on job-related traits, such as leadership, which may consist of courses in management, and progression to more responsible positions. Then a multiple-regression equation is used to rank candidates.

Cell 5: low job relatedness, surface characteristics, judgmental evaluation. A personal history index containing items on birth order, race, age, sex, and membership in civic groups, other family members working with firm, and socioeconomic class is evaluated by an interviewer who judges the extent of match with those patently required by the position.

Cell 6: low job relatedness, surface characteristics, statistical evaluation. A bio data blank containing information on race, age, sex, and membership in civic groups is empirically weighted by relationship to tenure.

Cell 7: low job relatedness, inferred traits, judgmental evaluation. A personal history questionnaire containing questions on childhood and family life and extra-curricular activities is reviewed to determine paranoid tendencies, ambitiousness, and aggressiveness. Patterns within applications are matched against presumed job requirements by a rater.

Cell 8: low job relatedness, inferred traits, statistical evaluation. A question-naire containing inquiries about sexual proclivities, membership in civic groups, and birth order is factor analyzed, and the pattern of scores on underlying traits such as leadership potential are evaluated by computer as against the desired pattern for the job.

The reader will probably agree that all cells have been represented in actual personnel selection practice despite the questionable legality and validity of some approaches.

When the research cited above is reviewed in light of this framework, it appears that there has been no attempt to assess quality of evaluation (for example, validity and reliability) as a function of the kind of information, job related or not, that has been gathered on application forms or resumes. However, accurate job information does appear to foster the creation of a stereotype comprised of job related and nonjob-related data that can lead to reliable ratings.[18] As to the importance of various kinds of information in evaluation, our judgment is that traditionally used personal history data is largely nonjob related. More direct evidence, provided by Hakel, Dobmeyer, and Dunnette, shows that by far the greatest weight in their study was given to nonjob-related information (scholastic standing).[19] However, subjects in the Langdale and Weitz study weighted job-related information most highly (for example, type of job sought, secretarial skills possessed).[20] Nor can it be stated with confidence that surface characteristics are superior to depth traits since the reported literature contains successful use of both.[21] Moreover, a comparison of application evaluation quality as a function of judgmental as compared with statistical combi-nation of information cannot be drawn, since successful instances of both ap-proaches have been reported, and unsuccessful instances generally will not appear in literature.[22]

As a first step in utilizing this conceptual framework, data were gathered to assess the interrater reliability of a cell 1 variant for evaluating applicants. The cell 1 approach utilized requires the development of nominal groups or categories, which are based on work experience and job-related education and ordinal scaling of these categories in terms of predictions as to which category will yield the best perform-ing candidates. The outcome is a formal rating protocol or catalog containing a full description of all categories and the scores associated with each. Applications are evaluated by assignment to one or another of the categories. This approach will be referred to as training and experience (T and E) evaluation.

Two factors that can be expected to have an impact on reliability are the experience of the raters and standardization in the scoring catalog and employment application. One might expect that the greater the experience of the T and E raters, the higher the reliability. However, it may be that less experienced raters can be utilized to achieve an adequate level of reliability. This, of course, would reduce administrative costs. To explore this possibility, the present study attempted, as one of its main objectives, to assess the effect of personnel analysts' experience on reliability.

Another influence on reliability, which is of interest in this study, is the degree of standardization in the rating "stimuli," job applications, and the scoring responses. Personnel systems may maintain a modicum of control over the standardization of job applications by using a standard form. However, it is almost impossible to control the wide range of mental sets and general lack of understanding of the evaluation procedure that applicants bring to the process of completing the application. Thus, an applicant usually does not list in full detail the appropriate information needed for an accurate assessment by a rater of the applicant's training and experience. More control is possible over the methods and procedures used in the evaluation. The development of formal T and E protocols referred to above represents an attempt to standardize the judgment process.

Although it was not possible in the context of the present study to vary standarization systematically, what was done was to control the impact of this variable by choosing for study fifteen widely disparate classes, which would guarantee a great degree of variation in job applicants and job types. In addition, the raters assigned to the job classes studied varied greatly in their background characteristics and experience. If reliability of evaluation for all classes could be demonstrated despite the variable conditions, then strong evidence for the reliability of the cell I T and E approach to application evaluation would be generated.

METHOD

Fifteen different job classes were selected with an average of nineteen applications per job. These classes were: wildlife management specialist, economist II, management analyst II, roadside rest area manager, medical records clerk, trades helper, civil engineering assistant I, park ranger I (general), park ranger I (selective), employment security intern, accountant III, teacher assistant, psychology assistant, drug abuse counselor, and statistical analyst II. In addition to diversity in duties, the jobs varied greatly in degree of complexity as demonstrated by differences in salary levels for each class, which ranged from $500 to over $1,000 per month. New training and experience evaluation scoring catalogs were developed for each job using a standard form.

In all, seven personnel analysts participated in this study. Their ages ranged from thirty to forty-four years. Three were women and four were Mexican-American. Their length of professional personnel experience varied from one month to over ten years. All had at least a bachelor's degree. Over the course of the study, it was determined by interviews that they all tended to have an average amount of familiarity with the class that they were evaluating at the time.

Prior to evaluation of applicants, an analyst would perform a rudimentary job analysis and develop the scoring catalog specifically for that position. The catalog was then reviewed by the second analyst. A conference between the two would take place to discuss the position and the catalog but not the applicants. Next, the applicants were rated independently by two analysts (rater 1 and rater 2) and assigned scores.

The results were analyzed in several ways. For each job, the independent scores were compared using a correlation coefficient. Another approach, which was perhaps more appropriate in view of the discontinuous, categorical nature of the data, was then taken to measure the degree of agreement corrected for chance utilizing Cohen's Kappa.[23] Also reported is the gross level of agreement or the percentage of all judgments of the raters for which they agreed. Finally, to assess the impact of experience, gross level of agreement between raters was correlated with their mean years of personnel experience. The data-gathering phase covered a three-month period from October to December 1973.

RESULTS

To illustrate the nature of the data, Table 2 contains the findings on park ranger I (general).

Table 2 Interrater reliability for the job class of park ranger I (general)

		Reject	70	80	90
Category score	90	0	0	0	1
Rater 2	80	0	0	1	0
	70	0	5	0	0
	Reject	14	1	0	0
		Reject	70	80	90
			Category score		
			Rater 1		

N = 22 applications
Correlation rater 1 with rater 2 = .96 (p < .005, one-tailed)
K (Cohen's Kappa) = .906

Correlational Data   All the correlations between rater 1 and rater 2 on all fifteen jobs were significant at the .05 level of confidence or better. The correlations ranged from .677 to 1.00, with a median of .96, indicating that there was a relatively high level of relationship between two independent ratings of applicants for any given position. Deviations from perfect correlations in the ratings of the jobs were usually explained in terms of a lack of clarity in the training and experience evaluation catalog or in the applications. From interviews with the raters, it was then determined that the more specific and standardized the materials, the more likely the correlations were to approach 1.00.

Level of Agreement Corrected for Chance (Kappa)   An analysis utilizing Cohen's Kappa indicated that there was a high level of agreement corrected for chance. This level of agreement ranged from .544 to 1.00 with a median of .91. This would indicate that there is a high proportion of joint judgments in which there is agreement after chance agreement has been excluded.

Gross Level of Agreement   Perhaps even more striking than the data reported above is the finding that the degree of agreement between rates was 100 percent for six of the fifteen classes, only one classification discrepancy per class appeared in another five of the classes, which represented a gross agreement rate of approximately 95 percent on median; and only two classification discrepancies per class appeared in another two job classes, which represents a gross agreement rate of approximately 89 percent on median. Thus, thirteen of fifteen job classes showed an 89 percent degree of agreement or better. The two job classes that had somewhat higher rates of disagreement were statistical analyst (gross agreement rate of 77 percent) and park ranger I (selective) (gross agreement rate 68 percent).

The Impact of Experience on Interrater Reliability   The data for the correlation between the gross levels of agreements for each job class and the mean of the personnel experience of the raters in each case is set forth in Table 3. The correlation of .82 (significant at $P < .05$, one-tailed) suggests that the amount of experience also appears to play a role over and above the lack of standardization in the scoring method and the applications. However, it should be noted that even though more experienced analysts seemed able to raise the agreement rate from "marginally acceptable" to "acceptable," the less experienced raters were able to agree substantially in their evaluations.

Table 3 The relationship between mean length of experience and degree of agreement

Degree of gross agreement (%)	Number of classes	Mean of experience of raters (months)
100	6	53.58
95.46	5	33.38
89.21	2	5.00
77.28	1	6.50
68.30	1	3.50
Total	15	

$N = 5$
Correlation between agreement and experience =
.82 ($p < .05$, one-tailed)

One further bit of information. The *seriousness* of the errors that were made should be explored. If one rater classified an applicant two or more categories higher or lower than the other, then this is even more cause for concern. It was found that such serious errors occurred only twice in the total 282 comparisons made, or aproximately seven-tenths of one percent of the time.

DISCUSSION

These findings tend to support the notion that the T and E categorical approach, a cell 1 variant, has a good degree of what Cattell has called "conspect" reliability.[24] The method also appears to have an acceptable degree of reliability in spite of varying experience among the raters and the marked lack of standardization in the application material evaluated. The reason for the outstanding degree of reliability is probably to be found in the relatively simplistic nature of the judgments to be made. Only two sources of information were used—training and experience—and these factors were compared with carefully defined standards for inclusion in one or another of the categories. The more complicated portion of the task is the actual construction of the catalog. A validity study is presently being planned on this T and E approach.

It also appears that experience of raters does affect reliability of application evaluation as Hakel, Dobmeyer, and Dunnette found.[25] The contrary results of Langdale and Weitz on the role of experience are perhaps a function of some particular aspect of their study.[26]

How does the method of application evaluation compare with the second most popular selection technique, the personal interview? As far as reliability and validity are concerned, this study—taken in conjunction with other available evidence—strongly suggests that application evaluation is the superior technique.[27] The complex dynamics of the interview perhaps place significant limits on effectiveness. Another probable cause of the superiority of application evaluation is that the accuracy of information provided by the applicant is better than that gathered in the interview, though Goldstein recently found sizable inaccuracies in both application and interview information.[28] (A sign of the times, perhaps?) Distortion of information in socially desirable directions may be more likely in the interview because of social pressures.[29] These pressures are further increased by the supposition that the interview is perceived by the applicant as the key component in the selection process.

At any rate, it is hoped that the data in the present study and the conceptual framework proposed will lead to a programmatic series of studies on application evaluation. Comparative evaluations of approaches with and between cells with respect to their reliability and validity across situations should prove useful to the personnel psychologist. The legality and administrative feasibility of the various approaches may also be studied.

NOTES

1. R. E. Carlson, "The Current Status of Judgmental Techniques in Industry," in *Alternatives to Paper and Pencil Testing*, eds. W. C. Byham and D. Bobin (Pittsburgh: University of Pittsburgh, Graduate School of Business, 1973). M. D. Dunnette, *Personnel Selection and Placement* (Belmont, Calif.: Wadsworth, 1966).

2. A. P. Maslow, "Evaluating Training and Experience," in *Recruitment and Selection in the Public Service*, ed. J. J. Donovan (Chicago: Public Personnel Association, 1968).

3. R. M. Guion, *Personnel Testing* (New York: McGraw-Hill, 1965). J. A. Langdale and J. Weitz, "Estimating the Influence of Job Information on Interviewer Agreement," *Journal of Applied Psychology* 57 (1973): 23–27.

4. Carlson.

5. Guion. E. A. Fleishman and J. Berniger, "One Way to Reduce Office Turnover," *Personnel* 37 (190): 63–69. R. W. Scollay, "Validation of Personal History Items Against a Salary Increase Criterion," *Personnel Psychology* 9 (1956): 325–36. R. H. Walther, "Self Description As a Predictor of Success or Failure in Foreign Service Clerical Jobs," *JAP* 45 (1961): 16–21.

6. D. P. Schwab and R. L. Oliver, "Predicting Tenure with Biographical Data: Exhuming Buried Evidence," *Personnel Psychology* 27 (1974): 125–28.

7. Scollay.

8. Langdale and Weitz.

9. P. M. Rowe, "Order Effects in Assessment Decisions," *JAP* 51 (1967): 170–73. M. D. Hakel, J. P. Ohnesorge, and M. D. Dunnette, "Interviewer Evaluations of Job Applicants' Resumes As a Function of the Qualifications of the Immediately Preceding Applicants: An Examination of Contrast Effects," *JAP* 54 (1970): 27–30.

10. R. E. Carlson and E. C. Mayfield, "Evaluating Interview and Employment Application Data," *Personnel Psychology* 20 (1967): 441–60.

11. J. W. Miller and P. M. Rowe, "Influence of Favorable and Unfavorable Information upon Assessment Decisions," *JAP* 51 (1967): 432–35. Langdale and Weitz, M. D. Hakel, T. W. Dobmeyer, and M. D. Dunnette, "Relative Importance of Three Content Dimensions in Overall Suitability Ratings of Job Applicants' Resumes," *JAP* 54 (1970): 65–71.

12. Hakel, Dobmeyer, and Dunnette.

13. Cf. Maslow, Guion.

14. G. J. Spencer and R. Worthington, "Validity of a Projective Technique in Predicting Sales Effectiveness," *Personnel Psychology* 5 (1952): 125–44. R. F. Peck and J. W. Parsons, "Personality Factors in Work Output: Four Studies of Factory Workers," *Personnel Psychology* 9 (1956): 49–79.

15. S. H. Cleff, "Computer-Assisted Job Matching," in *Alternatives to Paper and Pencil Testing*, eds. W. C. Byham and D. Bobin (Pittsburgh: University of Pittsburgh, Graduate School of Business, 1973).

16. Cf. J. Sawyer, "Measurement and Prediction, Clinical and Statistical," *Psychological Bulletin* 66 (1966): 178–200.

17. Carlson.

18. Langdale and Weitz.

19. Hakel, Dobmeyer, and Dunnette.

20. Langdale and Weitz.

21. Scollay, Peck and Parsons, Walther.

22. Spencer and Worthington.

23. J. Cohen, "A Coefficient of Agreement for Nominal Scales," *Educational and Psychological Measurement* 20 (1960): 37–46.

24. R. B. Cattell, *Personality and Motivation Structure and Measurement* (New York: Harcourt, Brace, and World, 1957).

25. Hakel, Dobmeyer, and Dunnette.

26. Langdale and Weitz.

27. Carlson, Guion.

28. J. N. Mosel and L. W. Cozan, "The Accuracy of Application Blank Work Histories," *JAP* 36 (1952): 365–69. Guion. D. J. Weiss and R. V. Davis, "An Objective Validation of Factua. Interview Data," *JAP* 44 (1960): 381–85. Carlson. I. L. Goldstein, "The Application Blank: How Honest Are the Responses? *JAP* 55 (1971): 491–92.

29. Cf. Carlson.

4

Directing,Controlling, and Public Personnel Management

In public personnel management directing and controlling involve the measurement and maintenance or increase of employee productivity. Several personnel activities are included. The first is productivity improvement through program budgeting, MBO, and program evaluation. Because these involve organizational rather than employee productivity, they have not traditionally been considered as part of the public personnel manager's domain. However, two factors do justify their inclusion: (1) the important contribution of human resources toward organizational productivity and (2) the link between organizational productivity and results-oriented job descriptions. Because these two factors have been discussed in previous articles (see Klingner, on the role of the personnel manager in Chapter 1 and Klingner on job descriptions in Chapter 3), they will not be dealt with here. Second, directing and controlling also involve the use of appraisal systems for evaluating employee performance. Because those evaluation methods that are most job related are also most expensive and difficult to develop, much experimentation and controversy exists within this area.

Performance evaluation is a controversial subject because it has an immediate impact on employees and because employees and managers often disagree as to which criteria and methods of evaluation are most fair. In the first article, Douglas McGregor takes an uneasy look at performance appraisal. He is afraid that evaluation systems that allow supervisors to rate employee personality traits are inequitable and ineffective. Supervisors lack the opportunity, ability, or desire to rate employees fairly. Also, personality traits are difficult to change and are not necessarily related to performance on the job.

Since 1957 when McGregor's article was written, other compelling reasons have developed for increasing the reliability and validity of performance appraisal. In the second article, William H. Holley and Hubert S. Feild discuss how appraisal systems can be developed that comply with affirmative action laws which prohibit discrimination on the basis of nonmerit factors. They suggest a number of techniques, such as behaviorally anchored rating scales (BARS) and tying performance evaluation to organizational objectives through MBO, which can make an appraisal system both more objective and performance oriented. Yet they admit that these systems are difficult and costly to develop and validate. Despite Douglas McGregor's warning, most public and private employers continue to utilize person-oriented criteria rather than performance-oriented criteria.

Finally, the improvement of employee performance requires personnel managers to assess training needs, develop training programs, and then judge their impact on employee behavior. Understandably, training is one of the most widely accepted personnel activities. Yet despite this, training is frequently used in inappropriate situations. Paul Thayer and William McGehee collaborate on a short article that touches upon the fundamental reasons for the success or failure of a training program. Training is only useful to improve performance in situations where employees lack the needed skills to do a job right. It is ineffective in situations where organizational or employee objectives are unclear, supervisory feedback is lacking, or rewards are inadequate to induce the desired performance. By using one training program to illustrate general conclusions about other similar programs, these authors show why proper assessment of training needs is important. Equally noteworthy, at least to many readers, is their ability to write with brevity and clarity.

Personnel management information systems are used to collect and evaluate data relating to organizational effectiveness. Because public personnel managers have traditionally tended to think in humanistic rather than quantitative terms, they have often not participated fully in the design or use of computerized information systems. The first of two articles on personnel information systems focuses on ways in which personnel can assist in the development of such a system. Sidney Simon stresses the importance of early involvement in the development of report requirements and systems design. If personnel managers do not make their data needs known, they will not be able to use the subsequent reports to evaluate the effectiveness of human resource utilization in their agency. Because of data system costs, he also considers it important that personnel managers collect and store only the data needed for employee records.

The other reason for carefully defining an organization's needs for employee information is, of course, employee privacy. Frank T. Cary, chief executive of IBM, describes the guidelines that restrict invasions of employee privacy yet permit supervisors to assist employees with work-related problems. The heart of this policy is to collect only needed data and to delete information that is either not germane to a particular user or may have an unwarranted implication for the employee.

Although the Cary and Simon articles are directed toward corporate personnel managers, they are equally useful to public agencies, which—with the exception of the federal government and large state personnel agencies—have tended to retain manual information systems. It will be easier for public personnel managers to use automated systems if they help in their development. Furthermore, traditional concepts of sovereignty and immunity from civil suit have made public agencies less cautious than most large private corporations about collecting data which could infringe upon their employees' right to privacy. Because IBM was primarily responsible for the development of automated personnel management systems, Cary's suggestions on preserving employee privacy are to the point. This article is also comforting for prospective personnel professionals—it shows that technological advances usually create unforeseen problems, which in turn require the development of different solutions.

An Uneasy Look at Performance Appraisal

Douglas McGregor

Performance appraisal within management ranks has become standard practice in many companies during the past twenty years and is currently being adopted by many others, often as an important feature of management development programs. The more the method is used, the more uneasy I grow over the unstated assumptions that lie behind it. Moreover, with some searching, I find that a number of people both in education and in industry share my misgivings. This article, therefore, has two purposes: to examine the conventional performance appraisal plan that requires the manager to pass judgment on the personal worth of subordinates and to describe an alternative that places on the subordinate the primary responsibility for establishing performance goals and appraising progress toward them.

CURRENT PROGRAMS

Formal performance appraisal plans are designed to meet three ends, one for the organization and two for the individual:

1. They provide systematic judgments to back up salary increases, promotions, transfers, and sometimes demotions or terminations.

2. They are a means of telling a subordinate how he or she is doing and suggesting needed changes in behavior, attitudes, skills, or job knowledge; they let

the employee know "where he or she stands" with the boss.

3. They also are being increasingly used as a basis for the coaching and counseling of the individual by the superior.

Problem of Resistance

Personnel administrators are aware that appraisal programs tend to run into resistance from the managers who are expected to administer them. Even managers who admit the necessity of such programs frequently balk at the process—especially the interview part. As a result, some companies do not communicate appraisal results to the individual, despite the general conviction that the subordinate has a right to know her or his superior's opinion so he or she can correct weaknesses. The boss's resistance is usually attributed to the following causes:

1. A normal dislike of criticizing a subordinate (and perhaps having to argue about it).
2. Lack of skill needed to handle the interviews.
3. Dislike of a new procedure with its accompanying changes in ways of operating.
4. Mistrust of the validity of the appraisal instrument.

To meet this problem, formal controls—scheduling, reminders, and so on—are often instituted. It is common experience that without them fewer than half the appraisal interviews are actually held. But even controls do not necessarily work. Thus: In one company with a well-planned and carefully administered appraisal program, an opinion poll included two questions regarding appraisals. More than 90 percent of those answering the questionnaire approved the idea of appraisals. They wanted to know how they stood. Some 40 percent went on to say that they had never had the experience of being told—yet the files showed that over four-fifths of them had signed a form testifying that they had been through an appraisal interview, some of them several times! The respondents had no reason to lie, nor was there the slightest supposition that their superiors had committed forgery. The probable explanation is that the superiors, being basically resistant to the plan, had conducted the interviews in such a perfunctory manner that many subordinates did not recognize what was going on.

Training programs designed to teach the skills of appraising and interviewing do help, but they seldom eliminate managerial resistance entirely. The difficulties connected with "negative appraisals" remain a source of genuine concern. There is always some discomfort involved in telling a subordinate he is not doing well. The individual who is "coasting" during the few years prior to retirement after serving his company competently for many years presents a special dilemma to the boss who is preparing to interview him.

Nor does a shift to a form of group appraisal solve the problem. Though the group method tends to have greater validity and, properly administered, can equalize varying standards of judgment, it does not ease the difficulty inherent in the interview. In fact, the superior's discomfort is often intensified when he or she must base the interview on the results of a *group* discussion of the subordinate's worth. Even if the final judgments have been the superior's, he or she is not free to discuss the things said by others which may have been an influence.

The Underlying Cause

What should we think about a method—however valuable for meeting organizational needs—that produces such results in a wide range of companies with a variety of appraisal plans? The problem is one that cannot be dismissed lightly. Perhaps this intuitive managerial reaction to conventional performance appraisal plans shows a deep but unrecognized wisdom. In my view, it does not reflect anything so simple as resistance to change or dislike for personnel technique or lack of skill or mistrust for rating scales. Rather, managers seem to be expressing very real misgivings, which they find difficult to put into words. This could be the underlying cause: The conventional approach, unless handled with consummate skill and delicacy, constitutes something dangerously close to a violation of the integrity of the personality. Managers are uncomfortable when they are put in the position of "playing God." The respect we hold for the inherent value of the individual leaves us distressed when we must take responsibility for judging the personal worth of a fellow man. Yet the conventional approach to performance appraisal forces us not only to make such judgments and to see them acted upon but also to communicate them to those we have judged. Small wonder we resist!

The modern emphasis upon the manager as a leader who strives to help subordinates achieve both their own and the company's objectives is hardly consistent with the judicial role demanded by most appraisal plans. If the manager must put on a judicial hat occasionally, she or he does it reluctantly and with understandable qualms. Under such conditions it is unlikely that the subordinate will be any happier with the results than will the boss. It will not be surprising, either, if the subordinate fails to recognize that he or she has been told where he or she stands.

Of course, managers cannot escape making judgments about subordinates. Without such evaluations, salary and promotion policies cannot be administered sensibly. But are subordinates like products on an assembly line, to be accepted or rejected as a result of an inspection process? The inspection process may be made more objective or more accurate through research on the appraisal instrument, through training of the "inspectors," or through introducing group appraisal; the subordinate may be "reworked" by coaching or counseling before the final decision to accept or reject her or him; but as far as the assumptions of the conventional appraisal process are concerned, we still have what is practically identical with a program for product inspection.

On this interpretation, then, resistance to conventional appraisal programs is eminently sound. It reflects an unwillingness to treat human beings like physical objects. The needs of the organization are obviously important, but when they come into conflict with our convictions about the worth and the dignity of the human personality, one or the other must give.

Indeed, by the fact of their resistance, managers are saying that the organization must yield in the face of this fundamental human value. And they are thus being more sensitive than are personnel administrators and social scientists whose business it is to be concerned with the human problems of industry.

A NEW APPROACH

If this analysis is correct, the task before us is clear. We must find a new plan—not a compromise to hide the dilemma but a bold move to resolve the issue.

A number of writers are beginning to approach the whole subject of management from the point of view of basic social values. Peter Drucker's concept of "management by objectives"[1] offers an unusually promising framework within which we can seek a solution. Several companies, notably General Mills, Incorporated, and General Electric Company, have been exploring different methods of appraisal that rest upon assumptions consistent with Drucker's philosophy.

Responsibility on Subordinate

This approach calls on the subordinate to establish short-term performance goals for him- or herself. The superior enters the process actively only after the subordinate has (a) done a good deal of thinking about the job, (b) made a careful assessment of personal strengths and weaknesses, and (c) formulated some specific plans to accomplish chosen goals. The superior's role is to help the person relate his or her self-appraisal, his or her "targets," and his or her plans for the ensuing period to the realities of the organization.

The first step in this process is to arrive at a clear statement of the major features of the job. Rather than a formal job description, this is a document drawn up by the subordinate after studying the company-approved statement. It defines the broad areas of employee responsibility as they actually work out in practice. The boss and employee discuss the draft jointly and modify it as may be necessary until both of them agree that it is adequate.

Working from this statement of responsibilities, the subordinate then establishes personal goals or "targets" for a period of, say, six months. These targets are specific actions the employee proposes to take, for example, setting up regular staff meetings to improve communication, reorganizing the office, completing or undertaking a certain study. Thus, they are explicitly stated and accompanied by a detailed account of the actions the individual proposes to take to reach them. This document is, in turn, discussed with the superior and modified until both are satisfied with it.

At the conclusion of the six-month period, the subordinate makes an appraisal of what he or she has accomplished relative to the targets set earlier. The subordinate substantiates it with factual data wherever possible. The "interview" is an examination by superior and subordinate together of the subordinate's self-appraisal, and it culminates in a resetting of targets for the next six months.

Of course, the superior has veto power at each step of this process; in an organizational hierarchy anything else would be unacceptable. However, in practice the superior rarely needs to exercise it. Most subordinates tend to underestimate both their potentialities and their achievements. Moreover, subordinates normally have an understandable wish to satisfy their boss and are quite willing to adjust their targets or appraisals if the superior feels they are unrealistic. Actually, a much more common problem is to resist the subordinates' tendency to want the boss to tell them what to write down.

Analysis versus Appraisal

This approach to performance appraisal differs profoundly from the conventional one, for it shifts the emphasis from appraisal to analysis. This implies a more positive approach. No longer is the subordinate being examined by the superior so that weaknesses can be determined; rather the subordinate is examining her- or himself in order to define not only weaknesses but also strengths and potentials. The importance of this shift of emphasis should not be underestimated. It is basic to each of the specific differences that distinguish this approach from the conventional one.

The first of these differences arises from the subordinate's new role in the process, in which she or he becomes an active agent, not a passive "object." The subordinate is no longer a pawn in a chess game called management development. Effective development of managers does not include coercing them (no matter how benevolently) into acceptance of the goals of the enterprise, nor does it mean manipulating their behavior to suit organizational needs. Rather, it calls for creating a relationship within which a person can take responsibility for developing personal potentialities, plan for her- or himself, and learn from putting these plans into action. In the process the person can gain a genuine sense of satisfaction, for she or he is utilizing her or his own capabilities to achieve simultaneously both personal objectives and those of the organization. Unless this is the nature of the relationship, "development" becomes a euphemism.

Who Knows Best?

One of the main differences of this approach is that it rests on the assumption that the individual knows—or can learn—more than anyone else about his or her own capabilities, needs, strengths and weaknesses, and goals. In the end, only the individual can determine what is best for his or her development. The conventional approach, on the other hand, makes the assumption that the superior can know enough about the subordinate to decide what is best for that person.

No available methods can provide the superior with the knowledge needed to make such decisions. Ratings, aptitude and personality tests, and the superior's necessarily limited knowledge of the person's performance yield at best an imperfect picture. Even the most extensive psychological counseling (assuming the superior possesses the competence for it) would not solve the problem because the product of counseling is self-insight on the part of the *counselee*.

Psychological tests are not being condemned by this statement. On the contrary, they have genuine value in competent hands. Their use by professionals as part of the process of screening applicants for employment does not raise the same questions as their use to "diagnose" the personal worth of accepted members of a management team. Even in the latter instance, the problem we are discussing would not arise if test results and interpretations were given to the individual, to be shared with superiors at the individual's discretion.

The proper role for the superior, then, is the one that falls naturally to her or him under the suggested plan: helping the subordinate relate career planning to the needs and realities of the organization. In the discussions the boss can use knowledge of the organization to help the subordinate establish targets and methods for achieving them that will (a) lead to increased knowledge and skill, (b) contribute to organizational objectives, and (c) test the subordinate's self-appraisal.

This is help that the subordinate wants. She or he knows well that the rewards and satisfactions sought from a career as a manager depend on her or his contribution to organizational objectives. The subordinate is also aware that the superior knows more completely what is required for success in this organization and *under this boss*. The superior, then, is the person who can help the subordinate test the soundness of chosen goals and the plans for achieving them. Quite clearly the knowledge and active participation of *both* superior and subordinate are necessary components of this approach.

If the superior accepts this role, he or she need not become a judge of the subordinate's personal worth. The superior is not telling, deciding, criticizing, or praising—not "playing God." Rather she or he listens, using knowledge of the organization as a basis for advising, guiding, and encouraging subordinates to develop their own potentialities. Incidentally, this often leads the superior to important insights about her- or himself and her or his impact on others.

Looking to the Future

Another significant difference is that the emphasis is on the future rather than the past. The purpose of the plan is to establish realistic targets and to seek the most effective ways of reaching them. Appraisal thus becomes a means to a *constructive* end. The sixty-year-old "coaster" can be encouraged to set performance goals and to make a fair appraisal of progress toward them. Even the subordinate who has failed can be helped to consider what personal moves will be best. The superior rarely faces the uncomfortable prospect of denying a subordinate's personal worth. A transfer or even a demotion can be worked out without the connotation of a "sentence by the judge."

Performance versus Personality

Finally, the accent is on *performance*, on actions relative to goals. There is less tendency for the personality of the subordinate to become an issue. The superior, instead of being in the position of a psychologist or a therapist, can become a coach helping the subordinate to reach individual decisions on the specific steps that will enable the subordinate to reach the chosen targets. Such counseling as may be required demands no deep analysis of the personal motivations or basic adjustment of the subordinate. To illustrate: Consider a subordinate who is hostile, short-tempered, uncooperative, insecure. The superior need not make any psychological diagnosis. The "target setting" approach naturally directs the subordinate's attention to ways and means of obtaining better interdepartmental collaboration, reducing complaints, winning the confidence of the people under him or her. Rather than facing the troublesome prospect of forcing a personal psychological diagnosis on the subordinate, the superior can, for example, help the individual plan ways of getting "feedback" concerning the individual's impact on associates and subordinates as a basis for self-appraisal and self-improvement. There is little chance that a person who is involved in a process like this will be in the dark about where he or she stands or that the individual will forget he or she is the principal participant in his or her own development and responsible for it.

A NEW ATTITUDE

As a consequence of these differences we may expect the growth of a different attitude toward appraisal on the part of superior and subordinate alike. Superiors will gain real satisfaction as they learn to help subordinates integrate their personal goals with the needs of the organization so that both are served. Once subordinates have worked out mutually satisfactory plans of action, superiors can delegate to them the responsibility for putting the plans into effect. The superiors will see themselves in consistent managerial roles rather than being forced to adopt the basically incompatible roles of either the judge or the psychologist.

Unless there is a basic personal antagonism between the two (in which case the relationship should be terminated), the superior can conduct these interviews so that both are actively involved in seeking the right basis for constructive action. The organization, the boss, and the subordinate all stand to gain. Under such circumstances the opportunities for learning and for genuine development of both parties are maximal.

The particular mechanics are of secondary importance. The needs of the organization in the administration of salary and promotion policies can easily be met within the framework of the analysis process. The machinery of the program can be adjusted to the situation. No universal list of rating categories is required. The complications of subjective or prejudiced judgment, of varying standards, of attempts to quantify qualitative data, all can be minimized. In fact, no formal machinery is required.

Problems of Judgment

I have deliberately slighted many problems of judgment involved in administering promotions and salaries. These are by no means minor, and this approach will not automatically solve them. However, I believe that if we are prepared to recognize the fundamental problem inherent in the conventional approach, ways can be found to temper our present administrative methods. And if this approach is accepted, the traditional ingenuity of management will lead to the invention of a variety of methods for its implementation. The mechanics of some conventional plans can be adjusted to be consistent with this point of view. Obviously, a program utilizing ratings of the personal characteristics of subordinates would not be suitable, but one which emphasizes *behavior* might be.

Of course, managerial skill is required. No method will eliminate that. This method can fail as readily as any other in the clumsy hands of insensitive or indifferent or power-seeking managers. But even the limited experience of a few companies with this approach indicates that managerial *resistance* is substantially reduced. As a consequence, it is easier to gain the collaboration of managers in developing the necessary skills.

Cost in Time

There is one unavoidable cost: the manager must spend considerably more time in implementing a program of this kind. It is not unusual to take a couple of days to work through the initial establishment of responsibilities and goals with each individual. And a periodic appraisal may require several hours rather than the typical twenty minutes. Reaction to this cost will undoubtedly vary. The management that considers the development of its human resources to be the primary means of achieving the economic objectives of the organization will not be disturbed. It will regard the necessary guidance and coaching as among the most important functions of every superior.

CONCLUSION

I have sought to show that the conventional approach to performance appraisal stands condemned as a personnel method. It places the manager in the untenable position of judging the personal worth of subordinates and of acting on these judgments. No manager possesses, nor could he or she acquire, the skill necessary to carry out this responsibility effectively. Few would even be willing to accept it if they were fully aware of the implications involved.

It is this unrecognized aspect of conventional appraisal programs that produces the widespread uneasiness and even open resistance of management to appraisals and especially to the appraisal interview.

A sounder approach, which places the major responsibility on the subordinate for establishing performance goals and appraising progress toward them, avoids the major weaknesses of the old plan and benefits the organization by stimulating the development of the subordinate. It is true that more managerial skill and the investment of a considerable amount of time are required, but the greater motivation and the more effective development of subordinates can justify these added costs.

NOTE

1. See Peter Drucker, *The Practice of Management* (New York: Harper & Brothers, 1954).

Performance Appraisal and the Law

William H. Holley

Hubert S. Feild

In today's economic environment, personnel productivity, efficiency, and account-ability have emerged as subjects of considerable interest to both public and private employers. Every organization aspires to develop management systems that con-tribute toward the objectives of productivity improvement and cost efficiency while at the same time rewarding its employees for high levels of effective performance. Performance appraisal or evaluation is one such system which serves as a basis for this commitment to organizational objectives and establishing personnel accoun-tability. However, in order to insure that the performance appraisal system meets it objectives while complying with EEOC, OFCC, and court requirements, more efforts and research must be devoted to the design of valid or job-related instru-ments and methods of performance appraisal. Without valid appraisal systems, the costs to an organization—both internal and external—easily become exorbitant.

An intricate part of the overall performance evaluation system is the ratings given by supervisors and used by management in making personnel decisions, for example, layoffs, promotions, transfers. Presently, performance ratings are receiv-ing more than just a passing interest from the EEOC, OFCC, and the courts because often they contain bias, are not reliable, and are not demonstrably job related.[1] As such, they do not meet the requirements and standards of the EEOC, OFCC, or other investigative agencies. Yet, as ironic as it may seem, supervisory ratings of em-ployee performance are commonly used as the performance measure or criterion in test validation studies.[2]

Industrial psychologists, through various methods such as behavioral expec-tancy rating scales and other critical incident techniques, have minimized some of the subjectivity of supervisory ratings in performance appraisal and have suc-ceeded in screening out some of the grossest aspects. However, a problem with ratings remains where there may be racial or sexual prejudice, conscious or uncon-scious, on the part of the supervisor.[3] Serious legal questions are being raised concerning the use of ratings in personnel decision making.

USE OF PERFORMANCE APPRAISAL SYSTEMS

Compliance with EEOC and OFCC standards and requirements would not be such a widespread problem if evaluation systems were not so common in industry and

William H. Holley and Hubert S. Feild are assistant professors of business at Auburn University.

government. A national study of 139 companies by the Bureau of National Affairs showed that performance appraisals systems using ratings were quite prevalent across a variety of job levels in industry.[4] Over 90 percent of the companies surveyed had formal performance evaluation programs for their supervisors, middle managers, and professional/technical personnel. Eight out of ten companies had programs for their office and sales personnel, while 59 percent included their production workers in their performance appraisal programs. A recent survey of state personnel directors showed that almost 80 percent of the states had statewide appraisal programs using some form of personnel rating.[5]

Table 1 summarizes the factors commonly used to appraise employees in industry and state government. It is interesting to note that many of the factors entail subjective judgments (for example, personal traits). With such widespread application of appraisal systems and the employment of ratings for factors such as those in Table 1, it can only be an understatement that much research on performance appraisal remains to be done.

The potential of the problem multiplies when one considers the purposes for which performance ratings are used in the private and public sectors. Table 2 reflects the purposes of their use in private industry and state governments. Since they serve as a basis for making these personnel decisions (for example, layoffs, promotions), performance ratings must comply with legal requirements.

EEOC GUIDELINES

The legal aspects of performance appraisal systems are reflected in the EEOC "Guidelines on Employee Selection Procedures," the requirements for establishing a prima facie case in shifting the burden of proof, and recent court cases regarding the use of performance ratings.

Several sections of the "Guidelines on Employee Selection Procedures" published in the *Federal Register* have a direct bearing on the use of performance ratings. In particular, these sections include the definition of a test, requirements for the use of selection techniques other than tests, and minimum standards for validation. Although by title the guidelines sound as if they apply only to tests commonly used in employee selection, it will be seen that they apply to any formal or informal device used to evaluate employees for such diverse purposes as layoffs, transfers, promotions, and salary adjustments.

For the purposes of the EEOC and the OFCC, a "test" is defined as

> ... any paper-and-pencil or performance measure used as a basis for any employment decision [which] ... includes all formal, scored, quantified, or standardized techniques of assessing job suitability including ... specific or disqualifying personal history or background requirements, specific educational or work history requirements, scored interviews, biographical information blanks, interviewers' rating scales, scored application forms, etc.[6]

In this sense, the definition of a test as used in the guidelines is not limited solely to the measurement of cognitive areas such as abilities, aptitudes, and intelligence, but it is extended into noncognitive domains as well, such as interests, attitudes, personality, and biographical data.

Table 1 Percentage of employers using selected factors in appraising employee performance

Factor	Private industry[a] Manufacturing	Nonmanufacturing	State government[b]
Managerial skills (knowledge, experience, ability to organize, etc.)	80	87	74
Achievement of goals (completion of programs, costs, production, etc.)	81	87	26
Job behaviors (as related to job duties)	64	65	80
Personal traits (attitudes, intelligence, dependability, etc.)	61	65	80
Potential (capacity to develop and advance, etc.)	58	61	8

Table 2: Percentage of employers using performance appraisal systems for selected purposes

Factor	Private industry[c]	State government[b]
Promotion	73	
Layoffs	27	58[d]
Discharge	46	
Wage and salary decisions	69	39
Training and development	61	38
Manpower planning and utilization	[e]	46

[a]Based on a study of 139 firms by the Bureau of National Affairs, *Managerial Performance Appraisal Programs*, Washington, D.C., 1974, pp. 4-5.
[b]Based on a study of 24 systems by H. S. Feild and W. H. Holley, "Performance Appraisal in Public Employment: An Analysis of State-Wide Practices," *Public Personnel Management* 4 (May-June 1975): 145.
[c]Based on a study of 166 firms by the National Industrial Conference Board, "Personnel Practices in Factory and Office: Manufacturing," *Studies in Personnel Policy* 194 (1964): 17.
[d]The categories of promotion, layoffs, and discharge were combined in the survey of state governments.
[e]Not reported.

In extending the jurisdictional purview of the EEOC and the OFCC to cover personnel devices other than tests to assure compliance with the Equal Employment Opportunity Act and Executive Orders 11246 and 11375, the requirements for such techniques are also specified.

> Selection techniques other than tests . . . may be improperly used so as to have the effect of discriminating against minority groups. Such techniques include, but are not restricted to, unscored or casual interviews and unscored application forms. Where there are data suggesting employment discrimina-

tion, the person may be called upon to present evidence concerning the validity of his unscored procedures as well as any tests which may be used.[7]

The guidelines also present additional evidence that performance appraisal methods are covered in their standards for use. "The work behaviors or other criteria of employee adequacy which the test is intended to predict or identify must be fully described; and additionally, in the case of rating techniques, the appraisal form(s) and instructions to the rater(s) must be included as a part of the validation evidence. Such criteria may include measures other than actual work proficiency, such as training time, supervisory ratings, regularity of attendance, and tenure. Whatever criteria are used, they must represent major or critical work behaviors as revealed by careful job analyses.

> In view of the possible bias inherent in subjective evaluations, supervisory rating techniques should be carefully developed and the ratings should be closely examined for evidence of bias. In addition, minorities might obtain unfairly low performance criterion scores for reasons other than supervisors' prejudice, as, when as new employees, they have had less opportunities to learn job skills. The general point is that all criteria need to be examined to insure freedom from factors which would unfairly depress the scores of minority groups.[8]

Most formal performance evaluation systems rely on paper-and-pencil measures to review employees' job performance (for example, ratings). These reviews are then used for personnel decision making and/or test validation purposes. It is, therefore, reasonable to conclude that performance appraisal systems fall under the purview of the EEOC. As will be seen, recent court cases support this contention.

PRIMA FACIE CASE AND BURDEN OF PROOF

The requirements for establishing a prima facie case and shifting the burden of proof are critical elements in understanding the legal processes of equal employment opportunity cases. To investigate the issues regarding a prima facie case and the burden of proof, the most reliable sources are the Supreme Court decisions and their interpretations by the lower courts. In *Griggs* v. *Duke Power Company*, the Court was specific in its position as it noted:

> Congress has placed on the employer the burden of showing that any given requirement must have a manifest relationship to the employment in question.[9]

Later, in 1972, the Supreme Court clarified its position further in *McDonnell Douglas Corporation* v. *Green*.

> The complainant in a Title VII trial must carry the initial burden under the statute of establishing a prima facie case of racial discrimination. This may be done by showing (i) that he belongs to a racial minority; (ii) that he applied and was qualified for a job for which the employer was seeking applicants, (iii) that despite his qualifications, he was rejected, and (iv) that, after his

rejection, the position remained open and the employer continued to seek applicants from persons of complainants' qualifications. [Once the prima facie case is established,] the burden then must shift to the employer to articulate more legitimate, nondiscriminatory reasons for the respondent's rejection.[10]

Other cases have shown that evidence of discrimination alone will establish a prima facie case of discrimination, and statistical data may not be needed.[11] In addition, lower courts have approved other ways to establish a prima facie case. In *Carter v. Gallagher*,[12] statistics showing that a certain group performed more poorly than others on a test were accepted as prima facie evidence. In *Western Addition Community Organization v. Alioto*,[13] a comparison of the percentage of a particular minority group among those employed by the defendant with the percentage of that minority group in the general population established a prima facie case. Lastly, in *Chance v. Board of Examiners*,[14] a comparison of the racial composition of the defendant's work force with that of a similarly situated work force was successfully used as evidence.

COURT CASES ADDRESSING PERFORMANCE APPRAISAL

For years the courts obviously considered performance rating systems as serving an accepted and legitimate function within the overall personnel management system. In fact, it was not until the 1970s that performance rating systems began to fall from grace. Coupled with the close reading of the guidelines, the employer's burden to show validity of personnel devices, and a more thorough investigation into the implementation and administration of performance rating systems, the courts, the EEOC, and OFCC have become highly critical of performance ratings and the manner in which they have been used.

The following cases indicate that performance appraisal results have been "inappropriately" used by employers in personnel decision making and that legal consequences await the employer found to be in violation.

A municipal police department violated the Civil Rights Act of 1866 and 1871 and the Equal Protection Clause of the Fourteenth Amendment when several black patrolmen were not promoted to sergeant. The court found that the regular service ratings of job performance were discriminatory, and a special service rating of applicants for promotion had racial effects (two Negroes who passed the promotion exam received a greater drop in their regular service ratings than white officers who also passed the exam). As a remedy, the judge required that evaluations be performed on a six-month basis, ratings be retained even though the person is not seeking promotion, potential for serving in the next rank be evaluated, explanations for any marked discrepancies between evaluation for promotion and regular service ratings be given, special ratings be performed by five persons—two of which are to be selected by the ratee—and raters support their evaluations with narrative reasons for their judgments.[15]

A municipal fire department violated the Equal Protection Clause of the Fourteenth Amendment by not proving that either the efficiency rating system or the use of seniority credits for promotion was necessary to the conduct of business of the department. The discrimination violation included: time-in-grade requirements to determine eligibility to take the exam, application of performance ratings differently for blacks, and penalizing effects of seniority credits to blacks. To correct the violation, the promotion list was voided and the defendant was required to design an efficiency rating system which would insure that blacks and whites were equally graded.[16]

A statewide cooperative extension service was found in violation of the law when its evaluation instrument to appraise performance discriminated against black employees in that evaluations were made by subjective judgments, scores of black employees averaged less than those of white employees, the evaluation instrument was not based on job analysis, and no data were presented to demonstrate that the evaluation instrument was a valid predictor of employee job performance. This organization was required to employ qualified blacks in substantial numbers at all levels without delay, and the court warned that lack of reasonable success would cause more stringent relief.[17]

PROMOTION AND TRANSFER

Two similar cases found employer discrimination in violation of Title VII of the Civil Rights Act. Neither employer was able to show that promotion and transfer procedures did not discriminate against black hourly employees. The court found the following as bases for discrimination: recommendations by foremen were based on standards that were vague and subjective and were made without written instructions concerning qualifications necessary for promotion; hourly employees were not notified of promotional opportunities or the qualifications necessary for promotion; and no safeguards to overt discriminatory practices were designed.

As an affirmative action, one company was required to offer training programs to upgrade personnel, to provide foremen with written insructions delineating objective criteria and specific qualifications necessary for promotion and/or transfer, and to establish a committee of managers to insure that no one was denied consideration for promotion or transfer.[18] The other company was ordered to post announcements of preforemen training classes, to post notices of qualifications required for salaried positions, and to insure that every hourly rated employee was considered for salaried employment when a position was available.[19]

Using performance ratings for determining personnel layoffs was found to be in violation of Title VII of the Civil Rights Act when an employer failed to validate the appraisal methods according to EEOC guidelines. The evaluations were judged invalid because they were based on subjective observations (two of three evaluators did not observe the employee on a daily basis), evaluations were not administered and scored under controlled and standardized conditions, and a disproportionate number of Spanish workers were laid off. The court ordered the company to reinstate the employees with nominal back pay and required the company not to use performance ratings until they had been validated.[20]

VALIDATION OF TESTS USING RATINGS

The court agreed with an EEOC ruling that an employer did not appropriately validate a selection test when it used ratings based on subjective and vague factors as the criteria for validation. Further, the employer did not comply with EEOC guidelines when it did not base the performance ratings on job analysis. As a result, the employer was enjoined from continuing the use of the selection test and was required to provide back pay to the employees and pay their attorney fees.[21]

These case analyses reveal that inappropriate use of evaluations *may* occur for any one or more of the following reasons:

1. The performance rating method has not been shown to be job related or valid.
2. The content of the performance rating method has not been developed from thorough job analyses.
3. Raters have not been able to consistently observe the ratees performing their work.
4. Ratings have been based on raters' evaluations of subjective or vague factors.
5. Racial, sexual, and so on, biases of raters may have influenced the ratings given to ratees.
6. Ratings have not been collected and scored under standardized conditions.

Although these six reasons are not meant to be mutually exclusive nor exhaustive, they do point out specific considerations to be given when using performance appraisals in personnel decision making.

CONCLUSIONS

As noted earlier, performance evaluation systems have enjoyed extensive application in both public and private organizations for a multitude of purposes, ranging from serving as a basis for promoting employees to serving as a criterion in test validation studies. Recently, however, serious legal questions have been raised concerning their use. In fact, of the available evidence to date, a significant number of cases brought to the courts involving performance evaluations have found them to be in violation of equal employment guidelines. Given the widespread use of these methods, the purposes for which they are used, and results of recent court cases, employers utilizing such data for personnel decisions may be in a precarious position. Thus, much research remains to be undertaken on the applicability of performance evaluation.

Clearly, a first step in this direction must be in terms of the validation of methods used in performance evaluation. In previous years, performance ratings were used as a criterion for evaluating the validity of predictors such as tests. Now, however, criteria are needed for validating ratings used in performance evaluation. Establishing empirical concurrent or predictive validity of ratings is likely to be quite difficult and, in some cases, perhaps impossible. Content validity, on the other hand, seems to be a reasonable step toward a validation effort.[22]

Newer evaluation techniques utilizing ratings must also be developed. Behavioral expectancy rating scales using specific job behaviors rather than subjective traits hold some promise.[23] These scales, however, are usually job specific and may be difficult to develop and apply in organizations having many different jobs. Techniques based on management by objectives (MBO), where measurable standards or objectives are set and the employee is judged on goal performance, represent another promising approach. An MBO program seems to be particularly relevant for managerial personnel but often has limited application to nonmanagerial jobs. Other techniques that base the ratings on output or quotas show possibilities, but comprehensive job analyses must precede their development. Regardless of the methods employed, the introduction of these newer evaluation techniques must be centered on research of the viability and effectiveness of the methods, and this research must be conducted within the framework of EEOC, OFCC, and court requirements.

NOTES

1. H. G. Heneman, "Research Roundup," *The Personnel Administrator* XIX (July-August 1974): 49.

2. R. M. Guion, *Personnel Testing* (New York: McGraw-Hill, 1965), 96.

3. G. Cooper and R. Sobol, "Seniority and Testing Under Fair Employment Laws: A General Approach to Objective Criteria of Hiring and Promotion," *Harvard Law Review* LXXXII (August 1969): 1662–63.

4. *Management Performance Appraisal Programs* (Washington: The Bureau of National Affairs, 1974), 2.

5. Ibid.

6. U. S. Government, "Guidelines on Employee Selection Procedures," *Federal Register* XXXV (August 1, 1970), 12333.

7. Ibid., 12336.

8. Ibid, 12334.

9. *Griggs v. Duke Power Company*, 401 U. S. 424 (1971), 3 EPD ¶ 8137.

10. *McDonnell Douglas Corporation v. Green*, 411 U. S. 792 (1972). 5 EPD ¶ 8607.

11. "Employment Testing: The Aftermath of *Griggs v. Duke Power Company*," *Columbia Law Review* LXXII (May 1972), 912.

12. *Carter v. Gallagher*, 3 FEP 900 (1971), 3 EPD ¶ 8205.

13. *Western Addition Community Organization v. Alioto*, 330 F. Supp. 536 (1972), 3 EPD ¶ 8327.

14. *Chance v. Board of Examiners*, 330 F. Supp. 213 (1972), 4 EPD ¶ 7600.

15. *Allen v. City of Mobile*, 331 F. Supp. 1134. (1971), 4 EPD ¶ 7582.

16. *Harper v. Mayor and City Council of Baltimore*, 359 F. Supp. 1187, (1973), 5 EPD ¶ 2650.

17. *Wade v. Mississippi Cooperative Extension Service*, 372 F. Supp. 126, (1974), 7 EPD ¶ 9186.

18. *Baxter v. Savannah Sugar Refining Company*, (DC Ga. 1972), 5 EPD ¶ 8009.

19. *Rowe v. General Motors Corp.*, 457 F. Supp. 348, (1972), 4 EPD ¶ 7687.

20. *Brito, et al. v. Zig Company*, 478 F. 2d 1200. (1973), 5 EPD ¶ 8626.

21. *Moody v. Albemarle Paper Co.*, 474 F. 2d 134 (CA-4, 1973), 5 EPD ¶ 8470. On June 25, 1975, the U.S. Supreme Court affirmed the decision of the Court of Appeals (Nos. 74-389 and 74-428). The Court concluded: ". . .[We] agree with the Court of Appeals that the District Court erred in concluding that Albemarle had proved the job relatedness of its testing program and that the respondents were consequently not entitled to equitable relief. The outright reversal by the Court of Appeals implied that an injunction should immediately issue against all use of testing at the plant. Because of the particular circumstances of this case, however, it appears that the more prudent course is to leave to the District Court the precise fashioning of the necessary relief in the first instance."

22. See, for example, S. J. Mussio and M. K. Smith, *Content Validity: A Procedural Manual*, (Chicago: International Personnel Management Association, undated); Selection Consulting Center, *Content Validity Manual* (Sacramento, California: Selection Consulting Center, undated); and R. M. Guion, "Content Validity Conference," *The Industrial Psychologist* XII (December 1974): 18.

23. J. P. Campbell, M. D. Dunnette, R. D. Arvey, and H. V. Hellervick, "The Development and Evaluation of Behaviorally Based Rating Scales," *Journal of Applied Psychology* LVII (July-August 1973): 15–22.

On the Effectiveness of Not Holding a Formal Training Course

Paul W. Thayer

William McGehee

The note that follows describes an event that occurred during the summer of 1953 at the Fieldcrest Mills, Incorporated plants in northern North Carolina. The note is being written by popular demand. The authors have related this anecdote frequently and have always been told, "You ought to write that up. That is the kind of thing our graduate students never get a chance to hear about. They should." So here we go, twenty-four years later.

During 1953, McGehee was under increasing pressure from various mill managers to fulfill his role as training director by holding a course for foremen on the union contract. The problem, the managers contended, was that the union stewards knew the contract from beginning to end. As a result, the stewards were constantly challenging the foremen's authority to assign specific jobs, discipline employees, or engage in other managerial behaviors. A foreman's request that a loom fixer fill in for an operator for a brief time, for example, might be challenged by an unsupported reference to certain clauses in the union contract. Stewards capitalized on the foremen's ignorance. Many managers suspected that stewards frequently ran bluffs just for sport.

McGehee was concerned that any standard course on the contract would be ineffective. Careful observation of mill managers and foremen suggested that the stewards' behaviors were a problem for the managers, not the foremen. While competent instruction, suitable classrooms, materials, and time were available, one essential condition for learning was missing—motivation. In addition, the textile

Paul W. Thayer teaches at North Carolina State University at Raleigh. William McGehee teaches at the University of North Carolina at Greensboro.

Reprinted from Paul W. Thayer and William McGehee, "On the Effectiveness of Not Holding a Formal Training Course," *Personnel Psychology*, Vol. 30 (1977) 455–456.

industry was in a slump, and every extra cost was examined with great care.

Rather than confront the managers with the probable fruitlessness of a training course, it was suggested that some baseline data should be gathered. A test revealing what is already known would result in a shorter course and more efficient use of foreman time. Boredom induced by covering already mastered material would be avoided. Obviously, since foremen could consult their pocket editions of the contract on the job, the exam should be of the open book type. Since consultation also occurred on the job, this, too, would be acceptable. Thayer got the job of preparing the test.

As an incentive for test taking, the company president agreed to host a steak dinner for the foreman who submitted the most correct answers in the shortest time period. He also promised that foreman's manager the same.

In the meantime, McGehee began to suggest to the various mill managers that other managers were willing to make substantial wagers that the number of their foremen getting high scores would exceed any other mill's record. In short order, bets were being placed at all levels among plants, from foreman to manager. Thayer prepared the most difficult and comprehensive multiple-choice exam possible. While only one alternative was correct for each question, a good deal of hairsplitting was done in creating the incorrect responses.

The stage was now set for the nontraining course. Exams were delivered simultaneously to all mills at exactly 8:00 A.M. one morning. Immediately, managers and chief foremen began holding joint exam-taking sessions before work, during breaks, at lunch, after work, at home, and so on. McGehee made sure that everyone knew who the test author was. At 8:05 A.M., Thayer's phone began to ring. It did not stop for a week. Everyone protested that there were two, three, and even four correct answers to various questions.

The activity could only be described as frenzied, in part because no one was sure of the exact means of determining the winner. And, as the authors didn't know either, all participants were left in ignorance.

Within a week, all exams were in, and all were perfect or near perfect. Two weeks later, the president hosted a steak dinner for seventy-five foremen and their managers.

Did the foremen learn? The reader may judge. During the predinner refreshment hour, through dinner, and after dinner, Thayer was surrounded by indignant foremen who quoted sections of the contract verbatim to support contentions as to the unfairness of certain exam questions.

Did the nontraining course work? It is hard to tell. Behavior at the dinner suggests that it did. At least as important, mill manager pressure for a course disappeared.

Essential learning conditions must exist. Do we look at those conditions first before—or instead of—building a course?

Personnel's Role in Developing an Information System

Sidney H. Simon

Most companies, regardless of size and regardless of the type of business they're in, will eventually implement some type of automated personnel system. And whatever they call it—personnel data system, human resource system, or employee information system—its basic purpose will be the same: effective and efficient management of the company's greatest asset, its people.

The vantage point taken here does not, as with most articles, provide much insight into the technical features and capabilities currently available in personnel information systems. This article tries, instead, to illuminate how personnel—the primary user of such systems—can best guide and participate in the development of employee information systems.

PERSONNEL SHOULD CAPTAIN THE PROJECT

This may seem fundamental, but how many personnel departments have ever chartered a specific group within their unit to be responsible for a personnel information system development cycle? A system development cycle will not be successful if personnel, the chief user, does not have an assigned responsibility, with the authority to speak for the organization. A well-defined systematic approach must be taken by this group, and throughout the development cycle, this group must continue to assume a leadership role, make binding decisions for personnel and any staff individuals important to the project. Group size may vary. Three to six people should be sufficient for personnel's purpose, and others can contribute as required on a part-time basis.

Throughout the system's development and implementation life cycle, three distinct groups may become involved—personnel, data processing, and possibly an external vendor. A data processing representative (systems analyst) must therefore be included in the new project organization within personnel but may still report to data processing management. The remainder of the group should consist of individuals from the personnel organization.

The group should be led by an individal who is from, or at least responsible to,

Sidney H. Simon is the manager of personnel systems for Bechtel Corporation in San Francisco, California.

the personnel organization. Since this project involves a complex systems development methodology, it is highly recommended that such a leader have some technical computer background. A data processing systems analyst would be such a candidate.

THE BASIC PHASES

There are a number of classical phases to be followed in the development and implementation of a personnel information system. These may be summarized as follows:

1. System Requirements—what the system must be able to do (not how, but what).

2. System Design—alernative solutions are reviewed and presented for accomplishing the requirements; a solution is selected, and the system designed to accomplish such.

3. System Development—programming and testing the system until all involved are satisfied that it is functioning according to design specifications.

4. Implementation—actually installing and initiating utilization of the system.

5. Documentation and Training—recording all relevant information concerning the system during all phases; ensuring that all individuals directly involved can utilize or operate the system as promised initially (documentation should also be included in each of the previous phases).

Planning is obviously a key function in all the previously mentioned phases. As most systems development plans are either unrealistic or just plain no good or both, personnel must ensure that adequate planning is initiated. Sufficient controls must also be established to provide a monitoring capability throughout all system phases.

DETAILED PLANNING SHOULD COME IN STAGES

An overall system's plan can only be, at best, extremely general in the beginning. Costs and time frames should be portrayed in general terms, for just as it is impossible to know how to design a system without having a firm requirements definition, it is equally impossible to know how long it will take and how much it will cost to develop a system that has not yet been designed. Each phase's output must include a detailed plan for accomplishing the next phase. You may decide that it is not worth going to the next phase. If the next phase requires $125,000 and you only have $50,000 left, then it is time to stop and reevaluate what you are doing. Perhaps you will have to accept less than you require or review your priorities to eliminate the lesser items. Also, while data processing should prepare the detailed plans for the next phase, it is personnel who should be totally responsible for the completion of the first phase—system requirements.

KEEP THE REQUIREMENTS
SEPARATE FROM THE SOLUTIONS

The system requirements phase involves defining what the system must be able to do. It should not include how the system can actually do it. At times, this is not easy, as the solution may be very obvious or there may not be any readily apparent alternatives. Nevertheless, data processing analysts should review the requirements and recommend solutions for the next phase. It is common for confusion to occur when personnel mixes requirements and solutions. For example, the requirement is to pay employees for services rendered. The usual solution is a paycheck—however, other solutions may also be considered, such as cash payments, automatic deposits, bonuses, and so forth.

ESTABLISH QUANTITATIVE MEASUREMENTS EARLY

Lack of quantitative measurement is another possible pitfall when defining requirements. When the system becomes operational, it should be compared to the requirements, but too often a valid comparison cannot be made if quantitative measurements have not been established. Without them, opinion becomes the only measure of whether the system is satisfying the requirements or not. This potential pitfall is compounded by the fact that requirements are usually stated in such broad general terms that it is difficult to determine whether they are ever satisfied. For instance, one requirement may be that the system should respond in a timely manner. What is a timely manner? A week, a day, ten months, or what? Another might call for an accessible system. How accessible? Accessible to whom? What is flexibility? What is reliability? And so on. Future system operational cost requirements cannot be flatly stated in general terms but should relate to transaction volumes such as cost per transaction. It is not easy to quantify all these in measurable terms, but it has to be done.

DISCARD ALL UNNECESSARY DATA

Personnel information worth keeping can be classified into three broad categories:

1. The information needed to conduct the business (organization, classification, salary, employee ID, and so on).
2. The information needed to comply with statutory and regulatory conditions (Social Security number, EEO, and so forth).
3. Other information (performance evaluation and so forth).

No information besides these types should be in the personnel information system. Privacy legislation will ensure that unnecessary data is not maintained by companies and private data banks, so think ahead and don't include it initially. Avoid maintaining subjective data relating to employees. Some data, such as a performance evaluation rating may be subjective but at least it is factual, and it should be included.

There are several philosophies regarding the level of data definition that is sufficient in the requirements phase. Some prefer to be very detailed, while others preach a summary approach. At some point, the data must be defined. It is not important whether you do it initially or later in the design phase, but the following data characteristics should be considered minimal for each data element:

1. Name
2. Description
3. Size and type (number of characters, numeric or alpha)
4. Origination source (directly input from a personnel source document or derived from other data in the system)
5. Edits and validations required (necessary tables)
6. Dependencies on other data
7. Valid number of occurrences per employee
8. Frequency of update
9. Data category
   ☐ Absolutely required
   ☐ Needed
   ☐ Nice to have, or
   ☐ Wish list
10. Special considerations
   ☐ Retention
   ☐ Security
   ☐ Other

The output products need not be defined in too much detail in this phase. Necessary system-generated products should be identified by purpose, content, volume, frequency and media. If an ad hoc information output capability is required, many detailed reports will not have to be defined.

When examining the basics of a personnel information system, we see that it is nothing but a sophisticated file cabinet. Aside from the data editing or validation at input, there is no complex processing until the data is captured and residing on file someplace. Using the data for personnel's functional applications, such as compensation trends, affirmative action tracking, and so on, may become extremely complex. These functions cannot be performed if appropriate data is not present. We therefore must concentrate on identifying the current and historical data that must be maintained to support all our personnel functions, while functional specialists should provide the data requirements for their unique needs.

We should also realize that the collection of the data must be feasible. If only 50 percent of the data is apt to be collected or may be valid, then perhaps it is not as important as everyone thinks that the amount of data to be collected must be consistent with the administrative efforts that can be allocated for such a purpose. A probability could be assigned for the collection of such data elements. Finally, there comes a time to ask the paramount question, "When are all the requirements completely defined?"

FINE TUNING THE TIME SCHEDULE

At some point, someone will cry out, "Hold it! I forgot such and such." This is normal and should be expected. In fact, all requirements will not be defined until system design and development start. The following graph (Fig. 1) depicts the relationship between the requirements percent complete to cost and time.

The time and cost curve is asymptotic to the requirements 100 percent complete level. This means we will never reach the 100 percent complete level no matter how much time and money we expend. To increase the percent complete from P_1 to P_2 (ΔP) requires an expenditure of time and cost of CT_1 to CT_2 (ΔCT). A greater percentage increase in cost and time (ΔCT) must be made to realize a small increase in percent complete (ΔP).

We must assume that the major requirements factors that will directly affect the overall system's architecture will be identified within a tolerable completion percentage level (P_1). Do not spend too much time and effort trying to tie down every last data element. These are the types of items that will usually fit into the established structure and will "pop out of the woodwork" at any time. If the group that was chartered within personnel is comprised of competent, knowledgeable individuals, the requirements will be defined well enough.

Few conflicts will probably arise during the requirements-definition phase. Those that do are usually within the personnel organization and can usually be resolved by the personnel manager. During the second phase, system design, the chance for conflict increases as another organizational group, data processing, begins to actively participate in the project. Since data processing is a more technical discipline than personnel and relies on an electro/mechanical device, it operates in a more pragmatic environment. Their recommendations are more apt to be based upon what data processing itself is able to provide, but sometimes that may not provide the best solution to the requirements. This may be due to a lack of equipment or lack of experience with the software that is available. In any case, it is well

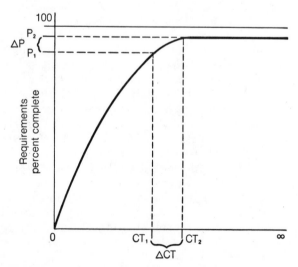

Figure 1 Cost and time

to remember that the requirements should be satisfied in the most feasible manner, and telling data processing people how it should be done is not apt to improve the chances.

The most important decision made during the system design phase is the "make or buy" decision. Does the in-house data processing organization develop the system from scratch, or are various components or even the total system purchased from an external vendor?

USE A SOFTWARE PRODUCT
THAT IS CURRENTLY AVAILABLE

Depending on your relationship with data processing, you may have problems purchasing external software. The argument usually advanced is that no available software package can satisfy the stated requirements, when in actuality, any vendor will modify their product to meet unique needs. The following should also be considered when examining available software: (a) Are all your requirements solid or is there some flexibility that would allow utilization of an already developed system? (After all, existing systems were developed to satisfy someone's requirements, and if it has had good success in the marketplace, it probably has been modified and expanded several times already.) (b) Would modification of your procedures or mode of operation be severely hampered if you changed to utilize an automated capability available in the marketplace? This does not mean you should change your whole method of operation. But if it cannot be modified to use existing software, the alternative of designing to suit it can involve extraordinary time and cost overruns.

A few of the factors to consider in arriving at a "make or buy" decision are:

1. Costs—Buying is usually at a fixed cost, including any modifications that are requested. If the vendor does not deliver, do not pay. An in-house data processing organization may expend several hundred thousand dollars and not produce anything of value.

2. Time Frames—Vendors have experience installing their system and can be fairly accurate regarding the time frame. An in-house data processing organization can give the best guess, depending on their experience with other systems of the same magnitude.

3. Product—If you buy a product, you can *see* what you will get before getting it. Yet even though you have a clear picture of your requirements and systems design, once the in-house development begins, strange things can happen. Changes and modifications can cause drastic changes in your costs.

4. Documentation—This is usually the most maligned aspect of a system's evolution. Lack of good documentation creates havoc when it comes time to maintain and modify the system. Be sure your vendors have adequate documentation for review prior to purchase, because documentation is costly and time consuming to develop in midstream. It is usually rushed, if prepared at all, during an in-house development cycle and may not ever satisfy personnel's or data processing's needs.

TAKING A FIX ON THE DESIGN PHASE

Data processing should be making the recommendations during the system's design phase, although all recommendations should be well documented, reviewed, and approved by personnel before proceeding with further work. Personnel should also ensure that the design recommendations meet all the stated requirements. If one is missing, don't settle for the excuse, "It will be added later, once the basics are operational . . . " There may never be a later. Remember, an output of the system design phase must be a detailed development and implementation plan. Personnel should insist that major milestones with defined events or products are established, and it is important that these events or products be very visible or measurable. Abstract or subjective items cannot be adequately monitored. An example of this:

1. Milestone x—complete documentation of program xyz specifications.
2. Milestone y—discuss functions that will be performed by program xyz.

Milestone x provides a product, a document, that has dimensions, content, and so on and can be reviewed and monitored. It is either complete or it is not complete. Milestone y, on the other hand, is kind of wishy-washy. There is nothing concrete that can be evaluated as to its adequate completion. There may also be a Task x detailing additional items that must be completed in a logical order to accomplish Milestone x. Data processing should ensure that this is properly planned.

Regularly scheduled review meetings should be held to monitor the project's progress, and personnel's role in the monitoring process should be an active rather than passive one. And although data processing is responsible for the development of the system, personnel should continuously concern itself with the details of requirements and interpreting ambiguous items.

WRAPPING UP THE FINAL DETAILS

Personnel should prepare the user manuals and guides for its own use. Successful operation of any system depends on following specified procedures, and these procedures must be well documented so qualified employees can be adequately trained to operate and utilize the system. Such documentation should include management overviews and summaries that detail the operational aspects for which personnel will be responsible. It is advisable for personnel to have as much control of the system as possible. This may include data entry and ad hoc report preparation and generation. In addition, the planning and preparation of system acceptance testing should be completed during the system development phase. Although components of the system are tested throughout the development cycle, final testing, with all components of the system working as a single unit, is usually poorly planned and conducted. The opposite should be the rule.

A large system will never be error free. However, most major and obvious errors must be eliminated before declaring the system to be operational. This is not an easy task. It was previously recommended that the system development group be led by an individual with some computer background. This is one area that particularly requires this experience. A systematic testing plan, involving the many combinations of transactions and functions performed, must be well prepared and executed.

Personnel must also ensure that test data bases and/or files are developed along with test transactions that have expected results. Much care should be taken to test all system functions and capabilities. Failure to do this will result in a poor systems implementation and perhaps cause problems that cannot be resolved immediately.

Systems errors will be encountered as the personnel system is being used. There must be formal procedures established to record the error conditions and provide feedback concerning the status of the corrections. It is also advisable with a newly operating system to continue the project review meetings to review system successes as well as failures.

Implementing a personnel system is not an easy job. They may all basically look alike, but the details are different. If you have persevered and brought a personnel system into operation, you will come to know, despite the frustrations, that it is well worth it—as you will discover when an information request is received from executive management and your system can provide answers.

IBM's Guidelines to Employee Privacy: An Interview with Frank T. Cary

David W. Ewing

Wanda A. Lankenner

Probably no organization in the world has taken the stance that IBM has on the question of employee privacy. The company has gone far beyond any legal requirements and the recommendations of most writers and legislators in protecting employees at all levels from the collection of unnecessary personal information and from improper use of personal data in the files. A remarkable aspect of this story is that IBM management established its policy not in response to any demands of activists or others but on its own initiative, out of a conviction that such steps are right. With the privacy issue on the mind of legislators, civil liberties authorities, and many other Americans, IBM's approach should be of practical interest to many business leaders. In this interview, Frank T. Cary describes the principal guidelines at IBM and their implementation.

Mr. Cary is chairman of the board and chief executive officer of IBM. He joined the company in 1948, became an assistant branch manager in San Francisco in 1954, and was named manager of the Chicago downtown office in 1956. He held a number of divisional and corporate posts before becoming president of the Data Processing Division in 1964. He was named senior vice-president in 1967 and elected to the board in 1968. In 1971 he was elected president of IBM, and in 1973 he

Frank T. Cary is chairman of the board and chief executive officer of IBM.

Reprinted by permission of the *Harvard Business Review*. "IBM's Guidelines to Employee Privacy" An Interview with Frank T. Cary (July-August 1971). Copyright ©1971 by the President and Fellows of Harvard College; all rights reserved.

became chairman and chief executive officer. He is a director or a trustee of several well-known organizations.

The interview with Mr. Cary was conducted by David W. Ewing, *Harvard Business Review's* executive editor-planning, and Wanda A. Lankenner, editorial assistant.

Harvard Business Review: Mr. Cary, you and other members of IBM's top management have spent a great deal of time working out an original approach to employee privacy. Why does this problem concern you so much?

Cary: Organizations have invaded people's privacy with steel file cabinets and manila folders for years. But computer systems with remote access have intensified both the problem and public concern. When I became chairman, it seemed to me that this subject was going to become an issue for us, as auto safety has become a major issue for Ford and General Motors. In years past we tended to step back, in the belief that others should take the lead—professors, politicians, lawyers. Now we have got to take some leadership and try to think our way through the subject. Privacy is not a passing fad.

Are the policies adopted by IBM applicable to business and government organizations in general?

Some of the things we've done are feasible in other organizations, but we have long recognized that we cannot solve many issues of individual privacy before the country solves them. We have to keep our efforts in the context of our business—we don't have any special competence to tell the world how legislators and privacy commissions and other groups should resolve all the questions being debated.

What part of the privacy issue, then, is of most concern to IBM?

Personal information about employees—the material that management keeps in files and data banks. This is a big part of the privacy issue but certainly not all of it. For instance, some hotly debated questions have to do with protection against intrusion by government agencies and the collection of census data. We don't have special competence in matters like those.

Have IBM employees influenced your concern with privacy?

Thomas Watson, Sr. and Jr., both had very strong beliefs in the dignity of the individual, but privacy in particular didn't begin to get special attention until the middle 1960s. That was when an IBM employee asked one day to see his personal folder. The question ended up in the office of Thomas J. Watson, Jr. After he reviewed it thoroughly his answer to the employee was yes. He then wrote to all IBM managers, saying that employees throughout the company ought to be able to see their personal folders. The subject has been growing with us ever since.

After becoming chief executive in 1973, you began giving privacy a higher priority than it had received in the past. How did you decide you had a problem?

When we looked at employee privacy in IBM from the top down, things appeared to be pretty good. We seemed to be handling personal data in a sensitive and careful way. But then we organized a corporate task force to look at the subject from the bottom up. At different IBM sites, local task forces were organized to find out what actually was being done. We found that in some cases information about employees was being handled in a way that we didn't like, that seemed to violate our principles.

What sort of things?

Oh, information in managers' informal files that shouldn't have been there, such as a piece of hearsay. Uses of information that shouldn't have been allowed, such as when an outsider requested more than routine facts about an employee.

Then how did you go about changing these practices?

I assigned some of our very best people to work on the problem. Also, I brought in Professor Alan Westin of Columbia, an authority on civil liberties, to serve as a consultant. After much creative thought and analysis, they would bring their ideas and proposals to me, and then I'd do what I like to call "put English on the ball." That is, I would give the recommendations some thought of my own and add my personal support in implementation—meetings with key management people, speeches, letters, and editorials in *Think*, our employee publication.

Was there much employee reaction to your efforts?

The changes we made weren't being demanded by employees and didn't come as any great surprise to them because in the past we had been paying attention to some of these needs. But I think that what we've done generally is considered by employees to be a good thing. Of course, we don't have all the answers even today. Our approach and thinking keep evolving.

What kind of feedback do you get from employees?

We use opinion surveys a lot in our business to find out how employees feel about certain things. Periodically we include a question about whether the employee feels that his or her manager and the IBM company in general treat personal information in a confidential enough way or appropriately—something like that. The great majority (close to 85 percent) feel that personal information is handled with sensitivity by IBM, and this feeling grows over time.

In a company with 160,000 employees in the United States, there are bound to be some people with legitimate grievances about privacy. Do you hear from these employees?

We do get some feedback on privacy questions through our "Speak Up!" program. "Speak Up!" is a system of communicating problems and questions to higher levels of management when they're not handled to an employee's satisfaction by his or her manager. The employee remains anonymous—no one knows the employee's name except the coordinator in the "Speak Up!" office. "Speak Up!" complaints about privacy have been minimal, but they indicate a widespread awareness of the issue.

After you decide on privacy guidelines, how do you make sure they're followed?

We try to make it very, very clear to managers what's expected of them. The rules for handling personal information are incorporated into our mangement training programs. We describe the principles we want followed, and we walk them through the specific do's and dont's of practicing the rules. We try to produce uniform understanding on this. Within thirty days of becoming a manager, every firstline manager begins to receive basic training.

In addition, we ask IBMers to help by bringing to mangement's attention infringements of personal privacy in their areas of the business. And we ask every employee to refrain from any practice that would unnecessarily invade the privacy of others.

What happens to a manager or other employee who violates a guideline?

Depending on the violation, the manager may be subject to dismissal. It's very clear-cut what we're trying to do, and I think everyone understands that we mean it. If there's confusion for some legitimate reason—and there may be because it's hard to anticipate all situations—we make allowances for error. But there have been cases when the manager has gotten into trouble.

Is it fair to say that people are penalized more severely for infractions of ethical standards at IBM than for, say, lapses in performance?

I think that failures in ethics and integrity here are less excusable than errors in performance. People can perform their jobs on a range from satisfactory to outstanding, but there's only one standard of ethics and integrity that we recognize. So, yes, there are two levels of assessment.

What kinds of problems has IBM had in developing general understanding of your privacy guidelines?

We've had little difficulty communicating the procedures. What information it is permissible to ask a job applicant for, what information goes where, who can use it, what is available to line managers versus what is available only to medical people—all of that has been formalized, and there's been little confusion about it. Where there's been a problem is in what the privacy rules mean for the manager-employee relationship. There was a tendency for some managers to think that privacy meant a change in the way they should be involved with their people.

What mistakes were your managers making?

They were withdrawing. This really worried me. We've always encouraged managers to have strong relationships with employees and to be interested and helpful to them. Partly because of the term *privacy*, I think, some managers began retreating from involvement. That wasn't what we wanted them to do.

Could you give us an example of managerial withdrawal?

I'll have to make it a hypothetical case. Suppose one of our managers got an anonymous letter giving strong indication that an employee was a child beater. The manager might judge this to be a private matter and not investigate. Of course he would be wrong. Humanitarian considerations aside, an accusation such as this, if true, might affect both the employee's performance and—if there were contact with customers—ability to represent IBM. The manager should not leave the problem unattended. He would have to investigate the situation.

The manager should not interpret privacy to mean "Let people alone"?

That's right. To give you a real, rather extreme example, a group of employees who listened to what we were saying about privacy mistakenly applied the idea to office design. They said we weren't respecting the privacy of employees because we weren't letting them have private offices. Finally, we realized what was happening. Some employees were reading into the word *privacy* their concerns for physical privacy. So we decided to be more precise by using the term *personal information*.

IBM employs some 130,000 people in countries overseas. Are they subject to the same guidelines as people in the United States?

The rules aren't applied formally in all other countries because of differing customs and traditions. For instance, it wouldn't make sense to apply the same rules to

IBMers in Japan. But the basic principles of our approach have been adopted in other countries like these, or are under review there, and I think these principles will be in practice in all countries before long.

Let's turn now to the specific everyday rules that IBM follows–the practices and policies that make this subject real from the standpoint of employees. We would like to start at the beginning, when information on an employee first accumulates. What personal information do you ask for from a job applicant?

Only what we think is necessary to make the employment decision—name, address, previous employer, education, and a few other basic facts. We don't even ask for date of birth at this time, although if the person is hired we will need to get his or her age. We don't ask about the employment of the applicant's spouse, about relatives employed by IBM, or for previous addresses. We don't ask about any prior treatment for nervous disorder or mental illness. We don't ask about arrest records or pending criminal charges or criminal indictments. We do ask about convictions—but only convictions during the previous five years.

IBM used to ask for some of the information now omitted. What made you change your mind?

We were getting a lot of data we really didn't need. It was cluttering up the files. Worse than that, it was tagging along after people. Particularly in the case of unfavorable information about an employee, there's a tendency for the material to follow the person around forever and to influence management decisions that it shouldn't. It's better not to have the data in the files in the first place.

But can you be sure in advance what personal information is going to be relevant?

No. But you know what you need at the time, for just this decision. Later you can collect more data as needed. This is part of the problem, you see. There's a common attitude that "It doesn't hurt to have all this information; it can't do any harm, so why not get it?" That's what we're working against. When we looked into this problem a few years ago, we found that it could indeed do harm to have information that wasn't of current relevance. For example, information about how young or how old a person is or about an arrest a couple of years ago—it shouldn't influence the hiring decision, but it might do so if it were on hand. So we decided the best thing to do was simply not to collect it.

What about appraisals of the applicant's strengths and weaknesses—do you cut back on that information, too?

Not at all. Just the opposite: Good interviewing becomes the key. Our people are very good at this, and we count on them to draw applicants out and understand their interests.

What about verifying the statements an applicant makes?

We used to employ outside credit agencies to do background checking on prospective employees, but not any more. When we feel that a reference on education or previous employment should be checked, our own people do it. Incidentally, they do it with the knowledge and consent of the applicant.

Inevitably there are some things we don't catch, but I don't think they are material enough to make it worthwhile to go through all the routines we used to have to go through. When we used to do background checks on applicants, for example, the information gathered would sometimes include data that just wasn't germane.

We're interested in employment testing. Some critics feel that tests can be an invasion of privacy. What's IBM's stance here?

We have stopped excursions into applicants' emotional and private lives through the use of personality tests. We don't use polygraphs in hiring or at any other time—we never have. But we use aptitude tests and consider them useful. Some tests have credibility, for instance, in forecasting a person's aptitude for programming or typing or certain other types of occupation. Also, this sort of information isn't so personal or sensitive. It's more job related than personality tests are.

What about tests of an applicant's general intelligence?

They don't help us much, either. Many of the people we hire have college backgrounds, and their records in college seem to be as good an indicator as any IQ test. So here again, since there are other ways of making the evaluation we need—ways that can't be called intrusions—we use them instead.

This brings us to the next stage. Do you try to control the buildup of personal information on an employee after he or she is hired?

Yes, we work pretty hard on that. We keep purging data that no longer seem relevant. Performance appraisals usually are kept for three years only—in unusual cases, for five years. All grades and appraisals from IBM course instructors are kept for three years only. A record of a conviction is thrown out after three years. Then there's all that information many managers keep on an employee's attendance, performance, vacation schedules, and so on. We tell managers to keep this material for a limited time only.

How much of the onus is on operating managers, rather than on the personnel department, to keep the files stripped down to essentials?

Since there are some files operating managers never examine, obviously the personnel department has to purge them of old data. But we hold individual managers responsible for seeing that job-related information, which they do see, is kept to a minimum. Now, the personnel department is responsible for developing guidelines, and it may check up on the manager to see that the purging is done, but he or she can't pass the buck. We say, in effect, "This is your job, and you know what the rules are—they're not terribly complex. It is up to you to see that the rules are followed."

Let's talk now about who can look at an employee's files. First, what can IBM line managers see?

Any job-related information they are allowed to see. The distinction between job related and nonjob related is important to the privacy question. An employee's performance appraisals, performance plans, letters of commendation, records of awards, sales records, production assignments, and so on—all such job-related information is kept available for the line manager to see. The manager needs to see it to make decisions. The only other people who can inspect this material are those with a need to know, such as a manager considering the employee for a new position.

Is there anything the line manager can't see?

Yes. Every large company has to have quite of bit of personal information on an employee that has little or nothing to do with work performance. So this information is out of bounds for the line manager. This file is open only to the personnel and financial departments. It includes medical benefits data, records of personal finances such as wage garnishments, payroll deductions, life insurance beneficiaries, payments for educational programs, house valuations, and so on. These items are required to administer benefit plans, to meet the company's legal obligations, and to carry out other aspects of personnel administration, but the operating manager does not need to know them. By this division, we protect the individual from having facts about his or her life accessible to people who should only be concerned with specific areas.

Numerous employees, attorneys, and civil liberties leaders are incensed because much personal information in the files of many employers may be released to outsiders—often without the employee's knowledge. How does IBM handle that issue?

If an outsider wants to verify that a person works for us, we will release the most recent job title the person has, the most recent place of work, and the date of employment at IBM. We'll do this much without contacting the employee. But if the outsider wants to know the person's salary or wants a five-year job chronology, we don't give out that information without written approval from the employee.

As for creditors, attorneys, private agencies, and others desiring nonjob-related information, we give out none of it without the employee's consent, unless the law requires disclosure by us.

We honor legitimate requests for information from government agencies, though we require the investigators to furnish proper identification, prove their legal authority, and demonstrate that they need the information sought. If a district attorney's office is making a criminal investigation, we cooperate within limits. It's hard to make rules to cover all situations that may arise, but we have specialists in the legal and personnel departments who use their judgment in an unusual situation, and they handle these problems pretty well.

Do you protect IBM's 600,000 or so stockholders in the same way?

Yes. Not long ago, for example, a U.S. senator wrote us asking for the names and holdings of IBM's 30 top stockholders. He had no subpoena. He would give no purpose for his inquiry, even after we asked. So we refused to give him the data he wanted. Suppose he had spelled out his purpose. Then, I suppose, we might have taken the next step and asked the permission of the 30 stockholders involved to release the facts.

Social Security numbers have been a sore spot with people concerned about privacy. How does IBM deal with this problem?

In 1973 we looked into the use of Social Security numbers and agreed that thereafter we would release them only to satisfy government and legal requirements—at least until some national consensus was arrived at on the use of universal identifiers or until new legislation was passed. So we don't give outside private organizations an employee's Social Security number without the person's consent; we don't even supply the number to the organization that administers our company scholarship program.

But Social Security numbers are useful for personal identification, aren't they?

Some organizations seem to think so, but we won't put Social Security numbers on company badges or identification cards. Also, we have taken them off all IBM medical cards; insurance companies get an IBM employee identification number when they process a medical or a dental claim.

We've discussed access to an employee's files by operating managers, the personnel department, and outsiders. What, if anything, can the employee himself or herself see?

With just a few exceptions, employees can see what's in their personnel folders—job-related information as well as nonjob-related. We want them to know what's there—no surprises. If they find something to quarrel with, they can ask for a correction. The key document, of course, is the performance appraisal. But there's less curiosity about this than you would think, and the reason is that the manager has already told the employee how he or she was rated. That was done when the appraisal session was held. In fact, the manager's appraisal that contains the ratings is reviewed by the employee, at which time he or she can add comments.

What are the exceptions—what data cannot be seen?

Employees can't see notes on "Open Door" investigations of complaints they made. At IBM, the "Open Door" is a system for allowing employees to take a grievance over their supervisors' heads to a higher management level. The employee identifies himself or herself (in this respect, the "Open Door" is different from "Speak Up!"), so the case goes into a special file, which, by the way, has very stringent access and retention standards. As chief executive, I'm the court of last resort, so to speak, and many cases come to me. I assign an executive to investigate each situation, and I personally review the findings. During the investigations, these senior managers talk to many people and get honest, frank answers to many tough questions. They couldn't get such candid answers if they didn't talk off the record, in strict confidence. So we don't allow an employee to see the notes made on a case he or she was concerned with. If we did, the "Open Door" system wouldn't work.

Can the employee learn anything at all about the investigation?

Oh, yes. The investigator sits down with the employee after the inquiries are completed and reports the conclusion. Some of the specific findings may be discussed. But the investigator doesn't quote the people interviewed and doesn't show the file to the employee concerned.

Do some of your assistants specialize in "Open Door" cases?

No one spends full time on them. We select different people on the basis of position occupied, objectivity, reputation for fairness, and so on. Also, we never ask the manager who has been criticized to do the investigation. We have strict ground rules for this, and I do have assistants who spend considerable time overviewing the system and seeing that the rules are followed. That the investigators start out taking the side of the complainants is an important rule. Quite often, they end up on that side—they find that the complainant is right.

Can an employee see information about salary plans for himself or herself?

Our managers make salary forecasts for their employees as a matter of course in business planning. In effect, a manager says, "I expect to increase so-and-so's salary by this much on such-and-such a date." We don't consider this personal information. It's business planning information and subject to change. Once the increase is acted on, the data become personal information, but until then the figures are not available to the employee concerned. In fact, such figures are not kept in the employee's file but in some place like the desk drawer of the manager.

Is information about an employee's promotion prospects handled in the same way?

Yes. Again, it's just good planning technique to know who is ready to take over the management jobs at certain levels. We prepare replacement tables with the names of, say, the top three candidates for every one of those jobs. Now, there are surely people who would love to see those tables and know who will be moved up if a certain individual gets hit by a streetcar the next day. But this, too, is business planning, not personal information, and so it's not available for employees to see. Besides, it would be misleading and misunderstood. We do not always do what is written in the replacement planning tables. Nor do we always give the amount of salary increase that is forecast.

Another thing many civil liberties spokesmen and others are unhappy about is the practice of recording employee conversations without the person's consent. What is IBM policy here?

There's absolutely no taping of a person's conversations on the telephone without express permission or at business meetings without prior announcement. I consider this a simple matter of respect for the individual.

Were conversations ever recorded in the past?

Yes, I think it was done sometimes. Some time ago, an employee had a hidden tape recorder he used for recording some sales calls he made on customers. He did it innocently, I think—for his own use to analyze what transpired. I think you just do not record conversations with customers or prospects or anyone else without telling them first. People act differently depending on the kind of talk they think they're having—recorded or not recorded, on the record or off, for a newspaper or for TV. As the saying goes, the medium is the message. I think it's the same principle that has influenced the courts to keep television out of the courtroom.

What about an employee's off-the-job behavior? Many Americans apparently feel that employers want to know too much about what an employee does after hours.

We're careful about that, too. In 1969 Thomas Watson, Jr., then chairman, wrote a letter to managers stating that management was concerned with off-the-job behavior only when it impaired a person's ability to perform regular job assignments—their own or others'—or when it affected the reputation of the company in a major way. The statement has continued to be our guideline.

Yet IBM has a reputation for being solicitious about employee welfare, as you pointed out earlier. Isn't it hard to draw the line?

Yes, because when a manager is trying to be helpful and when he's getting "nosey" is something that different people see in different ways. So you have to use judgment here. You can't have hard and fast rules. Certainly, spying of any kind is out. But what about a manager who visits an employee who is sick in the hospital or at home? Such a visit can be considered an invasion of privacy, given certain circumstances. So the manager has to be sensitive to the person and situation in order to do the right thing.

In Think, *IBM's publication for employees, an interesting problem was posed: An engineer goes on vacation and forgetfully leaves some confidential new product specifications in his desk drawer. Is his privacy being invaded if his manager goes into the drawer to get the specifications when needed?*

In one sense, there's no violation, because desks and files are IBM property. But the manager must have a very good reason for looking. No one should be fooling around in someone else's papers. Of course, it's important to try to avoid this sort of situation. When a person leaves on vacation or a trip, he or she should leave any business documents that might be needed in the hands of someone else who will carry on.

One hotly debated topic is management control of an employee's involvement with outside organizations. Could you comment on this question?

We ask employees who want to become involved in public problems and want to take a position on them to do so as private individuals, not on behalf of IBM. They should make that clear to the press. But only if there is a potential conflict of interest do we ask employees to excuse themselves from the discussion and any decision or to vote on it. This might be the case if, say, the employee sat on a board of education and the board were going to vote on an IBM proposal.

5

Rewarding and Public Personnel Management

The previous articles on results-oriented job descriptions, MBO, and objective performance evaluation standards have emphasized that there is a close relationship between employee productivity and organizational effectiveness. This in turn raises three questions that continue to perplex personnel managers and behavioral scientists:

1. What causes employee productivity to increase?
2. How is productivity related to employee job satisfaction?
3. What can managers and employees do to increase productivity?

Beginning with Frederick W. Taylor's research on the effect of work methods on productivity, behavioral scientists have investigated the factors that they believe affect employee productivity and job satisfaction: working conditions, economic rewards, group cohesion, individual growth, and organizational climate. Because satisfaction and productivity seem to depend on the interaction between individual needs and all the other factors, it is difficult to define their causes conclusively. It is not surprising, therefore, that the relationship between satisfaction and productivity remains unclear.

Charles N. Greene introduces this section with a review of the research on the relationship between job satisfaction and productivity. Unfortunately, researchers have reached contradictory conclusions, leading some commentators to conclude that the more they know about the relationship between job satisfaction and productivity, the less they understand it. While some studies have shown that happy employees are more productive, others have not confirmed this. Greene concludes that this confusion arises largely because of the effect of rewards as an intervening variable. In other words, employees who are rewarded for being productive are more satisfied with their jobs than are equally productive employees who are not equally rewarded. Because rewards are an important acknowledgment of productivity, the manager who can apply differential rewards equitably will reap the benefits of increased productivity.

If rewards do function as an intervening variable between satisfaction and productivity, it is important for the public personnel manager to design reward systems that meet employee and organizational goals. This leads to two problems. First, compensation systems must be flexible enough to provide the differing rewards desired by different employees and yet uniform enough to provide standardized rewards for the sake of administrative efficiency. A second problem is that the organization must distribute rewards fairly on the basis of relative employee productivity; yet employees and managers often define fairness differently.

Rewards can be given on the basis of three factors: job worth (more pay for jobs with greater responsibility), employee characteristics (more pay for seniority or education), and job performance.

Some evidence suggests that job satisfaction is caused by a combination of organizational rewards and organizational conditions. Job enrichment is one strategy for increasing both productivity and satisfaction by deliberately redesigning jobs to make them more inherently rewarding. It does so by increasing the variety, "wholeness," and significance of employee job tasks. Despite the success of job enrichment in many situations, it has failed where jobs, employees, or the demands on the organization make it an unsuitable solution to motivational problems. Richard Hackman and his associates suggest some techniques for determining the potential a job has for enrichment, thus enabling management to avoid improper planning or execution of a job enrichment program. In effect, they perceive job enrichment as a type of planned organizational change that may have unforeseen effects on the organization's job structure, authority patterns, and communications systems.

A second strategy for increasing employee job satisfaction is the use of flexible hours of work. By allowing employees to set their own work hours within certain limits coordinated by the agency, personnel managers hope to reduce absenteeism and abuse of sick leave. Robert T. Golembiewski and Carl W. Proehl, Jr., evaluate studies on the effectiveness of "flexitime." Many studies in this area are poorly designed in that they measure only employee reactions to flexible work hours rather than any actual objective changes in employee productivity. Also, many lack baseline data (collected before instituting flexitime) or control organizations that would serve to guard against intervening variables. Their conclusion is that while flexitime has been shown to increase productivity in some situations, it can also decrease productivity or increase administrative costs. Like other innovative methods of redesigning work, its effectiveness must be carefully assessed prior to adoption.

Another technique for improving productivity by increasing the flexibility of rewards to employees is "cafeteria compensation." Under such systems, the employer calculates the comparative value of different units of pay and benefits and allows employees to select different pay and benefit packages to meet their respective needs, providing that these packages have equal economic value. William B. Werther, Jr., explores some of the advantages and disadvantages of this method. The main advantage is that once a structure of equivalent benefits is established, each employee can select combinations of greatest desirability. This creates a climate of increased employee participation and acceptance of organizational policy. The two problems with this system are administration complexity and IRS regulations, which treat employee-elected benefits as taxable income rather than as an employer business expense. Despite these disadvantages, some agencies have reported success with flexible compensation programs.

Reward systems must be not only adaptable enough to meet the varying needs of different employees, they must also be sufficiently standardized to be easy for the organization to implement and administer. There is some conflict between standardization and flexibility, for the former emphasizes uniform pay and benefit packages that are easy to administer, while the latter emphasizes flexible compensation systems. The fairness of pay systems is always contested because the rewards are more limited than the demand for them, and then disagreements also exist over the relative value of job worth, employee characteristics, or employee performance as compensable factors. Most commentators agree that to be effective, rewards must be tied to employee productivity.

Henri van Adelsberg discusses ways of doing this. First, he attacks the misconception that public employees have a right to perpetual annual salary increases based on longevity. Second, he states that although base pay for a position should be competitive with pay rates for similar jobs in private industry, salary ranges above and below this point should be based on comparative employee productivity. Despite the fact that methods of determining absolute or relative employee productivity do exist, several conditions have prevented managers from consistently linking performance to compensation: resistance from employees, unions, and managers; lack of funds; and the absence of valid performance measurement systems. Third, he considers it important that agencies control "merit" increases in order to prevent gradual escalation of salaries above the midpoint of a position's salary range. And, finally, he approves of the trend toward compensation as a total package consisting of both pay and benefits. All of these efforts will result in increased ties between performance and compensation, as well as increased predictability and control by managers over agency personnel expenditures.

The last article, by Bernard Jump, Jr., discusses the problem of predictability and control over the cost of municipal pension plans. Jump is concerned that the funding of public employee retirement programs through current tax revenues represents a hidden problem for public agencies because of the unpredictable future cost of these programs. He urges cities to reevaluate their retirement system objectives to ensure that age, service, and disability retirement provisions are compatible with those of other governments. Retirement plans should also be more closely coordinated with Social Security, thereby controlling the total cost to the employer and, therefore, taxpayer. Most important for prudent fund management is determining that benefits not be increased unless funding sources that provide adequate revenue increases are identified and earmarked to finance growing demands on the pension fund.

In sum, these six articles explore the problems encountered by public personnel managers seeking to develop pay and benefit systems to meet organizational needs for increased employee productivity and administrative efficiency, as well as employee needs for flexibility and fairness. Needless to say, these goals are difficult to achieve.

The Satisfaction-Performance Controversy

Charles N. Greene

Current speculation continues to imply that satisfaction and performance are causally related. While the performance-causes-satisfaction proposition is a more recent development, the contention that satisfaction causes performance remains more widely held. Recent research findings, however, offer only moderate support of the former view and reject the latter. The evidence indicates that the relationship is more complex: *rewards constitute a more direct cause of satisfaction than does performance, and rewards based on current performance cause subsequent performance. Thus, the manager who wants to improve his subordinates' performance must first provide valued rewards of sufficient magnitude and then establish the necessary contingencies between effort and performance and between performance and rewards. Last, he or she needs to consider a range of nonmotivational factors.*

As Ben walked by smiling on the way to his office, Ben's boss remarked to a friend: "Ben really enjoys his job and that's why he's the best damn worker I ever had. And that's reason enough for me to keep Ben happy."

The friend replied: "No, you're wrong! Ben likes his job because he does it so well. If you want to make Ben happy, you ought to do whatever you can to help him further improve his performance."

Four decades after the initial published investigation on the satisfaction-performance relationship, these two opposing views are still the subject of controversy on the part of both practitioners and researchers. Several researchers have concluded, in fact, that "there is no present technique for determining the cause and effect of satisfaction and performance." Current speculations, reviewed by Schwab and Cummings, however, still imply—at least in theory—that satisfaction and performance are causally related although, in some cases, the assumed cause has become the effect, and in others the relationship between these two variables is considered to be a function of a third or even additional variables.[1]

Reprinted from Charles N. Greene, "The Satisfaction-Performance Controversy," *Business Horizons* (October 1972), 31–41.

THEORY AND EVIDENCE

Satisfaction Causes Performance

At least three fundamental theoretical propositions underlie the research and writing in this area. The first and most pervasive stems from the human relations movement with its emphasis on the well-being of the individual at work. In the years following the investigations at Western Electric, a number of studies were concluded to identify correlates of high and low job satisfaction. The interest in satisfaction, however, came about not so much as a result of concern for the individual as concern with the presumed linkage of satisfaction with performance.

According to this proposition (simply stated and still frequently accepted), the degree of job satisfaction felt by an employee determines her or his performance; that is, satisfaction causes performance. This proposition has theoretical roots, but it also reflects the popular belief that a happy worker is a productive worker and the notion that all good things go together. It is far more pleasant to increase an employee's happiness than to deal directly with his or her performance whenever a performance problem exists. Therefore, acceptance of the satisfaction-causes-performance proposition as a solution makes good sense, particularly for the manager because it represents the path of least resistance. Furthermore, high job satisfaction and high performance are both good, and, therefore, they ought to be related to one another.

At the theoretical level, Vroom's valence-force model is a prime example of theory-based support of the satisfaction-causes-performance case.[2] In Vroom's model, job satisfaction reflects the valence (attractiveness) of the job. It follows from his theory that the force exerted on an employee to remain on the job is an increasing function of the valence of the job. Thus, satisfaction should be negatively related to absenteeism and turnover, and, at the empirical level, it is.

Whether or not this valence also leads to higher performance, however, is open to considerable doubt. Vroom's review of twenty-three field studies that investigated the relationship between satisfaction and performance revealed an insignificant median static correlation of 0.14; that is, satisfaction explained less than 2 percent of the variance in performance. Thus, the insignificant results and absence of tests of the causality question fail to provide support for this proposition.

Performance Causes Satisfaction

More recently, a second theoretical proposition has been advanced. According to this view, best represented by the work of Porter and Lawler, satisfaction is considered not as a cause but as an effect of performance; that is, performance causes satisfaction.[3] Differential performance determines rewards which, in turn, produce variance in satisfaction. In other words, rewards constitute a necessary intervening variable, and thus satisfaction is considered to be a function of performance-related rewards.

At the empirical level, two recent studies—each utilizing time-lag correlations—lend considerable support to elements of this proposition. Bowen and Siegel, and Greene reported finding relatively strong correlations between performance and satisfaction expressed later (the performance-causes-satisfaction condition), which were significantly higher than the low correlations between satisfaction and performance which occurred during the subsequent period (the satisfaction-causes-performance condition).[4]

In the Greene study, significant correlations were obtained between performance and rewards granted subsequently and between rewards and subsequent satisfaction. Thus, Porter's and Lawler's predictions that differential performance determines rewards and that rewards produce variance in satisfaction were upheld.

Rewards as a Causal Factor

Closely related to Porter's and Lawler's predictions is a still more recent theoretical position that considers both satisfaction and performance to be functions of rewards. In this view, rewards cause satisfaction, and rewards that are based on current performance affect subsequent performance.

According to this proposition, formulated by Cherrington, Reitz, and Scott from the contributions of reinforcement theorists, there is no inherent relationship between satisfaction and performance.[5] The results of their experimental investigation strongly support their predictions. The rewarded subjects reported significantly greater satisfaction than did the unrewarded subjects. Furthermore, when rewards (monetary bonuses, in this case) were granted on the basis of performance, the subjects' performance was significantly higher than that of subjects whose rewards were unrelated to their performance. For example, they found that when a low performer was not rewarded, the worker expressed dissatisfaction but that his or her later performance improved. On the other hand, when a low performer was in fact rewarded for low performance, he or she expressed high satisfaction but continued to perform at a low level.

The same pattern of findings was revealed in the case of the high performing subjects with one exception; the high performer who was not rewarded expressed dissatisfaction, as expected, and his or her performance on the next trial declined significantly. The correlation between satisfaction and subsequent performance, excluding the effects of rewards, was 0.00; that is, satisfaction does not cause improved performance.

A recent field study, which investigated the source and direction of causal influence in satisfaction-performance relationships, supports the Cherrington-Reitz-Scott findings.[6] Merit pay was identified as a cause of satisfaction and, contrary to some current beliefs, was found to be a significantly more frequent source of satisfaction than dissatisfaction. The results of this study further revealed equally significant relationships between (1) merit pay and subsequent performance and (2) current performance and subsequent merit pay. Given the Cherrington-Reitz-Scott findings that rewards based on current performance caused improved subsequent performance, these results do suggest the possibility of reciprocal causation.

In other words, merit pay based on current performance probably caused variations in subsequent performance, and the company in this field study evidently was relatively successful in implementing its policy of granting salary increases to an employee on the basis of her or his performance (as evidenced by the significant relationship found between current performance and subsequent merit pay). The company's use of a fixed (annual) merit increase schedule probably obscured some of the stronger reinforcing effects of merit pay on performance.

Unlike the Cherrington-Reitz-Scott controlled experiment, the fixed merit increases schedule precluded (as it does in most organizations) giving an employee a monetary reward immediately after she or he successfully performed a major task. This constraint undoubtedly reduced the magnitude of the relationship between merit pay and subsequent performance.

IMPLICATIONS FOR MANAGEMENT

These findings have several apparent but nonetheless important implications. For the manager who desires to enhance the satisfaction of his or her subordinates (perhaps for the purpose of reducing turnover), the implication of the finding that rewards cause satisfaction is self-evident. If, on the other hand, the manager's interest in subordinates' satisfaction arises from a desire to increase their performance, the consistent rejection of the satisfaction-causes-performance proposition has an equally clear implication: increasing subordinates' satisfaction will have no effect on their performance.

The finding that rewards based on current performance affect subsequent performance does, however, offer a strategy for increasing subordinates' performance. Unfortunately, it is not the path of least resistance for the manager. Granting differential rewards on the basis of differences in subordinates' performance will cause subordinates to express varying degrees of satisfaction or dissatisfaction. The manager, as a result, will soon be in the uncomfortable position of having to successfully defend the basis for evaluation or having to put up with dissatisfied subordinates until their performance improves or they leave the organization.

The benefits of this strategy, however, far outweigh its liabilities. In addition to its positive effects on performance, this strategy provides equity since the most satisfied employees are the rewarded high performers and, for the same reason, it also facilitates the organization's efforts to retain its most productive employees.

If these implications are to be considered as prescriptions for managerial behavior, one is tempted at this point to conclude that all a manager need do in order to increase subordinates' performance is to accurately appraise their work and then reward them accordingly. However, given limited resources for rewards and knowledge of appraisal techniques, it is all too apparent that the manager's task here is not easy.

Moreover, the relationship between rewards and performance is often not as simple or direct as one would think, for at least two reasons. First, there are other causes of performance that may have a more direct bearing on a particular problem. Second is the question of the appropriateness of the reward itself; that is, what is rewarding for one person may not be for another. In short, a manager also needs to consider other potential causes of performance and a range of rewards in coping with any given performance problem.

Nonmotivational Factors

The element of performance that relates most directly to the discussion thus far is effort, that element which links rewards to performance. The employee who works hard usually does so because of the rewards or avoidance of punishment that he or she associates with good work. The employer believes tht the magnitude of the reward to be received is contingent on performance and, further, that performance is a function of how hard he or she works. Thus, effort reflects the motivational aspect of performance. There are, however, other nonmotivational considerations that can best be considered prior to examining the ways in which a manager can deal with the motivational problem.

Direction   Suppose, for example, that an employee works hard at the job, yet his or her performance is inadequate. What can the manager do to alleviate the problem? The manager's first action should be to identify the cause. One likely possibility is what can be referred to as a "direction problem."

Several years ago, the Minnesota Vikings' defensive end, Jim Marshall, very alertly gathered up the opponent's fumble and then, with obvious effort and delight, proceeded to carry the ball some fifty yards into the wrong end zone. This is a direction problem in its purest sense. For the employee working under more usual circumstances, a direction problem generally stems from a lack of understanding of what is expected or what a job well done looks like. The action indicated to alleviate this problem is to clarify or define in detail for the employee the requirements of the job. The manager's own leadership style may also be a factor. In dealing with an employee with a direction problem, the manager needs to exercise closer supervision and to initiate structure or focus on the task, as opposed to emphasizing consideration or relations with the employee.[7]

In cases where this style of behavior is repugnant or inconsistent with the manager's own leadership inclinations, an alternative approach is to engage in mutual goal setting or management-by-objectives techniques with the employee. Here, the necessary structure can be established but at the subordinate's own initiative, thus creating a more participative atmosphere. This approach, however, is not free of potential problems. The employee is more likely to make additional undetected errors before his or her performance improves, and the approach is more time consuming than the more direct route.

Ability   What can the manager do if the actions she or he has taken to resolve the direction problem fail to result in significant improvements in performance? The subordinate still exerts a high level of effort and understands what is expected—yet continues to perform poorly. At this point, the manager may begin, justifiably so, to doubt the subordinate's ability to perform the job. When this doubt does arise, there are three useful questions, suggested by Mager and Pipe, to which the manager should find answers before treating the problem as an ability deficiency: Could the subordinate do it if he or she really had to? Could the subordinate do it if his or her life depended on it? Are the subordinate's present abilities adequate for the desired performance?[8]

If the answers to the first two questions are negative, then the answer to the last question also will be negative; and the obvious conclusion is that an ability deficiency does, in fact, exist. Most managers, upon reaching this conclusion, begin to develop some type of formal training experience for the subordinate. This is unfortunate and frequently wasteful. There is probably a simpler, less expensive solution. Formal training is usually required only when the individual has never done the particular job in question or when there is no way in which the ability requirement in question can be eliminated from that job.

If the individual formerly used the skill but now uses it only rarely, systematic practice will usually overcome the deficiency without formal training. Alternatively, the job can be changed or simplified so that the impaired ability is no longer crucial to successful performance. If, on the other hand, the individual once had the skill and still rather frequently is able to practice it, the manager should consider providing the employee with greater feedback concerning the outcome of his or her efforts. The subordinate may not be aware of the deficiency and its effect on his or her performance, or he or she may no longer know how to perform the job. For example, elements of the job or the relationship between this job and other jobs may have changed, and the employee simply is not aware of the change.

Where formal training efforts are indicated, systematic analysis of the job is useful for identifying the specific behaviors and skills that are closely related with successful task performance and that, therefore, need to be learned. Alternatively, if the time and expense associated with job analysis are considered excessive, the critical incidents approach can be employed toward the same end.[9] Once training needs have been identified and the appropriate training technique employed, the manager can profit by asking one last question: "Why did the ability deficiency develop in the first place?"

Ultimately, the answer rests with the selection and placement process. Had a congruent person-job match been attained at the outset, the ability deficiency would never have presented itself as a performance problem.[10]

Performance Obstacles   When inadequate performance is not the result of a lack of effort, direction, or ability, there is still another potential cause that needs attention. There may be obstacles beyond the subordinate's control that interfere with performance. "I can't do it" is not always an alibi; it may be a real description of the problem. Performance obstacles can take many forms to the extent that their number, independent of a given situation, is almost unlimited.

However, the manager might look initially for some of the more common potential obstacles, such as a lack of time or conflicting demands on the subordinate's time, inadequate work facilities, restrictive policies or "right ways of doing it" that inhibit performance, lack of authority, insufficient information about other activities that affect the job, and lack of cooperation from others with whom the employee must work. An additional obstacle, often not apparent to the manager from face-to-face interaction with a subordinate, is the operation of group goals and norms that run counter to organizational objectives. Where the work group adheres to norms of restricting productivity, for example, the subordinate will similarly restrict his or her own performance to the extent that he or she identifies more closely with the group than with management.

Most performance obstacles can be overcome either by removing the obstacle or by changing the subordinate's job so that the obstacle no longer impinges on performance. When the obstacle stems from group norms, however, a very different set of actions is required. Here, the actions that should be taken are the same as those that will be considered shortly in coping with lack of effort on the part of the individual. In other words, the potential causes of the group's lack of effort are identical to those that apply to the individual.

The Motivational Problem

Thus far, performance problems have been considered in which effort was not the source of the performance discrepancy. While reward practices constitute the most frequent and direct cause of effort, there are also other less direct causes. Direction, ability, and performance obstacles may indirectly affect effort through their effects on performance. For example, an individual may perform poorly because of an ability deficiency and, as a result, exert little effort on the job. Here, the ability deficiency produced low performance, and the lack of effort on the individual's part resulted from his or her expectations of failure. Thus, actions taken to alleviate the ability deficiency should result in improved performance and, subsequently, in higher effort.

Effort is that element of performance which links rewards to performance. The relationship between rewards and effort is unfortunately, not a simple one. As indicated in Figure 1, effort is considered not only as a function of the (1) value and (2) magnitude of reward, but also as a function of (3) the individual's perceptions of the extent to which greater effort on his or her part will lead to higher performance, and (4) that his or her high performance, in turn, will lead to rewards. Therefore, a manager who is confronted with a subordinate who exerts little effort must consider these four attributes of reward practices in addition to the more indirect, potential causes of the lack of effort. The key issues in coping with a subordinate's lack of effort—the motivation problem—or in preventing such a problem from arising involve all four of the attributes of rewards just identified.[11]

Appropriateness of the Reward   Regardless of the extent to which the individual believes that hard work determines performance and subsequent rewards, she or he will obviously put forth little effort unless she or he *values* those rewards—that is, the rewards must have value in terms of the employee's own need state. An accountant, for example, may value recognition from the boss, an opportunity to increase the scope of her job, or a salary increase; however, it is unlikely that she will place the same value on a ten-year supply of budget forms.

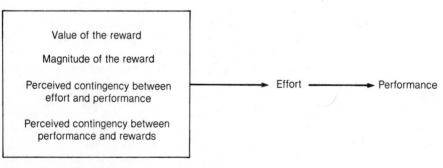

Figure 1   Reward practices

In other words, there must be consistency between the reward and what the individual needs or wants and recognition that there are often significant differences among individuals in what they consider rewarding. Similarly, individuals differ in terms of the *magnitude* of that valued reward they consider to be positively reinforcing. A 7 or 8 percent salary increase may motivate one person but have little or no positive effect on another person at the same salary level. Furthermore, a sizable reward in one situation might be considered small by the same individual in a different set of circumstances.

These individual differences, particularly those concerning what rewards are valued, raise considerable question about the adequacy of current organization reward systems, virtually none of which make any formal recognition of individual differences. Lawler, for example, has suggested that organizations could profit greatly by introducing "cafeteria-style" wage plans.[12] These plans allow an employee to select any combination of cash and fringe benefits he desires. An employee would be assigned "X" amount in compensation, which he may then divide up among a number of fringe benefits and cash. This practice would ensure that employees receive only those fringe benefits they value; from the organization's point of view, it would reduce the waste in funds allocated by the organization to fringe benefits not valued by its members. As a personal strategy, however, the manager could profit even more by extending Lawler's plan to include the entire range of nonmonetary rewards.

Rewards can be classified into two broad categories, extrinsic and intrinsic. Extrinsic rewards are those external to the job or in the context of the job, such as job security, improved working facilities, praise from one's boss, status symbols, and, of course, pay, including fringe benefits. Intrinsic rewards, on the other hand, are rewards that can be associated directly with the "doing of the job," such as a sense of accomplishment after successful performance, opportunities for advancement, increased responsibility, and work itself.

Thus, intrinsic rewards flow immediately and directly from the individual's performance of the job and, as such, may be considered as a form of self-reward. For example, one must essentially decide for himself whether his level of performance is worthy of a feeling of personal achievement. Extrinsic rewards, to the contrary, are administered by the organization; the organization first must identify good performance and then provide the appropriate reward.

Generally speaking, extrinsic rewards have their greatest value when the individual is most strongly motivated to satisfy what Maslow has referred to as lower-level needs, basic physiological needs and needs for safety or security, and those higher-level ego needs that can be linked directly to status. Pay, for example, may be valued by an individual because she believes it is a determinant of her social position within the community or because it constitutes a means for acquiring status symbols.

Intrinsic rewards are likely to be valued more by the individual after her lower-level needs have been largely satisfied. In other words, there must be an adequate level of satisfaction with the extrinsic rewards before intrinsic rewards can be utilized effectively. In order to make the subordinate's job more intrinsically rewarding, the manager may want to consider several actions.

Perhaps most important, the manager needs to provide meaningful work assignments, that is, work with which the subordinate can identify and become personally involved. He should establish challenging yet attainable goals or, in some cases, it may be more advantageous for him to create conditions that greatly enhance the likelihood that his subordinate will succeed, thus increasing the potential for attaining feelings of achievement, advancement, and recognition. The manager may also consider such means as increased delegation and job enlargement for extending the scope and depth of the subordinate's job and thereby increasing the subordinate's sense of responsibility and providing greater opportunity to make the job into something more compatible with his own interests.

In short, the manager should as best he can match the rewards at his disposal, both extrinsic and intrinsic, with what the subordinate indicates he or she needs or wants. Second, he should, by varying the magnitude and timing of the rewards granted, establish clearly in the subordinate's mind the desired effort-performance-reward contingencies.

Establishing the Contingencies   The contingency between effort and performance (that is, the extent to which the individual believes that by working harder, he will improve his performance) is largely a function of his confidence in his own abilities and his perceptions of the difficulty of the task and absence of obstacles standing in the way of successful task performance. When the effort-performance contingency is not clear for these reasons, the manager should consider several actions. She can reassign work or modify the task to be more consistent with the individual's perceptions of his own abilities, treat the problem as a "real" ability deficiency, remove the apparent performance obstacles, or simply reassure the individual.

The second contingency, the individual's belief that the rewards he receives reflect his accomplishments, is usually more difficult to establish. Here, two rather vexing predicaments are frequently encountered, both of which stem primarily from administration of extrinsic rewards. First, the instrument (usually a merit evaluation or performance appraisal device) may inaccurately measure the individual's contribution and thus his performance is rewarded in error. Reward schedules constitute the source of the second problem. Given fixed reward schedules (that is, the ubiquitous annual salary increase) adopted by the great majority of organizations, there is more frequently than not a considerable delay between task accomplishment and bestowal of the reward. As a result, the individual may not only fail to perceive the intended contingency but may incorrectly associate the reward with his behavior just prior to being rewarded. In other words, he may perceive a nonexistent contingency, and his subsequent behavior will reflect that contingency and, this time, go unrewarded.

Reward Schedules   The manner in which a given reward, or reinforcer, is scheduled is as strong a determinant of the effectiveness of that reward as is the value of the reward itself, or, for that matter, any other attribute of the reward. In organizations, the only plausible forms of reward schedules are intermittent as opposed to the continuous reward schedule in which the reward or punishment is administered after every behavioral sequence to be conditioned. In the case of the intermittent schedules, the behavior to be conditioned is reinforced only occasionally. There are four schedules of interest to the manager, each with varying effects on performance, as a number of investigations in the field of experimental psychology have revealed.

1. *Fixed-interval schedule:* Rewards are bestowed after a fixed period, usually

from the time the last reward was granted. This schedule is equivalent to the annual salary increase schedule in organizations, and its effects on performance are well-known. Typically, the individual "saves up," that is, she exerts a high level of effort just prior to the time of the reinforcement, usually her annual performance review. Her performance more than likely will then taper off until the time just prior to the next annual review.

2. *Variable-interval schedule:* Rewards are administered at designated time periods, but the intervals between the periods vary. For example, a reward may be given one day after the last rewarded behavior sequence, then three days later, then one week later, and so on, but only if the behavior to be conditioned actually occurs. This schedule results in fairly consistent rates of performance over long periods of time. Praise or other forms of social reinforcement from one's peers and superior, as an example, usually occur according to a variable-interval schedule not by intention, but simply because they are too involved with their own affairs to provide systematic reinforcement.

3. *Fixed-ratio schedule:* Reinforcement is provided after a fixed number of responses or performances by the individual. Incentive wage plans so frequently utilized in organizations constitute the prime example of this type of schedule. It is characterized by higher rates of effort than the interval schedules unless the ratio is large. When significant delays do occur between rewards, performance, much like in the fixed schedule, declines immediately after the reward is bestowed and improves again as the time for the next reward approaches.

4. *Variable-ratio schedule:* The reward is administered after a series of responses or performances, the number of which varies from the granting of one reward to the next. For example, an individual on a 15:1 variable-interval schedule might be reinforced after ten responses, then fifteen responses, then twenty responses, then ten responses, and so on, an average of one reinforcement for every fifteen responses. This schedule tends to result in performance that is higher than that of a comparable fixed-ratio schedule, and the variation in performance both before and after the occurrence of the reward or reinforcement is considerably less.

Virtually all managers must function within the contraints imposed by a fixed-interval schedule (annual salary schedule) or fixed-ratio schedule (wage incentives). However, this fact should not preclude consideration of the variable schedules, even within the framework of fixed schedules. Given their more positive effects on performance, such consideration is indeed highly desirable. It is conceivable, at least in a sales organization, for example, that monetary rewards (bonuses in this case) could be administered according to a variable-ratio schedule. From a more practical point of view, the entire range of nonmonetary rewards could be more profitably scheduled on a variable-interval basis, assuming that such scheduling was done in a systematic fashion.

CONCLUSIONS

This article has reviewed recent research concerning the relationship between satisfaction and performance and discussed the implications of the results of this research for the practicing manager. As noted at the outset, current speculation on the part of most practitioners and researchers continues to imply that satisfaction and performance are causally related, although confusion exists concerning the exact nature of the relationship. While the performance-causes-satisfaction proposition is a more recent development, the contention that satisfaction causes performance, nonetheless, remains the more widely held of the two beliefs, particularly among practitioners.

The recent research findings, however, offer only moderate support for the former view and conclusively reject the latter. Instead, the evidence provides rather strong indications that the relationship is more complex: (1) rewards constitute a more direct cause of satisfaction than does performance and (2) rewards based on current performance (and not satisfaction) cause subsequent performance.

For the manager who is concerned about the well-being of his subordinates, the implication of the finding that rewards cause satisfaction is self-evident. In order to achieve this end, the manager must provide rewards that have value or utility in terms of the subordinate's own need state and provide them in sufficient magnitude to be perceived as positively reinforcing. The manager whose goal is to increase a subordinate's performance, on the other hand, is faced with a more difficult task for two reasons. First, the relationship between rewards and performance is not a simple one. Second, there are other causes of performance—direction, the subordinate's ability, and existence of performance obstacles standing in the way of successful task performance—which the manager must deal also with.

The relationship between rewards and performance is complex because in reality there is at least one intervening variable and more than one contingency that needs to be established. An employee exerts high-level effort usually because of the valued rewards she associates with high performance. Effort, the intervening variable, may be considered a function of the value and magnitude of the reward and the extent to which the individual believes that high effort on her part will lead to high performance and that her high performance, in turn, will lead to rewards.

Therefore, the manager in addition to providing appropriate rewards, must establish contingencies between effort and performance and between performance and rewards. The first contingency, the extent to which the individual believes that "how hard he works" determines his performance, is perhaps the more readily established. This contingency is a function, at least in part, of the individual's confidence in his own abilities, his perceptions of the difficulty of the task, and the presence of performance obstacles. When a problem does arise here, the manager can take those actions indicated earlier in this article to overcome an apparent ability deficiency or performance obstacle. The performance-reward contingency requires the manager, by means of accurate performance appraisals and appropriate reward practices, to clearly establish in the subordinate's mind the belief that his own performance determines the magnitude of the rewards he will receive.

The establishment of this particular contingency, unfortunately, is becoming increasingly difficult as organizations continue to rely more heavily on fixed salary schedules and nonperformance-related factors (for example, seniority) as determinants of salary progression. However, the manager can, as a supplement to organizationally determined rewards, place more emphasis on nonmonetary rewards and both the cafeteria-style reward plans and variable-interval schedules for their administration.

It is apparent that the manager whose objective is to significantly improve subordinates' peformance has assumed a difficult but by no means impossible task. The path of least resistance—that is, increasing subordinates' satisfaction—simply will not work.

However, the actions suggested concerning reward practices and, particularly, establishment of appropriate performance-reward contingencies will result in improved performance, assuming that such improvement is not restricted by ability or direction problems or by performance obstacles. The use of differential rewards may require courage on the part of the manager, but failure to use them will have far more negative consequences. A subordinate will repeat that behavior which was rewarded, regardless of whether it resulted in high or low performance. A rewarded low performer, for example, will continue to perform poorly. With knowledge of this inequity, the high performer, in turn, will eventually reduce his or her own level of performance or seek employment elsewhere.

NOTES

1. Initial investigation by A. A. Kornhauser and A. W. Sharp, "Employee Attitudes: Suggestions from a Study in a Factory," *Personnel Journal* X (May 1932): 393–401.
   First quotation from Robert A. Sutermeister, "Employee Performance and Employee Need Satisfaction—Which Comes First?" *California Management Review* XIII (Summer 1971): 43.
   Second quotation from Donald P. Schwab and Larry L. Cummings, "Theories of Performance and Satisfaction: a Review," *Industrial Relations* IX (October 1970): 408–30.

2. Victor H. Vroom, *Work and Motivation* (New York: John Wiley & Sons, 1964).

3. Lyman W. Porter and Edward E. Lawler III, *Managerial Attitudes and Performance* (Homewood, Ill.: Richard D. Irwin, Inc., 1968).

4. Donald Bowen and Jacob P. Siegel, "The Relationship Between Satisfaction and Performance: The Question of Causality," paper presented at the annual meeting of the American Psychological Association, Miami Beach, September 1970.
   Charles N. Greene, "A Causal Interpretation of Relationship among Pay, Performance, and Satisfaction," paper presented at the annual meeting of the Midwest Psychological Association, Cleveland, Ohio, May 1972.

5. David J. Cherrington, H. Joseph Reitz, and William E. Scott, Jr., "Effects of Contingent and Non-contingent Reward on the Relationship Between Satisfaction and Task Performance," *Journal of Applied Psychology* LV (December 1971): 531–36.

6. Charles N. Greene, "Source and Direction of Causal Influence in Satisfaction-Performance Relationships," paper presented at the annual meetings of the Eastern Academy of Management, Boston, May 1972. Also reported in Greene, "Causal Connections Among Managers' Merit Pay, Satisfaction, and Performance," *Journal of Applied Psychology* 58, 1 (Jan.–Feb. 1973): 95–100.

7. For example, a recent study reported finding that relationships between the leader's initiating structure and both subordinate satisfaction and performance were moderated by such variables as role ambiguity, job scope, and task autonomy perceived by the subordinate. See Robert J. House, "A Path Goal Theory of Leader Effectiveness," *Administrative Science Quarterly* XVI (September 1971): 321–39.

8. Robert F. Mager and Peter Pipe, *Analyzing Performance Problems* (Belmont, Calif.: Lear Siegler, Inc., 1970), 21.

9. See, for example, J. D. Folley, Jr., "Determining Training Needs of Department Store Personnel," *Training Development Journal* XXIII (January 1969): 24–27, for a discussion of how the critical incidents approach can be employed to identify job skills to be learned in a formal training situation.

10. For a useful discussion of how ability levels can be upgraded by means of training and selection procedures, the reader can refer to Larry L. Cummings and Donald P. Schwab, *Performance in Organizations: Determinants and Appraisal* (Glenview, Ill.: Scott, Foresman & Co., 1972).

11. The discussion in this section is based in part on Cummings and Schwab, *Performance in Organizations*, and Lyman W. Porter and Edward E. Lawler III, "What Job Attitudes Tell About Motivation," *Harvard Business Review* LXVI (January-February 1968): 118–26.

12. Edward E. Lawler III, *Pay and Organizational Effectiveness: A Psychological View* (New York: McGraw-Hill, 1971).

A New Strategy for Job Enrichment

J. Richard Hackman

Greg Oldham

Robert Janson

Kenneth Purdy

Practitioners of job enrichment have been living through a time of excitement, even euphoria. Their craft has moved from the psychology and management journals to the front page and the Sunday supplement. Job enrichment, which began with the pioneering work of Herzberg and his associates, originally was intended as a means to increase the motivation and satisfaction of people at work—and to improve productivity in the bargain.[1, 2, 3, 4, 5] Now it is being acclaimed in the popular press as a cure for problems ranging from inflation to drug abuse.

Much current writing about job enrichment is enthusiastic, sometimes even messianic, about what it can accomplish. But the hard questions of exactly what should be done to improve jobs and how tend to be glossed over. Lately, because the harder questions have not been dealt with adequately, critical winds have begun to

J. Richard Hackman is associate professor of administrative sciences and psychology at Yale University. Greg Oldham is assistant professor of business administration at the University of Illinois. Robert Janson is vice-president of Roy W. Walters & Associates. Kenneth Purdy is a senior associate with Roy W. Walters & Associates.

The authors acknowledge with great appreciation the editorial assistance of John Hickey in the preparation of this paper and the help of Kenneth Brousseau, Daniel Feldman, and Linda Frank in collecting the data that are summarized here. The research activities reported were supported in part by the Organizational Effectiveness Research Program of the Office of Naval Research and the Manpower Administration of the U.S. Department of Labor, both through contracts to Yale University.

blow. Job enrichment has been described as yet another "management fad," as "nothing new," even as a fraud. And reports of job-enrichment failures are beginning to appear in management and psychology journals.

This article attempts to redress the excesses that have characterized some of the recent writings about job enrichment. As the technique increases in popularity as a management tool, top managers inevitably will find themselves making decisions about its use. The intent of this paper is to help both managers and behavioral scientists become better able to make those decisions on a solid basis of fact and data.

Succinctly stated, we present here a new strategy for going about the redesign of work. The strategy is based on three years of collaborative work and cross-fertilization among the authors—two of whom are academic researchers and two of whom are active practitioners in job enrichment. Our approach is new, but it has been tested in many organizations. It draws on the contributions of both management practice and psychological theory, but it is firmly in the middle ground between them. It builds on and complements previous work by Herzberg and others but provides for the first time a set of tools for *diagnosing* existing jobs and a map for translating the diagnostic results into specific actions step for change.

What we have, then, is the following:

1. A theory that specifies when people will get personally "turned on" to their work. The theory shows what kinds of jobs are most likely to generate excitement and commitment about work and what kinds of employees it works best for.

2. A set of action steps for job enrichment based on the theory, which prescribe in concrete terms what to do to make jobs more motivating for the people who do them.

3. Evidence that the theory holds water and that it can be used to bring about measurable—and sometimes dramatic—improvements in employee work behavior, in job satisfaction, and in the financial performance of the organizational unit involved.

THE THEORY BEHIND THE STRATEGY

What Makes People Get Turned on to Their Work?

For workers who are really prospering in their jobs, work is likely to be a lot like play. Consider, for example, a golfer at a driving range, practicing to get rid of a hook. His activity is *meaningful* to him; he has chosen to do it because he gets a "kick" from testing his skills by playing the game. He knows that he alone is *responsible* for what happens when he hits the ball. And he has *knowledge of the results* within a few seconds.

Behavioral scientists have found that the three "psychological states" experienced by the golfer in the above example also are critical in determining a person's motivation and satisfaction on the job.

1. *Experienced meaningfulness:* The individual must perceive his or her work as

worthwhile or important by some system of values he or she accepts.

2. *Experienced responsibility:* The individual must believe that he or she personally is accountable for the outcomes of his or her efforts.

3. *Knowledge of results:* The individual must be able to determine, on some fairly regular basis, whether or not the outcomes of his work are satisfactory.

When these three conditions are present, a person tends to feel very good about himself when he performs well. And those good feelings will prompt him to try to continue to do well—so he can continue to earn the positive feelings in the future. That is what is meant by "internal motivation"—being turned on to one's work because of the positive internal feelings that are generated by doing well, rather than being dependent on external factors (such as incentive pay or compliments from the boss) for the motivation to work effectively.

What if one of the three psychological states is missing? Motivation drops markedly. Suppose, for example, that our golfer has settled in at the driving range to practice for a couple of hours. Suddenly a fog drifts in over the range. He can no longer see if the ball starts to tail off to the left a hundred yards out. The satisfaction he got from hitting straight down the middle—and the motivation to try to correct something whenever he didn't—are both gone. If the fog stays, it's likely that he soon will be packing up his clubs.

The relationship between the three psychological states and on-the-job outcomes is illustrated in Figure 1. When all three are high, then internal work motivation, job satisfaction, and work quality are high, and absenteeism and turnover are low.

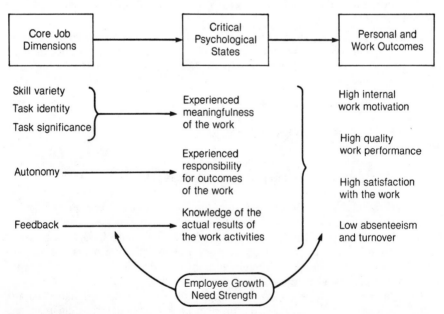

Figure 1   Relationships among core job dimensions, critical psychological states, and on-the-job outcomes

What Job Characteristics Make It Happen?

Recent research has identified five "core" characteristics of jobs that elicit the psychological states described above.[6,7,8] These five core job dimensions provide the key to objectively measuring jobs and to changing them so that they have high potential for motivating people who do them.

Toward Meaningful Work   Three of the five core dimensions contribute to a job's meaningfulness for the worker.

1. *Skill variety:* the degree to which a job requires the worker to perform activities that challenge skills and abilities. When even a single skill is involved, there is at least a seed of potential meaningfulness. When several are involved, the job has the potential of appealing to more of the whole person and also of avoiding the monotony of performing the same task repeatedly, no matter how much skill it may require.

2. *Task identity:* the degree to which the job requires completion of a "whole" and identifiable piece of work—doing a job from beginning to end with a visible outcome. For example, it is clearly more meaningful to an employee to build complete toasters than to attach electrical cord after electrical cord, especially if she never sees a completed toaster. (Note that the whole job, in this example, probably would involve greater skill variety as well as task identity.)

3. *Task significance:* the degree to which the job has a substantial and perceivable impact on the lives of other people, whether in the immediate organization or the world at large. The worker who tightens nuts on aircraft brake assemblies is more likely to perceive his work as significant than the worker who fills small boxes with paper clips—even though the skill levels involved may be comparable.

Each of these three job dimensions represents an important route to experienced meaningfulness. If the job is high in all three, the worker is quite likely to experience her job as very meaningful. It is not necessary, however, for a job to be very high in all three dimensions. If the job is low in any one of them, there will be a drop in overall experienced meaningfulness. But even when two dimensions are low, the worker may find the job meaningful if the third is high enough.

Toward Personal Responsibility   A fourth core dimension leads a worker to experience increased responsibility in his job. This is *autonomy*, the degree to which the job gives the worker freedom, independence, and discretion in scheduling work and determining how he will carry it out. People in highly autonomous jobs know that they are personally responsible for successes and failures. To the extent that their autonomy is high, then, how the work goes will be felt to depend more on the individual's own efforts and initiatives rather than on detailed instructions from the boss or from a manual of job procedures.

Toward Knowledge of Results   The fifth and last core dimension is *feedback*. This is the degree to which a worker, in carrying out the work activities required by the job, gets information about the effectiveness of his efforts. Feedback is most powerful when it comes directly from the work itself—for example, when a worker has the responsibility for gauging and otherwise checking a component he has just finished, and learns in the process that she has lowered his reject rate by meeting specifications more consistently.

The Overall "Motivating Potential" of a Job   Figure 1 shows how the five core dimensions combine to affect the psychological states that are critical in determining whether or not an employee will be internally motivated to work effectively. Indeed, when using an instrument to be described later, it is possible to compute a "motivating potential score" (MPS) for any job. The MPS provides a single summary index of the degree to which the objective characteristics of the job will prompt high internal work motivation. Following the theory outlined above, a job high in motivating potential must be high in at least one (and hopefully more) of the three dimensions that lead to experienced meaningfulness and high in both autonomy and feedback as well. The MPS provides a quantitative index of the degree to which this is in fact the case (see the Appendix at the end of this article for a detailed formula). As will be seen later, the MPS can be very useful in diagnosing jobs and in assessing the effectiveness of job-enrichment activities.

Does the Theory Work for Everybody?

Unfortunately not; not everyone is able to become internally motivated in his or her work, even when the motivating potential of a job is very high indeed. Research has shown that the *psychological needs* of people are very important in determining who can (and who cannot) become internally motivated at work. Some people have strong needs for personal accomplishment, for learning and developing themselves beyond where they are now, for being stimulated and challenged, and so on. These people are high in "growth-neeed strength."

Figure 2 shows diagrammatically the proposition that individual growth needs have the power to moderate the relationship between the characteristics of jobs and work outcomes. Many workers with high growth needs will turn on eagerly when they have jobs that are high in the core dimensions. Workers whose growth needs are not so strong may respond less eagerly—or at first even balk at being "pushed" or "stretched" too far.

Psychologists who emphasize human potential argue that everyone has within

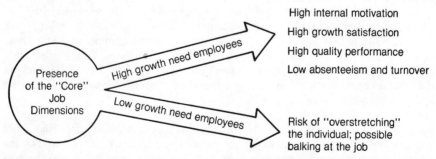

Figure 2   The moderating effect of employee growth-need strength.

him at least a spark of the need to grow and develop personally. Steadily accumulating evidence shows, however, that unless that spark is pretty strong, chances are it will get snuffed out by one's experiences in typical organizations. So, a person who has worked for twenty years in stultifying jobs may find it difficult or impossible to become internally motivated overnight when given the opportunity.

We should be cautious, however, about creating rigid categories of people based on their measured growth-need strength at any particular time. It is true that we can predict from these measures who is likely to become internally motivated on a job and who will be less willing or able to do so. But what we do not know yet is whether or not the growth-need "spark" can be rekindled for those individuals who have had their growth needs dampened by years of growth-depressing experience in their organizations.

Since it is often the organization that is responsible for currently low levels of growth desires, we believe that the organization also should provide the individual with the chance to reverse that trend whenever possible, even if that means putting a person in a job where she may be "stretched" more than she wants to be. She can always move back later to the old job—and in the meantime the embers of her growth needs just might burst back into flame, to her surprise and pleasure, and for the good of the organization.

FROM THEORY TO PRACTICE: A TECHNOLOGY FOR JOB ENRICHMENT

When job enrichment fails, it often fails because of inadequate *diagnosis* of the target job and employees' reactions to it. Often, for example, job enrichment is assumed by management to be a solution to "people problems" on the job and is implemented even though there has been no diagnostic activity to indicate that the root of the problem is in fact how the work is designed. At other times, some diagnosis is made—but it provides no concrete guidance about what specific aspects of the job require change. In either case, the success of job enrichment may wind up depending more on the quality of the intuition of the change agent—or his luck—than on a solid base of data about the people and the work.

In the paragraphs to follow, we outline a new technology for use in job enrichment that explicitly addresses the diagnostic as well as the action components of the change process. The technology has two parts: (1) a set of diagnostic tools that are useful in evaluating jobs and people's reactions to them prior to change—and in pinpointing exactly what aspects of specific jobs are most critical to a successful change attempt; and (2) a set of "implementing concepts" that provide concrete guidance for action steps in job enrichment. The implementing concepts are tied directly to the diagnostic tools; the output of the diagnostic activity specifies which action steps are likely to have the most impact in a particular situation.

The Diagnostic Tools

Central to the diagnostic procedure we propose is a package of instruments to be used by employees, supervisors, and outside observers in assessing the target job and employees' reactions to it.⁹ These instruments gauge the following:

1. The objective characteristics of the jobs themselves, including both an overall indication of the "motivating potential" of the job as it exists (that is, the MPS score) and the score of the job on each of the five core dimensions described previously. Because knowing the strength and weaknesses of the job is critical to any work-redesign effort, assessments of the job are made by supervisors and outside observers as well as the employees themselves; and the final assessment of a job uses data from all three sources.

2. The current levels of motivation, satisfaction, and work performance of employees on the job. In addition to satisfaction with the work itself, measures are taken of how people feel about other aspects of the work setting, such as pay, supervision, and relationships with co-workers.

3. The level of growth-need strength of the employees. As indicated earlier, employees who have strong growth needs are more likely to be more responsive to job enrichment than employees with weak growth needs. Therefore, it is important to know at the outset just what kinds of satisfactions the people who do the job are (and are not) motivated to obtain from their work. This will make it possible to identify which persons are best to start changes with and which may need help in adapting to the newly enriched job.

What, then, might be the actual steps one would take in carrying out a job diagnosis using these tools? Although the approach to any particular diagnosis depends upon the specifics of the particular work situation involved, the sequence of questions listed below is fairly typical.

Step 1. Are Motivation and Satisfaction Central to the Problem?   Sometimes organizations undertake job enrichment to improve the work motivation and satisfaction of employees when in fact the real problem with work performance lies elsewhere—for example, in a poorly designed production system, in an error-prone computer, and so on. The first step is to examine the scores of employees on the motivation and satisfaction portions of the diagnostic instrument. (The questionnaire taken by employees is called the Job Diagnostic Survey and will be referred to hereafter as the JDS.) If motivation and satisfaction are problematic, the change agent would continue to step 2; if not, she would look to other aspects of the work situation to identify the real problem.

Step 2. Is the Job Low in Motivating Potential?   To answer this question, one would examine the motivating potential score of the target job and compare it to the MPS's of other jobs to determine whether or not *the job itself* is a probable cause of the motivational problems documented in step 1. If the job turns out to be low on the MPS, one would continue to step 3; if it scores high, attention should be given to other possible reasons for the motivational difficulties (such as the pay system, the nature of supervision, and so on).

Step 3. What Specific Aspects of the Job are Causing the Difficulty?   This step involves examining the job on each of the five core dimensions to pinpoint the specific strengths and weaknesses of the job as it is currently structured. It is useful at this stage to construct a "profile" of the target job, to make visually apparent where improvements need to be made. An illustrative profile for two jobs (one "good" job and one job needing improvement) is shown in Figure 3.

Job A is an engineering maintenance job and is high on all of the core dimensions; the MPS of this job is a very high 260. (MPS scores can range from 1 to about 350; an "average" score would be about 125.) Job enrichment would not be recommended for this job; if employees working on the job were unproductive and unhappy, the reasons are likely to have little to do with the nature or design of the work itself.

Job B, on the other hand, has many problems. This job involves the routine and repetitive processing of checks in the "back room" of a bank. The MPS is 30, which is quite low—and indeed, would be even lower if it were not for the moderately high task significance of the job. (Task significance is moderately high because the people are handling large amounts of other people's money, and therefore the quality of their efforts potentially has important consequences for their unseen clients.) The job provides the individuals with very little direct feedback about how effectively they are doing it; the employees have little autonomy in how they go about doing the job; and the job is moderately low in both skill variety and task identity.

For Job B, then, there is plenty of room for improvement and many avenues to

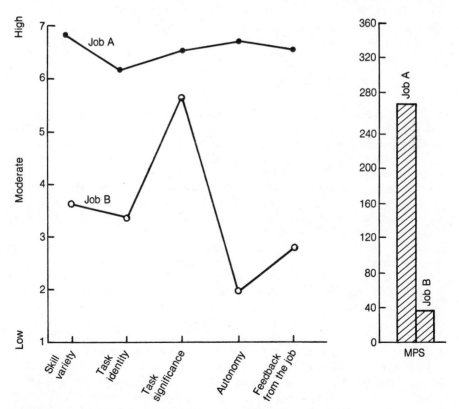

Figure 3   The JDS diagnostic profile for a "good" and a "bad" job

examine in planning job changes. For still other jobs, the avenues for change often turn out to be considerably more specific: for example, feedback and autonomy may be reasonably high, but one or more of the core dimensions that contribute to the experienced meaningfulness of the job (skill variety, task identity, and task significance) may be low. In such a case, attention would turn to ways to increase the standing of the job on these latter three dimensions.

Step 4. How "Ready" Are the Employees for Change?   Once it has been documented that there is need for improvement in the job—and the particularly troublesome aspects of the job have been identified—then it is time to begin to think about the specific action steps which will be taken to enrich the job. An important factor in such planning is the level of growth needs of the employees, since employees high on growth needs usually respond more readily to job enrichment than do employees with little need for growth. The JDS provides a direct measure of the growth-need strength of the employees. This measure can be very helpful in planning how to introduce the changes to the people (for instance, cautiously versus dramatically) and in deciding who should be among the first group of employees to have their jobs changed.

In actual use of the diagnostic package, additional information is generated which supplements and expands the basic diagnostic questions outlined above. The point of the above discussion is merely to indicate the kinds of questions we believe to be most important in diagnosing a job prior to changing it. We now turn to how the diagnostic conclusions are translated into specific job changes.

The Implementing Concepts

Five "implementing concepts" for job enrichment are identified and discussed below.[10] Each one is a specific action step aimed at improving both the quality of the working experience for the individual and his work productivity. They are: (1) forming natural work units, (2) combining tasks, (3) establishing client relationships, (4) vertical loading, and (5) opening feedback channels.

The links between the implementing concepts and the core dimensions are shown in Figure 4, which illustrates our theory of job enrichment, ranging from the concrete action steps through the core dimensions and the psychological states to the actual personal and work outcomes.

After completing the diagnosis of a job, a change agent would know which of the core dimensions were most in need of remedial attention. He could then turn to Figure 4 and select those implementing concepts that specifically deal with the most troublesome parts of the existing job. How this would take place in practice will be seen below.

Forming Natural Work Units   The notion of distributing work in some logical way may seem to be an obvious part of the design of any job. In many cases, however, the logic is one imposed by just about any consideration except jobholder satisfaction and motivation. Such considerations include technological dictates, level of worker training or experience, "efficiency" as defined by industrial engineering, and current workload. In many cases the cluster of tasks a worker faces during a typical day or week is natural to anyone *but* the worker.

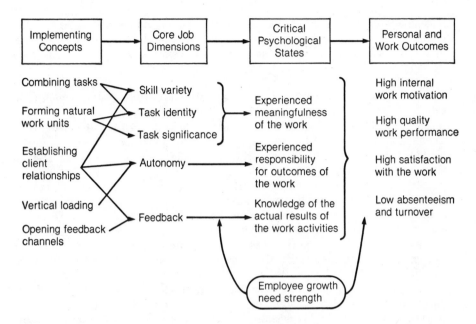

Figure 4   The full model: how use of the implementing concepts can lead to positive outcomes

For example, suppose that a typing pool (consisting of one supervisor and ten typists) handles all work for one division of a company. Jobs are delivered in rough draft or dictated form to the supervisor, who distributes them as evenly as possible among the typists. In such circumstances the individual letters, reports, and other tasks performed by a given typist in one day or week are randomly assigned. There is no basis for identifying with the work or the person or department for whom it is performed or for placing any personal value upon it.

The principle underlying natural units of work, by contrast, is "ownership"—a worker's sense of continuing responsibility for an identifiable body of work. Two steps are involved in creating natural work units. The first is to identify the basic work items. In the typing pool, for example, the items might be "pages to be typed." The second step is to group the items in natural categories. For example, each typist might be assigned continuing responsibility for all jobs requested by one or several specific departments. The assignments should be made, of course, in such a way that workloads are about equal in the long run. (For example, one typist might end up with all the work from one busy department, while another handles jobs from several smaller units.)

At this point we can begin to see specifically how the job-design principles relate to the core dimensions (compare with Figure 4). The ownership fostered by natural units of work can make the difference between a feeling that work is meaningful and rewarding and the feeling that it is irrelevant and boring. As the diagram shows, natural units of work are directly related to two of the core dimensions: task identity and task significance.

A typist whose work is assigned naturally rather than randomly—say, by departments—has a much greater chance of performing a whole job to completion.

Instead of typing one section of a large report, the individual is likely to type the whole thing, with knowledge of exactly what the product of the work is (task identity). Furthermore, over time the typist will develop a growing sense of how the work affects co-workers in the department serviced (task significance).

Combining Tasks   The very existence of a pool made up entirely of persons whose sole function is typing reflects a fractionalization of jobs that has been a basic precept of "scientific management." Most obvious in assembly-line work, fractionalization has been applied to nonmanufacturing jobs as well. It is typically justified by efficiency, which is usually defined in terms of either low costs or some time-and-motion type of criteria.

It is hard to find fault with measuring efficiency ultimately in terms of cost effectiveness. In doing so, however, a manager should be sure to consider *all* the costs involved. It is possible, for example, for highly fractionalized jobs to meet all the time-and-motion criteria of efficiency, but if the resulting job is so unrewarding that performing it day after day leads to high turnover, absenteeism, drugs and alcohol, and strikes, then productivity is really lower (and costs higher) than data on efficiency might indicate.

The principle of combining tasks, then, suggests that whenever possible existing and fractionalized tasks should be put together to form new and larger modules of work. At the Medfield, Massachusetts, plant of Corning Glass Works, the assembly of a laboratory hot plate has been redesigned along the lines suggested here. Each hot plate now is assembled from start to finish by one operator, instead of going through several separate operations that are performed by different people.

Some tasks, if combined into a meaningfully large module of work, would be more than an individual could do by herself. In such cases, it is often useful to consider assigning the new, larger task to a small *team* of workers, who are given great autonomy for its completion. At the Racine, Wisconsin, plant of Emerson Electric, the assembly process for trash disposal appliances was restructured this way. Instead of a sequence of moving the appliance from station to station, the assembly now is done from start to finish by one team. Such teams include both men and women to permit switching off the heavier and more delicate aspects of the work. The team responsible is identified on the appliance. In case of customer complaints, the team often drafts the reply.

As a job-design principle, task combination, like natural units of work, expands the task identify of the job. For example, the hot-plate assembler can see and identify with a finished product ready for shipment rather than a nearly invisible junction of solder. Moreover, the more tasks that are combined into a single worker's job, the greater the variety of skills he must call on in performing the job. So task combination also leads directly to greater skill variety—the third core dimension that contributes to the overall experienced meaningfulness of the work.

Establishing Client Relationships   One consequence of fractionalization is that the typical worker has little or no contact with (or even awareness of) the ultimate user of her product or service. By encouraging and enabling employees to establish direct relationships with the clients of their work, improvements often can be realized simultaneously on three of the core dimensions. Feedback increases, because of additional opportunities for the individual to receive praise or criticism of her work outputs directly. Skill variety often increases, because of the necessity to develop and exercise one's interpersonal skills in maintaining the client relationship. And autonomy can increase, because the individual often is given personal responsibility for deciding how to manage her relationships with the clients of her work.

Creating client relationships is a three-step process. First, the client must be identified. Second, the most direct contact possible between the worker and the client must be established. Third, criteria must be set up by which the client can judge the quality of the product or service he receives. And whenever possible, the client should have a means of relaying his judgments directly back to the worker.

The contact between worker and client should be as great as possible and as frequent as necessary. Face-to-face contact is highly desirable, at least occasionally. Where that is impossible or impractical, telephone and mail can suffice. In any case, it is important that the performance criteria by which the worker will be rated by the client must be mutually understood and agreed upon.

Vertical Loading   Typically the split between the "doing" of a job and the "planning" and "controlling" of the work has evolved along with horizontal fractionalization. Its rationale, once again, has been "efficiency through specialization." And once again, the excess of specialization that has emerged has resulted in unexpected but significant costs in motivation, morale, and work quality. In vertical loading, the intent is to partially close the gap between the doing and the controlling parts of the job, and thereby reap some important motivational advantages.

Of all the job-design principles, vertical loading may be the single most crucial one. In some cases, where it has been impossible to implement any other changes, vertical loading alone has had significant motivational effects. When a job is vertically loaded, responsibilities and controls that formerly were reserved for higher levels of management are added to the job. There are many ways to accomplish this:

1. Return to the job holder greater discretion in setting schedules, deciding on work methods, checking on quality, and advising or helping to train less experienced workers.

2. Grant additional authority. The objective should be to advance workers from a position of no authority or highly restricted authority to positions of reviewed, and eventually, near-total authority for his own work.

3. Time management—the job holder should have the greatest possible freedom to decide when to start and stop work, when to break, and how to assign priorities.

4. Troubleshooting and crisis decisions—workers should be encouraged to seek problem solutions on their own rather than calling immediately for the supervisor.

5. Financial controls—some degree of knowledge and control over budgets and other financial aspects of a job can often be highly motivating. However, access to this information frequently tends to be restricted. Workers can benefit from knowing something about the costs of their jobs, and potential effect upon profit, and various financial and budgetary alternatives.

When a job is vertically loaded it will inevitably increase in *autonomy*. And as shown in Figure 4, this increase in objective personal control over the work will also lead to an increased feeling of personal responsibility for the work, and ultimately to higher internal work motivation.

Opening Feedback Channels   In virtually all jobs there are ways to open channels of feedback to individuals or teams to help them learn whether their performance is improving, deteriorating, or remaining at a constant level. While there are numerous channels through which information about performance can be provided, it generally is better for a worker to learn about his performance *directly as he does his job*—rather than from management on an occasional basis.

Job-provided feedback is usually more immediate and private than supervisor-supplied feedback, and it increases the worker's feelings of personal control over his work in the bargain. Moreover, it avoids many of the potentially disruptive interpersonal problems that can develop when the only way a worker has to find out how he is doing is through direct messages or subtle cues from the boss.

Exactly what should be done to open channels for job-provided feedback will vary from job to job and organization to organization. Yet in many cases the changes involve simply removing existing blocks that isolate the worker from naturally occuring data about performances rather than generating entirely new feedback mechanisms. For example:

1. Establishing direct client relationships often removes blocks between the worker and natural external sources of data about his work.

2. Quality-control efforts in many organizations often eliminate a natural source of feedback. The quality check on a product or service is done by persons other than those responsible for the work. Feedback to the workers—if there is any—is belated and diluted. It often fosters a tendency to think of quality as "someone else's concern." By placing quality control close to the worker (perhaps even in her own hands), the quantity and quality of data about performance available to her can dramatically increase.

3. Tradition and established procedure in many organizations dictate that records about performance be kept by a supervisor and transmitted up (not down) in the organizational hierarchy. Sometimes supervisors even check the work and correct any errors themselves. The worker who made the error never knows it occurred and is denied the very information that could enhance both his internal work motivation and the technical adequacy of his performance. In many cases it is possible to provide standard summaries of performance records directly to the worker (as well as to his superior), thereby giving him personally and regularly the data he needs to improve his performance.

4. Computers and other automated operations can sometimes be used to provide the individual with data now blocked from her. Many clerical operations, for example, are now performed on computer consoles. These consoles can often be programmed to provide the clerk with immediate feedback in the form of a CRT display or a printout indicating that an error has been made. Some systems have even been programmed to provide the operator with a positive feedback message when a period of error-free performance has been sustained.

Many organizations simply have not recognized the importance of feedback as a motivator. Data on quality and other aspects of performance are viewed as being of interest only to management. Worse still, the *standards* for acceptable performance are often kept from workers as well. As a result, workers who would be interested in following the daily or weekly ups and downs of their performance and in trying accordingly to improve are deprived of the very guidelines they need to do so. They are like the golfer we mentioned earlier, whose efforts to correct his hook are stopped dead by fog over the driving range.

THE STRATEGY IN ACTION: HOW WELL DOES IT WORK?

So far we have examined a basic theory of how people get turned on to their work, a set of core dimensions of jobs that create the conditions for such internal work motivation to develop on the job, and a set of five implementing concepts that are the action steps recommended to boost a job on the core dimensions and thereby increase employee motivation, satisfaction, and productivity.

The remaining question is straightforward and important: *Does it work?* In reality, that question is twofold. First, does the theory itself hold water, or are we barking up the wrong conceptual tree? And second, does the change strategy really lead to measurable differences when it is applied in an actual organizational setting? This section summarizes the findings we have generated to date on these questions.

Is the Job Enrichment Theory Correct?

In general, the answer seems to be yes. The JDS instrument has been taken by more than 1,000 employees working on about one hundred diverse jobs in more than a dozen organizations over the last two years. These data have been analyzed to test the basic motivational theory and especially the impact of the core job dimensions on worker motivation, satisfaction, and behavior on the job. An illustrative overview of some of the findings is given below.[8]

1. People who work on jobs high on the core dimensions are more motivated and satisfied than are people who work on jobs that score low on the dimensions. Employees with jobs high on the core dimensions (MPS scores greater than 240) were compared to those who held unmotivating jobs (MPS scores less than 40). As shown in Figure 5, employees with high MPS jobs were higher on (a) the three psychological states, (b) internal work motivation, (c) general satisfaction, and (d) "growth" satisfaction.

2. Figure 6 shows that the same is true for measures of actual behavior at work—absenteeism and performance effectiveness—although less strongly so for the performance measure.

3. Responses to jobs high in motivating potential are more positive for people who have strong growth needs than for people with weak needs for growth. In Figure 7 the linear relationship between the motivating potential of a job and employees' level of internal work motivation is shown, separately for people with high versus low growth needs as measured by the JDS. While both groups of employees show increases in internal motivation as MPS increases, the *rate* of increase is significantly greater for the group of employees who have strong needs for growth.

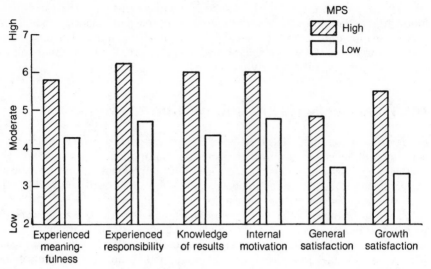

Figure 5   Employee reactions to jobs high and low in motivating potential for two banks and a steel firm

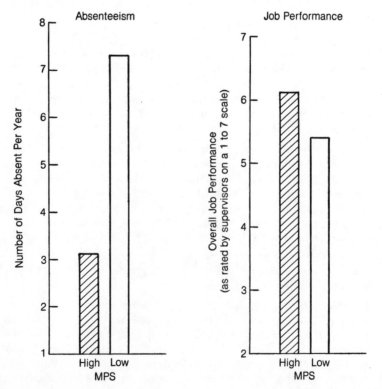

Figure 6   Absenteeism and job performance for employees with jobs high and low in motivating potential

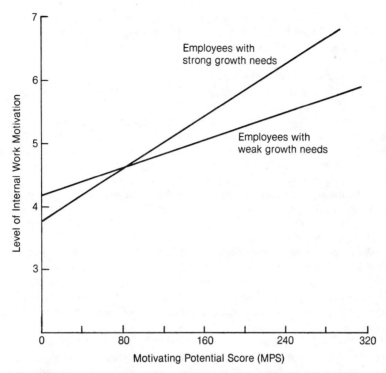

Figure 7. Relationship between the motivating potential of a job and the internal work motivation of employees (shown separately for employees with strong versus weak growth-need strength)

How Does the Change Strategy Work in Practice?

The results summarized above suggest that both the theory and the diagnostic instrument work when used with real people in real organizations. In this section, we summarize a job-enrichment project conducted at the Travelers Insurance Companies, which illustrates how the change procedures work in practice.

The Travelers project was designed with two purposes in mind. One was to achieve improvements in morale, productivity, and other indicators of employee well-being; the other was to test the general effectiveness of the strategy for job enrichment that we have summarized in this article.

The work group chosen was a keypunching operation. The group's function was to transfer information from printed or written documents onto punched cards for computer input. The work group consisted of ninety-eight keypunch operators and verifiers (both in the same job classification), plus seven assignment clerks. All reported to a supervisor who, in turn, reported to the assistant manager and manager of the data-input division.

The size of individual punching orders varied considerably, from a few cards to as many as 2,500. Some work came to the work group with a specified delivery date, while other orders were to be given routine service on a predetermined schedule. Assignment clerks received the jobs from the user departments. After reviewing the work for obvious errors, omissions, and legibility problems, the assignment clerk parceled out the work in batches expected to take about one hour. If the clerk found the work not suitable for punching, it went to the supervisor, who either returned the work to the user department or cleared up problems by phone. When work went to operators for punching, it was with the instruction, "Punch only what you see. Don't correct errors, no matter how obvious they look."

Because of the high cost of computer time, keypunched work was 100 percent verified—a task that consumed nearly as many man-hours as the punching itself. Then the cards went to the supervisor, who screened the jobs for due dates before sending them to the computer. Errors detected in verification were assigned to various operators at random to be corrected. The computer output from the cards was sent to the originating department, accompanied by a printout of errors. Eventually the printout went back to the supervisor for final correction.

A great many phenomena indicated that the problems being experienced in the work group might be the result of poor motivation. As the only person performing supervisory functions of any kind, the supervisor spent most of his time responding to crisis situations, which recurred continually. He also had to deal almost daily with employees' salary grievances or other complaints. Employees frequently showed apathy or outright hostility toward their jobs.

Rates of work output, by accepted work-measurement standards, were inadequate. Error rates were high. Due dates and schedules frequently were missed. Absenteeism was higher than average, especially before and after weekends and holidays.

The single, rather unusual exception was turnover. It was lower than the companywide average for similar jobs. The company has attributed this fact to a poor job market in the base period just before the project began and to an older, relatively more settled work force made up, incidentally, entirely of women.

The Diagnosis   Using some of the tools and techniques we have outlined, a consulting team from the Management Services Department and from Roy W. Walters & Associates concluded that the keypunch-operator's job exhibited the following serious weaknesses in terms of the core dimensions.

> Skill variety: there was none. Only a single skill was involved—the ability to punch adequately the data on the batch of documents.
>
> Task identity: virtually nonexistent. Batches were assembled to provide an even workload but not whole identifiable jobs.
>
> Task significance: not apparent. The keypunching operation was a necessary step in providing service to the company's customers. The individual operator was isolated by an assignment clerk and a supervisor from any knowledge of what the operation meant to the using department, let alone its meaning to the ultimate customer.
>
> Autonomy: none. The operators had no freedom to arrange their daily tasks to meet schedules, to resolve problems with the using department, or even to correct, in punching, information that was obviously wrong.
>
> Feedback: none. Once a batch was out of the operator's hands, she had no assured chance of seeing evidence of its quality or inadequacy.

Design of the Experimental Trial   Since the diagnosis indicated that the motivating potential of the job was extremely low, it was decided to attempt to improve the motivation and productivity of the work group through job enrichment. Moreover, it was possible to design an experimental test of the effects of the changes to be introduced: the results of changes made in the target work group were to be compared with trends in a control work group of similar size and demographic makeup. Since the control group was located more than a mile away, there appeared to be little risk of communication between members of the two groups.

A base period was defined before the start of the experimental trial period, and appropriate data were gathered on the productivity, absenteeism, and work attitudes of members of both groups. Data also were available on turnover, but since turnover was already below average in the target group, prospective changes in this measure were deemed insignificant.

An educational session was conducted with supervisors at which they were given the theory and implementing concepts and actually helped to design the job changes themselves. Out of this session came an active plan consisting of about twenty-five change items that would significantly affect the design of the target jobs.

The Implementing Concepts and the Changes   Because the job as it existed was rather uniformly low on the core job dimensions, all five of the implementing concepts were used in enriching it.

Natural units of work. The random batch assignment of work was replaced by assigning to each operator continuing responsiblity for certain accounts— either particular departments or particular recurring jobs. Any work for those accounts now always goes to the same operator.

Task combination. Some planning and controlling functions were combined with the central task of keypunching. In this case, however, these additions can be more suitably discussed under the remaining three implementing concepts.

Client relationships. Each operator was given several channels of direct contact with clients. The operators, not their assignment clerks, now inspect their documents for correctness and legibility. When problems arise, the operator, not the supervisor, takes them up with the client.

Feedback. In addition to feedback from client contact, the operators were provided with a number of additional sources of data about their performance. The computer department now returns incorrect cards to the operators who punched them, and operators correct their own errors. Each operator also keeps her own file of copies of her errors. These can be reviewed to determine trends in error frequency and types of errors. Each operator receives a weekly computer printout of her errors and productivity, which is sent to her directly rather than given to her by the supervisor.

Vertical loading. Besides consulting directly with clients about work questions, operators now have the authority to correct obvious coding errors on their own. Operators may set their own schedules and plan their daily work, as long as they meet schedules. Some competent operators have been given the option of not verifying their work and making their own program changes.

Results of the Trial   The results were dramatic. The number of operators declined from ninety-eight to sixty. This occurred partly through attrition and partly through transfer to other departments. Some of the operators were promoted to higher-paying jobs in departments whose cards they had been handling—something that had never occurred before. Some details of the results are given below.

Quantity of work. The control group, with no job changes made, showed an increase in productivity of 8.1 percent during the trial period. The experimental group showed an increase of 39.6 percent.

Error rates. To assess work quality, error rates were recorded for about forty operators in the experimental group. All were experienced, and all had been in their jobs before the job-enrichment program began. For two months before the study, these operators had a collective error rate of 1.53 percent. For two months toward the end of the study, the collective error rate was 0.99 percent. By the end of the study the number of operators with poor performance had dropped from 11.1 percent to 5.5 percent.

Absenteeism. The experimental group registered a 24.1 percent decline in absences. The control group, by contrast, showed a 29 percent *increase*.

Attitudes toward the job. An attitude survey given at the start of the project showed that the two groups scored about average, and nearly identically, in nine different areas of work satisfaction. At the end of the project, the survey was repeated. The control group showed an insignificant 0.5 percent improvement, while the experimental group's overall satisfaction score rose 16.5 percent.

Selective elimination of controls. Demonstrated improvements in operator proficiency permitted them to work with fewer controls. Travelers estimates that the reduction of controls had the same effect as adding seven operators—a saving even beyond the effects of improved productivity and lowered absenteeism.

Role of the supervisor. One of the most significant findings in the Travelers experiment was the effect of the changes on the supervisor's job and thus on the rest of the organization. The operators took on many responsibilities that had been reserved at least to the unit leaders and sometimes to the supervisor. The unit leaders, in turn, assumed some of the day-to-day supervisory functions that had plagued the supervisor. Instead of spending his days supervising the behavior of subordinates and dealing with crises, he was able to devote time to developing feedback systems, setting up work modules and spearheading the enrichment effort—in other words, managing. It should be noted, however, that helping supervisors change their own work activities when their subordinates' jobs have been enriched is itself a challenging task. And if appropriate attention and help are not given to supervisors in such cases, they can rapidly become disaffected—and a job-enrichment "backlash" can result.[11]

Summary   By applying work-measurement standards to the changes wrought by job enrichment—attitude and quality, absenteeism, and selective administration of controls—Travelers was able to estimate the total dollar impact of the project.

Actual savings in salaries and machine rental charges during the first year totaled $64,305. Potential savings by further application of the changes were put at $91,937 annually. Thus, by almost any measure used—from the work attitudes of individual employees to dollar savings for the company as a whole—the Travelers test of the job-enrichment strategy proved a success.

CONCLUSIONS

In this article we have presented a new strategy for the redesign of work in general and for job enrichment in particular. The approach has four main characteristics:

1. It is grounded in a basic psychological theory of what motivates people in their work.

2. It emphasizes that planning for job changes should be done on the basis of *data* about the jobs and the people who do them—and a set of diagnostic instruments is provided to collect such data.

3. It provides a set of specific implementing concepts to guide actual job changes, as well as a set of theory-based rules for selecting *which* action steps are likely to be most beneficial in a given situation.

4. The strategy is buttressed by a set of findings showing that the theory holds water, that the diagnostic procedures are practical and informative, and that the implementing concepts can lead to changes that are beneficial both to organizations and to the people who work in them.

We believe that job enrichment is moving beyond the stage where it can be considered "yet another management fad." Instead, it represents a potentially powerful strategy for change that can help organizations achieve their goals for higher quality work and at the same time further the equally legitimate needs of contemporary employees for a more meaningful work experience. Yet there are pressing questions about job enrichment and its use that remain to be answered.

Prominent among these is the question of employee participation in planning and implementing work redesign. The diagnostic tools and implementing concepts we have presented are neither designed nor intended for use only by management. Rather, our belief is that the effectiveness of job enrichment is likely to be enhanced when the tasks of diagnosing and changing jobs are undertaken *collaboratively* by management and by the employees whose work will be affected.

Moreover, the effects of work redesign on the broader organization remain generally uncharted. Evidence is now accumulating that when jobs are changed, turbulence can appear in the surrounding organization—for example, in supervisory-subordinate relationships, in pay and benefit plans, and so on. Such turbulence can be viewed by management either as a problem with job enrichment or as an opportunity for further and broader organizational development by teams of managers and employees. To the degree that management takes the latter view, we believe, the oft-espoused goal of achieving basic organizational change through the redesign of work may come increasingly within reach.

The diagnostic tools and implementing concepts we have presented are useful in deciding on and designing basic changes in the jobs themselves. They do not address the broader issues of who plans the changes, how they are carried out, and how they are followed up. The way these broader questions are dealt with, we believe, may determine whether job enrichment will grow up or whether it will die an early and unfortunate death, like so many other fledgling behavioral-science approaches to organizational change.

APPENDIX

For the algebraically inclined, the motivating potential score is computed as follows

$$\text{MPS} = \left[\frac{\text{Skill Variety} + \text{Task Identity} + \text{Task Significance}}{3} \right] \times \text{Autonomy} \times \text{Feedback}$$

It should be noted that in some cases the MPS score can be *too* high for positive job satisfaction and effective performance, in effect overstimulating the person who holds the job. This paper focuses on jobs which are toward the low end of the scale and which potentially can be improved through job enrichment.

NOTES

1. F. Herzberg, B. Mausner, and B. Snyderman, *The Motivation to Work* (New York: John Wiley & Sons, 1959).
2. F. Herzberg, *Work and the Nature of Man* (Cleveland: World, 1966).
3. F. Herzberg, "One More Time: How Do You Motivate Employees?" *Harvard Business Review* (1968): 53–62.
4. W. J. Paul, Jr., K. B. Robertson, and F. Herzberg, "Job Enrichment Pays Off," *Harvard Business Review* (1969): 61–78.
5. R. N. Ford, *Motivation Through the Work Itself* (New York: American Management Association, 1969).
6. A. N. Turner and P. R. Lawrence, *Industrial Jobs and the Worker* (Cambridge, Mass.: Harvard Graduate School of Business Administration, 1965).
7. J. R. Hackman and E. E. Lawler, "Employee Reactions to Job Characteristics," *Journal of Applied Psychology Monograph* (1971): 259–86.
8. J. R. Hackman and G. R. Oldham, *Motivation Through the Design of Work: Test of a Theory*, Technical Report No. 6, Department of Administration Sciences, Yale University, 1974.
9. J. R. Hackman and G. R. Oldham, "Development of the Job Diagnostic Survey," *Journal of Applied Psychology* (1975): 159–70.
10. R. W. Walters and Associates, *Job Enrichment for Results* (Cambridge, Mass.: Addison-Wesley, 1975).
11. E. E. Lawler III, J. R. Hackman, and S. Kaufman, "Effects of Job Redesign: A Field Experiment," *Journal of Applied Social Psychology* (1973): 49–62.

Public Sector Applications of Flexible Work Hours: A Review of Available Experience

Robert T. Golembiewski

Carl W. Proehl, Jr.

Programs of flexible workhours—henceforth, flexitime or F-T—have proliferated around the world, and most observers associate them with a broad range of positive effects for organizations as well as for their members, in personal life as well as at work. F-T may rightly be said to be a major managerial innovation, simple though it seems.

The innovation initially permeated business organizations and lately is getting much more public sector notice.[1] Paradoxically, the diffusion of this innovation has proceeded apace, in both arenas, without two crucial kinds of knowledge: a comprehensive review of the available F-T literature and a sophisticated understanding of why, when, and how F-T "works."

HOW GOES IT WITH F-T IN THE PRIVATE SECTOR?

The only available review of the literature[2] implies the common wisdom is quite justified in terms of global outcomes, especially in business-sector applications, even though we lack an understanding of the specifics of why and how F-T "works." The review covered twenty studies involving seventy-nine separate applications, with all but five coming from private-sector experience. Overall, F-T seems to generate positive effects under a broad range of conditions. The reviewers conclude in that summary effort.[3]

> Despite real limitations in available studies, both behavioral and attitudinal data encourage F-T applications. "Hard" data indicate that F-T is at least low-cost and may indeed imply handsome dividends on several critical organizational measures. "Soft" data strongly reinforce such a bias toward F-T applications, as seen from three organizational perspectives—that of employees, first-line supervisors, and managers.

These conclusions derive from a panel of studies which make a serious effort to track F-T effects and which report them in sufficient detail to permit some confidence about interpretations. This panel was selected from a mass of bibliographic citations—dominantly boosterish in tone and anecdotal and impressionistic when describing effects—which now run into the hundreds. The citations come from published sources, in the main, but also include in-house studies, dissertations, and studies by external consultants. Our definition of what constitues a "serious effort to track F-T effects" would not satisfy rigorous canons of empirical research, but it does exclude the more casual efforts.

The optimistic findings of the summary review have survived an additional eighteen months of search. Data concerning an additional 130 applications, again dominantly from business, have been found that meet our general criteria. They require no substantive changes in the interpretations of the original review.[4]

THE APPROACH TO PUBLIC SECTOR APPLICATIONS

What may be said of F-T applications in the public sector? Globally, the literature reflects two themes: hurry up and wait. The "hurry up" theme is well represented by Rubin's recent article,[5] which deftly describes the F-T notion, summarizes its anticipated advantages, suggests that now is the time to get on with more public sector applications but only gently reviews the available public sector experience. The "wait" theme gets profound expression in the ongoing research plans of the U.S. Office of Personnel Management, now into a three-year program of research on F-T even as applications burgeon.

This article proposes to slip between these two common public sector emphases. How? Our evolving panel of "serious" F-T studies now contains thirty-two public sector bibliographic items, involving seventy-four applications. These will be analyzed below basically via interpretation of four tabular summaries. In order, the tables

1. present an overview of major characteristics of the 32 public-sector studies;
2. review behavioral effects of F-T applications observed in public agencies;
3. summarize F-T's major effects on employee attitudes; and
4. provide perspective on the major supervisory attitudes related to F-T.

Generally, the model for analysis in the original review will be followed below.

Note that the thirty-two F-T citations are distinguished in the tables below in a major sense. Thirty citations deal with applications at one site or within one unit of government, applications about which we have been able to secure specific evaluation reports, either from published or internal sources. Two summary studies— each reviewing twenty-two applications—also are listed below the broken line toward the bottom of the several tables below. Of the latter forty-four applications, fourteen are described individually above the broken line. Original evaluations concerning the remaining cases in the two summary studies were not available to us.

MAJOR CHARACTERISTICS
OF PUBLIC SECTOR APPLICATIONS

The panel of public sector studies has at least seven major characteristics, as Table 1 helps establish. First, as an important preliminary note, F-T applications can differ significantly, as in the degree of employee discretion they permit. Many versions allow employees to change their hours of work without notice, day by day; but a few require prior clearance with supervisors and no subsequent change without notice. Similarly, some versions permit "banking" of excess hours, worked one day to be used to reduce hours worked another day or week or even month. Other plans permit no banking, in contrast, so starting time determines quitting time.

Table 1 does not distinguish these and other program variants, given the small number of cases. Possibly, perhaps even probably, such distinctions may isolate significantly different clusters of effects in larger data batches or in research comparing alternative ways in which individuals can influence their work hours.[6]

Second, public sector studies provide little specific insight about desirable models of implementation. Hence Table 1 stands moot on this critical point. This deficiency also characterizes the private sector literature, albeit in lesser degree. Some may even argue that it does not make much difference, in that we have been able to unearth only two F-T applications that "did not work" and those in organizations which saw F-T autocratically and foolishly imposed.

While holding out the possibility that even autocratic and top-down implementation may succeed, more often than not we encourage building into F-T applications numerous opportunities for involvement, participation, and even broadly based veto. Illustratively, in a major business application, the full implementation cycle had these major features *from the outset*:[39]

All line managers in a large R and D operation were presented several options for increasing employee freedom and discretion at work, including the F-T concept

Possible advantages/disadvantages of the several options were discussed in terms of how each option "would work here"

All managers committed to try a lengthy pilot study with one F-T variant within a part of R and D, which variant they helped design

All managers helped develop an evaluation effort whose data they agreed would permit them to determine the success or failure of the pilot *in their eyes*

Several of the managers volunteered their units as experimental and comparison groups for the duration of the pilot study, after checking with their subordinates

At the conclusion of the pilot study, and utilizing both attitudinal and performance measures, managers decided about continuation and further diffusion of the F-T variant.

When word about the experiment and its subsequent diffusion to all of R and D spread, corporate officials at first wanted to extend the F-T variant throughout headquarters' operations in one fell-swoop. Consistent with the design above, however, they were urged alternatively to specify only the maximum F-T properties to which they were willing to commit. With the help of corporate personnel, major cost centers then could variously decide on specific F-T variants—to suit different kinds of work, employee preferences, and so on. Almost all cost centers decided to implement F-T, using basically four variant designs, which variously approached the maxima authorized by corporate officials.[40]

Third, existing F-T applications in the public sector clearly cluster in a narrow range: they often relate to professional and clerical jobs in white-collar settings and

Table 1 Overview of panel of public-sector studies reporting specific flexitime effects

Study	Setting	Union involved?	Study design	Comparison group(s)?	Hard/soft data?	Statistical treatment?
Air University, Maxwell A.F.B. Alabama (1975)[7]	100 employees	?	Post only	No	S	None
Atlanta Regional Commission (1969)[8]	All employees (approx. 60) in metro planning agency	No	Post/long post	No	S	None
Crawford (1979)[9]	Four departments, Prince George, Maryland County government	Yes	Post only	No	S	None
District of Columbia (1975)[10]	300 employees in Department of Human Resources	?	Generally post only; some pre/post comparisons	No	H/S	None
Environmental Protection Agency (1977, 1978)[11]	Headquarters, Environmental Protection Agency	?	Generally post only; some pre/post comparisons	No	H/S	None
Finegan (1977); Bureau of Government Financial Operations (1975, 1976)[12]	1450 employees, U.S. Treasury Department	?	Generally post only; some pre/post comparisons	No	H/S	None
Finkle (1979)[13]	950 employees in five New Jersey State agencies	?	Pre/post	No	H/S	None
General Services Administration (1977)[14]	100 employees of National Personnel Records Center 26 employees of Central Reference Division of Office of National Archives	?	Pre/post	No	H/S	None
Giammo (1977); Social Security Administration (1974)[15]	Eight offices and bureaus of the Social Security Administration	Yes	Pre/post	Yes	H/S	None
Harvey & Luthans (1979)[16]	27 employees in a human services agency	?	Pre/post	Yes	H/S	Analysis of variance

Study	Description		Design			
Mueller & Cole (1977); U.S. Geological Survey (1977)[17]	2700 employees; Washington, D.C. offices of a federal agency	Yes	Generally post only; some pre/post comparisons	No	H/S	None
Naval Ship Engineering Systems Command, Port Hueneme, California (1975)[18]	1,700 employees	?	Generally post only; some pre/post comparisons	?	H/S	None
Office of Accounting, Department of Labor (1977)[19]	All 112 employees in the office	Yes	Pre/post/long post	No	H/S	None
Osteen (1979)[20]	46 offices of the Library of Congress	Yes	Pre/post	No	H/S	None
Port Authority (1975)[21]	850 nonunionized employees	No	Pre/Post	No	H/S	None
Reutter (1973)[22]	250 employees in three agencies of Baltimore city government	Yes	Post only	No	S	None
Salvatore (1974)[23]	110 employees in a Canadian federal agency	Yes	Generally post only; some pre/post comparisons	No	H/S	None
Santa Clara (1975)[24]	Juvenile-Adult Probation Department	Yes	Pre/post/long post	No	S	None
Seattle Civil Service Commission (1975)[25]	167 employees	?	Post only	No	S	None
Shulman (1979)[26]	Federal Home Loan Bank; 20 departments with 225 employees	No	Post only	No	S	None
Stevens & Elsworth (1979)[27]	90 clerical workers in three Australian government departments	?	Pre/post	No	S	F-test; multiple discriminant analysis procedure

Table 1 (continued)

Study	Setting	Union involved?	Study design?	Comparison group(s)?	Hard/soft data?	Statistical treatment?
Swart (1974)[28]	33 employees in Inglewood, California; all but police and fire personnel	?	Post only	No	H/S	None
Thornton (1973)[29]	50 members of Personnel Department in a Canadian federal agency	?	Pre/post	No	H/S	None
Transportation Systems Center (1979)[30]	Employees at Transportation Systems Center of the Department of Transportation's Research and Special Programs Administration	?	Pre/post	No	H/S	None
Uhlmann (1977)[31]	Denver regional office, HEW	?	Pre/post	No	H/S	None
U.S. Army Natick Laboratories (1974)[32]	1,200 laboratory employees	?	Generally post only; some pre/post comparisons	No	H/S	None
U.S. Army Tank Automotive Command (1975)[33]	400 employees	?	Pre/post	No	H/S	None
U.S. Information Agency (1975)[34]	33 employees	?	Pre/post	No	H/S	None
Vieth (1977)[35]	1,335 civilian administrative employees, Tinker A.F.B.	?	Post only	No	H/S	None
Walker, Fletcher & McLeod (1975)[36]	125 employees in two British Civil Service offices	?	Post only	No	S	None
Ronen, Primps & Cloonan (1978)[37]	Summary of 22 U.S. federal applications	Yes	Pre/post	?	H/S	?
U.S. Army (1977)[38]	22 FT experiments in various army units	?	Pre/post	No	H/S	None

they usually involve small numbers of employees. Both factors may simplify socialization and informal controls, making such applications an easier piece. One can reasonably raise the question of the generalizability of F-T effects to thing-processing or production settings, consequently, and perhaps also to work sites with large numbers of employees.

Fourth, some of the available studies detailed in Table 1 exclude various categories of employees. Thus the Port Authority's application excluded all union employees, and Inglewood's application did not cover fire or police services.

We lack knowledge about what effects such exclusions generate, but we can be certain that—as in the case of teaching, fire, and police personnel—there will be numerous public jobs to which only restricted F-T variants may be appropriate or none at all. Morale problems may inhere in such exclusions, whether they are necessary or merely convenient.

Fifth, available studies deal with an important source of variability in that they occur in both union and nonunion settings. But the research is all but moot concerning the specific characteristics of appropriate hosts, whether management or union. Of course, willingness to experiment with F-T implies a definite preference for influence-sharing versus authoritarian systems. And F-T applications clearly do not require the range of skills associated with many other approaches to participative management, such as team building. Plainly, however, we cannot specify the characteristics as a "culturally prepared" host organization from the available research.

Sixth, about half of the sources in Table 1 give attention to behavioral as well as attitudinal measures, to "hard" as well as "soft" data. Much organizational research gets justly criticized for its basic reliance on "soft" data, and bottom-line effects are often neglected in idealistic visions of a new humanism. So both hard and soft data are desirable in F-T studies.

Seventh, and most prominently, F-T research may be criticized on technical grounds as deficient in several obvious particulars. For example, only two studies in Table 1 utilize control or comparison groups. Despite the great problems of providing real "controls" or "comparisons," especially in the field, they do help eliminate hypothetical explanations for observed effects alternative to the treatment.

Moreover, about half of the individual studies in the panel use a posttest-only design, and they permit only such weak conclusions: X percent of respondents after Z months of experience with F-T report that they are satisfied with effects. More robust interpretations would be supported by observations made just before and some time after an F-T installation, in contrast. Such pre/post designs were used in about half of the individual studies reported in Table 1. Longitudinal studies are rare. These report observations at several points surrounding an F-T treatment and permit substantial confidence about F-T effects. Table 1 contains two pre/post/long-post cases—which convention means that three or more observations were made, at least one before an F-T intervention, another shortly thereafter, and one or more additional observations over an extended period of time.

Finally, at best, virtually all public sector F-T studies use only straightforward data arrays without any statistical treatment. Statistical methods only serve to aid choice processes, of course. But they can usefully help distinguish mere randomness in the data from noteworthy variations. Only two of the present panel of public sector studies utilize statistical methods for comparing data.

These technical criticisms do not reflect mere methodological fussiness. Not all managerially useful research need follow the natural science model. Indeed, following Porras and Roberts, we need to distinguish at least four kinds of useful and legitmate "research."[41]

1. implementation research, as in the use of diagnostic interviews or surveys to permit choice of appropriate interventions;
2. evaluation research, which tests for global outcomes to assess the potency of interventions;
3. assessment research, which focuses on global outcomes as well as on the processes inducing them; and
4. theory-building research, which is oriented toward discovering fundamental relationships, as by testing hypotheses.

F-T studies basically provide examples of only the first and second types, and quite weak examples at that. More assessment and theory-building research are much needed, given that implementation and evaluation research will predominate for most practical purposes.

MAJOR BEHAVIORAL EFFECTS

Along with their obvious contributions to increased employee discretion, proponents typically argue that F-T applications will induce a number of organizationally attractive behavioral outcomes. Illustratively, most propose that F-T tends to reduce tardiness, as well as absenteeism and sick leave, especially those of the one-day variety. What rationale supports such a view? An employee under conventional work hours who oversleeps or who succumbs to an urge to take advantage of a sale might "call in sick" even if only an hour or so of lateness is contemplated. Such white lies would not be necessary under F-T. F-T also is often thought to reduce turnover by making conditions at work more attractive. Many also argue that overtime will be reduced, with the flexible hours permitting longer (or shorter) workdays when the situation requires. Relatedly, flexing employees could provide longer service days for users without overtime, a consideration of some magnitude in the public sector in these Proposition 13 days.

Critics doubt these sunny prospects. For example, they maintain that F-T will only increase costs. Thus more employees might be necessary to provide coverage, costs of supervision might increase, and overtime charges might rise, particularly as hourly workers remain to provide support services to salaried employees who are flexing a workday longer than normal.

The ayes have it, quite decisively, when the total F-T literature is surveyed.[42] Favorable behavioral effects dominate in these studies, which basically reflect business sector experience.

What does the slimmer public sector literature reveal about the behavioral effects of F-T applications? Table 2 summarizes the available data, reported as specific magnitudes whenever possible. General terms also are used—for example, "no appreciable effect" or "reduced"—to provide the most suitable summary of results.

What do the public sector data suggest? Five conclusions seem appropriate,

Table 2 Overview of behavioral effects reported in public-sector studies

Study	Sick leave or absenteeism	Tardiness	Turnover	Overtime	Trends in costs	Measured productivity
District of Columbia (1975)	Both reduced (one-hour sick leave down 68% and one- to two-hour sick leave down 16%, one-hour absenteeism down 77% and one- to two-hour absenteeism down 42%)					No increases
Environmental Protection Agency (1977, 1978)	Both reduced				Decreased	
Finegan (1977); Bureau of Government Financial Operations (1975, 1976)	Both reduced	Eliminated		Reduced		
Finkle (1979)	Both reduced	Reduced			Some increases in direct overhead costs	
General Services Administration (1977)	Both reduced					
Giammo (1977); Social Security Administration (1974)	Both reduced	Reduced or eliminated	Reduced	Reduced		No difference found in one bureau; increase of 11.6% in Bureau of Data Processing
Harvey & Luthans (1979)	"Favorable effect"		No change			

Table 2 (continued)

Study	Sick leave or absenteeism	Tardiness	Turnover	Overtime	Trends in costs	Measured productivity
Mueller & Cole (1977); U.S. Geological Survey (1977)	Sick leave decreased by 7%; annual leave decreased by 10%	Reduced	Lowest turnover rate in 5 years	39% of the offices reported small decrease; 23% a substantial decrease; 15% a small increase	Slight increase of $7,400 in extra salaries	*Map Production*—decrease of 3.6% in one area and 14.3% increase in another area. *Map Distribution*—11.5% decrease *Finance*—13.5% increase in vouchers processed. *Technical Reports*—6.3% increase.
Naval Ship Engineering Systems Command, Port Hueneme, California (1975)					Decrease in energy consumption	
Office of Accounting, Department of Labor (1977)	Absenteeism reduced by 70—75%	"Almost eliminated"		Reduced	No substantial costs, only those required for installing time recorder	Increased 3% in 3 work units
Osteen (1979)	"Significantly decreased"	81% of managers stated there was a decrease; 8% found increases; 11% found no change				
Port Authority (1975)	"No appreciable effect"			"No appreciable effect"		

Salvatore (1975)			Reduced			
Swart (1974)	Both reduced		Reduced		Decreased by $20,000 in 9 months	
Thornton (1973)	Both reduced		Reduced		Reduced	
Transportation Systems Center (1979)	Both reduced				"No net change"	
Uhlmann 1977	Both reduced		"Eliminated"			
U.S. Army, Natick Laboratories (1974)	Both reduced					
U.S. Army Tank Automotive Command (1975)	Sick leave reduced by 29%					2% increase
U.S. Information Agency (1975)		Reduced	"No longer a problem"			Accounts Payable and Claims Section improved 4.5% in vouchers processed; reduced backlog 16%
Vieth (1977)	Both reduced	Reduced				
Ronen, Primps & Cloonan (1978)	Decrease in 12 agencies; no change in 2 agencies; increase in 1 agency	Decrease in 10 agencies	Decrease in 2 agencies; no change in 1 agency; mixed results in 6 agencies			8 agencies reported increased measured productivity; 2 reported inconclusive results
U.S. Army (1977)	Both reduced	Reduced	No change	Reduced	Some net savings	5% increase at Detroit Engineer District; 10.7% increase at Regional Dental Activities (Alameda,) California)

relying basically but not exclusively on Table 2. First, the literature may surprise many when it comes to reporting behavioral or "hard" effects. Thus about 70 percent of the studies report such data, and Table 2 has one entry of an effect for each empty cell. That is to say, the definite majority of studies reporting behavioral or "hard" data each utilized several indicators, on the average.

Second, Table 2 implies that the benefits of F-T applications far outweigh their costs, as determined by behavioral measures. For sick leave, absenteeism, tardiness, and turnover, the record implies almost universal improvement, with a few notices of "no appreciable effect" or "no change" adding only a little variety to the results. Trends in overtime and other costs, moreover, seem at least unchanged. Indeed, they trend downward in almost all cases.

This strong trend attracts attention, especially since it coincides with trends in the full family of F-T studies. At the very least, then, the data imply that F-T does not worsen major features of the work site, as critics warn. Of course, one might argue that this feature of the F-T literature reveals that "negative findings" do not get published. Even if true, this does not account for the substantial number of unpublished sources included in our evolving F-T panel that unanimously report similar effects.

Third, just as almost all of the private sector studies, Table 2 provides few specific data concerning objective measures of productivity. Note that Tables 3 and 4 below show that both employees and first-line supervisors often report that productivity does increase under F-T. These opinions receive strong support from seven studies in Table 2, which measure productivity effects in terms of dollars and cents, measures of amount and quality of work completed, and so on.

That only about one-quarter of the studies provide objective data about productivity may be interpreted diversely. At the very least, this betters the record of private sector studies. Moreover, productivity measurement is often difficult, and especially so in many public agencies. In addition, the results can be questionable even when measurement is attempted. Witness the various ways of emphasizing what reporting systems seek—as by "balloon-squeezing," inflated estimates, and neglect of major "intangibles." Perhaps paramountly, many see F-T as a low-cost fringe benefit—as improving the quality of work and as impacting on employee attitudes and turnover but as not especially relevant to productivity.

To be sure, public sector studies can be faulted on grounds of research design, but the trends above are consistent with the best available private sector study.[43] Details would be burdensome here, and their interpretation cannot be certain. In capsule, however, five work units in a financial firm were studied for specific effects of F-T applications on productivity. The results? Two of the five units reflected significant productivity increases, and three units showed no major change. The authors conclude:

> Given the differing outcomes of the experimental groups, as well as experimental design limitations, no clear-cut conclusions with regard to the impact of flexible working hours on productivity can be made. The results based on five units are mixed.

This conclusion probably understates the case. For many F-T proponents would emphasize that productivity did not significantly *decrease* in any of the five cases. Since F-T is no cost or low cost, and given a stable level of productivity, positive effects on employee attitudes would be sufficient to encourage F-T applications.

Table 3 Overview of attitudinal effects reported by employees in public-sector studies

Study	% urging F-T be continued	% reporting productivity increased	% reporting morale improved	% reporting greater control of work and personal life	% reporting decreases in availability of others, communication efficiency	% reporting resentment of timekeeping system	% reporting abuse of F-T	% reporting favorable effects on commuting
Air University Maxwell A.F.B. Alabama (1975)		25% increase; 10% decrease; 65% no change	61% increase 8% decrease					Effect cited
Atlanta Regional Commission (1979)	95%	31%	39%	76%	17%	80%		46%
Crawford (1979)	Effect cited		Effect cited			Effect cited		
District of Columbia (1975)			92%					59%
Environmental Protection Agency (1977)	87.1%; 3.1% no, and 9.8% undecided	48%	67%					50%
(1978)	91.3%; 4.6% no, and 4.1% undecided	60%						54%
Finegan (1977); Bureau of Governmental Operations (1975, 1976)	100%	Effect cited	86.5%	96.2%	Effect cited			83.5%

Table 3 (continued)

Study	% urging F-T be continued	% reporting productivity increased	% reporting morale improved	% reporting greater control of work and personal life	% reporting decreases in availability of others, communication efficiency	% reporting resentment of time-keeping system	% reporting abuse of F-T	% reporting favorable effects on commuting
Finkel (1979)		Effect cited	Effect cited	Effect cited				Effect cited
General Services Administration (1977)								
Giammo (1977); Social Security Administration (1974)		33%	68%	90%		5%		75%
Harvey & Luthans (1979)				Effect cited				
Mueller & Cole (1977); U.S. Geological Survey (1977)		36%; 2% cite adverse effects	Effect cited	68%	Effect cited		10%	Effect cited
Naval Ship Engineering System Command, Port Hueneme, California (1975)		64%; 4% report decrease; and 32% no change	89%; 2% report decrease and 9% no change	Effect cited				

Office of Accounting, Department of Labor (1977)		Effect cited	Effect cited	Effect cited		Effect cited	Effect cited
Osteen (1979)	100%	Effect cited	Effect cited	Effect cited			
Port Authority (1975)	85%; 4% support discontinuance	Effect cited	Effect cited	47%; 2% report less	6%	53%; 2% cite adverse effects	67%
Reutter (1973)	Effect cited	Effect cited		Effect cited		Effect cited	
Salvatore (1974)	100%		Effect cited	Effect cited		8%	Effect cited
Santa Clara (1975)						Effect cited	Effect cited
Seattle Civil Service Commission (1975)		Effect cited	Effect cited	Effect cited			Effect cited
Shulman (1979)		Effect cited	Effect cited	Effect cited		Effect cited	Effect cited
Stevens & Elsworth (1979)			Effect cited	Effect cited		Effect cited	
Swart (1974)		Effect cited	Effect cited	Effect cited			
Thornton (1973)	98%	Effect cited	Effect cited	Effect cited		Effect cited	Effect cited
Transportation Systems Center (1979)	94%	55%; 19% report no change; 2% decrease; and 24% no opinion	85%	Effect cited	Effect cited	3%	Effect cited
U.S. Army Natick Laboratories (1974)	100%						Very favorable effect

Table 3 (continued)

Study	% urging F-T be continued	% reporting productivity increased	% reporting morale improved	% reporting greater control of work and personal life	% reporting decreases in availability of others, communication efficiency	% reporting resentment of time-keeping system	% reporting abuse of F-T	% reporting favorable effects on commuting
U.S. Army Tank Automotive Command (1975)		74%; 12% report decrease; and 14% uncertain						Effect cited
U.S. Information Agency (1975)			Effect cited	Effect cited				
Vieth (1977)				Effect cited				
Walker, Fletcher & McLeod (1975)	96%	25%; 1% report adverse effects	28%; 1% report deterioration	Effect cited	7%; 15% report increased communication efficiency			Efffect cited
Ronen, Primps & Cloonan (1978)	100% of 6 reporting agencies	Effect cited	Effect cited	8 of 8 reporting agencies	Opposite effect cited in one agency	Both positive and negative attitudes cited		12 of 12 agencies reporting
U.S. Army (1977)	86%		100%	100%				77%

Table 4 Overview of attitudinal effects reported by direct supervisors in public-sector studies

Study	% urging F-T be continued	% reporting productivity increased	% reporting morale increased	% reporting increased problems scheduling employee work	% reporting increased problems scheduling personal time	% reporting increased problems in communicating with colleagues	% reporting increased problems in accounting for employee's time	% reporting abuse of F-T	% reporting favorable effects on commuting
Atlanta Regional Commission (1978)	100%	22%	56%		39%	27%			61%
Crawford (1979)	Effect cited								
District of Columbia (1975)		Effect cited							
Environmental Protection Agency (1977)	100% of males 94% of females	40.1%						85% had seen none	
(1978)		51.2%						65% had seen none	
Finegan (1977); Bureau of Government Financial Operations (1975, 1976)	100%	Effect cited	100%	Effect cited	Effect cited	Effect cited	Effect cited		Effect cited
Finkle (1979)				More effective planning possible		Improved			
General Services Administration (1977)				Less problems	Less problems				
Giammo (1977); Social Security Administration		Effect cited	68%	Effect cited	Effect cited				Effect cited

Table 4 (continued)

Study	% urging F-T be continued	% reporting productivity increased	% reporting morale increased	% reporting increased problems scheduling employee work	% reporting increased problems scheduling personal time	% reporting increased problems in communicating with colleagues	% reporting increased problems in accounting for employee's time	% reporting abuse of F-T	% reporting favorable effects on commuting
Harvey & Luthans (1979)		Effect cited							
Mueller & Cole (1977); U.S. Geological Survey (1977)		27%	79%	1.5% report major problems; 21.5% minor problems; 77% no problems	6%	8.8% increase; 15.3% decrease; 75.9% no change		10%	Effect cited
Office of Accounting, Department of Labor (1977)		Effect cited	Effect cited	Effect cited			Effect cited		
Osteen (1979)	100%	Effect cited	Effect cited	Effect cited	Effect cited	Effect cited	Effect cited	Effect cited	
Port Authority (1975)		Effect cited	Effect cited						
Reutter (1973)	Some resistance to program								
Salvatore (1974)		Effect cited	Effect cited		Effect cited	Effect cited		Minor abuse	
Shulman (1979)				Effect cited	Effect cited				Effect cited

Thornton (1973)						Effect cited
Transportation Systems Center (1979)		59%; 41% report no change; 10% no opinion	91%; 5% report no change; 4% no opinion		Less problems		
Uhlmann (1977)	Effect cited			Effect cited		Effect cited	
U.S. Army Natick Laboratories (1975)	100%	Effect cited					Very favorable effect
U.S. Army Tank Automotive Command (1975)		Effect cited					Effect cited
Ronen, Primps & Cloonan (1978)	Effect cited	Effect cited	3 of 3 agencies reporting	Opposite effect cited in one agency	Opposite effect cited in one agency	Opposite effect cited in one agency	2 of 2 agencies reporting

The attitudinal impacts of F-T—as the section below demonstrates—are over-whelmingly positive.

Fourth, F-T can have important bottom-line effects external to the employing organization, which effects Table 2 does not cover. Consider the effects on an urban transit property when 51,000 public employees in one Canadian city went on F-T. To simplify, F-T had several positive effects, at "marginal cost" to the transit property. Illustratively:[44]

> Peak demand for service was significantly "flattened" and demand was dis-tributed more broadly on both sides of the previous peak
>
> Bus operating speeds in the downtown area were improved
>
> Improvements occurred in the efficiency of the utilization of both operators and vehicles

MAJOR EMPLOYEE ATTITUDINAL EFFECTS

The sketch above of F-T's behavioral effects has a special salience, given that the common wisdom has always seen F-T's most powerful effects acting on employee attitudes. Note that critics have been restrained when it comes to predicting awk-ward "soft" outcomes—on employee satisfaction, morale, and so on—even when they aggressively deny any positive effects on output, costs, or other "hard" indi-cators. To be sure, critics do worry that with F-T, co-workers may be less available, communication may become more difficult, etc.

The total F-T literature—again, predominantly business oriented—provides very strong support for the rosy view. Indeed, the reported attitudinal effects are all-but-unanimously positive.[45]

But what of public sector F-T effects on employee attitudes or feelings? Five points seem most relevant concerning Table 3, which summarizes governmental experience with F-T. Where possible, actual percentages are cited in Table 3. Where such magnitudes are not provided by researchers who nonetheless report a conse-quence, Table 3 uses such conventions as "effect cited."

First, public sector F-T studies give more attention to "soft" than "hard" effects. Thus Table 3 has substantially more columns and more entries than Table 2.

Second, the positive effects have it, on overwhelming balance. The negative effects seem tolerable—as in the percentage reporting abuse of F-T, which probably approximates the level of abuse of other systems of work hours. Note one exception—the whopping 80 percent of respondents who report resentment with the time-keeping system adopted at the Atlanta Regional Commission. Even there, 95 percent of all employees want F-T to continue, including all of the supervisors.

Third—as is true of the full F-T literature, with only one exception—the panel of public sector studies deals only with individual attitudinal items. The psychometric properties of the data—whether they constitute scales or generate independent factors and so on—do not get explored. This leaves the findings summarized in Table 3 open to serious criticism. Specifically, the eight attitudinal items reported there are the most frequently referred to. But those eight items might tap eight orthogonal dimensions, or some smaller number. Those eight items might even only measure the same phenomenal domain eight different ways. It makes a great difference, on technical and substantive grounds.

Fourth, public sector F-T studies resemble their broad family in an important and related regard. As we concude elsewhere, F-T studies do not utilize available scales or instruments—tapping involvement, tension at work, satisfaction, and so on—that would provide insight concerning why and how F-T applications "work." This conclusion seems appropriate, then.[47]

> Such scales or instruments often constitute relatively known quantities in terms of their dimensionality, reliability, validity, and so on. . . . Altogether, the failure to use conventional effects reflects the primitive state of the available F-T literature.

Fifth, the overall thrust of the data trends cannot be reasonably doubted, whatever the lack of elegance in design and methods. Table 3 implies profound and positive shifts in attitudes following F-T applications, which provide major motivation for F-T applications in the public sector, on their own and especially as reinforced by the apparently positive effects of F-T on behavior sketches in Table 2.

MAJOR SUPERVISORY ATTITUDINAL EFFECTS

In the speculation about F-T effects, both proponent and critic emphasize the first-line supervisory role. The issues related to this critical linking role are significant ones. Does F-T deprive the immediate supervisor of a significant control point? Does it complicate the scheduling and monitoring of work? Does it make communications more difficult? Such questions relate to both organizational traditionalists as well as humanists. The former often see F-T as implying a loss of leverage for keeping employees in line, and organizational humanists, are mindful of the literature that stresses the first-line supervisor's central role in influencing the quality of working life, which role they have no desire to complicate.

What does the full record show? For the full family of F-T studies, optimism seems definitely appropriate. The balance of effects clearly favors positive outcomes. As we summarized the available evidence.[48]

> Overall, no more than a fifth of the direct supervisors surveyed ever report that F-T complicated their job—in scheduling employee work, in communicating, etc. Typically, the percentages of first-line supervisors reporting such negative effects are substantially lower than 20 percent—more like 5 to 10 percent.
>   . . . first-line supervisors imply that F-T has desirable effects that seem to more than counterbalance any negative effects. For example, at least 70 percent of each population of first-line supervisors wanted their F-T programs to continue, with the average being closer to 90 percent. . . . Forty percent or more see a lessening of commuting problems under their F-T programs.

And what of the public sector experience, as summarized in Table 4? Note that the nine items referred to there are the most frequently cited ones in the panel of studies. We highlight only four points implied in Table 4.

First, actual research attention belies the avowed criticality of the first-line supervisors. About a third of the public sector panel of studies fail to provide any data about impacts on the first-line supervisory role, and most studies deal with only one or a few issues of relevance, typically in generalized terms rather than specific magnitudes.

Second, the weight of the available data clearly supports the view that the direct supervisors, at worst, report only modest negative effects of F-T. The paucity of entries in columns 4–8 suggests the point. And even in the case of the Atlanta Regional Commission—which reports the highest proportion of negative effects in Table 4—the full description of the application does not generate alarm.

Third, reports from first-line supervisors also imply that F-T's desirable effects more than counterbalance any negative effects. For example, even in the Atlanta Regional Commission—the exceptional case where approximately 20–40 percent of first-line supervisors reported greater problems in scheduling and in communicating with colleagues—all supervisors urged the continuance of F-T beyond a trial period. Consistently, substantial majorities report increases in morale: the crude average approximates 55 percent, even including one case of an agency reporting no overall increase which was entered in the calculation as 0 percent. This seems a positive effect, whatever the individual meanings attributed to "morale" by respondents. Finally, many supervisors report a lessening of commuting problems under their F-T programs.

Fourth, although the panel of public sector applications does not reflect the point, longitudinal research implies that first-line supervisory attitudes about F-T might lag behind those of employees. In one case, for example, supervisors remained initially cautious about F-T. In contrast, employees were highly positive about F-T from the start. After six months, however, the supervisors had climbed on the bandwagon, while employees maintained or even raised their enthusiasm for F-T.[49]

The supervisory lag has a credible explanation. F-T implies some changes in supervisory behaviors/attitudes that require time for working through.[50] Sooner rather than later, however—the slim data imply—almost all supervisors have the skills and patience to develop any changes appropriate for F-T. And then supervisory caution or suspicion dissipates. This adaptive process is encouraged and reinforced, one suspects, by the employee's positive response to F-T.

Note that, if some such learning lag does exist for first-line supervisors, Table 4 understates the favorableness of supervisory reactions to F-T. As Table 1 implies, longitudinal studies are rare. Almost all studies use pre/post or post-only designs—the former compared observations before a F-T application with observations at a later time, usually a matter of no more than a few months and the latter design makes observations only after a F-T application, as when respondents are asked how satisfied they are with F-T and perhaps to estimate whether they are then more or less satisfied than they were before F-T.

CONCLUSION

Overall, then, public sector F-T applications have the same pattern of positive versus negative effects as business applications. Both "hard" and "soft" data, relating to both employees and supervisors, strongly support such a conclusion. Very real questions can be raised about the number and quality of public sector studies, however.

The bottom line provides adequate support for two conclusions, then. Based on what we know, diffusion of the F-T concept seems appropriate. At the same time, much remains to be learned about F-T effects, as well as about the conditions of application that especially encourage positive effects.

NOTES

1. As in Richard S. Rubin, "Flexitime: Its Implementation in the Public Sector," *Public Administration Review* 39 (May-June 1979): 277–82.

2. Robert T. Golembiewski and Carl W. Proehl, Jr., "A Survey of the Empirical Literature on Flexible Workhours: Character and Consequences of a Major Innovation," *Academy of Management Review* 3 (October 1978): 837–53.

3. Ibid., 852.

4. Robert T. Golembiewski and Carl W. Proehl, Jr., "A Survey of the Empirical Literature on Flexible Workhours: An Update." A paper prepared for delivery at the Annual Meeting of the American Psychological Association, New York City, September 4, 1979.

5. Rubin, "Flexitime: Its Implementation."

6. Such differentiating effects are attributed by Harvey and Luthans to "staggered hours" versus "flexible hours" as the term is used here. See Barron H. Harvey and Fred Luthans, "Flexitime: An Empirical Analysis of its Real Meaning and Impact," *MSU Business Topics* 27 (Summer 1979): 31–36.

7. Air University, Maxwell Air Force Base, Alabama, "Summary Report of Flexitime Program in the Federal Government," Bureau of Policies and Standards, U.S. Civil Service Commission, December 5, 1975.

8. Atlanta, Georgia, Regional Commission, "Proposed Flexible Hours Plan," internal memo, July 1978; and "Flexible Hours Program: Evaluation Survey Results," internal memo, January 1979.

9. Robert Bruce Crawford, untitled report, a draft. Prepared by the Office of Personnel, The Prince George's County Government, 1979.

10. District of Columbia Department of Human Resources, Washington, D.C., "Summary Report of Flexitime Program in the Federal Government," Bureau of Policies and Standards, U.S. Civil Service Commission, December 5, 1975.

11. Environmental Protection Agency, "Flexitime in EPA Headquarters," internal memo, October 1976: "Semi-Annual Headquarters Flexitime Evaluation," internal memo, August 1977; and "Final Headquarters Flexitime Evaluation," internal memo, July 1978.

12. James R. Finegan, Testimony before Subcommittee on Employee Ethics and Utilization of the Committee on Post Office and Civil Service on H.R. 2732, Part-Time Employment and Flexible Working Hours, October 4, 1977, pp. 155–65; Bureau of Government Financial Operations, "Summary Report of Flexitime Program in the Federal Government," Bureau of Policies and Standards, U.S. Civil Service Commission, December 5, 1975; and "Evaluation of Experimental Flexitime Program," internal memo, September 1976.

13. Arthur L. Finkle, "Flexitime in Government," *Public Personnel Managment* 8 (May-June 1979): 152–55.

14. General Services Administration, "Flexitime Report," internal memo, April 21, 1977.

15. Thomas Giammo, Testimony before Subcommittee on Employee Ethics and Utilization of the Committee on Post Office and Civil Service on H.R. 2732, Part-Time Employment and Flexible Work Hours, October 4, 1977, 150–52; and Social Security Administration, "Federal Offices Try Flexible Hours," *The Office* (December 1974), 70.

16. Harvey and Luthans, "Flexitime," 27: 31–36.

17. Oscar Mueller and Muriel Cole, "Concept Wins Converts at Federal Agency," *Monthly Labor Review* 100 (February 1977): 71–74.

18. Naval Ship Engineering Systems Command, Port Hueneme, California, "Summary Report of Flexitime Program in the Federal Government," Bureau of Policies and Standards, U.S. Civil Service Commission, December 16, 1975.

19. Office of Accounting, Department of Labor, "Pilot Flexitime Project in the Office of Accounting," internal memo, October 1977.

20. Cicily P. Osteen, "Library of Congress Managers Assess Their Experiences with Flexitime," internal memo, August 30, 1979.

21. Port Authority of New York and New Jersey, Planning and Development Department, "Flexible Workhours Experiment at the Port Authority of New York and New Jersey," December 1977.

22. Mark Reutter, "Baltimore's Changing Work Styles: Employees Determine Own Working Schedule under Innovative Program Begun in City by Insurance Company," *The Sunday Sun*, Baltimore, Maryland, November 25, 1973, 1d.

23. P. Salvatore, "Flexible Working Hours: The Experiment and Its Evaluation," Personnel Branch, The Department of Communications of the Government of Canada, internal memo, January 1974.

24. Santa Clara County, California, Juvenile and Adult Probation Departments, "Flexitime Summary Report," internal memo, 1975.

25. Seattle Civil Service Commission, "Summary Report of Flexitime Program in the Federal Government," Bureau of Policies and Standards, U.S. Civil Service Commission, December 5, 1975.

26. Jill E. Shulman, "Flexitime as an OD Intervention," *OD Practitioner* 11 (October 1979): 11–15.

27. Errol D. Stevens and Rod Elsworth, "Flexitime in the Australian Public Service: Its Effect on Non-Work Activities," *Public Personnel Management* 8 (May-June 1979): 196–205.

28. J. Carroll Swart, "What Time Shall I Go to Work Today? *Business Horizons* 17 (October 1974): 19–26.

29. L. V. Thornton, "Report on Flexible Hours Experiment in the Personnel Branch," Ottawa, Canada: Personnel Branch, Department of Consumer and Corporate Affairs, April 1973.

30. Transportation Systems Center, "Evaluation of Flexitime Model at TSC," internal memo, August 1979.

31. Gary J. Uhlmann, Testimony before Subcommittee on Employee Ethics and Utilization of the Committee on Post Office and Civil Service on H.R. 2732, Part-Time Employment and Flexible Work Hours, July 8, 1977, 87–95.

32. U.S. Army Natick Laboratories (Massachusetts), "Summary Report of Flexitime Program on the Federal Government," Bureau of Policies and Standards, U.S. Civil Service Commission, December 1974.

33. U.S. Army Tank Automotive Command (Michigan),"Summary Report of Flexitime Program in the Federal Government," Bureau of Policies and Standards, U.S. Civil Service Commission, December 1975.

34. U.S. Information Agency, "Summary of Flexitime Program in the Federal Government," Bureau of Policies and Standards, U.S. Civil Service Commission, December 1975.

35. Warren Vieth, "Tinker Employees Drift into Flexitime," *Oklahoma City Times*, August 29, 1977, 5.

36. James Walker, Clive Fletcher, and Donald McLeod, "Flexible Working Hours in Two British Government Offices," *Public Personnel Management* 4 (July-August 1975): 216–22

37. Simcha Ronen, Sophia Primps, and John Cloonan, Testimony before the Senate Committee on Governmental Affairs on S.517, Flexitime and Part-Time Legislation, June 29, 1978.

38. U.S. Army, "Flexitime Experience in the Department of the Army," internal memo, September 1977.

39. Robert T. Golembiewski, Rick Hilles, and Munro Kagno, "A Longitudinal Study of

Flexi-Time Effects, *Journal of Applied Behavioral Science* 10 (July 1974): 503–32; and Robert T. Golembiewski, Samuel Yeager, and Rick Hilles, "Factor Analysis of Some Flexitime Effects," *Academy of Management Journal* 18 (September 1975): 500–09.

40. For details, consult Golembiewski, Hilles and Kagno, "A Longitudinal Study," 10:503–32. See also Robert T. Golembiewski, *Approaches to Planned Change* (New York: Marcel Dekker, 1979), Vol. 2, esp. 215–53.

41. Jerry I. Porras and Nancy Roberts, "Toward a Typology of Organization Development Research," Research Paper No. 470, Stanford University, Graduate School of Business, 1978.

42. Golembiewski and Proehl, "A Survey of Flexible Workhours," 845–47.

43. Virginia E. Schein, Elizabeth H. Maurer, and Jan F. Novak, "Impact of Flexible Working Hours on Productivity," *Journal of Applied Psychology*, 62 (No. 4, 1977): 463–65.

44. John Bonsall, "Flexible Hours: Progress Report No. 1," internal memo, OC Ottawa-Carleton TRANSPO. April 2, 1974, 15.

45. Golembiewski and Proehl, "A Survey of Flexible Workhours," 847–49.

46. Golembiewski, Yeager, and Hilles, "Factor Analysis," 18: 500–09.

47. Golembiewski and Proehl, "A Survey of Flexible Workhours," 849.

48. Ibid., 850–51.

49. Golembiewski, Hilles, and Kagno, "A Longitudinal Study," 10: 519–26.

50. For example, see Lee A. Graff, *An Analysis of the Effect of Flexible Working Hours on the Management Function of the First-Line Supervisor.* Ph.D. dissertation, Mississippi State University, 1976.

Flexible Compensation Evaluated

William B. Werther, Jr.

All organizations are faced with a common dilemma. On the one hand, every enterprise requires structure, rigidity, and the constraints of objectives if organizational goals are to be achieved. On the other hand, each member of the organization requires varying degrees of autonomy in order that his or her personal needs may be satisfied. To pursue either of these extremes to the exclusion of the other results in diminished organizational performance.

In recent years, this dilemma has been obfuscated by the growing concern for the quality of life in general and the quality of work in particular. Although each student of the problem defines quality differently, individual autonomy does appear to be a common ingredient in most definitions. That there is a constant, albeit gradual, drift toward increased autonomy for workers can be illustrated by the greater acceptance of job enrichment, implementation of flexible manpower

William B. Werther, Jr., is an associate professor of management at Arizona State University.

schedules, incorporation of participative goal setting in management-by-objectives programs, legislation such as the Williams-Steiger Occupational Safety and Health Act of 1970, and —still earlier—the Hawthorne studies during the Depression. Even a cursory study of business history reveals that the move toward greater awareness of employee desires is not a recent trend—nor is it likely to diminish. Thus, meeting the dual challenges of individual needs and organizational performance confronts decision makers with a difficult set of constraints to balance. It is an arduous task because the constraints are constantly changing; today's optimal solutions become suboptimal tomorrow because the work environment is dynamic. To succeed, organizations must continually seek innovative techniques to satisfy employee needs—and these techniques must also enhance organizational performance.

Unfortunately, there is no definite method, or even a reasonable methodology, to determine what the proper balance should be for any organization. Instead, the solution to this organizational dilemma is contingent upon an optimal balance of both employee needs and organizational goals—a balance that must necessarily be an individual one for each organization and for each person within the organization. Thus, the search for this optimal balance can only be resolved atomistically by each individual within the guidelines of organizational policy.

This dilemma creates problems when organizational policies are out of balance and too strongly favor either organizational goals or individual needs. When this occurs, employee satisfaction or organization performance, or both, are diminished. In virtually all firms, this imbalance can be observed in the policies surrounding compensation. Traditionally these policies have been biased in favor of organizational goals to the detriment of employee needs. Obviously, such an imbalance can only serve to increase individual dissatisfaction and, in turn, decrease organizational performance.

TRADITIONAL COMPENSATION SYSTEMS

Employee compensation represents an important determinant of employee satisfaction; unfortunately, present compensation policies are antithetical to the trend of greater employee autonomy. Instead, programs are established to ensure the efficiency of payroll administration; little consideration is given to the individuality of the employees who receive the remuneration. Admittedly, procedures had to be standardized when manual systems were used to compile payrolls. Today, however, all but the smallest firms have automated their payroll systems. As a result, the rigid constraints left over from manual systems are archaic and dysfunctional. They are dysfunctional because the organization receives few direct or indirect advantages from present methods, except for minor economies in payroll compilation. Those savings seem relatively insignificant when compared with the average of $2,500 spend (according to the United States Chamber of Commerce) by industry on each worker's fringe benefits. In return for payroll efficiencies, the company forfeits employee awareness of fringe benefits. For example, if the results of one study are representative, the average employee can recall less than 15 percent of the fringe benefits to which he is entitled.[4]

This employee ignorance—or, more correctly, apathy—stems from the near total uninvolvement by the recipient in his benefit program. Instead, each "participant" is granted benefits with few, if any, options. He is given specified holidays, a vacation of a predetermined length, and other fixed or relatively fixed benefits. That is, he is offered no control over the mix of wages and benefits given to him by the organization. Not only does this approach deny the fundamental differences between workers, it squanders organizational resources. It is wasteful because there are not inherent inducements for the wage earner to perform in ways that are advantageous to the organization. Furthermore, the structure of common benefit programs contrasts unfavorably with company pronouncements of concern over employee welfare and individuality.

The rigidity of traditional compensation procedures exacerabates still another problem: high costs. And the present system ensures that fringe-benefit expenses will remain the fastest growing component of the total labor bill. Since current procedures limit benefit selection, those employees or union leaders who seek new fringes must do so by trying to expand the already bulging list of company benefits. This leads to several different but overlapping groups within the organization vying for the addition of new benefit programs. Younger workers, for example, are more likely to seek higher company life insurance or maternity benefits because they are faced with growing families. At the same time, older employees favor improved retirement benefits. Each of these factions represents an important force within the organization. This is especially true of firms in which a union represents workers. The inevitable result is that employees seek increases in both retirement *and* insurance benefits. If granted in lieu of additional wage increases, these benefits are usually noncontributory (paid by the employer). Since the cost of many benefits, especially those dealing with medical or disability insurance, are increasing as rapidly as the rate of inflation (and sometimes even faster), the organization not only ends up providing fringe benefits that are costly, but it also becomes committed to escalating outlays in the future. Inherent in traditional compensation procedures, therefore, are the seeds for still larger increases in the cost of fringe benefits.

FLEXIBLE COMPENSATION SYSTEMS

Flexible compensation offers a viable alternative to these shortcomings. It is a system that permits individual employees to determine the relative mix of their fringe benefits and wage package. Though the employer must limit discretion because of Internal Revenue Service rulings, even a moderate increase in compensation flexibility permits the organization to maintain better control over fringe benefit costs while concurrently eliminating many of the deficiences of present compensation techniques.

Implementation

Flexible compensation plans begin with the premise that the individual worker can improve the mix of her total remuneration (wages and benefits) over the fixed relationship that commonly prevails in most firms. Each employee is unique; only he or she can optimize the compensation package.

With this assumption accepted, the first step is to determine employee interest. A brief questionnaire is an appropriate vehicle for this purpose. Questionnaire-based inquiries would determine whether employees are willing to forego some benefits in order to improve others and whether they are willing to buy supplemental benefits through payroll deductions. Further questions seek to determine which benefits employees wish to have increased, which benefits they are willing to decrease in order to improve others, which new benefits they want added, and which benefits they are willing to abandon completely. Information generated from this survey would determine worker interest in the implementation of a flexible benefit program within the organization. A significant number of unfavorable responses to the idea would terminate any further consideration of the program.

The second step would be to estimate the cost of changing payroll procedures based upon employee input. Included here are software modifications, employee counseling, and redesign of specific benefit packages. The third step involves a policy decision as to which minimum benefits should be required for all employees, if any. For example, workers might elect a combination of benefits that leaves their financial security in jeopardy. Some may decline to take any medical insurance or life insurance or retirement contributions. Thus, minimum participation in each of these crucial areas might be established. The organization, for example, may decide all employees will be covered by a major medical policy with a $1,000 deductible per family per year. Supplemental insurance up to and including "first-dollar" coverage would then be made an option that the employee could elect. Or company pension plans might become mandatory at the beginning of the employee's third or fifth year of employment. This would assure that each employee has some provisions for his or her retirement.

The fourth step requires a determination of the total amount of money spent on fringe benefits for each worker. (Given the standardization of benefits within organizations, this information could be compiled by job type.) This total includes outlay for health, life, and disability insurance; holiday, vacation, and sick pay; jury pay; retirement contributions; and other employer expenditures associated with fringe benefits. This base figure for each worker is then credited by the company to the worker's benefit account. The result is an individual fund against which each employee charges the cost of his or her benefits.

The fifth step is to develop a schedule of prices containing the cost of each benefit. This detailed price list shows the employee the cost of each benefit and the cost of supplements. For example, the price of the required major medical coverage would be listed along with the charge for first-dollar coverage, maternity coverage, and other health insurance options.

A determination of whether to increase, decrease, or leave unchanged the amount of money now spent by the organization for each employee's benefits is the next step. This is an important decision because it will affect the acceptability of the plan to employees and because it obviously affects the organization's costs. The rationale for decreasing the amount of money spent for each employee's benefits could be that the enterprise needs to recover at least some of the implementation and administrative costs. Or, decision makers may elect to increase the outlays for benefits because the possibility of adverse selection and the smaller number of employees electing any one option will raise the costs of insurance benefits. The cost of time-off benefits (holidays, vacations, sick pay, and jury pay) are unchanged, however. Such an increase would probably not be large, since employees would be able to offset the additional charges for one benefit (life insurance) by dropping another benefit (jury pay).

Of course the company may elect to take the middle road and simply not change the figure currently spent on employees. This could be done with the understanding that higher costs can be defrayed through reallocation of monies. That is, each year the organization's fringe benefit costs change by some determinable amount. This amount is almost always upward. By putting a freeze for one or two or possibly three years on the amount of monies allocated for each worker's benefits, the organization may be able to recoup a substantial amount of the implementation and administrative costs of the program.

Once the basic structure of the benefits and costs has been established, the next step is to communicate the new program to the employees. The simplest method consists of developing an order form. The order form—a computer printout— would list the benefits, associated costs, and the amount in the employee's fringe benefit account. The printout would also indicate which coverages, such as major medical, are automatically provided to every employee.

The worker (who has all the cost information, available funds, and the basic limitations on an individualized computer printout) can select the mix of benefits that most effectively satisfies her needs. She then submits this information to the personnel department, where it is automatically evaluated. A printout showing benefits provided and funds remaining would be returned for her final approval. If the employee has overdrawn her account, the return statement would show the amount necessary to make up this deficiency—both as a total and as an amount to be deducted from each paycheck during the period. The worker could then make her final decision about her fringe benefit package for the upcoming time period. (The election would have to be made one year in advance of the actual receipt of benefits, judging from current Internal Revenue Service rulings.)

A heavy commitment by the personnel department in time and computer services would be initially required to establish the program. To alleviate this problem, implementation could be extended over the period of one year—on each employee's anniversary date; current fringe benefits would continue until that time. Subsequently, new elections of benefits could be made on the employee's anniversary date each year to avoid a serious overload on the personnel department at any one time. Changes in the employee's status (new dependents, change in marital status, or the like) could be handled in several ways. In the case of marriage or childbirth, the company might elect to absorb the increased employee costs during the first year. (Though this would involve some additional costs, these nominal expenses would probably be more than offset by the goodwill inherent in company recognition of the employee's changed status.) Similarly, increases in premium charges during the year could be handled by direct payroll deductions from the employee's wages, by a debit against next year's account, or by the company's absorbing the increase until the expiration of the covered year. The deduction from the employee's wages, however, would probably be the most equitable manner of handling changes in status or increases in premiums.

OPPORTUNITIES AND PITFALLS

Are the advantages of flexible compensation sufficient to overcome the time, effort, and organizational resources required to implement it? Unfortunately, no definitive answer exists. The solution depends solely on an analysis of the advantages and disadvantages when compared with the cost of implementation within the context of each organization.

Advantages

One obvious advantage of flexible compensation is that this concept is congruent with managerial philosophies of employee individuality. In and of itself, this congruity offers no direct gain to the organization; however, implementation may create a higher degree of acceptance toward other management changes. Thus, cost reduction, quality improvement, motivational, and other beneficial programs may gain greater employee support.

Not only is each worker more cognizant of the benefits that are available, but the documentation of company outlays also provides him with a picture of his total compensation—something few workers appreciate. Understanding is especially important at the time of pay raises; indicating to every employee his total increase in remuneration (raises *and* benefits) enhances individual feelings of fair treatment. Under flexible compensation techniques, total remuneration is an appropriate figure since the recipient can allocate the increase between wages and benefits. Companies that adopt flexible compensation methods can properly emphasize total compensation; and in this way, such firms will get more—more loyalty, more stable employment relationships, more performance, more applicants—for their money.

Along these same lines, the use of total compensation makes "selling" company contract proposals to union members easier. Fewer contract ratification assemblies become contract rejection meetings if the total compensation approach is applied. Obviously union leaders and management stand to benefit. With the allocation of benefit monies an individual prerogative, fewer internal pressure groups emerge within the union and the company in order to expand or add benefits. Therefore, labor officials and management can concentrate on the primary issues (responsibilities, objectives, and performance) and not on the secondary ones (allocating limited funds to an array of benefit demands). When pressure for a new benefit does arise, management can make it available at little cost to the company since it would be paid by workers through benefit account deductions.

Thus, new fringes become a personal—not a corporate—trade-off. Benefits that are optimized by each recipient may enable him or her to achieve a higher level of satisfaction even though the total company outlay per worker is the same. The improved satisfaction and the probable disappearance of pressure groups seeking new benefits may allow the organization to slow—even stop—the growth in fringe benefit costs as a percentage of total compensation.

In addition to improved morale, turnover, loyalty, and labor relations, there is a significant opportunity to reduce absenteeism. With flexible compensation, every absence results in a transfer of dollars from the employee's benefit account to his or her wage account; nonhealth-related absences would decline because truancy means a reduction in benefit monies for the absent employee. At present, most organizations permit a specified number of paid absences. Since there is no direct cost to the worker, there is an incentive to use sick days. Flexible compensation programs include an identifiable cost associated with absenteeism. Thus, an employee faces no disruption in his or her short-term income pattern, and the company does not suffer because the absence is not wholly without penalty to the employee.

Disadvantages

Partially counteracting the advantages and opportunities of flexible compensation are some significant disadvantages and pitfalls. The major pitfall at the present time is the Internal Revenue Service position in regard to flexible compensation. Under the doctrine of constructive receipt, the IRS views all discretionary payments of value to employees as taxable income. This means that the amount of money now spent by an employer to secure benefits for employees is not subject to income tax because the company's contribution is controlled by the employer. The employer buys the benefits for workers; for tax purposes it is an expense to the firm. Since the employee is not allowed discretionary control over how his benefit monies are spent, the value of such benefits is not included in his tax liability. The fact that the company can write off the expense against revenue and that workers acquire benefits without using after-tax dollars has been the great appeal of company-provided fringe benefits. However, if a flexible compensation program is adopted under present IRS guidelines, the dollar value of the employee's benefit account would be added to his income for purposes of income tax computation unless certain preconditions are satisfied. This obviously represents a potentially significant drawback.

Those companies that have experimented with flexible compensation programs have been required to seek advisory rulings *before* implementing their plan. At present IRS reaction to any specific proposal is uncertain. It does appear, however, that flexible compensation will be permitted provided that the employee election of benefits is irrevocably made prior to the actual receipt of benefits. Moreover, it appears that the election must be for at least one year at a time. With these two constraints satisfied, flexible compensation plans will—barring any future unfavorable IRS rulings—qualify for the preferential tax treatment now accorded traditional benefit programs.

The second major disadvantage of flexible compensation schemes is the cost of implementation and administration. Although these expenses may be recovered directly (through a reduction in total outlays at present or in the future) or indirectly (through improved morale, lower absenteeism and turnover, or greater employee awareness of benefits), certain implementation costs are unavoidable. Basically, these outlays fall into four categories. First, there is the cost of determining the employee interest. Next, there is the expense of developing the price list of benefits under the less favorable actuarial assumptions. (This outlay is minimal since insurers who plan to bid on the system can provide this information.) Third, there is the cost of developing the computer software to process employee requests. And finally, there are the day-to-day administrative costs of operating the program. The availability of surplus computer time, size of company, varying complexity of benefit programs, and necessary management policy decisions require that estimates of these expenditures be made on an individual company basis.

To minimize the initial outlays, however, the flexible program may be designed and implemented for a small group (such as workers at a field location, top management, or one plant). A careful accounting of the associated costs incurred in these pilot programs would generate an accurate estimate of costs for company-wide implementation before the organization's resources are finally committed. Such an approach would also allow management to develop additional guidelines to facilitate full-scale operation of flexible compensation.

The third pitfall is less tangible but equally important to the success of new compensation approaches: management resistance. Confronted by uncertain economic conditions, the need for action in personnel-related activities often takes second place. This does not mean improvements in the company's employee relations must wait for a more tranquil economic environment. Planning, cost estimates, and clarifications from the Internal Revenue Service can be undertaken with little expense. If the program is executed gradually, the initial costs are spread over a longer period and are less disruptive to organizational and personnel department budgets. With a clear understanding of the problems—especially those related to implementation and administration costs—more definitive proposals can be offered to top management, union leaders, and government officials. The implication for personnel specialists is to begin these preliminary activities now. Action begun at this time will be unclouded by union demands and competitive pressures (from other companies that will surely use flexible compensation to lure away top workers).

The constant development of improved programs for employees is an observable historic fact. Since the 1930s—and before—increased attention has been paid to employee needs through new programs. There is no reason to expect this trend to change. Thus, the most important disadvantage associated with flexible compensation programs may well become present-day inaction.

CONCLUSIONS

Traditional compensation systems provide organizations with economies in payroll computation and benefit administration. In exchange for these savings, the enterprise forfeits employee awareness of corporate benefit expenditures, an opportunity to reduce turnover and absenteeism, any hope of mitigating future cost increases in fringe benefits, and an effective method of instilling greater employee autonomy.

Flexible compensation is not without its problems. The Internal Revenue Service has not clarified its determination of "constructive receipt" in light of flexible compensation proposals, and the cost of implementation and administration must be considered. The applicability of flexible compensation is contingent, therefore, upon an evaluation of the relative advantages and disadvantages for each organization. The changeover costs are of special importance. Can they be defrayed? If not, does the balance between opportunites and pitfalls justify absorbing these expenses? Is employee interest high enough for implementation to be a building block toward higher morale, improved motivation, or better labor-management relations? These are tough questions. Answers can be found only on an organization-by-organization basis.

The potential corporate and employee gains from a flexible compensation system cannot be long ignored in the face of rising outlays for benefits. Further underscoring the need for a new approach are trends toward greater employee autonomy. Leaders who espouse a belief in Theory Y or situational management philosophies must see traditional compensation techniques as incongruent.

Though it is difficult to enhance employee autonomy and organizational performance concurrently, the two are not mutually exclusive; on the contrary, they are interdependent. Future corporate success will increasingly depend upon advances in the management of personnel. The alternative is corporate atrophy.

NOTE

1. William H. Holley, Jr. and Earl Ingram II, "Communicating Fringe Benefits," *Personnel Administrator* (March-April 1973): 21–22.

Relating Performance Evaluation to Compensation of Public Sector Employees

Henri van Adelsberg

The following discussion addresses one of public personnel management's most vexing and emotional issues—that of linking employee performance to salary administration. Performance evaluation per se is difficult enough, but "pay-for-performance" is traumatic. The following comments will assume the existence of a valid performance measurement, recording, and calculation device.

COMMON MISCONCEPTIONS IN PUBLIC SECTOR COMPENSATION

Some Myths about Governmental Salary Administration

The most pervasive fallacy is that public employees have a quasi-property right to perpetual annual salary increases. It is easy to understand how that misconception has arisen, since lax public employers have permitted the concept of "merit" to become synonymous with "in-range longevity." The mania for the perpetual in-

Henri van Adelsberg is director of state and local government services for the management consulting firm of Hay Associates.

Printed from Henri van Adelsberg, "Relating Performance Evaluation to Compensation of Public Sector Employees," *Public Personnel Management* (March-April 1978), 72–79.

crease has destroyed any vestige of true "pay-for-performance" in the public sector and is the cause of many abuses of classification plans as well. The annual national fiscal impact of this phenomenon is incalculable, but it is probably in the billions of dollars.

A second major misconception about "merit" increases is that the amount is normally the next precalculated step in the incumbent's respective salary grade. This reduces the concept of merit compensation to a binary process of determining whether or not the incumbent will be advanced to the next step in the salary grade. Since most governmental agencies neither have a policy nor supervisors with sufficient strength to deny an individual the next "merit" step, the process has become one of automatic in-range longevity movement until the incumbent reaches the maximum step in the respective salary range.

Reaching the maximum step in the salary range, negatively described as "peaking out," creates the illusion of finality of career opportunity. It is at this point that pressure for unwarranted position reclassifications begins. Linking the maximum of a salary range to limitations on career opportunity or upward mobility is absurd, because that should be directly related to individual qualifications and the agency's selection process.

Private Sector Compensation Practices

Public employees continously express envy over the additional compensation opportunities afforded to employees in the private sector, such as stock options, profit sharing, commissions, bonuses, and so on. To a substantial extent, that envy is unwarranted. Field sales and executive personnel do have opportunities for additional compensation, such as commissions, but these are directly related to their own extraordinary efforts. Commissioned sales personnel generally are totally on commission and do not receive a salary but a modest draw against future commissions. Stock options have to be exercised by a purchase of the stock; the option is merely a guaranteed price for future purchase. Bonuses have to be earned through special efforts, and profit sharing is a company-wide benefit which pays out generally very modest annual amounts, and only when the company makes a profit.

In reality, public employees, with their year-around guaranteed jobs, solid fringe benefit programs, rapid in-range salary acceleration, longevity bonuses, and generally desirable working conditions, have a compensation advantage over their private sector counterparts. This is not true for public management and executive positions, whose total compensation levels generally are below that of their private sector counterparts.

Public employees have several additional advantages not enjoyed by the private sector. The first is that, with unusual exceptions, such as New York City, most public employers have been able to increase wages commensurate with the prevailing rates without layoffs. Private employers who, by the nature of their products, cannot increase their prices to keep salaries moving up, either have to lay off workers to make up the difference or go out of business. Recent events in the newspaper industry are pertinent examples.

The other major advantage, not well understood by many public employees and administrators since it is difficult to obtain information about internal salary administration in the private sector, is the extent to which individual public employees can influence compensation policy and specific administrative decisions, especially at the municipal and county level. Too many city councils and county boards live in greater fear of their employees than their constituents. Each public employee has appeal and grievance rights far in excess of their private counterparts, and the record of adjudication of their appeals tends to be more liberal than in the private sector.

BASIC RELEVANT CONCEPTS OF SALARY ADMINISTRATION

Before linking performance evaluation to compensation, a few basic concepts of compensation must be stated. This presentation is limited to the base salary component of compensation.

Competitive Employment Market Influence

Base salaries are the device by which public employers obtain and retain qualified individuals to deliver the services the agency is charged with providing to its community. It is not a method of providing and controlling a particular quality and level of lifestyle for a certain segment of that community—its employees. The base salaries must be internally equitable, which means "equal-pay-for-equal-work," to the maximum extent possible. Additionally, base salaries must be competitive with an agency's relevant employment market. The latter is often decribed as a "prevailing rate" philosophy.

The salary rate prevailing in the market place is not the beginning rate but is the *average* of what employers are paying their entire work force, composed of beginners and seasoned individuals, performing at an assumed level of competence. In-range longevity pay, in addition to base salary, is a concept peculiar to the public sector and, therefore, not normally reflected in prevailing rate data which includes private employers.

In-Range Salary Administration

Assuming an internally equitable and externally competitive base salary range, the next step is to explore the basic concepts of administering that range. Stated another way, it is the process of periodically determining where an employee's salary should be placed within that range. It is not, as professed by some in the public sector, a question of how an employee moves from the first step to the last step in the range, with all of its implications. There really are not too many options to effective in-range salary administration. It is either on the basis of individual job performance or not.

A valid and useful tool for public agencies to maintain and increase the level of service they provide their communities, and the level of productivity of their employees, is a "pay-for-performance" system. There is very little dispute over that concept, but it is somewhat like motherhood these days—people are for it but are reluctant to become pregnant. The principal issue is that no one wants their compensation affected by the judgment of others, even if it could result in higher salary increases than possible under current procedures. By cooperating with this resistance, public managers have deleted the principal mechanism for encouragement and reward of exceptional performance and productivity, negative performance sanctions short of suspension or termination, and a substantial degree of control over salary expenditures.

Nature of the Salary Range

The linkage between individual job performance and salary takes place within the salary range but not necessarily at the specific amounts which constitute the range. Table 1 contains illustrations of various types of salary ranges and demonstrates their limitations and capabilities for reflecting unique amounts.

Example 1 is the most common found in government, the interlocking salary grade/step schedule. It provides really only three steps for reflecting performance, since the second step normally is automatically linked to the first and awarded at the completion of the probationary period. The traditional six-month postprobationary increase is a valid concept and reflects to a degree the "learning curve" concept. Its major weakness is that it provides only three choices at 5 percent

Table 1 Various types of salary ranges

Example 1—Grade step salary range—5 x 5 system

	Step 1	½ year	1½ years	2½ years	3½ years
Grade 17	$500	$525	$551	$579	$608
Grade 18	$525	$551	$579	$608	$638

Example 2—Grade/step salary range—opened range 5 x 10

	Minimum	Midpoint	Maximum
Grade 17	$500	$551	$608
Grade 18	$525	$579	$638

Example 3—Labor/trades salary range—5 x 5

	Entrance step	Competent step	Exceptional performance step
Grade 17	$525	$551	$579
Grade 18	$551	$579	$608

Example 4—Ungraded management salary plan—50% open range

	Minimum	Midpoint	Maximum
Job X	$1,600	$2,000	$2,400
Job Y	$2,226	$2,782	$3,338

intervals for performance increase amounts—five if the agency has a seven step plan, and so on.

Example 2 demonstrates how a traditional salary range can be opened up to provide a wider range of performance award choices. Inasmuch as the illustrative salary range is approximately 35 percent wide, it provides 35 1 percent choices or 70 choices at ½ percent intervals. The first step, then, is to enable a salary range to realistically reflect the wide variety of performance capabilities of individual employees and the agency's fiscal capabilities.

Example 3 is a shortened grade/step salary range used for blue collar or other occupations in which salaries are set by collective bargaining. It shows how a traditional grade/step salary range can be utilized to reflect performance levels under such circumstances. The shorter range reflects a shorter learning curve, and advancement from entrance step to the fully competent step could be in three months.

Example 4 is an example of the complete "open range" concept, where the minimum and maximum of the salary range are automatic extensions of the range midpoint. In the example, the minimum is 80 percent and the maximum is 120 percent of the midpoint amount, to create a 50-percent-wide management/ executive salary range. Variations can be made to shorten the range, such as 85 percent and 115 percent of midpoint will provide a 35 percent wide range, and so on.

The foregoing illustrations are indicative of the basic nature and variety of salary ranges but not an exhaustive treatment. The following discussion centers on the determination, within the range, of an individual's specific salary amount, on the basis of performance.

ABSOLUTE VERSUS RELATIVE PERFORMANCE EVALUATION CALCULATION

A salary range can reflect differences in performance only in numerical terms. The ultimate term is a specific dollar amount, but one or more calculations must precede it. The degree to which those calculations reflect absolute or relative performance controls the extent to which an agency possesses an "in-range longevity" or "pay-for-performance" system.

Absolute Performance Calculation

This refers to the common public sector of inverted performance evaluation, by which an employee merely has to be certified eligible for a merit increase (that is, not yet at maximum step in range) and not found to be incompetent. In fact, some agencies even go to the extreme of requiring written documentation from a supervisor only when a merit increase is to be denied. Thus, the calculation is binary— yes or no—measured against whatever criterion an agency utilizes. This approach is not capable of any subtle differentiation between the absolutes, yes or no.

The absolute decision is reflected in the salary range by moving the individual's salary to the next available precalculated step. Only in rare instances is a mechanism available to move an individual two steps at once for extraordinary performance. Equally rare, if not extinct, are mechanisms to move an employee to a lower step in the range than currently held due to poor performance. Although the binary absolute calculation is workable, it is the least desirable of all possible formal approaches.

Even within the absolute system, agencies should not limit themselves to the precalculated amount of the next step but explore the possibility of utilizing half steps or indeterminate amounts based on the agency's fiscal capabilities. Such a variation, of course, requires modification of the static grade/step salary range tables. It also may require the very desirable concept of severing performance pay from the static grade/step salary range schedule altogether.

The fiscal impact of the absolute approach results in predictable, but uncontrollable, expenditures. For instance, an agency with a $10,000,000 payroll which has 50 percent of its employees eligible for a one-step "merit" increase of 5 percent would have to spend $250,000 in addition to its annual prevailing rate increase. Assuming that the prevailing rate increase was 6 percent, the total salary adjustment would be 8.5 percent. Illustrative of the status of the "merit" increase are agencies which, during periods of fiscal austerity when no prevailing rate increases were granted, still provided the automatic in-range increase.

Relative Performance Calculation

This refers to the practice of ranking individuals according to their relative internal performance evaluation. This requires that the agency's performance measurement procedure be capable of generating a numerical total. The agency then has a mechanism for identifying the best and most productive employees, the competent employees, the mediocre employees, and the incompetent employees. After the relative performance identification process, it remains to develop a procedure for determining and distributing varying amounts of merit salary.

First, however, an agency must come to grips with the critical and primary issue that "merit" salary amounts are not over and above base salary amounts, but the merit principle is a way of administering the base salary range. In other words, the salary range is administered on the basis of relative performance, that is, "pay-for-performance." The annual performance measurement becomes the method of determining the position or step at which incumbents will be placed in their respective salary range.

The basic difference between the "relative" and the "absolute" procedure is that under the "relative" approach incumbents are not automatically advanced to the next available precalculated step. Incumbents might be advanced more than the equivalent of one step, if they are in the top X percent in the agency; they might not move at all, even if they were competent, since that is what the middle portion of the salary range is for; or they might be reduced within the salary range if their performance was at the very bottom of the relative evaluations but not so incompetent that they should be terminated.

There are many possible variations. The open range method permits performance compensation decisions at 1 percent intervals, while the grade/step method has only 5 percent intervals. Thus, the open range method has the greatest flexibility and responsiveness to fiscal capabilities. Variations on the grade/step ranked performance evaluation approach include: *upper half adjustment only*—which provides a one-step merit advancement only to the top 50 percent of the employees; *lower steps group adjustment only*—which provides an increase only to those who are eligible and whose current position in range is below step 4.

PRINCIPAL IMPEDIMENTS TO
LINKING PERFORMANCE TO COMPENSATION

There is one principal impediment to the true linking of actual evaluated performance to compensation and that is the pervasive unwillingness of managers and supervisors to accept responsibility for such discretionary duties. Procedurally, technically, and legally, linking evaluated job performance to compensation is immediately possible. The common reasons given for its absence include:

employee and union resistance

department head and supervisory resistance

lack of enabling rules or statutes

insufficient precedent

other agencies don't do it

lack of funds

absence of valid performance measurement system

previously tried and did not work

not necessary

CONTROLLING "MERIT" EXPENDITURES

Most agencies must annually budget at least three salary cost items to arrive at the projected personnel cost total: prevailing rate increases, promotions through reclassification, and "merit" increases. Merit increases are quite difficult to calculate since a number of employees will be at the maximum of their range and have no merit steps remaining. In any event, the public employer's annual salary increase budget most often reflects not only increases in the external prevailing rate, but also another 2–3 percent for internal "merit" increases.

Fiscal Impact of Current Procedures

Most agencies' current salary practice exceeds the middle of their salary range (grade) system by 5–10 percent. If the agency is a prevailing rate employer, then the middle of their salary range system should approximate the external prevailing rate. Thus, such public employers tend to exceed the prevailing rate by 5–10 percent annually through the "merit" step approach. Financially, this ranges from a $50–100,000 annual overexpenditure for a small agency or from $50–100,000,000 for a billion dollar employer such as the State of Maryland.

Since base salary plus "merit" is normally the total salary amount used for payment of premiums for certain fringe benefits and retirement, the fiscal impact of "merit" is even more extensive than illustrated above. It is possible that some agencies have unknowingly overpaid the prevailing rate for a ten-year period, equivalent to an entire year's payroll.

Midpoint Budgeting

The external prevailing salary rate is the total of what other employers are paying for similar work including "merit," productivity, seniority, and so on. There is no need for public employers to exceed the prevailing rate for their annual salary policy. The agency need only budget for all its positions at the midpoint of their respective salary range to achieve the fiscal equivalent of its entire salary practice at the prevailing rate.

On the department level, this means each department should budget only an amount equal to the midpoint of all of its salaries, minus anticipated savings from vacancies, turnover, and so on. Thus, each department head will be accountable for implementing the performance evaluation plan on a "relative" basis. To place someone at 5 percent over midpoint, someone will have to be placed at 5 percent below midpoint in an equivalent salary range to make up the difference.

The midpoint budgeting approach is not difficult to implement on an agency-wide budgeting basis. It simultaneously brings a higher degree of responsible fiscal control to the salary expenditure process and permits a conversion from the automatic in-range longevity concept of merit to a relative pay-for-performance approach to salary administration.

Limited Access Approach

The variations of this approach center on limiting access to higher in-range salary amounts, both to distinguish superior performance from other levels and to limit the fiscal impact.

Step Limit: Many agencies limit for superior performance access to the last one or two steps in a range. This is only meaningful if movement to the range maximum is not automatic.

Percentage Limit: The most effective limited-access approaches for grade/step plans combine a prededication of the last two steps of a grade for superior performance, with a specified maximum percentage of total employees, either agency-wide or department-wide, that can occupy those steps at any time. If the percentage and step limits are coupled with midpoint budgeting, an agency will have a very effective approach.

Open Range Limits: In addition to midpoint budgeting, agencies can limit their performance expenditures by predetermining at what percentage of salary range midpoint they wish to administer their salary ranges.

Agencies can forecast, limit, and control salary expenditures inclusive of performance at very precise interval funding through open range systems. Thus, if Agency X adjusts its salary policy 6 percent across the board, and the previous compa-ratio was 100, then the new compa-ratio is 94, prior to any adjusted expenditures under the new policy.

If an agency only wished to spend 4 percent across the board, then it can fund the new 6 percent policy at 4 percent for a 98 compa-ratio. As long as all employees are above the minimum of the range, the prevailing rate and internal equity concepts remain intact. This concept can be applied in greater degrees to both sides of the mid-point, that is 90 compa-ratio or 110 compa-ratio. Thus, an agency, can develop its base salary policy and funding at 95 compa-ratio, plus declare an additional 5 compa-ratio for "merit" and achieve compa-ratio 100.

MANAGEMENT/EXECUTIVE COMPENSATION PLANS

There is a growing trend toward viewing compensation for governmental managers as a total compensation concept rather than in salary terms only. Total compensation includes noncash compensation composed of fringe benefits and perquisites. Let us concentrate on the cash compensation (base salary) component. The principal salary-related facet of the trend toward recognizing the need for a different approach to recruiting and retaining qualified public managers is the open salary range. Good examples of this approach at the municipal level include Kansas City, Missouri; Phoenix, Arizona; and Madison, Wisconsin.

The key difference in the linkage of management performance to salary is that all goals, measurements, and performance level definitions are prenegotiated between the incumbent and immediate executive or elected organizational superior. Excluded from this approach are elected positions such as mayor, governor, sheriff, and so on. The performance topics are normally MBO types of specifics, objectively measured in quantitative terms.

Table 2 depicts two examples expressing premeasured performance standards. The five performance levels divide the total salary range into five available in-range salary positions expressed as percent of midpoint, on a 50 percent salary range, as follows:

Table 2 Management objectives with predetermined performance standards

Individual objectives			Standards of performance				
			1 Marginal	2 Adequate	3 Competent	4 Commendable	5 Distinguished
A	Weight in percent	25%	75	80	85	90	95

Process claims for unemployment compensation.
Measure: Workload/available man-hours/difficulty/quotient as determined by workload analysis report.

Individual objectives			Standards of performance				
			1 Marginal	2 Adequate	3 Competent	4 Commendable	5 Distinguished
B	Weight in percent	25%	2/1/78	1/1/78	12/1/77	11/1/77	10/1/77

Expand data processing service capability by 20%.
Measure: Install RMX computer by 12/1/77.

The difference between A and B is the degree of absoluteness or discretion to be utilized. A is semiautomatic in that it limits final compa-ratio decisions to the minimum and maximum of the respective salary range zones achieved by the incumbent. For example, a "competent" rating results in a 95–105 percent of midpoint salary opportunity under A, while it generates an 80–105 percent opportunity under B. Both A and B require a final act of subjective discretion—that of specifying the exact in-range (in-zone) position that an incumbent will receive, that is, 97 percent or 103.5 percent, etc.

B also has the option of limiting the possible salary increase to a predetermined maximum percentage, thus minimizing bizarre possibilities. For example, a new incumbent might achieve a "distinguished" performance level, but an immediate 50 percent salary increase, from 80 percent of midpoint to 120 percent of midpoint, would be unreasonable. In such an instance, a decision to award a 15 percent increase, from 80 to 95 percent of midpoint may be sufficient and realistic.

Midpoint budgeting is not recommended for an agency's management/ executive salary plan, as it would defeat the purpose of the MBO or accountability management plan.

OTHER TYPES OF
PERFORMANCE-RELATED COMPENSATION

Up to this point, we have discussed salary-related performance compensation, primarily on a within-salary range basis. There is, of course, a wide variety of formal and informal performance-related compensation (cash and noncash) now being awarded by public agencies, such as:

   accelerated step increase(s)

   discretionary time off

   longevity compensation

   marksmanship pay and/or awards

   reclassification for certification or licensing

   suggestion awards

   tuition reimbursement

In many instances, the existence of these opportunities is incentive enough for superior performance from success-oriented employees. They also provide a crutch for weak supervisors who do not want to make discriminating performance choices amongst their subordinates, since access to this type of performance-related compensation is virtually automatic and entirely employee-generated.

Exceptional Performance Bonus

One tool, relatively untried in the public sector, is the cash bonus for superior performance. Such an approach is free from procedural limitations of the grade/step system and provides a more substantial amount of flexibility for managers and supervisors. The exceptional performance bonus plan could provide up to $500 for extraordinary and exceptional single-event performance or for consistent exceptional performance. The bonus is not a perpetual item as is step in grade, and funds for such a procedure should be limited by department to a percentage of its total budget, and so forth.

The basic factor inhibiting these more innovative approaches to performance incentives is that public sector managers and supervisors do not want to assume responsibility for such discretionary duties.

Compensating City Government Employees: Pension Benefit Objectives, Cost Measurement, and Financing

Bernard Jump, Jr.

As urban fiscal problems have intensified in recent months, increasing attention is being paid to public employee compensation and its role in the fiscal difficulties of cities. The news media frequently report charges and countercharges being exchanged by those who contend that public employee compenstion gains have been excessive and are a primary cause of cities' problems and by others who argue that public employees are being made the scapegoat for problems attributable to inflation, recession, and severe economic base deterioration in older urban areas.

Unfortunately, this controversy is not likely to be resolved soon, if only because of enormous inadequacies and ambiguites in the relevant data. As matters stand, it is possible to find evidence consistent with each of the views described above.

For example, Commerce Department wage data by industry have long indicated that average wages of state and local government employees have exceeded those of private industry employees (see Table 1). This relationship continued to exist during 1974, the latest year for which the Commerce Department data are available, with average state and local wages and salaries equaling slightly more than $10,000, or a little more than $200 greater than average salaries of private

This paper draws heavily on the author's "State and Local Government Pension Plans and Their Financing: Emerging Problems and Issues for Policymakers," a paper prepared for the Academy for Contemporary Problems' Conference on Public Pensions, Denver, Colorado, June 7, 1976.

Bernard Jump, Jr., "Compensating City Government Employees: Pension Benefit Objectives, Cost Measurement and Financing," *National Tax Journal*, Vol. 29, No. 3 (September 1976), 240–256.

Table 1 Average annual wages and salaries and supplements per full-time employee equivalent, state and local government and private industry, 1962–1974

	Wages and salaries		Supplements		Total compensation		Supplements as a % of wages and salaries	
	State and local government	Private industry	State and local government	Private industry	State and local government	Private industry	State and local government	Private industry
1962	$ 5,017	$ 5,081	$ 432	$ 482	$ 5,449	$ 5,564	8.6%	9.5%
1967	6,324	6,231	617	667	6,940	6,898	9.8	10.7
1972	8,922	$ 8,409	980	1,110	9,902	9,519	11.0	13.0
1973	9,425	8,900	1,080	1,253	10,504	10,153	11.5	14.1
1974	10,069	9,839	1,384	1,469	11,453	11,308	13.7	14.9
Average annual growth rates								
1962–1972	5.9%	5.2%	8.5%	8.7%	6.2%	5.5%		
1962–1974	6.0	5.7	10.2	9.7	6.4	6.1		
1972–1973	5.6	5.8	10.2	12.9	6.1	6.7		
1973–1974	6.8	10.6	28.1	17.2	9.0	11.4		
Average growth per 1% increase in CPI[a]								
1962–1972	1.8%	1.6%	2.6%	2.6%	1.9%	1.7%		
1962–1974	1.4	1.4	2.4	2.3	1.5	1.5		
1972–1973	.9	.9	1.6	2.1	1.0	1.1		
1973–1974	.6	1.0	2.6	1.6	.8	1.0		

[a]Equal to ratio of compound annual growth rates of wages and salaries, supplements and total compensation to the compound annual growth rates of the Consumer Price Index.

Sources: U.S. Department of Commerce, Office of Business Economics, The National Income and Product Account of the United States, 1929–1965, Statistical Table: A Supplement to the Survey of Current Business (Washington, D.C.: USGPO, 1966). U.S. Department of Commerce, Bureau of Economic Analysis, Survey of Current Business, July, 1974. Unpublished data furnished by U.S. Department of Commerce, Bureau of Economic Analysis.

industry employees. Importantly, however, wages of private industry employees grew more rapidly between 1972 and 1974 than did those of state and local government employees. Similarly, real wages of the average state and local government employee have declined since 1972, as wage gains have lagged behind growth in prices; whereas the average private industry employee just about held his own in relation to prices.

The picture is just about reversed in the case of supplements to wage and salaries or fringe benefits other than those included in wages. The average costs of employee supplements in private industry has consistently exceeded the cost for state and local government employee supplements. But the cost of these supplements has been growing faster in state and local government than in private industry, and it surged dramatically between 1973 and 1974. As a result, the average cost of supplements per employee equaled almost $1400 in 1974 or less than 10 percent below that for private industry employees.

However, there are risks in drawing inferences about comparative compensation levels on the basis of aggregate wage and compensation data. For example, the aggregate data are averages based on compensation for a wide variety of skill levels and job classifications. Hence, it is to be expected that state and local government pay levels show up higher in analyses of aggregates because the proportion of professional and highly skilled employees is probably greater in state and local government than in private industry.[1] Moreover, to speak of the average wage or compensation of state and local government employees is to overlook differences that may exist between particular government units within a region and between geographic regions.[2]

Second, reported state and local government expenditures for employee fringe benefits might understate the true cost because of the common tendency among governments to defer making full contributions for the cost of accruing pension benefits.[3]

It is not the purpose of this paper to try to resolve the issue of whether state and local employee compensation is in some sense too high, too low, or at the proper level. Instead, the balance of this paper will focus on public employee retirement benefits, the fringe benefit that accounts for the majority of the cost of wage supplements.[4] The next section examines the retirement income packages provided to employees in selected cities. Of central importance in the analysis is the relative adequacy of the benefits provided both in comparison with those provided to private industry employees and in comparison with the preretirement income of the state and local employees. Attention is given to the pivotal role of Social Security as an element of retirement income, to the appropriate age when employees become eligible to retire, to pensions at early ages for policemen and firemen, and to the desirability of postretirement cost of living adjustments.

Following the examination of retirement benefits is a review of major problems connected with pension cost measurement and finance. Since some states and local governments have systematically failed to make full provision in current operating budgets for retirement benefits as they accrue to employees on the payroll, and since it is frequently claimed that this practice has been responsible for overly generous pension benefits and for future budgetary commitments that have been labeled "financial time-bombs,"[5] this section will review the basics of actuarial cost measurement and funding that are essential for evaluating a city's pension finance situation.

PUBLIC EMPLOYEE RETIREMENT BENEFITS

Although the "typical" pension plan consists of a variety of distinct elements,[6] the central benefit in all pension plans is the benefit payable for so-called normal or regular retirement. With few exceptions, it is the quality or richness of this benefit that determines whether a particular plan is thought to be good or poor. Similarly, this benefit is usually the single most costly element of a pension package. Therefore, it is useful to begin any analysis of the pension element of public employee compensation by looking at regular retirement benefits.

Most public employee pension plans are of the defined-benefit type, in which the benefit is the product of the employee's years of service and some percentage of a final average salary. In some plans the percentage of salary is fixed, regardless of years of service; while in others the percentage may increase for years of service beyond a specified minimum. Some plans require only that the employee attain a specified age in order to qualify for regular retirement benefits; others add a minimum years-of-service requirement or even substitute it entirely for an age minimum. Virtually all plans make provision for early retirement benefits that are equal to less than the actuarial present value of the regular retirement benefits already accrued by the employee.

Replacement Rates

The nature of many pension plan benefit formulas is such that one cannot easily generalize about how generous a particular plan is, either in the absolute or relative to other plans. The more practical approach is to focus on specific age and years of service combinations and to compare across plans the benefits that would be paid under each circumstance, given a specified salary at retirement and a specified salary history. The resulting ratios of retirement benefits to salary at retirement are known as replacement rates or ratios.

Replacement rates at several age and years of service combinations are reported in Table 2 for eight large city general employee pension plans and for three private industry plans.[7] Among the significant points is the substantial range in benefits provided by the various cities, especially at earlier retirement ages and with fewer years of service. Second, a city's ranking in the group of eight cities varies with the age and years of service combination, and no city is either first or last in every instance. Third, benefits paid by all eight public plans are superior to those provided by any of the three private plans. Finally, no plan, public or private, provides a pension benefit that is even remotely close to salary at time of retirement.

Replacement Rates,
Social Security Benefits, and Spendable Income

Though useful as crude measures of the absolute and relative richness of pension plans, gross benefit to gross salary replacement rates are deficient as true measures of total retirement income. For one thing, they do not reflect the availability to virtually all private industry employees and to some public employees of Social Security benefits beginning at age 62.[8]

Table 2 Regular service retirement benefits as a percentage of final year's salary for various ages and years of service, selected cities—general employees[a]

	20 years service, age 60	25 years service, age 55	25 years service, age 60	30 years service, age 60
Atlanta	[b]	34.9%	38.7%	46.5%
Chicago	33.2%	30.1	43.0	52.8
Dallas	38.1	[b]	47.7	57.2
Detroit	32.6	[b]	40.6	48.5
Los Angeles	40.0	N/A[d]	50.0	60.0
New York City[c]	33.3	43.0	48.2	57.5
Philadelphia	45.5	52.3	52.3	59.1
Washington, D.C.	34.5%	[b]	44.1	53.6
Eastman Kodak	17.5	14.6	21.8	35.0
IBM	19.2	20.4	23.9	28.7
New York Telephone	21.9	27.4	27.4	32.9

N/A-Information not available

[a]Estimates are based on $15,000 salary in final year and past salary increases of 5 percent annually.

[b]Not possible. Does not meet age and/or service requirements.

[c]Estimates are for Career Pension Plan members. Benefits for sanitation and transit workers are generally higher.

[d]Reduced benefit.

Source: Plan descriptions for each city's and private firm's pension system.

Furthermore, replacement rates should be adjusted to reflect differential income taxes before and after retirement, as well as the employee's share of the Social Security payroll tax and the employee's own contribution for his or her pension, both of which are required only during an employee's working years. The net effect of these adjustments is almost always that a given gross income will yield more spendable or take-home income after retirement than before. In other words, the amount of retirement income that must be provided to maintain a retiree at his or her preretirement standard of living will be less than the salary received by the employee during his or her final year of employment.[9]

To illustrate the general nature of the adjustment procedure and to demonstrate the significance of Social Security benefits vis-à-vis preretirement income, derivation of the preretirement spendable income and the public pension benefit required to produce an equivalent postretirement spendable income for general city employees in New York City and Washington, D.C., is shown in Table 3. Prior to retirement, the spendable income of a Washington, D.C., employee earning a gross salary of $15,000 is virtually identical to that of her New York City counterpart. However, largely because Washington, D.C., does not participate in the Social Security program while New York City does, the Washington, D.C., employee must receive a gross pension benefit that is 121 percent (at age sixty-two) to 183 percent (at age sixty-five) larger than that required by a New York City employee if she is to

Table 3 Retirement income required to maintain city employee[a] in New York City and Washington, D.C. at the spendable income earned during final year of employment

	Before retirement			
	Age 62		Age 65 and above	
	New York City	Washington, D.C.	New York City	Washington, D.C.
1. Gross salary	$15,000	$15,000	$15,000	$15,000
2. Less: federal income tax[b]	2,002	2,002	1,672	1,672
3. Less: city income tax[b]	202	650	177	580
4. Less: state income tax[b]	590	N/A	490	N/A
5. Less: employee pension contribution	—	1,050	—	1,050
6. Less: FICA (social security tax)	878	—	878	—
7. Equals: spendable income	$11,328	$11,298	$11,783	$11,698

	After retirement			
8. Spendable income required after retirement to equal spendable income received during final year of employment	$11,328	$11,298	$11,783	$11,698
9. Less: social security benefits received[c]	$ 5,587	$ —	$ 6,984	$ —
10. Equals: retirement benefit (after tax) required	$ 5,741	$11,298	$ 4,799	$11,698
11. Retirement benefit before tax required	$ 6,147	$13,588	$ 4,799	$13,588
12. Less: federal income tax[b, d]	406	1,739	—	1,409
13. Less: local income tax[b,d]	—	551	—	481
14. Equals: retirement benefit (after tax) required	$ 5,741	$11,298	$ 4,799	$11,698

Table 3 (continued)

	After retirement			
	Age 62		Age 65 and above	
	New York City	Washington, D.C.	New York City	Washington, D.C.
15. Retirement benefit (before tax) required as percentage of final year gross salary (line 11 plus line 1)	41.0%	90.6%	32.0%	90.6%

[a]Married employee with no children

[b]Based on 1975 tax rates with standard deduction, joint return, two exemptions, and two extra exemptions at age 65.

[c]Estimate for employees who work during 1976 and begin collecting benefits in 1977.

[d]Tax on retirement benefit computed as if entire benefit financed by employer.

have a postretirement spendable income equal to her preretirement spendable income.[10]

Following the general procedure just described, net or spendable income replacement rates were computed for employees (at ages sixty-two and sixty-five and who were earning $15,000 at retirement) of each of the eight cities and three private firms (see Table 4). The results are striking. First, net replacement rates for public employees in each of the three cities that provide Social Security coverage—Detroit, New York City, and Philadelphia—are substantially above 100 percent; that is, spendable income after retirement exceeds spendable income before retirement. Second, net replacement rates for the private industry employees come very close to 100 percent. Finally, retired public employees in the five cities that do not provide Social Security coverage receive considerably less spendable income during retirement than they received in their year prior to retirement—and this is true even when a city's basic pension plan is superior to that of the typical public pension plan.[11]

Significance of Social Security Coverage

The existence of such a wide range of net replacement rates among the eight cities points up the pivotal role played by Social Security in determining whether retirement incomes at age 63 and later are unequivocally adequate. And in the case of governments that do provide Social Security coverage in addition to a staff pension plan, it is becoming increasingly obvious that there is a need to take Social Security into account in designing the staff pension plan.

The Social Security program has become highly dynamic in the sense that current benefit formulas are producing increasing replacement rates—with attendant increases in the dollar cost to employers and employees. Necessarily then, a

Table 4 Annual service retirement benefit (after tax) and social security benefit (where applicable) as a percentage of disposable income in final year of employment for general employees with 30 years service and $15,000 final year's salary, selected cities[a, b]

	Age 62[d]	Age 65[d]
Atlanta[c]	53% (46%)	54% (46%)
Chicago[c]	61 (53%)	62 (53%)
Dallas[c]	64 (57%)	64 (57%)
Detroit	106 (48%)	116 (48%)
Los Angeles[c]	67 (60%)	68 (60%)
New York City	118 (58%)	127 (58%)
Philadelphia	118 (59%)	129 (59%)
Washington, D.C.[c]	63 (54%)	64 (54%)
Eastman Kodak	90 (35%)	101 (35%)
IBM	84 (28.7%)	94 (28.7%)
New York Telephone	88 (32.9%)	100 (33.6%)

[a]Disposable income before retirement based on $15,000 gross salary less federal income taxes, pension contributions and social security contributions (where applicable). Estimates for New York City and Washington, D.C. also reflect deductions for state and /or local income taxes.

Both before-and-after-retirement disposable income based on assumption of married couple with no children, joint return, standard deduction, and extra exemption at age 65.

[b]Social Security payments are estimates for employees who work during 1976 and begin collecting benefits in 1977. Payments are inclusive of both primary and spouse's benefit.

[c]Employees are not covered by social security.

[d]Percentages in parentheses are gross pension benefits divided by $15,000.

SOURCE: Plan descriptions for each city's and private firm's pension system.

participating government, once it has decided that the total replacement rate of its staff pension plan and Social Security is as high as it should be, must take account of the likelihood that Social Security replacement rates will continue to increase by devising a method whereby the replacement rate produced by its pension plan will decline so as to maintain a fixed total replacement rate. The alternative is to lose all control of both the overall costs of providing retirement income to employees and the replacement rate provided by that retirement income.

Surprisingly, if not inexcusably, most states and local governments providing both a staff pension plan and Social Security coverage have not designed their pension plans so that the maximum total replacement rate is fixed.[12] As a consequence, it is practically certain that their employees who retire after a long career of, say, twenty-five to thirty years, will receive retirement income that produces replacement rates above 100 percent. Clearly, there is something very wrong with such a result, particularly when it is achieved at substantial cost to the taxpayer.

Instead of speculating about the possible reasons why so few public pension plans are integrated or coordinated with the Social Security program, it will suffice to say that the reason is not because of technical barriers relating to benefit formulas. Indeed New York has recently enacted a retirement income plan for certain of its employees that will coordinate pension and Social Security benefits, the general objective being to provide a thirty-year employee who retires at age sixty-five with spendable income equal to preretirement spendable income. The key to the proposed plan is that an amount equivalent to 50 percent of any primary Social Security payment becomes an offset or deduction from the basic pension benefit provided by New York's pension plan.[13] Thus, if Social Security replacement rates for future retirees increase, the share of a fixed total retirement income replacement rate furnished by New York's pension plans will decrease.

What Are Appropriate Replacement Rates?

Irrespective of whether Social Security coverage is provided or whether the public pension plan is linked to the Social Security benefit package, there is the fundamental issue of what a state or local government should set as a target net replacement rate. Presumably there is no cogent case for spendable retirement income in excess of preretirement spendable income, especially if provision is made for a deceased retiree's dependent survivors and if the retiree has adequate medical coverage. But assuming a consensus exists with respect to an upper limit of 100 percent on replacement rates from publicly financed retirement programs, should 100 percent be the target or standard for measuring the adequacy of benefits? And regardless of the replacement rate standard adopted, at what age and after how many years of service should the benefits be available, and should some portion of the cost be borne by an employee's contributions during his working career?[14]

Although the income of most retired persons never comes close to 100 percent of preretirement income, largely because so many private industry employers provide no pension plan, such a goal is certainly attractive.[15] However, this is a costly goal. Depending on the precise assumptions made about such matters as life expectancy after retirement, future inflation and interest rates, and the extent to which retirees are to share in national productivity gains thus maintaining their relative income position throughout retirement, the cost of 100 percent net replacement rates could require 30 to 40 percent individual savings rates (or their equivalent in employer pension contributions and intergenerational transfers to finance Social Security benefits).[16] When one considers both that the typical state and local employee is currently contributing about 11 percent of his or her gross earnings for pension and Social Security benefits[17] and that he or she would be hardpressed to raise that savings rate substantially, it is clear that the public's share of the cost to provide 100 percent replacement rates is extraordinarily high—perhaps far higher than society is prepared to go.

The full scope and complexity of the issues involved in trying to determine socially acceptable and economically feasible retirement income standards are rather more than we can explore fully here. Our principal objective in raising the matter at all is to suggest that the question of how generous public employee retirement income should be has nuances and ramifications far broader than are reflected in the usual debate about whether public pensions are too high relative to private industry pensions and whether a particular governmental unit can afford the pensions it provides. For present purposes, it is sufficient to observe that aiming for retirement income standards as high as those implied by the better public employee retirement plans—where a staff pension plan is added on a noncoordinated basis to Social Security—has important financial implications for society in general. In fact, the implications are probably so important that the locus of ultimate decisions as to the size of public employee retirement income should not reside exclusively in the conventional employer-employee bargaining process.

What is the Appropriate Retirement Age?

Returning to the matter of the ability of individual governments to afford particular pension arrangements, we question the merits of the widespread tendency to set regular retirement ages below even the age minimums set by the Social Security program and prevailing in private industry. Similarly, we are skeptical as to the justification for the spreading practice of awarding benefits at any age to employees who have served some minimum years of service. Judging from the paucity of carefully reasoned arguments on behalf of such practices, it is difficult not to conclude that normal retirement before age sixty-two and normal retirement eligibility based only on years of service neither directly serves a useful public objective nor is it equitable in relation to private industry practices. We have been singularly unsuccessful in finding objective evidence to support pension policies that encourage voluntary retirement at age sixty or even earlier for public employees in nonhazardous occupations.[18] Similarly, the idea that employees should be rewarded, regardless of age, for putting in a specified number of years of service seems equally indefensible.

Extraordinary Pensions for Police and Firemen

Whereas the trend toward declining retirement ages without reduction in benefits for general public employees may just be the result of increased employee strength in bargaining and/or excessive generosity on the part of acquiescent government officials, the long-standing practice of providing one-half of pay pensions at very early ages to policemen and firemen who have rendered twenty to twenty-five years of service is the result of more explicit governmental policy objectives and assumptions about the purpose of pensions.[19] In general, the purpose of generous pensions for uniformed employees who have completed comparatively short work careers is to insure the maintenance of youthful and vigorous forces. The objective appears to have at least a glimmer of logic.

Unfortunately, the objective of pensioning off members of the uniformed forces at middle age is proving to be extraordinarily expensive, the cost of some police and fire pension plans being close to 50 percent of payroll.[20] Not only is the cost high, it has shown a tendency to increase rather steadily as police and firefighter salaries have grown and pension benefit improvements have been forthcoming.

Even if the cost of these pensions were not approaching prohibitive levels, there would still be reason to question whether uniformed employees should be released from employment just because they reach an age when they are no longer thought to be physically able to meet the full demands of their jobs. At a minimum, it would seem essential that governments begin to explore the possibility of moving uniformed employees in their middle years out of the physically demanding job classifications and into jobs they could perform successfully until they reach the normal retirement age for general employees.[21] Implicitly, this suggestion carries the assumption that pension benefits should not be viewed as a compensation premium for taking on hazardous duty. Presumably that premium is already built into the salary base of uniformed employees.[22]

Retirement Income and Inflation

With some justification, public employee groups are apt to respond to suggestions that their pensions are too high by pointing out that inflation can quickly dissipate the purchasing power of benefits if the plan does not include some mechanism to adjust payments to offset price increases. And while it is true that some cost of living adjustment (COLA) provision is far more common in public pension plans than in private plans, the bulk of the adjustment provisions are either ad hoc or capped so they generate benefit increments below those that would be required to maintain real income during inflationary surges such as we have experienced during the 1970s. For example, of the eight cities whose replacement rates were reviewed above, only one formally guarantees an uncapped COLA, one has a guaranteed COLA with a 5 percent annual ceiling, three others have COLAs of 3 percent or less, and the remaining three guarantee no COLA whatsoever (see Table 5).

Despite the merits of the principle that retirees deserve some protection from inflation, uncertainty as to the rate of future inflation makes it fiscally unwise for governments to attempt to totally insulate their employees from inflation. Even with COLA provisions capped in the range of 3 percent inflation rates, the cost implications are not insignificant.[24] Nevertheless, the outside limit of the potential costs of a capped COLA can be estimated just as precisely as any other element of the pension package, and a determination can be made in the context of the overall benefit package and the financial circumstances of the city regarding whether such a benefit provision will be granted.[25]

Table 5 Postretirement cost of living adjustment provisions for the pension plans of general employees in selected cities

	Maximum annual benefit increase
Atlanta	0%
Chicago	2
Dallas	5
Detroit	2
Los Angeles	3
New York City	0
Philadelphia	0
Washington, D.C.	No limit[a]

[a]Adjustment made whenever CPI increases for three consecutive months by at least 3 percent over the CPI used for the last adjustment increase. Adjustment equals (a) highest percentage increase in CPI during the three consecutive months plus (b) an additional 1 percent.

SOURCE: Plan descriptions for each city's pension system.

PENSION COST MEASUREMENT AND FINANCE

This section is concerned with the measurement of benefit costs and how these costs are financed. We will first review briefly some of the fundamentals of pension cost measurement and financing or funding since these are so troublesome to nonspecialists. Following that will be an explanation of how the interested observer can go about evaluating the pension financing practices of a jurisdiction and how policymakers can be alerted to incipient pension finance problems before they result in fiscal crises. Finally, we will enumerate some safeguards that jurisdictions can use to help insure that future pension costs remain under control.

The Deferred Nature of Pension Benefit Claims

It is frequently alleged that public pension benefits have not reached their current levels as the result of conscious decisions that particular benefit levels meet a community's notion of adequacy or that their cost is acceptable within the context of the community's overall financial commitments. Rather, critics suggest that public pension benefits have grown so generous either because legislators are unaware of the full budgetary implications of what they are asked to approve or because they are able to conceal the full costs from an unsuspecting public until long after the benefit liberalization has taken place.

Regardless of why pensions benefits have been permitted to reach their present levels and regardless of whether benefits are too high in some absolute sense, current levels of pension contributions in many jurisdictions are high enough to suggest that some might choose to have considerably less generous benefits now had they been required from the time of plan inception to charge all accruing benefit costs to current operating expenditures. Unfortunately, the retirement benefit component of employee compensation costs is unique among the various elements that make up a jurisdiction's current operating outlays, and herein is the problem.

The uniqueness arises because of the deferred nature of the pension liabilities being accrued. Unlike salaries that must be paid as they are earned, pension benefit claims are earned throughout an employee's working career, but these claims are not collected until sometime after the career ends.

Given the deferred nature of the pension obligation, a jurisdiction may avoid paying for some or even all of the accruing benefits until an employee retires and becomes eligible to collect. When such practices are followed, cost allocations are distorted over time as is the distribution of the cost burden among different generations of taxpayers. Moreover, the stage may be set for sudden and catastrophic increases in current operating costs when the work force matures and large waves of employees reach retirement age.

In addition, the failure to recognize accruing pension costs and to reflect them immediately in the operating budget may distort the overall employee compensation decision. In other words, if the burden of pension costs does not have to be borne simultanous with their accrual, the total compensation package may be larger than if pension costs were paid immediately as they accrue to employees. Wage packages and pension packages with identical total costs (in present value terms) over the working lives of an employee group may not be treated as perfect substitutes. Both employees and shortsighted public officials may be biased toward pensions and away from forms of compensation that have more immediate budgetary and tax consequences.

Fundamentals of Actuarial Funding

Clearly then, the case for funding pension benefits as they accrue, a practice known as actuarial funding, is persuasive.[26] Formally, *actuarial funding* refers to a procedure whereby the estimated cost—*the actuarial present value*—of pension benefits accruing to active employees is systematically paid by the employer into a fund (perhaps with a share paid in by the employee as well). In turn, the retirement fund makes payments to retirees and invests surplus funds.

The *actuarial* in actuarial funding reflects the fact that the exact cost of retirement benefits for an employee group cannot be known with certainty until the last member of the eligible group and his or her beneficiaries die. Hence, pension costs allocated or attributed to each year of an employee's work career must be estimated on the basis of *actuarial assumptions* that reflect the actuary's (and others') best guesses about the probabilities that a variety of contingencies will occur. Among the required actuarial assumptions are: whether and when the employee will quit; whether and when the employee will retire; whether and when the employee will become disabled; the age when the employee will die; the employee's career salary progression; and the rate of interest earned on invested funds.

At the inception of a pension plan or at a time when a benefit improvement is being contemplated, an actuary—equipped with a set of actuarial assumptions and an actuarial cost method—can estimate the cost of the benefits and allocate that cost among the years during which each plan member will be accruing benefit claims. But, based as they are on assumptions about future events, actuarial cost estimates are never precisely correct and must be revised from time to time as experience unfolds.

The Inexact Nature of Actuarial Assumptions

Although there are better and worse actuarial assumptions in terms of the quality of the analysis and data used to derive them, even the best actuaries cannot predict future events with certainty. Thus, actuarial assumptions have to be monitored against unfolding experience and modified from time to time when they are found to depart substantially and consistently. Necessarily then, when a new assumption about a relevant event replaces an old assumption, the cost estimate for a particular pension plan and set of participants is likely to change. As such, these changes are the inevitable product of uncertainty about the future and not a weakness of the general procedure.

Barring major and frequent improvements in the pension plan, the inevitable cost adjustments that result from changed actuarial assumptions should not be large enough to have a major impact on a jurisdiction's annual budget—if the unfolding experience is monitored closely. But if there are major benefit improvements or if actuarial assumptions are too liberal (that is, financially more favorable than actual experience), the actuary's *plan valuation* or *valuation of liabilities* will reveal an increase in accrued liabilities for which the funding plan has made no provision. When this occurs, contributions will have to be increased if the jurisdiction is to continue funding (making provision for) liabilities at the rate contemplated when the funding plan is adopted.[27]

The Measurement of Pension Plan Liabilities

The nuances of pension plan liability measurement are widely misunderstood and often unrecognized by nonspecialists. They lead to a great deal of confusion about a retirement system's condition and about the fiscal implications for the governmental unit responsible for meeting the liabilities. Although demanding, a mastery of the basics of liability measurement is worth the effort to anyone concerned with understanding the fiscal condition of a retirement system.

The first essential point is that liability growth is what an expanding retirement system is all about. An employee is added to the jurisdiction's work force and immediately begins accruing retirement benefits which are conceptually, if not always legally, his assets. The concomitant of this asset creation process is a liability creation process affecting the employer. An employee's pension assets are his employer's pension liabilities. Assuming the governmental unit recognized the full cost implications when it agreed to the pension plan and determined that it could afford to meet the cost, the growth of pension liabilities should not be a cause for alarm. If an appropriate funding plan has been adopted, the employer's annual contributions to the retirement system will assure the availability of sufficient funds to meet the full pension liability owed to the employee. In effect then (and with some oversimplification), a fund is built up during an employee's working years, and the value of the fund at any moment is equal to the present value of the liabilities accrued by the employer on behalf of the employee.

Unfunded Accrued Liability

One of the most troublesome barriers to understanding government pension obligations and one that is, at times, the cause of needless alarm among public officials, taxpayers, and members of the financial community involves *unfunded accrued liabilities* (that is, liabilities for which there are as yet no assets). As a practical matter, most pension plans will have some unfunded accrued liabilities at various points in their evolution. And as such, the existence of these liabilities does not indicate fiscal irresponsibility or impending trouble.

For example, when a pension plan is launched, it is customary to make the benefits retroactive for service prior to plan inception. Hence, there will immediately be an unfunded accrued liability. But since not all of the employees then on the payroll will retire immediately, the initial unfunded accrued liability need not be paid for immediately.[28] Rather, a sound funding plan will usually include provision for amortizing the unfunded accrued liability over several years in much the same way that a person pays off a home mortgage. If all unfunded accrued liabilities are ever totally amortized, the pension plan is described as *fully funded*.

Unfortuntely, much confusion exists with respect to unfunded accrued liabilities. For one thing, many nonspecialists seem to view full funding—meaning no unfunded accrued liabilities—as the *sine qua non* of soundly financed pension systems. Many reports emanating from the offices of public officials and members of the municipal finance community generate more heat than light about the significance of some communities' unfunded accrued liabilities. The risks of confusion and erroneous inferences are particularly great where attempts are made to convert reported aggregate unfunded accrued liabilities into per capita figures and to use the results for intercommunity comparisons of pension liability burdens. As we explain below, different pension systems use different actuarial cost methods, and the size of a pension system's liabilities at any point in time is a function of the particular actuarial cost method used. Furthermore, a system's record in funding its accrued liabilities and in limiting growth in these liabilities is likely to be a far better indicator of the adequacy of its pension funding program than is the absolute size of unfunded accrued liabilities at a single point in time.

Just as there are some analysts who are sometimes inclined to exaggerate the importance of unfunded accrued liabilities, there are others—including some actuaries and other pension specialists—who are too sanguine about the need to make provision for unfunded pension liabilities. Some in the latter group go as far as to argue that the unfunded accrued pension liability of a community "is not in fact comparable to bonded indebtedness."[29] However, such liabilities are equivalent to bonded debt if state law makes pension commitments binding obligations of the community, whether or not the formal requirements for amortizing these liabilities are as inflexible as is the usual case with bonded indebtedness.

Measuring Funding Program

In any event, while the notion of full funding is valuable as an attribute that distinguishes the exceptionally well-financed pension system, its operational utility is minimal because there may be good reasons for the existence of unfunded accrued liabilities. All of which suggests the need for some other measures or techniques to distinguish systems in trouble from those following sound funding plans.

One such measure is the *funding ratio*—the ratio of a pension plan's assets to its accrued liabilities. Obviously, a full-funded plan would have a ratio of 1. But what can be concluded about a plan whose ratio is ¾, ½, or 0? One generalization is that a funded ratio within striking distance of 1 indicates that the plan has been soundly financed so far. Predictably, then, it follows that warning bells should go off if any but a brand new plan has a ratio close to 0. But this is not to say that calamity is imminent, for the plan may have few members near retirement age, and employer contributions at current levels may be sufficient to pay for all benefits due in the next few years. Nevertheless, a ratio indicating little or no funding progress is a signal that the situation should be reviewed carefully, because a system without assets and no immediate prospect for having any is sooner or later certain to require sharply higher increases in employer outlays.[30]

Few other generalizations about a plan's condition can be made on the basis of no more than the funded ratio for a single year. The careful analyst will want to look at the ratio's trend. If examination of the trend reveals a history of increasing ratios and few instances of declines, the system is probably being soundly financed. Conversely, there would be grounds for concern if the ratio has deteriorated steadily during recent years. Obviously then, it must be recognized that retirement systems with identical funded ratios may not have equally favorable (or unfavorable) financial prospects. Furthermore, it is essential to understand that both this method and the one described immediately below use estimates of the liability measure that will vary according to which actuarial cost method is used in the plan variation. Thus it is possible that two actuaries could evaluate the same retirement system and arrive at substantially different totals for unfunded accrued liabilities.

Another version of the funded-ratio technique involves comparing a system's assets with the several components that comprise accrued liabilities. In effect, this approach distributes assets among their claimants: current retirees and other beneficiaries, active and former members with vested rights to benefits, and active employees with accrued but not yet vested rights. Since the sum of the total claims of these groups is by definition equal to the accrued liability, a system that is fully funded would have assets in an amount sufficient to cover all of the claims. Consequently, the conclusions that can be reached by this approach are not unlike those that can be inferred when funded ratios are studied. The special value of this approach is that it provides more refined information and it may be helpful to think of funding in terms of accumulating assets for identifiable groups of claimants.

There is a variation of the method just described that is free of the ambiguities that arise because different actuarial cost methods yield different estimates of accrued liabilities. In this method, liabilities are computed as if the plan were going to terminate at once, and these liabilities are then compared with assets on hand. "If the accumulated assets, properly valued, equal the plan termination liability, the plan could on the date of valuation discharge all of its obligations for accrued benefits without further contributions."[31] But here, as in the methods described earlier, the technique does no more than relate one kind of information to another; the job of drawing conclusions remains for the analyst.

Actuarial Funding Methods

Reference has been made to the desirability of allocating, over the period of each employee's service, the total cost of providing his pension benefits. This process produces a cost estimate for each year's accruing benefit liability that should be charged against the jurisdiction's general budget. By appropriating for these costs as they accrue, assets can be accumulated by the time an employee retires that are equal to the then-present value of all benefits he or she will collect. If this is done and if the accumulated assets are managed safely,[32] the employee can be confident that the benefits will be paid.

Despite its conceptual clarity, the allocation process presents some practical difficulties that make it confusing to the nonspecialist. One difficulty is that there is no universally recognized "best" or "correct" actuarial funding or cost method, although certain methods are inappropriate for a given type of pension plan. By substituting one appropriate funding method for another, the actuary can produce dramatically different costs for any given year and for a series of years. Equally dramatic changes in the rate of asset accumulation can also result. Similarly, the discretion permitted in adopting an actuarial cost method can mean that the reported annual costs of two pension plans will not be identical, even though the plans are identical in every material way.

As a further complication, the same funding method can produce different costs, depending on the duration over which accrued liabilities are being funded or amortized—that is, if the liabilities are being amortized at all. The details behind these complications are sufficiently involved that their exegesis is best left to an actuarial treatise. However, their flavor can be sensed by looking briefly at two funding methods in wide use by state and local government systems.

Entry-age normal funding involves an annual contribution (cost) consisting of a *normal cost* and a *supplemental cost*. Normal cost is the level amount or percentage of an employee's salary that would be required yearly during an employee's entire work career. If normal cost were actually contributed each year beginning with the year of entry, and if no unfunded accrued liabilities (supplemental liabilities) were created along the way, the present value of accumulated contributions at the time of retirement would equal the actuarial present value of all benefits owed to the retiree. In other words, the employee's pension would be fully funded when she retired. A corollary of entry-age normal's leveling of costs is that contributions in the early years of an employee's career are higher than the accruing value of her benefits, and they are lower than accruing values in the years near the age of retirement.

Since unfunded supplemental or accrued liabilities will almost certainly be created at various points during a plan's operation, a supplemental cost contribution may be made to amortize them. But as noted earlier, even actuaries don't speak with one voice about the proper period for amortizing liabilities. Some argue that the period should not be longer than the average remaining work life of current employees. Others argue that the period can be as long as forty to fifty years or even longer. There are even those who see no reason to amortize at all. It is in large part because the amortization period can vary according to who makes the choice that different actuaries, using the same actuarial cost method, can arrive at widely different cost estimates for the same plan.

Although a close relative of entry-age normal funding, *aggregate funding* requires an annual contribution, measured as a percentage of payroll, that is the ratio of the actuarial present value of all unfunded future benefits to be collected by current employees and retirees to the actuarial present value of all future salaries of the same group. Initial contributions required with aggregate funding will be higher than those required with the usual approach to entry-age normal funding or with practically every other method of funding.[33] This is because aggregate funding effectively allocates the costs connected with a particular group's pension benefits over the group's average remaining work life. If no subsequent accrued liabilities are created, contributions as a percentage of payroll will decline over time, a result of the rapidity with which this approach builds up assets.[34]

To reiterate, there are alternative ways by which the costs of a pension plan can be estimated and distributed over time. This means that there can be a faster or slower rate of asset accumulation, depending on the actuarial funding method selected. And since asset accumulation is what funding is about, it is important that the actuarial funding method be selected with some predetermined funding objectives in mind.

Criteria for Choosing a Funding Plan

Some may find it hard to accept the idea that funding objectives are judgmental matters, arguing instead that the proper objective is axiomatic—a retirement system should be fully funded. However, as noted above, even the notion of full funding is not without ambiguities. Widely used and quite respectable funding methods can yield differing estimates of pension liabilities and costs. Similarly, a single funding method can yield differing estimates, depending on the amortization period selected and the actuarial assumptions used, and not even the expert may be able to say which estimate is the correct one. Under these circumstances, one is well-advised not to make full funding the single guiding standard.

A related source of difficulty in setting funding objectives is the troublesome matter of paying off supplemental liabilities such as those incurred when a pension plan is launched or when benefits are enriched. To require immediate funding might mean that a community could never afford a respectable pension plan. Additionally, there is reason to question whether the pension plan's entire "start-up" costs should be borne by only one set of taxpayers. Perhaps it is fairer to spread the cost between present and future taxpayers.

Conventional practice is to treat subsequent increments to supplemental liabilities, such as the liabilities created when a benefit plan is liberalized, in the same manner as liabilities created at plan inception. That is to say, when benefit improvements are made retroactive for the past service of current members, the resulting unfunded accrued liabilities are amortized over several years. The effect of this procedure is to minimize the immediate cost of a benefit improvement.

But in view of the mounting evidence that pension costs are becoming a serious burden to many states and local governments, in part precisely because there has been a history of successive benefit liberalizations, we question the merits of spreading these costs over a generation or more. If improvements in pension benefits have come to be viewed as regular events, and if they are always to be made retroactive for past service of current members, then it seems fiscally prudent to require that the resulting unfunded accrued liability be immediately and fully charged against the current operating budget. With due allowance for enough time to work off the burden of current levels of unfunded accrued laibilities, one could confidently predict that such a requirement would minimize the chances that a government would ever again have serious pension finance troubles.

Along these same lines, governments might consider earmarking some revenue component as the primary source of financing for at least any increments to pension costs that result from benefit liberalization. By requiring that, say, property tax rate or income tax rates be raised as necessary to finance the obligations, public officials and taxpayers would be sure that their retirement systems were being soundly financed, and all would quickly be aware of the fiscal implications of proposed benefit improvements.

Given the differing views even among responsible persons as to how rapidly pension liabilities should be paid for, it is unlikely that many governments will soon adopt such stringent funding requirements. But it is to be hoped that public officials and employees, too, recognize the dangers of adding pension improvement upon pension improvement, in part because these require only small immediate expenditures. Although it is unlikely that many governmental units will go bankrupt in the way that thousands of private firms do every year, the experience of the last couple of years should remind everyone that even large states and local governments do not have an unlimited capacity to generate additional revenues. In turn, this suggests that in matters of pension finance it is well to err on the conservative side and to accumulate assets rapidly. At a minimum, following this course provides the community with a cushion in the event of unexpected economic adversity.

CONCLUSIONS

The cost of providing retirement benefits to their employees is a growing burden to many cities. And while the retirement benefits furnished to employees by cities that do not provide Social Security coverage are seldom excessive relative to retirees' needs, the same cannot be said for the benefits provided by cities participating in the Social Security program. There is a definite need for cities in the latter group to devise methods to coordinate their pension plans with Social Security, thus controlling the total cost of their retirement income programs. Cities should also review the overall objectives of their retirement income programs, giving special attention to their income replacement rate objectives, their age and service requirements for pension eligibility, and their retirement policies for employees in hazardous occupations.

On the pension financing side, the prudent course for cities might be to force themselves to fund accruing employee pension benefits more rapidly and with the assistance of less liberal actuarial assumptions—at least for future service pension liabilities. The conventional practice of making benefit improvements retroactive for past service and of funding the resulting past service liabilities over thirty or more years should be reexamined in the context of what may be a deteriorating general economic and fiscal outlook for many cities. If particular revenue sources were earmarked to finance accruing pension obligations and if new post service liabilities had to be financed as they were incurred, public officials, taxpayers, and employees might be forced to give more careful attention to the community's employee retirement policies and commitments.

NOTES

1. Neal R. Peirce, "Federal-State Report/Public Workers Pay Emerges as Growing Issue," *National Journal* (August 23, 1975): 1200.

2. See Peirce, "Federal-State Report," p. 1200; and Edward H. Friend, *1973 National Survey of Employee Benefits for Full-Time Personnel of U.S. Municipalities*, (Washington, D.C.: Labor-Management Relations Service of the National League of Cities, United States Conference of Mayors, and National Association of Counties, 1974).

3. Friend, 1973 National Survey, 3.

4. Friend, *1973 National Survey*, 6. Also see U.S. Bureau of Labor Statistics, "State Government Employee Compensation: U.S. Summary, 1972," Report 433, February 1975.

5. "City Pension Plans Go Deeper in the Hole," *Business Week* (September 15, 1975): 80. Also see, for example, John C. Perham, "The Mess in Public Pensions," *Dun's Review* (March 1976): 48–50.

6. For a good summary of typical provisions for state and local government employee pension plans, see Robert Tilove, *Public Employee Pension Funds*; A Twentieth Century Fund Report (New York: Columbia University Press, 1975), chap. 2. For a comparable analysis of private industry pension plan provisions, see Bankers Trust Comany, *1975 Study of Corporate Pension Plans* (New York: Bankers Trust, 1975), 6–33.

7. The cities were selected to provide some diversity with respect to city size and geographic

location, and the private firms chosen all employ large numbers of clerical and professional personnel somewhat comparable to the clerical and nonteaching professional work force of large urban governments. Moreover, the benefits provided by the private firms used in this analysis are among the best in private industry. Some of the cities and all three private firms used here were also used by the author in an analysis prepared in connection with the New York State Permanent Commission on Public Employee Pension and Retirement System's report *Recommendations for a New Pension Plan for Public Employees: The 1976 Coordinated Escalator Retirement Plan* (New York: The Commission, 1976).

8. Of the eight cities included here, Social Security coverage is provided to some or all employees in Detroit, New York City, and Philadelphia.

9. Although not taken account of in our calculations, a retiree's living costs will also be lower because of savings on job-related expenses. For some general estimates of savings resultng from retirement, see Peter Henle, "Recent Trends in Retirement Benefits Related to Earnings," *Monthly Labor Review* (June 1972): 18.

10. Another important factor affecting the postretirement spendable incomes of former New York City employees is that their pension benefits are not subject to either New York City or State income taxes.

11. As the numbers in parentheses in Table 4 show, the gross pension benefit for a Los Angeles general employee with thirty years service is 60 percent, and this is superior to the typical pension plan. See Tilove, *Public Employee Pension Funds*, chap. 2.

12. Tilove, *Public Employee Pension Funds*, 339.

13. Although the precise terms were modified in the final legislation enacted in June 1976, the general outline of the arrangement is described in Permanent Commission on Public Employee Pension and Retirement Systems, *Recommendation for a New Pension Plan*. See New York State Senate Bill No. 10799 (1976) and Assembly Bill No. 13139 (1976).

14. Ideally, replacement rates used in plan comparisons should be standardized by excluding the share of total benefits financed by employee contributions. Although most public employee pension plans require employee contributions, the rate of contribution varies among plans from 0 to as much as 8 or 9 percent of an employee's salary. Hence, some of the difference between public plans' replacement rates can be justified by differences in the share of benefits financed by employees. Similarly, lower replacement rates in private industry plans seem reasonable because private industry employees usually do not contribute toward their pensions.

15. A. J. Jaffe, "Pension Systems—How Much Myth? How Much Reality?" Paper presented at the Tenth International Congress on Gerontology, Jerusalem, June 1975, 9; and Henle, "Recent Trends in Retirement Benefits," 20.

16. Jaffe, "Pension Systems," pp. 4–5. Jaffe's estimates are also discussed in Juanita M. Kreps, "Social Security in the Coming Decade: Questions for a Mature System," *Social Security Bulletin* (March 1976): 23.

17. This is a crude estimate based on the assumption that the average employee pension contribution is in the range of 5 percent. Adding this to the 5.85 percent contribution rate for Social Security leads to total contributions of nearly 11 percent.

18. Here we are ignoring arguments of a macro nature that are based on the notion that forced or induced retirements are necessary to make room for persons entering the labor force.

19. But not all cities grant one-half pay pensions after twenty or twenty-five years regardless of age. Likewise, not all cities that do grant such benefits did so on a unilateral basis. In other words, employee bargaining strength plays a role here as well as in the case of retirement provisions for employees in nonhazardous classifications.

20. Tilove, *Public Employee Pension Funds*, 237.

21. For a similar proposal, see Edward H. Friend, "A Proposal: An Approach to the Rising Costs of Police and Fire Pension Systems," Appendix 1 in Philip M. Dearborn, Jr., *Pensions for Policemen and Firemen* (Washington, D.C.: Labor Management Relations Service of the National League of Cities, National Association of Counties, and the United States Conference of Mayors, 1974), 18–20.

22. But this point should not be pushed too far because it is not clear what the response of affected police and firemen would be. After all, the essence of our proposal amounts to a reduction in total compensation, and it is unlikely that implementation of such a benefit cutback would be accepted without a whimper—or more.

23. Tilove, *Public Employee Pension Funds*, 43, 45.

24. For a good discussion of the cost implications of postretirement cost of living adjustments, see Edward H. Friend, "Hidden Bombshells in Cost-of-Living Adjusted Pension Benefits and Post Retirement Health and Welfare Benefits," *1974 Annual Conference Proceedings of Internationl Foundation of Employee Benefit Plans*, 92–99.

25. Friend, "Hidden Bombshells," 94.

26. An excellent summary of the basics of actuarial funding is contained in Tilove, *Public Employee Pension Funds*, chaps. 8 and 9. For a more technical discussion, see Dan M. McGill, *Fundamentals of Private Pensions*, 3d ed. (Homewood, Ill.: Richard D. Irwin, Inc. for the Pension Research Council, 1975).

27. The most extreme example of the fiscal implications of allowing actuarial assumptions to become grossly obsolete involves New York City's five actuarial retirement systems. For reasons that can fairly be labeled as utterly irresponsible, the trustees of these plans failed for as long as fifty years to revise actuarial assumptions that were financially far more favorable than actual experience. As a consequence, when New York finally got around to recomputing pension liabilities with realistic actuarial assumptions, it found that its contribution for fiscal 1976 would have to be increased by about $460 million or 38 percent if it were to continue following the dictates of its current cost measurement method. Relative to its payroll, this would represent an increase in cost from 26 percent to 36 percent. See *Pensions: A Report of the Mayor's Management Advisory Board*, New York City, April 1976, 9.

28. Indeed, to insure equity between generations of taxpayers might require that some portion of the initial liability be borne by future taxpayers.

29. Tilove, *Public Employee Pension Funds*, 166.

30. One of the most extreme examples of the consequence of failing to make advance provisions for accruing benefits is Washington, D.C. The District's current pay-as-you-go cost for the police and fire system is nearly 50 percent of payroll, and this percentage will continue growing for the next several decades. Depending on the assumptions made for salary growth and inflation, the cost may ultimately exceed 100 percent of payroll. See Hearings before the Senate Committee on the District of Columbia on Fiscal Pressures on the District of Columbia, Ninety-Fourth Congress, 2nd session, part 3, Pension Systems, at 85 (1976).

31. McGill, *Fundamentals of Private Pensions*, 378.

32. The risk that assets won't be managed prudently is a matter that deserves close attention. Such attention is especially important now that governments (for example, New York State and City) have rediscovered the "virtues" of borrowing from their own retirement systems. See Louis M. Kohlmeier, *Conflicts of Interests: State and Local Pension Fund Assets Management* (New York: Twentieth Century Fund, 1976).

33. For example, it has been estimated that the 1976 New York City contribution would be about $1.7 billion under aggregate funding and about $1.4 billion under entry-age normal with a forty-year amortization of past service liability. *Pensions: A Report of the Mayor's Management Advisory Board*, 9.

34. Strictly speaking, unfunded accrued liabilities need not be calculated when liabilities are valued by means of the aggregate funding technique.

6

Equity and Public Personnel Management

Equity functions are an important addition to public personnel management. Equity functions include employee rights, labor-management relations, grievance procedures, affirmative action, and career/life planning. They represent the efforts of employees, unions, and outside groups to affect personnel practices. But because the objectives and values of these forces often differ from those of agency management, equity functions frequently conflict with other personnel activities, and in many cases, controversial objectives must be imposed from outside on organizations by courts or regulatory agencies.

David H. Rosenbloom's article on equity functions suggests that the emergence of grievance and appeal systems augers a fundamental expansion of constitutional rights offered to public employees on the job. In particular, employees have an increased property interest in their jobs, requiring due process before the organization can institute disciplinary action, and increased freedom of speech, association, and thought. All of this requires personnel managers to modify previous rules regarding political association and private conduct or belief, and because it is becoming more difficult to discipline employees, agencies may accord increased responsibility to unions in the development of personnel policies.

No area reflects the changes in public personnel management more than labor-management relations. Managers and legislators have been forced into sharing responsibility with employees for determining such issues as pay, benefits, and working conditions. The article by Richard H. Allen describes the differences between the legal contexts of private sector and public sector bargaining, primarily the absence of uniform enabling legislation in the latter. While public employees have the right to organize, they do not have the right to strike in most jurisdictions. The lack of nationwide collective bargaining legislation means that each state is free to define crucial issues independently for itself and subservient counties—unit determination, the scope of bargaining, bargaining procedures, and impasse procedures. One additional problem is that public unions must often bargain with agency managers who are powerless to impose settlements on a legislature, and this confuses the definition of "good faith bargaining."

Lanning S. Mosher states that public managers have the responsibility of using labor-management relations for the public interest. In particular, they should seek neither to destroy unions nor to abdicate their role as spokespersons for employee interests in favor of the union. This requires that managers be tough prepared negotiators, who are at the same time willing to address employee concerns directly and honestly. Though some commentators may feel that this approach is an impossible ideal, the author considers it necessary if both sides are to win at the bargaining table.

The diversity and complexity of public sector labor-management relations are shown by the fourth article, in which Richard S. Rubin discusses the particular context of labor-management relations for police officers and fire fighters. Because of their importance to the public safety, states and municipalities have been reluctant to extend collective bargaining rights to them. Even when this conflict is resolved, other characteristics of public safety positions make collective bargaining difficult: (1) the presence of supervisors in a bargaining unit could be detrimental to the paramilitary chain of command of these organizations; (2) public safety employees generally have an earlier retirement age and more liberal pension benefits than do their "civilian" counterparts in other agencies; and (3) it is difficult to resolve bargaining impasses if enabling legislation forbids strikes by public safety employees. Although "job actions" and arbitration have been suggested as alternatives to strikes, municipal officials are still undecided as to how they can best meet the needs of these employees while still protecting the interests of the public.

Disciplinary actions and grievances represent opposing sides in the struggle to preserve equity for employees and management. The former are used by managers to penalize employees for violations of work rules or low productivity. The latter are used by employees, working with or without a union contract, to protest unfair actions on the part of management. Because of the conflicting values involved, these activities are the focal points of controversy among managers, employees, and outside groups.

Any discussion of employee complaints or grievances must consider what types of employees file grievances and what impact grievances can have on an organization. W. W. Ronan and his associates conclude that grievants can be identified on the basis of other work-related behaviors. They show a higher rate of terminations and other adverse indicators, yet also have a higher level of education. Regardless of this, the authors do feel that several kinds of grievances are good in that they may point out poor management practices. For this reason, it may be more desirable to have employees file grievances than not.

Affirmative action and equal employment opportunity are critical equity areas because they define the conditions under which public employees are selected, promoted, and rewarded. As we have seen with selection and promotion, changes in the law have an immediate and direct effect on the personnel practices of public organizations.

Affirmative action law and compliance procedures are complex, confusing, and controversial. An easy way to start an argument among personnel managers is by suggesting that affirmative action is nothing but good (or bad) personnel management. Convincing arguments can be made on either side. Proponents of affirmative action consider it an important method of utilizing all human resources more fully by increasing the equity of recuitment, selection, promotion, training, compensation, and career/life planning. Opponents consider it a variation on the old "political" practice of using personnel rules to favor one race or sex at the expense of others. In addition, they decry the cost of compliance procedures and reporting requirements.

In the first of four articles on affirmative action, Elliot M. Zashin discusses its impact on federal employment. He evaluates a number of major criticisms of affirmative action and concludes that it is necessary, has been to some extent successful, is not necessarily in conflict with merit system standards, does not necessarily lead to reverse discrimination, and does not require quotas. While many whites criticize affirmative action because they believe it leads to preferential selection, he feels it should be supported because this criticism has not been validated.

David E. Robertson discusses the implications of the 1978 changes in EEOC selection guidelines that employers must follow. In particular, he feels that reliance on the 80-percent rule and the "bottom-line" strategy to assess adverse impact may reduce an employer's incentive to validate tests at all. On the other hand, the increased acceptance given to nonempirical validation methods may make validation easier for small agencies. However, the cautious nature of his conclusions shows that all these regulations are subject to continual interpretation and modification by federal courts.

The third article on affirmative action, by James A. Craft, discusses the impact of seniority on reassignment and promotion. Unions and many managers support seniority because it makes promotion decisions simpler. Yet seniority systems may be in violation of civil rights laws if they were originally established for discriminatory purposes. Furthermore, such systems usually affect minorities and women adversely, even if this was not their intent, because employees in these categories lack seniority compared to white males. Lastly, in the event of organization-wide layoffs or transfers, seniority systems may lead to the retention of employees with lesser job skills.

Francine S. Hall addresses a problem faced by many public personnel managers—how to meet hiring and promotion goals under an affirmative action program when a recessionary economy results in a stable or declining work force. Her suggestions include providing training and encouraging personal growth for minorities and women, redesigning jobs, conducting career planning, and creating job lattices to reduce the number of dead-end positions.

Career/life planning is the last equity function. It involves meeting the employee's need for greater information with which to make choices among alternative career patterns. The objective here is not primarily to increase the quality of organizational forecasting, but rather to improve the rationality and satisfaction behind individual career patterns within the agency. The article by Edgar Schein (in Chapter 2) provided a good theoretical introduction to the objectives and techniques of career/life planning. Here, Cary B. Barad describes an in-house interest-inventory system developed and used by the Social Security Administration. Employees respond to a number of statements about organizational job activities and are matched with clusters of occupations based on the extent to which their responses are similar to those of satisfied employees in each of the occupational groups.

Public Personnel Administration and the Constitution: An Emergent Approach

David H. Rosenbloom

During the past decade the courts have almost completely transformed the nature of the constitutional position of public employees in the United States. This transformation has largely resulted in an expansion of the constitutional rights and protections afforded public employees in their relationship with government in its role as employer. In the early stages of change, judicial decisions tended to destroy prevailing doctrines without replacing them with much more than a demand that the balance between the rights of public employees and public employers be redressed. It is now possible, however, to identify a consistent line of judicial reasoning that has been emerging and to assess, in a preliminary way, its importance for public personnel administration.

NEW FOUNDATIONS

Historically, the constitutional position of public employees in the United States was governed by what has become known as the doctrine of privilege.[1] Under this line of interpretation it was generally accepted that because there was no constitutional right to public employment and because such employment was voluntary rather than compulsory, public employees had few constitutional rights which could not be legitimately abridged by the state in its role as employer. That this doctrine has now been completely discarded is common knowledge. The Supreme Court, for example, has stated, ". . . the Court has fully and finally rejected the wooden distinction between 'rights' and 'privileges' that once seemed to govern the applicability of procedural due process rights.[2] It is easier to note the demise of the doctrine of privilege, however, than to comprehend its replacement.

It is impossible to summarize briefly the content of the line of constitutional interpretation that has superseded the doctrine of privilege. It is still emerging, generally vague, and sometimes contradictory in several of its facets. At its foundation, however, are a new set of assumptions. First, the courts currently approach the constitutional position of public employees from the premise "... that a state [or the federal government] cannot condition an individual's privilege of public employment on his nonparticipation in conduct which, under the Constitution, is protected from direct interference by the state."[3] Thus, for example, it is now generally agreed that:

> A citizen's right to engage in protected expression or debate is substantially unaffected by the fact that he is also an employee of the government, and as a general rule, he cannot be deprived of his employment merely because he exercises those rights. This is so because dismissal from government employment, like criminal sanctions or damages, may inhibit the propensity of a citizen to exercise his right to freedom of speech and association.[4]

Perhaps more fundamentally, from the viewpoint of public personnel administration, it is also currently accepted that, "... whenever there is a substantial interest, other than employment by the state, involved in the discharge of a public employee, he can be removed neither on arbitrary grounds nor without a procedure calculated to determine whether legitimate grounds do exist."[5] These principles create a new set of facts for public employees; but in the absence of further elaboration by the courts, they cannot provide sufficient guidance for a corresponding adjustment of public personnel practice. Although there has been little additional theoretical development of the current constitutional approach, an analysis of judicial decisions over the past five years or so indicates that at least one central strand of thought is running through most of the cases and that it is likely to have a considerable impact on public personnel theory and practice in the years to come.

THE DEVELOPMENT OF AN IDIOGRAPHIC APPROACH

Analysis of judicial decisions involving the procedural and substantive constitutional rights of public employees indicates that the courts have, with only one major exception, demonstrated a marked reluctance to uphold flat, general, across-the-board special restrictions on their rights. The judiciary has largely demanded, rather, that in applying general personnel regulations and principles to individual employees, public employers address the merits of the specific cases at hand. In other words, while it may sometimes be permissible to take adverse action against public employees in such a fashion that it infringes upon their ordinarily held constitutional rights as citizens, such action cannot be taken in all areas and generally cannot be applied without reference to the specific set of facts in each case.

Procedural Due Process

In terms of procedural due process, the emergent principle is evident in a number of recent cases. Prior to the Supreme Court's decisions in *Roth* v. *Board of Regents* and

Perry v. Sindermann (1972),[6] the lower courts were widely divided on the questions of whether a dismissed or nonrenewed public employee had a constitutional right to a statement of reasons for the adverse action and an opportunity to attempt to rebut them. Roth established the rule that although there is no general constitutional right to either a statement of reasons or a hearing, both of these might be constitutionally required in individual instances. This would be the case under any one of four conditions. One is the instance of removal or nonrenewal in retaliation for the exercise of constitutional rights such as freedom of speech or association. A second ground is impairment of reputation. The Court held that:

> The State, in declining to rehire the respondent, did not make any charge against him that might seriously damage his standing and associations in his community. It did not base the nonrenewal of his contract on a charge, for example, that he had been guilty of dishonesty or immorality. Had it done so, this would be a different case. For "[w]here a person's good name, reputation, honor, or integrity is at stake because of what the government is doing to him, notice and an opportunity to be heard are essential." [Citations omitted] ... In such a case, due process would accord an opportunity to refute the charge before University officials.[7]

Third, and perhaps not fully distinguishable, a public employee would have a right to procedural due process if a dismissal or nonrenewal "... imposed on him a stigma or other disability that foreclosed his freedom to take advantage of other employment opportunities."[8]

Finally, if one had a property right or interest in a position, procedural due process would be required before employment could be terminated. But, "To have a property interest in a benefit, a person clearly must have more than an abstract need or desire for it. He must, instead, have a legitimate claim of entitlement to it."[9] In the closely related Sindermann case, the Court indicated that such a claim need not necessarily be based on a written contract or statutory protection, but might also be based on "... an unwritten 'common law' ... that certain employees shall have the equivalent of tenure."[10]

In avoiding an across-the-board approach, Roth and Sindermann make it necessary for public personnel administrators and the courts to determine whether a dismissal or nonrenewal is such that it constitutes an infringement upon liberty, including impairment of reputation or future employment possibilities, or upon property interests. This approach requires a good deal of individual judgment in individual cases. For example, what constitutes a charge that might seriously and adversely affect one's reputation or chances of earning a livelihood in a chosen occupational area? Thus far, it has been held that removals or nonrenewals for fraud,[11] racism,[12] lack of veracity,[13] and, at least in connection with high-level urban employment, absenteeism and gross insubordination[14] can violate procedural due process in the absence of a hearing. It has also been strongly suggested that removal at an advanced age tends to preclude subsequent employment and therefore requires the application of procedural due process.[15] On the other hand, a charge of being "anti-establishment" has been found not to create a sufficient impairment of reputation so as to afford constitutional protection.[16] The point is not to ask whether these holdings are consistent or reasonable, but rather to note that a public employee's right to procedural due process protections in adverse actions, where reasons for the action are supplied, must be evaluated on a multidimensional basis including an assessment of the nature of the charge, the type and level of position, and the age of the individual. Under these circumstances it is evident that each case is largely a separate one.

The same individualized tendency prevails with regard to the issue of what constitutes a constitutionally cognizable property interest. In *Sindermann* the length of employment was about ten years. In other cases, twenty-nine and eleven years of employment were found to create enough of a property interest to warrant the application of procedural due process.[17] It has also been held that, ". . . regulations or standards of practice governing nontenured employees which create an expectation of reemployment[18] can establish a property interest. On the other hand, eight years of employment on a series of one-year certificates was found to be insufficient to require procedural due process in a nonrenewal.[19]

A final question with regard to procedural due process involves the nature of the protections that must be provided when a hearing is required or held. The law here is ambiguous, and its ambiguity is such that prudent public personnel administrators will probably tend to develop considerably more elaborate hearing procedures than have generally prevailed in the past. Confrontation and cross-examination have been required in some cases[20] but not in others of a similar nature.[21] The courts are also divided on whether a strict separation of prosecutorial and judicial functions is constitutionally required.[22] There is also a question as to whether hearings can constitutionally be closed to the press and the public.[23] If there is any prevailing precept, it is that the more severe the injury to the individual, the greater the procedural protections that must be provided; but again this is a factor that must be weighed with reference to the specifics of each case.

Freedom of Expression, Association, and Thought

Recent holdings regarding substantive constitutional rights reveal a similar tendency. Here the major issues have been the extent to which public employees can exercise the rights of freedom of expression, association, and thought. The most important case currently governing public employees' rights to freedom of speech is *Pickering v. Illinois* (1968). There the Supreme Court held that although ". . . it cannot be gainsaid that the State has interests as an employer in regulating the speech of its employees that differ significantly from those it possesses in connection with regulation of the speech of the citizenry in general,"[24] the proper test is whether the state's interest in limiting public employees' ". . . opportunities to contribute to public debate is . . . significantly greater than its interest in limiting a similar contribution by any member of the general public."[25] The Court identified six elements which would generally enable the state to abridge legitimately public employees' freedom of expression. These can be paraphrased as follows:

1. The need for maintaining discipline and harmony in the work force.

2. The need for confidentiality.

3. The possibility that an employee's position is such that his or her statements might be hard to counter due to his or her presumed greater access to factual information.

4. The situation in which an employee's statements impede the proper performance of duties.

5. The case where the statements are so without foundation that the individual's basic capability to perform his or her duties comes into question.

6. The jeopardizing of a close and personal loyalty and confidence.

In applying *Pickering*, the courts have developed a fairly consistent pattern requiring individualized judgment. In addition to the above factors, it has been held that the nature of the remarks or expression,[26] degree of disruption,[27] and likelihood that ". . . the public will attach special importance to the statements made by someone in a particular position . . ."[28] must be weighed. In general, only discussions of matters of public concern, as opposed to those primarily of interest to co-workers, are subject to protection under *Pickering*.

There is one major exception to all of this—partisan expression and activity. Without in any way attempting to deny its great importance, however, it should be recognized that the Supreme Court has treated regulations for political neutrality differently than others affecting the constitutional position of public employees. Such regulations were initially upheld in *United Public Workers* v. *Mitchell* (1947).[29] Since that time several federal and state courts have held political neutrality provisions to be unconstitutional.[30] The *Mitchell* decision, for example, was held to have been ". . . vitiated by the force of subsequent decisions,"[31] and placed ". . . among other decisions outmoded by the passage of time."[32] However, in *Civil Service Commission* v. *National Association of Letter Carriers* (1973) and *Broadrick* v. *Oklahoma* (1973),[33] a companion case, the Supreme Court decided to ". . . unhesitatingly reaffirm the Mitchell holding. . . ."[34] The Court argues that such a judgment simply confirmed

> . . . the judgment of history, a judgment made by this country over the last century that it is in the best interest of the country, indeed essential, that federal service should depend upon meritorious performance rather than political service, and that the political influence of federal employees on others and on the electoral process should be limited.[35]

In terms of *Pickering*, therefore, the government had an obviously much greater interest in limiting the partisan activities of its employees than it did in limiting those of its other citizens. Moreover, *Broadrick* indicated that the Court is willing to allow great leeway in terms of the wording of restrictions on the political participation of public employees. In this area, therefore, sweeping restrictions on the constitutional rights of public employees, even loosely worded and without regard to position, are legitimate. Elsewhere this is not the case.

The law regarding public employees' rights of freedom of association and thought falls into the predominant idiographic pattern. Their right to freedom of association was broadly guaranteed by the Supreme Court in *Shelton* v. *Tucker* (1960).[36] The case left open the questions of whether public employees could have membership in subversive organizations, organizations with illegal objectives, and unions. Their right to join the latter was guaranteed in *American Federation of State, County, and Municipal Employees* v. *Woodward* (1969).[37] With regard to the former, it was held in *Elfbrandt* v. *Russell* (1966)[38] that there could be no general answer, but rather that each case had to be judged on the basis of whether a public employee actually supported an organization's illegal aims since "[t]hose who join an organization but do not share its unlawful purposes and who do not participate in its unlawful activities surely pose no threat, either as citizens or as public employees."[39]

Similarly, in terms of freedom of thought, adverse actions based on almost anything more than simple refusal to pledge support for the federal and state constitutions are unconstitutional in the absence of a hearing to determine the beliefs an individual holds and how these can negatively and seriously affect governmental interests. Thus, in *Connell* v. *Higginbotham* (1971), for example, the Supreme Court held that a loyalty oath requiring public employees to swear that they ". . . do not believe in the overthrow of the Government of the United States or of the State of Florida by force or violence"[40] falls ". . . within the ambit of decisions of this Court proscribing summary dismissal from public employment without hearing or inquiry required by due process. . . ."[41] Therefore, exclusion from public employment on the basis of association or thought is to be effectuated for the most part only on a case by case basis in which specific factors are taken into account.

Equal Protection

There have also been several cases in the area of equal protection that have required an idiographic approach. In *Baker* v. *City of St. Petersburg* (1968),[42] twelve black policemen contested the constitutionality of police department practices under which all blacks were assigned to a zone that was predominantly black in population. The district court found that the ". . . assignment of Negro officers to the predominantly Negro Zone 13 was not done for the purpose of discrimination but for the purpose of effective administration."[43] The police department argued that blacks could better identify and communicate with blacks than could whites. The circuit court of appeals, however, reversed on the ground that ". . . a Department's practice of assigning Negroes solely on the basis of race to a Negro enclave offends the equal protection clause of the Fourteenth Amendment."[44] Yet the court went on to say, "We do not hold that the assignment of a Negro officer to a particular task because he is a Negro can never be justified."[45]

The Supreme Court followed this line of reasoning in *Sugarman* v. *Dougall* (1973), a case involving discrimination against aliens. The Court held that ". . . a flat ban on the employment of aliens in positions that have little, if any, relation to a state's legitimate interest, cannot withstand scrutiny under the Fourteenth Amendment."[46] At the same time, however, "A restriction on the employment of noncitizens, narrowly confined, could have particular relevance to this important state responsibility, for alienage itself is a factor that reasonably could be employed in defining 'political community.' "[47]

Although the Supreme Court chose to treat the issue under due process rather than equal protection, a somewhat similar line of reasoning was adopted concerning mandatory maternity leaves. In *Cleveland Board of Education* v. *LaFleur* (1974), the Court found policies requiring pregnant school teachers to leave their jobs four and five months before the expected date of birth to be unconstitutional because "There is no individualized determination by the teacher's doctor—or the school board's—as to any particular teacher's ability to continue at her job."[48] The Court indicated, however, that mandatory leaves applying only in the last few weeks of pregnancy might present a different set of issues and conclusions.

Implications for Public Personnel Administration

Public personnel administration in the United States still retains a paradigm that was largely developed by the civil service reform movement. With strict regard to public employment, as opposed to wider political interests, the reformers stood for political neutrality, a higher level of morality, and greater administrative efficiency. Each of these goals has left a significant legacy for contemporary public personnel administration that is likely to undergo modification as a result of the emergence of an idiographic approach to the constitutional status of public employees.

The reformers' emphasis on political neutrality led to the enactment of restrictions on the partisan political activity of public employees in a large number of jurisdictions. It also encouraged the development of a position-oriented public personnel administration which attaches rank and salary to positions rather than individuals and thereby makes it somewhat more difficult to exercise political favoritism. Regulations concerning public employees' membership and belief in subversive organizations and causes are also partially subsumed under the goal of political neutrality. However, the idiographic approach seems certain to foster significant changes in this area.

Although the Supreme Court has left no doubt that, in general, regulations for political neutrality are constitutionally permissible, it has also created a presumption that *nonpartisan* political expression by public employees is constitutionally protected. Under *Pickering* and the cases following it, the latter can be abridged only when a government has demonstrable and compelling interests in so doing. Moreover, exclusion from public employment on the basis of political association or political belief is no longer constitutionally legitimate in the absence of procedural due process protections. These strictures require modification of the position orientation because thinking in terms of "classified," "excepted," "sensitive," and "nonsensitive" positions and position levels is no longer consititutionally viable or useful with regard to some adverse actions.

While the type of position still retains importance in determining the nature of permissible expression, association, and thought, each public employee has a constitutional right to be heard on the merits of his or her individual case. Broad exclusions, except for partisan activity, can no longer withstand constitutional scrutiny. Therefore, the public service may remain largely nonpartisan, but insofar as the Constitution is concerned, public employees as a group cannot be required to be *apolitical* as well. Moreover, it is possible that the partisan/nonpartisan distinction, which is clearly a legacy of reform, may prove untenable under conditions of increasing political activity by public employees[49] and that consequently both public personnel administrators and the judiciary will have to rethink many of the issues involved.

The morality of public employees has also been an important concern of public personnel administration in the postreform period. Removals or exclusions for " . . . infamous, dishonest, immoral, or notoriously disgraceful conduct"[50] have not been uncommon. The idiographic approach is also likely to have a considerable impact in this area. The *Roth* decision would require a hearing before a public employee could be removed or not renewed on any of the above grounds. Elsewhere it has been held that ". . . a finding that an employee has done something immoral or indecent could support a dismissal without further inquiry only if all immoral or indecent acts of an employee have some *ascertainable deleterious* effect on the efficiency of the service."[51] Together, these decisions, and the idiographic approach generally, make it necessary to determine: (1) whether an employee has engaged in an alleged act; (2) whether the act can be considered immoral, indecent, or so on, both in general and in connection with injury to the employee's reputation and chances for future employment; and (3) whether the act, even if committed and immoral or indecent, is such that the individual's employment would have a demonstrable adverse effect on legitimate objectives of the public services. These requirements not only make it necessary to treat each case separately, but they also introduce a stringency that makes it very probable that many forms of behavior which once served as a basis for exclusion from the public service for immorality or indecency will prove insufficient for this purpose in the future.[52]

The implications of the idiographic approach for the objective of greater administrative efficiency are less clear. "Efficiency" has been used as a justification for many practices, including some, such as racial and sexual discrimination, that are no longer constitutionally acceptable. Techniques for measuring efficiency, however, are still very crude, and it appears that in time the idiographic approach will compel public personnel administrators either to develop better ones or to forfeit a good deal of their authority over public employment to the judiciary. The case by case approach to the constitutional status of public employees requires the courts to play a far greater role in overseeing public personnel administration than was previously the case. Indeed, the demise of the doctrine of privilege and the development of the idiographic approach have coincided with a broadening of the ". . . scope of [judicial] review to include a judicial determination as to whether the administrative findings were capricious, arbitrary, or unreasonable, or whether such findings were supported by the record."[53] In order to justify many of their regulations before the courts in the future, therefore, public personnel administrators will be increasingly required to demonstrate how these effectuate efficiency.

More general implications of the idiographic approach for public personnel administration follow from its more limited implications for each of the foregoing areas. In its pursuit of political neutrality, higher morality, and greater efficiency, public personnel administration has developed a very considerable policing function. Even though this has declined somewhat in the face of more recent developmental approaches, a large part of the responsibility of most central personnel agencies in the United States is still to ensure compliance with personnel regulations.

The idiographic approach, however, is likely to make many aspects of policing more difficult and costly. In requiring a case by case approach to many questions involving the constitutional position of public employees, by affording public employees greater constitutional protection, and by broadening the scope of judicial review of administrative determinations, the courts have obviously made adverse actions more difficult to justify. Hearings must be more frequently held, and their procedures must be more elaborate. Open hearings with counsel, confrontation, and cross-examination will become more common. In practice this will almost inevitably lead to a decline in the coercive power of public employers over their employees. The psychological, economic, and time costs of taking adverse actions will often outweigh the benefits that might be gained by removing an employee. Personnel administration by adversary proceeding is not likely to be efficient or effective. The specter of super- and subordinates facing each other at hearings and in lawsuits and perhaps then returning to work together seems unattractive from almost all perspectives. As a leading civil service reformer expressed it, "If it were necessary to establish unfitness or indolence, . . . by such proof as would be accepted in a court of law, sentence would seldom be pronounced, even against notorious delinquents . . . "[54] Thus, insofar as public personnel administrators desire to regulate the on-the-job behavior of public employees, they will have to rely less on policing activities and punishment and turn more toward other means of inducing compliance.[55]

A decline in public personnel administration's policing function may also be forthcoming as a result of the peculiar nature of the hearings required by the idiographic approach. In the past the function of most quasi-judicial administrative hearings involving personnel matters has been to determine factually whether a public employee violated a regulation or failed to perform adequately on the job. Constitutional questions were seldom raised and almost always deferred to the courts. In instances where liberty or property, as defined in *Roth* and *Sindermann*, are involved, however, the idiographic approach requires that hearing officials—often employed by central personnel agencies—no longer assume the validity of personnel regulations. Instead, they must assess the relationship of regulations to legitimate personnel goals and to injury to individual employees. Therefore a constitutional question is quickly raised, and the hearing process must become more judgmentally independent than has generally been the case. This not only shifts much of the burden of proof from the public employee to the public employer, but it also creates an important, often internal, check on the policing function of public personnel administration at the hearing stage.

Relatedly, one of the most important effects of the idiographic approach may be to reinforce the ongoing process of granting unions a larger role in public personnel administration. In some jurisdictions, unions have already secured a right to be present at grievance proceedings and adverse action hearings. They may also be authorized to represent employees regardless of the employees' union membership. Expansion of the requirements of procedural due process and the emergence of new substantive constitutional guarantees on a case by case basis obviously point in the direction of increasing union attention to the provision of counsel and other legal services. More significantly, to the extent that unions are interested in the security and freedom of public employees, they may further develop their role as judicial pressure groups by actively seeking out and bringing litigation. Such developments would probably strengthen their bargaining position with regard to public personnel matters of constitutional concern and make public personnel administration a more shared enterprise between management and unions.

In sum, then, an analysis of recent cases involving the constitutional position of public employees indicates that although there is still a good deal of ambiguity in some areas, at least one consistent line of judicial reasoning has emerged. The doctrine of privilege has been replaced by an approach requiring that constitutional questions concerning public employees be decided largely on a case by case basis. Although an idiographic approach is natural for the judiciary in applying due process, it requires significant modification of public personnel administrative practice. Political neutrality is becoming more narrowly defined as partisan neutrality. Regulations intended to ensure a high level of morality among public servants will have to be more carefully formulated, applied, and related to other personnel objectives. In order to justify regulations designed to foster greater administrative efficiency, public personnel administrators will have to develop better measurement techniques. More generally, the idiographic approach lessens the utility of public personnel administration's policing function, and this will probably be compensated through the development of other means of securing compliance.

The last two points suggest that while the idiographic approach does require some difficult rethinking of public personnel administrative questions, it may well encourage the development of a more satisfying public personnel administration.[56] A decline in the policing function, the expansion of public employees' constitutional guarantees, and a larger role for unions in the formulation of personnel policy may make public employment a more attractive work environment and more competitive with private employment. Public personnel administration will be more technically satisfying if it becomes grounded on a more conscious effort to separate real from presumed relationships and more cognizant of what is not known about employee and organizational behavior. Finally, the emergent constitutional approach requires public personnel administration to be in greater political and social harmony with contemporary behavior and values.

NOTES

1. For a historical analysis of the constitutional position of federal employees in the United States, see David H. Rosenbloom, *Federal Service and the Constitution* (Ithaca: Cornell University Press, 1971). The "idiographic" approach elaborated upon in this article can be seen as the judiciary's method of applying the doctrine of "substantial interest" discussed in the earlier work.
2. *Roth v. Board of Regents*, 33 L. Ed. 2d 548, 557 (1972).
3. *Gilmore v. James*, 274 F. Supp. 75, 91 (1967).
4. *Pickering v. Board of Education*, 391 U.S. 563, 574 (1968).
5. *Birnbaum v. Trussell*, 371 F 2d 672, 678 (1968).
6. *Roth*, cited supra, n. 2; *Perry v. Sindermann*, 33 L. Ed. 2d 570 (1972).
7. *Roth v. Board of Regents*, 33 L. Ed. 2d 548, 558.
8. *Ibid.*, 559.
9. *Ibid.*, 561.
10. *Perry v. Sindermann*, 33 L. Ed. 2d 570, 580.
11. *United States v. Rasmussen*, 222 F. Supp. 430 (1963).
12. *Birnbaum v. Trussell*, cited supra, n. 5.
13. *Hostrop v. Board of Junior College District No. 515*, 471 F 2d 488 (1972).
14. *Hunter v. Ann Arbor*, 325 F. Supp. 847, 854 (1971).
15. *Olson v. Regents*, 301 F. Supp. 1356 (1969).
16. *Lipp v. Board of Education*, 470 F 2d 802 (1972).
17. *Johnson v. Fraley*, 470 F 2d 179 (1972), and *Lucas v. Chapman*, 430 F 2d 945 (1970).
18. *Ferguson v. Thomas*, 430 F 2d 852, 856 (1970).
19. *Patrone v. Howland Local Schools Board of Education*, 472 F 2d 159 (1972).

20. See, among others, *U.S.* v. *Rasmussen*, cited *supra*, n. 11; *Kelley* v. *Herak*, 252 F. Supp. 289 (1966), subsequently overruled in *Herak* v. *Kelley*, 391 F 2d 216 (1968); *Ahern* v. *Board of Education*, 456 F 2d 339 (1972).

21. See, among others, *Polcover* v. *Secretary of Treasury*, 477 F 2d 1223 (1973), and *Bishop* v. *McKee*, 400 F 2d 87 (1968).

22. See *Camero* v. *United States*, 375 F 2d 777 (1967); *Taylor* v. *New York Transit Authority*, 433 F 2d 665 (1970); *Allen* v. *City of Greensboro*, 452 F 2d 489 (1971); and *Simard* v. *Board of Education*, 473 F 2d 988 (1973).

23. In *Fitzgerald* v. *Hampton*, 467 F 2d 755 (1972), it was held that the Constitution requires that a quasi-judicial administrative proceeding involving personnel matters to be open to the press and public, at least under the specific circumstances involved.

24. *Pickering* v. *Illinois*, 391 U.S. 563, 568.

25. *Ibid.*, 573.

26. See, among others, *Clark* v. *Holmes*, 474 F 2d 928 (1972); *Childwood* v. *Feaster*, 468 F 2d 359 (1972); *Duke* v. *North Texas State University*, 469 F 2d 829 (1973); and *Goldwasser* v. *Brown*, 417 F 2d 1169 (1969).

27. See *Peale* v. *United States*, 325 F. Supp. 193 (1971); *James* v. *Board of Education*, 461 F 2d 566 (1972); *Rozman* v. *Elliott*, 467 F 2d 1145 (1972); *Russo* v. *Central School District*, 469 F 2d 623 (1972); *Hanover* v. *Northrup*, 325 F. Supp. 170 (1971); and *Donahue* v. *Stauton*, 471 F 2d 75 (1972).

28. *Donovan* v. *Reinbold*, 433 F 2d 738, 743 (1970); see also *Fisher* v. *Walker*, 464 F2d 1147 (1972).

29. 330 U.S. 75 (1947).

30. *Mancuso* v. *Taft*, 341 F. Supp. 574 (1972); *Hobbes* v. *Thompson*, 448 F 2d 456 (1971); *Fort* v. *Civil Service Commission*, 61 Cal. 2d 331 (1964); *Kinnear* v. *San Francisco*, 61 Cal. 2d 341 (1964); *Minielly* v. *Oregon*, 242 Ore. 490 (1966); and *Bagley* v. *Hospital District*, 421 F 2d 409 (1966). Political neutrality regulations were upheld in *Northern Virginia Regional Park Authority* v. *Civil Service Commission*, 437 F 2d 1347 (1971) and *Kearney* v. *Macy*, 409 F 2d 847 (1969).

31. *Mancuso* v. *Taft*, 341 F. Supp. 574, 577 (1972).

32. *National Association of Letter Carriers* v. *Civil Service Commission*, 346 F. Supp. 578, 585 (1972).

33. 37 L. Ed. 2d 796, and 37 L. Ed. 2d 830 (1973).

34. 37 L. Ed. 2d 796, 804.

35. Ibid.

36. 364 U.S. 479 (1960).

37. 406 F 2d 137 (1969).

38. 384 U.S. 11 (1966).

39. Ibid., 17.

40. 403 U.S. 207, 208 (1971).

41. Ibid., 208-209.

42. 400 F 2d 294 (1968).

43. Ibid., 296.

44. Ibid., 300.

45. Ibid., 300-301.

46. 37 L. Ed. 2d 853, 862 (1973). See also *Jalil* v. *Hampton*, 460 F 2d 923 (1972).

47. 37 L. Ed. 853, 864. In passing it should be noted that this decision brings into question the legitimacy of statutes, such as the Foreign Service Act, which prohibit the employment of citizens whose naturalization did not take place prior to a specific number of years before their application for employment was made.

48. 39 L. Ed. 2d 52, 62. Such issues have generally been treated under equal protection. See *Shattmann v. Texas*, 459 F 2d 32 (1972); *Cohen v. Chesterfield County School Board*, 474 F 2d 395 (1973); *LaFleur v. Cleveland Board of Education*, 465 F 2d 1184 (1972); *Buckley v. Coyle Public School System*, 475 F 2d 92 (1973); and *Green v. Waterford Board of Education*, 473 F 2d 629 (1973).

49. For a discussion of increasing political involvement by federal employees, see D. H. Rosenbloom, "Some Political Implications of the Drift Toward a Liberation of Federal Employees," *Public Administration Review* XXXI (July/August 1971): 420–26.

50. U.S. Civil Service Commission Rule V. section 3. See Civil Service Commission, *Civil Service Act, Rules, Statutes, Executive Orders, and Regulations* (Washington, D.C.: U.S. Government Printing Office, 1941), 37.

51. *Norton v. Macy*, 417 F 2d 1161, 1165 (1969), emphasis added.

52. In *Norton v. Macy, supra* n. 51, and *Scott v. Macy*, 349 F 2d 182 (1965), it was held that homosexuality was not sufficient grounds for removal in the absence of a showing that it was adversely related to competence or the efficiency of the federal service. Similarly, it is questionable whether it would still be constitutionally possible to dismiss a policeman for living with an unmarried woman. See *The New York Times*, August 1, 1968, 27. There have been too few cases to indicate clearly what forms of "immorality," if any, might still provide the basis for general exclusion from public service.

53. *West v. Macy*, 284 F. Supp. 105 (1968).

54. U.S. Civil Service Commission, "Reform of the Civil Service: A Report to the President, December 18, 1971," *Orations and Addresses of George Wilson Curtis*, Vol II, ed., Charles E. Norton (New York: Harper and Bros., 1894), 51.

55. For a discussion of compliance in organizations, see Amitai Etzioni, *Complex Organizations* (New York: The Free Press, 1961).

56. For a general discussion of how public personnel administration might be further developed, see D. H. Rosenbloom, "Public Personnel Administration and Politics: Toward a New Public Personnel Administration," *Midwest Review of Public Administration* VII (April 1973): 98–110.

Collective Bargaining in the Public Sector

Richard H. Allen

INTRODUCTION

It is the purpose of this article to examine labor relations in the public sector and to identify some of its special characteristics and problems. To do so, there will be a brief examination of employee rights in the private sector, against which the corresponding rights of employees in the public sector will be compared and contrasted: first, where there is no statute governing public employees and, secondly, where such a statute does exist. This article is not intended to be an in-depth analysis of public sector labor relations. Rather, it is intended as an overview and a springboard from which further research into this rapidly developing field may be commenced.

Private employee rights are governed by the National Labor Relations Act.[1] Under this act, private employees are given certain basic rights, among which are the right to organize,[2] to bargain collectively,[3] and to engage in concerted activity for the purpose of collective bargaining or other mutual aid or protection, that is, the right to strike.[4] In addition, the act provides a mechanism for holding elections to determine if the employees want to organize;[5] if the union wins, it will be certified by the NLRB as the exclusive bargaining agent for all of the employees in the bargaining unit.[6]

The act further describes a series of employer and union unfair labor practices, which the NLRB is empowered to restrain.[7] Various unfair labor practices in which the employer is prohibited from engaging are: (1) interfering with employee's exercise of Section 7 rights,[8] (2) dominating, interfering, or supporting a labor organization,[9] (3) encouraging or discouraging union membership by discrimination,[10] (4) discriminating against an employee for filing unfair labor practice charges,[11] and (5) refusing to bargain collectively with the employee representative.[12] There are corresponding unfair labor practices for unions[13] and prohibitions against certain secondary boycotts,[14] featherbedding,[15] and organizational and recognitional picketing.[16]

Public employees and their employer, on the other hand, have no comprehensive federal statutory scheme to define their rights and duties. They are specifically excluded from coverage under the NLRA. By definition an "employer" does "not include the United States or any wholly owned government corporation or any Federal Reserve Bank, or any state or political subdivision thereof."[17] Since the

Richard H. Allen has been an attorney for the National Labor Relations Board and is vice-chairman of the Labor Law Committee of the General Practice Session of the American Bar Association.

Reprinted from Richard H. Allen, "Collective Bargaining in the Public Sector," *Barrister*, Vol. 3, No. 3 (Fall 1976), 65–70. Copyright 1976 American Bar Association.

federal government and the states are not employers under the NLRA, their employees are not covered by the act because the act excludes "any individual employed ... by any other person who is not an employer as herein defined."[18] Consequently, public employees are subject to a variety of judicial and legislative rules depending on the state where they are located.

CONSISTENT TREATMENT OF PUBLIC EMPLOYEES

Despite the varied treatment of public employees, there are two areas of consensus. The first is that public employees have a constitutionally protected right to organize;[19] and the second is that public employees *do not* have the constitutional right to strike,[20] or even demand that the employer bargain. There are of course exceptions to the prohibition of strikes, but for the most part it is accepted in all jurisdictions. The great divergence of treatment of public employees comes in the collective bargaining realm. There it makes a significant difference whether the particular state has adopted a statute governing public employees. Before dealing with these differences, however, the right to organize and the prohibition of strikes will be examined.

Right to Organize

Although the right of public employees to organize is generally accepted, it is not a long established right. Initially, most states prohibited public employees from forming or joining unions on various rationales, among which were (1) that wide discretion should be given municipal authorities to discipline employees to preserve public order; (2) that public servants gave up certain rights enjoyed by private citizens; (3) that public employees owed the state undivided allegiance; and (4) that allowing public employees membership in unions could lead to strikes and disrupt essential public services.[21] However, over the last ten years the federal courts have established that public employees, even policemen and firemen, have the right to organize or join a labor union.[22] The basic rationale of these decisions is that any prohibition of union membership is an abridgement of the right of free association guaranteed by the First Amendment[23] and made applicable to the states through the Due Process Clause of the Fourteenth Amendment.[24] At the same time, however, the courts have taken pains to point out that a state does have a valid interest in prohibiting strikes and collective bargaining.[25]

It is the prohibition of association that renders a particular statute invalid as an overbroad means of accomplishing proscription of strikes and collective bargaining, not the forbidding of strikes by public employees and contracts between public employee unions and government agencies. As a result, a state may not prevent public employees from organizing or joining a labor organization. It can, however, as a general rule, prevent its agencies from recognizing and contracting with the organization, and it can prohibit strikes by the employees.

Prohibition against Strike

The other area where most states agree on treatment of public employees concerns the right to strike. With few exceptions,[26] the states either by judicial decision[27] or by statute[28] have prohibited strikes in the public sector. These decisions and statutes have been based on one or more of the following reasons: (1) society needs uninterrupted rendition of essential services; (2) a public employee strike is a strike against the government and as such amounts to rebellion or treason; (3) because of the difference between private and public employees, a public employee strike would have impermissible effects on the economy and government efficiency; (4) the immediate employer is unable to respond to the financial demands of the striking employees because the power to increase wages rests with the legislature; (5) the government does not operate to make a profit; and (6) to allow public employees the right to strike would give them inordinate power to enforce their will upon the legislature to the detriment of less organized seekers of government appropriations.[29]

The no-strike rules in the various states have been attacked on constitutional grounds on several occasions. It has been alleged that the prohibition of strikes amounts to involuntary servitude in violation of the Thirteenth Amendment. However, this argument was met with the answer that the employee could quit at any time.[30] Other attacks have been founded on alleged violations of the Due Process Clause and Equal Protection Clause of the Fourteenth Amendment. These arguments met with similar lack of success. The due process argument was dismissed on the ground that the Constitution does not guarantee the right to strike.[31] The equal protection argument was met with the response that there is a valid distinction between private and public employees and that there is a rational relationship between this distinction and the denial of the right to strike.[32] Despite the repeated failures of such constitutional attacks, these arguments may be successful in the future, particularly for employees who serve the government in a "proprietary" function.

DISPARATE TREATMENT OF PUBLIC EMPLOYEES

Having established the areas where the states are in virtual agreement, in allowing organization but prohibiting strikes, it is necessary to turn to the area where each state's treatment of public employees is a little different—the area of collective bargaining. As noted earlier, a state is under no constitutional duty to recognize or bargain with a public employee union once it is organized. Therefore, each state is free to deal with collective bargaining as it sees fit. It is this choice that results in the variety of treatment. The various approaches range from complete prohibition of collective bargaining[33] to compulsory arbitration of disputes resulting from a negotiation impasse.[34] For the purposes of discussion, the states and their different schemes will be divided into two categories: states with no statute regulating collective bargaining and states that do have a statutory plan.

Nonstatutory Approach

In the states where there is no statute allowing or prohibiting collective bargaining, it has been left up to the judicial system to define its limits. The initial judicial response, and still the law in some jurisdictions, was that an agreement to bargain collectively was an illegal delegation of legislative authority.[35] However, a trend is discernible to judicially tolerate voluntary recognition of public employee organizations and collective bargaining agreements.[36] Even in those states that allow an employer to enter into agreements with the union, such employer has no duty to do so. Although gaining initial recognition would appear a significant obstacle to overcome, public opinion may eventually compel the public employer to recognize the collective bargaining agent.[37]

Since the employer can grant recognition and enter into a collective bargaining agreement which may be enforced by the employees through the judiciary, it is incumbent upon the employer to make several vital decisions before granting recognition and entering into negotiations. An initial decision the employer must make is whether it wants to enter into a written agreement or to have a de facto type of arrangement. Although a de facto arrangement would appear to give the employer more control, it may be held to have bound itself to things it would not have agreed to in writing on a theory of promissory estoppel.[38] Secondly, the employer must determine whether to recognize the union as the exclusive bargaining agent for all its employees, a fragmented portion, or for those joining as members. In making this decision it would have to examine a possible conflict with a state's right-to-work law.[39]

Another related decision pertains to the size of the bargaining unit. While fragmenting the bargaining units would appear to minimize the effect of an illegal strike, the employer could find himself with numerous agreements, a cohesive union overlapping several augmented bargaining units, and the possibility of sympathetic employees honoring a picket line of other employees, thereby continuing to deliver a crippling blow.

A different problem in states that have no statutory scheme regulating collective bargaining is what to do about an issue not covered by the original collective bargaining agreement. (As mentioned earlier, subjects covered under the agreement may be resolved by the courts.) Yet, where the agreement does not cover the disputed issue, the public employee is subject to the discretion of her or his employer unless the employer agrees to submit to mediation, fact-finding, and/or arbitration.

The above considerations emphasize the employer's control over collective bargaining in states without statutory regulations. The employer can define the rules under which bargaining will take place, it can limit the issues over which it must bargain, and it can unilaterally enact its own proposals on issues excluded from the collective bargaining agreement. All of this results from the fact that it is under no duty to recognize or to bargain with public employee unions.

Civil Service Statutes

Before turning to statutory approaches to collective bargaining, some states have utilized a civil service system to serve as a gap filler where there is no statute compelling collective bargaining. Although originally conceived to implement the merit principle, it has been expanded to cover aspects of employee relations that extend beyond eliminating patronage and rewarding merit such as grievance disputes, labor management relations, employee training, safety, moral and attendance control problems.[40]

The difficulty with civil service statutes arises in those states that do have a public employee statute. In the event of conflict between the civil service law and the public employee law, which one prevails? Some public employee laws specifically provide that it should control. However, few legislatures[41] foresee this problem when enacting public sector bargaining laws, and the conflict must be settled by the courts.

In determining the probable scope of each statute, the courts must seek to determine legislative intent. In the view of some jurisdictions, courts should not permit preexisting statutes to supersede the employer's duty to negotiate over rates of pay, hours of work, and other terms and conditions of employment described in the act as subjects of bargaining.[42] At most, civil service statutes should be controlling as to recruitment, hirings, promotions, and demotions.[43] The conflict will probably be resolved by holding that the state's collective bargaining law shall prevail where it is in conflict with the civil service statutes.

Statutory Approaches

The different statutory approaches to collective bargaining among the states present a wide variety of approaches to collective bargaining in the public sector. However, the various statutes can be classified into two categories or modifications thereof; "meet and confer" statutes and "collective negotiation" statutes.[44] Meet and confer statutes[45] have not enjoyed the wide adoption that collective negotiation statutes[46] have, and the present trend seems to be toward the collective negotiation model.[47] In final form, most statutes do not adopt either model in its pure form, with a majority appearing to be of the latter,[48] while some meet and confer statutes require more negotiation than an initial glance would indicate.[49]

In its pure form, a meet and confer statute does not impose any obligation on the employer to bargain with the employee representative.[50] It only requires a discussion of proposals prior to the unilateral adoption of policy by the employer.[51] Moreover, these discussions are usually held with multiple employee representatives, instead of an exclusive bargaining agent.[52]

The collective bargaining model, on the other hand, imposes a statutory duty on the employer to bargain collectively with the employee representative, who is generally the exclusive bargaining agent for all of the employees in the appropriate unit.[53] In addition, many of them define the subjects of bargaining, as well as impose a mutual requirement of bargaining in good faith.[54] Frequently, they are patterned after the National Labor Relations Act with respect to subjects of bargaining.[55]

To compensate for the prohibition of public employee strikes, most collective bargaining statutes provide for some form of negotiation impasse procedure. These various procedures include (1) fact-finding, (2) mediation and/or (3) arbitration. By imposing a duty to bargain, defining the scope of bargaining, and providing post impasse procedures subsequent to negotiating, these statutes give to the public employee rights similar to those enjoyed by the private sector, excepting the right to strike.

Before addressing the special problems created by these statutes, a brief description of the various post impasse settlement procedures is necessary. Fact-finding is essentially the use of the arbitration procedure with recommendations instead of a decision. The parties present their case to the fact finder(s), who in turn prepares a report with advisory recommendations, with which the parties may or may not comply. The advisory recommendations are made public in hopes that public opinion will force the parties to comply with the recommendations.[56]

Mediation is the most common of the post impasse procedures. The main function of mediation is to keep the lines of communication open by bringing in a neutral third party. The mediator listens to both sides and helps the parties get to the crux of the dispute at a time when the parties have been unable to resolve their differences in earlier negotiations.[57] The mediator proposes solutions in hopes that the parties will reach a settlement.

Compulsory arbitration is also being used by a growing number of jurisdictions[58] and has been hailed as "the wave of the future"[59] and the only acceptable alternative to the strike.[60] Under this procedure, once impasse is reached, the parties submit their proposal to the arbitrator, and he or she then renders a decision which binds the parties. One potential drawback of binding arbitration is that the parties will hold back their best offers if they foresee an impasse and leave it to the arbitrator to decide, thereby "chilling" negotiations.[61] Whether this is actually the case or not is the subject of much debate.[62] However, one variation on compulsory abritration that has evolved is final offer arbitration.[63] Under this procedure, each side submits a final offer to the arbitrator who in turn chooses between the two offers and selects one as his or her decision without modification. Supporters of this approach state it eliminates any holding back in anticipation of arbitration. Some states have adopted this procedure.[64]

FORESEEABLE PROBLEMS

Having laid the groundwork of the statutory regulation of collective bargaining, it is now necessary to consider the problems[65] they create. One of the foremost problems created by the duty to bargain in the public sector is one of determining exactly who the employer is that is required to bargain. Unlike the private sector, the immediate employer of the bargaining unit does not always have control of the employees' wages, hours, and other terms and conditions of employment. This is often left up to the legislature or some other governmental agency.[66] As a result, not only is it difficult to ascertain the particular employer the statute requires to bargain, but also many agreements entered into by the immediate employer must be subsequently approved by department heads or the legislature.[67]

In addition, it is often not exactly clear whether the immediate employer has the authority to enter into such conditional agreements and/or bind the legislature to such agreements.[68] Thus, it is difficult to impose statutory sanctions for refusal to bargain in good faith when there is so much doubt as to the identity of the employer required to bargain. One approach to solving this problem is for the legislature to define "employer" with more specificity. Although it is probably the more sound approach, few states have done so.[69] The more common approach is to leave it up to the state labor boards and the courts to resolve.[70]

A closely related problem concerns the scope of bargaining in the public sector. In the private sector, the NLRB has developed guidelines concerning mandatory subjects of bargaining over which the parties must bargain, in comparison to subjects which are merely permissive—that is, where the parties may bargain about them, but neither party may insist on them.[71] Many statutes have adopted the language of the NLRA and leave it to the state board or the courts to define mandatory and permissive subjects with the NLRB decisions as precedent.[72] Yet some courts have rejected the NLRB decisions and have devised their own tests.[73]

A final point to consider is how long an employer must negotiate before instituting unilateral changes. Most collective negotiation statutes have been interpreted to require exhaustion of the enumerated post impasse procedures before the employer can take unilateral action.[74] Despite the criticisms of the various post impasse procedures,[75] they seem to be fairly effective in resolving collective bargaining disputes.[76]

One last caveat should be stressed before leaving the subject. Most of this article has been based on the assumption that the right to strike is still denied to the public employee and that federal regulation will not preempt the field. Therefore, it is important to note that a few states are experimenting with allowing public employees, or at least certain types of public employees, a limited right to strike.[77] Also, it is important to point out that there are advocates for a federal scheme closely akin to the private sector's NLRA and that Congress has considered legislation on the subject.[78]

CONCLUSION

In recent years the rights of public employees have developed to a position similar to those of employees in the private sector. While most states are in consensus that public employees have the right to organize but do not have the right to strike, there exists a wide variety of legislative and judicial responses as to exactly what obligations and commitments the public employer has to the collective bargaining agent. The legislature and courts have the difficult task of fitting together the collective bargaining process with other governmental processes. Hopefully the accommodation that is made will be one that deals fairly with all competing interests.

NOTES

1. 29 U.S.C. §§ 151–68 (1970).
2. NLRA, § 7, 29 U.S.C. § 157 (1970).
3. Idem.
4. Idem.
5. NLRA, § 9, 29 U.S.C. § 159 (1970).
6. Idem.
7. NLRA, § 8, 29 U.S.C. § 158 (1970).

8. NLRA, § 8(a)(1), 29 U.S.C. § 158(a)(1) (1970).

9. NLRA, § 8(a)(2), 29 U.S.C. § 158(a)(2) (1970).

10. NLRA, § 8(a)(3), 29 U.S.C. § 158(a)(3) (1970).

11. NLRA, § 8(a)(4), 29 U.S.C. § 158(a)(4) (1970).

12. NLRA, § 8(a)(5), 29 U.S.C. § 158(a)(5) (1970).

13. NLRA, § 8(b)(1-3), 29 U.S.C. § 158(b)(1-3) (1970).

14. NLRA, § 8(b)(4), 29 U.S.C. § 158(b)(4) (1970).

15. NLRA, § 8(b)(6), 29 U.S.C. § 158(b)(6) (1970).

16. NLRA, § 8(b)(7), 29 U.S.C. § 158(b)(7) (1970).

17. NLRA, § 2(2), 29 U.S.C. § 152(2) (1970).

18. NLRA, § 2(3), 29 U.S.C. § 152(3) (1970).

19. United Fed'n of Postal Workers v. Blount. 325 F. Supp. 879 (D.D.C.) aff'd, 404 U.S. 802 (1971) [hereinafter cited as *Postal Workers*]; American Fed. of State, County & Municipal Employees v. Woodward, 406 F.2d 137 (8th Cir. 1969) [hereinafter cited as *Woodward*]; McLaughlin v. Tilendis, 398 F.2d 287 (7th Cir. 1968) (teachers) [hereinafter cited as *McLaughlin*]; Melton v. City of Atlanta, 324 F. Supp. 315 (N.D. Ga. 1971) (policemen) [hereinafter cited as *Melton*]; Atkins v. City of Charlotte, 296 F. Supp. 1068 (W.D.N.C. 1969) (firemen) [hereinafter cited as *Atkins*].

20. For an exhaustive listing of decisions denying the right to strike absent statutory prohibition, see Duff, *Labor Law: Right of Public Employees to Strike or Engage in Work Stoppage*, 37 A.L.R. 3d 1147, 1156 (1971). For an exhaustive listing of statutes prohibiting the right to strike, see Revelos, *Strikes by Public Employees: Is Tweedledee the Answer*, 15 S. Tex. L.J. 14, 16 n.10 (1974).

21. King v. Priest, 357 Mo. 68, 206 S.W.2d 547, *appeal dismissed*, 333 U.S. 852, *reh. denied*, 333 U.S. 878 (1947); Hutchinson v. Magee, 278 Pa. 119, 122 A. 234 (1923); McNutt v. Lawther, 223 S.W. 503 (Texas, 1920); San Antonio Fire Fighters' Union v. Bell, 223 S.W. 506 (Texas, 1920); Carter v. Thompson 164 Va. 312, 180 S.E. 410 (1935); Perez v. Board of Police Comm'rs, 78 Cal. App. 2d 638, 178 P. 2d 537 (1947); Jackson v. McLeod, 199 Miss. 676, 24 So. 2d 319, *cert. denied*, 328 U.S. 863 (1946).

22. See note 19 *supra*.

23. *Postal Workers* at 883; *Woodward* at 139; *McLaughlin* at 289; *Melton* at 319; *Atkins* at 1075.

24. *Postal Workers* at 883; *Woodward* at 139; *McLaughlin* at 288; *Melton* at 319; *Atkins* at 1076.

25. *Postal Workers* at 882; *Melton* at 320; *Atkins* at 1077.

26. ALAS. STAT. § 23.40.200 (1972); HAWAII REV. STAT. § § 89-11, -12 (1970); MINN. STAT. ANN. § 179.64(7) (Supp. 1974); MONT. REV. CODES ANN § 41-2209 (Supp. 1974); ORE. REV. STAT. § 243.725 (1973); PA. STAT. ANN. tit. 43, § 1101.1003 (Supp.1974-75); VT. STAT. ANN. tit.21, § 1730 (Supp. 1974).

27. See note 20 *supra*.

28. See note 20 *supra*.

29. See generally Anderson, *Strikes and Impasse Resolution in Public Employment*, 67 MICH. L. REV. 943 (1967); Revelos, *Strikes by Public Employees: Is Tweedledee the Answer*, 15 S. TEX. L.J. 14, 21 (1974); Duff, *Labor Law: Right of Public Employees to Strike or Engage In Work Stoppage*, 37 A.L.R.3d 1147, 1150-51 (1971).

30. City of Evanston v. Buick, 421 F.2d 595 (7th Cir. 1970); Trustees of Calif. State Colleges v. Teachers Local 1352, 13 Cal. App. 3d 863, 92 Cal. Rptr. 134 (1970); Pinellas County Classroom Teachers Ass'n v. Board of Public Instruction, 214 So. 2d 34 (Fla. 1968); City of Holland v. Holland Educ. Assn. 380 Mich. 314, 157 N.W.2d 206 (1968); DiMaggio v. Brown, 19 N.Y.2d 283, 279 N.Y.S.2d 161, 225 N.E.2d 871 (1967); Pawtucket v. Teachers Local 930,101 R.I. 243,221 A.2d 806 (1966).

31. *Postal Clerks* at 882; New York v. DeLury, 23 N.Y.2d 175, 295 N.Y.S.2d 901, 243 N.E.2d 128, *application denied*, 23 N.Y.2d 766, 296 N.Y.S.2d 958, 244 N.E.2d 472, *app. dismissed*, 394 U.S. 455, *reh. denied* 396 U.S. 872 (1968). Adkins v. Myers, 15 Ohio Misc. 91, 239 N.E.2d 239 (1968).

32. *Postal Clerks* at 883; School Dist. v. Holland Educ. Assn. 380 Mich. 314, 157 N.W.2d 206 (1968); New York v. DeLury, note 29 *supra*.

33. N.C. GEN STAT. § 95-98 (validity upheld in *Atkins*, see note 20 *supra*.)

34. MINN. STAT. ANN. § 179.70 (Supp. 1973); NEB. REV. STAT. § § 48-801 et. seq. (Reissue 1974); ORE. REV. STATE. § 243.743 (1973). The federal government has also provided for compulsory arbitration of disputes in the postal service. 29 U.S.C. § 1207 (1970).

35. Miami Water Works v. Miami, 157 Fla. 445, 26 So. 2d 194 (1946); Mugford v. Mayor of Baltimore, 185 Md. 266, 44 A.2d 745 (1945); Hagerman v. City of Daytona, 147 Ohio St. 313, 71 N.E.2d 246 (1947).

36. Norwalk Teachers' Assn. v. Board of Educ., 138 Conn, 269, 83 A.2d 482 (1951); Springfield v. Clause, 356 Mo. 1239, 206 S.W.2d 539 (1947); Youngstown Educ. Assn. v. Youngstown City Bd. of Educ., 36 Ohio App. 35 (1973); Foltz v. Dayton, 270 Ohio App. 2d 35 272 N.E. 2d 169 (1970); Cincinnati Metro. Housing Auth. v. Cincinnati Dist. Council, 17 Ohio Misc. 134, 244 N.E.2d 898 (1969).

37. Alley and Facciolo, *Concerted Public Employee Activity in the Absence of State Statutory Authorization: I*, 2 J. LAW & ED. 401, 404–05 (1973).

38. Idem.

39. Dade County Classroom Teachers' Assoc. v. Dade County Educ. Assn., 225 So. 2d 903 (Fla. 1969).

40. Edwards, *The Developing Labor Relations Law in the Public Sector*, 10 DUQUESNE L. REV. 357. 370-371 (1972), *citing*, REPORT OF TASK FORCE ON STATE AND LOCAL GOVERNMENT LABOR RELATIONS 18 (1967).

41. For states that did forsee the conflict see, HAWAII REV. STAT. § 89-9(d) (Supp. 1972); KAN. STAT. ANN. ch 75-4330, § 10(a) (Supp. 1972); MASS. ANN. LAWS ch 149, § 1781 (Supp. 1972): ME. REV. STAT. ANN. tit. 26, § 969 (Supp. 1972), MICH. COMP. LAWS ANN. §§ 423.201-.216 (Supp. 1973).

42. Civil Service Comm'n v. Wayne County Bd. of Supervisors. 384 Mich. 363, 184 N. W. 2d 201 (1971); Edwards, *supra* note 40, at 371; and Edwards, *The Emerging Duty to Bargain in the Public Sector*, 71 MICH. L. REV. 885, 911 (1973); Anderson, *The Impact of Public Sector Bargaining*, 1973 WIS. L. REV. 986, 1004 (1973).

43. Edwards, *supra* note 40, at 371; Anderson, *supra* note 42, at 1004.

44. Edwards. *The Emerging Duty to Bargain in the Public Sector*, 71 MICH. L. REV. 885, 895 (1973); Moberly, *Public Sector Labor Relations Law in Tennessee*, 42 TENN. L. REV. 235, 257-8 (1975).

45. See, for example, ALA. CODE tit. 37, § 450(3) (Supp. 1969).

46. See, for example, MICH. COMP. LAWS ANN. § 423.215 (1967).

47. Edwards, *The Emerging Duty to Bargain in the Public Sector*, 71 MICH. L. REV. 885, 896 (1973).

48. Idem.

49. Idem. at 897.

50. GOVERNMENT EMPLOYMENT RELATIONS REPORT REFERENCE FILE (Glossary) 91:02-03 (1970).

51. Idem.

52. Idem.

53. See, for example, MICH. COMP. LAWS ANN. § 423.215 (1967).

54. See, for example, PA. STAT. ANN. tit. 43, § 1101.701 (Supp. 1972).

55. Compare Mich. and Pa. Statutes cited in notes 53 and 54 with NLRA § 8(d), 29 U.S.C. § 148(d) (1970).

56. See Word, *Fact-Finding in Public Employee Negotiations*, 95 MONTHLY LABi REVi (Feb. 1972).

57. Moberly, *supra* note 44, at 262.

58. States presently using compulsory arbitration include Alaska, Massachusetts, Nebraska, New York, Oregon, Pennsylvania, Rhode Island, Wisconsin, and Wyoming.

59. Anderson, *A Survey of States with Compulsory Arbitration Provisions for Fire and Police*, as cited in Nelson, *Final Offer Arbitration: Some Problems*, 30 ARB. J. 50 (1975).

60. Nelson, *Final Offer Arbitration: Some Problems*, 30 ARB. J. 50 (1975).

61. Stevens, *Is Compulsory Arbitration Compatible with Bargaining*, 5 IND. REL. 44, 44–45 (1966).

62. Kheel, *Strikes and Public Employment*, 67 MICH. L. REV. 931, 938 (1969); Moberly, *supra* note 44, at 263–64; Nelson, *supra* note 60.

63. Moberly, *supra* note 44, at 264; Nelson, *supra* note 60, at 51.

64. Massachusetts, Michigan, Minnesota, and Wisconsin.

65. Many of the problems discussed will be common to those states allowing collective bargaining by voluntary recognition and states having "meet and confer" statutes. However, because those states do not impose a duty to bargain nor define mandatory subjects of bargaining or impose past impasse resolutions procedures, several of the problems discussed will apply only to those states having "collective negotiation" statutes.

66. Mack, *Public Sector Collective Bargaining*, 2 FLA. ST. U.L. REV. 281, 282 (1974).

67. See, for example, *the New York Taylor Act*, N.Y. Civil Service Law §§ 200–212 (McKinney Supp. 1971), which requires the agreement to contain a provision stating it is subject to legislative approval.

68. Edwards, *supra* note 47, at 904.

69. See, for example, WIS. STAT. ANN. § 111.81(16) (Supp. 1973).

70. See, Typographical Union v. Personnel Division, Gov't Employment Relations Report No. 400, (Case No. C39, March 31, 1971).

71. NLRB v. Wooster Division of Borg-Warner Corp., 356 U.S. 342 (1958).

72. See, notes 53 and 54 *supra*. See also Westwood Community Schools, 7 Mich. E.R.C. Lab. Op. 313, 317 (1972).

73. Education Assn. v. Decourcy, 295 A.2d 526, 535-36 (Conn. 1972); Labor Relations Bd. v. Richlard School Dist., Government Employment Relations Report No. 485, at B-3 (Pa. L.R.B. Jan. 8. 1973).

74. City of Dearborn, 7 Mich. Employment Relations Commission Labor Opinions 749 (1972); East Hartford Educ. Assn. v. East Hartford Bd. of Educ., Govt. Employment Relations Report No. 484, at B-8 (No. 17, 82, 87, Hartford County Conn. Super. Ct., Nov. 10, 1972). And in one case even after the contract had expired, see Board of Educ. v. Conn. Teachers' Assn., 81 L.R.R.M. 2253 (1972); Triborough Bridge and Tunnel Authority, 5 New York Public Employment Relations Board 3064 (1972).

75. See Revelos, *supra* note 29, at 26.

76. See Rhemus, *Is a 'Final Offer' Ever Final?* 97 MONTHLY LAB. REV. 43 (Sept. 1974); Stern, *Final Offer Arbitration—Initial Experience in Wisconsin*, 97 MONTHLY LAB. REV. 39 (Sept. 1974).

77. See note 26 *supra*.

78. S. 3294 and 3295, 93d Cong., 1st Sess. (1974); H.R. 8677 and 9730, 93d Cong., 1st Sess. (1974).

Facing the Realities of Public Employee Bargaining

Lanning S. Mosher

Public employees and their unions have recently been blamed for almost everything but Vietnam and Watergate. It's really ridiculous! In a recent *Newsweek* feature, James Farmer of CORE acknowledged that public employees had become the new "Niggers" of the 1970s. For too many public officials and politicians, they have become an excuse for poor policies, failure to define achievable goals, too little courage, and too much managerial incompetence. Let's not let unions become the excuse that budgets—"if we only had more money"—have become. Let's accept the challenge and manage!

First, let me identify my own prejudices about the role of collective bargaining in public management. I believe that collective bargaining can be used as a method to improve the overall quality of management in the public sector. It is one method of managing relations with employees. It is a process that should yield benefits for all concerned—management, taxpayers, and employees—if public management is willing to recognize that it is a system through which employees can have a meaningful say in decisions that affect their working lives *and accept their obligation to act as managers in the public interest.* It is not the only system, but it can work. However, it will not serve the interests of all the people if officials seek to destroy unions, nor will it succeed where public management and officials abdicate their leadership role and let public employee unions come completely between them and their employees.

The advent of collective bargaining in the public sector is a normal extension of a socially acceptable process which has been used successfully in the private sector to handle conflict. The Supreme Court's decision in *Usery* v. *National League of Cities* does not herald the end of the spread of collective bargaining. Public employees will continue to seek additional power. Paternalism is passe. The demands of public employees will conflict with demands of others. Also, organized labor has realized that the public sector is ripe for organization. Labor has recognized that the public sector can set patterns which private industry will have to match in order to compete. Labor's objectives mandate the organization of the public sector. Also, the organizing is easy. There is usually little employer opposition after a bargaining law is passed. "Fraternal" employee associations evolve into or are replaced by real unions. Collective bargaining is one way of handling this conflict.

Lanning S. Mosher is director of employee relations for the state of Maine.

Reprinted from Lanning S. Mosher, "Facing the Realities of Public Employee Bargaining," *Public Personnel Management* (July-August 1978), 243–248.

NEW PROBLEM

Collective bargaining is a "new problem" to most public managers. Most public managers are used to working with two basic management tools: the law which establishes their agency and gives them certain powers and duties and a budget within which they are expected to operate. Questions about performance have come from above, usually about how well one stays within his budget and about how well he complies with his agency's law without violating anyone else's law. The challenges which public management will face in the bargaining process, from below as well as above and through increased public exposure resulting from mediation, fact-finding, and arbitration, will force management to begin to sharpen its skills and fulfill its managerial role. New skills, and in some cases whole new approaches, will be required as employees press for joint determination of terms and conditions of employment and for input into program and policy determination.

THE OBVIOUS "COST" IMPACT

There is no conclusive research on the amount of money that collective bargaining and public employee unions is costing taxpayers. However, of the research done in the field of public employee labor relations, the best research has been on salary levels, the most obvious cost. In *Public Sector Labor Relations: An Evaluation of Policy-Related Research*, the principal investigator, Dr. Ralph Jones, concluded that "although a variety of research designs are used in a broad range of environments, the study's findings are remarkably consistent. On balance, they indicate that the public sector unions do, in fact, increase wages but that these increases are relatively small." In addition, they find that "the mere existence of union organization has no discernible impact on wages. Rather, it is the right of the union to negotiate contracts that really matters." Most studies would lead one to the conclusion that the overall effect is a differential of between 1 and 5 percent. However, recent developments in New York and elsewhere indicate that the parties to the bargaining process are responsive to the economic realities of the times. The pressures of the labor market, the economy, and politics will exist with or without collective bargaining. Also, employee salary levels are only one factor in determining total costs and unit costs.

POTENTIALLY BENEFICIAL EFFECTS

There are other aspects of the bargaining process which must be considered in addition to the impact on salary levels. First, collective bargaining can act as a catalyst in improving overall management. Challenges to management's positions, including possible review by factfinders and arbitrators, strengthens the management process by identifying management as a group and as a function and demanding that it act accordingly. Managers who make poor decisions in employee relations areas frequently make poor decisions in other areas. The training in managerial techniques, including leadership and grievance handling which often follows the commencement of collective bargaining, usually improves performance in all areas. It is unfortunate that in all too many cases supervisors and managers are recognized as a group needing special training and deserving special attention and treatment only after a bargining law has passed. Even so, legislative bodies resist providing any financial incentives for managerial performance similar to those provided in the private sector.

How successfully management emerges as a counterbalancing power to public employee unions will determine what benefits the public reaps from public employee bargaining. Schlicter, Healy, and Livernash reached similar conclusions concerning collective bargaining in the private sector in their classic book, *The Impact of Collective Bargaining on Management*. Perry and Wildman, *The Impact of Negotiations in Public Education –The Evidence from the Schools*, published in 1970, concluded "The adversary role of the bargaining process requires that someone play the role of adversary. To the extent that administrative personnel control resources or rewards sought by teachers, they will be cast in that role and will lose their status as colleagues. The result will be a tendency for school administrators to become managers in the traditional bureaucratic sense." Losing a grievance can be an incentive to learn: to get all the facts and check the policy and contract carefully. The decision-making process is essentially the same on employee problems as it is for other problems.

Second, collective bargaining encourages a close review of terms and conditions of employment and should help control these costs. Without collective bargaining, costly inefficiencies and practices may easily avoid close scrutiny and may survive and grow. It is in this area in which public managers with a "can do" attitude will find the opportunites for personal growth and advancement. They will be the ones willing to tackle the problems unearthed by collective bargaining.

Third, collective bargaining provides machinery to standardize and stabilize costs and relations with employees. Ad hoc decisions increasing benefits on a piece-meal basis are easily made through existing administrative and legislative machinery without adequate evaluation of the long-range impacts on costs and operations. How many cases do you know of where decisions have been made administratively to extend a certain benefit—for example, minimum pay for call-in for court appearances—without any consideration of the costs? Similarly, many decisions are made locally or departmentally that result in dissimilar practices which tend to piggyback themselves across agency lines and are never subject to any centralized review or long-range planning. Legislatures do the same sort of thing. They may pass laws setting up a special retirement plan for employees in certain categories and then leave it to a board of trustees of the retirement system to decide which particular classes fall within the categories. Other special benefits may be extended to special groups solely due to political clout. Bargaining on such issues gives public management the *opportunity* to clearly define what changes are being made and assign proper and reasonable costs to them. The process, if properly managed, forces each party to justify the changes it seeks and make thoughtful selections.

Finally, collective bargaining centralizes power with the chief public executive, providing him or her with the tools with which to balance the growing power of employee organizations. Under many collective bargaining laws, the chief executive becomes involved—with clout—in decisions formerly made by Civil Service Boards. Under most bargaining laws, unions must make agreement with the chief executive before going to the legislative body. More than one public employee union official in different states has admitted that it was easier to get some things through the political process than it is through collective bargaining.

GETTING THE MOST OUT OF PREPARING FOR BARGAINING

Collective bargaining should be a boon to all aggressive public managers, whether they work in staff or operating agencies. They should play an important role in the analysis of employee relations policies and programs and the costs which should precede the commencement of bargaining.

Essentially, three questions need to be answered in specific detail: (1) Where are we now? (2) How did we get here? (3) Where should we be going? This is essentially the same agenda that should be used in any management decision. Unfortunately, the normal tendency to accept things as they are and to do them the way we have always done them, coupled with a maintenance of current services approach to the budgeting process, has made it easy for public managers (and politicians) to get along without going through a detailed analysis of programs, policies, and costs. There have been situations where no one knew how many worked on shifts, who was actually getting overtime pay, the time spent in nonwork activities, or the costs of the standard benefits. This needs to change. Prior to the start of bargaining there is a need to identify such things as payments for court appearances, reporting pay, and other practices which may not show up in formal state policies. Management should do its homework before the unions turn over all the rocks. The type of analysis that is needed here is not unique. It requires the kind of expertise which should be possessed by any good systems or management analyst. There is no substitute in collective bargaining, as well as in any other managerial decision, for doing your homework thoroughly. If you don't know where you should be going, how can you expect to get there? If you haven't done your homework well, the innocent little "benefits guaranteed clause," which almost any union will try and get in its first agreement, may wind up costing you untold millions if you are naive enough to agree to it. Someone needs to write a book for your jurisdiction called, "Everything You Wanted to Know about Personnel Practices in Government, but Were Afraid to Ask."

Resource committees composed of operating and staff agency personnel may be helpful in analyzing programs, policies, and procedures. They should be asked to recommend solutions to any problems that they find in existing policies and procedures, whether or not these areas may be legally negotiable. Whether the problems need solving at the bargaining table or through some other means is a technical decision. What is important is that real problems are addressed in a serious and realistic manner. Quite often employee relations, both in the public and private sectors, are improved mostly as a result of activities which occur outside the narrow limits of negotiations and the processing of grievances. In the writer's personal experience, the greatest improvements in employee relations at an overseas mine grew out of a training program that was developed for indigenous supervisory staff. For the first time, they began to understand what the company was doing and how well it was or was not doing. The changes that resulted from their new skills and attitude helped immensely in improving production and relations with employees and their unions. Similarly, grievances at one institution were substantially reduced by holding periodic labor-management meetings.

WORKING WITH THE NEGOTIATOR

The chief negotiator need not be someone who is knowledgeable in all areas of your operations and administration. He or she is often someone hired for special technical skills. He or she will want to learn all time permits about programs and operations. However, the spokesperson is only a part of the management team and cannot be expected to have all the answers. Public managers must realize that their chief negotiator will be placed in situations calling for hard and fast decisions. If the preparation has been inadequate, the negotiator, with the blessing of his or her principal—usually the chief executive—will not hesitate to use his or her judgment to fill any voids which result from poor preparation or abdication of responsibility on the part of others. The result may be a bad decision which costs and causes operating problems over the life of an agreement. In one situation, an agency refused to acknowledge the existence of a problem, and their refusal to recognize the problem and take action resulted in a clause being inserted in the first agreement which they later found very unsatisfactory. In subsequent years, that clause became a crutch on which they blamed many of their problems. When forced to document the alleged problems, they were unable to do so in most cases. However, their attempts at documentation enabled them to define the real problem, which they addressed with some success in the next round of negotiations. Adequate preparation the first time—objective analysis of the facts and recognition of their emotional effect on employees—could have avoided many unnecessary problems.

WHAT THE FUTURE REQUIRES

Public management needs to accept collective bargaining and the social pressures that have led up to collective bargaining as being real and valid. They are the manifestations of problems in human needs which are recognizable in all human organizations, whether it is the church, the Communist Party or A.T.&T. As our society becomes increasingly technical, almost to the point that we need interpreters to talk to people in other fields, we need to recognize that each of us represents, to some extent, a special interest group. In public management we must continually pause and reflect on the long-range implications of our own actions and objectives and try to bring them into perspective with the need of the public for efficient delivery of necessary governmental services.

The needs of individuals in all groups for a meaningful work experience, a sense of belonging and personal worth, and some control over their destinies will be increasingly important in the future. The increasing complexity of society will contribute to this.

We all work for many reasons. If the public well is dry and salary increases are not available, we will look for more satisfaction and recognition in other ways. For these reasons, I think we can expect to see more employee organization interest in program and policy development, staffing patterns, and indeed, the services that are to be provided.

Interestingly enough, Tom Donahue, executive assistant to AFL-CIO Chief George Meany, expressed some aspects of the basic philosophy of American unionism in an address made at the International Conference on Trends in Industrial Labor Relations in Montreal in May of 1976. He said, in part, "Union's first and principal function is to organize workers and represent these workers . . . to improve their job conditions . . . to bargain collectively. Only when this function is successful can unions pursue their secondary function—the expression of social unionism. People join unions primarily because they want to express their human dignity on the job. It means more than dollars negotiated in the wage package. That dignity is the foundation on which a social program can be built to improve the worker's relative position in society . . . that equality is established through the collective bargaining process where equals talk with equals." Mr. Donahue was comparing American unionism with some forms of unionism in Europe. He felt that American unions were much stronger and more effective than some of their European counterparts, which are represented on corporate boards. It is also interesting to note that in this same talk one of the objectives and trends that he saw for the labor movement in the future was "new patterns of collective bargaining in the public sector on an area or regional basis and with a closer correlation between public and private sector bargaining."

All of these forces, including the development of collective bargaining as an institution, need to be understood in historical perspective. The public manager needs to understand this and realize that the objectives he or she sets for collective bargaining must be realistic. We must understand that for collective bargaining to work, it must be handled in such a way that all parties benefit—public management, the public employee, and the taxpayer. In short, everyone must win. The "I win, you lose" approach in the short run will come back to wreack havoc in the long run. Organizations, like human beings, can be healthy as well as unhealthy, and we will get out of them exactly what we put into them.

Apart from the specific responses to the actual problems of conducting negotiations themselves, public management must meet the challenge to pull itself up by its own bootstraps. This will require more attention to management development and training and getting the public and legislators to recognize that management is a bona fide special interest within governmental administration.

Management has long been recognized in the private sector as the essential ingredient in making the capitalist system work. Unfortunately, public sector management enjoys no similar reputation for making government work. We need to find substitutes for the profit and loss statement by which we can evaluate the success of public management. We need incentives to perform and new ways to measure performance. We need to shift the emphasis from protecting the employee against political spoils and patronage to demanding that the taxpayer receive proper value for the payments rendered. In short, managers and politicians must accept their responsibilities for managing government.

Labor Relations for Police and Fire: An Overview

Richard S. Rubin

Police officers and fire fighters are a breed apart from other municipal workers. The public singles out these two professions from other municipal employees in its strong opposition to granting them collective bargaining rights. The belief is that society cannot afford to let its protective service workers be unionized because any halt in police or fire protection would endanger the public welfare. Other opponents of their unionization point to the way police and fire departments are structured, saying their paramilitary organization does not lend itself to collective bargaining—that a tight chain of command and strict discipline cannot coexist with unionization.[1]

Despite the public expectation for police and fire fighters to place duty to society above their right to bargain collectively, thirty-four states and the District of Columbia grant fire fighters the right to bargain collectively, while twenty-six states and the District of Columbia give police officers the right to do so.[2] Collective bargaining is fast becoming the accepted way to determine wages, hours, and working conditions in police and fire departments.

Police and fire fighters make up one-fourth of all municipal employees in the United States. They are the most highly organized of all municipal workers—not necessarily in organizations for collective bargaining purposes but in employee associations which may have no connection with organized labor but wield tremendous political power because of their large memberships.[3]

STRUCTURE OF PROTECTIVE SERVICES

The typical protective service employee is a police officer or fire fighter who works with about fifteen others in a department. The majority of protective service employees work in police or fire departments, physically separated from other public sector employees. The average police department has ten to twenty sworn employees; the average fire department is small, but exact numbers are not available because of the heavy reliance on volunteers.[2]

Figures in 1968 showed about 409,000 full-time civilian and sworn personnel working in the 40,000 police departments in the United States. Of these 409,000 police workers, only 23,000 worked at the federal level in fifty agencies; another 50,000 worked at the state level divided up into two hundred agencies. The remaining 336,000 police workers were employed at the local level.[4]

Richard S. Rubin is an associate professor in the School of Public and Environmental Affairs at Indiana University and director of the Midwest Center for Public Sector Labor Relations.

Reprinted from Richard S. Rubin, "Labor Relations for Police and Fire: An Overview," *Public Personnel Management* (September-October 1978), 337–345.

About 26,000 paid and volunteer fire departments were operating in the United States in 1974. A few operated at the federal level, none at the state level. The only exception occurred in some states that hired a state fire marshal to investigate arson and incendiary fires and to enforce fire prevention regulations.[2]

HISTORY OF POLICE ORGANIZATION

Despite the general acceptance within the last decade of the protected right of public employees to organize and bargain collectively, there has been a reluctance to extend these rights to police officers. Until police gained statutory protection through collective bargaining legislation in the 1960s, their rights to organize and join employee organizations for the purposes of collective bargaining were restricted by state statutes, municipal ordinances, and/or departmental regulations.

There were restrictions on a police officer's rights to belong to the Fraternal Order of Police, to join an association affiliated with organized labor, and to belong to labor groups that admitted members other than police officers. Prior to 1968, state courts upheld these restrictions on the basis that police, because of their unique role in society, could be denied their First Amendment right to freedom of association. It wasn't until 1968 that several federal circuit court decisions reversed these state court decisions and statutes.[2,5,7]

Opponents of collective bargaining for police officers contend that police should not be involved in any process that has the potential of interrupting vital public services—that allows the possibility of a strike or any form of work stoppage. These opponents argue that:

> Affiliation with organized labor conflicts with an officer's sworn duty to carry out impartial law enforcement. For instance, the police officers' neutrality might be compromised in a situation where it would be necessary to break up picket lines, acting against fellow union members.[1]

> Unionization is inconsistent with the discipline that is necessary in a quasi-military organization—thus, there is the possibility of undermining public safety.[1]

> Police are "professionals" and should not use the tools of laborers.[6]

> Unionization threatens the trend to make police departments more "professional" because unions push to recruit, promote, and reassign police on the basis of seniority rather than merit.[7]

> The sovereignty of the police chief would be undermined, thereby threatening management's ability to manage.[6]

> Sergeants and lieutenants would want to bargain; and, as vital links in the chain of command, their organization would cause all kinds of problems. The implementation of policies, orders, and programs would be upset.[6]

Although there is strong resistance to police unionization, it is sometimes ignored that police and fire fighters have been highly organized since the late 1800s. These early organizations, however, were far different from present-day employee organizations, functioning more as social benefit societies for their members.[8] They sometimes served as lobbying agents, working to influence legislators to favor police officers and fire fighters by passing advantageous legislation. These long-established organizations for police and fire fighters have gradually evolved to take on the function of collective bargaining. Sometimes the change has occurred against strong opposition from government officials and the public.

Police officers have suffered a tumultuous history in their attempts to join organized labor. Even today, there is no nationwide police union, with most of the organizations being independents or local affiliates of regional organizations limited to police only.[2] The Fraternal Order of Police comes the closest to being a national police union.[7] Often there are separate organizations for patrolmen, sergeants and lieutenants, and top managers. And many police officers hold membership in more than one organization.[2]

Police first tried to organize in 1897 when a special group in Cleveland, Ohio, petitioned the American Federation of Labor for a charter. The AFL turned down their request and continued to reject the requests of other police officers until 1919. In June of that year, the AFL began to charter police unions and by September it had thirty-seven locals including ones in Boston, Los Angeles, and St. Paul, Minnesota.[5]

One of these locals was the Boston Social Club whose police officers went on strike September 9, 1919, after a feud with the mayor of Boston and the governor of Massachusetts over wages and fringe benefits. The governor called in the state militia. A riot ensued and seven persons died. The 1,200 police who struck were fired and never rehired. As news of the Boston strike spread, police unions all over the country were forced to relinquish their charters, and police efforts to unionize were stopped for more than twenty years.[5]

In the 1940s and 1950s efforts to unionize police were revived by the American Federation of State, County and Municipal Employees (AFSCME). Forty locals were organized by AFSCME, but most were small and inactive. Furthermore, they were bound by "no strike" clauses. No matter how weak, however, these locals were at least allowed to exist. In thirty-eight other cities, local authorities halted any attempt to form police unions.[8]

Although police were for the most part thwarted in their attempts to unionize for collective bargaining, organization was going on behind the scenes at this time. Police continued to form local associations throughout the whole period, many of which were affiliated with large state or national groups. These groups functioned primarily as lobbying and social benefit societies. So when police militancy erupted in the 1960s, most urban police were already organized into some association that could serve as a vehicle for expressing discontent.[9]

During the 1960s, these associations began to change from mere social benevolent societies to unions aimed at better wages and working conditions through collective bargaining. Police strikes or work stoppages occurred in several major cities across the United States, including Detroit; Youngstown, Ohio; and Pontiac, Michigan.[10]

Police discontent reached its peak in the 1960s for several reasons:

1. The public was showing increased hostility toward the police, which made officers doubt the status and prestige of their profession. This public hostility was expressed in attacks on police by blacks and student demonstrators, in U.S. Supreme Court decisions which seemed to restrict the personal discre-

tion of the police officer, in the public clamor for civilian review boards, in increased violence directed at the police, and in the mounting crime rate.[9]

2. Public demands for law and order frustrated police officers when they came at a time of increased hostility toward police. These two seemingly conflicting demands compounded the police task.[9]

3. Police felt they were not receiving enough money to compensate for the increased hazards of their work in the face of public hostility and more demanding work loads. In fact, police salaries seemed to be declining in relation to salaries for other occupations. Wages for police officers were not keeping pace with inflation.[9]

4. Methods of resolving grievances did not exist, and channels of communications were often blocked.[9]

5. Job requirements were upgraded to include college education, and police wanted the respect and salary commensurate with these higher level requirements.[11]

These deep sources of dissatisfaction spurred police officers into action. They were further encouaged to unionize when they saw how successful other public employees were when they used confrontation tactics. A greater percentage of young police officers who were employed were more willing than older police officers to take overt action. Moreover, state statutes were being passed making the effort to unionize less difficult for the police.[9]

HISTORY OF FIRE FIGHTER ORGANIZATION

Fire fighters organized more quietly than police officers did. They made the transition from social benefit societies to modern public employee unions with less resistance from the public. Fire fighters began to form social and benefit societies in the early 1900s for security because they had no institutionalized pension and insurance programs. This was the time when many cities, especially the larger ones, were beginning to pay their fire fighters and organize them into fire departments instead of relying on volunteer squads. In an effort to increase their political clout, many of these local fire organizations applied to the American Federation of Labor for charters. The AFL accepted the applications on an individual basis.[2]

A national union of fire fighters was proposed by the AFL in 1915, and three years later the International Association of Fire Fighters (IAFF) was formed. At first some fire fighters opposed the large national union. But opposition weakened when the AFL charter emphasized how unique fire fighters were because they could not use economic sanctions to gain concessions and influence management in collective bargaining. The formation of the IAFF gave fire fighters access to local labor councils. The fire fighters thereby gained leverage to grant or withhold funds or endorsements in political campaigns. Thus, fire fighters gained new leverage to influence candidates to raise their wages and improve their working conditions.[2,3]

Today the International Association of Fire Fighters is the largest and most influential organization of fire department employees.[9] Its only competitor for membership is AFSCME, and it does not appear to be a major competitor.[2] A 1973 survey of fire departments in cities with 50,000 population or more revealed that only 1 percent of the 271 cities responding said that AFSCME represented the majority of its fire fighters in wage and related employment concerns.[12] The survey revealed the following breakdown:

> 1 percent had the AFSCME
> 77 percent had the IAFF
> 17 percent had a local association
> 5 percent responded "Other"

All ranks of professional fire fighters can belong to the IAFF except those who work in shipyards. It is not uncommon for all the uniformed employees of a fire department including the fire chief to belong to the local of the IAFF. However, a fire chief's participation in the union is limited to passive membership.[3]

The IAFF functions to provide various types of insurance, to improve methods of fighting fires, and to hold collective bargaining seminars and promote collective bargaining among the locals. The IAFF has very low dues. It is decentralized, giving the locals a great deal of autonomy in determining policy and making decisions. The IAFF contained a "no strike" clause until it was deleted in 1968.

DIFFICULTIES IN COLLECTIVE BARGAINING

Once police and fire fighters are given the right to organize and engage in collective bargaining, several questions unique to the protective services arise:

> Should supervisors and rank and file employees be placed in the same bargaining unit?
>
> Should police officers and fire fighters have the same wage scale?
>
> What is adequate in terms of pensions, disability insurance, and death benefits?
>
> How can impasses be resolved most effectively in the face of "no strike" clauses?

Determining which employees belong in a bargaining unit is a real problem with police officers, and to a lesser extent with fire fighters. The problem centers on determining who is a supervisor. Supervisors are traditionally excluded from collective bargaining because their job duties clearly fall within the responsibilities of management. But in police departments, the lines blur between supervisors and rank and file officers.

Definitions of supervisors sometimes exclude lieutenants from bargaining but usually do not exclude sergeants, who are more likely to do investigation and technical work than hire and fire employees in the lower ranks.[6] But if common interests are a criterion for being placed in the same bargaining unit, sergeants and even lieutenants who have been promoted through the ranks would have mutual interest in wages, hours, and working conditions that should place them in the same unit.[5]

However, to combine sergeants and lieutenants in the same bargaining unit with rank and file employees might create havoc in the chain of command within the police or fire department. Because of this possibility, there is a tendency to break up the various job classifications in the authority structure of the police department into different bargaining units. Police are usually divided into different bargaining units by rank. Moreover, labor relations boards have been reluctant to place every employee of the police department below the chief in the same bargaining unit.[2]

In fire departments, on the other hand, it is common for everyone under the assistant chief to be in the same bargaining unit. Supervisors in fire departments do have bargaining rights but they must be placed in separate bargaining units. In Michigan, for instance, the law limits the title of supervisor to "the fire commissioner, safety director, or other similar administrative agency or administrator." In Minnesota, only the "administrative head and assistants of police and fire departments" are considered to be supervisors and thus placed in a separate bargaining unit.[3]

In Wisconsin, bona fide supervisors in the public sector are not allowed to bargain collectively. The Wisconsin law specifies who is a supervisor in its fire departments. "As to fire fighters employed by municipalities with more than one fire station, the term *supervisor* shall include all officers above the rank of the highest ranking officer at each single station. In municipalities where there is but one fire station, the term *supervisor* shall include only the chief and the officer in rank immediately below the chief. No other fire fighter shall be included under the term *supervisor* . . ."[13]

Other considerations that complicate police and fire fighter labor relations are:

1. Should uniformed employees be included in the same bargaining unit with nonuniformed employees?
2. Should police and fire employees be placed in the same bargaining unit?
3. Should police and fire employees be placed in the same bargaining units with other city employees or in separate bargaining units?

In all of these cases, the trend has been toward separation.

WAGE PARITY BETWEEN FIRE FIGHTERS AND POLICE

Bargaining for parity between police and fire fighters sets these occupations apart from other public sector jobs. Wage parity for police and fire employees means that within any one jurisdiction that assumes responsibility for law enforcement and fire protection, the wages of employees who perform one task will be similar or equal to the wages of employees who perform the other task. Parity does not mean that the wages for police officers or for fire fighters in one city must be the same as in the next city.

Parity between police officers and fire fighters dates back to a period before collective bargaining began. From 1927 to 1967 the salaries of police officers and fire fighters did not diverge more than two points, according to a recent survey. Another survey showed that police and fire fighters wages in Indiana are at parity in thirty-four of the forty-eight cities in the state.[14]

However, the latest trend has been to pay police more than fire fighters. Municipalities justify this difference, saying that the requirements for recruiting, training, and maintaining the professional standards of police officers have been elevated.[7]

Fire fighters argue for parity; police officers argue against it. Fire fighters say their wages should at least be equal to police officers', citing the following reasons:[7]

1. Fire fighters work more hours than police do.
2. Fire fighters need a high degree of technical training to fight fires.
3. Fire fighters are subject to a great number of hazards.

Police officers argue against parity with fire fighters on the grounds that:[7]

1. Police incur more job-related injuries than fire fighters.
2. Police spend more hours performing official duties than fire fighters.
3. Police departments lose more personnel than fire departments because of low salaries.
4. Police must deal with people while fire fighters deal with things. Police officers contend that more skills are needed to work with hardened criminals, militant youths, and irate citizens. Although police admit that fire fighting is dangerous, they say the knowledge and skills needed are mostly mechanical and are therefore less valuable than the skills needed by police officers.

POLICE AND FIRE FIGHTER PENSIONS

Pensions for police and fire fighters are established to maintain a public safety force that is young, alert, and able to meet the emergency demands of the job. Thus pensions encourage men and women in the protective service to retire early by offering substantial benefits at an early age. In this sense, police and fire fighters have more in common with the military than they do with other municipal employees.

Police and fire fighter pensions are expensive. They often amount to 50 percent of a city's payroll. These pension funds, most of which are locally administered, are often seriously underfunded. Many cities and counties are committed to relatively expensive benefits, and the full cost of these benefits is not reflected in current budgets but must be confronted ten to twenty years from now.[15]

A typical pension plan for police and fire fighters includes the following features:

Normal benefits are payable at age fifty or fifty-five, after twenty to twenty-five years of service.

Normal benefit is 50 percent of final pay, plus 1.67 percent for each year of service over the minimum service required for a normal pension. Final pay varies in its definition from the amount paid over the last year to the average paid over the last five years.

There are no early retirement benefits; a vested right to a deferred pension is acquired after fifteen years of service.

Disability benefits are payable after five years of service, equal in amount to one-third to one-half of final salary if disability is not service connected; half to three-quarters of salary if service connected.

Annuities are provided widows and surviving minor children ranging from 25 to 50 percent of pay if death is not service connected, up to two-thirds final pay if service connected.

There is no automatic cost of living adjustment of pensions.

Employees contribute about 6 percent of pay to the plan.

There is no companion Social Security coverage.

The trend among police and fire fighters to retire early after short periods of service compounds the problem of pensions in the public sectors. Many police and fire fighters are able to retire after only twenty years of service at which time they begin to receive 50 percent of their final salary as a yearly pension, according to a special Labor-Management Relations Service report. The costs of such benefits can approach 50 percent of the total payroll cost of a municipality.[16]

Inflation further complicates the problem of pensions. Most pension plans for police and fire fighters gauge retirement payments according to the final year's salary or to an average of salaries over the last several years. This causes retirement payments to reflect inflated wages and to soar beyond the actuarial expectations on which contribution rates were based.[16] In Indiana, for instance, fire and police pension benefits are tied to the current base wage resulting in inflationary costs for local governments.

Most police and fire fighters use their pensions for disability or early retirement, not for retirement after the normal number of years of service. Many police and fire fighters retire at the age of forty-five to fifty-five, rather than at sixty-five. This complicates the problem of providing these employees with a pension program. Many pensions for police and fire fighters who are disabled cost twice as much as for all other state and local employee pensions. This calculation is based on the percentage of total payments.[15]

JOB ACTIONS ALTERNATIVE TO STRIKES

It is illegal in every state for police and fire fighters to strike. Since their services are considered essential, it is unlikely that police officers and fire fighters will ever be allowed to strike. This restriction contrasts with the right to strike among private employees and among public workers in some states.

Despite the prohibition of strikes, police officers and fire fighters have struck and initiated other job actions. Mild forms of protest to pressure employees have included the following:[7]

Work slowdown—all tasks are performed but in a slow, deliberate manner so that work piles up. An example is painstaking safety checks on vehicles and equipment.

Work speedup—a particular type of work is accelerated, all rules and regulations are literally enforced such as in a "ticket blizzard."

Lobbying in state legislature.

Picketing to embarrass the city administration.

Filing civil law suits.

Concertedly refusing to work overtime voluntarily.

More disruptive forms of protest include striking and work stoppage in which employees disrupt work on a selected basis. An example of work stoppage would be police employees not writing any tickets. Another job action is for all police or fire employees to call in sick with headaches or backaches, called the "blue flu" or the "red rash." In other cases, all employees stage a mass resignation or remain absent claiming that they are "attending a professional seminar."[7]

IMPASSE RESOLUTION TECHNIQUES

No-strike laws or laws that impose harsh penalties for striking are not enough to prevent disruption in the delivery of services to the public. The need for effective alternatives to resolve impasses has resulted in mediation, fact-finding, and arbitration.

Arbitration has been the most successful in resolving impasses in the protective services. Supporters of arbitration claim that the process provides for reasonable bids from both sides in the dispute. It allows the parties to reach agreement without interrupting essential services. Its critics say that arbitration undermines the bargaining process, creates a dependency on the third-party arbitrator, and establishes a split-the-difference syndrome.[17]

Police and fire fighters in states that require arbitration seem to be satisfied with this method, but municipal employers are not. Arbitration has been used for police and fire fighter disputes for six years in Pennsylvania, five years in Michigan, and two years in Wisconsin. During this time, none of the unions in these states has lobbied for any drastic changes, and there has been almost complete compliance with the law.[17]

The dissatisfaction of municipal employers with arbitration dates back to before the collective bargaining laws were passed. The employers' opposition rests on the belief that arbitrators grant wage increases that are too high, ignoring the city's ability to pay and whether such an increase is comparable with wages in other appropriate jurisdictions. Public managers still begrudge a system in which a third party tells them how much to pay their police and fire fighters. In fact, a few municipal managers have privately said that they would prefer giving police and fire fighters the right to strike rather than submit to arbitration. However, the majority of public employers feel arbitration is here to stay. They find the system is undesirable but not as bad as they thought it would be.[17]

CONCLUDING REMARKS

Despite a long history of opposition to collective bargaining for police officers and fire fighters, the nationwide trend is to grant protective service workers these rights. Traditionally highly organized groups, the police and fire-fighting professions are changing their long-established benevolent societies into unions for the purposes of collective bargaining. The majority of fire fighters are represented by the International Association of Fire Fighters, with all employees under the assistant chief usually belonging to the same bargaining unit. However, there is no nationwide police union, and the trend has been to separate police officers into different bargaining units according to rank within the department. The major problems of management with protective service employees is financing early-retirement pensions, accepting arbitration as an impasse resolution technique, balancing the demands of fire fighters for wage parity with police against police opposition to wage parity, and recognizing job actions without disrupting essential police and fire-fighting protection of the public.

Several options have been discussed to make the police and fire-fighting services less costly and more effective and efficient. These include combining police and fire departments, creating a metropolitan police authority, subcontracting for police and fire-fighting services, and demilitarizing the police and fire-fighting forces. Each of these options has been tested with varying degrees of success in different cities across the country. It remains to be seen if any of these proposals will become the trend in the future.

NOTES

1. Hervey Juris, "Police Personnel, Police Unions, and Participating Management," *Proceedings of the 22nd Annual Winter Meeting* (Madison, Wisconsin: Industrial Relations Research Association, 1969) 311–20.

2. Mollie H. Bowers, *Labor Relations in the Public Safety Services* (Chicago, Illinois: International Personnel Management Association, 1974). (PERL 46)

3. J. Joseph Loewenberg, "Policemen and Firefighters," in *Emerging Sectors of Collective Bargaining*, ed. Seymour L. Wolfbein (Morristown, New Jersey: General Learning Corporation, 1970) 129–72.

4. George D. Eastman, ed., *Municipal Police Administration* (Washington, D.C.: International City Management Association, 1971).

5. M. W. Aussieker, Jr., *Police Collective Bargaining* (Chicago, Illinois: Public Personnel Association, 1969). (PERL 18)

6. Charles W. Maddox, *Collective Bargaining in Law Enforcement* (Springfield, Illinois: Charles C. Thomas, 1975).

7. John H. Burpo, *The Police Labor Movement* (Springfield, Illinois: Charles C. Thomas, Publisher, 1971).

8. Allen Z. Gammage, and Stanley L. Sachs, *Police Unions* (Springfield, Illinois: Charles C. Thomas, Publisher, 1972).

9. Hervey A. Juris, and Peter Feuille, *Police Unionism* (Lexington, Massachusetts: D.C. Heath and Co., 1973).

10. Robert E. Alexander, "Municipal Police Labor Relations: Impasse Resolution Procedures," *Public Safety Labor Reporter* (January 1975) Features: 4–1–4–9.

11. Joseph D. Smith, "Police Unions: An Historical Perspective of Causes and Organizations," *The Police Chief* (November 1975): 24–28.

12. "Police and Fire Personnel Policies in Cities Over 50,000," *Municipal Year Book, 1974* (Washington, D.C.: International City Management Association, 1974) 222–52.

13. Wisconsin Municipal Employment Relations Act, *Wisc. Stat. Ann.* Sect. 111.70 through 111.71, as amended.

14. Indiana Association of Cities and Towns. *1975 Salaries and Wage Schedules and Proposed 1976 Salaries and Wage Schedules for Appointed City Officials and Employees* (Indianapolis, Indiana: Indiana Association of Cities and Towns, 1975.

15. Robert Tilove, "Pension Plans for Policemen and Firemen," *Public Employee Pension Funds* (New York: Columbia University Press, 1976).

16. Philip M. Dearborn, *Pensions for Policemen and Firemen*. (Washington, D.C.: Labor-Management Relations Service, 1974).

17. James L. Stern et al. *Final-Offer Arbitration*. (Lexington, Massachusetts: D.C. Heath and Co., 1975).

Three Studies of Grievances

John Price

James Dewire

John Nowack

Kenneth Schenkel

William Ronan

As Ash (1) has pointed out, grievances—despite their heavy cost and disruptiveness—have received relatively little research study. In fact, Slichter et al.(11) thought it necessary to distinguish between employee grievances and complaints because of the general misunderstanding of the two.

The grievance is a specific complaint that the union-management labor contract has been violated by one of the parties, although management grievances against a union member are virtually unheard of. A union member, filing a grievance, is charging management with a labor contract violation. Complaints are more general and may or may not be accepted for action. Persons lodging formal complaints are the subjects of this study.

BACKGROUND RESEARCH

Only five studies were found in the literature pertaining to grievances. Three of these studies dealt with the nature of grievants; the other two with different aspects of grievances.

John Price is an air force colonel. James Dewire is an army captain. John Nowack is an army major. Kenneth Schenkel is a personnel research specialist with Southern Bell Telephone. William Ronan is a faculty member of the School of Psychology at Georgia Tech.

"Three Studies of Grievances" by W. W. Ronan, James Dewire, John Price, John Nowack, and Kenneth Schenkel. Reprinted with permission *Personnel Journal* copyright January 1976.

Fleishman and Harris (5) found a correlation of 0.37 between grievances and turnover when they studied fifty-seven production groups in a motor truck manufacturing plant. Ronan (9) compared grievance activity from 1957 to 1961 between two plants manufacturing heavy processing equipment for the metals industry. He found that the particular plant did have a significant effect on the number of grievances submitted, but kind of work did not. Also, highly skilled workers received favorable settlement of their grievances a significantly higher percentage of the time than did unskilled workers. Both groups submitted grievances for similar reasons and seemed to follow the same pattern in terms of rate of grievance submission. Ronan concluded from the study that the most important factor in grievances for this concern was the particular plant. From the foregoing it appears that grievance activity may be influenced by the causes of turnover and plant characteristics. Additionally, the evidence indicates that successful settlement of grievances may be associated with the skill level of employees. Additional study has shown that grievances may be related to certain traits of employees.

Eckerman (4) hypothesized significant personal differences between grievants and nongrievants. He found that foundry and machine shop workers who had submitted grievances started working for the company at a lower rate, had larger wage increases, were in better physical condition, had more children, and were less likely to have been born in the South than a random sample of nongrievants.

Sulkin and Pranis (12) conducted a pilot study to determine the feasibilty of gathering limited data from personnel records and of using these data to generate hypotheses for a more extensive investigation of whether a typical grievant exists. Subjects for this study were fifty-eight grievant workers compared with a random sample of fifty-three nongrievant employees. The results indicated that grievants had more education, were more active in the union, had a higher absentee rate, had a higher late rate, and received lower wages with fewer net increases than nongrievants.

Ash (1) analyzed some of the factors associated with grievances in an industry employing over 10,000 production and maintenance workers. A selection of 159 grievants was matched with a sample of 159 nongrievants in terms of being hired for a job within the same bargaining unit, year hired, and current employment status with the company. Ash found that grievants were younger, predominantly male, less likely to be married, and more likely to be American citizens, and more often rehires than were nongrievants.

The above conflicting results might be attributed to several sources. For example, the studies were conducted with limited populations in terms of size , occupations, and geographical locations. Eckerman and Sulkin and Pranis apparently did not match their subjects on presumably relevant variables. Further, it is not clear whether variables were indexed to compensate for the different periods of service among the subjects. Whatever the case, there is a clear need for further research both because of the past conflicting results and the limited number of studies conducted.

METHOD

The studies to be described are based upon a six-year grievance file (over 4,000 grievances) of one plant of a major manufacturing corporation employing, at the time of the grievances, some 25,000 persons. These grievances were sorted and classified, and during this process it appeared that there were different groups of grievants.

One large group was composed of persons who had submitted only one or two grievances; another was a group who had submitted a large number of grievances; and another group had submitted grievances because of some disciplinary action by the company against them. These groups are the samples of the following studies.

An attempt was made to match grievant groups with nongrievant on sex, seniority, and job classification. The latter necessarily entailed matching by work unit. Exact correspondence of matching could not be achieved for all subjects. Consequently, a two-year range of seniority was used for matching. Subjects who could not be satisfactorily matched were dropped from any sample.

RESULTS—SAMPLE 1

The subject sample was defined as persons who had submitted a grievance during the six-year period of the grievance files. From a listing of names of those submitting grievances, a 250-person random sample was selected—approximately every seventeenth individual on the list.

A matching group was selected on the personal variables previously described by locating a grievant on a seniority list. This seniority list ordered individuals by seniority within job classification. The persons selected had not submitted a grievance during the time period under study.

The definitions are: *grievant*—an individual employee who had submitted at least one grievance during the six-year period; *nongrievant*—an individual employee who had not submitted a grievance during the same time period.

Data for the variables were obtained solely from company records. No individuals were contacted. A numerical identification system was developed for individuals included in the study to ensure their protection from any possible adverse effects from the study. All variables were indexed over time where this seemed indicated. Forty variables were selected from the information available in the personnel records:

1.   Wage increases—hourly rate of pay increase expressed in dollars. Determined by subtracting initial hourly rate paid at hiring from the rate of pay received at the termination of the period during which an employee must have filed a grievance to be classified as a grievant. This was divided by total service years with the company as of that termination date.
2.   Marital status—whether or not married at hire.
3.   Exemptions—number of exemptions claimed at hire for income tax withholding purposes.
4.   Owns home—renting versus own or buying home, at hire.
5.   Height/weight ratio—height in inches divided by weight in pounds.
6.   Birthplace—employee born within or out of state.
7.   Birth year—year of birth minus 1900.
8.   Hiring age—age of an employee at the time he was hired expressed in years.
9.   Veteran—any active military duty prior to hiring.

10. Military status—whether or not employee was a member of either National Guard or Reserves at hire.

11. Education—number of years of formal education at hire.

12. Jobs held—total number of jobs held during a ten-year period prior to hire, excluding military service but including self-employment such as farming.

13. Residences—number of residences occupied during a five-year period prior to hire (not military).

14. Police record—arrests for offenses other than minor traffic violations prior to hire.

15. Whether an employees was white or nonwhite.

16. Derogatory information—whether any letters of recommendation from former employers or acquaintences furnished by the prospective employee contained information of a derogatory nature such as quit without notice, drinking, and so on.

17. Employee performance notices (EPN)—number of such notices divided by total years of company service. EPNs are given for violations of company rules or policies.

18. Commendations—number of commendations received per year. These include letters from outside the employee's department, awards for cost reduction, and awards for excellent performance or perfect attendance for a specified period.

19. Garnishments—number of times employee's wages were garnished per year.

20. Courses—training courses successfully completed both on and off duty divided by years of company service.

21. Sick leaves—number of leaves divided by years of service.

22. Days sick—number of days divided by years of service.

23. Injuries—occupational injuries per year.

24. Physical limitations—whether or not an employee indicated some physical limitation at time of hire.

25. Layoffs—number of times laid off per year.

26. Days laid off—number of days off per year of service.

27. Permanent promotions—promotions received per year.

28. Merit increases—increases in pay per year as recommended by employee's supervisor.

29. Temporary promotions—number of temporary promotions received per year of service, including jobs performed at a higher rate, and number of field trips for company.

30. Demotions—number of downgrades received per year.

31. Promotions refused—number of promotions refused plus number of self-requested downgrades per year.

32. Change requests—number of requests per year including shift, department, and job classification.

33. Changes directed—number of changes directed by the company as (32) above.

34. Absentee rate—number of times employee absent per year excluding vacations, layoffs, and so forth.

35. Late rate—number of times late per year of service including failure to complete shift.

36. Grievance rate—number of grievances submitted per year prior to the period of this study.

37. Letter of indebtedness (LOI)—letters on file soliciting company aid in collecting overdue debt by years' service.

38. Medical limitations—number of medical notices restricting performance of some tasks per year.

39. Leaves requested—absences for personal reasons per year.

40. Days absent—days off per year for above leaves.

The collected data were analyzed using a one-way multivariate analysis of variance program developed by Clyde, Cramer, and Sherin (2). The program yields an overall F test (Wilks' Lambda) between groups, means, standard deviations, and a two-tailed test between each of the variables (10) if the overall F test is significant. The data analysis method was used for the two samples described later.

The results of the analysis for sample 1, grievants, are shown in Table 1. Only the mean differences, estimated standard errors of differences, and the t values are shown. It should be pointed out that the sequence of t tests performed on the forty variables does not represent a sequence of independent tests because of some correlation among the variables. The procedure was justified on a heuristic basis since this is considered an exploratory study. Of the variables, thirteen of forty were found significantly different at the .01 level of confidence with several others near that level.

On the basis of such significance the grievants:

1. Received more wage increases.

2. Were younger and hired at a younger age (difference between birth date and hiring age smaller for grievants).

3. Had higher educational levels.

4. Had more derogatory information in their personnel files.

5. Had fewer sick leaves.

6. Had more self-reported physical limitations.

7. Were laid off more (probably because of lower seniority).

8. Received more permanent and temporary promotions.

9. Received more demotions (likely due to seniority and 8 above).

10. Had a higher grievance rate.

11. Requested more leaves.

12. Had higher absence rates.

Table 1 Grievants versus non-grievants

	Mean difference	Standard error of difference	t-value
1. Wage increases	.03	.01	3.95[a]
2. Marital status	.03	.04	.89
3. Dependents	.24	.14	1.77
4. Home ownership	.08	.04	1.88
5. Ht-Wt ratio	.00	.01	.92
6. Birthplace (in-out of state)	.01	.04	.22
7. Year born	3.28	.68	4.83[a]
8. Hiring age	2.69	.62	4.36[a]
9. Military veteran	.06	.04	1.45
10. Military reserve member	.05	.04	1.30
11. Educational level	.71	.27	2.58[a]
12. Number previous jobs	.16	.16	1.00
13. Times change residence	.21	.11	1.90
14. Police record	.04	.02	1.48
15. Race	.03	.02	1.53
16. Derogatory information	.07	.02	3.01[a]
17. Employee/personnel notice	.01	.01	1.43
18. Commendations	.00	.01	.22
19. Garnishments	.01	.01	1.10
20. Company training courses	.03	.02	2.08
21. Sick leaves	.02	.01	2.63[a]
22. Days sick	.57	.67	.88
23. Work injuries	.01	.00	1.65
24. Physical limitations	.09	.02	4.27[a]
25. Layoffs	.01	.01	1.65
26. Days (layoffs)	3.63	1.08	3.35[a]
27. Permanent promotions	.04	.01	3.09[a]
28. Merit increases	.01	.01	.80
29. Temporary promotions	.04	.02	2.43[a]
30. Demotions	.04	.01	2.84[a]
31. Promotions refused	.01	.01	1.16
32. Job changes refused	.01	.01	.80
33. Changes DI	.03	.08	.35
34. Absence rate	1.07	.52	2.04
35. Tardiness rate	.74	.40	1.84
36. Grievance rate	.06	.02	4.01[a]
37. Letters of I and S	.01	.01	1.45
38. Medical limitations	.03	.04	.77
39. Leaves requested	.01	.00	3.19[a]
40. Absence rate	2.34	.89	2.63[a]

[a]Significant at .01 level

RESULTS—SAMPLE II

For this sample a "multiple grievant" was defined as an employee who had submitted three or more grievances during the period under study. A total of 117 such individuals was identified and, of these, suitable data were located for 97. None of these persons was found in sample I, and they were matched with nongrievants as described above.

The results of the tests between the multiple grievant and nongrievant groups are shown in Table 2.

The tests indicated only one variable—grievants receiving more permanent promotions—significant at the .01 level. If the .05 level of confidence were used, the

Table 2 Multiple grievants versus non-grievants

	Mean difference	Standard error of difference	t-value
1. Hiring age	.09	.07	1.24
2. Year born	.13	.06	2.31
3. Marital status	.19	.23	.79
4. Education level	.01	.09	.12
5. High school diploma	.02	.09	.23
6. Dependents	.15	.09	1.70
7. Military veteran	.10	.05	1.99
8. Military discharge (type)	.01	.05	.22
9. Birthplace (in-out of state)	.25	.15	1.62
10. Derogatory information	.25	.22	1.14
11. Police record	.48	.27	1.17
12. Times change residence	2.20	.96	2.29
13. Number previous jobs	2.67	1.04	2.57
14. Height	.73	.77	.95
15. Weight	.55	.28	1.92
16. H/W ratio	1.11	3.35	.33
17. Absence rate	.00	.01	.08
18. Employee personnel notice	.00	.02	.28
19. Commendations	.00	.02	.15
20. Permanent promotions	.06	.02	3.13[a]
21. Company training courses	.01	.02	.69
22. Work injuries	.01	.01	1.10
23. Sick leaves	.01	.02	.66
24. Garnishments	.00	.01	.22
25. Wage increases	.00	.01	.22
26. Beginning wage	.02	.04	.57
27. Race	.00	.03	.04

[a]Significant at .01 level

same age and hiring relationships as found for sample I obtain. In addition, grievants changed residence more often, and more grievants had military service. These results seem to be chance.

RESULTS—SAMPLE III

Subjects for this analysis were those who submitted grievances because of disciplinary action by management directed at them, usually discharge. The 125 grievants were compared with a matched sample. The results are shown in Table 3.

Of the variables, sixteen of thirty-two were significantly different at the .01 level of confidence. On the basis of these differences, it is indicated that the greivants:

1. Showed the same birth date—hiring age relationship as found with sample I.
2. Had a higher level of education.
3. Had higher grievance rates.
4. Had other disciplinary grievances.
5. Had more terminations.
6. Had more suspensions.
7. Had more employee personnel notices (absences and others).
8. Had fewer commendations.
9. Had refused more promotions.
10. Had more derogatory information in files.
11. Had more arrests.
12. Had more sick leaves.
13. Had more absences.

Variables included here but not for the other samples were:

1. Born in the United States versus foreign birth.
2. Other disciplinary grievances.
3. Termination from company service.
4. Suspension from company service.
5. Promotions/demotions before and after disciplinary grievances.
6. Previous Employee Personnel Notices for absence.

DISCUSSION AND CONCLUSIONS

From these data it appears that grievants and nongrievants do differ on various demographic and behavioral characteristics, for samples I and III, particularly.

With sample II, multiple grievants, the differences are not as many as those in the other two groups. At the .05 level of confidence only five of twenty-seven tests were significant. While this is well above the chance level, it does not compare with the results of the other two evaluations in both percentage and size of significant

Table 3 Disciplinary grievants versus non-grievants—t-values

	Mean difference	Standard error of difference	t-value
1. Year born	2.48	.89	2.78[a]
2. Hiring age	2.39	.86	2.78[a]
3. Educational level	.78	.24	3.31[a]
4. Birthplace (U.S.-foreign)	.01	.01	1.00
5. Birthplace (in-out of state)	.07	.05	1.45
6. Marital status	.06	.05	1.24
7. Military veteran	.01	.06	.14
8. Height	.03	.34	.09
9. Weight	1.88	3.02	.62
10. H/W ratio	.01	.01	.93
11. Grievance rate	.98	.21	4.69[a]
12. Other disciplinary grievances	.37	.06	6.29[a]
13. Terminations	.55	.07	7.46[a]
14. Suspensions	.66	.08	7.93[a]
15. Employee personnel notices	2.12	.27	7.80[a]
16. Commendations	.93	.25	3.68[a]
17. Promotions refused	.46	.15	3.11[a]
18. Promotions prior to grievance	.08	.23	.34
19. Demotions prior to grievance	.21	.21	.91
20. Promotions after grievance	.28	.19	1.50
21. Demotions after grievance	.26	.15	1.79
22. Temporary promotions	.39	.23	1.70
23. Race	.08	.04	2.27
24. Number previous jobs	.12	.22	.55
25. Company training courses	.75	.41	1.83
26. Derogatory information	.14	.05	3.20[a]
27. Police record	.19	.07	2.91[a]
28. Work injuries	.88	.22	3.97[a]
29. Sick leaves	.70	.30	2.31
30. Physical limitations	.02	.05	.46
31. Employee personnel notice (Absences)	.93	.15	6.34[a]
32. Absence rate	2.27	.42	5.39[a]

[a]Significant at .05 level

differences. It appears these results are suggestive and further study could lead to better understanding of grievants and grievances.

The sample l persons, who seemingly are regarded as better workers since they received both more wage increases and promotions, are younger in both age and seniority. However, they missed more work by requested leaves and absences. Possibly they were engaged in other activities, perhaps another job. They were better educated and had a higher grievance rate together with more physical limitations at the time of hiring. The general picture appears to be one of individuals who are more able both in terms of job skills and perceptions of contract violations. The derogatory information variable would indicate people who are possibly ambitious, outspoken, and somewhat resistant to conventions and other people.

The sample III group, discipline, seems to be the euphemistically named "problem employee" recognized in industrial relations work. With this group, there is a history of personal difficulties both at work and in other settings. With the former, grievances, terminations, suspensions, sick leaves, and absence are higher, and with the latter, derogatory information and a police record. There is also a record of more promotions and higher educational level, indicating relatively higher ability together with a propensity for personal difficulties. It could be hypothesized that a personality disorder of a more or less serious nature exists.

With regard to other work, the results of this study appear to be most in agreement with the findings reported by Ash (1). Both studies found that grievants were about three years younger than nongrievants and that this difference was significant. Race and veteran status, Ash's other two discriminating variables, were not verified in the present study, although the difference patterns were the same.

Eckerman's (4) findings conflict with the results of the present study in terms of wage increases, educational level, age of grievants, marital status, number of exemptions, and number of jobs held prior to hire. Not significant but in the same direction were veteran status, race, letters of indebtedness, and routine personnel changes. It is important to note that Eckerman did not compare matched samples of grievants and nongrievants. One of his significant findings was that grievants had more net service with the company than nongrievants.

The Sulkin and Pranis (12) findings conflict with the results here in terms of days of sick leave and wage increases. Points of agreement include age, late and absentee rates, and educational level. The only variables significantly different in both studies were wages and educational level.

Several factors may account for the above differences. The classification of grievants by kind of grievance is probably most important. As was shown, there were differences in discriminating variables in such groups. Here too the nongrievant sample was matched to the grievant sample on the basis of sex, seniority, and job classification; the other studies used random samples of employees as the matched group. Additionally, the operational definitions of the variables were not the same. In the Sulkin and Pranis study, for example, net totals were used for work record data, whereas in the present study these data were expressed in terms of rates. Finally the Sulkin and Pranis study had only fifty-eight subjects in their nongrievant group and fifty-three in the grievant. Other local conditions, such as plant location, kind and size of plant (9), work situation, and union activity may have had an influence on grievance activity; such conditions may account for the research differences found.

Generally, grievants do seem to constitute at least two identifiable groups that are to a large extent mutually exclusive. The results above obviously need cross-validation in other organizations along with studies of the personal traits and characteristics that might describe other kinds of grievants. See Mulder (8) for a study that seems to correspond to the result for sample III. A further point seems indicated: Not all grievances are "bad," as they are generally regarded by management. The grievants in sample I seem to be more able persons who perceive and will protest actual contract violation. From any point of view, this would seem to be more desirable than passive acceptance of possibly poor management practices.

NOTES

1. The opinions expressed in this article are those of the authors and in no way reflect those of the Department of Defense or the Department of the Army.

REFERENCES

1. Ash, P. "The Parties to the Grievance." *Personnel Psychology* (1970) 23: 13–37.
2. Clyde, D. J., E. M. Cramer, and R. J. Sherin. *Multivariate Statistical Programs.* (Coral Gables, Florida: University of Miami Biometric Laboratory, 1966).
3. DeWire, J. E. *Comparison of Multiple Grievants Versus Non-grievants in Industry.* (Atlanta, Georgia: School of Psychology, Georgia Institute of Technology, 1972).
4. Eckerman, A. C. "An Analysis of Grievances and Aggrieved Employees in a Machine Shop and Foundry." *Journal of Applied Psychology.* 32 (1948): 255–69.
5. Fleischman, E. A., and E. F. Harris. "Patterns of Leadership Behavior Related to Employee Grievances and Turnover." *Personnel Psychology,* 15 (1962) 43–56.
6. Hays, W. L. *Statistics for Psychologists.* (New York: Holt, Rinehart & Winston, 1963).
7. McKersie, R. B., and W. W. Shropshire. "Avoiding Written Grievances: A Successful Program." *The Journal of Business* 35 (1962): 135–52.
8. Mulder, F. "Characteristics of Violators of Formal Company Rules." *Journal of Applied Psychology* 55 (1971): 500–02.
9. Ronan, W. W. "Work Group Attributes and Grievance Activity." *Journal of Applied Psychology* 47 (1963): 38–41.
10. Roscoe, J. T. *Fundamental Research Statistics for the Behavioral Sciences.* (New York: Holt, Rinehart & Winston, 1969).
11. Slichter, S. H., J. Healy, and E. R. Livernash. *The Impact of Collective Bargaining on Management.* (Washington, D.C.: The Brookings Institution, 1960).
12. Sulkin, H. A., and R. W. Pranis. "Comparison of Grievants in a Heavy Machine Company." *Personnel Psychology* 20 (1967): 111–19.

Affirmative Action, Preferential Selection, and Federal Employment

Elliot M. Zashin

Despite the ambiguities created by the variety of opinions in the *Bakke* decision, the constitutionality of federal affirmative action (AA) programs for equal employment opportunity (EEO) seems reasonably secure. A majority of the Court decided that the Equal Protection Clause does not bar taking race into consideration in selection procedures; whether setting aside slots *exclusively* for members of minority groups (particularly where the institution in question does not have a record of past discrimination) is unconstitutional remains somewhat problematic.[1] Affirmative action as it has been formulated by the Civil Service Commission (CSC) for federal employment falls comfortably within those vague boundaries. Commission policy with respect to the use of numerical goals is merely permissive, not mandatory, and goals are defined as clearly different from quotas. Although competitive agencies under CSC jurisdiction *must* design and implement AA plans and programs, no finding of prior discrimination is required. However, it seems likely that a case of discrimination could be made by showing the differential effects on minorities and women of federal personnel procedures that lack justification in organizational necessity.

Nonetheless, the ambiguous resolution of consititutionality leaves other objections to AA standing: (1) that AA in federal employment is unnecessary; (2) that it is ineffective; (3) that it conflicts with merit standards; (4) that it leads to reverse discrimination and imposes unfair burdens on white males; (5) that it threatens, through quota systems, to create fixed racial/ethnic categories for the distribution of public employment; and (6) that it is misdirected. Before examining these criticisms, I will describe the emergence of AA in federal EEO efforts to provide a context and to help clarify what AA means, at least in terms of federal personnel policy and its implementation. I will then discuss some of the controversial concepts.

When President Nixon used the term "affirmative action program" in his Executive Order 11748 (1969) concerning EEO he was referring to such measures as assuring that recruitment reach all sources of job candidates, utilizing present skills of employees to the fullest extent, maximizing employees' opportunities to enhance their skills, and participating at the local level with other employers, schools, and public and private groups in cooperative efforts to improve community conditions affecting employability. This EO reaffirmed the notion stated in President Johnson's

Elliot M. Zashin is an associate professor of public management at the Graduate School of Management, Northwestern University.

Reprinted from Elliot M. Zashin, "Affirmative Action, Preferential Selection, and Federal Employment," *Public Personnel Management* (November-December 1978), 378–393.

EO 11246 (1965)[2] that equal opportunity had to be applied to all aspects of the personnel process; it spelled out in greater detail than previous orders what affirmative action meant. Earlier in the decade President Kennedy emphasized "affirmative" steps in his EO 10925 (1961), but the measures specified were general. The order did call for the collection of data on minority employment in the Executive Branch; apparently until that time, there had been no systematic information collected about minority employment and no quantitative basis on which to estimate progress in eliminating discrimination.

Prior to Kennedy's statement, EEO or fair employment was interpreted to mean nondiscrimination; that is, exclusion of individuals from employment or promotion on the basis of race was impermissible. However, the policy was at best a symbolic commitment because there was no meaningful enforcement mechanism. Thus, it was not surprising that Kennedy Administration officials realized that nondiscrimination was not significantly increasing the numbers of blacks in federal employment, especially in the higher grades.

Although nothing resembling goals and timetables were incorporated into federal equal employment opportunity programs at this time, opponents of such programs revealed that they were concerned about the possibility of preferential selection. The 1964 Civil Rights Act contains the following provisions:

> Nothing contained in this title shall be interpreted to require any employer, employment agency, labor organization, or joint labor-management committee subject to this title to grant *preferential treatment to any individual or to any group because of the race, color, religion, sex or national origin* of such individual or group on account of an *imbalance which may exist with respect to the total number of percentage of persons of any race, color, religion, sex, or national origin employed by any employer,* referred or classified for employment by any employment agency or labor organization, admitted to membership or classified by any labor organization, or admitted to, or employed in, any apprenticeship or other training program, *in comparison with the total number or percentage of persons of such race, color, religion, sex, or national origin in any community, State, section or other area, or in the available work force in any community, State, section or other area.*[3]

It was not until 1968 that goals and timetables were officially employed by a government agency as part of EEO. The Office of Federal Contract Compliance (OFCC), in its 1968 guidelines, required contractors to develop "specific goals and timetables for the prompt achievement of full and equal opportunities" and utilization of minority personnel. The most notable example of the use of goals and timetables was the Philadelphia Plan, instituted in 1969; here the OFCC "established annually increasing proportions for minority employment in the skilled trades."[4] Rendering a decision on the Philadelphia Plan, a federal circuit court ruled that the above quoted provision of Title VII of the 1964 Civil Rights Act was a limit on other state or federal remedies dealing with discrimination in employment.[5]

In 1971, the Department of Defense decided to implement an affirmative action plan using goals and timetables—with the approval of the Office of Management and Budget. This decision put the Civil Service Commission, which opposed the use of such devices, under pressure to be consistent with this major federal employer. When it appeared that responsibility for the Federal EEO program might be transferred to the Equal Employment Opportunity Commission (EEOC), the CSC yielded on this point. It had resisted taking this step because CSC officials considered goals and timetables to violate the principles of open competition and merit selection. The CSC did not view EEO as "a program to offer special privilege to any one group of persons because of their particular race, religion, sex, or national origin."⁶ Compensatory treatment was seen to violate the EEO principle of nondiscrimination. Preferential selection was not acceptable if based on racial or ethnic group membership; other criteria, for example, economic disadvantage, should be used. Thus, in yielding on this point, the CSC did so reluctantly and attempted in its regulations and procedures to restrict the circumstances in which goals and timetables would be used.

> Employment goals and time tables should be established in problem areas where progress is recognized as necessary and where such goals and timetables will contribute to progress, i.e., in those organizations and in those occupations and grade levels where minority employment is not what should reasonably be expected in view of the potential supply of qualified members of minority groups in the work force and in the recruiting area and available opportunities within the organization.⁷

At that time, the information necessary to make such judgments was not available to the CSC, so affirmative action problem areas would have been hard to pinpoint. Moreover, goals and timetables were permitted, not required, in federal agency EEO programs; the CSC also did not require that agencies submit work-force profiles each year so that progress in hiring and promoting minorities could be quantitatively assessed.

In 1972, congressional amendments to Title VII of the 1964 Civil Rights Act extended to federal employees the same basic protections private sector employees had been granted. The CSC was directed to review and approve federal agency AA plans annually and to evaluate agency EEO programs on a regular basis. During the Congressional debate, the question of quotas and preferential hiring was raised in both houses and specifically discussed in the Senate. The Philadelphia Plan and the federal court decisions upholding it (and similar EEO devices) were cited. The Senate twice defeated amendments to the act which proposed explicit prohibition of quotas and preferential hiring. Congress appeared to be giving tacit sanction to the use of such devices in certain circumstances.

In the Executive Branch, the agencies charged with monitoring EEO compliance recognized that quotas generally were considered objectionable and developed a consensual position distinguishing them from permissible goals. A 1973 memorandum issued by the CSC, EEOC, OFCC, and the Department of Justice defined the two in the following way:

> A quota system, applied in the employment context, would impose a fixed number or percentage which must be attained, or which cannot be exceeded; the crucial consideration would be whether the mandatory numbers of persons have been hired or promoted. Under such a quota system, that number would be fixed to reflect the population in the area, or some other numerical base, regardless of the number of potential applicants who meet necessary qualifications. If the employer failed, he would be subject to sanction. It would be no defense that the quota may have been unrealistic to start with,

that he had insufficient vacancies, or that there were not enough qualified applicants, although he tried in good faith to obtain them through appropriate recruitment . . .A goal, on the other hand, is a numerical objective, fixed realistically in terms of the number of vacancies expected and the number of qualified applicants available in the relevant job market. Thus, if through no fault of the employer, he has fewer vacancies than expected, he is not subject to sanction, because he is not expected to displace existing employees or to hire unneeded employees to meet his goal. Similarly, if he has demonstrated every good faith effort to include persons from the group which was the object of discrimination into the group being considered for selection but has been unable to do so in sufficient numbers to meet his goal, he is not subject to sanction.[8]

In August 1976, the Equal Employment Opportunity Coordinating Council issued an affirmative action policy statement that was agreed to by all its members, including the Department of Justice, the Department of Labor, the Equal Employment Opportunity Commission, the Civil Service Commission, and the Commission on Civil Rights. The statement, which represented a reconciling of important differences among the members on affirmative action, recommended the use of work-force profiles and goals and timetables:

> The first step in the construction of any affirmative action plan should be an analysis of the employer's work force to determine whether percentages of sex, race, or ethnic groups in individual job classifications are substantially similar to the percentages of those groups available in the work force in the relevant job market who possess the basic job related qualifications. When substantial disparities are found through such analyses, each element of the overall selection process should be examined to determine which elements operate to exclude persons on the basis of sex, race, or ethnic group. . . When an employer has reason to believe that its selection procedures have the exclusionary effect described . . . above, it should initiate affirmative steps to remedy the situation. Such steps, which in design and execution may be race, color, sex, or ethnic "conscious," include . . . establishment of a long-term goal and short-range, interim goals and timetables for the specific job classifications, all of which should take into account the availability of basically qualified persons in the relevant job market . . . establishment of a system for regularly monitoring the effectiveness of the particular affirmative action program, and procedures for making timely adjustments in this program where effectiveness is not demonstrated. . . .The Council recognizes that affirmative action cannot be viewed as a standardized program which must be accomplished in the same way at all times in all places.[9]

One of the problems encountered in analyzing the AA controversy is the ambiguity and inconsistency with which key terms are used. Many persons consider AA more or less equivalent to preferential treatment or selection for minorities and/or women, and preferential treatment is often equated with reverse discrimination. Numerical goals are repeatedly treated as synonymous with quotas. Preferential treatment, reverse discrimination, and quotas are terms to which strong emotions and normative connotations are attached, so it is difficult to make coherent, dispassionate assertions about AA without first clarifying one's usage.

Let's begin with quotas. The statement quoted above on goals and quotas provides a useful basis for clarifying the distinction. While opponents of AA tend to view goals as semantic camouflage for quotas, there are two clear differences in theory and, one, I would argue, holds in practice too. In the definitions cited, the key concepts used to distinguish quotas from goals are "mandatory requirements" versus "good faith efforts" and "fixed numbers or percentages" versus "targets based on the number of qualified applicants in the relevant job market." The General Accounting Office (GAO) report, "Problems in the Federal Employee Equal Employment Opportunity Program Need to Be Resolved," which used these definitions found that agencies set their numerical employment objectives and implemented them in such various ways that they ended up being neither goals nor quotas. For example, the objective might be set arbitrarily (like a quota) but not made mandatory (like a goal), or it might be set realistically in light of anticipated vacancies and potential supply of qualified candidates (like a goal) but then required (like a quota).[10] Such outcomes suggest that the conceptual distinctions break down in practice, but I suggest this result comes about because the distinction has two parts and only one of them (that is, mandatory versus good faith) is required.

The availability of qualified candidates (the key to formulating goals according to the definitions above) may appear nonproblematic, but the issue of what qualifications are job related is both complex and controversial. Most federal selection devices have not been statistically validated as job related. Furthermore, there is a paucity of information about the presence of presumably qualified minorities and women in the work force. According to the GAO, the CSC does not now provide useful labor market information to appointing authorities so that their hiring goals *can* be based realistically on availability considerations. It appears that most agencies rely on 1970 Census data and this is not adequate to deal with the task. Thus, goals of this kind may be a chimera now. In other words, the formulation of numerical employment objectives is generally in too primitive and inchoate a state to use it as one key to distinguishing goals from quotas. This is one reason why advocates of vigorous AA propose using standards not related to the availability of qualified minorities, but rather minority percentage of population or minority percentage of work force.

If the potential danger critics see in quotas is reverse discrimination or preferential selection (see below), it would appear that these are more likely to occur because of the pressure of sanctions behind the quotas.[11] I would argue that the crucial difference in practice now between goals and quotas is what happens when they are not fulfilled. This is basically what Deborah Greenberg, counsel for the NAACP Legal Defense and Education Fund, contends when she says that the crux of the difference is "where the burden of proof lies when the numbers are not attained and the weight of that burden."

> A quota exists if, when the designated number or percentage is not reached, the employer has a heavy burden of proving inability to find sufficiently qualified persons from the group previously subjected to discrimination. If the employer merely has to demonstrate some efforts and the burden of proof is on the party pressing for the numerical target to show bad faith, then the target can be said to be a goal.[12]

In other words, one may not be sure whether a goal is a quota until the target number or percentage is not met. Then the difference turns on what circumstances will be considered extenuating, who has to demonstrate their existence (or absence), and what sanctions can be imposed for failure to make the case. In practice, the line between goals and quotas may not be easy to draw, but persons who know the specific circumstances should be able to agree whether a numerical objective was a goal or a quota.

Judging by recent GAO, CRC, and Federal Personnel Management Project (FPMP) reports, I believe it is unlikely that any significant sanctions are applied to agencies or managers and supervisors when numerical employment objectives are not met. As already indicated, the CSC never has encouraged the use of goals,[13] and it has not penalized agencies that do not use them. Moreover, even when agencies formulated numerical objectives—and the 1974 CRC report on federal EEO enforcement indicated that most did not—the CSC does not appear to pressure those agencies whose AA Plans reveal that their goals have not been met.[14] These reports suggest that supervisors are not evaluated on their EEO performance and that EEO evaluations, when they do occur, do not play any significant role in one's being considered for promotion. The reports note repeated instances in which supervisors were not disciplined despite findings (after formal complaints were filed and investigated) that they had discriminated in personnel matters. The FPMP points to "the apparent absence of . . . sanctions for agency failures and shortcomings in assuring equal employment opportunity" and notes that "the monitoring and evaluation systems of both CSC and the agencies . . . are ineffective both in assessing program deficiencies and as a tool to delineate authority, responsibility, and accountability."[15] In sum, the implementation of numerical employment objectives in federal EEO programs apparently has not involved the widespread use of sanctions that would convert these objectives into quotas.

The concept of quota is usually taken to imply that relative qualifications of candidates will be put aside and the mandatory requirement of fixed numbers or percentages will result in preferential selection. Yet neither goals nor even quotas necessarily imply preferential selection. That term can have at least the following three meanings:

1. Where applicants are rated more or less equally on selection criteria, a minority candidate is given preference;

2. In the process of ranking candidates on selection criteria, positive credit is given minority status;

3. Giving preference to a minority candidate regardless of relative qualifications (assuming these are relevant) or giving preference to a minority candidate even when his or her qualifications are clearly inferior.

Although goals (or quotas) can be applied in such a way that any of these three forms of preferential selection occur, implementation can proceed without them. By focused recruiting, employee development and training, and changes in selection devices, far larger numbers of women and minorities can be brought into the pool of eligible candidates in many occupational areas, making it possible for employers to find qualified women and minorities for jobs that traditionally have had few of them. Such measures do require investing more resources in personnel management and/or allocating more resources to activities which may disproportionately benefit previously disadvantaged groups. Nonetheless, preferential selection per se need not occur.

Alan Goldman[16] has questioned the need for goals in addition to other AA requirements: why, if the latter are designed to eliminate discriminatory treatment, have goals at all? Pressure can be applied by regulators to ensure good faith; the imposition of goals seems likely to create pressure for preferential selection. It may be that the "real" impetus behind goals is a desire for proportional shares of employment to compensate certain groups for handicaps imposed by discrimination. Are proponents of AA dubious that elimination of discrimination from the federal employment process will soon create a "representative bureaucracy?" Do they believe that only the implementation of specific goals can achieve a parity that will recompense disadvantaged groups?

Perhaps, but there are pragmatic reasons for wanting to retain goals along with AA. Goals provide a relatively easy method of evaluating AA programs and techniques; how do the actual results compare with what seemed realistic and/or with what may become realistic (as other changes in society occur)? Moreover, goals can be a means of preventing managers and supervisors from setting their sights too low or merely going through the motions. While good faith efforts are acceptable in a goal system, pro forma efforts may at times be virtually indistinguishable from them—unless the monitoring agency is able to observe closely what occurs in the process. Clearly this is not feasible considering present CSC recources and the personnel management evaluations now made of competitive agencies. So goals can, to some extent, serve as a proxy for evaluating the "good faith" of AA efforts. Furthermore, the labor market availability information developed in the goal-setting process can be used diagnostically to determine where underutilization of minorities and women is occurring within federal occupations.

Now let us look systematically at the major criticisms of affirmative action.

1. "AA in EEO is not necessary. The policy of nondiscrimination in employment in the federal government has substantially increased the number of blacks who are employees; additional measures are not required."[17] Like the goals-quotas issue, this objection poses the question of baselines; against what standard is EEO progress to be measured? Advocates of vigorous AA propose baselines such as disadvantaged group percentage of total population or of overall work force. Others have suggested that the appropriate standard is the availability of qualified female or minority individuals in the relevant work force. Recent CSC figures on female and minority representation in the higher CS grades indicate that the first two standards have generally not yet been attained,[18] as I have already indicated, data on availability is usually inadequate, so it is very difficult to decide whether the government employs its share of the qualified women and minorities. Obviously, there can be no agreement here unless there is agreement on a baseline, but these imply different ultimate goals or values. Using a disadvantaged group's percentage of total population as a standard suggests that one seeks to make the federal work force representative (passively or actively) of the national population. If one uses a group's percentage of the overall work force, a "fair share" of national employment may be the ultimate goal. If one argues for a standard based on the current capability of a group to provide required skills, one's ultimate value may be conventional merit standards and a concept of equity based upon them. In short, this criticism of AA quickly dissolves into a debate about values, whereas initially it appears to be an assertion of fact.

2. "AA in federal EEO programs has not been effective." A judgment of effectiveness implies a standard of measurement and quickly we are back to some of

the same issues raised by the first criticism. However, more can be said. One test, sometimes applied, of the impact of AA is a comparison of black representation in higher GS grades, for example, 9 and above, pre- and post-1972, the year Congress directed the CSC to see that competitive agencies implemented AA and the first year numerical goals had CSC permission. The aggregate figures for civil service employment in the higher grades overall do not show marked differences between the percentage gains per year before and after 1972. For the period from November 30, 1970 to May 31, 1972, the per year percentage gains for blacks in GS 9–11 and 12–18 averaged 0.40 and 0.27 respectively; for the period from May 31, 1972 to May 31, 1974, the average figures were 0.65 and 0.30.[19]

The data presented suggest that the onset of AA did not produce dramatic employment increases for blacks in the higher grades, where their percentages were far below those attained in lower grades; however, the data do not permit detailed evaluation of A A. Indeed, year-to-year percentage changes in disadvantaged group representation, viewed in relation to changes in total federal work force, can be a misleading indicator of the potential for increased employment of these groups. For example, the increase in the number of blacks in a certain grade may even exceed the increase in the overall work force in that grade, but unless we examine total vacancies in that grade, we do not have a feel for the total chances agencies had to increase the representation of disadvantaged groups. Of course, the availability of those groups in the labor market has to be considered in evaluating the potential for increases. However, we soon realize that availability is not determined just by the credentials members of those groups possess but also by the requirements the CSC and specific agencies attach to positions they are seeking to fill.

This realization takes us a step further into the personnel process, and ultimately we must recognize that any adequate assessment of AA requires us to examine federal personnel operations as a system, not as separate actions with separate results. Even with the few intensive studies of agency personnel operations that exist, it is possible to show that policies, procedures, and practices can produce differential outcomes for disadvantaged groups whether or not individual acts of discrimination occur or individuals of different sex or race are given equal treatment, that is, the same criteria are applied to them as to white males. Aspects of the personnel system screen in or screen out members of certain groups, not necessarily on the basis of their sex and/or race, but because of characteristics they possess which are generally associated with their race and/or sex. This is why it is unreasonable to conclude that the rates of change so far achieved constitute virtually all that is feasible; we need to know much more about the system. It seems more likely that AA has not been effectively implemented. This conclusion is supported by the numerous GAO, CRC, and FPMP studies, which provide a long list of deficiencies in the formulation and implementation of EEO/AA programs. It may be too facile to suggest that AA like Christianity, has never been tried, but it seems fair to suggest that the possibilities of AA have not yet been exhausted in an overall good faith effort.

3. "AA is in conflict with meritocratic standards." Critics claim that under AA programs, individuals will be selected for higher education, employment, or promotion on the basis of a group characteristic rather than in terms of "relative" qualifications or ability. As a result, "less qualified minority individuals will be selected over better qualified majority (white) persons." This was the basic contention in the *Bakke* case. This criticism makes certain crucial assumptions about the

validity of present measures of relative merit and the present qualifications of minorities. In principle, AA need not be antithetic to meritocratic standards, but in practice it does imply some change in measures. Should conventional measures of cognitive aptitude or previous learning be the primary basis for making selection decisions?[20] Effective AA probably requires reducing the emphasis on conventional selection devices, for example, years of formal education, IQ, and other pencil-and-paper tests, and so on, and relying more heavily on skills, experience, ability to perform, and job aptitude.

The widespread use of conventional criteria and devices has been based on the assumption that these were satisfactory means of applying meritocratic standards. In the last few years, a number of serious criticisms have been made. First, it has been shown that tests of cognitive aptitude may be culturally biased. Second, such tests may not be an accurate or relevant measure of future performance. Few job tests have been validated as performance-related. In *Griggs* v. *Duke Power Company*, the Supreme Court ruled that if an employer uses a selection practice which operates to exclude a minority from employment opportunities, the burden of proof is on the employer to show that the requirement is manifestly related to the job in question. Third, radical critics contend that meritocratic criteria and selection devices actually serve primarily to *legitimate* the allocation of a scarce value, that is, higher occupational status, instead of rationally allocating human resources within the existing division of labor. If meritocratic standards and selection devices are problematic with respect to job performance, and in many cases they appear to be, one cannot say with certainty that AA programs have selected minority candidates who are less qualified than white candidates.

4. "AA leads to reverse discrimination and imposes unfair burdens on white males." If we define reverse discrimination as choosing a member of a disadvantaged group when his or her qualifications are clearly inferior to other candidates, it would be extremely difficult to determine whether this has occurred with any frequency in federal employment systems. Quite possibly, federal managers and supervisors have passed over white males with better qualifications to select or promote eligible (that is, qualified) members of disadvantaged groups. An EEO officer in one agency indicated to me that this was a major means his agency has used to make significant improvements in its work force EEO profile. Moreover, there have apparently been a number of formal discrimination complaints filed by white males in recent years.[21] Nonetheless, how often such treatment occurs and to what extent it can be attributed to AA programs is problematic.

Assuming that such preferential selection occurs, is an unfair burden being imposed on the better qualified white male who is being passed over? More generally put, can the adverse effects of preferential selection on such individuals be justified? Since they are unlikely to be the cause of the disadvantages women and minorities have experienced, is it fair for them to bear the cost of neutralizing the handicaps? George Sher contends that "unless reverse discrimination is practiced, they [that is, the better qualified white candidates passed over] will *benefit* more than the others [that is, other white candidates] from [the effects of past discrimination] on their [black] competitors."[22] He suggests that the better qualified white candidates who are passed over by preferential selection are, in effect, losing an *unfair* advantage which they have gained from prior discrimination by others. Normally, they would be attaining positions without serious competition from talented blacks, whom discrimination has, in various ways, put out of the competition. Preferential selection can eliminate that unfair benefit by putting minority members back into the pool of those who potentially qualify for selection—by giving them credit for special experience or by lowering certain entry standards for them. Some of the black candidates will be selected from the pool, reducing the number of places left for whites, assuming the total number is fixed.

While one cannot say that the effects of past discrimination on present competition will be neatly canceled in any particular instance by a preferential selection system, Sher may be making this kind of assumption at the societal level. In other words, *at any particular time*, the preferential selection systems take away from whites roughly the same number of positions blacks, for example, would have obtained on the basis of open competition, absent past discrimination. If so, one can say that overall the better qualified (Sher's assumption) whites are only losing an advantage (at least a rough approximation) they would *not* have had if there had been no prior discrimination. However, in practice a key consideration is the number of minorities or women the employer (or admissions office or EO agency regulating them) would like or is willing to see selected. Implementing a selection system for employment (or admissions) that "advantages" members of disadvantaged groups may not seem worth the effort if it does not achieve an increase in the actual number selected. If significant results are desired in the short run, the selection device (or admissions formula) will have to be adjusted to produce more preferential selection. The problem with a policy of neutralizing the handicaps of disadvantaged groups is that results from a preferential selection program can approximate or even exceed minority percentage of the general population (or minority percentage of the work force or school population or of the portion of the general population seeking employment or school admission) over a period of years and still not change the percentage of disadvantaged groups in the particular occupation, grade level, or profession as a whole very rapidly. Thus, if a significant increase in the latter, rather than in the intake rates, is the real goal of AA, higher annual targets at the entry level will be necessary. If achieved, the result might impose a disadvantage on current white male candidates that is greater than the advantage they gain from previous discrimination because the effects of discrimination over a long period of years are being eliminated in a much shorter time span. If this situation occurs, Sher's defense of preferential selection is undermined, but how do we determine that this point has been reached? In the case of federal employment, I would argue that, viewed in toto, the system still provides considerable opportunities for white males, especially at the levels and in the occupations where there are large numbers of them seeking federal jobs. This is not to say that other factors do not limit the impact of conventional merit standards; for example, nonveterans may often lose out to veterans because of preference points for military service, and at the highest levels, those without connections may often lose out because of preselection.

5. "AA threatens, through quota systems, to create fixed racial/ethnic categories for the distribution of public employment (as well as other public goods). Groups other than those now considered disadvantaged by the Government (blacks, Hispanics, native Americans, Asian-Americans, and women) will demand that AA programs be applied to them as well, and a rigid system of allocating public employment according to group shares may well result." This objection is much like 3; it suggests that individual initiative will be sapped by eliminating considerations of merit, achievement, and motivation from employment decisions. An

advocate of AA could reject this criticism by saying that AA does not entail rigid quotas, but the basic contention can be controverted on other grounds. First, the prospect of such a rigid system seems remote enough. The likelihood that other groups will demand inclusion in AA programs is not insignificant, but there are criteria for drawing the line between disadvantaged groups and "others." Each of the groups so far singled out as officially disadvantaged has been the victim of pervasive discrimination, both recent and long standing. While orientals seem a deviant case, in that they have prospered socioeconomically relative to the others, their being included reflects in part at least a national attitude that they are ethnically outside the bounds of the heterogeneous majority. Obviously other groups have been victims of discrimination, but I do not think that comparable cases can be made for additional groups in terms of intensity, duration, and impact of discrimination. If such a case can be made for another group, then including it with the others will be legitimate. This "solution" may seem facile, but the same kinds of indicators that supported the case for including the present groups can be used to justify omitting them (or dropping certain AA programs) when significant progress has been made. Critics of AA may say that we will have by then a "representative bureaucracy" with specific percentages of places assigned to specific groups. However, achieving a representative federal civil service need not entail permanent establishment of rigid distributional quotas for employment.

6. "AA in federal employment is misdirected, especially for blacks. Blacks have already achieved overrepresentation in the lower federal employment grades. The number of positions that blacks and other minorities can gain at the higher levels are severely constrained by the limited number of such positions in toto, and the minority individuals who can hope to qualify are already relatively well off. Thus, assessed in terms of helping those minorities whose economic need is greatest, AA can have little impact. In view of the opposition such programs appear to be causing, the federal government might do more to help disadvantaged minorities by concentrating 'remedial' efforts elsewhere." This argument has merit, but it ignores certain considerations. It would be nice if the funds allocated to AA could be transferred into other programs that would aid more economically disadvantaged minorities, but bureaucratic and political constraints undermine the practicality of the idea. The present costs of AA programs are not really known. The GAO repeatedly recommends better cost reporting in its evaluations of agency EEO/AA programs. Moreover, it would be difficult to decide—based on presently available information and standards—which programs are clearly least effective and thus proper candidates for phasing out. More significant perhaps is the fact that AA programs, particularly the special emphasis programs (FWP, SSP), have developed constituencies and there would probably be at least covert resistance to resource shifts. Supporters of AA might argue that an anti-AA campaign will be used by opponents to shut down the whole EEO effort and that the end result will be absolute cuts in civil rights expenditures, not transfers. These considerations argue against the *practicability* of diverting resources from AA in employment to other areas of equal opportunity. However, defenders of AA would want to make the case for maintaining and even expanding present efforts in positive terms.

Advocates defend continuation of AA programs on a variety of grounds. (1) The federal government's commitment to affirmative action is a very important symbol for the nation as a whole, a symbol of the national purpose to bring blacks, women, and other disadvantaged groups into full participation in all aspects of our society.

The tangible and intangible effects of this commitment are hard to measure, but to abandon it now—when these groups are not yet close to full equality, particularly in the area of employment—would signal an official end to the national civil rights effort of the last two decades. (2) While the number of higher level positions in federal employment systems is relatively small, these positions are particularly significant for policy formulation and implementation. Increased numbers of persons from disadvantaged groups in the clientele-related functions of federal service agencies will facilitate access of these groups to those services. (3) AA programs can help create a middle class of blacks and Hispanics with high occupational status, a class of persons who will be politically and socially influential in their own racial/ethnic communities and in the cities in which these are concentrated. (4) Greater racial/ethnic balance in critical institutions, such as the federal government, will help increase tolerance for racial differences in the society at large. (5) The federal government must demonstrate that it can overcome the long-standing exclusion or absence of women, blacks, and other minorities from the highest levels of public service if it is to be credible in its efforts to gain compliance with EEO mandates from the private sector. Like the criticisms of AA, these defenses deserve some scrutiny, particularly in terms of their assumptions and implications.

1. If one defends continued federal affirmative action on the grounds that it represents a necessary public commitment, that it symbolizes the national commitment to justice and equity for minorities, then the ambiguity of the ultimate goals of affirmative action—the ultimate implications of justice and equity—needs to be addressed. Equality of opportunity is the principle we ostensibly espouse as a nation, but many supporters of AA consider it a misleading phrase because it is difficult to specify just what is to be made equal and, therefore, difficult to determine when opportunities are actually equal regardless of race. Equal opportunity has been defined as everyone's having the same chances to succeed, but what does this mean in practice? What does "chances" include? In other words, how equal must the circumstances of individuals be made so that we can feel reasonably confident that the only remaining significant cause of differential results is differences in individual ability. If equality of results were the standard applied, as some recommend, then the problematics of equal opportunity are obviated. So far, most Americans seem hesitant to sever the alleged link between different rewards and differences in ability. This is why critics of AA have a point—though misconceived—when they conjure up gloomy visions of a society in which public goods are distributed by proportional quotas to specified groups. The point is not that AA is moving us inexorably toward that kind of society, but rather that one option to be considered in implementing AA is whether to sever that link explicitly and provide population shares of certain public goods to historically disadvantaged groups without making them pass over the barriers of conventional standards of merit or worth.

Americans and their political representatives usually are reluctant to openly confront the controversial questions that AA as a national policy poses. How much inequality do we actually have in this society? How much and what kinds of equality do most Americans really want? What differences in the quality of American life would greater socioeconomic equality make? What sacrifices are the politically, economically, and socially advantaged willing to make to achieve greater equality? While silence on these questions may be politically expedient, we cannot pursue AA broadly and indefinitely without making critical value choices, and if we do not make these choices explicitly, they will still get made.

2. One cannot assume that members of disadvantaged groups who attain higher level positions in the federal government will automatically identify with their own racial/ethnic/sex group and seek to represent their interests in policy formulation and implementation. Rosenbloom and Kinnard[23] point out that there has been very little study done on the impact of an individual administrator's social identity on his or her actions in office. Data from their respondents—elite minority administrators in the Department of Defense—indicated that, for the sample at least, "members of minority groups in high ranking bureaucratic positions generally feel a responsibility to try to serve the needs of other minorities." At the least, I would contend that these persons are more likely to understand the disadvantages members of their groups have experienced and can communicate that understanding to others in positions of influence. To the extent that members of disadvantaged groups fill a significant number of high ranking positions, they may be more apt to openly advocate policies that will be beneficial to other members of their group.

Similarly, the presence of significant numbers of minorities in agencies dealing with minority clienteles should serve to produce better understanding of the peculiar needs of the group, more confidence on the part of clienteles that their needs will be treated sympathetically, and thus increased incentive to make use of services to which members of the group are entitled.

3. The presence of such persons in minority communities may serve to fill a leadership and "role model" gap that some commentators believe contributes significantly to the political and economic weaknesses of these communities. Governments have historically served as avenues of upward mobility for groups disadvantaged in other areas of endeavor. While this function has not always been consciously undertaken, its end result can be a legitimate objective of public policy. If such upward mobility is achieved as a by-product of affirmative action, it may work to obviate the need for such programs in the long run because the newly advantaged members of the group will pass on these advantages in some form to the next generation.

These assertions are plausible, but they lack substantial empirical support. Do high ranking federal employees from minority groups play a vital role in their racial/ethnic communities? Or do they become a privileged minority within a minority—for example, members of a black bourgeoisie—separating itself from less fortunate members of the group and identifying more in attitude and aspiration with white members of the same class? There is evidence that blacks as a group are increasingly split into distinct socioeconomic classes, and it may be that AA merely works to increase the division.

4. That greater racial/ethnic/sex integration of federal agencies will increase tolerance of group differences seems plausible, but empirical research on tolerance among federal employees is scarce or nonexistent. Social-psychological studies of prejudice indicate that individuals who have experienced equal-status contacts with members of other races are more likely to show increased acceptance of them, particularly if they seek common goals, are cooperatively dependent upon each other, and their interactions are supported by authorities or laws.[24] These conditions could be met within the higher levels of the federal service.

5. Successful affirmative action in the area of federal employment may be a necessary condition for effective action in the private sector both as to inspiration

and specific methods. If the government cannot organize to implement AA effectively within its own agencies, its demand on the private sector will appear hypocritical. Indeed, EEO requirements placed on large segments of the private sector (and monitored by the EEOC and the OFCC) are more stringent than those the CSC has mandated for federal appointing authorities. On the other hand, statistical comparisons of wages and employment probabilities indicate that the record of the federal government with respect to blacks and women is superior to that of the private sector.[25] This result is not altogether a result of AA by any means (for example, the federal pay comparability system works to benefit all federal employees relative to private sector workers), but it suggests that the probability of effective AA is greater in the public sector.

The government appears to have a number of advantages in this area. The broad policy goals of many federal agencies are compatible with the goals of AA. This is particularly true of several major departments that already have relatively high percentages of blacks in higher level GS grades, for example, Labor, Health, Education and Welfare (HEW), and Housing and Urban Development (HUD). In the private sector, AA is an externally mandated policy with which an enterprise is expected to comply. Generally it has very little to do with the private firm's primary goals. The firm must absorb the costs of an AA program whether or not there are compensating benefits that have economic payoffs. In that regard, there do not appear to be any *typical* incentives for private firms to eliminate individual acts of discrimination or hiring and promotion methods which produce and maintain differential results for whites and minorities and women.[26] Moreover, private firms practicing discrimination have not had to bear the social costs of their policies and practices,[27] for example, underutilization of human resources, subsidization of persons excluded from labor markets, as well as less tangible social and psychological detriments. Those costs are more obvious to federal agencies because many federal programs are designed to remediate problems partly caused by discriminatory exclusions in the labor market.

Cost/effectiveness of AA is not likely to be a crucial factor in the federal EEO programs—even though program evaluation and productivity are growing concerns of legislators and public administrators—but in the private sector, the costs of implementing EEO/AA requirements are already causing considerable displeasure.

The sheer number of enterprises in which EEO/AA must be implemented in the private sector (even considering only major ones) is very large, and the monitoring task itself is terribly formidable. While there are many federal departments and agencies with numerous subdivisions, the number of different AA programs necessary to deal with them would appear considerably smaller relative to the total number of employees affected. Furthermore, federal agencies provide a useful testing ground for new strategies and techniques. Since most private firms are reluctant to incur significant costs in a nonprofit-related endeavor, little private sector experimentation in the EEO area seems likely. The government has already developed a number of techniques and programs whose results could be evaluated in terms of private sector applicability.

By establishing the special emphasis programs, the government has provided a base—albeit not a potent one—from which advocates of AA can work from within. There is nothing really comparable in the private sector, especially since many unions have not distinguished themselves from an EEO perspective.

CONCLUSION

It appears that most of the criticisms of AA stem from a belief that it leads to preferential selection. Many white Americans do not believe that blacks are still victims of discrimination, and thus they view preferential selection with skepticism or even hostility. Since it is problematic whether discrimination within the government is as responsible for differentials in federal employment among race and sex groups as past discrimination in other social institutions, critics of AA might urge policymakers to consider whether AA should be used at all within the government to help rectify the effects of discrimination that has occurred outside it. Why pressure federal agencies to hire minorities, rather than increase the numbers of minorities with appropriate work and educational experience? The latter approach, from the critics' vantage point, would reduce the probability that preferential selection will occur. To raise this question does not necessarily imply that AA should be taken out of government EEO efforts. The crux of the matter may be whether federal AA programs can be developed that will find, train, and promote members of disadvantaged groups who have the best chance of succeeding in higher level administrative positions.

While critics may be dubious that this can be done without detriments more weighty than the gains, I submit that the case against AA in public employment has not been made in any rigorous sense, that the weight of evidence is *not* clearly against the continued necessity for and the usefulness, past or future, of these programs. Furthermore, in the absence of assurance about the qualifications necessary for most forms of employment and with provisions for training on the job and performance evaluation, preferential selection in AA programs need *not* be a threat to the quality of public servants. There are already some important deviations from ostensibly meritocratic standards in the public service, and no one knows what impact they have had on productivity and quality of performance. It has not been shown that when AA "succeeds," it does so only at the cost of deteriorating the quality of federal personnel.

It would be helpful to have a better sense of the changes, if any, AA has produced in federal agency EEO programs, not in terms of paper procedures or organization charts but in terms of measurable practices, for example, changes in outreach, interviewing, selection devices, skill-upgrading programs, promotion reviews, and, of course, what impact these changes have had on hiring and promotions.[28] We need to know whether changes have been implemented successfully in some agencies and not in others and, if so, why.

At the same time, it is important to recognize that AA has been in existence for only about five years and that is a relatively limited time on which to base substantive conclusions. What supporters fear is that the potential in AA will never be realized because public opinion will too readily accept the arguments against it and that the federal government will yield up its civil rights-inspired commitment to improve the status and condition of disadvantaged groups. The *Bakke* decision is reassuring in one respect—the constitutionality of AA is no longer suspect—but that hardly suggests there will be no challenges to AA in other forums.

NOTES

1. Four Justices said that the 1964 Civil Rights Act itself prohibited the use of a quota plan; five Justices said that the case could not be decided on the basis of the Civil Rights Act, that the constitutional issue had to be reached. One of these five ruled that reserved places violated the Equal Protection Clause unless certain conditions were met.

2. This EO transferred responsibility for monitoring EEO in federal agencies to the CSC.

3. Title VII, Sec. 703 (j) [42 USC 2000e et seq.], (emphasis added).

4. Quoted in Charles S. Bullock III, "Expanding Black Economic Rights," ed. in *Racism and Inequality*, (San Francisco: W. H. Freeman, 1975), 78. Harrel Rodgers, Jr.

5. *Contractors Association of Eastern Pennsylvania* v. *Secretary of Labor*, 442. F. 2nd. 159 (1971).

6. Quoted in David H. Rosenbloom, "The Civil Service Commission's Decision to Authorize the Use of Goals and Timetables in the Federal Equal Employment Opportunity Program," *Western Political Quarterly* 26, (June 1973): 237.

7. Quoted in Rosenbloom, 248.

8. "Memorandum-Permissible Goals and Timetables in State and Local Government Employment Practices in Affirmative Action Planning for State and Local Governments," United States Civil Service Commission, December 1973.

9. *Intergovernmental Personnel Notes*, September-October 1976.

10. The report indicates that lower level personnel may sometimes have resorted to techniques (to achieve numerical objectives) that top management did not intend.

11. This is not to say that the use of goals does not put some pressure on managers and supervisors; goals provide regulators with a more tangible basis for evaluating the effectiveness of an AA program, and this may act as a constraint on the persons responsible for implementing it. Nonetheless, this does not seem equivalent to the sanctions behind a quota.

12. "Public Policy Issues in the Quota Controversy," *Education and Urban Society* 8, 1 (November 1975): 74.

13. Indeed, it tried to discourage their use prior to 1972.

14. There are indications that AA plans often fail to indicate who is responsible for the fulfillment of specific objectives, thereby making it difficult to hold any individuals accountable.

15. *Personnel Management Project*, Vol 1: Final Staff Report (Washington, D.C., December 1977), 88; *Federal Personnel Management Project, Option Paper Number One* (Washington, D.C., September 7, 1977), 40.

16. "Affirmative Action," in *Equality and Preferential Treatment*, eds., Marshall Cohen, Thomas Nagel, and Thomas Scanlon (Princeton, N.J.: Princeton University Press, 1977), 192–209. Goldman's argument is made in the context of AA in hiring of university faculty and goal implementation under HEW supervision; however, his *general* contention applied to federal AA efforts, as well.

17. This criticism usually predates the establishment of the Federal Women's Program (FWP) and the Spanish Speaking Program (SSP). It appears that women, like blacks, are well represented at the lower GS levels, but Hispanic employment falls short of population parity even in the lower GS grades.

18. The following table includes 1976 data on women and minorities in the general schedule positions of Civil Service and in the national labor force.

	Women	All Minorities
GS9	33.7%	14.8%
GS18	2.8%	3.2%
National work force Employed (20 years and older for women, 16 and older for minorities)	39.9%	11.5%
National work force (20 years and older for women, 16 and older for minorities)	39.6%	10.8%

SOURCE: *Equal Employment Opportunity Statistics: November 1976*, SM 70-76B, US CSC, Bureau of Personnel Management Information Systems; *Handbook of Labor Statistics 1977*, US Department of Labor, Bureau of Labor Statistics.

19. The table below includes data from several major agencies which had relatively low black representation in the higher GS grades prior to 1972. See also Winfield Rose and Tiang Chia, "The Impact of the EEO Act of 1972 on Black Employment in the Federal Service: A Preliminary Analysis," *Public Administration Review* 38 (May-June 1978): 245–51.

20. They are not at present the sole basis for such decisions, but formal education appears to be an important criterion in federal accessions.

21. The 1975 CRC report—*The Federal Civil Rights Enforcement Effort-1974, Volume V: To Eliminate Employment Discrimination*—states that male sex discrimination complaints increased from 3.6 percent of the total in FY 1972 to 6.3 percent in FY 1974. However, it is impossible to determine what percentage of these were filed by white males since the CSC tabulation did not indicate how many complaints alleged both sex and race discrimination.

22. "Justifying Reverse Discrimination in Employment," in Cohen, Nagel, and Scanlon, p. 54. I should note that I have taken Sher's argument in its baldest form; he indicates that he does not think it applies to reverse discrimination for women and that his argument justifies reverse discrimination "in favor of only those group members whose abilities have actually been reduced; and it would be implausible to suppose that every black (or every woman) has been affected in this way," 59.

23. David Rosenbloom and Douglas Kinnard, "Bureaucratic Representation and Bureaucrats' Behavior: An Exploratory Analysis," *Midwest Review of Public Administration* 11 (March 1977): 35–42.

24. See Thomas F. Pettigrew, "Racially Separate or Together?" *Journal of Social Issues* 25 (January 1969): 54–57.

25. See James Long, "Employment Discrimination in the Federal Sector," *Journal of Human Resources*, 11 (Winter 1976) 86–97; and Sharon Smith, "Government Wage Differentials by Sex," *Journal of Human Resources* (Spring 1976), 185–99.

26. Assuming that the labor supply (including both whites and blacks) is relatively elastic. The economics of discrimination are complex; on the one hand, if most firms discriminate against minorities, other firms may be able to hire minority workers at lower wages than would ordinarily prevail; on the other, there may be costs of changing one's own employment policies to take advantage of this differential.

27. Other than as taxpayers along with the rest of us.

28. The reports cited above do not cause me to be optimistic about the extent of these changes.

Percentage of black employees in federal agencies by GS grade

GS	May 1975	Nov. 1974	Nov. 1973	Nov. 1972	Nov. 1971	Nov. 1970	Agency
9-11	11.0	10.5	10.2	9.0	7.9	7.5	Commerce
12-13	6.8	6.0	5.7	5.2	4.6	4.6	
14-15	4.1	4.0	3.8	3.2	2.8	2.6	
16-18	1.4	0.8	0.5	0.5	0.3	0.5	
9-11	10.4	10.2	10.0	9.8	9.7	9.6	Veteran's
12-13	5.6	5.4	4.9	4.2	3.9	3.8	Administration
14-15	4.2	4.2	3.5	3.9	3.3	2.0	
16-18	3.4	2.5	0.8	2.8	2.6	2.5	
9-11	16.1	15.4	13.5	12.8	10.7	9.6	General
12-13	6.9	6.4	5.9	5.1	4.3	3.6	Services
14-15	4.2	4.2	3.5	3.9	3.3	2.0	Administration
16-18	4.0	3.8	2.4	2.9	2.7	2.8	
9-11	3.9	3.6	3.2	3.2	2.9	2.8	NASA
12-13	2.0	2.0	1.8	1.7	1.7	1.6	
14-15	0.9	0.8	0.6	0.5	0.4	0.4	
16-18	0.0	0.0	0.0	0.4	0.3	0.3	
9-11	6.2	6.3	6.0	4.8	3.8	3.0	Transportation
12-13	3.5	3.2	2.8	2.6	2.2	2.0	
14-15	2.6	2.4	2.1	2.2	1.6	1.4	
16-18	4.9	5.0	5.7	7.2	4.7	4.9	
9-11	6.5	6.1	5.0	4.1	3.3	2.9	Justice
12-13	2.6	2.5	2.3	2.2	1.6	1.5	
14-15	2.7	2.7	2.0	1.8	1.8	1.7	
16-18	2.8	2.7	2.7	2.6	1.2	1.2	

SOURCE: U.S. Civil Service Commission, Bureau of Manpower Information Systems, *Minority Group Employment in the Federal Government* (series begun in November 1969).

New Directions in EEO Guidelines

David E. Robertson

Most people believe there has been significant progress toward achieving the goal of equal employment opportunity. Minority participation in employment has almost doubled during the past decade.[1] Employers are more aware these days that selection decisions must not result in adverse impact on any minority group. But in spite of this progress, there are still real problems as enforcement agencies and the courts attempt to put the mandate of Title VII into effective practice.

Opinions have been advanced that the government has gone too far in protecting the rights of minorities and that preferential treatment of such groups has resulted in discrimination against nonminorities.[2] At the minimum, it has been argued that government overregulation of the employment process has resulted in unreasonable demands being placed on the small employer.[3] It now remains to be seen precisely how the revised uniform guidelines on employee selection procedures will affect the situation, but some hypotheses can certainly be drawn at this time.

REGULATION OF THE SELECTION PROCESS

The Tower Amendment to the 1964 Civil Rights Act specifically approves the use of "professionally developed ability tests," provided that such tests are not "designed, intended, or used to discriminate because of race, color, religion, sex, or national origin."[4] The Equal Employment Opportunity Commission charged with enforcing the act published a set of guidelines in 1966, with extensive revisions in 1970, which were intended to spell out, in general terms, the employer's obligation regarding testing and selection procedures as they relate to equal employment opportunity. Shortly after the 1970 guidelines were issued, the Supreme Court in the landmark case of *Griggs* v. *Duke Power* established a legal framework for employment testing, citing with approval the procedures contained in the guidelines.[5] These guidelines became the model for another set of guidelines issued by the Office of Federal Contract Compliance for those employers subject to regulation under Executive Order (EO) 11246, as amended by EO 11375.

Both sets of guidelines were not only complex and difficult to understand for lay practitioners, but they also contained provisions that severely limited the use of employment tests. In a few instances, the guidelines were in conflict with each other and with federal law as developed through case litigation. As a consequence

David E. Robertson is an associate professor of management at Northeast Louisiana University in Monroe.

of this legal complexity and confusion, many companies abandoned employment testing altogether in favor of more subjective selection procedures designed to avert challenges and hire enough minority candidates to avoid enforcement agency intervention. The more objective procedures were abandoned because few employers were able to prove the validity of their selection procedures under the 1970 guidelines, and most didn't wish to risk charges of noncompliance.[6]

The federal government has been severely criticized for not setting more realistic selection procedure standards. Part of the difficulty may be due to divergent efforts of various enforcement agencies. Commissioner Daniel E. Leach of the EEOC recently commented:

> In looking at the anti-bias efforts today, I am a little reminded of the old circus act with five clowns in a tiny car. One honking the horn, one turning and spinning the wheel, one with a foot on the brake, another with a foot on the gas, and a fifth sitting on top shouting and waving.[7]

In the years after adoption of the original guidelines, the need for a uniform philosophy among federal EEO agencies became more evident. In November 1976, the Labor Department, the Justice Department, and the Civil Service Commission agreed to issue new guidelines for public sector employers and employers subject to EO 11246. The Equal Employment Opportunity Commission, however, did not sign the new Federal Executive Agency Guidelines and instead republished the 1970 guidelines for use in the private sector. It wasn't until December 1977 that a revised "Uniform Guidelines on Employee Selection Procedures" was finally approved by all four major agencies responsible for EEO concerns. A draft of the proposed rules was subsequently published in the Federal Register for comments, and they are expected to go into effect with very little revision on approximately July 1, 1978.[8] While the final version may contain a few changes from the provisions discussed here, enforcement agency officials do not anticipate any substantive changes. Yet there are many differences between these guidelines and the 1970 guidelines, as can be seen by examining the 80-percent rule, bottom-line strategies, fairness of tests, alternate procedures, and other validation approaches.

THE 80-PERCENT RULE

One of the requirements imposed on employees by the original guidelines and the *Griggs* decision was that tests be job related. The only way job relatedness can be proven is through the validation process, a statistical comparison of test scores with some measure of job success. Validation under the new rules is not required in all cases. It is essential only in instances where the test or other selection device produces an adverse impact on a minority group. Under the new guidelines, adverse impact has been defined in terms of selection rates, the selection rate being the number of applicants hired or promoted divided by the total number of applicants.

Under the new guidelines, a selection rate for any minority group which is less than 80 percent of the rate for the group with the highest rate will generally be regarded as evidence of adverse impact.[9] A rate of more than 80 percent will generally be regarded as evidence that there is no adverse impact. Employers who hoped for an explicit specification of conditions having adverse impact will be disappointed with the extensive use of the term *generally*, for this wording gives government enforcement agencies the right to define adverse impact as they choose. The notion of providing a specific operational definition of adverse impact seems good except that the difference in the selection rate between the minority group in question and the group with the highest rate is not fixed. This difference would be only 2 percent if the majority group's selection rate is as low as 10 percent. In other words, the 80-percent rule suggests a tolerance of 20 percent difference, but this 20 percent tolerance holds only if the majority group's selection rate is 100 percent, a very rare occurrence. Since selection rates in most actual situations will run closer to 10 percent in many instances, there will be situations in which a selection device will result in a slightly smaller percentage of minority candidates being hired. Such a device will then be judged as having adverse impact instead of simply reflecting the kind of normal variation one gets in dealing with small samples.

Revising the guidelines to require validation in the event of adverse impact presumably gives some relief to the smaller employer, inasmuch as a full-fledged longitudinal validation study may cost $25,000 or more.[10] Still, it seems likely that the small percentage difference permitted between the selection rates of majority and minority groups will not materially reduce the requirements for validation nor reduce the extent of government involvement. The 80-percent rule may even encourage more challenges and interventions since the point where a violation exists is clearer than before.

BOTTOM-LINE STRATEGIES

The so-called bottom-line strategy is another new provision apparently intended to reduce the burden of coneucting separate vaidation studies for each step in the selection process. The original guidelines contained a very broad definition for tests as any formally scored quantified, or standardized technique for assessing job suitability. The new guidelines are even broader, covering unstandardized, informal, or unscored selection procedures. It is specified that where such procedures result in adverse impact, employers should take steps to correct the adverse impact or standardize and validate the procedure.[11] It would appear on the surface that the new bottom-line provision would offer some relief to employers by excusing them from separately validating each procedure so long as the combined effect of the entire selection process does not produce adverse impact,. This theoretically saves the employer a great deal of trouble because if he/she uses many devices—weighted application blanks, interviews, tests, reference checks, and so forth—there is no longer any need to validate each one separately.

There is a fly in the ointment, however. The employer, in order to prove the entire selection process does not result in adverse impact on any minority group, must now keep records of the numbers of applicants and hires by sex and by racial and ethnic group, including separate figures for blacks, Indians, Hispanic people, and whites.[12] Any time and expense that is saved by using the bottom-line concept will surely be consumed in the new record keeping obligations. It is ironic that government formerly admonished employers not to be conscious of sex and racial classifications, yet now requires them to maintain records on such classifications.

FAIRNESS OF TESTS

While the federal government, in adopting the new uniform guidelines, has failed to relieve the burden on employers, it has also ignored the advice of authorities on test validation. The 1970 guidelines contained a provision to which many testing authorities have objected. This provision states that where technically feasible, a separate validation study must be conducted for each minority group to check on the possible existence of what has been called differential validity. A selection device with differential validity is a device that predicts accurately for one sub-group but not another.[13] The original guideline authors believed that it is possible for a racial, ethnic, or sex group to regularly score lower than members of another group on a selection procedure while still performing the job equally well. The controversy over this issue set off a flurry of research about the possiblility of differential or single group validity.[14, 15, 16] While the results are still coming in, it appears that differential prediction is a discredited concept. Most psychologists seem to believe that if a selection device is carefully constructed and is predictive in the overall, then it will be equally predictive for any or all subgroups. Contrary results are attributed to poorly selected criteria and sampling error.

The new guidelines, rather than taking into account the results of recent research, not only continue to recognize the concept of differential prediction, but also call for users to make special "studies of fairness" and describe the procedures for making such studies in substantial detail.[17] The fairness studies call for separate validation for each subgroup as required in the original guidelines. The inclusion of these requirements in the new guidelines seems to be another instance where the federal government has ignored recent research results and the advice of personnel specialists and practitioners.

ALTERNATE PROCEDURES

The alternate procedures provisions of the new guidelines are inconsistent with an earlier court decision. The earlier ruling suggested that if a selection procedure is properly validated, it is not considered discriminatory, even though it may have an adverse impact.[18] It has also been pointed out that Congress has not commanded that the less qualified be preferred over the better qualified simply because of minority origins.[19]

The new guidelines seem to ignore these court holdings in indicating that users may choose alternate selection procedures to eliminate adverse impact. Alternate procedures include, but are not limited to, affirmative action programs plus "measures of superior scholarship; culture, language, or experience factors; selected use of established registers; selection from a pool of disadvantaged persons who have demonstrated their general competency; [or] use of registers limited to qualified persons who are economically disadvantaged."[20] No mention is made of how one determines that a person has "general competency" or is "qualified" in the absence of measures normally determined through regular selection procedures.

The employer who chooses to use these preferential hiring procedures runs the risk of violating both the Civil Rights Act and the Constitution.[21] The substitution of a numbers approach for proper test validation was not intended by Congress or the courts, and its inclusion in the new guidelines will certainly lead to legal challenges. It took a long time for the personnel profession to recognize the importance of validating selection devices, and the *Griggs* decision finally made validation mandatory. Some people apparently believe that employers primarily validate tests so that they can legally exclude minorities.[22] If one believes this, it is not hard to conclude that the only way to ensure the hiring of minorities in sufficient numbers is not through validation but through permitting and encouraging selection procedures that guarantee equal hiring results. The new uniform guidelines have in many ways abandoned the concept of equal opportunity in favor of the concept of equal results.

As noted previously, the new guidelines apparently allow an employer to substitute an affirmative action program complete with goals and timetables for a validated selection procedure if the program eliminates adverse impact. While the encouragement of affirmative action programs is laudable, a primary criterion should be based on the actual proportion of minorities in the relevant labor market, a different criterion than comparative selection provides. These multiple standards of what constitutes discrimination will surely lead to confusion.

The alternate procedures section also fails to take into account previous court decisions indicating that the employer has a right to select the most qualified candidate for a job.[23] The numerous references to selection of "qualified persons" indicates that the guideline authors see no distinction between marginally qualified and highly qualified candidates. The whole merit system is based on the assumption that there are demonstrable differences in merit among those who are qualified and that selection should be made from among the "best-qualified" applicants. While the availability of alternate procedures in theory will provide some much needed flexibility, the mixture of selection procedures and affirmative action programs seems to add needless complication.

OTHER VALIDATION APPROACHES

In the past, the EEOC and the courts have permitted either content or construct validity to be used as a substitute for empirical or criterion-related validity, but only where it was not feasible or practical to prove empirical validity.[24] Content validity refers to the extent to which a selection device accurately samples the tasks to be performed on a job. Construct validity refers to the extent to which a selection device measures a specific theoretical construct or trait which is known to be essential to successful job performance. There is less agreement among professionals in the testing field about content and construct validity than about empirical validity. Both content and construct validity are developing concepts, and there are disagreements among authorities as to how evidence of these qualities should be determined.[25] This has not prevented EEOC examiners and judges from plunging into the field and making their own assessments.

The net effect of the new rules is to elevate content and construct validity to a coequal status with empirical validity, rather than giving preference to the latter. There may be nothing wrong with permitting any of the three types of validity to be used, but certainly the admission of less structured concepts will result in more and more elaboration of special conditions and requirements as cases begin to progress through the courts. Fortunately, a number of specific requirements and applications of content and construct validity are spelled out to discourage employers from selecting either of these strategies merely because validation is less time consuming, costly, or difficult to achieve than empirical validity. Of course, not all testing authorities agree that construct and content validity are independent of each other and viable alternatives to empirical validity.[26]

The new uniform guidelines will obviously have a substantial effect on the employee selection process in both the public and private sector. Of the five procedural changes that have been discussed, it is likely that the 80-percent rule and the alternate procedure provisions will have the greatest impact.

The 80-percent rule represents a step toward simplifying the standards by which selection procedures are judged, and to this extent its adoption may help clarify rather than confuse. This will be particularly true if the standard is used in ruling out claims of adverse impact as well as defining instances where it exists. Professionals continue to claim that a fixed percentage should not be used and that the only acceptable method of testing differences in selection rates is statistical analysis. Time will tell whether the new "rule of thumb" will prove to be a workable standard.

The future prospects of the alternate procedures provisions do not seem nearly so bright. The new guidelines go far beyond specifying minimum legal standards for selection procedures. They call for voluntary affirmative action programs which in design and execution may be conscious of race, color, sex, or ethnic origin. There are two major problems in encouraging affirmative action programs as part of the uniform guidelines on selection. First, there is danger that employers might read these provisions and conclude that having a voluntary affirmative action program is an appropriate defense for charges resulting from use of selection procedures with an adverse impact on one group.[27] Second, the use of unvalidated procedures to produce race, ethnic, or sex-conscious decisions may violate Title VII or the Constitution, as mentioned previously. The legality of preferential hiring may be resolved when the *Bakke* case is decided.[28]

There appear to be no easy solutions to the complex question of how much regulation is appropriate. Government involvement in the selection process has increased greatly over the last decade, and if the new guidelines are any indication, the future will bring even greater involvement. In retrospect, the requirement of proper selection process validation has improved personnel practices and also helped achieve the goal of promoting equal employment opportunity. Congress intended to preserve the merit principle and envisioned that equal opportunity would be realized from the use of truly objective selection procedures, not a classifications-conscious or numerical approach, which is the direction we seem to be headed. Personnel professionals, and in particular the Ad Hoc Group on Employee Selection Procedures, could do much to help government agencies draft a workable set of guidelines. Employers can only hope that some attention is paid to the suggestions of this group as the final version is implemented.

NOTES

1. W. Perry Lowell, "The Mandate and Impact of Title VII,"*Labor Law Journal*, 26, 12 (December 1975).
2. Ernest Van Den Haag, "Reverse Discrimination: A Brief Against It," *National Review* 19, 16 (April 29, 1977): 492–95.

3. David E. Robertson, "Employment Testing and Discrimination," *Personnel Journal* 54, 1 (January 1975): 18–21.

4. David E. Robertson, "Update on Testing and Equal Opportunity," *Personnel Journal* 56, 3 (March 1977): 144–47.

5. *Employment Practices Decisions* Vol. 3 (Chicago: Commerce Clearing House, Inc., 1971) 6430–36.

6. C. Paul Sparks, "Guidance and Guidelines," *The Industrial-Organizational Psychologist* 14, 3 (May 1977): 30–33.

7. Virgil B. Day, ed., "Comments of the Ad Hoc Group on Employee Selection Procedure," (mimeographed), American Psychological Association, February 17, 1978.

8. Civil Service Commission. Telephone conversation with Assistant Director, Personnel Research, Development Center, Civil Service Commission, 1900 E Street NW, Washington, D.C. 20415, May 23, 1978.

9. "Uniform Guidelines on Employee Selection Procedures," *Federal Register* 42, 251 (December 30, 1977): 65544.

10. F. L. Schmidt and J. E. Hunter, "The Future of Criterion-Related Validity Studies in Title VII Employment Discrimination Cases," *The Personnel Administrator* (September 1977).

11. "Uniform Guidelines on Employee Selection Procedures," 65545.

12. Ibid., 65543.

13. D. W. Bray and J. L. Moses, "Personnel Selection," *Annual Review of Psychology* 23 (1972): 545–76.

14. V. R. Boehm, "Negro-White Differences in Validity of Employment and Training Selection Procedures: Summary of Research Evidence," *Journal of Applied Psychology* 56 (1972): 33–39.

15. E. J. O'Connor, K. N. Wexley, and R. A. Alexander, "Single-Group Validity: Fact or Fallacy?" *Journal of Applied Psychology* 60 (1975): 352–55.

16. F. L. Schmidt, J. S. Berner, and J. E. Hunter, "Racial Differences in Validity: Fact or Fallacy?" *Journal of Applied Psychology* 58 (1973): 5–9.

17. "Uniform Guidelines on Employee Selection Procedures," 65547.

18. David E. Robertson, "Employment Testing and Discrimination."

19. G. Cooper and R. B. Sobol, "Seniority and Testing Under Fair Employment Laws: A General Approach to Objective Criteria of Hiring and Promotion," *Harvard Law Review* 82, 8 (June 1969): 1650.

20. "Uniform Guidelines on Employee Selection Procedures," 65546.

21. David E. Robertson, "Employment Quotas and the New Equality," *Proceedings: American Institute for Decision Sciences*, Midwest Division (May 1978).

22. Virgil B. Day, "Comments of the Ad Hoc Group."

23. Ibid.

24. David E. Robertson, "Update on Testing and Equal Opportunity."

25. Robert L. Ebel, "Comments on Some Problems of Employment Testing," *Personnel Psychology* 30 (1977): 55–63.

Equal Opportunity and Seniority: Trends and Manpower Implications

James A. Craft

Seniority, broadly defined as an employee's length of continuous service with an employer, has enjoyed increasing acceptance and use in organizational manpower decisions since World War II. It has become an integral part of the institutionalized web of rules that affects the administration of human resources in the internal labor market. Specifically, seniority has come to represent an enforceable priority under a collective bargaining agreement which qualifies an employee for benefits from the employer and provides a common basis for employees to estimate their relative status in terms of job security and opportunities for advancement.[1] However, while seniority remains a core concept in manpower management, the context in which it is applied and the rules for application are undergoing challenges and important changes. This has basically come about through pressures and decisions from parties external to the collective bargaining relationship with the intent to promote equal employment opportunities for minority groups. Given the importance of seniority as an element of manpower management, the purpose of this article is to briefly identify some of the major trends and controversies currently affecting the use of seniority and, also, to examine the implications for human resources management that these imply.

In the attempt to eliminate illegal employment discrimination, the courts, various federal and state administrative agencies, and labor arbitrators have rendered decisions, decrees, and guidelines that have restructured seniority as a manpower allocation mechanism. In general, changes can be broadly examined in terms of (1) the effective unit of seniority for internal manpower allocation decisions and (2) the use of seniority as a basis for layoffs during a reduction in an employer's work force.

Unit of Seniority

The size of the unit in which an employee can effectively exercise seniority rights has important implications for both the employee and management. Traditionally, by narrowing the unit wherein an employee earned and exercised her or his seniority rights, workers could often eliminate competition for better paying jobs. It has not been unheard of, for example, for powerful union members to formulate grievances or demands to obtain more favorable seniority units for themselves through restricting lines of promotion or in other ways narrowing seniority units.[2]

James A. Craft is an associate professor of business administration at the University of Pittsburgh.

Reprinted from James A. Craft, "Equal Opportunity and Seniority: Trends and Manpower Implications," *Labor Law Journal* (December 1975), 750–758, published by Commerce Clearing House, Inc., copyrighted 1975.

Also, management has in the past sometimes preferred rather narrow seniority units. Such units would more likely insure adequate training for employees in the job progression line and would minimize any disruptions due to transfers and/or bumping during a layoff.[3] While the actual size and number of seniority units will tend to vary with the industry, type of union, economic conditions of the industry, and so on, there are many firms with rather narrow departmental or occupational units. In the steel industry in the 1960s, for example, some plants had from three to four hundred seniority units—with one case where there were only two jobs per unit.[4]

A problem has arisen due to the fact that in many organizations black workers had traditionally been hired into a few predominately black departments or jobs—in which generally less desirable work was performed and, on the average, they received lower pay. The use of narrow departmental or job seniority units, while insuring those in the units of better opportunities, effectively excluded blacks from access to the higher paying jobs and reduced chances for their promotion to higher job classifications.[5] If a black worker, for example, wished to transfer to another unit with better job and promotional opportunities, he or she was required to start at an entry level job and begin to accumulate seniority in that unit to bid for further jobs. His or her accumulated seniority in the plant in a different department mattered for naught in the new unit.

With the advent of a proactive national policy on equal employment opportunity and its accompanying enforcement agencies, the narrow exclusionary seniority unit structures were challenged. The result of a number of court cases, an arbitration ruling, and a major consent decree clearly tend to indicate that the effective unit of seniority is to be broadened.[6] In effect, for major manpower allocation decisions, such as transfer, promotion, and layoff, the effective unit of seniority is to be *plant-wide* seniority. Usually, affected minorities have the opportunity to exercise plant-wide seniority to transfer to jobs in more desirable departments—assuming that they can perform the work satisfactorily, either initially or with some training. For later job bidding in the department, only plant-wide seniority, not departmental or job seniority, is considered as the length of service factor in the selection decision. This, of course, has a major impact in restructuring the entire competitive seniority hierarchy for all employees.

Perhaps the single most dramatic illustration of the magnitude of the movement to plant-wide seniority comes from the steel industry, which traditionally has employed departmental seniority as a basis for promotion and other manpower allocation decisions. In the recent Consent Decree entered into by nine major companies and the Steelworkers Union, over 300,000 people (including an affected class of about 40,000 minorities) in about 250 plants were affected. Under the conditions of the decree, these employees now are accorded plant-wide seniority, which will be utilized in future decisions relating to promotions, step-ups, demotions, layoffs, and so forth.

Seniority in Layoffs

In a seniority unit structured by collective bargaining agreements (or in some cases by custom or administrative fiat), regardless of size, it is customary that length of service be used as a major factor in determining who is to be laid off during a reduction in force.[7] Generally speaking, the employee with the least seniority is laid off first. The rule tends to be "last hired, first fired."

Many employees prefer the seniority principle in layoffs since it provides an objective standard to govern job retention, and it is equitable in the sense that it provides greater job security for those who have held the jobs the longest.[8] Management, while emphasizing the need to consider employee ability and plant efficiency in layoffs, has recognized a certain value in the use of seniority in layoffs. For example, in some cases, seniority tends to be related to productivity. In addition, the use of seniority does provide protection for loyal long-time employees and may lead to better morale and less turnover among experienced employees. Therefore, seniority has been widely accepted by unions and management as one important criterion for determining layoffs—especially where the seniority units are narrow and seniority layoffs reduce inefficiency from excessive bumping.[9]

The conflict between this widely accepted use of seniority and equal employment opportunity has become apparent with the recent economic recession. Many companies that currently have affirmative action programs did not hire or only hired a few blacks prior to the late 1960s. With the advent of the economic downturn, these companies were compelled to reduce their work forces. Applying the well-established and generally accepted seniority principle in layoffs led to a disproportionate reduction of blacks, females, and other minorities recently hired under affirmative action programs. Therefore, an employer faced the unenviable dilemma of possibly violating his affirmative action agreement if he used seniority in layoffs or alternatively, violating the collective bargaining agreement (or administrative custom) if he retained minorities with less seniority than white workers who were laid off.

The emergence of this conflict has led to two divergent viewpoints on what action should be taken by the employer. The first viewpoint, which apparently has been supported by the Equal Employment Opportunity Commission and a few other groups, is that even if a seniority system is plant-wide, layoffs based on reverse seniority may be inappropriate since they perpetuate the effects of past discrimination, that is, blacks and other minorities are disproportionately affected because they have been most recently hired.[10]

In such cases, it has been suggested that the employer could maintain separate seniority lists for minorities and whites. During a layoff period, she or he could then maintain the racial ratio that existed when the last new employee was hired. Another suggestion related to maintaining an acceptable racial ratio has been that the employer use methods such as work sharing, elimination of overtime, voluntary early retirement, payless holidays, payless workdays, rotating layoffs, reduction in hours, and so forth, so there would not be a disproportionate effect on minorities.[11]

A second and apparently predominant point of view, endorsed by several circuit courts of appeal, the Civil Rights Department of the AFL-CIO, the Solicitor of Labor, and others, is that if a plant-wide seniority system is "facially neutral" (that is, it is not designed to affect people on the basis of race or sex), it is a bona fide and legal system for layoffs based on reverse seniority.[12] In such an interpretation, even if the seniority system continued the effects of past discrimination, it would still be used in layoffs, since it is not designed purposefully to affect any minority. In addition, by not using it, the inequities would be excessive for those who had built up rights in the neutral system but had no part in the discriminatory activities of the firm.

SOME MANPOWER MANAGEMENT IMPLICATIONS

The current changes and conflicts in the status and use of seniority have direct implications for organizational human resource management. The implications appear to be most significant in terms of the operations of internal labor markets, employee morale and worker attitudes, and with regard to the stability in union organizations and the consequent effect on labor relations.

Internal Labor Market Operations

One of the concerns about the use of seniority as a major factor in manpower allocation decisions has been that it restricts the flexibility in the use and mobility of the internal work force and leads to a closed market system. With the implementation of plant-wide seniority systems, one of the mobility barriers (that is, narrow seniority units) is alleviated. This should have the impact of increasing the movement of personnel among jobs in the internal market. While this will quite likely be helpful in opening more opportunities for minorities and providing a larger human resource base to draw from for any specific job, it can also have deleterious effects. For example, employer costs are likely to increase, at least in the short run, due to a number of problems which would have been minimized with retention of narrower seniority units.

First, there will most likely be a number of persons who, in their enthusiasm to get a new and more desirable job, will transfer to a different department. If they cannot perform effectively in the new position by the end of the trial period, they will have to be returned to their original job. Second, training (for example, safety, skill, and so on) beyond that usually required by the employer for persons entering a specific job will involve increased operating outlays. Finally, most consent decrees and court decisions require that a transferee be able to retain her previous wage rate if the new job pays less than her previous job, that is, rate retention. This will, in some cases, put the wage structure out of line, and the employer will be faced with paying higher rates than normal while the employee learns a job and exhibits lower productivity than the average.

The actual problems of dislocation, retraining, and inefficiency and their concomitant costs will depend directly on the extent of transfers that take place in the internal labor market. A few early reports indicate that, perhaps surprisingly, such transfers may not be extensive in some organizations.[13] This may reduce the scope of disruption and the immediate costs of implementing the plant-wide seniority concept in certain of those facilities where it has not been historically used.

With regard to the question of layoffs, if regular seniority-based procedures are used (only substituting plant-wide seniority instead of departmental or job seniority), the immediate effect is likely to be the retention of less skilled employees while higher skilled employees are laid off. For example, a minority worker could transfer, on the basis of plant-wide seniority, to a new department. Initially, it is most likely that he will take a lower level job that is available to gain job skills and operating knowledge before he can bid on better jobs in the department as they open up. Subsequently, in a layoff, a person in a more skilled job might have to be laid off due to the fact that he has less plant seniority than the transferee. The result is the retention of a less skilled worker who previously would have been bumped by the more skilled worker who had more departmental seniority.

The racial ratio approach to a reduction in force can also lead to the outcome of retaining less skilled employees, while more highly skilled employees from the white seniority list are laid off. If some type of work-sharing procedure is used, it would result in an underutilization of many if not all of the employer's work force.

Employee Morale and Attitudes

Employee morale and job attitudes are important considerations, since they tend to affect manpower problems such as grievances, turnover, recruitment, and absenteeism. Seniority, which is directly related to job security and promotional opportunity, has been cited by some as an important factor in the development and maintenance of satisfactory employee morale. The implementation of plant-wide seniority for promotion and layoff purposes or the possible use of some racial ratio or modified seniority system as a basis for layoffs poses a direct and obvious threat to job security and the advancement opportunities perceived by the majority of employees.

The security and promotional potential built up by departmental personnel over long periods of time are now diluted since the competition is now based on plant-wide seniority. For example, with the implementation of a plant-wide seniority system, employees with long plant service can enter a department and take a position in line for the more desirable jobs. Even though they are newcomers to the department (so called "outsiders"), they may outrank the present workers and can move past them in bidding for a future opening in the job progression line. Also, as we have seen, recent transfers to a department may be retained during a layoff while employees with less total plant seniority but more departmental seniority will be laid off. Apparently such things are happening with less than happy results for employee morale.[14]

Another consequence seems to have resulted from the implementation of systems that allow blacks with greater plant seniority to "leapfrog" over whites with more departmental seniority and/or allow junior black workers to be retained while senior white workers are laid off: increased racial animosity among employees.[15] Such emotional responses can lead to high levels of tension and anxiety on the job with the result of lowered morale and its consequent problems.

Union Stability and Labor Relations

Management, by law, is required to deal with the employees' union over substantive issues relating to the work situation. Generally speaking, managers would prefer to deal with a politically stable union. Such stability can provide a more "businesslike" basis for labor relations. For example, the union leadership is likely to enjoy reasonable tenure in office, and they may be able to make some decisions and commitments for the union. In an enduring relationship of respect, management and union leaders can conduct forthright discussions of pressing problems affecting the parties. In addition, where there is internal stability within the union, there is less likelihood that infighting and conflict of union politics among employees will affect operating efficiency (for example, wildcat strikes, grievance, and so on).

However, new programs and policies affecting basic "bread and butter" issues (for example, job security, wages, and so forth) which *differentially* impact on the membership and challenge vested interests, can be expected to arouse strong feelings among the rank and file. Such issues affecting a broad base of the membership can create factions within the union resulting in political instability and a less secure position for the leadership. The operating manifestations of this instability for management might include increased numbers of grievances submitted by employees who feel slighted by the policy, more pressures on all parties in contract negotiations to meet the demands of the several union factions with potentially conflicting objectives, and more difficulty securing ratification by the membership when a tentative agreement is reached in negotiations. The less secure and more questionable status of the union leadership as representative of the membership makes candid discussions and commitments more difficult to obtain.

The recent decisions and decrees affecting the unit of seniority and the use of seniority in layoff situations seem to incorporate much of what is needed to create the factionalism and instability in a number of local unions and possibly in a national union. Clearly, as we have seen, one basic factor stimulating this type of response is that changes in a basic job right, such as seniority, have tremendous potential effects on the security and opportunities of thousands of workers who presumably had accepted and invested substantial portions of their work lives in a reasonably stable seniority system with generally accepted rules to be used in manpower allocation decisions.

Also, perhaps to add insult to injury, the new seniority requirements have been imposed from outside the collective bargaining relationship with virtually no consultation or input from the rank and file members of the union. Given the importance of the issue, this can be expected to result in the discontent of the members who perceive themselves as adversely affected. In the light of trade union history, it is not unlikely that such animosity and discontent will be directed at the union leadership as well as other factions in the union which are potential beneficiaries of the new plan.

While it is still too early to be able to determine completely the effects of the changes and conflicts in seniority application, there are indications of emerging internal problems in some unions that may lead to internal instability and the concomitant problems. For example, there are illustrations in the steel industry. In the Steel Workers union, a group called the "Steel Workers Justice Committee" has been formed to fight the Consent Decree in the industry.

This committee has, with several hundred persons, picketed the USW headquarters in Pittsburgh on several occasions, demanding meaningful discussions with the union leadership on the issue. The committee, in addition to other dissident groups, has challenged the decree and its implementation in the courts—with little success to date. In addition, there have been increasing numbers of open meetings opposing the decree. Some local officers are highly skeptical of it and are participating in the implementation committees more because they are required to do so than due to personal support or by choice.[16]

CONCLUSIONS AND DISCUSSION

In the attempt to promote equal employment opportunity, it appears clear that most authoritative indicators point to the use of the plant as the effective unit in which seniority is to be accumulated and in which it can be exercised. In many plants and industries, plant-wide seniority will replace seniority in traditionally narrower departmental or occupational units as the basis for manpower allocation decision making.

Upon transferring into a new department, for example, an employee will use his or her plant-wide seniority as the basis for bidding for better jobs which later become available in the department. Such use of plant-wide seniority would appear to be a useful and perhaps a minimally disruptive approach (considering alternatives) to aiding minorities in attaining their "rightful place" in certain organizational manpower systems.[17]

However, it seems clear that management must be ready for some increased costs and new personnel problems with the resulting changes in the structure of the internal labor market. There will be a strong likelihood of lowered morale and racial animosity among employees as the new system is implemented. Potentially disruptive instabilities emerging in some unions could affect the collective bargaining relationship.

With regard to layoffs, where collective bargaining agreements exist, the trend appears to have turned strongly in favor of using plant-wide seniority systems as a basis for layoff of personnel. The proposed alternative of using some mechanism (for example, separate seniority lists, work sharing, and so on) to maintain a racial ratio and reduce the "disproportionate impact" of layoffs on affected minorities appears not to have spread far beyond the prodding of the EEOC, a few related agencies, and some early district court decisions following the EEOC line of reasoning.

Frankly, in my view, the momentum that this position once seemed to enjoy would appear to be rapidly diminishing. For example, the EEOC has proposed to come forward with a set of guidelines for layoffs affecting minorities (presumably using some aspect of the racial ratio approach), but its projected date of delivery has long since passed and there is little evidence to indicate that such formal guidelines will be forthcoming in the near future. The EEOC also has a new chairman, an industrial practitioner with labor-relations experience and an appreciation of the emotional and practical meaning of seniority in manpower decision making. He appears to be efficiency oriented and, in contrast to his predecessor, has taken no stand on the issue of seniority in layoffs.[18]

In addition, several recent and widely publicized circuit court of appeals decisions have reversed the district courts and have supported the use of seniority systems in making layoffs (as long as plant-wide seniority is used). Also, as we have indicated, there are strong institutional forces arguing for the use of seniority in layoffs in terms of equity for all employees. Finally, while it may take a Supreme Court decision to finalize the matter, the entire issue may dwindle in importance as we appear to be moving out of the recession and into the recovery phase of the current business cycle. As employees are brought back onto the payroll, the major questions will center on the use of plant-wide seniority for job transfer and bidding for better jobs and less on the problems of administering a general reduction in force.

NOTES

1. For an excellent discussion of the development and use of the seniority principle in internal manpower management, see the following sources: John W. McCaffrey, "Development and Administration of Seniority Provisions," in *NYU Second Annual Conference on Labor*, ed. Emanuel Stein (New York City: NYU, 1949) 131–54; Sumner H. Slichter, et al., *The Impact of Collective Bargaining on Management* (Washington, D.C.: The Brookings Institution, 1960) chapters 5, 6, and 7; and John T. Dunlop and James J. Healy, *Collective Bargaining: Principles and Cases*, rev. ed. (Homewood Illinois: Richard D. Irwin, Inc., 1955), 229–241.

2. For a discussion of the activities of union members to manipulate seniority units to their personal benefit, see Leonard R. Sayles, "Seniority: An Internal Union Problem" *Harvard Business Review* 30, (January-February 1952): 55–61.

3. Layoffs, for example, can entail much cost and inefficiency through bumping and extensive reallocation of persons and jobs. George Taylor has noted a situation where "in contracting the work force by 10 percent, over 40 percent of the people had to be reassigned." See George W. Taylor, "Seniority Concepts," in *Arbitration Today*, ed. J. T. McKelvey (Washington, D.C.: Bureau of National Affairs, 1955) 127–37.

4. See James J. Healey, ed., *Creative Collective Bargaining* (Englewood Cliffs, New Jersey: Prentice-Hall, Inc., 1965) 214.

5. For data and illustrations on this point, see the following: Cary D. Thorp, Jr., "Racial Discrimination and Seniority," *Labor Law Journal*, 23 (July 1972): 407; and "U.S. Orders Bethlehem Steel to Give Blacks Pay, Seniority Changes at Maryland Mill," *Wall Street Journal*, January 17, 1973, 5.

6. For the basic court cases on this subject see *Quarles v. Philip Morris, Inc.*, 279 F. Supp. 505, 57 LC ¶9109 (DC Va., 1968); *Local 189, United Papermakers and Paperworkers, AFL-CIO v. United States*, 416 F. 2d 980, 60 LC ¶9289 (CA-5, 1969), cert. denied, 397 U.S. 919 (1970); *United States v. Bethlehem Steel Corporation*, 446 F. 2d 652 3 EPD ¶8257 (CA-2, 1971). For an arbitrator's decision on the matter see the decision by J. D. Dunn printed in 64 LA 310; for the Consent Decree, see *United States v. Allegheny Ludlum Industries, Inc. et al.*, Civil Action No. 74P339 (DC Ala., 1974).

7. For a classic discussion of the use of seniority in layoffs and the nature of the seniority unit, see Sumner H. Slichter, *Union Policies and Industrial Management* (Washington, D.C.: The Brookings Institution, 1941) 98–163 and C. Wilson Randle, *Collective Bargaining: Principles and Practices* (New York: Houghton Mifflin Co., 1951) 410–53.

8. The moral underpinning of this has been called the "ethics of queue." See Melvin W. Reder, "Job Scarcity and the Nature of Union Power," *Industrial and Labor Relations Review* (April 1960): 353–57.

9. For a recent survey regarding seniority use in manpower decisions where collective bargaining agreements are in effect, see the following bulletins of the Bureau of Labor Statistics: *Administration of Seniority* (Bulletin 1425-14, 1972); *Layoff, Recall, and Worksharing Procedures* (Bulletin 1425-13, 1972); and *Seniority in Promotion and Transfer Provisions* (Bulletin 1425-11, 1970). Seniority has also been widely used in nonunion firms as a basis for personnel decisions. See, for example, National Industrial Conference Board, *Seniority Practices in Nonunionized Companies*. Studies in Personnel Policy, No. 110 (New York: National Industrial Conference Board, 1950).

10. The position of the former EEOC Chairman, John H. Powell, Jr., is one of opposition to the use of traditional seniority in layoffs in cases where its use would negatively affect the employment of minorities. Powell was chairman during much of the controversy and litigation on the issue. See Earnest Holsendolph, "Recession Layoffs and the Civil Rights of Minorities," *New York Times*, January 29, 1975, 17, and Paul Delaney, "Action Reviewed on Bias Charges," *New York Times*, February 12, 1974, 36. Also, see letter by EEOC Executive Director Harold S. Fleming sent on December 31, 1974 to chief executive officers of the two hundred largest U.S. corporations requesting special efforts to protect minorities during the recession cited in IRRC, *News for Investors*, II (February, 1975): 41. The seminal court case taking this approach is *Watkins v. Steel·*

workers, *Local 2369 and Continental Can Company*, 369 F. Supp. 1221 7 EPD ¶9130 (DC La.,1974). The Watkins doctrine has recently been rejected by the Fifth Circuit Court of Appeals. See "Seniority System in Employment Upheld by Court," *Wall Street Journal*, July 18, 1975, 17.

11. See Charlayne Hunter, "Last Hired, and Usually the First Let Go," *New York Times*, January 29, 1975, 17; Eileen Shanahan, "Women Advocate Option on Layoffs," *New York Times*, February 14, 1974, p. 10; BNA, *What's New in Collective Bargaining Negotiations and Contracts*, April 10, 1975, p. 3; BNA, "EEOC Deferral of Action on Layoff Guidelines," *Labor Relations Reporter* 88 (April 21, 1975): 313–14.

12. The basic court cases related to this position include: *Waters v. Wisconsin Steel Works*, 502 F. 2d 1309 8 EPD ¶9658 (CA-7, 1974) and *Jersey Central Power and Light v. IBEW Local Unions*, 9 EPD ¶9923 (CA-3, 1975). The opinion of the Solicitor of Labor can be found in BNA, "Legality of Fictional Seniority Rights," *Labor Relations Reporter* 84 (June 16, 1975): 139–40 and Marylin Bender, "Job Discrimination, 10 Years Later," *New York Times*, November 10, 1974, sec. 3, pp. 1, 5. The position presented by the director of the AFL-CIO Civil Rights Department, William Pollard, can be found in "Seminar on Corporate EEO Compliance Problems," *Labor Relations Reporter* 84 (June 23, 1975): 166–67. It is of consequence to note that Section 703 (h) of the Civil Rights Act of 1964 as amended allows differential compensation, terms, and conditions of work in a "bona fide seniority or merit system."

13. For example, in the Bethlehem Steel Lackawanna, N.Y., mill only about one-quarter of the blacks eligible signed up to transfer. Apparently, only about 16 percent of these persons actually changed jobs. See "Some Transfer Statistics on Concluded Steel Case," *Wall Street Journal*, August 8, 1973. Later experience indicates that this is not an isolated example.

14. For an example of some early experiences, see Maia Licker, "Bringing Racial Equality to Nation's Steel Mills Is Long and Bitter Task," *Wall Street Journal*, August 8, 1973, 1, 12.

15. Ibid. Also see "Police Layoffs Shaking Up Detroit," *The Pittsburgh Press*, August 11, 1975, and James C. Hyatt, "Courts' Protection Against Job Layoffs Sought by Minorities," *Wall Street Journal*, November 5, 1974, and John Egenton, "How Job Layoffs can Heighten Racial Tension," *The Philadelphia Inquirer*, (August 5, 1975).

16. See, for example, John P. Moody, "Civil Rights Panel Costs USW Officers Here," *Pittsburgh Post-Gazette*, October 28, 1974 and John P. Moody, "Steel Workers Protest Court Decree on Job Seniority," *Pittsburgh Post-Gazette*, June 18, 1975; "Steel's Antibias Pact Draws Some Plant Level Criticim," *Industry Week* 181 (May 20, 1974): 16–17.

17. The approach of the courts seems to be what has been called the "rightful place" approach. This generally entails the use of plant-wide seniority by affected minorities to bid for jobs when openings occur. This would not include bumping white employees out of jobs they currently hold. For other possible approaches, see "Title VII, Seniority Discrimination and the Incumbent Negro," *Harvard Law Review* 80 (April 1967): 1260–83.

18. For useful information on the background and approach of Lowell W. Perry, the new chairman of EEOC, see the following: "Labor Letter," *Wall Street Journal*, June 10, 1975, BNA, "New EEOC Chairman's Emphasis on Conciliation," *Labor Relations Reporter* 89 (June 16, 1975): 137–38; BNA, "Ford's Choice to Head EEOC," *Labor Relations Reporter* 88 (April 21, 1975): 314.

Gaining EEO Compliance with a Stable Work Force[1]

Francine S. Hall

Work force stability has recently emerged as one aspect of a recessionary economy that is causing new EEO problems for personnel administrators. Their attempts to implement goals and timetables during such a period are complicated by two factors. First, their companies are not increasing the number of positions in many job categories. In fact, they may be cutting back and laying off. Second, people themselves are less likely to voluntarily resign. With a lack of expansion and low turnover rates, the work force stabilizes. The result is a situation in which an organization's path to compliance is not through recruitment and selection. Faced with a stable work force, companies increasingly realize that their best chances for compliance lie with more effective utilization of women and minorities currently employed.

This route to affirmative action, however, presents many problems for the personnel manager. For example, consider some of the problems uncovered during interviews with people in two Midwest manufacturing organizations. The first organization is a container plant employing approximately three hundred people. The second is a diversified firm in the electronics industry with approximately six thousand employees.

PROBLEM IDENTIFICATION

Acting Affirmatively May Translate into "Reclassification" and "Lateral Transfers"

Typically, this involves moving women and minorities into positions that have traditionally been held by whites or males. These moves do not represent promotions or necessarily desirable shifts. In fact, they may be perceived as undesirable by the employees involved. An example would be attempting to move women from light assembly or packing positions into jobs such as forklift truck drivers or heavy machine operators. In both companies, managers reported that females did not respond positively to these efforts and often openly resisted such moves. We can label this the problem of resistance to lateral mobility.

Francine S. Hall is an assistant professor of management science at the University of Wisconsin-Parkside in Kenosha.

Acting Affirmatively May Require Accelerated
Movement of Women and Minorities into Management Positions

In many organizations the typical upward mobility pattern involves a "career track." To be eligible for a supervisory position, a person may be required to have a specified amount of experience and expertise in various technical positions. In addition, union contracts may cover bidding procedures and binding on the minimum time required to move through the track. In the companies interviewed, this created several problems, especially as affirmative efforts were directed to female employees.

Managers reported a second type of resistance—resistance to upward mobility—among women. This was documented in one case by statistics on the number of women electing to take advantage of a "presupervisory" training program the company offered. Only one woman volunteered despite special efforts to recruit women into the program. Anecdotal data reported by the managers suggested several possible reasons for this resistance. The common theme, however, centered on the females' perceptions of the supervisory role. As one woman reported when queried as to why she would not want to assume a management position: "I thought a supervisor had to be a 'Two-Ton Tony!' "

Many of the minorities, but especially the women employees, lacked the technical expertise to qualify for positions that would allow them to move up in these career tracks. Again, this appears to be a special problem for organizations where career mobility is tied to the technology. Females have generally not been directed toward developing their mechanical aptitudes to the same extent that males have in our culture.

Another issue that was being considered as a possible problem in one company was the potential discriminatory effects of the career track itself. Richard D. Sibbernsen has discussed this problem in detail in the Labor Law Journal. As he points out, unions may be liable along with companies for creating tracks that ". . .erect artificial, arbitrary, and unnecessary barriers to the hiring and advancement of minorities or females."[2] The corresponding issue in institutions of higher education is the legality of the Ph.D. requirement for faculty positions and the granting of faculty tenure. It has been argued that this should not be used as a necessary requirement for teaching and presents a discriminatory barrier to entrance and advancement in the academic professions among minorities.

Problems with Attitudes Toward
Preferential and Acceleration Programs

In their efforts to act affirmatively to implement the law, companies may unwittingly defy it, creating a situation in which affirmative action equals discrimination for nonminority males. Even when reverse discrimination is not a problem, affirmative efforts often engender discriminatory attitudes on the part of managers and co-workers. Without the technical and psychological support of the employee's supervisor and peers, success may be difficult, if not impossible, to achieve.

What can be done about these problems? One of the basic techniques for better understanding how to tackle any problem situation can be found in Kurt Lewin's classic "Force Field Analysis." In essence, this is a technique for examining the relationship between forces "pushing" to change the status quo and the forces acting to "resist" the change. When the strength of resisting forces equals the strength of pushing forces, the status quo remains unchanged. Since most efforts to push in the direction of a change will engender resistance, pushing harder is not the answer. It is generally easier and more effective to reduce resistance to change than to increase the push for it. This is a basic principle which can be referred to when trying to resolve EEO problems such as those described above. In utilizing this principle, the focus should be on identifying ways to decrease barriers and resistance to compliance-related changes.

THE DIAGNOSTIC SURVEY

The first approach a company should consider is one basic to effective planned change. This is the diagnostic survey, utilizing three types of diagnoses relating to the identified problems.

The first type involves diagnosing barriers within the individual. Several intraindividual barriers to both lateral and upward mobility opportunities may cause resistance. Some of those that were identified as possible causes of resistance in company interviews were: (1) the individual's perceptions of job qualifications and required role behavior; (2) the individual's needs and need satisfaction on the present job; (3) the individual's self-image; (4) the individual's perceptions of organizational opportunities, management's attitudes, and so on; (5) the individual's career aspirations or lack of them; and (6) personal and family conflicts.

An employee who either does not possess or believes he or she does not possess the skills or abilities perceived to be required by a position could be expected to have low motivation to move into that position. The example of a woman's perception of a supervisory position would be an instance of this.

If a person fulfills social needs on the job, then moving into a position that requires a great deal of solitary time would probably engender resistance. Again, the women in light assembly and packing jobs are a good example. Frequently they work sitting down in small groups or along an assembly line. This may allow for a great deal of verbal and social interaction, a source of job satisfaction. Clearly, they would not be motivated to move to a position that would not provide the opportunity to meet their needs.

Finally, personal and family conflicts may be real. These can be managed, however, if people are given help in problem solving, using coping strategies and support.

IDENTIFYING BARRIERS

The second type of diagnosis involves identifying barriers within the job. The type of work involved in a reclassification may not "fit" with the individual's skills, attitudes, needs, or self-image. Organizations that do not consider job-related variables that impose real barriers (skill requirements, role definition, and so on) may have difficulty both in identifying candidates and/or preparing and training them to move into these positions. Here, again, the diagnosis should examine both the technical and the social or behavioral aspects of the job as it is currently defined or carried out.

The third type of diagnosis involves identifying barriers within career tracks. The critical questions to be asked in such a diagnosis are: (1) Is the time required in a particular position necessary and directly tied to competence? and (2) Are the skill requirements to move up skills that can only be acquired on the job? Could someone be trained to move through the track more rapidly?

STRUCTURAL REDESIGN

While it is difficult, in many cases, to change the technical skill requirements, it is possible to redesign work to reduce some of the inherent social and psychological barriers that create resistance. Some of the more successful job enrichment experiments, for example, have involved "team" assembly units. If this approach is not feasible, other approaches should be explored. Rotating teams that shift people through several positions (for example, light assembly, solo assignment, and so on) may be possible. This would also expand the repertoire of job-related skills for an individual and increase flexibility within the organization.

A second type of structural change would involve redesigning career tracks. The nature of career tracks may be a touchy one in many organizations. Not only do they have historical precedence in many cases, but they are usually written into union contracts. Given a potential dual liability, however, that companies and unions face, several steps are suggested by Sibbernsen to review and eliminate their potential discriminatory effects.

1. All jobs in lines of progression should be assessed to determine if they are functionally related. Do they afford training and experience necessary to perform at the next level? If they are not related in this way, they should be removed from the line of progression and put in a special job pool.

2. Lines of progression should be evaluated to determine if the operation is more efficient as a result of a person's service in a lower, functionally related position. If not, then job or department seniority should be replaced, and total length of service in all jobs should be used.

3. Jobs should be evaluated to determine if a person can obtain equivalent experience in another position. If he or she can, then the justification for residence requirements should be negated.[3]

While these suggestions may not apply in all cases, the purpose of redesigning career tracks is to remove artificial and unrelated promotion prerequisites that have been built into advancement patterns.

CAREER PLANNING

A third approach to reducing resistance to mobility involves working with the individual employee to plan a career. This is particularly important where resistance to upward mobility appears to be the problem.

Frequently, employees join an organization without giving much thought to where they are going, where they want to be, or how to get there. This is often the case for hourly employees who view the relationship with a company as a "job" rather than a career. When an advancement opportunity arises, there may be a perceived "identity gap" between the job and the employee. The gap may not be real. It may simply be the result of a lack of information about job opportunities, awareness of one's self (and capabilities), preplanning, and so on. Put simply, people who haven't thought about what a higher position entails, what they want out of their work, or how they are going to manage their work life to achieve this may be psychologically unprepared to respond positively to equal opportunity. Taking advantage of employment opportunity requires a certain degree of vocational maturity!

In his work with adolescents, John O. Crites suggests five "career competencies" that contribute to a person's career maturity. These are: (1) self-appraisal (assessing one's interests and abilities); (2) occupational information (obtaining knowledge about occupations, organizations, and specific jobs); (3) goal selection (selecting career goals consistent with one's career capabilities); (4) planning (specifying the means through which to achieve career goals—identifying action steps one has to take); and (5) problem solving (developing the ability to identify, evaluate, and select among alternative solutions and coping strategies). As D. T. Hall states in *Careers in Organizations*, "These are . . . specific skills that can be developed. Of all the personal guidelines for career growth, these five competencies are the most basic. . . ."[4]

The above competencies are but one example of the type of career capabilities that persons need in order to take advantage of the expanding opportunities available to them. Virginia O'Leary has pointed out in her article in *Psychological Bulletin* that many of the barriers to upward mobility among women lie within the individual herself.[5]

For the personnel administrator attempting to reduce and eliminate these barriers, one of the most promising techniques appears to be career planning and development programs. Companies such as Weyerhauser have already undertaken such efforts. For readers interested in learning more about their program, the film *Women in Management: Threat or Opportunity* (Bureau of National Affairs, Washington, D.C.) is a suggested resource.

TRAINING AND PREPARATION

A fourth and final approach involves training programs to develop and prepare *both* the employee and the manager for the realities of EEO.

In a survey of a random sample of members of the American Society for Personnel Administration conducted in 1975, training and preparation for implementing EEO emerged as one of the strongest correlates of managerial commitment. In a current survey, interviews with personnel administrators in Wisconsin organizations suggest that lack of training and preparation for EEO is one of the chief problems encountered by people in line management.

The potential impact of training programs is not limited to better preparing managers. All of the problems stated above can be alleviated through appropriate types of training, for training enables employees to prepare for lateral as well as upward mobility. Prepared to face new opportunities, people can then take advantage of them. For the company, the payoff is simple: More qualified women and minorities willing to respond to the challenge of EEO.

A SUMMARY OF TECHNIQUES

The above discussion suggests three problem areas that emerge when an organization attempts to implement EEO with the resources of its existing work force: resistance among women and minorities, career track barriers, and attitudinal barriers. It was suggested that the most effective approach to solving these types of problems is not to push people into compliance. Effective change needs to be accomplished through a reduction of barriers to compliance.

Table 1 summarizes the four techniques that companies can employ and the problem areas where these would be most appropriate. The table shows one technique—training—is applicable to all three types of problems.

Up to now, training has been a voluntary approach to enhancing EEO compliance. Is it effective? Apparently the government believes it is. In a recent court decision in North Carolina (*Johnson v. Ryder*), the court required one company to provide EEO training for supervisors.[6] Does this action predict yet another set of compliance problems about to emerge? The answer appears to depend on the individual company and whether it has the foresight to self-select and employ problem-solving techniques of the type discussed in this article.

Table 1 Techniques for reducing barriers to EEO compliance

	Techniques						
	Diagnostic Survey			Structural Redesign		Career Planning	Training and Preparation	
Problem areas	Indiv.	Job	Track	Jobs	Path		Empl.	Mgrs.
I. Resistance among women and minorities								
A. To lateral moves and reclassification	X	X		X			X	X
B. To upward mobility	X	X				X	X	X
II. Career Track Barriers								
A. Adverse effect track			X	X				X
B. Technical and behavioral requirements				X			X	X
III. Attitudinal barriers								
A. Reverse effects							X	X
B. Managerial attitudes								X

NOTES

1. This article is based, in part, on a presentation given at a symposium, "Effect of Affirmative Action Programs on Traditional Organizational Behavior Patterns," Rossal S. Johnson, Chair, Midwest Academy of Management, St. Louis, Mo., April 23, 1976. Part of the article refers to a study conducted in 1975 with the support of a Faculty Research Grant and Fellowship from Western Michigan University.
2. *Labor Law Journal* (October, 1975): 666.
3. Ibid.
4. D. T. Hall, *Careers in Organizations* (Pacific Palisades, California: Goodyear, 1947) p. 181.
5. Virginia O'Leary, *Psychological Bulletin* 81 1974: 802–26.
6. *Business Week*, May 3, 1976, p. 107.

Developing and Using an In-House Interest Inventory

Cary B. Barad

From the standpoint of cost to benefits and effective manpower utilization, matching the worker with the job obviously makes good business sense. Employees whose jobs are congruent with their measured interests and abilities will more likely benefit from job-related training, produce at optimum levels, and experience satisfaction with work and self. Further, they will be less likely to leave the organization in search of a better job.

Fortunately, objective and valid measures of occupational aptitude and ability are not in short supply. Unfortunately, according to organizational placement specialists and counselors attempting to assist their employees in preparing for long-term career objectives and/or job changes, the commercially published interest tests are of limited practical usefulness.

At the Social Security Administration (SSA), for example, career development counselors found that measures such as the Kuder Preference Record and Strong Vocational Interest Blank mostly covered job areas that were completely unrelated to the job families that typified the work of the agency. Measuring an employee's preference for outdoor, musical, or artistic kinds of activities was useless since in-house outlets for these interests were nonexistent. SSA therefore decided to develop its own in-house interest inventory, which perhaps can serve as a useful model for other large public and private institutions faced with similar problems.

Cary B. Barad is a senior personnel psychologist at the Social Security Administration Office of Human Resources in Baltimore, Maryland.

THE SETTING

SSA, a nationwide social insurance complex, endeavors to provide its eighty thousand employees with counseling and placement services aimed at facilitating self-development and in-house career advancement. The thrust of SSA's employee development program is directed toward the lower-graded, less well-educated members of the work force who are seeking to improve their job status within the agency.

Although the number of employees working for SSA is relatively large, the nature of the agency restricts variation in its job-family structure. Further, of the twenty-two basic occupational areas that have been identified thus far, only twelve of them are realistically "within reach" of the employee/client population from the standpoint of both job vacancies and education/work experience requirements. Most of these areas encompass clerical, insurance claims, and data processing jobs.

PHASES OF DEVELOPMENT

To meet the needs of the agency's central office counselors and employees for a new job-related interest inventory, SSA's human resources psychologists constructed what may be the first work-preference schedule geared specifically toward local in-house jobs. This new paper-and-pencil career planning aid, called the SSA Career Interest Profile (CIP), was developed in three phases.

In the content validation phase, SSA psychologists first developed a pool of tentative items using a job analysis of the twelve focal occupations. This phase involved both on-site observations and consultations with experienced employees and supervisors. The initial item pool was carefully screened to ensure the gender neutrality of all terms and to verify that the covered experiences and activities would be equally familiar to both men and women. The items were then administered to a small sample of GS-4-level volunteers for comments on content, readability, and item clarity.

In the scale construction phase, an experimental form of the CIP was administered on a confidential "no name" basis to a total of seven hundred male and female journeyman-level employees in all twelve job areas. Participants were asked to indicate the extent to which each individual item accurately described their own duties and whether they liked, disliked, or were unsure of their feelings about the activity described in the item. Prior to statistical analysis, a special job attitude index was used to eliminate the responses of those participants ($N=50$) who were dissatisfied with or neutral toward their jobs. The responses of the satisfied participants were then used to assign items statistically to the specific job areas under study.

An item was assigned to a particular scale when the percentage of participants who worked in a particular job area and who indicated that the item accurately described their own work was at least twice as great as the percentage of all participants in the twelve job areas combined who indicated that the item accurately described their own work. In effect, the response patterns of the different occupational groups—in terms of tasks performed—determined the specific scale for which each item was weighted. For example, 92 percent of the participants working in public contact claims jobs said that CIP item 31 accurately described their work. In contrast, only 15 percent of all participants employed in the twelve areas combined did so. Therefore, item number 31 was assigned to and weighted for Scale I: Public Contact Claims (see Figure 1).

In the final norming phase, participants' like, dislike, and unsure responses to the items in their own scale were quantified, tabulated, and transformed into standard scores. Percentiles were also derived for each of the twelve scales on the basis of the responses of the appropriate criterion group of employees. The Career Interest Profile was then ready for general application by SSA's human resources psychologists.

THE CIP APPROACH TO CAREER COUNSELING

Under the CIP approach to career counseling, the employee/client is presented with 240 numbered statements, each corresponding to a specific SSA job activity. The employee is asked to indicate whether or not he or she would like to perform each activity on a regular basis, using a like, dislike, or unsure response format. Next, each respondent's answer sheet is scored, either by hand or by computer, and his or her responses are compared with those of satisfied journeyman-level employees in each of the twelve covered SSA occupations.

Thus the direction of an employee/client's interests is first determined by the extent to which he or she responds positively to those items that have been weighted for specific occupational scales. As noted earlier, an item is weighted for an occupational scale when it accurately reflects the tasks performed by members of that occupation. The strength or "height" of the employee/client's interest within a given scale is then measured by summing the numerical equivalents of his or her item responses across all the items comprising the scale and comparing this sum—on a percentile basis—with the sum obtained for employees on whose responses the scale was specifically constructed. A graphic self-interpreting profile (Figure 2) is then constructed and returned to the employee along with information on how to contact a career counselor for follow-up discussions.

RELIABILITY

The internal consistency reliability coefficients for the twelve scales range from .86 to .96—well within the limits established for instruments of this type. Therefore, an individual's CIP scores can be expected to remain stable, consistent, and accurate over time. Plans are currently under way to collect and analyze follow-up data on test-retest reliability and to study the relationship between CIP scores, job satisfaction, and career movement and entry.

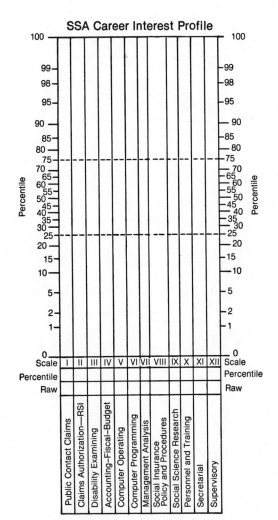

Figure 1 Selected CIP items by occupational scale

SSA Career Interest Profile

Your Career Interest Profile is designed to help you plan your career at SSA. It should help you decide what type(s) of work you would enjoy doing.

The following key will assist you in interpreting your Career Interest Profile.

Percentile

75–100   Your interest in doing things involved in this work area matches that of those people presently working in positions of this type who *most like what they are doing.*

25–75   Your interest in doing things involved in this work area matches that of those people presently working in positions of this type who *like what they are doing moderately well.*

0–25   Your interest in doing things involved in this work area matches that of those people presently working in positions of this type who *least like what they are doing.*

Important

Your Career Interest Profile is not used in any agency personnel actions, nor does it indicate ability or potential to succeed in different types of work.

Figure 2 Self-interpreting profile sheet

Index

414

416

Intergovernmental Personnel Act, 53–56, 58n, 59n
Internal Revenue Service, 217, 279, 281, 284
International Association of Fire Fighters, 350, 351, 355
International City Mangers Association (ICMA), 50
Interview, 169, 176. See also Recruitment; Selection

Jackson v. McLeod, 338n
Jaffe, A. J., 314n
Jakus, Larry, 77, 128
Jalil v. Hampton, 329n
James v. Board of Education, 329n
Janson, Robert, 230
Jeanneret, P. R., 150, 154n
Jenkins, G. W., 86n
Jersey Central Power and Light v. IBEW Local Unions, 401n
Job actions. See Labor management relations
Job analysis, 142, 149–54; and performance evaluation, 191; defined, 155. See also Job classification; Job evaluation
Job application, 169–77. See also Selection; Recruitment
Job classification, 155–56. See also Job analysis; Job evaluation
Job description, 39–43, 154–63, 215. See also Job analysis
Job design, 32–39, 405. See also Flexitime; Job enrichment
Job enlargement, 32–33. See also Job design
Job enrichment, 32–35, 216, 230–50; product-oriented, 35–39. See also Job design
Job evaluation, 141–55, 156. See also Job analysis; Job classification
Job satisfaction, 215–17, 218–30; and flexible compensation, 281–85; and flexitime, 264–71, 271–73; and job enrichment, 243–45
Johnson, Lyndon B., 368
Johnson, Rossal S., 408n
Johnson v. Fraley, 328n
Johnson v. Ryder, 407
Jones, M. A., 154n
Jones, Ralph, 342
Jones, William A., Jr., 60–61, 68n

Jump, Bernard, Jr., 217, 295
Juris, Hervey, 356n

Kagno, Munro, 277n
Kalish, R. A., 102n, 103n
Kantner, R. M., 103n
Katz, Robert, 102n, 104n
Kaufman, S., 250n
Kearney v. Macy, 329n
Kegan, Daniel L., 127n
Kelley v. Herak, 329n
Kendall, L. M., 163n
Kennedy, John F., 50, 369
Kheel, Theodore W., 62n, 340n
Kimberly, John R., 77, 112, 127n
Kindall, Alva F., 105, 111n
King, Albert S., 127n
King v. Priest, 338n
Kinnard, Douglas, 385n
Kleisath, S. W., 126n
Klingner, Donald E., 4, 5, 69, 75n, 142, 154, 178
Knudsen, Steven, 77, 128
Kohlmeier, Louis M., 315n
Koontz, H., 87n
Kornhauser, A. A., 229n
Krislov, Samuel, 58n

Labor management relations, 317, 331–57; and civil service reform act of 1978, 133–34; and merit system, 51, 53; and seniority, 397–98; arbitration, 335–36; collective bargaining, 333–36, 341–46; enabling legislation, 50–51; impasse resolution techniques, 335–36, 355; job actions, 354–55; negotiation, 345; police and fire, 347–57; problems with, 336–37; 351–52; public sector growth of, 50–51; public v. private sector, 331–37; strikes, 333, 354–55. See also Employee rights; Grievances
Labor Relations Board v. Richland School District, 340n
Langdale, J. A., 172, 176n, 177n
Lankenner, Wanda A., 206
Lawler, Edward E., III, 219, 229n, 220, 230n, 250n
Lawrence, Paul R., 127n, 250n
Lawshe, C. H., 151, 154n
Layoffs, 394–95. See also Affirmative action; Seniority; Reduction in force
Leach, Daniel E., 387